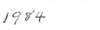

Major Problems in American Foreign Policy

Major Problems in

American Foreign Policy

SECOND EDITION

DOCUMENTS AND ESSAYS

Volume II: Since 1914

Edited by
Thomas G. Paterson
UNIVERSITY OF CONNECTICUT

D. C. Heath and Company • Lexington, Massachusetts • Toronto

FOR *Aaron Matthew*

International Standard Book Number: 0-669-06449-1

Library of Congress Catalog Card Number: 83-80923

Preface

The invitation to offer a second edition of this volume has afforded me the enviable opportunity to review the rich literature in diplomatic history. The goal remains: to provide students and instructors with the most distinguished, readable, and stimulating writing in the field. Since the first edition, the body of scholarly studies has grown tremendously, and new documents have become available to the curious historian. In this edition, new chapters appear, and many of the chapters carried over from the first edition have been revised to include new research, fresh and changed interpretations, recently declassified documents, and topics that have loomed in the last few years as especially helpful in understanding current foreign policy. At the same time, the core of the best scholarship from the first edition has been retained.

Each chapter addresses a major theme or question over which contemporaries and later scholars and writers have differed. The primary documents in each chapter introduce the problem, outline issues, reveal the flavor of the times, and convey the level of intelligence and intensity with which people held their positions and tried to persuade others. The questions were momentous—sometimes abstract, sometimes deadly concrete, but always consequential—and people like us defined and debated them. They suffered in their confusion and defeat, and they prospered in their success. This book attempts to capture and reveal that human dimension—that *people* struggled to make decisions. The essays in each chapter also reflect these qualities. Thus we learn not only *what* happened but *why* alternative policies were rejected. Joining studies by past masters are contributions by younger voices. Varying points of view are represented, and care has been taken to avoid contriving debates to fit a false either-or format. The chapter introductions and section headnotes set the readings in historical and interpretive perspective. Further Reading sections, highlighting recent scholarship, suggest other books and articles for continued research.

In the late 1970s the People's Republic of China adopted a new system for rendering Chinese phonetic characters into the Roman alphabet. This new method, the Pinyin, replaced the Wade-Giles technique. The Pinyin system is now commonly used, but we are in a transition stage in which the old spellings still appear. Because the documents and essays in this volume were written originally in the old manner, I have retained their Wade-Giles spellings. In the introductions and headnotes, however, the old spellings are followed by the Pinyin spellings in parentheses.

Many people have helped me prepare this anthology. My friend and colleague J. Garry Clifford, as always, gave valuable advice. For suggestions and other courtesies I thank Harold Barto, Richard Dean Burns, Bruce Cummings, Joe Decker, John Dobson, Michael Ebner, Gerald Gordon, Gregg Herken, James Hindman, Michael Hunt, Donald Johnson, Lawrence Kaplan, Warren Kimball, Melvyn Leffler, Douglas Little, James Matray, John Merrill, Charles Neu, Stephen Pelz, Carol Petillo, Sister Eileen Rice, Kenneth Shewmaker, Mark Stoler, William Stueck, and John Sylvester. My colleagues Karen Kupperman and Harry Stout shared their expertise with me, as did doctoral students Harlow Sheidley and Thomas Zoumaras. Ellen P. Kerley, an undergraduate History major, provided indispensable assistance. Jean Manter, my departmental secretary, assisted in many ways, and Holly Izard Paterson once again favored the book with her help.

TGP

Contents

9 Mao's China and the Chances for Sino-American Accommodation

10 The Korean War

The Characteristics of Modern American Foreign Policy

1

Scholars have identified several key characteristics of recent American foreign policy. Whether called motives or roots, these characteristics are fundamental and enduring. Which are most important in generating American foreign policy is a question of much debate. Some students of history stress an American ideological quest for democratic political principles and equal opportunity as well as a humanitarian, reformist sense of mission fueled by an unbounded American optimism. Others point to national security, economic needs, capitalism, or an anti-revolutionary penchant for order. Words like "democracy," "moralism," "national security," "capitalism," "economic expansion," and "open door" have frequently been used to describe the roots of American behavior in international relations. A study of these various factors helps to explain why the United States became an interventionist, global power in the twentieth century. In short, what is the mainspring of American foreign policy?

ESSAYS

The first essay, written by Dexter Perkins, one of the deans of diplomatic history and an author of major books on the Monroe Doctrine, reflects a viewpoint that has often been called "nationalist." Indeed, Perkins is seldom critical of American foreign policy; rather, he strongly commends the American record, finding it characterized by a sincere attempt to implant abroad the best of America—its democratic principles.

The second essay, by George F. Kennan, is critical of such an interpretation and of the characteristic itself. As an historian and career diplomat who helped to articulate

1

the containment doctrine in the late 1940s, Kennan has consistently argued in his many position papers and publications, especially in *American Diplomacy, 1900– 1950,* that a streak of "moral-legalism" has characterized United States foreign policy, making it abruptly changeable whenever fickle public opinion shifted.

The final essay, by William Appleman Williams of Oregon State University, who has been a major influence in the development of a critical interpretation of United States foreign policy, argues that American diplomacy has amounted to a "tragedy," because the American people, driven by an "open door" economic expansionism that has meant coercion abroad, have violated their best ideals.

Democracy

DEXTER PERKINS

It is a truism, but one that needs to be constantly reiterated, that words are often used by men to arouse emotion and fortify prejudice, rather than to describe exactly or appeal to reason. The language of politics, national and international, is full of clichés which serve these convenient purposes. To many of those who lean towards the left, the partisans of the right are always "reactionaries"; while no other word than "radical" or "socialist" or perhaps "Communist" will satisfy some conservatives in describing the friends of moderate change. In international affairs, "honor" and "justice" and the "interests of humanity" are likely to be the exclusive concern of one nation, while sinister motives are unvaryingly ascribed to its rival, together with what is usually described since the days of Hitler as "warmongering." Among the convenient terms of abuse in the vocabulary of contemporary international politics is the term "imperialism." To the Soviet Union the peoples of the West and, particularly, the United States are imperialists. The cliché has wide influence; beyond question, along with many other Russian propaganda devices, it produces a certain degree of confusion in the minds of excellent people who are not free from a touch of masochism; and it reminds the newborn nations of the world of the "oppression" which preceded their liberation. It is well worth while, then, to examine what is termed American imperialism, to determine its character and its limitations, and to assess the strength of the imperialist motive in American foreign policy historically and in the present day.

At the outset of this analysis it is important to draw a clear distinction between expansion and imperialism. Expansion, in the view that will be taken in the following pages, is the process by which the political control of a given nation is extended over territory which then becomes assimilated and incorporated in the political and constitutional system of the expanding state. The cession of Louisiana by France to the United States in 1803, or even the acquisition of California by conquest from Mexico in 1848, are examples of expansion. The

Reprinted by permission of the publishers from *The American Approach to Foreign Policy,* Revised Edition, by Dexter Perkins, Cambridge, Mass.: Harvard University Press, Copyright © 1962 by the President and Fellows of Harvard College.

regions thus acquired became a part of the federal union, and whatever moral judgment we may wish to make with regard to these acquisitions, we shall naturally recognize the fact that today the regions so acquired present no special problem, so far as their political status is concerned, but constitute parts of a united nation.

The question of how to deal with territories acquired outside the continental area of the United States did not arise until the end of the nineteenth century. Not that there was no appetite for such territories. Americans had had their eyes on Cuba since the days of Jefferson; on at least two occasions the purchase of the island was seriously discussed, and once, in the case of the well-known Ostend Manifesto, its seizure, in the event that Spain refused to sell, was somewhat blatantly advocated. After the Mexican War there was a movement for the annexation of all of Mexico, and in 1848 President Polk proposed the occupation of Yucatan. Just after the Civil War Secretary Seward negotiated a treaty for the purchase of the Danish West Indies; and President Grant proposed the annexation of the Dominican Republic. But none of these projects came to fruition. Down to 1860 Northern antagonism to slavery put a damper on the acquisition of any territory which might increase the influence of the South; and in the twenty years after the Civil War the country was primarily concerned with the problems of reconstruction and with its own remarkable internal development. In the period of the Spanish-American War, however, as we have already seen, the United States acquired dominion over Puerto Rico, Guam, and the Philippines, and in 1899 it acquired title to a part of the Samoan islands. In 1903, taking advantage of the revolution which gave birth to the independent republic of Panama, the American government established a virtual protectorate over the new state and secured the Panama Canal Zone. In 1916 it bought the Virgin Islands. And in the twenty-year period between 1898 and 1918, it intervened in the affairs of Cuba for a brief period (1906–1909) and occupied for longer intervals the territory of three independent states, Nicaragua, Haiti, and the Dominican Republic. It would seem reasonable to describe this period as one of American imperialism, and it is well worth while to examine what this "imperialism" was like in practice.

There is one essential generalization with which we ought to begin. American rule over other peoples has always been rule with an uneasy conscience. Implicit in it at all times has been faith in the democratic process, the belief that it was the duty of an imperial power to prepare the way to self-government for the peoples over whom it exercised control. This is something that ought never to be forgotten in any discussion of the whole problem. Indeed, it means that "imperialism," as it is conceived by the Americans, can be only a passing phase. We can see this principle at work in the discussions at the end of the Spanish-American War. The very assumption of imperial rule over the territories acquired from Spain was bitterly contested in principle. The idea of such rule was regarded by substantial numbers of Americans—including some eminent members of the dominant Republican Party—as inconsistent with the Declaration of Independence and the Constitution. The treaty for the acquisition of these territories passed the Senate with a single vote to spare, after vigorous congressional and public debate and, although the imperialists won, the anti-imperialists, in a sense, called the tune. The establishment of a wide measure of self-government for the peoples brought under American sway was regarded as desirable by both parties and became the basis of American policy. Let us look at the record in this respect, first of all in the case of the Philippines.

After a brief period of military rule and the unsavory episode of American repression of a Filipino insurrection, a civil government was established in the islands in 1901, and the Filipinos were admitted to not a few administrative offices. By 1907 a Filipino Assembly had been created, with complete legislative power, a commissioner elected to the United States House of Representatives to watch over the interests of the islands, and a majority of Filipinos established on the Filipino Commission, which carried on the work of the administration under the direction of the governor and which also exercised legislative powers. In 1916 a two-chamber legislature was created and, though the right of veto existed in the governor, under the Wilson administration wide authority was given to the new body, and it was left free to formulate general policies with little interference. There was a reaction under the governorship of General Leonard Wood, who displayed a somewhat autocratic temper, but this was short-lived. Finally, in 1934, Congress provided for the calling of a constitutional convention and for the complete independence of the islands. There was to be an interim period during which the United States was represented in the islands by a high commissioner, with strictly limited powers; but this lasted for only ten years, and in 1946 the independent Filipino Republic came into being. While the United States, with the consent of the Filipino government, retains bases in the islands, it no longer exercises any direct political authority over the conduct of Filipino affairs.

Let us look next at Puerto Rico. For a short time the island remained under military government. But in 1900 there was set up a civil regime which provided for a legislature, the lower house of which was elected by the Puerto Ricans themselves, and which gave to the island a civil governor. This very moderate measure of popular control was enlarged by the Jones Act of 1917. By this legislation, both houses of the Puerto Rican legislature were to be chosen by the inhabitants of the island, a substantial number of the administrative posts were placed in their hands, a bill of rights was enacted, and a Puerto Rican commissioner was given a seat in the House of Representatives. Thus the way was provided for a greater degree of self-rule. In 1947, still another step was taken. The governor of the island, instead of being chosen by the President of the United States, was henceforth to be elected by the Puerto Ricans and was to hold office for a fixed term. Virtually the whole administrative machinery was placed in native hands, leaving only the judges of the supreme court to be chosen by the President of the United States. And while, in theory, the power of veto over Puerto Rican legislation exists, and can be exercised either by the President or through congressional enactment, in practice the inhabitants of the island enjoy a wide degree of self-government.

The other territories acquired by the United States are Samoa, Guam, and the Virgin Islands, all of them small ones, with populations in each case under

60,000. The first two have been under naval rule, but even here there has been some representation accorded to the native population, and Guam has been transferred to civil authority. The third enjoys today the status accorded to Puerto Rico before the legislation of 1947. Even in these instances, then, the principle of self-government has been given expression.

In addition to controlling the territories mentioned, the United States exercised supervision and control over various Caribbean republics, setting up governments there which, in one form or another, were under the control of the American marines. Though a variety of motives explain these interventions (and we shall have more to say of this later), among them was the hope of bringing about orderly government based on a respect for constitutional and democratic processes. It may be instructive to see how much success was achieved. Indeed, by an analysis of the situation in these communities today, we may gain some insight into the fundamental question as to whether democratic institutions can be exported successfully and made to function efficiently.

The situation has varied in the five states under review (Panama, Cuba, Haiti, the Dominican Republic, and Nicaragua). In the Dominican Republic, for example, the departure of the Americans was soon followed by the establishment of a military dictatorship which was one of the most ruthless and cruel in the history of the Caribbean. Rafael Leonidas Trujillo, until his death in 1961, governed the state with a rod of iron for more than thirty years. He certainly brought peace to the Dominicans, but to speak of democracy is out of the question. A somewhat milder autocratic rule was that established by Anastasio Somoza in Nicaragua. In Haiti, there have been better and worse rulers since American evacuation in 1934, but hardly popular government. In Cuba, there have also been better and worse periods. Interspersed with administrations which observed, to a substantial extent, democratic forms, there have been the dictatorships of Gerardo Machado, Fulgencio Batista, and Fidel Castro. The hope for genuine democracy in Cuba has never seemed less bright than it does as these words are written. Furthermore, even in the better eras, the venality and corruption of Cuban politicians has been notorious. The most hopeful picture presented has been that of Panama. There popular processes have been reasonably democratic. Yet there were revolutions in Panama in 1949 and 1951, and rule by a virtual dictator from 1951 to 1955.

As we look at the record as a whole we shall find in it some reason for questioning the universal validity of the democratic idea. We may well ask whether popular institutions are adapted to peoples with a very different tradition and a very different social composition from our own. We may well ask whether something does not depend upon political habit, whether something does not depend upon the diffusion of knowledge, whether something does not depend upon the existence of a broadly based middle class which desires order and peace and which, from its very position, practices those arts of compromise which are of the essence of democratic rule. The story of American interventions demonstrates that the imposition of a brief period of tutelage by no means guarantees the solidity of popular government, as we understand it in this country.

Whether one accepts these conclusions or not, however, the experiment carried on in the second two decades of the century was short-lived. With relation to Latin America, there has been a strong current of feeling that conducts the United States in a very different direction, and that was manifest even in the palmy days of the imperialist idea. In the period between 1910 and 1917, Mexico was in chronic disorder. The temptation to teach the Mexicans a lesson, to "clean up" a bad situation, was most certainly present. Yet neither the Taft nor the Wilson administration attempted to do anything of the kind. In the broad sense they let the Mexican peoples decide their own destinies. Wilson, it is true, found himself led by his prejudice against the Mexican dictator Victoriano Huerta to the occupation of Vera Cruz, a step which resulted in Huerta's overthrow, but he never desired full-scale intervention in Mexico. Even when the end of the war in Europe freed American hands from foreign complications, there was no attempt to police Mexico into good democratic behavior. The restraint shown by the United States was a remarkable example of the strength of the anti-imperialist impulse in American politics at a time when there was substantial pressure for another course of action. Policing little nations, rather than comparatively big ones, was as far as the United States was ready to go even in the imperialist decades.

Moreover, government by marines, inaugurated in Nicaragua in 1912, in the Dominican Republic in 1915, and in Haiti in 1916, did not long prove to be very popular with the American people. As early as the campaign of 1920, Senator Warren G. Harding, then a candidate for the presidency, actuated (it is fair to assume) by political motives rather than by profound knowledge of the situation in the Caribbean, sharply criticized the acts of the previous administration. And, with the advent of the Republican regime into power, the first steps were taken towards the liquidation of one of these military governments, that of the Dominican Republic, and the evacuation of Dominican territory was consummated in 1925. In the same year an attempt was made at withdrawal from Nicaragua and, though unsettled conditions again brought about American intervention, the way was soon prepared for a new withdrawal. In the meantime, important modifications were taking place in the view held by the United States with regard to the Roosevelt corollary of the Monroe Doctrine, which, as we have seen, formed a justification of interference in the affairs of other states. The State Department at this time (1928) drew up the famous Clark memorandum which, after analyzing the history of the Doctrine, came to the conclusion that it did not justify the use of force for the chastisement of unruly republics and the setting up of military rule. The next year the Senate of the United States, in ratifying the Kellogg-Briand Pact for the outlawry of war, adopted a kind of declaration or gloss on that instrument as to the limits to be placed on the principles of Monroe. At the time the Clark memorandum had not yet been published. Thus the Senate vote of 1929 was the first public repudiation by a body that was a part of the treaty-making power of the doctrine of intervention which had been practiced scarcely more than a decade before.

The change in American opinion was accelerated by the pressure of the Latin American republics themselves. At the Pan-American conference in Havana in

1928, the American delegation was made aware of the intensely critical attitude of most of our southern neighbors with regard to the whole problem of intervention. The administration, indeed, foreseeing what would be the tone of discussion there, had drawn Charles Evans Hughes from retirement to justify the position of the United States. But Hughes, though he was successful in postponing a vote on a resolution condemning all interventions, could not exorcise the essential hostility of the Latin American republics to the claims of the United States to exercise international police power. And the net result of the conference was probably to strengthen the movement away from imperialism.

It seems probable that the Great Depression also accentuated this tendency. The nation was in no mood, with the advent of the thirties, to use its physical power to protect American investors abroad. The hostility of the New Deal to the great financial interests made it relatively easy for the Roosevelt administration to forswear the habits of the past and place our relationship with Latin America on a new basis. At the Conference of Montevideo in 1933, Secretary Hull put his name to a protocol which bound the signatory states to abstain from all interference in the domestic concerns of any one of them. True, the Secretary boggled slightly at the proposed formula, and he even made a reservation intended to leave the door open for positive action for the protection of American interests. But the Senate of the United States, amazingly enough, ratified this protocol unanimously, and in 1936, when at Buenos Aires a new declaration was drawn up asserting the same principle in stronger terms, it was accepted without difficulty by the American delegation and ratified, like its predecessor, without a dissenting vote in the Senate.

In 1948 the United States went further. At the Conference of Bogota it put its name to a protocol which declared: "no state or *group of states* has the right to intervene, directly or indirectly, in the internal or external affairs of any other state. The foregoing principle prohibits not only armed force but also any other form of interference or attempted threat against the personality of the state or against its political or economic or cultural elements." It would hardly have been possible to make a more sweeping commitment of an anti-imperialistic character.

At no time since the signing of these three agreements has the American government intervened by force of arms at any place in the New World. In 1938 it bore tolerantly the expropriation of American oil interests in Mexico and in Bolivia. In 1940 it made no protest against the Cuban constitution, which dealt harshly in some respects with American interests. Only once has the pledge given in the Montevideo, Buenos Aires, and Bogota protocols, even by a broad construction, been violated: this was in 1961. At that time there had been established in Cuba a government under Fidel Castro which formed a close connection with Communist Russia and Communist China, and which was itself Communist or proto-Communist in character. In April 1961, the American government gave encouragement and some measure of actual military and economic support to an attempted invasion of the island by counterrevolutionaries. Its action failed; it met with considerable criticism at home; and the Kennedy administration, notwithstanding provocations of an extreme character, reiterated previous pledges that it would take no direct hostile action against the Castro regime. This episode might raise the question (which only the future will resolve) as to whether the United States is bound to stand by while American governments are subverted with the encouragement and open aid of its avowed antagonists. It can hardly serve to shake the thesis that in its relation with its Latin American neighbors the United States has demonstrated a restraint such as has only rarely been practiced by a nation possessed of great physical power. Moreover, it is one thing to abstain from interference with the freedom of action of the New World republics; it is another thing to permit the subversion of the free and independent states of the New World by international Communism.

A second aspect of United States relations with its "southern neighbors" should be mentioned. During the Second World War, by arrangement with other governments, notably Guatemala, Ecuador, Panama, and Brazil, its armed forces were stationed on the soil of these states. Today they are to be found in none of them. Even in the case of Panama, where an important security interest is plainly at stake, the American government, after long negotiations, withdrew its forces from Panamanian territory.

What was the record of the United States towards its conquered enemies at the end of the Second World War? What of Germany and Japan? In both cases the American government smiled upon the establishment of democratic regimes. In no way, once these regimes had been established, did it attempt to control them. True, American troops remain on German and Japanese soil. But they are there by agreement with the states concerned. They are there not as agents of control, but as symbols of the readiness of the American government to sustain the forces of popular rule. To speak of this as imperialism would be an absurdity.

One reservation must be made. In the islands of the Pacific conquered from Japan (of which Okinawa is the most important), the concern of our own military and naval men for security has resulted in the continuation of American administration. The treaty of peace with Japan, however, provided for the establishment of a United Nations trusteeship. As of the present writing, this provision has not been implemented. Yet the very willingness of the United States, in theory at least, to accept something less than unlimited sovereignty is a partial answer to its critics, and if the country follows precedents established, let us say, in the case of Guam, it will give a substantial voice to the inhabitants of these territories in the determination of their own affairs.

Up to this point we have been considering imperialism only in its political aspects. Now we must examine it on the economic side. Here, the questions that call for an answer are these: Where American political control or supervision has been extended, have the results been beneficial to the inhabitants of the area concerned, looking at the matter from the economic point of view? Second, have American business interests exercised—and do they exercise—a substantial and noxious control over the governments of other states in which they do business? And third, are the policies of the United States today, in America, in Europe, or in Asia, justly to be criticized as examples of "economic imperialism"?

To the first of these questions the answer seems clear. Such countries as Puerto Rico and the Philippines could almost certainly not have found the capital for their own development if they had operated as independent governments from 1898 thenceforward. They would have remained, as they then were, relatively backward communities. American rule gave to American capitalists the assurance of peace and order, and indeed of protection against arbitrary exaction, and thus contributed powerfully to encourage investment on a substantial scale. The case becomes still stronger when we are talking of regions in which chronic misgovernment existed before American control. You cannot expect foreign money to enter a country where disorder is virtually endemic. Whatever else American rule in the Dominican Republic may have done, to cite one example, it most certainly paved the way for a period of domestic tranquillity and opened the door to American entrepreneurs. The progress of the island since the American occupation has been remarkable, and it has had a far larger national income than before. Though the gain was less spectacular in Nicaragua or in Haiti, there, also, the net result of the American occupation was undoubtedly an economic advance.

It will be said that the profits from a situation of this kind go to a very few. That they are equitably distributed (assuming that we could agree upon what the word "equitably" implies), I should not for a moment attempt to assert. But that *some* benefit trickles down to a portion of the masses is certain. In the countries we have mentioned, American entrepreneurs usually pay higher wages than native employers and take better care of those who work for them. By their expanding activities, the number of workers is increased. The taxes which are levied upon them may go, if the government is honestly administered, or even if it is not, to serve the public interest and to make social progress possible without imposing an undue burden upon the less fortunate class in the community. There is, undeniably, a net economic gain which extends beyond the narrow circle of the entrepreneurs themselves.

Nor can we entirely neglect other contributions that are sometimes made by an occupying power which indirectly promote the welfare of those temporarily under its rule. The United States, in its brief period of control in Cuba, did much to set going a system of public instruction and to check the ravages of yellow fever. It did something for education in the Dominican Republic. It did much for the building of roads in both the Dominican Republic and Haiti. It reorganized the railroad system in Nicaragua. And it provided in every case a domestic tranquillity which could hardly fail to be of value to the mass of the population, for it certainly means something to relieve the average man of the plunder of revolutionary armies and the depredations of civil war. In addition to all this, the United States has often expended its own funds on a very substantial scale to assist the economies of such communities as the Virgin Islands, Puerto Rico, and the Philippines.

The second question which we posed concerned the influence of American business corporations in countries where they do business but where there is no political control by the United States itself. There are undeniably shoddy episodes in the American past in this regard. The most reprehensible have to do with the fomenting of revolution or with the giving of support to revolutionary factions, of course with the hope of return if these factions come into power. The revolution of 1910 in Nicaragua, to cite a case, was beyond much question instigated by American interests on the east coast of the republic, and there was a connection, though a tenuous one, between these interests and the State Department. In the course of the next year, the revolution which broke out in Honduras was financed from New Orleans, and those who promoted it naturally had interested objects in view. In the Mexican turmoil of the period 1910 to 1917, the oil companies at times maintained private armies which bid defiance to the authority of the state, and some of them heavily backed the so-called Constitutionalists, participating actively in what was virtually a civil war. Less reprehensible, no doubt, but still not to be defended, are the cases, not innumerous in the history of the Central American republics in the same and in an earlier period, when fantastic privileges were secured by foreign corporations from complacent or corrupt legislatures, and when corporate influence was often powerful enough to permit the circumvention or defiance of the law.

To judge from the surface evidence, this kind of thing is far less likely to occur today. In the first place, the standard of American business morals, while not so high as to please the exacting, has undeniably improved. In the second, since the Latin American states (in which most of these episodes have occurred) are now protected against intervention by the United States by the protocols of Montevideo and Buenos Aires, they can make a more effective resistance to the exactions of foreign capitalists. To state the matter in another way, the capital-receiving state can and does prescribe the terms under which the foreign entrepreneur operates. The American government has left and does leave to other countries wide latitude in the fixing of these terms. It has, invariably, contented itself with formal protests and demands for compensation, even in cases of expropriation. It is bound not to intervene by physical force. It rests, then, with the capital-receiving state to form its policies so that, on the one hand, by inordinate exactions it does not kill the goose that lays the golden eggs and, on the other hand, it appropriates for its own people a reasonable part of the profits that come from foreign enterprise.

It is entirely wrong to regard the export of American capital to other lands as in itself immoral or exploitative. On the contrary, it is of the very essence of economic progress that states with a surplus of fluid capital use it to develop the economies of those which do not, that those who have the best managerial skills and technological know-how use these skills and this knowledge to develop the resources of lands less fortunate in their capacity to act for themselves. Certainly, there must be some basis of understanding between the foreign entrepreneur and the state in which he operates. The entrepreneur must not be grasping; he must operate his business with some regard for the climate of opinion and for the social interests inevitably connected with his activities; the state must, on its part, not be oppressive in its policies and must recognize that those who invest their funds within its borders must not be prevented from making a fair profit on their investment. But with these things understood, the practice of capital export is beneficent, not maleficent—more, we repeat, it is indispensable to world progress. This fact should be self-evident. Unhappily it is not. The cliché "economic imperialism" is used to make odious what is normal and desirable. We need very emphatically to put this cliché in its place and to analyze very carefully the thought of those who put it forward.

This brings us to the third question asked at the beginning of our discussion: are American public policies today on the economic side rightly subject to criticism as imperialistic?

In the course of the last few years, the export of private capital has been supplemented—or supplanted—by the export of *public* capital. Should such capital export fall under moral condemnation? Was the Marshall Plan reprehensible, as our enemies asserted? I do not see how this question can be answered in the affirmative. True, the American grants of aid to European states implied some concession to American opinion on the part of the receiving states. But how could aid be given on any other terms? Is it not reasonable to ask assurances that it be used for the ends for which it is granted, and in a way that will assist the purposes we have in view? When and by what government would aid be given on any other basis? Is there any evidence that majority opinion in the countries aided, fully and freely expressed, regarded the conditions as unduly onerous? Was the national independence of the states concerned seriously curtailed? Was there any great national revolt against the acceptance of our support? Or is it not more likely that Europeans would say of the Marshall Plan, as Churchill did of Lend-Lease, that it was one of the most unsordid acts in history? It is a distortion of terms to apply the word "imperialism" to such an expedient of European recovery as the Marshall Plan.

What applies to the Marshall Plan applies no less to the military and economic grants made by the American government in various parts of the world. It is elementary that these grants should be something more than mere handouts; their beneficiaries can hardly object to provisions which guard against misuse and ensure the attainment of the purpose the United States has in view. It would indeed be a verbal topsy-turvydom in which arrangements freely entered into for the defense or economic stimulation of other states were represented as "imperialism." The fact that some confused minds accept such a definition proves nothing, except the melancholy ability of some of us to accept the illogical.

There is, finally, the vague term "moral imperialism." It is difficult to invest this phrase with exact content. Perhaps the nearest we can come to it is to deal with the problem of recognition. Historically, the American government has sometimes abstained from recognition of regimes whose moral origins it did not approve. The Central American treaties of 1907, negotiated with the encouragement of the State Department, called for the withholding of recognition of Revolutionary regimes until free elections had taken place. Woodrow Wilson declined to recognize the Mexican ruler, Victoriano Huerta, because his rise to power was stained by the murder of his enemies. The Roosevelt administration refused to deal in 1944 with an Argentine government it did not believe representative of the Argentine people. The Soviet regime was recognized by the United States only in 1933, nearly sixteen years after its establishment. Other examples might be cited, including the consistent refusal of Washington to acknowledge the Chinese government at Peiping. Such pressure, it may be conceded, has in most instances been rather futile. Indeed, the practice of withholding recognition on moral grounds has been very largely abandoned. Only in the case of Communist China, which is still technically at war with the United States and which has violated many of the terms entered into for a truce in Korea, has the American government steadily refused to enter into formal relations with a regime of which it disapproves. Whatever one may think of the practice, the record of experience does not suggest that this type of moral imperialism constitutes a serious danger to the integrity or the continuance or the effective international action of the state against which it is directed.

In this review of American policy, it is not pretended that the record is above reproach. In the Philippines sharp hostilities preceded the establishment of American rule. In Haiti, Santo Domingo, and Nicaragua there was substantial local resistance to American authority. Our relations with Cuba are not without blemish. But, nonetheless, by the comparative standard, the United States has no reason to apologize for its record.

One other aspect of the problem of imperialism may be mentioned. What has been the attitude of the United States towards the imperialism of others? Has it been the stalwart defender of rule imposed from above, or has it been the champion of wider freedom? On the whole, it has been the latter. It favored the independence of India and of Indonesia. It has not been unfriendly to the establishment of the new and independent states of Africa. Its influence was exerted to encourage British withdrawal from Egypt. On occasion, caught between the interests of its European allies and its sympathy with self-determination, it has not always spoken so clearly. Yet its own example pleads strongly in its behalf. Its own imperialist impulse came late and, as we have seen, was soon exhausted. It does not lie with the Soviet Union to direct reproaches against it.

Powerful nations, by the ineluctable necessities of international politics, almost inevitably make their power felt. The question is, how do they exert it? Do they exert it with utter ruthlessness, as did Hitlerian Germany? Do they assert the universal validity of the principles on which their own governments are founded, as the Russian government does today? Do they intrigue to subvert regimes which they do not find attractive? Or are they led towards tolerance, as the United States has clearly been in accepting the doctrine of non-intervention in Latin America, and as it has shown in its attitude towards other forms of government in various parts of the world, until some issue of national security was involved? Have they used their economic power harshly, or towards good ends? The answer to those questions suggests that, in the moderation that ought to go with strength, the United States on the whole has played and is playing a creditable role.

Moralism-Legalism

GEORGE F. KENNAN

After many years of official duty in the Foreign Service of the United States, it fell to me to bear a share of the responsibility for forming the foreign policy of the United States in the difficult years following World War II. The Policy Planning Staff—it was my duty to set up this office and direct it through the first years of its existence—was the first regular office of the Department of State to be charged in our time with looking at problems from the standpoint of the totality of American national interest, as distinct from a single portion of it. People working in this institutional framework soon became conscious of the lack of any general agreement, both within and without our government, on the basic concepts underlying the conduct of the external relations of the United States.

It was this realization of the lack of an adequately stated and widely accepted theoretical foundation to underpin the conduct of our external relations which aroused my curiosity about the concepts by which our statesmen had been guided in recent decades. After all, the novel and grave problems with which we were forced to deal seemed in large measure to be the products of the outcome of these past two world wars. The rhythm of international events is such that the turn of the century seemed a suitable starting point for an examination of American diplomacy and its relation to these two great cycles of violence. One and a half decades elapsed between the conclusion of the war with Spain and the dispatch of the first "Open Door" notes, on the one hand, and the outbreak of World War I, on the other. Measured against what we know of the relationships between cause and effect in the great matters of international life, this is a respectable period of time and one in which the influence of a country as powerful as the United States of that day could, if exerted consistently and with determination, have affected perceptibly the course of world affairs. The same was plainly true of the interval between the two world wars. By 1900 we were generally aware that our power had world-wide significance and that we could be affected by events far afield; from that time on our interests were constantly involved in important ways with such events.

By what concepts were our statesmen animated in their efforts to meet these new problems? What assumptions had they made concerning the basic purposes of this country in the field of foreign policy? What was it they felt they were trying to achieve? And were these concepts, in the light of retrospect, appropriate and effective ones? Did they reflect some deeper understanding of the relationship of American democracy to its world environment—something which we, perhaps, had forgotten but ought to resurrect and place again at the foundation of our conduct? Or had they been inadequate and superficial all along? . . .

It is surely a curious characteristic of democracy: this amazing ability to shift

George F. Kennan, *American Diplomacy, 1900–1950* (Chicago: University of Chicago Press, 1951), pp. v–vi, 65–66, 95–101. Copyright © 1951 by The University of Chicago Press.

gears overnight in one's ideological attitudes, depending on whether one considers one's self at war or at peace. Day before yesterday, let us say, the issues at stake between ourselves and another power were not worth the life of a single American boy. Today, nothing else counts at all; our cause is holy; the cost is no consideration; violence must know no limitations short of unconditional surrender.

Now I know the answer to this one. A democracy is peace-loving. It does not like to go to war. It is slow to rise to provocation. When it has once been provoked to the point where it must grasp the sword, it does not easily forgive its adversary for having produced this situation. The fact of the provocation then becomes itself the issue. Democracy fights in anger—it fights for the very reason that it was forced to go to war. It fights to punish the power that was rash enough and hostile enough to provoke it—to teach that power a lesson it will not forget, to prevent the thing from happening again. Such a war must be carried to the bitter end.

This is true enough, and, if nations could afford to operate in the moral climate of individual ethics, it would be understandable and acceptable. But I sometimes wonder whether in this respect a democracy is not uncomfortably similar to one of those prehistoric monsters with a body as long as this room and a brain the size of a pin: he lies there in his comfortable primeval mud and pays little attention to his environment; he is slow to wrath—in fact, you practically have to whack his tail off to make him aware that his interests are being disturbed; but, once he grasps this, he lays about him with such blind determination that he not only destroys his adversary but largely wrecks his native habitat. You wonder whether it would not have been wiser for him to have taken a little more interest in what was going on at an earlier date and to have seen whether he could not have prevented some of these situations from arising instead of proceeding from an undiscriminating indifference to a holy wrath equally undiscriminating. . . .

As you have no doubt surmised, I see the most serious fault of our past policy formulation to lie in something that I might call the legalistic-moralistic approach to international problems. This approach runs like a red skein through our foreign policy of the last fifty years. It has in it something of the old emphasis on arbitration treaties, something of the Hague Conferences and schemes for universal disarmament, something of the more ambitious American concepts of the role of international law, something of the League of Nations and the United Nations, something of the Kellogg Pact, something of the idea of a universal "Article 51" pact, something of the belief in World Law and World Government. But it is none of these, entirely. Let me try to describe it.

It is the belief that it should be possible to suppress the chaotic and dangerous aspirations of governments in the international field by the acceptance of some system of legal rules and restraints. This belief undoubtedly represents in part an attempt to transpose the Anglo-Saxon concept of individual law into the international field and to make it applicable to governments as it is applicable here at home to individuals. It must also stem in part from the memory of the origin of our own political system—from the recollection that we were able, through acceptance of a common institutional and juridical framework, to reduce to harmless dimensions the conflicts of interest and aspiration among the original thirteen colonies and to bring them all into an ordered and peaceful relationship with one another. Remembering this, people are unable to understand that what might have been possible for the thirteen colonies in a given set of circumstances might not be possible in the wider international field.

It is the essence of this belief that, instead of taking the awkward conflicts of national interest and dealing with them on their merits with a view to finding the solutions least unsettling to the stability of international life, it would be better to find some formal criteria of a juridical nature by which the permissible behavior of states could be defined. There would then be judicial entities competent to measure the actions of governments against these criteria and to decide when their behavior was acceptable and when unacceptable. Behind all this, of course, lies the American assumption that the things for which other peoples in this world are apt to contend are for the most part neither creditable nor important and might justly be expected to take second place behind the desirability of an orderly world, untroubled by international violence. To the American mind, it is implausible that people should have positive aspirations, and ones that they regard as legitimate, more important to them than the peacefulness and orderliness of international life. From this standpoint, it is not apparent why other peoples should not join us in accepting the rules of the game in international politics, just as we accept such rules in the competition of sport in order that the game may not become too cruel and too destructive and may not assume an importance we did not mean it to have.

If they were to do this, the reasoning runs, then the troublesome and chaotic manifestations of the national ego could be contained and rendered either unsubstantial or subject to easy disposal by some method familiar and comprehensible to our American usage. Departing from this background, the mind of American statesmanship, stemming as it does in so large a part from the legal profession in our country, gropes with unfailing persistence for some institutional framework which would be capable of fulfilling this function.

I cannot undertake in this short lecture to deal exhaustively with this thesis or to point out all the elements of unsoundness which I feel it contains. But some of its more outstanding weaknesses are worthy of mention.

In the first place, the idea of the subordination of a large number of states to an international juridical regime, limiting their possibilities for aggression and injury to other states, implies that these are all states like our own, reasonably content with their international borders and status, at least to the extent that they would be willing to refrain from pressing for change without international agreement. Actually, this has generally been true only of a portion of international society. We tend to underestimate the violence of national maladjustments and discontents elsewhere in the world if we think that they would always appear to other people as less important than the preservation of the juridical tidiness of international life.

Second, while this concept is often associated with a revolt against nationalism, it is a curious thing that it actually tends to confer upon the concept of nationality and national sovereignty an absolute value it did not have before. The very principle of "one government, one vote," regardless of physical or political differences between states, glorifies the concept of national sovereignty and makes it the exclusive form of participation in international life. It envisages a world composed exclusively of sovereign national states with a full equality of status. In doing this, it ignores the tremendous variations in the firmness and soundness of national divisions: the fact that the origins of state borders and national personalities were in many instances fortuitous or at least poorly related to realities. It also ignores the law of change. The national state pattern is not, should not be, and cannot be a fixed and static thing. By nature, it is an unstable phenomenon in a constant state of change and flux. History has shown that the will and the capacity of individual peoples to contribute to their world environment is constantly changing. It is only logical that the organizational forms (and what else are such things as borders and governments?) should change with them. The function of a system of international relationships is not to inhibit this process of change by imposing a legal strait jacket upon it but rather to facilitate it: to ease its transitions, to temper the asperities to which it often leads, to isolate and moderate the conflicts to which it gives rise, and to see that these conflicts do not assume forms too unsettling for international life in general. But this is a task for diplomacy, in the most old-fashioned sense of the term. For this, law is too abstract, too inflexible, too hard to adjust to the demands of the unpredictable and the unexpected.

By the same token, the American concept of world law ignores those means of international offense—those means of the projection of power and coercion over other peoples—which by-pass institutional forms entirely or even exploit them against themselves: such things as ideological attack, intimidation, penetration, and disguised seizure of the institutional paraphernalia of national sovereignty. It ignores, in other words, the device of the puppet state and the set of techniques by which states can be converted into puppets with no formal violation of, or challenge to, the outward attributes of their sovereignty and their independence.

This is one of the things that have caused the peoples of the satellite countries of eastern Europe to look with a certain tinge of bitterness on the United Nations. The organization failed so completely to save them from domination by a great neighboring country, a domination no less invidious by virtue of the fact that it came into being by processes we could not call "aggression." And there is indeed some justification for their feeling, because the legalistic approach to international affairs ignores in general the international significance of political problems and the deeper sources of international instability. It assumes that civil wars will remain civil and not grow into international wars. It assumes the ability of each people to solve its own internal political problems in a manner not provocative of its international environment. It assumes that each nation will always be able to construct a government qualified to speak for it and cast its vote in the international arena and that this government will be acceptable to the rest of the international community in this capacity. It assumes, in other words, that domestic issues will not become international issues and that the world community will not be put in the position of having to make choices between rival claimants for power within the confines of the individual state.

Finally, this legalistic approach to international relations is faulty in its assumptions concerning the possibility of sanctions against offenses and violations. In general, it looks to collective action to provide such sanction against the bad behavior of states. In doing so, it forgets the limitations on the effectiveness of military coalition. It forgets that, as a circle of military associates widens in any conceivable political-military venture, the theoretical total of available military strength may increase, but only at the cost of compactness and ease of control. And the wider a coalition becomes, the more difficult it becomes to retain political unity and general agreement on the purposes and effects of what is being done. As we are seeing in the case of Korea, joint military operations against an aggressor have a different meaning for each participant and raise specific political issues for each one which are extraneous to the action in question and affect many other facets of international life. The wider the circle of military associates, the more cumbersome the problem of political control over their actions, and the more circumscribed the least common denominator of agreement. This law of diminishing returns lies so heavily on the possibilities for multilateral military action that it makes it doubtful whether the participation of smaller states can really add very much to the ability of the great powers to assure stability of international life. And this is tremendously important, for it brings us back to the realization that even under a system of world law the sanction against destructive international behavior might continue to rest basically, as it has in the past, on the alliances and relationships among the great powers themselves. There might be a state, or perhaps more than one state, which all the rest of the world community together could not successfully coerce into following a line of action to which it was violently averse. And if this is true, where are we? It seems to me that we are right back in the realm of the forgotten art of diplomacy from which we have spent fifty years trying to escape.

These, then, are some of the theoretical deficiencies that appear to me to be inherent in the legalistic approach to international affairs. But there is a greater deficiency still that I should like to mention before I close. That is the inevitable association of legalistic ideas with moralistic ones: the carrying-over into the affairs of states of the concepts of right and wrong, the assumption that state behavior is a fit subject for moral judgment. Whoever says there is a law must of course be indignant against the lawbreaker and feel a moral superiority to him. And when such indignation spills over into military contest, it knows no bounds short of the reduction of the law-breaker to the point of complete submissiveness—namely, unconditional surrender. It is a curious thing, but it is true, that the legalistic approach to world affairs, rooted as it unquestionably is in a desire to do away with war and violence, makes violence more enduring, more terrible, and more destructive to political stability than did the older motives of national interest. A war fought in the name of high moral principle finds no early end short of some form of total domination.

The Open Door Policy

WILLIAM APPLEMAN WILLIAMS

A re-examination of the history of twentieth-century American foreign relations
(and the relationship between foreign policy and the domestic economy) offers
the most promising approach to . . . a reconsideration of our assumptions. First,
we thereby confront directly what happened. We learn the ideas and the actions
of the men who made or influenced policy, and the consequences of those
events at home and abroad. Second, at the end of such a review of the past,
we return to the present better informed. Finally, that increased knowledge
and understanding may help us to muster the nerve to act in ways that can
transform the tragedy into a new beginning.

For history is a way of learning, of getting closer to the truth. It is only by
abandoning the clichés that we can even define the tragedy. When we have
done that, we will no longer be merely acquiescing in the deadly inertia of the
past. We will have taken the first and vital step in making history. Such a reexamination of history must be based upon a searching review of the way
America has defined its own problems and objectives, and its relationship
with the rest of the world. The reason for this is simple: realism goes nowhere
unless it starts at home. Combined with a fresh look at Soviet behavior, such
an understanding of American policy should help in the effort to outline new
programs and policies designed to bring America's ideals and practical objectives closer to realization.

In the realm of ideas and ideals, American policy is guided by three conceptions. One is the warm, generous, humanitarian impulse to help other people
solve their problems. A second is the principle of self-determination applied at
the international level, which asserts the right of every society to establish its
own goals or objectives, and to realize them internally through the means it
decides are appropriate. These two ideas can be reconciled; indeed, they com-
plement each other to an extensive degree. But the third idea entertained by
many Americans is one which insists that other people cannot *really* solve their
problems and improve their lives unless they go about it in the same way as the
United States.

This feeling is not peculiar to Americans, for all other peoples reveal some
degree of the same attitude toward the rest of the world. But the full scope and
intensity of the American version is clearly revealed in the blunt remark of
former Secretary of State Dean G. Acheson. He phrased it this way in explaining and defending the American program of foreign aid as it was being evolved
shortly after the end of World War II: "We are willing to help people who
believe the way we do, to continue to live the way they want to live."

This insistence that other people ought to copy America contradicts the
humanitarian urge to help them and the idea that they have the right to make

Specified excerpts from pp. 9–11, 49–50, 53–58, 303–308 in *The Tragedy of American
Diplomacy* by William Appleman Williams (Thomas Y. Crowell Company). Copyright
© 1959 by William Appleman Williams. Reprinted by permission of Harper & Row,
Publishers, Inc.

such key decisions for themselves. In some cases, the American way of doing things simply does not work for the other people. In another instance it may be satisfactory, but the other society may prefer to do it in a different way that produces equally good results—perhaps even better ones. But even if the American way were the *only* effective approach, the act of forcing it upon the other society—and economic and political pressure are forms of force— violates the idea of self-determination. It also angers the other society and makes it even less apt to accept the American suggestion on its own merits. Hence it is neither very effective nor very idealistic to try to help other people by insisting from the outset that they follow closely the lead and the example of the United States on all central and vital matters.

The same kind of difficulty arises in connection with the economic side of American foreign policy. The United States needs raw materials and other goods and services from foreign countries, just as it needs to sell some of its own goods and services to them. It might be able literally to isolate itself and survive, but that is not the issue. Not even the isolationists of the late 1920's and early 1930's advocated that kind of foreign policy. The vital question concerns instead the way in which America gets what it needs and exports what it wants to sell.

Most Americans consider that trade supplies the answer to this problem. But trade is defined as the exchange of goods and services between producers dealing with each other in as open a market as it is possible to create, and doing this without one of them being so beholden to the other that he cannot bargain in a meaningful and effective way. Trade is not defined by the transfer of goods and services under conditions established and controlled largely by one of the parties.

Here is a primary source of America's troubles in its economic relations with the rest of the world. For in expanding its own economic system through- out much of the world, America has made it very difficult for other nations to retain any economic independence. This is particularly true in connection with raw materials. Saudi Arabia, for example, is not an independent oil pro- ducer. Its oil fields are an integrated and controlled part of the American oil industry. But a very similar, if often less dramatic, kind of relationship also develops in manufacturing industries. This is the case in countries where estab- lished economic systems are outmoded or lethargic, as well as in the new, poor nations that are just beginning to industrialize. American corporations exercise very extensive authority, and even commanding power, in the political economy of such nations.

Unfortunately, there is an even more troublesome factor in the economic aspect of American foreign policy. That is the firm conviction, even dogmatic belief, that America's *domestic* well-being depends upon such sustained, ever- increasing overseas economic expansion. Here is a convergence of economic practice with intellectual analysis and emotional involvement that creates a very powerful and dangerous propensity to define the essentials of American welfare in terms of activities outside the United States.

It is dangerous for two reasons. First, it leads to an indifference toward, or a neglect of, internal developments which are nevertheless of primary importance. And second, this strong tendency to externalize the sources or causes of good things leads naturally enough to an even greater inclination to explain the lack of the good life by blaming it on foreign individuals, groups, and nations. This kind of externalizing evil serves not only to antagonize the outsiders, but further intensifies the American determination to make them over in the proper manner or simply push them out of the way.

The over-all result of these considerations is that America's humanitarian urge to assist other peoples is undercut—even subverted—by the way it goes about helping them. Other societies come to feel that American policy causes them to lose their economic, political, and even psychological independence. . . .

In summation, the true nature and full significance of the Open Door Policy can only be grasped when its four essential features are fully understood.

First: it was neither a military strategy nor a traditional balance-of-power policy. *It was conceived and designed to win the victories without the wars.* In a truly perceptive and even noble sense, the makers of the Open Door Policy understood that war represented the failure of policy. Hence it is irrelevant to criticize the Open Door Policy for not emphasizing, or not producing, extensive military readiness.

Second: it was derived from the proposition that America's overwhelming economic power would cast the economy and the politics of the poorer, weaker, underdeveloped countries in a pro-American mold. American leaders assumed the opposition of one or many industrialized rivals. Over a period of two generations the policy failed because some of those competitors, among them Japan and Germany, chose to resort to force when they concluded (on solid grounds) that the Open Door Policy was working only too well; and because various groups inside the weaker countries such as China and Cuba decided that America's extensive influence in and upon their societies was harmful to their specific and general welfare.

Third (and clearly related to the second point): the policy was neither legalistic nor moralistic in the sense that those criticisms are usually offered. It was extremely hard-headed and practical. In some respects, at any rate, it was the most impressive intellectual achievement in the area of public policy since the generation of the Founding Fathers.

Fourth: unless and until it, and its underlying *Weltanschauung,* were modified to deal with its own consequences, the policy was certain to produce foreign policy crises that would become increasingly severe.

Once these factors are understood, it becomes useful to explore the way that ideological and moralistic elements became integrated with the fundamentally secular and economic nature of the Open Door Policy. The addition of those ingredients served to create a kind of expansionism that aimed at the marketplace of the mind and the polls as well as of the pocketbook.

Taken up by President Theodore Roosevelt and his successors, the philosophy and practice of secular empire that was embodied in the Open Door Notes became the central feature of American foreign policy in the twentieth century. American economic power gushed into some underdeveloped areas within a decade and into many others within a generation. It also seeped, then trickled, and finally flooded into the more developed nations and their colonies until, by 1939, America's economic expansion encompassed the globe. And by that time the regions where America's position was not extensively developed were precisely the areas in which the United States manifested a determination to retain and expand its exploratory operations—or to enter in force for the first time.

Throughout these same years, the rise of a new crusading spirit in American diplomacy contributed an outward thrust of its own and reinforced the secular expansion. This righteous enthusiasm was both secular, emphasizing political and social ideology, and religious, stressing the virtues (and necessities) of Protestant Christianity. In essence, this twentieth-century Manifest Destiny was identical with the earlier phenomenon of the same name.

Americans assumed a posture of moral and ideological superiority at an early date. Despite the persistence of the Puritan tradition, however, this assertiveness took predominantly secular forms. Supernatural authority was invoked to explain and account for the steady enlargement of the United States, but the justifications for expansion were generally based on standards derived from this world. The phrase "Manifest Destiny," for example, symbolized the assertion that God was on America's side rather than the more modest claim that the country had joined the legions of the Lord. As that logic implied, the argument was that America was the "most progressive" society whose citizens made "proper use of the soil." For these and similar reasons, it was added, the laws of "political gravitation" would bring many minor peoples into the American system.

Though it had appeared as early as the eve of the American Revolution, the assertion that the expansion of the United States "extended the area of freedom" gained general currency after the War of 1812. President Andrew Jackson seems to have coined the phrase, with his wildcatting intellectual supporters making many variations. One of the more persuasive and popular, which won many converts during and after the war with Mexico, stressed America's responsibility to extend its authority over "semi-barbarous people." By thus taking up the duty of "regeneration and civilization," America could perform the noble work of teaching inferiors to appreciate the blessings they already enjoyed but were inclined to overlook. In turn, this would prepare them for the better days to follow under America's benevolent leadership.

Near the end of the century, American missionaries and domestic religious leaders began to impart a more theological tone to this crusading fervor. This resulted in part from the effort by the clergy to marry traditional Christianity with the new doctrine of evolution and in that way adjust their theology to the latest revelations, and also to sustain their influence in the age of science. Josiah Strong was an innovator of that kind. As a Congregationalist minister in whom the frontier experience and outlook exercised an important influence, Strong concluded that the theory of evolution only substantiated the doctrine of predestination. America had been hand-picked by the Lord to lead the Anglo-Saxons in transforming the world. "It would seem," he explained with reference to the American Indians and other benighted peoples, "as if these inferior tribes were only precursors of a superior race, voices in the wilderness crying: Prepare ye the way of the Lord."

Ever since New England ministers had accepted the challenge of saving the heathens of Hawaii, a crusade that began in the eighteenth century, American missionaries had been noticeably concerned about Asia—and in particular China. As the Reverend Hudson Taylor explained in 1894, there was "a great Niagara of souls passing into the dark in China." Though they never lost faith, a growing number of missionaries did get discouraged enough to question whether hell-fire sermons on the dangers of damnation were an approach sufficient unto the need. Some thought fondly of the sword of righteousness, and toyed with the idea of a "Society for the Diffusion of Cannon Balls." That kind of crusade was never organized, but the missionaries did begin in the 1890's to demand formal support and protection from the American Government.

This request, while never acted upon with the same vigor as those from business groups, did receive sympathetic and favorable consideration. For one thing, the religious stake in China was significant: America had over 500 missionaries in that country, and their schools claimed a total student body of nearly 17,000 Chinese. Many churches had also supported intervention in Cuba. But the most important factor was the way that the missionary movement began to evolve an approach that offered direct support to secular expansion.

Missionaries had always tended to operate on an assumption quite similar to the frontier thesis. "Missionaries are an absolute necessity," explained the Reverend Henry Van Dyke of Princeton in 1896, "not only for the conversion of the heathen, but also, and much more, for the preservation of the Church. Christianity is a religion that will not keep." Religious leaders began to link the missionary movement with economic expansion in what the Reverend Francis E. Clark of the Christian Endeavor organization called "the widening of our empire." The Board of Foreign Missions also welcomed such expansion as "an ally."

Then, beginning in the mid-1890's, the missionaries began to change their basic strategy in a way that greatly encouraged such liaison with secular expansionists. Shifting from an emphasis on the horrors of hell to a concern with practical reform as the lever of conversion, they increasingly stressed the need to remake the underdeveloped societies. Naturally enough, they were to be reformed in the image of the United States. Such changes would lead to regeneration identified with Christianity and witnesses for the Lord would accordingly increase.

Not only did this program mesh with the idea of American secular influence (how else were the reforms to be initiated?), but it was very similar to the argument that American expansion was justified because it created more progressive societies. Missionaries came to sound more and more like political leaders, who were themselves submerging their domestic ideological differences at the water's edge in a general agreement on expansion as a reform movement.

The domestic reformer La Follette offers an excellent example of this convergence of economic and ideological expansion that took place across political lines. He approved taking the Philippines because it would enable America "to conquer [its] rightful share of that great market now opening [in China] for the world's commerce." Expansion was also justified because the United States had a "bounden *duty* to establish and *maintain* stable government" in the islands. Pointing out that from the beginning "the policy of this government has been to expand," La Follette justified it on the grounds that "it has *made men free.*" Thus, he concluded, "we can legally and morally reserve unto ourselves perpetual commercial advantages of priceless value to our foreign trade for all time to come" by taking the Philippines.

Theodore Roosevelt's outlook reveals an even more significant aspect of this progressive integration of secular and ideological expansionism. His concern for economic expansion was complemented by an urge to extend Anglo-Saxon ideas, practices, and virtues throughout the world. Just as his Square Deal program centered on the idea of responsible leaders using the national government to regulate and moderate industrial society at home, so did his international outlook revolve around the idea of American supremacy being used to define and promote the interests of "collective civilization."

Thus it was necessary, he warned in his Presidential Message of December 1901, to exercise restraint in dealing with the large corporations. "Business concerns which have the largest means at their disposal . . . take the lead in the strife for commercial supremacy among the nations of the world. America has only just begun to assume the commanding position in the international business world which we believe will more and more be hers. It is of the utmost importance that this position be not jeopardized, especially at a time when the overflowing abundance of our own natural resources and the skill, business energy, and mechanical aptitude of our people make foreign markets essential."

Roosevelt integrated that kind of expansion with ideological considerations and imperatives to create an all-inclusive logic and set of responsibilities which made peace itself the consequence of empire. In his mind, at any rate, it was America's "duty toward the people living in barbarism to see that they are freed from their chains, and we can free them only by destroying barbarism itself." Thus, he concluded, "peace cannot be had until the civilized nations have expanded in some shape over the barbarous nations."

The inherent requirements of economic expansion coincided with such religious, racist, and reformist drives to remake the world. The reason for this is not difficult to perceive. As they existed, the underdeveloped countries were poor, particularistic, and bound by traditions which handicapped business enterprise. They were not organized to link up with the modern industrial system in a practical and efficient manner. It was economically necessary to change them *in certain ways and to a limited degree* if the fruits of expansion were to be harvested. As with the missionaries, therefore, the economic and political leaders of the country decided that what was good for Americans was also good for foreigners. Humanitarian concern was thus reinforced by hard-headed economic requirements.

The administrations of Theodore Roosevelt understood this relationship between economic expansion and overseas reform, and explicitly integrated it into the strategy of the Open Door Policy. It was often commented upon in dispatches and policy statements concerning China and Latin America. In his famous Corollary to the Monroe Doctrine, for example, Roosevelt (who thought of the Open Door Policy as the Monroe Doctrine for Asia) stressed the need for reforms and asserted the right and the obligation of the United States to see that they were made—and honored. . . .

America can neither take its place in nor make its contribution to the world community until it believes and demonstrates that it can sustain prosperity and democracy without recourse to open-door imperial expansion. The central issue of the mid-twentieth century is how to sustain democracy and prosperity without imperial expansion and the conflicts it engenders. The reason is obvious: the sparks from those collisions now fall into a nuclear tinderbox. It is all very well to converse bravely, seriously, and learnedly about surviving such a holocaust, but that is like sitting around the evening fire talking about what to do in the morning after the horse has been stolen instead of discussing ways and means of barring the barn door that night.

It is true that there are no completely foolproof locks, but it does not follow from that quite mundane observation that the risks of using the ones we have are greater than the risks and costs of getting along without the horse—or of buying another one. Yet this is precisely what we are doing when we give up on disarmament on the grounds that it cannot be 100 per cent guaranteed in advance, and turn instead to discussions of how to intimidate the Soviets with superweapons, or of how to rebuild the United States after a nuclear war.

One of the most disturbing features of international affairs between 1952 and 1962 was the extent to which it was the Russians, rather than the Americans, who sensed and appreciated this essential aspect of reality. For this is the real meaning of the Soviet doctrine of coexistence. They are proposing that the existing political and military balance be accepted as the foundation of world politics for an indefinite period. It is ironic, but in a deadly way, that it has been the United States and China which have refused to agree to this proposition.

The American nonrecognition of Mao Tse-tung's government has served in this sense to mask an unspoken entente between them on this crucial point of policy. There is not even any conscious thought—let alone any conspiracy—involved on the American side of this agreement. For that matter, American policy-makers seem wholly deaf and unconscious to the point despite the very broad hints that have been shouted from the Kremlin. As far as Washington is concerned, it could in this respect be called the best-kept secret treaty in the nation's entire history. The only way that the United States can break free of this entangling alliance with the Red Chinese is by accepting the Soviet doctrine of coexistence.

Americans must do this, not only to make it possible to slow down the dangerous momentum of the cold war toward thermonuclear war, not only to strengthen the advocates of coexistence in China, but even more in order that Americans themselves can apply their intelligence and humanitarianism to the very real and serious problems in the United States. This proposal has nothing to do with reviving and embracing either the theory or the practice of isolationism. There is no longer any question of whether or not we shall have relations with the rest of the world; there is the far more significant one of the kind of relations we shall have. That problem cannot be discussed intelligently to any relevant conclusions so long as it is defined in the narrow terms of the existing approach. We need to ask questions about the very *nature* of the traditional foreign policy of the United States, not questions concerning merely the *means* of putting it into operation. The right kind of questions are admittedly those that make us squirm. But isn't it time to find out whether we can still take that kind of question?

Isn't it time to stop defining trade as the control of markets for our surplus products and control of raw materials for our factories? Isn't it time to stop depending so narrowly—in our thinking as well as in our practice—upon an informal empire for our well-being and welfare?

Isn't it time to ask ourselves if we are really so unimaginative that we have to have a frontier in the form of an informal empire in order to have democracy and prosperity at home? Isn't it time to say that we can make American society function even better on the basis of equitable relationships with other people?

Isn't it time to stop defining trade as a weapon against other people with whom we have disagreements? Isn't it time to start thinking of trade as a means to moderate and alleviate those tensions—and to improve the life of the other people?

Isn't it time to stop trying to expand our exports on the grounds that such a campaign will make foreigners foot the bill for our military security? Isn't it time instead to concern ourselves with a concerted effort to halt and then cancel the armaments race?

Isn't it time to stop saying that all the evil in the world resides in the Soviet Union and other communist countries? Isn't it time to admit that there is good as well as evil in those societies, and set about to help increase the amount of good?

Isn't it time to admit that our own intelligence reports mean that the Russians have been following a defensive policy in nuclear weapons? Isn't it time to take advantage of that attitude on their part, break out of our neurosis about a Pearl Harbor attack, and go on to negotiate an arms control measure?

Isn't it time to admit, in short, that we can avoid living with communist countries only by embarking upon a program that will kill millions of human beings? Isn't it time, therefore, to evolve and adopt a program that will encourage and enable the communist countries to move in the direction of their own utopian vision of the good society as we endeavor to move in accordance with our own ideals?

For beyond acceptance of coexistence, the United States must embark upon a patient and concerted effort to establish and maintain by continued negotiation and development a *modus vivendi* with the Soviet Union, the People's Republic of China, and their allies. To this effort, economic agreements, involving normal credits and loans and a continuing increase of trade in consumer items and goods needed for general economic development, are basic. Such an approach will facilitate two processes essential to continued peace. First, it will open the way for continued reform within communist countries. That will make it easier, secondly, for the United States to allocate its aid and assistance to other nations through the appropriate agencies of the United Nations. Future requests to the United States for aid should be referred to such committees of the United Nations for mutual discussion and decision. If approved, such grants should be administered by the United Nations. For if America's objective is the improvement of life throughout the world, then there is no better way to speed that process. Such a policy would also strengthen America's own position. For it is true, as Thucydides is reputed to have remarked, that the greatest exercise of power lies in its restraint.

Once freed from its myopic concentration on the cold war, the United States could come to grips with the central problem of reordering its own society so that it functions through such a balanced relationship with the rest of the world, and so that the labor and leisure of its own citizens are invested with creative meaning and purpose. A new debate over the first principles and practices of government and economics is long overdue, and a statement of a twentieth-century political economy comparable to *The Federalist* papers would do more to enhance America's role in the world than any number of rockets and satellites. The configuration of the world of outer space will be decided on the cool green hills of earth long before the first colonizing spaceships blast free of the atmosphere.

Having structured a creative response to the issue of democracy and prosperity at home, the United States could again devote a greater share of its attention and energy to the world scene. Its revamped foreign policy would be geared to helping other peoples achieve their own aspirations in their own way. The essence of such a foreign policy would be an open door for revolutions. Having come to terms with themselves—having achieved maturity—Americans could exhibit the self-discipline necessary to let other peoples come to terms with themselves. Having realized that "self-righteousness is the hallmark of inner guilt," Americans would no longer find it necessary to embark upon crusades to save others.

In this fashion, and through a policy of an open door for revolutions, Americans would be able to cope with the many as yet unknown revolutions that are dependent upon peace for their conception and maturation. Only in this way can either the general or the specific tragedy of American diplomacy be transcended in a creative, peaceful manner. Otherwise the next Cuba may very well be the last. For unless the existing attitudes and policies are changed, another Cuba will clearly be dealt with through military intervention involving American troops. And that—even without direct Soviet or Chinese retaliation in kind—could insure the final catastrophe.

Of course, such an American intervention would have profound and reactionary consequences in Russia and China, and hence upon the relationship between them. The result would be a further acceleration of the already very serious momentum toward thermonuclear war. It would very probably, and whatever the outcome of the specific intervention by the United States, produce an increasing loss of control on both sides.

The way to transcend tragedy is to reconcile the contrasting truths which define the tragedy. Left instead to run out the string of their own logic, as they were and did in Cuba, the clashing truths will sooner rather than later kindle a global nuclear fire. To transcend tragedy requires the nerve to fail. But a positive effort to transcend the cold war would very probably carry the United States and the world on into an era of peace and creative human endeavor.

For the nerve to fail has nothing at all to do with blustering and self-righteous crusades up to or past the edge of violence. It is instead the kind of quiet confidence that comes with and from accepting limits, and a concurrent understanding that accepting limits does not mean the end of existence itself or of the possibility of a creative life. For Americans, the nerve to fail is in a real sense the nerve to say—and mean—that we no longer need what Turner called "the gate of escape" provided by the frontier. It is only in adolescence or senility that human beings manifest a compulsive drive to play to win. The one does not yet know, and the other has forgotten, that what counts is how the game is played. It would actually be pathetic rather than tragic if the United States jumped from childhood to old age without ever having matured. Yet that is precisely what it will do unless it sloughs off the ideology of the Open Door Policy and steps forth to open the door to the revolutions that can transform the material world and the quality of human relationships.

Perhaps it is by now apparent to the reader that there is a basic irony involved in this conception and interpretation of American foreign policy as tragedy. This irony arises from, and is in that sense caused by, the truth that this essay is in two respects written from a radical point of view.

First, it is radical in that it seeks to uncover, describe, and analyze the character and logic of American foreign policy since the 1890's. It is therefore critical in the intellectual sense of not being content with rhetoric and other appearances, and of seeking instead to establish by research and analysis a fuller, more accurate picture of reality.

Second, it is radical in that it concludes from the research and reflection, that American foreign policy must be changed fundamentally in order to sustain the wealth and welfare of the United States on into the future. This essay recommends that the frontier-expansionist explanation of American democracy and prosperity, and the strategy of the Open Door Policy, be abandoned on the grounds that neither any longer bears any significant relation to reality.

FURTHER READING

Richard J. Barnet, *Roots of War* (1972)

William P. Bundy, ed., *Two Hundred Years of American Foreign Policy* (1977)

Edward M. Burns, *The American Idea of Mission* (1957)

Robert Dallek, *The American Style of Foreign Policy: Cultural Politics and Foreign Affairs* (1983)

Charles DeBenedetti, *The Peace Reform in American History* (1980)

Alexander DeConde, ed., *Encyclopedia of American Foreign Policy*, 3 vols. (1978)

Arthur A. Ekirch, Jr., *Ideas, Ideals, and American Diplomacy* (1966)
Lloyd C. Gardner, *Imperial America* (1976)
Norman A. Graebner, *Ideas and Diplomacy* (1964)
Morrell Heald and Lawrence S. Kaplan, *Culture and Diplomacy* (1977)
Akira Iriye, "Culture and Power: International Relations as Intercultural Relations," *Diplomatic History* 3 (1979), 115–128
Gabriel Kolko, *The Roots of American Foreign Policy* (1969)
Walter Lippmann, *U.S. Foreign Policy: Shield of the Republic* (1943)
Frank Merli and Theodore A. Wilson, eds., *Makers of American Diplomacy* (1974)
Hans J. Morgenthau, *In Defense of the National Interest* (1951)
Robert E. Osgood, *Ideals and Self-Interest in America's Foreign Relations* (1953)
Robert A. Packenham, *Liberal America and the Third World* (1973)
Thomas G. Paterson, J. Garry Clifford, and Kenneth J. Hagan, *American Foreign Policy: A History* (1983)
Dexter Perkins, *The Evolution of American Foreign Policy* (1948)
David Potter, *People of Plenty* (1954)
Arthur M. Schlesinger, Jr., *The Imperial Presidency* (1973)
Franz Schurmann, *Logic of World Power* (1974)
Robert Tucker, *The Radical Left and American Foreign Policy* (1971)
E. L. Tuveson, *Redeemer Nation* (1968)
Albert K. Weinberg, *Manifest Destiny* (1935)
Rubin F. Weston, *Racism in U.S. Imperialism* (1972)
William A. Williams, *The Contours of American History* (1966)
———, *Empire as a Way of Life* (1980)

United States Entry into World War I

2

In August 1914 Europe became engulfed in war. Because the United States was a world power and a major trader on the high seas, it was drawn into the catastrophic event. Until early 1917, the Wilson administration struggled to define a policy that would end the bloodshed in Europe, protect America's interests and ideals, and keep the United States out of the conflagration. But in April of that year, President Woodrow Wilson chose war.

Why did Wilson decide to enter the conflict? Most historians point to the German U-boat as the catalyst, but disagree on why the President reacted to submarine warfare the way he did. Did the United States enter the war to ensure its national security? Or its economic well-being? That is, did realism characterize American diplomacy? Or did idealism, a defense of principles and honor, govern Wilson's decision for war? And was American entry inevitable or could Wilson have compromised and followed alternative policies? Finally, how "neutral" was American diplomacy?

DOCUMENTS

The German submarine, the U-boat, loomed as a major obstacle in German-American relations when U-20 sank the British liner *Lusitania* on May 7, 1915, killing 1,198 people, 128 of them Americans. The first document is a firm note that Woodrow Wilson sent to Berlin on May 13 warning it to disavow submarine warfare and to respect the right of Americans to sail on the high seas. The second document, a failed resolution by Senator Thomas P. Gore and Representative Jeff: McLemore, sought in February 1916 to prevent Americans from traveling on armed belligerent vessels, thereby reducing the chances for a clash with the Germans. The third document is the memorandum of a conversation between Secretary of State Robert Lansing and Count Johann-Heinrich Bernstorff, the German Ambassador to the United States. The meeting took place on April 20, 1916, less than a month after the torpedoing of the *Sussex.* The conversation helped produce a German pledge not to attack merchant vessels and liners without warning.

The Zimmermann Telegram of January 1917 caused a serious deterioration of relations between Berlin and Washington. Intended for Mexico, the message was intercepted by the British and turned over to American authorities. Germany now seemed a threat in America's own backyard. When the Germans initiated unrestricted submarine warfare in February, Wilson broke diplomatic relations. On April 2, after the sinking of several vessels, the President asked Congress for a declaration of war. One of the few dissenters in the Senate (the vote for war was 82 to 6) was Robert LaFollette. The senator from Wisconsin, in a speech of April 4, feared the consequences of American entry into the First World War.

The First *Lusitania* Note, 1915

In view of the recent acts of the German authorities in violation of American rights on the high seas which culminated in the torpedoing and sinking of the British steamship *Lusitania* on May 7th, 1915, by which over 100 American citizens lost their lives, it is clearly wise and desirable that the Government of the United States and the Imperial German Government should come to a clear and full understanding as to the grave situation which has resulted.

The sinking of the British passenger steamer *Falaba* by a German submarine on March 28, through which Leon C. Thrasher, an American citizen, was drowned; the attack on April 28 on the American vessel *Cushing* by a German aeroplane; the torpedoing on May 1 of the American vessel *Gulflight* by a German submarine, as a result of which two or more American citizens met their death; and, finally, the torpedoing and sinking of the steamship *Lusitania,* constitute a series of events which the Government of the United States has observed with growing concern, distress, and amazement. . . .

The Government of the United States has been apprised that the Imperial German Government considered themselves to be obliged by the extraordinary circumstances of the present war and the measures adopted by their adversaries in seeking to cut Germany off from all commerce, to adopt methods of retaliation which go much beyond the ordinary methods of warfare at sea, in the proclamation of a war zone from which they have warned neutral ships to keep away. This Government has already taken occasion to inform the Imperial German Government that it cannot admit the adoption of such measures or such a warning of danger to operate as in any degree an abbreviation of the rights of American shipmasters or of American citizens bound on lawful errands as passengers on merchant ships of belligerent nationality; and that it must hold the Imperial German Government to a strict accountability for any infringement of those rights, intentional or incidental. It does not understand the Imperial German Government to question those rights. It assumes, on the contrary, that the Imperial Government accept, as of course, the rule that the lives of noncombatants, whether they be of neutral citizenship or citizens of one of the nations at war, can not lawfully or rightfully be put in jeopardy by the capture or destruction of an unarmed merchantman, and recognize also, as all other nations do, the obligation to take the usual precaution of visit and search to ascertain whether a suspected merchantman is in fact of belligerent nationality or is in fact carrying contraband of war under a neutral flag.

The Government of the United States, therefore, desires to call the attention of the Imperial German Government with the utmost earnestness to the fact that the objection to their present method of attack against the trade of their enemies lies in the practical impossibility of employing submarines in the destruction of commerce without disregarding those rules of fairness, reason, justice, and humanity, which all modern opinion regards as imperative. It is practically impossible for the officers of a submarine to visit a merchantman at sea and examine her papers and cargo. It is practically impossible for them to make a prize of her; and, if they can not put a prize crew on board of her, they can not sink her without leaving her crew and all on board of her to the mercy of the sea in her small boats. These facts it is understood the Imperial German Government frankly admit. We are informed that, in the instances of which we have spoken, time enough for even that poor measure of safety was not given, and in at least two of the cases cited, not so much as a warning was received. Manifestly submarines can not be used against merchantmen, as the last few weeks have shown, without an inevitable violation of many sacred principles of justice and humanity.

American citizens act within their indisputable rights in taking their ships and in traveling wherever their legitimate business calls them upon the high seas, and exercise those rights in what should be the well-justified confidence that their lives will not be endangered by acts done in clear violation of universally acknowledged international obligations, and certainly in the confidence that their own Government will sustain them in the exercise of their rights. . . .

Long acquainted as this Government has been with the character of the Imperial German Government and with the high principles of equity by which they have in the past been actuated and guided, the Government of the United States can not believe that the commanders of the vessels which committed these acts of lawlessness did so except under a misapprehension of the orders issued by the Imperial German naval authorities. It takes it for granted that, at least within the practical possibilities of every such case, the commanders even of submarines were expected to do nothing that would involve the lives of non-combatants or the safety of neutral ships, even at the cost of failing of their object of capture or destruction. It confidently expects, therefore, that the Imperial German Government will disavow the acts of which the Government of the United States complains, that they will make reparation so far as reparation is possible for injuries which are without measure, and that they will take immediate steps to prevent the recurrence of anything so obviously subversive of the principles of warfare for which the Imperial German Government have in the past so wisely and so firmly contended.

The Government and people of the United States look to the Imperial German Government for just, prompt, and enlightened action in this vital matter with the greater confidence because the United States and Germany are bound together not only by special ties of friendship but also by the explicit stipulations of the treaty of 1828 between the United States and the Kingdom of Prussia.

Expressions of regret and offers of reparation in case of the destruction of neutral ships sunk by mistake, while they may satisfy international obligations, if no loss of life results, can not justify or excuse a practice, the natural and necessary effect of which is to subject neutral nations and neutral persons to new and immeasurable risks.

The Imperial German Government will not expect the Government of the United States to omit any word or any act necessary to the performance of its sacred duty of maintaining the rights of the United States and its citizens and of safeguarding their free exercise and enjoyment.

The Gore-McLemore Resolution, 1916

Whereas a number of leading powers of the world are now engaged in a war of unexampled proportions; and

Whereas the United States is happily at peace with all of the belligerent nations; and

Whereas it is equally the desire and interest of the American people to remain at peace with all nations; and

Whereas the President has recently afforded fresh and signal proofs of the superiority of diplomacy to butchery as a method of settling international disputes; and

Whereas the right of American citizens to travel on unarmed belligerent vessels has recently received renewed guaranties of respect and inviolability; and

Whereas the right of American citizens to travel on armed belligerent vessels rather than upon unarmed vessels is essential neither to their life, liberty, or safety, nor to the independence, dignity, or security of the United States; and

Whereas Congress alone has been vested with the power to declare war, which involves the obligations to prevent war by all proper means consistent with the honor and vital interest of the Nation:

Now, therefore, be it

Resolved by the Senate (the House of Representatives concurring), That it is the sense of the Congress, vested as it is with the sole power to declare war, that all persons owing allegiance to the United States should, in behalf of their own safety and the vital interest of the United States, forbear to exercise the right to travel as passengers upon any armed vessel of any belligerent power, whether such vessel be armed for offensive or defensive purposes: and it is the further sense of the Congress that no passport should be issued or renewed by the Secretary of State or by anyone acting under him to be used by any person owing allegiance to the United States for purpose of travel upon any such armed vessel of a belligerent power.

Lansing and Bernstorff Discuss Submarine Warfare, 1916

L. Good morning.

B. Good morning, Sir. You handed me a copy of the note yesterday, and in the present state of affairs of course my chief object is to find a way how this break can be avoided, because I hope it can be avoided. My idea is to find a way out of it, but of course I had to telegraph my Government that this Government seemed to offer little opportunity for settlement. If it means the entire stopping of the use of submarines, I am afraid that it cannot be arranged.

L. You will recall that we said in the first *Lusitania* note that we thought it was impossible to use submarines in a really humane way and that later, in our note of July 21, we said that the way submarine warfare had been conducted for the past two months showed that it was possible and therefore we hoped that course would be pursued. Then we had the sinking of the *Arabic* right on top of that, which was another great disaster. Our position is that, if submarine warfare had been conducted in that way, that possibly there would have been no further question raised. But it has not. It has been conducted in the most indiscriminate way and we cannot help but believe that it is ruthless. In those conditions submarine warfare should stop against commercial vessels, unless visit and search is observed.

B. That, of course, is impossible. Germany cannot abandon submarine warfare. No government could come out and say—"We give up the use of submarines." They would have to resign.

L. What possible methods in the use of submarines, that are effective from a belligerent standpoint, can be suggested which will comply with the law?

B. I had always supposed that warning was to be given.

L. We do not consider that the people on board—the non-combatants on board the vessels—are in a place of safety when put into an open boat a hundred miles from land. It might be calm there, but in the two days it would take them to reach land there might be a severe storm. That is one of the grounds of complaint.

B. That, of course, speaking of neutral vessels—

L. The fact that we do not have Americans on these vessels does not remove the menace to American lives. The sinking of neutral vessels shows that Americans cannot travel with safety on neutral vessels even. That is the serious part of it and I do not know how your Government can modify submarine warfare and make it effective and at the same time obey the law and the dictates of humanity.

B. Humanity. Of course war is never humane.

L. "Humanity" is a relative expression when used with "war" but the whole tendency in the growth of international law in regard to warfare in the past 125 years has been to relieve non-combatants of needless suffering.

B. Of course I think it would be an ideal state of affairs, but our enemies violate all the rules and you insist on their being applied to Germany.

L. One deals with life; the other with property.

B. Yes.

L. The German method seems reckless to me. It is as if a man who has a very dim vision should go out on the street with a revolver in search of an enemy and should see the outline of a figure and should immediately fire on him and injure him seriously and then go up and apologize and say he made a mistake. I do not think that would excuse him. That seems to be the course pursued by your submarine commanders—they fire first and inquire afterwards.

B. I myself cannot at all explain how it comes that so many neutral vessels have been attacked. I have not the slightest evidence. I do not know anything about it from our communications.

L. Of course we are gradually collecting the evidence. We have not in all the cases but we have in certain ones. The *Tubantia,* for example, seems to have been torpedoed by a German torpedo—a Schwartz kopf.

B. She was at anchor.

L. No. I do not think she had let her anchor down but she was preparing to anchor. She was at rest.

B. Yes, I know. And then there was a Spanish vessel which—

L. Of course there is this, Mr. Ambassador, that any discussion of the submarine and its present method of attack cannot go on indefinitely.

B. What was your idea to prevent the break—that we should for the time being stop?

L. I think the only way is to declare an abandonment and then if the German Government desires to discuss a method of renewal—

B. An absolute abandonment, to my mind, is impossible. It might be possible to announce stopping for a time for discussion and giving the reason plainly for the purpose of quieting our public opinion, that might be possible.

L. I understand you are speaking entirely without instructions.

B. I am not at all instructed. I am speaking to you purely from my desire to prevent a break.

L. In view of our note I would not want to say that that would be satisfactory, but if it was made—

B. I am only trying to see what can be done because a declaration to my Government to absolutely abandon submarine warfare would make a break absolutely necessary. To abandon it would mean the overthrow of the Chancellor.

L. Probably you would get a more radical man. I realize that.

B. So the question is what we can do.

L. There would have to be a complete abandonment first and then if the German Government desires to discuss the matter—

B. I want to do what I can, because I am perfectly convinced they do not want to break; quite apart from the sentimental side I think they do not want a break. A break would prolong the war. It would last for years.

L. We do not any of us want to prolong the war.

B. That is exactly why I want to get out of this present difficulty. From the present state of affairs it looks as if the end is coming and if now there was a break and the United States was brought into the war it would prolong it. It would cause new complications.

L. New complications?

B. New economic difficulties.

L. I think that would be Germany's problem. The only possible course is an abandonment of submarine warfare, whether limited or not would depend on the terms. I would want to see an abandonment first and then possibly a discussion could follow as to how submarine warfare can be conducted within the rules of international law and entire safety of non-combatants, because, of course, in my viewpoint that is the chief question of international law in regard to attacks by belligerents on enemy's commerce.

B. Then I am to understand that you do not recognize the law of retaliation?

L. We do not recognize retaliation when it affects the rights of neutrals.

B. The British retaliate by stopping all commerce to Germany.

L. It is a very different thing. The right to life is an inherent right, which man has from birth; the right of property is a purely legal right.

B. Only in this case, England's methods affect the lives of non-combatants of Germany.

L. Not neutrals.

B. No, but it affects non-combatants.

L. Does it affect their lives? I thought from the statements which have been made that Germany was not suffering from want of food.

B. But they are trying to starve them. You do not stop England but insist we must stop our retaliation.

L. But you must appreciate that we care more for the lives of our people than we do for the property.

B. We have the same difficulty—our people are getting to care more for lives. That is the whole difficulty—we are dealing with a warlike population.

L. I realize that. I appreciate that you have great difficulty with your public.

B. If you and I were to have the say in settling the case it would be an easy matter, because one can discuss the matter without heat.

L. I realize that. It makes it very difficult, but I do not think there is any other course. That certainly may be an impossible course for your Government to pursue, yet I see no other way, and I think I am as anxious to preserve peace as anyone.

B. I wanted to find out what I could do, because I do not see how they can do it though they might do it temporarily. I am sure that in the first place they would say they believed in the submarine entirely and that secondly the rules of international law must be modified by conditions. Your idea is that the submarine cannot be used if it does comply with the rules.

L. That is true. My view is that certain instruments of war are not proper to use under certain conditions, and that is the viewpoint that has largely been held in regard to the submarine as a commerce destroyer. You can not and do not know the nationality of the boat attacking. It attacks without being seen and so avoids responsibility. It gives every opportunity to kill indiscriminately and recklessly.

B. I perfectly agree with you that sinking without warning would have to stop entirely, sinking without warning is an international offense, and that is why I thought possibly my Government might give up the retaliation, but I do not think it would be possible to say we would give up submarine warfare. I do not think we would do it.

L. And if they should now sink another vessel it would be very serious—that is the way I look at the situation.

B. And if they continue the submarine warfare and an instance should happen directly after the break of diplomatic relations, if that should come, it would be still more serious.

L. That is logical.

B. That is why I look at it so seriously.

L. I do not feel that breaking off of diplomatic relations necessarily means war.

B. I do not say it myself but I do not see how it can be avoided. If we refuse it will be because we are to continue submarine warfare and then something might happen which would mean war. I came to see if something could not be done.

L. I am very much obliged to you for coming in, sir.

B. Good bye, Mr. Secretary.

L. Good bye.

The Zimmermann Telegram, 1917

It is our purpose on the 1st of February to commence the unrestricted U-boat war. The attempt will be made to keep America neutral in spite of it all.

In case we should not be successful in this, we propose Mexico an alliance upon the following terms: Joint conduct of the war. Joint conclusion of peace. Ample financial support and an agreement on our part that Mexico shall gain back by conquest the territory lost by her at a prior period in Texas, New Mexico, and Arizona. Arrangement as to details is entrusted to your Excellency.

Your Excellency will make the above known to the President [Carranza] in strict confidence at the moment that war breaks out with the United States, and you will add the suggestion that Japan be requested to take part at once and that he simultaneously mediate between ourselves and Japan.

Please inform the President that the unrestricted use of our U-boats now offers the prospect of forcing England to sue for peace in the course of a few months.

Confirm receipt.

Woodrow Wilson's War Message, 1917

I have called the Congress into extraordinary session because there are serious, very serious, choices of policy to be made, and made immediately, which it was neither right nor constitutionally permissible that I should assume the responsibility of making.

On the third of February last I officially laid before you the extraordinary announcement of the Imperial German Government that on and after the first day of February it was its purpose to put aside all restraints of law or of humanity and use its submarines to sink every vessel that sought to approach either the ports of Great Britain and Ireland or the western coasts of Europe or any of the ports controlled by the enemies of Germany within the Mediterranean. That had seemed to be the object of the German submarine warfare earlier in the war, but since April of last year the Imperial Government had somewhat restrained the commanders of its undersea craft in conformity with its promise then given to us that passenger boats should not be sunk and that due warning would be given to all other vessels which its submarines might seek to destroy, when no resistance was offered or escape attempted, and care taken that their crews were given at least a fair chance to save their lives in their open boats. The precautions taken were meagre and haphazard enough, as was proved in distressing instance after instance in the progress of the cruel and unmanly business, but a certain degree of restraint was observed. The new policy has swept every restriction aside. Vessels of every kind, whatever their flag, their character, their cargo, their destination, their errand, have been ruthlessly sent to the bottom without warning and without thought of help or mercy for those on board, the vessels of friendly neutrals along with those of belligerents. Even hospital ships and ships carrying relief to the sorely bereaved and stricken people of Belgium, though the latter were provided with safe conduct through the proscribed areas by the German Government itself and were distinguished by unmistakable marks of identity, have been sunk with the same reckless lack of compassion or of principle.

I was for a little while unable to believe that such things would in fact be done by any government that had hitherto subscribed to the humane practices of civilized nations. International law had its origin in the attempt to set up some law which would be respected and observed upon the seas, where no nation had right of dominion and where lay the free highways of the world. By painful stage after stage has that law been built up, with meagre enough results, indeed, after all was accomplished that could be accomplished, but always with a clear view, at least, of what the heart and conscience of mankind demanded. This minimum of right the German Government has swept aside under the plea of retaliation and necessity and because it had no weapons which it could use at sea except these which it is impossible to employ as it is employing them without throwing to the winds all scruples of humanity or of respect for the understandings that were supposed to underlie the intercourse of the world. I am not now thinking of the loss of property involved, immense and serious as that is, but only of the wanton and wholesale destruction of the lives of noncombatants, men, women, and children, engaged in pursuits which have always, even in the darkest periods of modern history, been deemed innocent and legitimate. Property can be paid for; the lives of peaceful and innocent people cannot be. The present German submarine warfare against commerce is a warfare against mankind.

It is a war against all nations. American ships have been sunk, American lives taken, in ways which it has stirred us very deeply to learn of, but the ships and people of other neutral and friendly nations have been sunk and overwhelmed in the waters in the same way. There has been no discrimination. The challenge is to all mankind. Each nation must decide for itself how it will meet it. The choice we make for ourselves must be made with a moderation of counsel and a temperateness of judgment benefitting our character and our motives as a nation. We must put excited feeling away. Our motive will not be revenge or the victorious assertion of the physical might of the nation, but only the vindication of right, of human right, of which we are only a single champion.

When I addressed the Congress on the twenty-sixth of February last I thought that it would suffice to assert our neutral rights with arms, our right to use the seas against unlawful interference, our right to keep our people safe against unlawful violence. But armed neutrality, it now appears, is impracticable. Because submarines are in effect outlaws when used as the German submarines have been used against merchant shipping, it is impossible to defend ships against their attacks as the law of nations has assumed that merchantmen would defend themselves against privateers or cruisers, visible craft giving chase upon the open sea. It is common prudence in such circumstances, grim necessity indeed, to endeavour to destroy them before they have shown their own intention. They must be dealt with upon sight, if dealt with at all. The German Government denies the right of neutrals to use arms at all within the areas of the sea which it has proscribed, even in the defense of rights which no modern publicist has ever before questioned their right to defend. The intimation is conveyed that the armed guards which we have placed on our merchant ships will be treated as beyond the pale of law and subject to be dealt with as pirates would be. Armed neutrality is ineffectual enough at best; in such circumstances and in the face of such pretensions it is worse than ineffectual: it is likely only to produce what it was meant to prevent; it is practically certain to draw us into the war without either the rights or the effectiveness of belligerents. There is one choice we cannot make, we are incapable of making: we will not choose the path of submission and suffer the most sacred rights of our nation and our people to be ignored or violated. The wrongs against which we now array ourselves are no common wrongs; they cut to the very roots of human life.

With a profound sense of the solemn and even tragical character of the step I am taking and of the grave responsibilities which it involves, but in unhesitating obedience to what I deem my constitutional duty, I advise that the Congress declare the recent course of the Imperial German Government to be in fact nothing less than war against the government and people of the United States; that it formally accept the status of belligerent which has thus been thrust upon it; and that it take immediate steps not only to put the country in a more thorough state of defense but also to exert all its power and employ all its resources to bring the Government of the German Empire to terms and end the war. . . .

While we do these things, these deeply momentous things, let us be very clear, and make very clear to all the world what our motives and our objects are. My own thought has not been driven from its habitual and normal course by the unhappy events of the last two months, and I do not believe that the thought of the nation has been altered or clouded by them. . . . Our object now, as then, is to vindicate the principles of peace and justice in the life of the world as against selfish and autocratic power and to set up amongst the really free and self-governed peoples of the world such a concert of purpose and of action as will henceforth ensure the observance of those principles. Neutrality is no longer feasible or desirable where the peace of the world is involved and the freedom of its peoples, and the menace to that peace and freedom lies in the existence of autocratic governments backed by organized force which is controlled wholly by their will, not by the will of their people. We have seen the last of neutrality in such circumstances. We are at the beginning of an age in which it will be insisted that the same standards of conduct and of responsibility for wrong done shall be observed among nations and their governments that are observed among the individual citizens of civilized states.

We have no quarrel with the German people. We have no feeling towards them but one of sympathy and friendship. It was not upon their impulse that their government acted in entering this war. It was not with their previous knowledge or approval. It was a war determined upon as wars used to be determined upon in the old, unhappy days when peoples were nowhere consulted by their rulers and wars were provoked and waged in the interest of dynasties or of little groups of ambitious men who were accustomed to use their fellow men as pawns and tools. Self-governed nations do not fill their neighbour states with spies or set the course of intrigue to bring about some critical posture of affairs which will give them an opportunity to strike and make conquest. Such designs can be successfully worked out only under cover and where no one has the right to ask questions. Cunningly contrived plans of deception or aggression, carried, it may be, from generation to generation, can be worked out and kept from the light only within the privacy of courts or behind the carefully guarded confidences of a narrow and privileged class. They are happily impossible where public opinion commands and insists upon full information concerning all the nation's affairs.

A steadfast concert for peace can never be maintained except by a partnership of democratic nations. No autocratic government could be trusted to keep faith within it or observe its convenants. It must be a league of honour, a partnership of opinion. . . .

Does not every American feel that assurance has been added to our hope for the future peace of the world by the wonderful and heartening things that have been happening within the last few weeks in Russia? Russia was known by those who knew it best to have been always in fact democratic at heart, in all the vital habits of her thought, in all the intimate relationships of her people that spoke their natural instinct, their habitual attitude towards life. The autocracy that crowned the summit of her political structure, long as it had stood and terrible as was the reality of its power, was not in fact Russian in origin, character, or purpose; and now it has been shaken off and the great, generous Russian people have been added in all their naive majesty and might to the forces that are fighting for freedom in the world, for justice, and for peace. Here is a fit partner for a League of Honour.

One of the things that has served to convince us that the Prussian autocracy was not and could never be our friend is that from the very outset of the present war it has filled our unsuspecting communities and even our offices of government with spies and set criminal intrigues everywhere afoot against our national unity of counsel, our peace within and without, our industries and our commerce. . . . That it means to stir up enemies against us at our very doors the intercepted note to the German Minister at Mexico City is eloquent evidence.

We are accepting this challenge of hostile purpose because we know that in such a government, following such methods, we can never have a friend; and that in the presence of its organized power, always lying in wait to accomplish we know not what purpose, there can be no assured security for the democratic governments of the world. We are now about to accept gauge of battle with this natural foe to liberty and shall, if necessary, spend the whole force of the nation to check and nullify its pretensions and its power. We are glad, now that we see the facts with no veil of false pretense about them, to fight thus for the ultimate peace of the world and for the liberation of its peoples, the German peoples included: for the rights of nations great and small and the privilege of men everywhere to choose their way of life and of obedience. The world must be made safe for democracy. . . .

It is a distressing and oppressive duty, Gentlemen of the Congress, which I have performed in thus addressing you. There are, it may be, many months of fiery trial and sacrifice ahead of us. It is a fearful thing to lead this great peaceful people into war, into the most terrible and disastrous of all wars, civilization itself seeming to be in the balance. But the right is more precious than peace, and we shall fight for the things which we have always carried nearest our hearts,— for democracy, for the right of those who submit to authority to have a voice in their own governments, for the rights and liberties of small nations, for a universal dominion of right by such a concert of free peoples as shall bring peace and safety to all nations and make the world itself at last free. To such a task we can dedicate our lives and our fortunes, everything that we are and everything that we have, with the pride of those who know that the day has come when America is privileged to spend her blood and her might for the principles that gave her birth and happiness and the peace which she has treasured. God helping her, she can do no other.

Robert M. LaFollette Dissents, 1917

The poor, sir, who are the ones called upon to rot in the trenches, have no organized power, have no press to voice their will upon this question of peace or war; but, oh, Mr. President; at some time they will be heard. I hope and I believe they will be heard in an orderly and a peaceful way. I think they may be heard from before long. I think, sir, if we take this step, when the people to-day who are staggering under the burden of supporting families at the present prices of the necessaries of life find those prices multiplied, when they are raised a hundred per cent, or 200 per cent, as they will be quickly, aye, sir, when beyond that those who pay taxes come to have their taxes doubled and again doubled to pay the interest on the nontaxable bonds held by Morgan and his combinations, which have been issued to meet this war, there will come an awakening; they will have their day and they will be heard. It will be as certain and as inevitable as the return of the tides, and as resistless, too. . . .

Just a word of comment more upon one of the points in the President's address. He says that this is a war "for the things which we have always carried nearest to our hearts—for democracy, for the right of those who submit to authority to have a voice in their own government." In many places throughout the address is this exalted sentiment given expression.

It is a sentiment peculiarly calculated to appeal to American hearts and, when accompanied by acts consistent with it, is certain to receive our support; but in this same connection, and strangely enough, the President says that we have become convinced that the German Government as it now exists— "Prussian autocracy" he calls it—can never again maintain friendly relations with us. His expression is that "Prussian autocracy was not and could never be our friend," and repeatedly throughout the address the suggestion is made that if the German people would overturn their Government it would probably be the way to peace. So true is this that the dispatches from London all hailed the message of the President as sounding the death knell of Germany's Government.

But the President proposes alliance with Great Britain, which, however liberty-loving its people, is a hereditary monarchy, with a hereditary ruler, with a hereditary House of Lords, with a hereditary landed system, with a limited and restricted suffrage for one class and a multiplied suffrage power for another, and with grinding industrial conditions for all the wageworkers. The President has not suggested that we make our support of Great Britain conditional to her granting home rule to Ireland, or Egypt, or India. We rejoice in the establishment of a democracy in Russia, but it will hardly be contended that if Russia was still an autocratic Government, we would not be asked to enter this alliance with her just the same. Italy and the lesser powers of Europe, Japan in the Orient; in fact, all of the countries with whom we are to enter into alliance, except France and newly revolutionized Russia, are still of the old order—and it will be generally conceded that no one of them has done as much for its people in the solution of municipal problems and in securing social and industrial reforms as Germany.

Is it not a remarkable democracy which leagues itself with allies already far overmatching in strength the German nation and holds out to such beleaguered nation the hope of peace only at the price of giving up their Government? I am not talking now of the merits or demerits of any government, but I am speaking of a profession of democracy that is linked in action with the most brutal and domineering use of autocratic power. Are the people of this country being so well represented in this war movement that we need to go abroad to give other people control of their governments? Will the President and the supporters of this war bill submit it to a vote of the people before the declaration of war goes into effect? Until we are willing to do that, it illy becomes us to offer as an excuse for our entry into the war the unsupported claim that this war was forced upon the German people by their Government "without their previous knowledge or approval."

Who has registered the knowledge or approval of the American people of the course this Congress is called upon to take in declaring war upon Germany? Submit the question to the people, you who support it. You who support it dare not do it, for you know that by a vote of more than ten to one the American people as a body would register their declaration against it.

In the sense that this war is being forced upon our people without their knowing why and without their approval, and that wars are usually forced upon all peoples in the same way, there is some truth in the statement; but I venture to say that the response which the German people have made to the demands of this war shows that it has a degree of popular support which the war upon which we are entering has not and never will have among our people. The espionage bills, the conscription bills, and other forcible military measures which we understand are being ground out of the war machine in this country is the complete proof that those responsible for this war fear that it has no popular support and that armies sufficient to satisfy the demand of the entente allies can not be recruited by voluntary enlistments.

ESSAYS

In the first essay, Daniel M. Smith argues that the United States went to war to preserve its security; Germany constituted a serious danger and Woodrow Wilson grasped that reality. Ross Gregory of Central Michigan University questions this emphasis on "realism" and suggests instead that Wilson took the nation to war to preserve American principles. Finally, Otis L. Graham, Jr., of the University of North Carolina, Chapel Hill, does not think the United States should have entered the war, is skeptical about Wilson's "realism," and suggests that the best way to have ensured American security was not war abroad, but an intensification of the progressive reform movement at home. He discusses some alternative policies that he suggests might have prevented American entry into World War I.

Realism and National Security

DANIEL M. SMITH

In recent years historians have examined closely the role of national self-interest in propelling the United States into World War I. For two decades after that war ended, the scholarly debate was centered on the question of whether the country had been genuinely neutral in 1914–1917, with the defenders of the Wilson administration contending that hostilities had resulted only because of German submarine attacks on American rights and lives on the high seas, while critics ("revisionists") attributed involvement to the administration's allegedly unneutral policies favoring the Allied cause. The coming of World War II, when the Axis powers posed a manifest threat to American security and national values, suggested the need for a reevaluation of the causes of the earlier struggle. Wartime books, like Walter Lippmann's *U. S. Foreign Policy: Shield of the Republic,* reinterpreted the decision for war in 1917 as necessitated by the German challenge to Anglo-American control of the north Atlantic and to the security of the United States in the Western Hemisphere. A decisive German victory would have supplanted British with German naval power and would have constituted a real and immediate danger to North America. Since 1945 a number of scholars have reexamined President Wilson's foreign policies and have inquired into the role of considerations of the national economic and security interests in the decision for war. The answers reveal that realistic concepts of the national interests were held by Wilson and his principal advisers and were involved to a degree in the formulation of basic neutrality policies and the ultimate transition to belligerency.

In the years after the Spanish-American War, a number of influential Americans began to view Germany as a dynamic and imperialistic power potentially dangerous to the United States. Both countries were relatively new to the ranks of great world powers, and were rapidly industrializing and seeking overseas markets and coaling stations. A measure of rivalry was virtually inescapable. During the war with Spain, the German government had indicated a definite interest in acquiring a share of the Philippine Islands in case the United States relinquished them, and the conduct of the German naval squadron observing American military operations in Manila Bay gave rise to a legend of a hostile plot to intervene in Spain's behalf. After the brief war, some American naval and army officers were convinced that German economic and territorial ambitions constituted a threat to the nation's security and its hegemony in Latin

From *The Great Departure: The United States and World War I, 1914–1920,* by Daniel M. Smith. Copyright © 1965 by John Wiley & Sons, Inc. Reprinted by permission of John Wiley & Sons, Inc.

America. The Navy General Board in 1901 emphasized the imperative necessity of controlling the Caribbean Sea and the approaches to the Panama Canal,
and opposed acquisition of territory in the area by any foreign power as a
menace to American security. The Board recommended purchase of the Danish
West Indies, since "In view of the isthmian canal and the German settlements
in South America, every additional acquisition by the United States in the West
Indies is of value." Rumors of alleged German attempts to acquire naval bases
in the Galapagos Islands and in Haiti brought repeated objections by the military departments to the State Department in 1910–1912. The vital Panama
Canal, nearing completion, would be endangered by such foreign lodgments.

During these years, naval planners contended that Germany and Japan
offered the most serious potential danger to American interests. The navy,
therefore, should be sufficiently enlarged to cope with all eventualities. The Navy
League of the United States, founded by civilian enthusiasts in 1902 with Navy
Department approval and patterned after European organizations, clamored
for a larger navy to cope with threats to the Monroe Doctrine. Germany was
viewed as the principal challenger of that sacred national policy and the press
releases of the Navy League pointed out the ominous portents of American
naval inferiority to the Kaiser's fleets. Although its efforts were only moderately
successful, a recurrent theme of the League's publications prior to 1914 was the
possible German menace to American security. The Navy General Board concurred and a confidential estimate in 1910 depicted Germany as thwarted in its
expansionist drives both in the Pacific and in Latin America: "it is seen that
there are latent causes that render a break with Germany more probable than
with either of the other two great maritime powers. . . ." The War Department
shared these views and drafted plans for repelling a German attack on North
America. A War College paper in 1909–1910 described Germany as surpassing
the United States in many areas of economic competition in Latin America and
the Far East and as colonizing extensively in Brazil in an apparently well-
planned move. Because France and Great Britain had preempted most of Africa
and the United States had blocked expansion in the Far East and Latin America, the author of the paper concluded that "while war may never result between the United States and Germany yet the student of history must recognize
the existence of causes [economic] which tend to produce it. . . ."

Apprehension of Germany existed outside military circles. A. T. Mahan,
advocate of naval expansion, published books and articles on America's interest in seapower and in the world balance of power. Theodore Roosevelt and
members of his circle were greatly influenced by Mahan's realistic appraisals of
world politics and his emphasis on an Anglo-American community of interest.
Roosevelt wrote his friend Henry Cabot Lodge in 1901 that only Germany
might be "a menace to us in anything like the immediate future," whereas "we
are closer to her [England] than to any other nation; and . . . probably her interest and ours will run on rather parallel lines in the future." His friends Henry
and Brooks Adams concurred that Anglo-American interests coincided, with
the United States probably destined eventually to assume the leadership as
British power slowly deteriorated.

Other informed citizens also began to view Germany as a potential enemy, while envisioning Great Britain with its sea power as fulfilling a benevolent and protective role. The editors of the *New York Times,* after 1898, advocated closer ties with England as the one great power that shared a community of interests with America, and they called for at least naval parity with Germany. American periodicals from time to time carried articles expressing great distrust of German ambitions as they affected the Western Hemisphere. Comparisons of the German and American navies were occasionally made. *Munsey's Magazine* in 1901 recommended increased naval construction and cooperation with Great Britain to meet the German challenge to the new world.

Articles from English journals on the same themes were reprinted in American periodicals. One of the most prophetic essays was written by an Indiana University professor of political science, Amos S. Hershey, in 1909 for *The Independent.* Professor Hershey depicted Germany as endangering both world peace and American economic and security interests, and he urged that the menace be countered by the formation of an Anglo-American alliance. If an Anglo-German war should occur, he predicted that America could hardly remain neutral if Germany seemed about to triumph and to wrest naval supremacy from Great Britain: "A blockade of the British Isles by German cruisers and submarine mines, or the loss involved in the dangers to contraband trade would be severely felt in this country." Writing in the same year, the well-known English commentator Sydney Brooks noted that a growing number of Americans were aware that isolationism was no longer feasible and that Germany was as much an American as a British problem. In a war between England and Germany, he concluded that the United States would be benevolently neutral toward the British cause and might enter the struggle if Germany threatened to halt the export of American foodstuffs to the British Isles. On the eve of the great war, the American career diplomat Lewis Einstein joined this small group of writers in emphasizing the importance to the United States of a friendly British naval power and the dangers that would ensue if Germany achieved naval supremacy. In an article entitled "The United States and Anglo-German Rivalry," published anonymously in Britain in 1913, Einstein examined the probable results of a German victory, which he believed would affect adversely American economic and political interests in the Caribbean and the Far East. He predicted that the United States might find it necessary to intervene in order to prevent a British defeat and the consequent creation of an unfavorable balance of power.

The outbreak of war in 1914 enhanced the belief of a number of citizens that the national interest required an Allied victory. Editorials and letters in the *New York Times,* and several articles by historians George Louis Beer, George Burton Adams, and Albert Bushnell Hart, contended that security and maintenance of the Monroe Doctrine required the preservation of British naval supremacy. To Beer, "German ambitions in South America have been dormant only because the British fleet was an insuperable barrier. . . . Similar dangers threaten our economic interests in the Far East." Hart pointed out the nation's stake in the existing world equipoise, which affected the country's ability to defend the Monroe Doctrine: "Peace can be maintained only by convincing Germany and Japan, which are the two Powers most likely to be moved by an ambition to possess American territory." To Adams, apart from valid idealistic and ideological factors, "political and military expediency" justified intervention to preclude a German triumph over the Allies. A sweeping German success would leave no power in Europe able to restrain its ambitions; the United States at the minimum would have to exist in a hostile world as a result and probably would face direct Teutonic challenges. Other well-known scholars and commentators, such as Walter Lippmann of the *New Republic,* presented papers on these themes at the 1916 assembly of the American Academy of Political and Social Science. Books and articles by H. H. Powers, Roland G. Usher, and Hudson Maxim also warned of the dangers of a German victory.

The great majority of Americans, however, were not accustomed to the contemplation of foreign policy based on realistic appraisals of economic and political interests. Instead, popular reactions in 1914–1917 largely reflected traditional isolationist attitudes, modified by some emotional and ideological sympathy with the Allies. It is clear, nevertheless, that for over a decade a minority of informed citizens had been exposed to repeated warnings that an aggressive Germany potentially endangered an Anglo-American community of interests. They had come to view Great Britain as the bulwark standing between the Western Hemisphere and Europe, whose removal would expose the United States to great peril. Such views were particularly prevalent in the eastern part of the United States, and were held by people with considerable influence in the molding of public opinion. Existence of these attitudes and convictions made it inestimably easier to condemn Germany on moral and idealistic grounds and probably facilitated the ultimate entry into war.

The most influential advisers of President Wilson shared a "realistic" appraisal of the significance of the European war for the United States. Robert Lansing, counselor of the State Department and its second in command, presidential adviser Edward M. House, and ambassadors Walter Hines Page in London and James W. Gerard in Berlin, together with several cabinet members, fused pro-Ally sentiments and ideological considerations with apprehensions that a German victory would affect adversely American economic and political interests. . . .

A descendant of a distinguished New York family and trained in international law, Lansing had traveled extensively abroad and by 1914 had participated in more international arbitrations than probably any other living American. As a result of training and experience, he was eminently practical and "hard-headed" in his approach to world affairs and questions of foreign policy. Although he shared the American faith in the efficacy and future of democracy and as a devout Presbyterian believed in the moral imperative, Lansing recognized that amoral physical power was the underlying reality in international relations. Moral law did and should govern domestic society, but unfortunately relations between states were characterized by materialistic and selfish motives and conflicts usually were resolved by violence. In essence a nation dealt with other nations in a savage manner, regardless of how enlightened the conduct of its domestic affairs might be. To assume otherwise, to believe that foreign policy should be founded solely on altruistic motives, was fallacious and a grave error. Idealism had an important place in American foreign policy but it needed to be harmonized with common sense.

The initial response of Lansing to the war was one of relief that his country was spared the waste and sufferings of the conflict. Yet he was pro-Ally from the first, in part because of emotional and cultural attachments to Great Britain, and in part because of his conviction that the Allies represented the democratic impulse against the aggressive autocracy of the Central powers. He assumed, as many others, that the war would soon end in an Allied triumph, and at first he concentrated on perfecting American neutrality. By early 1915, however, he perceived that the war would be a long and bitter one seriously affecting the economic and political interests of the United States. Submarine warfare, a novel and rude challenge to trade and past international practices, seemed to Lansing to portend a possible German victory. The destruction of British passenger liners with American travelers aboard removed all doubt from his mind and underscored America's interest in the outcome of the war. Germany, he believed, was a very real danger to American ideals and to its economic interests and security.

On July 11, 1915, a few days after he had succeeded Bryan as secretary of state, Lansing recorded in his private notebook his views on policy:

> I have come to the conclusion that the German Government is utterly hostile to all nations with democratic institutions because those who compose it see in democracy a menace to absolutism and the defeat of the German ambition for world domination. Everywhere German agents are plotting and intriguing to accomplish the supreme purpose of their Government. . . . Germany must not be permitted to win this war and to break even, though to prevent it this country is forced to take an active part. This ultimate necessity must be constantly in our minds in all our controversies with the belligerents. . . .

If Germany should win, the United States would be confronted with a hostile naval power threatening its interests in the Caribbean, in Latin America generally, and perhaps in the Far East as well. The United States had already experienced sharp controversies with an expansionist Japan, frequently rumored to be on the verge of deserting the Allies and realigning with the Central powers. Lansing could envision, therefore, the possibility of a future grand alliance between the three autocratic empires of Germany, Russia, and Japan, which would isolate the United States in a menacing world.

The new secretary was also imbued with the American faith in democracy and its eventual universal triumph. Democratic states were inherently peace-loving, he believed, because the ordinary citizen presumably never desires war and its costly sacrifices, which fall heaviest on the average man, whereas autocratic states with dynastic rivalries were basically aggressive and militaristic. From the point of view of Lansing and others similarly inclined, imperial Germany, the leading representative of a militaristic and statist philosophy, could be said to be a triple threat to the United States: ideologically it menaced democratic institutions and values, militarily it endangered the nation's security, and it was the most serious rival of the United States for economic and political influence in Latin America. To cope with these dangers, Lansing resolved to endeavor to watch carefully German activity in Latin America, especially in turbulent Mexico and the Caribbean area, to take steps to forestall possible German acquisition of bases by American purchase of the Danish West Indies (done in 1916–1917), to keep the submarine issue clearly defined, and to enter the war if it became necessary to avert a Teutonic victory.

Although ideological factors figured prominently in Lansing's thought, at least as important were considerations of the country's economic and security needs. In his private memoranda he repeatedly recorded the conviction that a German conquest in Europe would dangerously expose the United States. On the eve of America's entry into the war, he wrote: "The Allies must *not* be beaten. It would mean the triumph of Autocracy over Democracy; the shattering of all our moral standards; and a real, though it may seem remote, peril to our independence and institutions." In 1915–1916, however, he appreciated the fact that public opinion was divided, with pacifist and isolationist traditions still strong, and that the president was most reluctant to contemplate actual hostilities. Insofar as he was able, therefore, he tried to shape the American course so that dangerous disputes with the Allies would be avoided, while the submarine issue was clearly delineated and the American people were slowly prepared by events for the great leap into belligerency. Lansing usually did not speak to Wilson directly of his belief that the nation's vital self-interests required preparation for war, but with an understanding of the presidential psychology he instead used moralistic and legalistic arguments to justify what he viewed as the correct policy. Often working in close cooperation with the similarly inclined Colonel House, Lansing was able to achieve a large measure of influence on Wilsonian foreign policy.

Other officials within the State Department and the foreign service held comparable views on the meaning of the war. James Brown Scott, William Phillips, and Frank L. Polk (later undersecretary) were also pro-Ally in sympathies and were persuaded that a German triumph would endanger America. Chandler P. Anderson, a legal adviser on problems of neutrality, remarked after a discussion with Lansing of a recent German note that it was surly in tone and "a good example of the sort of lecturing and regulating that all nations might expect if Germany succeeded in its ambition to rule the world." From London, Ambassador Walter Hines Page sought to convince Wilson and top administration figures that Britain's fight against Germany was in the best interests of the United States. Only if the Allies won, he wrote, would a favorable power balance be preserved in the Far East and in the Atlantic. Ambassador James W. Gerard in Berlin had similar apprehensions and predicted that if the Central powers emerged victorious "we are next on their list." . . .

President Wilson entered office surprisingly uninformed about foreign affairs. What was striking about this was not its novelty, since most presidents after the Civil War had been similarly ill-equipped, but was, as Arthur Link has pointed out, that it should have been true of Wilson, a professional historian and political scientist, author of a number of books and former president of Princeton University. Yet his publications indicated little interest in foreign affairs, and prior to 1898 he had written of diplomatic problems and machinery as almost a minor aspect of government. After the "passing" of the frontier and the Spanish-American War, he like others was made aware that the isolation of the nineteenth century was no longer possible and that the nation would perforce play an ever larger role in world affairs. Nothing indicated, however, that his knowledge and interest in international relations was more than perfunctory and superficial. In an oft-quoted remark, on the eve of his presidential inauguration, Wilson confessed to a friend that his primary interests were in domestic reform and that it would be "the irony of fate" if he should be compelled to concentrate on foreign affairs.

Wilson has been described by many scholars as primarily an idealist unresponsive to practical considerations in foreign relations and as unusually independent of his pro-Ally advisers in shaping America's course during the great war. Later studies have substantially modified such estimates. He was deeply moralistic in his approach, the result of being steeped in Calvinistic piety and training during his youth. Idealism usually meant for him, however, not the ignoring of practical considerations but the exalting of noble purposes and goals. He has been aptly described [by Arthur S. Link] as a "romantic moralist, who . . . raised every issue and conflict to a high stage. . . ." He was capable of sometimes being blinded to reality by his faith and goals, as was painfully clear after the 1919 peace conference, but in the neutrality period his moralistic impulses usually were reenforced rather than contradicted by practical considerations of the national interest. Recent historians have revealed also that Wilson was by no means impervious to the counsel of his close advisers and that he shared to a degree their analyses of the meaning of the war to America's economic, security, and ideological interests.

When the war began, Wilson's first reactions were based on emotional sympathy for England and its allies, and he tended to attribute to Germany primary responsibility for beginning the struggle. Within a few months, however, he had recovered emotional balance and had come to realize that the causes of the war were complex and that guilt was more evenly distributed than he had at first suspected. Yet he remained sympathetic toward the Allies, especially Great Britain and its leaders in whom he had much trust and whom he long believed were pursuing more reasonable goals than were the other belligerents. He also came to appreciate the view that a decisive German victory would pose some danger for the United States. He indicated agreement with House that "if Germany won it would change the course of our civilization and make the United States a military nation." Later in the fall of 1914, he told his private secretary Joseph Tumulty, that he would not pressure England to a dangerous point on the issue of neutral rights because Britain was fighting for the life of the world. During the *Arabic* crisis in mid-1915, he surprised House by stating that he had never been certain that America would not have to intervene in order to prevent a German victory. In 1916, in an effort to promote greater defensive military preparedness, Wilson repeatedly revealed in his public addresses serious concern for the national security and the long-range safety of Latin America. In these speeches he justified heavier expenditures on the army and navy as necessitated in part to protect American trade on the high seas and to avert possible dangers to the Western Hemisphere. Thus at Pittsburgh he asked rhetorically:

> What is it that we want to defend? . . . We want to defend the life of this Nation against any sort of interference. We want to maintain the equal right of this Nation as against the action of all other nations, and we wish to maintain the peace and unity of the Western Hemisphere.

Again, at Cleveland, he warned his audience that the United States "must play her part in keeping this conflagration from spreading to the people of the United States; she must also keep this conflagration from spreading on this side of the sea. These are matters in which our very life and our whole pride are embedded. . . ."

It must be emphasized, however, that in general Wilson did not believe that a German victory, undesirable though it would be, would pose an immediate threat to the United States. Like most of his fellow citizens, he was confident of an eventual Allied triumph. But if the opposite should result, he thought that Germany probably would be too weakened by the European war to offer more than a future menace to the security of the Western Hemisphere. He remarked to a sceptical Colonel House, in late 1914, that Germany would need at least several years for recuperation before it could undertake a direct challenge to the United States. He adopted policies, therefore, which protected those national interests that were immediately affected by the war (commerce, legal rights, and prestige), and relied upon such measures as purchase of the Danish West Indies and increased military preparations to ward off future dangers to the national security and to the Monroe Doctrine. He was long convinced, in fact, that neutrality was the wisest course for America and that peace without victory for either belligerent side would alone make possible a just and stable postwar world. The mission of the United States, therefore, was to stand as a bastion of liberty and peace, and to serve all mankind by helping to mediate this terrible struggle whenever events proved favorable. Not until early 1917, after the failure of his two peace overtures and the renewal of submarine warfare, did he accept the necessity for intervention in the war. . . .

American involvement in World War I, as in most other wars, defies simplistic explanations. In the 1930's the historical debate was polarized into the "submarine school," best represented by Charles Seymour, and the "revisionists," with Charles C. Tansill as the most effective spokesman. Seymour dismissed political and economic factors as at most peripheral causes of the war entry and instead emphasized the submarine challenge to American rights and lives. Tansill overlooked security aspects of the war and emphasized American unneutrality, the economic and sentimental ties to the Allies, as pulling the United States into conflict. Neither approach suffices to explain so complex an event. Seymour probably was right in the contention that there would have been no war without the submarine issue, for otherwise Germany and America would not have had a direct clash of interests and power. But the U-boat challenge alone does not explain why the United States adopted the strict accountability policy, since other alternatives were at least theoretically possible. As for the revisionist charges of unneutrality, it seems clear that American neutrality in fact was benevolent toward the Allies and grudgingly technical toward Germany. This did not result from deliberate planning, however, but rather from previous emotional and cultural affinities and from wartime economic connections with the Allies. In any case, Germany did not launch unrestricted submarine warfare merely from anger at the United States or just to cut off the arms trade. Although a different American posture perhaps could have influenced German policy along a more moderate course, the final decision for full underseas warfare was undertaken as the best remaining hope for decisive victory over the Allies through starving Britain into submission.

Just as clearly the hypothesis that the United States went to war in 1917 primarily to protect an endangered security against an immediate threat is not satisfactory. Although Lansing and House, and occasionally Wilson, thought of Germany as a menace to American security and stability, it was primarily as a future danger rather than an imminent peril. Yet Wilson was indeed far more practical in his policies and thinking than many scholars formerly believed, and he sought to promote the national interests as he envisioned them. Aided by his advisers, who exerted considerable influence on him, Wilson adopted policies that embodied economic and prestige interests, as well as moral considerations. The tacit acquiescence in the war trade and the permission of credits and loans to the belligerents reflected primarily economic interests; whereas the strict accountability policy toward U-boat warfare combined economic and moralistic factors with a desire to uphold the nation's prestige and honor as essential to any worthwhile diplomatic endeavors in the future including mediation of the war. Thus policies toward the Allies were favorable or benevolent because America's basic interests were essentially compatible with British control of the seas and Allied utilization of the American market. The course adopted toward Germany, on the other hand, was firmly nonacquiescent. Submarine warfare endangered American economic connections with Europe and as well violated moral sensibilities and affronted the national honor.

Among high administration officials, Lansing appears to have held the clearest conviction that American security would be endangered by a German triumph and that intervention in the struggle might be necessary—by late 1916 he believed it *was* necessary—to prevent that possibility. Although he sometimes indicated complete concurrence with Lansing's views, Colonel House believed that the most desirable culmination of the war would be enough of an Allied victory to check German ambitions but with Germany left sufficiently strong to play its proper role in the balance of power and to check Russian expansionism. A desire to preserve the balance of power, in the sense of ending the war short of victory for either side, was a factor behind the mediation plans of House and Wilson in 1915 and 1916.

Why did the reluctant president finally decide that belligerency was the only possible answer to unrestricted U-boat warfare? Why did he not rest content with the diplomatic rupture, or with armed neutrality or a limited naval war? The answer seems to have been that the prestige and honor of the nation were so committed as the result of previous policies that nothing less than a diplomatic break and a forceful defense of American interests were possible. By 1917 the evidence suggests that Wilson feared that a German victory was probable and that it would disturb the world balance, and although he was not apprehensive about an immediate threat to the United States, he did believe that such a result would endanger his idealistic hopes for a just peace and the founding of a new and stable world order. He referred to Germany as a madman who must be restrained. He finally accepted the necessity for actively entering the war, it would appear, with the submarine as the precipitant, only because he believed that larger reasons of national prestige, economic interests, and future security so demanded, and above all because of his commitment to the cause of an enduring world peace.

In Defense of Rights and Honor

ROSS GREGORY

In light of the controversy which later surrounded America's entry into the First World War, and the momentous effect that war had on the future of the world, it seems appropriate here to offer some final observations about Wilsonian diplomacy and the factors responsible for intervention. Wilson asked Congress to declare war in 1917 because he felt Germany had driven him to it. He could find no way, short of an unthinkable abandonment of rights and interests, to avoid intervention. He briefly had tried armed neutrality, and as he said in the war message, that tactic had not done the job. Germany was making war on the United States, and Wilson had no reasonable alternative to a declaration of hostilities. Hence submarine warfare must bear the immediate responsibility for provoking the decision for war. It nonetheless is not enough to say that the United States went to war simply because of the submarines, or that the events of January–March 1917 alone determined the fate of the United States, for a number of factors helped bring the nation to that point where it seemed impossible to do anything else. During the period of neutrality the American government made certain decisions, avoided others, found itself pulled one way or another by national sentiment and need and by the behavior of the belligerent nations.

Any account of American intervention would go amiss without some reference to the pro-Ally nature of American neutrality. American money and supplies allowed the Allies to sustain the war effort. While Wilson did not act openly partial to the Allies, he did promote American economic enterprise and declined to interfere—indeed showed no signs of dismay—when the enterprise developed in ways that were beneficial to Britain and France. Although Wilson did experience a considerable hardening of attitude toward the Allies in 1916 (his major advisers did not), he could not bring himself to limit the provisioning of Britain and France; and it was this traffic that brought on submarine warfare. Without American assistance to the Allies, Germany would have had no reason to adopt policy injurious to the interests of the United States.

There were several reasons why American policy functioned in a manner which favored the Allies. The first was a matter of circumstances: Britain controlled the sea, and the Allies were in desperate need of American products —conditions which assured that most American trade would go to Britain and France. The second factor was an assumption by much of the American population, most members of the administration, and the president that the political and material well-being of the United States was associated with preservation of Britain and France as strong, independent states. Germany unintentionally confirmed the assumption with the invasion of Belgium, use of submarines, and war tactics in general. While pro-Ally feeling was tempered by a popular desire to stay out of the conflict and by the president's wish to remain fair and formally neutral, it was sufficiently strong to discourage any policy that would weaken the Allied war effort. House, Lansing, and Page were so partial to the Allies that they acted disloyally to the president. Wilson frequently complained about Britain's intolerable course; he sent notes of protest and threatened to do more. He grumbled about Page's bias for the British and questioned the usefulness of his ambassador in Britain. Yet he did nothing to halt Britain's restrictions on trade with continental Europe, and Page stayed on in London until the end of the war. Wilson declined to press the British because he feared that such action would increase Germany's chances of winning and lead to drastic economic repercussions in the United States. Favoritism for the Allies did not cause the United States to go to war with Germany. It did help create those conditions of 1917 in which war seemed the only choice.

The United States (or much of the population) preferred that Britain and France not collapse, and the nation was equally anxious that Germany not succeed, at least not to the extent of dominating Europe. A prewar suspicion of German militarism and autocratic government, and accounts, during the war, of "uncivilized" German warfare influenced Wilson and a majority of the American people to believe that the United States faced an evil world force, that in going to war with Germany the nation would be striking a blow for liberty and democracy. This general American attitude toward the war of 1914–18 probably influenced Wilson's decision to resist submarine warfare, and thus affected his neutrality policies. More important, it made the decision to intervene seem all the more noble and did much to determine the way the United States, once it became belligerent, prosecuted the war. It was not, however, the major reason for accepting intervention. For all the popular indignation over the invasion of Belgium and other allegedly atrocious German warfare, there still did not develop in the United States a large movement for intervention. Even in 1917 Wilson showed the utmost reluctance to bring the nation into the war. Americans evidently were willing to endure German brutality, although they did not like it, as long as it did not affect their interests; and one must wonder what the American response—and the response of the president—would have been had no Americans been aboard the *Lusitania*. Wilson's vilification on April 2 of the German political system was more a means of sanctifying the cause than a reason for undertaking it. He was a curious crusader. Before April 1917 he would not admit that there was a need for America to take up the sword of righteousness. Against his will he was driven to the barricades, but once he was in the streets he became the most thorough and enthusiastic of street fighters.

The most important influence on the fate of the United States 1914–17 was the nation's world position. National need and interests were such that it was nearly impossible to avoid the problems which led the nation into war. Even if the administration had maintained a rigidly neutral position and forced Britain to respect all maritime rights of the United States, it is doubtful that the result would have been different. Grey testified that Britain would have yielded rather than have serious trouble with the United States, which means that, faced with American pressure, Britain would have allowed a larger amount of American trade through to Germany. This was the most the Germans could have expected from the United States, and it would not have affected the contraband trade with the Allies. Germany used submarines not because of the need to obtain American supplies, but from a desire to prevent the Allies from getting them.

The course that would have guaranteed peace for the United States was unacceptable to the American people and the Wilson administration. Only by severing all its European ties could the nation obtain such a guarantee. In 1914 that act would have placed serious strain on an economy that already showed signs of instability; by 1916 it would have been economically disastrous. At any time it would have been of doubtful political feasibility, even if one were to premise American popular disinterest in who won the war. The British understood this fact and reacted accordingly. If such thoughts suggest that the United States was influenced by the needs of an expanding capitalist economy, so let it be. It is by no means certain that another economic structure would have made much difference.

One might argue that measures short of a total embargo, a different arrangement of neutral practices—for instance, stoppage of the munitions traffic, and/or a ban on American travel on belligerent ships—would have allowed a profitable, humane, yet nonprovocative trade with Europe. Though a reply to that contention can offer no stronger claim to truth than the contention itself, one can offer these points: Wilson argued that yielding one concession on the seas ultimately would lead to pressure to abandon all rights. The pragmatic behavior of belligerents, especially the Germans, makes that assessment seem fair. Lest the German chancellor appear a hero to opponents of American intervention, it is well to remember that Bethmann's views on submarine warfare were not fashioned by love of the United States, or by the agony of knowing his submarines were sending innocent victims to their death. He was guided by simple national interest and the desire to use submarines as fully as circumstances allowed. It also is worth noting that Germany, when it reopened submarine warfare in 1917, was interested not merely in sinking munitions ships, but wanted to prevent all products going to Britain and was especially anxious to halt shipments of food. Had the United States wished to consider Bryan's proposals, keeping people and property out of the danger zone, it would have been easier early in the war, perhaps in February 1915, than after the sinkings began, and above all after the *Lusitania* went down. Yielding in the midst of the *Lusitania* crisis involved nothing short of national humiliation. If Bryan's proposals would have eliminated the sort of incident that provoked intervention, they also would have required a huge sacrifice— too great, as it turned out, for Wilson to accept. The United States would have faced economic loss, loss of national prestige, and probably the eventual prospect of a Europe dominated by Hindenburg, Ludendorff, and Wilhelm II.

No less than the nation as a whole, Wilson found himself accountable for the world standing of the United States. He felt a need and an obligation to promote economic interests abroad. When dealing with Germany he usually spoke in terms of principle; in relations with the Allies he showed awareness of practical considerations. In the hectic days of August 1914, he took steps to get American merchant ships back to sea. In the summer of 1915, advisers alerted him to the financial strain Britain had come to experience, the weakening of the pound sterling and the need to borrow funds in the United States. The secretary of the treasury recommended approval of foreign loans. "To maintain our prosperity we must finance it," he said. Lansing, who believed similarly, wrote the president: "If the European countries cannot find the means to pay for the excess of goods sold them over those purchased from them, they will have to stop buying and our present export trade will shrink proportionately. The result will be restriction of output, industrial depression, idle capital, idle labor, numerous failures, financial demoralization, and general unrest and suffering among the laboring masses." Shortly afterward the administration acquiesced as the House of Morgan floated loans of $500 million for the British and French governments. War traffic with the Allies prompted the German attempt to stop it with submarines. Submarine warfare led to destruction of property and loss of American lives. What had started as efforts to promote prosperity and neutral rights developed into questions of national honor and prestige. Wilson faced not merely the possibility of abandoning economic rights but the humiliating prospect of allowing the Germans to force him to it. The more hazardous it became to exercise American rights, the more difficult it was to yield them.

Wilson's definition of right and honor was itself conditioned by the fact that he was president of the United States and not some less powerful nation. His estimate of what rights belonged to the United States, what was for belligerents fair and humane warfare, rested not simply on a statement of principle, but on the power of the United States to compel observance of these principles. He could not send demands to the German government without some reason for believing the Germans would obey. Interpretation of national honor varies with national economic and military strength. The more powerful the nation, the more the world expects of it and the more the nation expects of itself. Such small seafaring states as Denmark and the Netherlands suffered extensive losses from submarine warfare, and yet these governments did not feel themselves honor bound to declare war. Wilson credited his right to act as a mediator to his position as leader of the most powerful neutral state. Indeed, he sometimes felt obligated to express moral principle. He could not, and would not, have acted these ways had he been, let us say, president of the Dominican Republic. It is thus possible to say that despite Wilson's commanding personality, his heavy-handedness in foreign policy and flair for self-righteousness, American diplomacy in final analysis was less a case of the man guiding affairs of the nation than the nation, and belligerent nations, guiding the affairs of the man.

It is tempting to conclude that inasmuch as the United States was destined to enter the conflict, it might as well have accepted that fact and reacted accordingly. Presumably this response would have involved an earlier declaration of war, certainly a large and rapid rearmament program. In recent years some "realist" scholars, notably George F. Kennan, have considered that this course would have been practical. However wise that policy might have been, it did not fit conditions of the period of neutrality. Wilson opposed entering the war earlier, and had he thought differently, popular and congressional support were highly questionable. People did not know in 1914 that commercial relations would lead them into the World War; most of them believed during the entire period that they could have trade and peace at the same time. The body of the United States was going one way during the period of neutrality, its heart and mind another. For a declaration of war there needed to be a merging of courses.

Then, too, it was not absolutely certain that the United States had to enter the conflict, for the nation after all did avoid intervention for over two and one-half years, two-thirds of the war's fighting time. That same strength which eventually brought the nation into the war for a while helped it avoid intervention. From this perspective the campaign for mediation might have represented some of Wilson's soundest thinking. German officials never were certain about American strength, and the longer they had to endure a costly, indecisive conflict, the more they were willing to consider the type of gamble taken in 1917. American intervention was all but certain unless the United States made a drastic change in policy—which, as we have seen, it was unwilling to do— or unless someone beforehand brought the war to an end. It incidentally also seems fair to say that an indecisive settlement, a "peace without victory," would have better served the interests of the United States, not to mention the interests of the world, than the vindictive treaty drawn up in 1919. These thoughts, of course, are hindsight, but it is ironic that Wilson made the same observations weeks before the United States entered the war. . . .

One of the most provocative features of Wilsonian diplomacy was the president's apparent obsession with moral principle and international law. To critics this tendency suggested blindness to realistic goals, ignorance of the way nations deal with one another, if not a profession of personal superiority. In some ways the critics were right. Wilson was dedicated to principle. He thought the old system of interstate relations was unsatisfactory and looked to a time when nations would find rules to govern relations among themselves no less effective than laws within individual states. He wished to have a large part in making those rules. His propensity to quibble about shipments of cargo and techniques of approaching ships at sea seemed a ridiculous and remote abstraction at a time when the fate of nations hung in balance. It was naïve to expect nations to respect legal principles when they had so much at stake. If they obeyed Wilson's command, their obedience was due less to principle than to his nation's ability to retaliate. At the same time international law was to Wilson more than an ideal; it was a manifestation of neutral intent and a device for defining American neutrality. Unless the United States decided to declare war or to stay out of the mess entirely, it would have to deal with complicated questions of neutral rights. International law was not merely convenient, it was the only device available. There fortunately was no conflict between Wilsonian principle and American rights and needs—the principle could be used to uphold the need. That the United States found an attraction for international law is not surprising: the restraints the law placed on belligerents would benefit any nation wishing to engage in neutral wartime commerce. International law looked to an orderly international society, and the United States, a satisfied nation, would profit from order. The chaos of 1914–17 strengthened feeling in the United States that American interests coincided with world interests, or, put another way, that what was good for the United States was good for the world.

Even so, it is not adequate to say that Wilson was a realist who clothed practical considerations with moral rhetoric. He was both practical and idealistic, at least during the period of American neutrality. If he believed that upholding principle would advance American interests, he also hoped that promoting American interests would serve the cause of international morality. By demonstrating that the United States would not condone brutality, disorder, and lawlessness, he hoped to set a standard for other nations to follow. Wilson wanted to help reform the world, but he would have settled for protecting the interests of the United States and keeping the nation at peace.

Evidence from various quarters supports these final conclusions: there is no indication that Wilson went to war to protect American loans to the Allies and large business interests, although these interests, and economic factors in general, helped bring the United States to a point where war seemed unavoidable. There is no evidence that Wilson asked for war to prevent the defeat of Britain and France. It could well have been, as several scholars have written, that preservation of Britain and France was vital to the interests of the United States. American neutrality, incidentally or by design, functioned to sustain that thesis. Even so, Wilson did not intervene to prevent these nations' collapse; the Allies, while not winning, were not on the verge of losing in the spring of 1917. Nor did Wilson go to war to preserve American security. This is not to say that he was not concerned with security; he simply did not see it in jeopardy. The president did ask his countrymen for war as a means of protecting American honor, rights, and general interest—for both moral and practical reasons. He saw no contradiction between the two. But Wilson's idea of right and interest grew out of what the nation was at the time, and the First World War made clear what had been true for some years: the United States was in all respects a part of the world, destined to profit from its riches and suffer from its woes.

Wilson's Wrong Choices

OTIS L. GRAHAM, JR.

This desire to end the emotional and political division of the country was prominent among the factors leading Wilson to ask for war. Now, with the step taken, the war required unity for its prosecution. The wave of relief and enthusiasm that greeted his war message could not be expected to last beyond a few days. The articulate people who had never believed that the issues between Europeans were worth one American life would surely not be silenced by the Declaration of War by Congress. And their arguments might have a certain effect: we were not under attack, no official person had declared that our national security was in jeopardy, we would have to travel thousands of miles even to become involved in the war, and the war was sure to have its unpleasant costs, particularly in lives and money. To preserve a workable majority against such divisive thoughts would require that the war have a powerful, simple, emotionally appealing, and durable justification. Wilson may have asked for war, as a leading historian has said, because he had no other choice, but it would not do to attempt to prepare the nation for its exertions with such flimsy stuff. In April, 1917, and for the months ahead, the entry of the nation into the European war must have an explanation to enlist the energies and loyalties of a democratic people—simple, emotional, a tiny bit skeptical, deeply romantic. For this task it is impossible to imagine a more appropriate citizen than Woodrow Wilson. At calling men to sacrifice, at simplifying the complex, at extracting principle from secular confusion, no man of that generation was his equal. He understood from the start the need for public education of the most dramatic effectiveness (although he had some doubts of its side effects), and made his April 2 address the most impressive justification for American belligerency ever offered.

Wilson's war message . . . repays close reading. His first and presumably chief reason for calling America to arms was to defend the rights of all mankind, now imperiled by German submarine warfare. The human rights under attack were broader than the right to travel safely on the seas even during a world war; they were the rights to peace and justice, of which the present German government had shown itself to be an implacable foe. The United States fought also for ends that were closely related to American self-interest and security, although Wilson did not state the matter quite in those terms—to defend the American form of

Otis L. Graham, Jr., *The Great Campaigns: Reform and War in America, 1900–1928* (Englewood Cliffs, N.J.: Prentice-Hall, Inc., 1971). Reprinted by permission of the author.

government against authoritarianism (the Russian Revolution of March made this construction possible), to avoid those naval humiliations that would have eliminated the nation's status as a great power, and to construct a postwar "concert of free peoples as shall bring peace and safety to all nations."

When Wilson left the joint session to a deafening applause, when his old enemy Senator Lodge gripped his hand and thanked him for expressing the "loftiest . . . sentiments of the American people," he must have known that the message was a superb success. He had provided the vocabulary for, and started in motion, that avalanche of "moist and numerous language," to borrow Mr. Dooley's phrase, which informed the American people why they must now become involved in a war that three years, and in some cases even days earlier, they had regarded with disgust. Editorial writers, preachers, stump speakers, teachers, and professors would see to it in the days ahead that the reasons we fought—simple, noble, overwhelming—were communicated throughout the country. The average draftee who was not a close reader of the *New York Times* or the *Congressional Record* now could be expected to understand why we were in the World War, and not to bother himself very much about it. But Wilson's success at framing convincing and communicable goals did as much as anything else to defeat those goals for which he had contended since foreign affairs began to claim so much of his attention in 1914.

It is hard in retrospect to approve either Wilson's timing or his reasoning in the fateful, difficult foreign policy decisions forced on him by the Great War in Europe. He argued that the United States could no longer tolerate non-belligerency because to submit to humiliations would be to permit the destruction of human rights and national prestige. If the national prestige was involved at all it was because he willed it so; neither law, economic necessity, nor tradition required a guarantee of rights of travel on armed belligerent vessels. As for the notion that human rights were somehow in jeopardy if Americans died on the high seas, the less said about that mystical idea the better for Wilson's reputation as an incisive thinker. Yet intelligent men have found reason to defend Wilson's decision to ask for intervention, not as the best of poor alternatives, but as a wise and proper step. In the view of the Realists, armed intervention was justified by a rational calculation of the national interest. America could not tolerate the domination of Europe by an undemocratic, expansionist Germany, and her vital interests now required armed intervention in a European war to secure the balance of power and construct an unprecedented union of nations for collective security. This view of international affairs was held as early as 1914 by men like Lewis Einstein and Walter Lippmann and has been adopted by most scholars since the 1940s. Some feel that Wilson stumbled accidentally onto the right course, others that despite his abstract language about principles, he intuitively understood that a German victory constituted a threat to American security and so conducted American foreign policy as to refuse to permit it. If he did not use phrases like "balance of power" and "American vital interests," it was because he faced a public of implacable naïveté and uninformed idealism, one which could only be motivated to the necessary sacrifices through the thrilling language of Protestant evangelism. But his drive to put himself and his country in a commanding position to mediate was strong from the beginning; it was one of the reasons he finally decided to intervene, and the sort of peace he wished to mediate did bear a close resemblance to the balance-of-power compromise the Realists approve.

Respected scholars have repeatedly made this argument for Wilson's intuitive realism, even though it requires some redefinition of his terminology and some careful scrutiny of the spaces between the lines. But if the president saw that our security was involved in the contest going on in Europe, as a few of his private remarks suggest, he made no effort to explain the matter to the American public. This may be credited to his own uncertainty rather than to political timidity. Wilson proved in the Brandeis appointment and later in the League fight that he was not afraid of political risks. But whether he was a slightly confused half-realist or a secret realist with exaggerated fears of the political risks involved in candor, Wilson spent the years from 1914 to 1917 talking about ideals, rights, and proper naval behavior. When he wrote state papers with his unrivaled eloquence, they were usually for the purpose of educating the Germans in their human and Christian responsibilities, not in educating his countrymen in the hard realities of modern geopolitics. When he asked for military preparedness, a logical step for one who wished his country to be in a position to influence events, he shaped a program of naval rearmament and left the army still puny—exactly what one would do who was in fact concerned with maritime rights rather than with European power dispositions. When he finally asked for intervention, he came across as a pure idealist on a mission of rescue for high, unassailable, but somehow precious ideals.

Guided by their president's words, which were repeated many times by pulpit and press, the boys went to beat the hell out of Germany for sinking our ships and for not being peace loving and democratic. Apparently the thrashing would be educational for the Germans, would produce great moral improvement among them, and would not only restore threatened human rights to their rightful place but would vindicate them forever. The attractiveness of this high enterprise, along with a general boredom, a habit of obedience, and perhaps above all an unrealistic expectation of what war would be like (Wilson himself thought the war would be over in six months and that our part in it would be primarily naval, and he was not alone) was enough to call the nation to arms.

Of course, it is almost certain that he could not have persuaded the country to enter the war for realistic reasons. He could never have convinced an isolationist and parochial society to participate in history's most horrible war for such uninspiring goals as the restoration of the balance of power and the defense of England's security on the novel grounds that both had a close relation to our own *vital* interests. The number of Americans who thought in such terms was so small that the entire group could easily be locked into a White House bathroom. Many wished to declare war, but merely wishing a declaration of war on Germany did not make one a Realist. Even those around the president who favored war did not know until after April that the Allies were in grave danger of losing. They, too, in the days before April 2, had talked of principles and human rights. Wilson himself might have tried over the months from August, 1914, to create a realistic public understanding of the American stake in the war, but no sensible person argues that this would have been enough. Twenty years later another persuasive president tried, and never convinced a majority of his countrymen. But if an effort to achieve limited but attainable goals was ruled out by American tradition and the state of popular education, by what logic does one take the nation into war for goals that are unattainable and in fact hardly coherent, and whose only virtue has not to do with their connection to reality but their ability to move public opinion behind belligerency? Wilson got the country to act, but for the wrong reasons at the wrong time.

There were men, like Theodore Roosevelt, who thought that war had no costs of any consequence, that fighting was in some way a beneficial experience for men and nations. But Wilson was wiser than that. There is an apocryphal story, told by the journalist Frank Cobb, in which Wilson on the eve of the war message predicted that going into the war would cost the country most of the New Freedom gains and much of its internal tolerance and sanity. Although Cobb's story has recently been challenged, we know that Wilson reckoned the costs of war much more realistically than most contemporaries, especially the domestic costs. In addition, he knew that the language and ideas he must employ to create a large, enthusiastic majority out of the refractory isolationists and temporary pacifists who surrounded him would create a type of fervor that would probably make his goals unattainable. For Wilson, whatever his talk of moral absolutes and "force without stint or limit," went to Europe basically to effect a compromise. He remained more interested in diplomacy than in victory, and while he led the nation against the forces of darkness he was sure the guilt in Europe was not all on one side and insisted that the United States be designated an "associated power," not an ally. Three times in his war message he spoke of restraint, of the necessity to fight without passion or vindictiveness. But Americans listened to the Wilson they preferred: the moralist, not the conciliator. To get the nation into the war he had proclaimed war aims that made restrained action and limited involvement impossible and made reaction inevitable among a people who had not been dealt with candidly.

The disappointments he feared—but did not fear enough—came in full measure. Germany was beaten, but she did not learn the moral lessons Wilson intended. If human rights were better off for American entry, no man has yet found a way to measure the improvement. Nor did the American influence at Versailles create a lasting peace. Because we were there, the settlement was a bastard compromise, "fairer" than the one the Germans would have dictated if the United States had not entered, but by no means more conducive to the stability of Europe and the avoidance of the horrors of 1939–45. The democracies won the war, but their victory did not stem the slide of Western civilization into dictatorship and philosophic malaise.

These disappointments came to Wilson's international aspirations, and there is no evidence that he foresaw the possibility of such defeats, although a number of hardened cynics were predicting them. Domestically, the costs of American involvement were far, far beyond even Wilson's relatively astute premonitions: 130,000 American lives lost in combat, 35,000 permanently disabled, approximately 500,000 influenza deaths in the U.S. in the winter of 1918–19 from a virus imported from the battlefields; an expenditure of $33.5 billion by

1919, to which may be added at least the $13 billion spent as of 1931 (according to economist John M. Clark) on veterans' pensions and interest on the war debt; 20 million person-years of labor diverted to war, or six months' work by every American; the 25 race riots of 1919; the stimulus to private indulgence and social irresponsibility; the decimation of the liberal center and the hobbling of the Left.

Such a brief sketch of the high costs and low yields of American participation in the war suggest an error in judgment. While Wilson had nothing like the influence over events that either he or his critics assumed, many doors of history hinged on his decisions. If it is too much to ask of any mortal political leader that, given the circumstances of spring, 1917, he choose division and national humiliation over unity and pride, it is not too much to ask for a different line of diplomacy reaching back to 1914, one that would not allow such restricted and self-defeating alternatives to hem him in.

It might be objected that a concentration on Wilson's decisions from 1914 forward ignores the historic trend toward a more active world role for the United States that commenced in the 1890s, and that this short-sighted perspective exaggerates his freedom. True, the United States in the twenty years before Wilson's Presidency had acquired an empire, intervened militarily in four countries where affairs had not gone to our liking and exerted diplomatic pressure in countless others, had built a modern navy, and had steadily expanded her international commercial contacts. But while this trend meant the inexorable approach of world power and involvement, it did not imply intervention in World War I. Our early military interventions had been limited in scope, had occurred in Latin America and the Far East, and had not been wildly popular.

Another argument with which I am not sympathetic holds that progressivism had an affinity for war. Progressives were activists, moralists, and had a strong sense of mission. They were therefore especially prone to foreign crusades, so the indictment runs. Those advancing this argument point to the fact that wars followed hard upon the reform eras of the 1890s, the Wilson years, the New Deal, the Fair Deal, the New Frontier. Further, they point to progressive Theodore Roosevelt's activist role in Panama and elsewhere, to Wilson's bellicose Mexican policy and his strong internationalism after World War I was over. A progressive President, a progressive country in 1914–1917—war was inevitable! But as plausible as these associations may appear, the case fails to convince. Close studies of progressive attitudes toward foreign policy consistently fail to detect a "progressive" position, whether activist, isolationist, or any other. Progressive T.R. wanted to intervene early, progressive Wilson tried for three years to stay out, and progressives LaFollette and Bryan fought intervention before 1917 and disapproved of it later. Reformers were of diverse minds on American foreign policy, and while some were quite jingoistic, the most opposition to the war came from the Left, liberal as well as radical.

Nonetheless, there is a tendency among modern students of Wilson to be so impressed with the long-term trend toward international involvement, and the supposed predisposition of the reform mind to crusades, not to mention the

President's political and diplomatic difficulties, that Wilson's policies are presented as virtually inevitable. Sympathetic scholars point out that Wilson presided over often uncontrollable tides of passion and group interest and that he was forced many times to drift and wait, passive before forces he knew to be beyond his Constitutional and personal powers to shape. But he also acted decisively many times, channeling events within a reasonably wide belt of possibility. Where he had no alternatives or no reasonable ones, we cannot be revisionists. Where he had them we must make judgments, so long as they are tempered with a respect for historic forces which always dwarf men, and with sympathy for this brilliant, patriotic Christian who inherited such baffling dilemmas.

Perhaps no other president would have seen the importance of the early decisions regarding the British blockade and the Declaration of London. The way was politically clear for the administration to insist on the declaration, but most men would have weakened and let it go. No one expected a long war. But many of the decisions of the spring of 1915 bore Wilson's personal stamp. Demands on the belligerents could have been linked, and Germany could have been held to the same postwar accounting reserved for the Allies. Bryan requested a passenger ban at that time, and Wilson was not on principle opposed. Yet he declined to suggest one, insuring that the idea would come from Congress and require his opposition.

The loan decision is an interesting case. Charles Beard showed some years ago that Bryan himself flinched before the bankers' arguments. The country was in an economic recession in 1914, a recession that produced "the largest number of business failures in our country's history," according to *Bradstreet's Journal,* and that brought Andrew Carnegie to write Wilson on 23 November, 1914: "The present financial and industrial situations are very distressing. I have never known such conditions, such pressing calls upon debtors to pay. . . ." No one, from the Harvard Economics Department through the entire range of federal agencies, had any idea how to cope with it beyond maintaining a happy investment climate for the men who hired other men. We now know that recovery could have been achieved by having the government borrow funds from New York banks and reemploy people by a program of spending—on ships and tanks if it wished, but preferably on schools, hospitals, and housing. But this was advocated only by a few unbelievable socialists. The bankers showed Wilson a golden opportunity to put idle funds to work by simply *allowing* Europeans to borrow in New York and spend the money in this country. The pressure was enormous, and there were no real counterpressures and no constructive countersuggestions. Here was an apparently painless cure for America's economic troubles, and the enthusiasm for Allied loans and trade would certainly have broken Wilson politically had he blocked it only with arguments drawn from moral repugnance. *The New York Times* editorialized in early 1915:

We have oversupplied ourselves with forces of production and they are idle in unusual proportion. . . . The Promise of the new year is that we shall accomplish a peaceful penetration of the world's markets to an extent we have never dreamed of. What others have shed blood to obtain through politics and force we shall obtain while bestowing our benevolence. . . . It is a new translation of the old beatitude, revised: blessed are the keepers of the peace for prosperity shall be within their homes and palaces.

Well might British ambassador Spring-Rice write to Grey in October: "When it became apparent that a loan was necessary, many secret forces began to act in its favour." It may now seem incredible that to achieve recovery the United States must ship to Europe both money and goods and call it a sharp bargain. But it made sense in a capitalistic order with only a rudimentary economic science, and there was literally no other plausible way in 1915 to get idle funds to work. The loan decision, while not inevitable, must be seen sympathetically in this light. Keynes' *General Theory* was twenty-one years away.

But if Wilson could hardly have been expected to maintain the ban against loans to good customers abroad, he might have eliminated munitions from the resulting trade. The Hitchcock bill of December, 1914, would have accomplished that, and there was ample precedent and political support for it. Embargoes on munitions were imposed by Denmark, Sweden, Italy, the Netherlands, Spain, and Norway. The United States itself had embargoed munitions to Mexico in 1913. A passenger ban might have easily been added in the spring of 1916, if not earlier. When the liner *Persia* was sunk on January 3, the principal Congressional reaction was anger that *American citizens had been aboard.* That month Wilson left for a speaking tour to gain support for preparedness and learned that the Congress accurately reflected the country's mood. A passenger ban was his for the asking; and while this would not have diminished the Allied trade, there would be no loss of American life to inflame the issue if Germany eventually resorted to unrestricted submarine warfare despite a ban on munitions, as she well might.

These two changes in policy taken together would have vastly altered the equation of forces. There were no other good alternatives of comparable importance, although Wilson passed up some minor opportunities for a more neutral course. The Lansing modus vivendi on armed ships could have been put into effect, but probably would not have made cruiser warfare the rule. Britain had been sending few armed ships to America anyway, and with Q-ships operating in British waters the submarines were still in danger on the surface. Yet the move would have been helpful. As for Wilson's mediation efforts, it is hard to fault his intentions or his persistence, except to wish that his general appeal had been issued earlier, and from a position of greater neutrality. But there was never much interest in a negotiated peace. Some small things he might have done. He might have fired Page and secured an ambassador to London who would not weaken protests against the blockade. He might, as some progressives urged, have dampened some enthusiasm in important quarters by declaring that, in the event of war, he would draft capital as well as men.

But the passenger ban and the munitions embargo were probably enough, and they were politically possible. Naval troubles with Germany would have arisen, but would have been manageable. With Wilson's rhetorical power and discipline of mind, the road to neutrality was diplomatically and politically passable.

Had Wilson acted along these lines the result would almost certainly have been a German victory, either in the form of a negotiated or a dictated peace. Hohenzollern Germany would dominate the continent—a nation adept in the industrial arts, astonishingly vigorous, nominally Christian, capitalistic, racially arrogant, militaristic, deep in its own internal struggle between the socialists and the entrenched and unimaginative conservatives of land and industry. At least the last years of the war and perhaps more, with their relentless butchery and crippling moral and political consequences, would have been averted. One is permitted to doubt the November, 1917 success of Lenin. Speculation could go on. It should also be noted that the education the American people supposedly received in their new international responsibilities would not have taken place, or at least not in the same way. In view of American foreign policy attitudes from 1919 through 1941, one contemplates the loss of this schooling with relative calm.

The allure of a different American diplomacy springs not from a blind aversion to warfare but from a reasoned conception of the nature of American security. Wilson was sure that our security lay in a respect for law, in the spread of parliamentary governments, in the prestige that comes to nations that do not tolerate the infringement of their rights, in a defeated Germany, in a just peace, and in a postwar league of nations. Much of this is silly, but some of it represents the deepest insight into modern international relations. His mistake lay not in his instincts, a compound of the profound and the harmless, so much as in his judgment of the circumstances. Given the circumstances—the uncontrollable passions of Europe and the ignorance that gripped his own great democracy—there was only one *sure* way to pursue American security, a familiar way, without staggering risks, and without death. It was by an intensification of that surge of internal reform to which he had already become committed: the purification of our own democracy, the diversion of more resources to the education and physical well-being of our people, the broadening of the sway of equality, the conservation of our resources, the humanizing of our hours and conditions of work, the enhancement of the efficiency of our industry, the beautification and ordering of our cities, the narrowing of the gap between the classes. But a decision was reached to interrupt this work for a different approach to national unity, a different approach to economic prosperity, a different approach to the respect of nations.

Ernest May has guessed that Wilson would have chosen differently if he had foreseen the casualties of the Argonne and Chateau-Thierry. In the last speech before his stroke, delivered at Pueblo, Colorado, on 25 September 1919, Wilson said, his face streaked with tears, "What of our pledges to the men that lie dead in France . . . ? There seems to me to stand between us and the rejection or qualification of this treaty the serried ranks of those boys in khaki, not only those boys who came home, but those dear ghosts that still deploy upon the fields of France." We have seen much more of the twentieth century than Woodrow Wilson, and the doubts grow stronger.

FURTHER READING

Thomas A. Bailey and Paul B. Ryan, *The* Lusitania *Disaster* (1975)

Paul Birdsall, "Neutrality and Economic Pressure, 1914–1917," *Science and Society,* 3 (1939), 217–228

John M. Blum, *Woodrow Wilson and the Politics of Morality* (1956)

Edward H. Buehrig, ed., *Wilson's Foreign Policy in Perspective* (1957)

John Garry Clifford, *The Citizen Soldiers* (1972)

John W. Coogan, *The End of Neutrality* (1981)

John M. Cooper, Jr., " 'An Irony of Fate': Woodrow Wilson's Pre-World War I Diplomacy," *Diplomatic History,* 3 (1979), 425–437

————, *The Vanity of Power* (1969)

Patrick Devlin, *Too Proud to Fight* (1975)

Alexander and Juliette George, "*Woodrow Wilson and Colonel House:* A Reply to Weinstein, Anderson, and Link," *Political Science Quarterly,* 96 (1981–82), 641–665

Ross Gregory, "To Do Good in the World: Woodrow Wilson and America's Mission," in Frank J. Merli and Theodore A. Wilson, eds., *Makers of American Diplomacy* (1974)

————, *Walter Hines Page* (1970)

N. Gordon Levin, *Woodrow Wilson and World Politics* (1968)

Arthur S. Link, *Wilson,* 5 vols. (1947–1965)

————, *Woodrow Wilson: Revolution, War, and Peace* (1979)

Ernest R. May, *The World War and American Isolation, 1914–1917* (1959)

Walter Millis, *Road to War* (1935)

Charles E. Neu, "The Search for Woodrow Wilson," *Reviews in American History,* 10 (1982), 223–228

Daniel M. Smith, "National Interest and American Intervention, 1917: An Historiographical Appraisal," *Journal of American History,* 52 (1965), 5–24

————, *Robert Lansing and American Neutrality, 1914–1917* (1958)

Charles C. Tansill, *America Goes to War* (1938)

Barbara Tuchman, *The Zimmermann Telegram* (1958)

Edwin A. Weinstein, *Woodrow Wilson: A Medical and Psychological Biography* (1981)

————, James W. Anderson, and Arthur S. Link, "Woodrow Wilson's Political Personality," *Political Science Quarterly,* 93 (1978–79), 585–598

Woodrow Wilson, Henry Cabot Lodge, and the League Fight

3

During the First World War, President Woodrow Wilson said he wanted a "peace without victory"—a lenient peace—and some historians have in fact suggested that Wilson asked for war in April 1917 to ensure himself a place at the peace table. In January 1918 he issued his peace program of Fourteen Points. To Wilson, the fourteenth point proposing a League of Nations was the most important. The war ended on November 11, 1918, a few days after the Republicans captured both Houses of Congress in the fall elections. In January of the following year, the President attended the Paris Peace Conference at Versailles and, over several months, made compromises in order to secure a peace treaty and his cherished Covenant of the League of Nations.

At home, however, many Americans began to question Wilson's handiwork and to offer amendments and reservations to protect United States sovereignty, which they claimed was threatened, especially by Article 10 of the Covenant prescribing collective security. The President battled back in a vigorous national debate, generally refused to compromise, and ultimately witnessed the defeat, in the United States Senate, of the treaty and American membership in the League in November 1919 and again in March 1920.

Historians disagree in their explanations for the rejection. Some concentrate on the personal feud between Wilson and Republican Senator Henry Cabot Lodge, whereas others stress the President's arrogance and stubbornness in the face of overwhelming political odds. Still others note that the debate centered on key questions about the national interest and that the final verdict was determined by American nationalists who were not willing to throw off their tradition of unilateralism in favor of collective security.

DOCUMENTS

Wilson issued his Fourteen Points in a speech on January 8, 1918. The League of Nations was created at Versailles and its Article 10, reprinted here, aroused heated controversy in the United States; Wilson considered the article the heart of the Covenant and the key to collective security. In a speech on September 17, 1919, in San Francisco, the President defended the League against mounting criticism. Led by Senator Henry Cabot Lodge of Massachusetts, critics offered a number of reservations to the Covenant and incorporated them in a Lodge resolution dated November 19, 1919.

The Fourteen Points, 1918

We entered this war because violations of right had occurred which touched us to the quick and made the life of our own people impossible unless they were corrected and the world secured once for all against their recurrence. What we demand in this war, therefore, is nothing peculiar to ourselves. It is that the world be made fit and safe to live in; and particularly that it be made safe for every peace-loving nation which, like our own, wishes to live its own life, determine its own institutions, be assured of justice and fair dealing by the other peoples of the world as against force and selfish aggression. All the peoples of the world are in effect partners in this interest, and for our own part we see very clearly that unless justice be done to others it will not be done to us. The programme of the world's peace, therefore, is our programme; and that programme, the only possible programme, as we see it, is this:

I. Open covenants of peace, openly arrived at, after which there shall be no private international understandings of any kind but diplomacy shall proceed always frankly and in the public view.

II. Absolute freedom of navigation upon the seas, outside territorial waters, alike in peace and in war, except as the seas may be closed in whole or in part by international action for the enforcement of international covenants.

III. The removal, so far as possible, of all economic barriers and the establishment of an equality of trade conditions among all the nations consenting to the peace and associating themselves for its maintenance.

IV. Adequate guarantees given and taken that national armaments will be reduced to the lowest point consistent with domestic safety.

V. A free, open-minded, and absolutely impartial adjustment of all colonial claims, based upon a strict observance of the principle that in determining all such questions of sovereignty the interests of the populations concerned must have equal weight with the equitable claims of the government whose title is to be determined.

VI. The evacuation of all Russian territory and such a settlement of all questions affecting Russia as will secure the best and freest cooperation of the other nations of the world in obtaining for her an unhampered and unembarrassed opportunity for the independent determination of her own political development and national policy and assure her of a sincere welcome into the society of free nations under institutions of her own choosing; and, more than a welcome, assistance also of every kind that she may need and may herself desire. The treatment accorded Russia by her sister nations in the months to come will be the acid test of their good will, of their comprehension of her needs as distinguished from their own interests, and of their intelligent and unselfish sympathy.

VII. Belgium, the whole world will agree, must be evacuated and restored, without any attempt to limit the sovereignty which she enjoys in common with all other free nations. No other single act will serve as this will serve to restore confidence among the nations in the laws which they have themselves set and determined for the government of their relations with one another. Without this healing act the whole structure and validity of international law is forever impaired.

VIII. All French territory should be freed and the invaded portions restored, and the wrong done to France by Prussia in 1871 in the matter of Alsace-Lorraine, which has unsettled the peace of the world for nearly fifty years, should be righted, in order that peace may once more be made secure in the interest of all.

IX. A readjustment of the frontiers of Italy should be effected along clearly recognizable lines of nationality.

X. The peoples of Austria-Hungary, whose place among the nations we wish to see safeguarded and assured, should be accorded the freest opportunity of autonomous development.

XI. Rumania, Serbia, and Montenegro should be evacuated; occupied territories restored; Serbia accorded free and secure access to the sea; and the relations of the several Balkan states to one another determined by friendly counsel along historically established lines of allegiance and nationality; and international guarantees of the political and economic independence and territorial integrity of the several Balkan states should be entered into.

XII. The Turkish portions of the present Ottoman Empire should be assured a secure sovereignty, but the other nationalities which are now under Turkish rule should be assured an undoubted security of life and an absolutely unmolested opportunity of autonomous development, and the Dardanelles should be permanently opened as a free passage to the ships and commerce of all nations under international guarantees.

XIII. An independent Polish state should be erected which should include the territories inhabited by indisputably Polish populations, which should be assured a free and secure access to the sea, and whose political and economic independence and territorial integrity should be guaranteed by international covenant.

XIV. A general association of nations must be formed under specific covenants for the purpose of affording mutual guarantees of political independence and territorial integrity to great and small states alike. . . .

We have spoken now, surely, in terms too concrete to admit of any further doubt or question. An evident principle runs through the whole programme I have outlined. It is the principle of justice to all peoples and nationalities, and their right to live on equal terms of liberty and safety with one another, whether they be strong or weak. Unless this principle be made its foundation no part of the structure of international justice can stand. The people of the United States could act upon no other principle; and to the vindication of this principle they are ready to devote their lives, their honor, and everything that they possess. The moral climax of this the culminating and final war for human liberty has come, and they are ready to put their own strength, their own highest purpose, their own integrity and devotion to the test.

Article 10 of the League Covenant, 1919

Article 10. The Members of the League undertake to respect and preserve as against external aggression the territorial integrity and existing political independence of all Members of the League. In case of any such aggression or in case of any threat or danger of such aggression the Council shall advise upon the means by which this obligation shall be fulfilled.

The Lodge Reservations, 1919

Resolved . . . That the Senate advise and consent to the ratification of the treaty of peace with Germany . . . subject to the following reservations and understandings . . . which ratification is not to take effect or bind the United States until the said reservations and understandings . . . have been accepted by . . . at least three of the four principal allied and associated powers. . . .

1. . . . in case of notice of withdrawal from the league of nations, as provided in said article [Article 1], the United States shall be the sole judge as to whether all its international obligations . . . have been fulfilled, and notice of withdrawal . . . may be given by a concurrent resolution of the Congress of the United States.

2. The United States assumes no obligation to preserve the territorial integrity or political independence of any other country . . . under the provisions of article 10, or to employ the military or naval forces of the United States under any article of the treaty for any purpose, unless in any particular case the Congress, which . . . has the sole power to declare war . . . shall . . . so provide.

3. No mandate shall be accepted by the United States under article 22 . . . except by action of the Congress of the United States.

4. The United States reserves to itself exclusively the right to decide what questions are within its domestic jurisdiction. . . .

5. The United States will not submit to arbitration or to inquiry by the assembly or by the council of the league of nations . . . any questions which in the judgment of the United States depend upon or relate to . . . the Monroe doctrine; said doctrine is to be interpreted by the United States alone and is . . . wholly outside the jurisdiction of said league of nations. . . .

6. The United States withholds its assent to articles 156, 157, and 158 [Shantung clauses]. . . .

7. The Congress of the United States will provide by law for the appointment of the representatives of the United States in the assembly and the council of the league of nations, and may in its discretion provide for the participation of the United States in any commission. . . . no person shall represent the United States under either said league of nations or the treaty of peace . . . except with the approval of the Senate of the United States. . . .

9. The United States shall not be obligated to contribute to any expenses of the league of nations . . . unless and until an appropriation of funds . . . shall have been made by the Congress of the United States.

10. If the United States shall at any time adopt any plan for the limitation of armaments proposed by the council of the league . . . it reserves the right to increase such armaments without the consent of the council whenever the United States is threatened with invasion or engaged in war. . . .

14. The United States assumes no obligation to be bound by any election, decision, report, or finding of the council or assembly in which any member of the league and its self-governing dominions, colonies, or parts of empire, in the aggregate have cast more than one vote.

Wilson Defends the League, 1919

It is my purpose, fellow citizens, to analyze the objections which are made to this great League, and I shall be very brief. In the first place, you know that one of the difficulties which have been experienced by those who are objecting to this League is that they do not think that there is a wide enough door open for us to get out. For my own part, I am not one of those who, when they go into a generous enterprise, think first of all how they are going to turn away from those with whom they are associated. I am not one of those who, when they go into a concert for the peace of the world, want to sit close to the door with their hand on the knob and constantly trying the door to be sure that it is not locked. If we want to go into this thing—and we do want to go into it—we will go in it with our whole hearts and settled purpose to stand by the great enterprise to the end. Nevertheless, you will remember—some of you, I dare say—that when I came home in March for an all too brief visit to this country, which seems to me the fairest and dearest in the world, I brought back with me the first draft of the Covenant of the League of Nations. I called into consultation the Committees on Foreign Affairs and on Foreign Relations of the House and Senate of the United States, and I laid the draft of the Covenant before them. One of the things that they proposed was that it should be explicitly stated that any member of the League should have the right to withdraw. I carried that suggestion back to Paris, and without the slightest hesitation it was accepted and acted upon; and every suggestion which was made in that conference at the White House was accepted by the conference of peace in Paris. There is not a feature of the Covenant, except one, now under debate upon which suggestions were not made at that time, and there is not one of those suggestions that was not adopted by the conference of peace.

The gentlemen say, "You have laid a limitation upon the right to withdraw. You have said that we can withdraw upon two years' notice, if at that time we shall have fulfilled all our international obligations and all our obligations under the Covenant." "Yes," I reply; "is it characteristic of the United States not to fulfill her international obligations? Is there any fear that we shall wish to withdraw dishonorably? Are gentlemen willing to stand up and say that they want to get out whether they have the moral right to get out or not?" I for one am too proud as an American to debate that subject on that basis. The United States has always fulfilled its international obligations, and, God helping her, she always will. There is nothing in the Covenant to prevent her acting upon her own judgment with regard to that matter. The only thing she has to fear, the only thing she has to regard, is the public opinion of mankind, and inasmuch as we have always scrupulously satisfied the public opinion of mankind with regard to justice and right, I for my part am not afraid at any time to go before that jury. It is a jury that might condemn us if we did wrong, but it is not a jury that could oblige us to stay in the League, so that there is absolutely no limitation upon our right to withdraw.

One of the other suggestions I carried to Paris was that the committees of the two Houses did not find the Monroe Doctrine safeguarded in the Covenant of the League of Nations. I suggested that to the conference in Paris, and they at once inserted the provision which is now there that nothing in the Covenant shall be construed as affecting the validity of the Monroe Doctrine. What is the validity of the Monroe Doctrine? The Monroe Doctrine means that if any outside power, any power outside this hemisphere, tries to impose its will upon any portion of the Western Hemisphere the United States is at liberty to act independently and alone in repelling the aggression; that it does not have to wait for the action of the League of Nations; that it does not have to wait for anything but the action of its own administration and its own Congress. This is the first time in the history of international diplomacy that any great government has acknowledged the validity of the Monroe Doctrine. Now for the first time all the great fighting powers of the world except Germany, which for the time being has ceased to be a great fighting power, acknowledge the validity of the Monroe Doctrine and acknowledge it as part of the international practice of the world.

They are nervous about domestic questions. They say, "It is intolerable to think that the League of Nations should interfere with domestic questions," and whenever they begin to specify they speak of the question of immigration, of the question of naturalization, of the question of the tariff. My fellow citizens, no competent or authoritative student of international law would dream of maintaining that these were anything but exclusively domestic questions, and the Covenant of the League expressly provides that the League can take no action whatever about matters which are in the practice of international law regarded as domestic questions. We did not undertake to enumerate samples of domestic questions for the very good reason, which will occur to any lawyer, that if you made a list it would be inferred that what you left out was not included. Nobody with a thoughtful knowledge of international practice has the least doubt as to what are domestic questions, and there is no obscurity whatever in this Covenant with regard to the safeguarding of the United States, along with other sovereign countries, in the control of domestic questions. I beg that you will not fancy, my fellow citizens, that the United States is the only country that is jealous of its sovereignty. Throughout these conferences it was necessary at every turn to safeguard the sovereign independence of the several governments who were taking part in the conference, and they were just as keen to protect themselves against outside intervention in domestic matters as we were. Therefore the whole heartiness of their concurrent opinion runs with this safeguarding of domestic questions.

It is objected that the British Empire has six votes and we have one. The answer to that is that it is most carefully arranged that our one vote equals the six votes of the British Empire. Anybody who will take the pains to read the Covenant of the League of Nations will find out that the assembly—and it is only in the assembly that the British Empire has six votes—is not a voting body. . . .

Not a single affirmative act or negative decision upon a matter of action taken by the League of Nations can be validated without the vote of the United States of America. We can dismiss from our dreams the six votes of the British Empire, for the real underlying conception of the assembly of the League of Nations is that it is the forum of opinion, not of action. It is the debating body; it is the body where the thought of the little nation along with the thought of the big nation is brought to bear upon those matters which affect the peace of the world, is brought to bear upon those matters which affect the good understanding between nations upon which the peace of the world depends; where this stifled voice of humanity is at last to be heard, where nations that have borne the unspeakable sufferings of the ages that must have seemed to them like æons will find voice and expression, where the moral judgment of mankind can sway the opinion of the world. That is the function of the assembly. The assembly is the voice of mankind. The council, where unanimous action is necessary, is the only means through which that voice can accomplish action.

You say, "We have heard a great deal about Article X." I just now said that the only substitute for the League of Nations which is offered by the opponents is a return to the old system. What was the old system? That the strong had all the rights and need pay no attention to the rights of the weak; that if a great powerful nation saw what it wanted, it had the right to go and take it; that the weak nations could cry out and cry out as they pleased and there would be no hearkening ear anywhere to their rights.

ESSAYS

Woodrow Wilson's perspective on the League of Nations and the American debate over it is developed by Arthur S. Link of Princeton University. A major Wilson biographer, Link explains the politics of the question and lauds Wilson as a prophet. William C. Widenor of the University of Illinois, in a selection from his *Henry Cabot Lodge and the Search for an American Foreign Policy* (1980), studies the Massachusetts senator's opposition to Wilson's League and his recommended changes. Widenor disputes the view of a demonic Lodge locked in a personal feud with the President; he stresses instead the importance of ideas in the debate.

Woodrow Wilson's Perspective

ARTHUR S. LINK

Wilson returned to the United States in June 1919 to face the crucial task of winning the support of the American people and the approval of the Senate for the Versailles Treaty, the underpinning of the Paris settlements. During the months following Wilson's homecoming, indeed until the election of 1920, there ensued in the United States a debate no less important than the great debate of 1787–1789 over ratification of the Constitution. At stake was the issue of American participation in a new world order capped by the League of Nations, an instrumentality designed to promote world co-operation and peace and armed with sanctions (including military force) to prevent aggression.

Some details of the well-known parliamentary struggle and of the bitter personal controversy between Wilson and his chief antagonist, Senator Henry Cabot Lodge of Massachusetts, cannot be ignored. However, the emphasis of this chapter will be upon what has often been obscured by too much focus on the dramatic details—how the great debate of 1919–1920 revealed differences in opinion concerning the role that the United States should play in world affairs. These differences were fundamental and authentic because they transcended partisanship and personality. They also are as relevant to Americans in the latter part of this century as they were in Wilson's day.

Arthur S. Link, *Woodrow Wilson: Revolution, War, and Peace* (Copyright © 1979 by Harlan Davidson, Inc., Arlington Heights, IL), pp. 104–113, 119–128. Reprinted by permission of the publisher.

The general lines of battle over ratification of the Treaty of Versailles were drawn before Wilson went to Paris, and largely by Wilson himself. Wilson's appeal during the congressional campaign had given a partisan coloration to the whole process of peacemaking. Many Republicans had regarded Wilson's appointment to the American Peace Commission of only one nominal Republican—Henry White, a career diplomat—as a slap in the face. By ignoring the Senate in his appointment of the commission, moreover, Wilson made it inevitably certain that the fight over the Treaty would renew in virulent form the old conflict between the President and the upper house for control of foreign policy.

It would be a great mistake to assume, as some historians have done, that the fate of the Treaty was foreordained by the injection of partisanship into the question of peacemaking or by Wilson's failure to appoint senators to the commission. In the subsequent controversy, Wilson had the warm support of the League to Enforce Peace, composed mainly of prominent Republicans, including former President William Howard Taft. The debate in the country over the Treaty was not a partisan one; and, in the final analysis, the votes in the Senate were partisan only to the degree that a large number of Democratic senators followed Wilson's demands. The important point is that the country at large and the Senate, to a large degree, divided over profoundly important issues, not along party lines. Finally, the fact that Wilson took no senators with him to Paris was of no consequence for the final result.

While Wilson was in Paris, there were unmistakable signs at home that he would encounter significant opposition in the Senate. The most ominous of these was the so-called Round Robin resolution that Lodge read to the Senate on March 4, 1919. It was signed by thirty-seven senators, more than enough to defeat the Treaty, and declared that the Covenant of the League of Nations, "in the form now proposed to the peace conference," was unacceptable. At the same time, isolationists in the Senate were already beginning a furious rhetorical attack against the Covenant.

Although Wilson was defiant in a speech in New York just before he sailed for Paris, he did accept the advice of his friends who urged him to conciliate his critics. He first tried, through Henry White, to ascertain precisely why the Covenant was not acceptable to Lodge and the signers of the Round Robin. Then, when Lodge refused to give any specifics, Wilson consulted Taft and other Republican supporters of the League and, in response to their suggestions, obtained changes in the Covenant. They provided for the right of member nations of the League to withdraw after giving due notice, exempted domestic questions from the League's jurisdiction, permitted member nations to refuse to accept a colonial mandate, and, most important, accorded formal recognition to the Monroe Doctrine.

Wilson was exhausted by the end of the peace conference and showed numerous indications of an unwillingness to compromise further with his senatorial critics. Colonel House, on the day that Wilson left Paris, urged him to meet the Senate in a conciliatory spirit. "I have found," Wilson is alleged to have replied, "that one can never get anything in this life that is worthwhile without fighting for it." This self-referential statement suggests that Wilson felt a great burden of guilt because of the compromises that he had made. If this was true, then the guilt feelings were reinforcing his determination to make no further compromises.

Refreshed by the return voyage, Wilson returned to Washington on July 8 in a confident mood. And with good reason. Much of the senatorial criticism of the Treaty was captious. Most important, by this time thirty-two state legislatures had endorsed the Covenant in concurrent resolutions; thirty-three governors had expressed their approval; and a *Literary Digest* poll indicated overwhelming support for the Covenant among editors of newspapers and magazines. Indeed, the whole country seemed to be in a fever of excitement about the League.

Wilson was, therefore, in the mood of a triumphant leader presenting his adversaries with a *fait accompli* when he laid the Treaty formally before the Senate on July 10. He did not refer to the senators, as he had often done, as his "colleagues," and he did not use his favorite phrase "common counsel," that is, the necessity of reasonable give and take before arriving at a final decision. On the contrary, he "informed" the senators that a world settlement had been made and then took the highest possible ground to urge prompt and unqualified approval. The League of Nations, he exclaimed, was the best hope of mankind. "Dare we reject it and break the heart of the world?" He gave the answer in an impromptu peroration at the end:

> The stage is set, the destiny disclosed. It has come about by no plan of our conceiving, but by the hand of God who led us into this way. We cannot turn back. We can only go forward, with lifted eyes and freshened spirit, to follow the vision. It was of this that we dreamed at our birth. America shall in truth show the way. The light streams upon the path ahead, and nowhere else.

Wilson met reporters in an informal press conference after delivering this address. He was relaxed and confident. There had been much talk of reservations to the Treaty. What did the President think of that idea? Wilson replied that he was determined to oppose all reservations, for they would require a two-thirds vote of the Senate and necessitate renegotiation of the Treaty. It is significant that a constitutional scholar should have made such a mistake. He had no doubt that the Treaty would be ratified just as it stood.

Actually, the situation was far less simple and reassuring than Wilson imagined at the beginning of the great debate. For one thing, powerful voices were already raised in outright and violent condemnation of the Treaty on various grounds. Idealists, who had thrilled at Wilson's vision of a new world, condemned the Treaty because it failed to establish a millennial order. The German-Americans believed that the Treaty was a base betrayal of the Fatherland; the Italian-Americans were angry over Wilson's opposition to Italy's demands. Most important, the several million Irish-Americans, inflamed by the civil war then raging in Ireland, were up in arms because Wilson had refused to win Irish independence at Paris and because the Treaty allegedly benefited the hated English. The powerful chain of Hearst newspapers was marshaling and inciting all the hyphenate protests. Out-and-out isolationists believed that American membership in the League of Nations would mean entanglement in all of Europe's rivalries and wars. They had powerful advocates in a small group of so-called irreconcilables or bitter-enders in the Senate, led by Hiram W. Johnson of California, William E. Borah of Idaho, and James A. Reed of Missouri, who opposed the Treaty for various deeply rooted reasons—nationalism, chauvinism, and idealism.

These were the major groups who opposed ratification of the Treaty. In the ensuing debate, they were the loudest and busiest participants of all. They were, however, a minority among the leaders of thought and political opinion, and they spoke for a minority of the people, at least before 1920, if not afterward. This is a simple point but a vital one, because, in its important aspects, the debate over the Treaty was not a struggle between advocates of complete withdrawal on the one side and proponents of total international commitment on the other. It was, rather, a contest between the champions of a potentially strong system of collective security and a group who favored a more limited commitment. It was a choice between these alternatives, and not between complete isolation or complete internationalism, that Wilson, the Senate, and the American people eventually had to make. We will, therefore, let the arguments of the isolationists pass without analysis and concentrate our attention upon the two main and decisive courses of the debate.

Differences of opinion in the United States over the territorial and other provisions of the Treaty were insignificant as compared to the differences evoked by the Covenant of the League and its provisions to prevent aggression and war. Those provisions were clear and for the most part unequivocal. Article 10 guaranteed the political independence and territorial integrity of every member nation throughout the world. Articles 11, 12, 13, 15, 16, and 17 established the machinery of arbitration for all international disputes susceptible to that procedure and decreed that an act of war against one member nation should "*ipso facto* be deemed to . . . [be] an act of war against all the other Members" and should be followed automatically by an economic blockade against the aggressor and by Council action to determine what military measures should be used to repel the aggression. These were almost ironclad guarantees of mutual security, meant to be effective and unencumbered by the right of any nation involved in a dispute to veto action by the League's Council. Whether such a worldwide system could work, and whether the American people were prepared at this stage of their development to support such a system even if it did work—these were the two main issues of the great debate of 1919–1920.

The decisive opposition to the Versailles Treaty came from a group of men who, to a varying degree, would have answered no to both these questions. This group included some of the most distinguished leaders in and out of the Senate, like Senator Frank B. Kellogg of Minnesota, President Nicholas Murray Butler of Columbia University, former Secretary of State Elihu Root, and Charles Evans Hughes, Republican presidential candidate in 1916. Most of them were Republicans, because few Democrats active in politics dared to incur the President's wrath by opposing him. They were not isolationists but limited internationalists who believed that the United States should play, in a varying degree, an active role in preserving the peace of the world. Most of them favored, for example, arbitration, the establishment of something like a World Court to interpret and codify international law, and international agreements for disarmament, economic cooperation, and the like. Some of them even supported the idea of alliances with certain powers for specific purposes.

On the other hand, all the limited internationalists opposed any such approval of the Treaty as would commit the United States unreservedly to the kind of collective security the Covenant of the League had created. Their arguments might be summarized as follows:

First, a system of collective security that is worldwide in operation is not likely either to work or to endure the strains that will inevitably be put upon it, because in practice the great powers will not accept the limitations that the Covenant places upon their sovereignty, and no nation will go to war to vindicate Article 10 unless its vital interests compel it to do so. Such sweeping guarantees as the Covenant affords are, therefore, worse than no guarantees at all because they offer only an illusory hope of security.

Second, the Covenant's fundamental guarantee, embodied in Article 10, is impossible to maintain because its promise to perpetuate the *status quo* defies the very law of life. As Elihu Root put it:

> If perpetual, it would be an attempt to preserve for all time unchanged the distribution of power and territory made in accordance with the views and exigencies of the Allies in this present juncture of affairs. It would necessarily be futile. . . . It would not only be futile; it would be mischievous. Change and growth are the law of life, and no generation can impose its will in regard to the growth of nations and the distribution of power upon succeeding generations.

Third, the American people are not ready to support the Covenant's sweeping commitments and in fact should not do so unless their vital interests are involved in a dispute. They would and should be ready to act to prevent the outbreak or any conflict that threatened to lead to a general war, but it is inconceivable that they would or should assume the risk of war to prevent a border dispute in the Balkans, or to help maintain Japanese control of Shantung Province or British supremacy in Ireland and India. Unconditional ratification of the Treaty by the United States would, therefore, be worse than outright rejection, for it would mean the making of promises that the American people could not possibly honor in the future.

Fourth, unqualified membership in the League will raise grave dangers to American interests and the American constitutional system. It will menace

American control over immigration and tariff policies, imperil the Monroe Doctrine, increase the power of the President at the expense of Congress, and necessitate the maintenance of a large standing army for the fulfillment of obligations under the Covenant.

Fifth, and most important, full-fledged participation in such a system of collective security as the Covenant establishes will spell the end of American security in foreign affairs, because it will mean transferring the power of decision over questions of peace and war from the President and Congress to an international agency which the United States could not control.

The limited internationalists, voicing these objections day in and day out as the great debate reached its crescendo in the autumn of 1919, made their purposes and program indelibly clear. They would accept most of the provisions of the Treaty unrelated to the League and acquiesce in the ones that they did not like. They would also sanction American membership in the League of Nations. But they would also insist upon reserving to the United States, and specifically to Congress, the power of decision concerning the degree of American participation in the League; and they would make no binding promise to enforce collective security anywhere in the future. This strategy was devised by Elihu Root in July 1919.

This was also the final, public position of Senator Lodge, the man who devised and executed the Republican strategy in the upper house during the parliamentary phase of the Treaty struggle. Personally, Lodge had little hope for the success of the League, a profound contempt for Wilson, and almost a sardonic scorn for Wilson's international ideals. The Massachusetts Senator was an ardent nationalist, almost a jingoist. He was no isolationist, but a believer in a strong balance of power. His solution would have been harsh terms, including dismemberment of Germany, and the formation of an Anglo-Franco-American alliance as the best insurance for future peace. But, as chairman of the Foreign Relations Committee and leader of his party in the Senate, it was his duty to subordinate his own strong feelings and to find a common ground upon which most Republicans could stand. That common ground, that program acceptable to an overwhelming majority of Republicans inside the Senate and out, was, in brief, to approve the Treaty and to accept membership in the League. This would be subject to certain amendments and reservations that would achieve the objectives of the limited internationalists.

Amendments and reservations designed to satisfy the moderate internationalists were embodied in the report that the Republican majority of the Foreign Relations Committee presented to the Senate on September 10, 1919. During the following weeks, that body rejected the amendments (on the ground that they would require renegotiation of the Treaty) and adopted most of them in the form of reservations, fourteen in all. Most of them were unimportant, but there was one that constituted a virtual rejection of the kind of collective security that Wilson had envisaged. It was Reservation 2, which declared that the United States assumed no obligations to preserve the territorial integrity or political independence of any other country, unless

Congress should by act or joint resolution specifically assume such an obligation. In addition, the preamble to the reservations provided that American ratification of the Treaty should not take effect until at least three of the four principal Allied powers had accepted the reservations in a formal exchange of notes.

This, then, was the program to which most of Wilson's opponents stood committed by the time that the Senate moved toward a formal vote on the Versailles Treaty. Whether Lodge himself was an irreconcilable who desired the defeat of the Treaty, or whether he was merely a strong reservationist, is an important question but an irrelevant one at this point. The significant fact is that he had succeeded in uniting most Republicans and in committing them to a program that affirmed limited internationalism at the same time that it repudiated American support of a tentative collective security system.

Meanwhile, despite his earlier show of intransigence, Wilson had been hard at work in preparation for the impending struggle. In an effort to split the Republican ranks, he held a series of conferences in late July with eleven Republican senators who he thought would favor approval of the Treaty after the adoption of a few interpretive reservations. On August 19, the President met the Foreign Relations Committee at the White House for a three-hour grilling on all phases of the settlement. The interchange produced no new support for the Treaty. What Wilson did not know, and never did seem to know, was that virtually all of the so-called mild reservationists had already coalesced into the central hard-core Republican pro-League group in the Senate. They were the men who voted with Democrats to convert Lodge's amendments into reservations. They were the ones who forced Lodge, for the sake of party unity, to support the treaty with reservations. Finally, they were the real authors of the reservations. Thus, confer as much as he could, Wilson made no headway in winning the support that would be vital when the Senate voted on the Treaty.

In response, Wilson made one of the most fateful decisions of his career. It was, as he put it, to go to the people and purify the wells of public opinion that had been poisoned by the isolationists and opponents of unreserved ratification. He was physically weakened by his labors at Paris, and his physician warned that a long speaking tour might endanger his life. Even so, he insisted upon making the effort to rally the people, the sources of authority, who had always sustained him in the past.

Wilson left Washington on September 3, 1919, and headed for the heartland of America, into Ohio, Indiana, Missouri, Iowa, Nebraska, Minnesota, and the Dakotas—into the region where isolationist sentiment was strongest. From there he campaigned through the Northwest and the major cities of the Pacific Coast. The final leg of his journey took him through Nevada, Utah, Wyoming, and Colorado, where the tour ended after Wilson's partial breakdown on September 25 and 26. In all he traveled 8,000 miles in twenty-two days and delivered thirty-two major addresses and eight minor ones. It was not only the greatest single speaking effort of Wilson's career, but also one of the most notable forensic accomplishments in American history.

Everywhere that he went, Wilson pleaded in good temper, not as a partisan, but as a leader who stood above party strife and advantage. He was making his tour, he explained, first of all so that the people might know the truth about the Treaty of Versailles and no longer be confused by the misrepresentations of its enemies. . . .

There remained the greatest threat of all to the integrity of the Covenant, the challenge of the reservation to Article 10. This reservation, Wilson warned, would destroy the foundation of any collective security, because it was a notice to the world that the American people would fulfill their obligations only when it suited their purposes to do so. "That," the President exclaimed at Salt Lake City, "is a rejection of the Covenant. That is an absolute refusal to carry any part of the same responsibility that the other members of the League carry." "In other words, my fellow citizens," he added at Cheyenne,

> what this proposes is this: That we should make no general promise, but leave the nations associated with us to guess in each instance what we were going to consider ourselves bound to do and what we were not going to consider ourselves bound to do. It is as if you said, "We will not join the League definitely, but we will join it occasionally. We will not promise anything, but from time to time we may cooperate. We will not assume any obligations. . . ." This reservation proposes that we should not acknowledge any moral obligation in the matter; that we should stand off and say, "We will see, from time to time; consult us when you get into trouble, and then we will have a debate, and after two or three months we will tell you what we are going to do." The thing is unworthy and ridiculous, and I want to say distinctly that, as I read this, it would change the entire meaning of the Treaty and exempt the United States from all responsibility for the preservation of peace. It means the rejection of the Treaty, my fellow countrymen, nothing less. It means that the United States would take from under the structure its very foundations and support.

The irony of it all was, Wilson added, that the reservation was actually unnecessary, *if the objective of its framers was merely to reserve the final decision for war to the American government.* In the case of all disputes to which it was not a party, the United States would have an actual veto over the Council's decision for war, because that body could not advise member nations to go to war except by unanimous vote, exclusive of the parties to the dispute. Thus, Wilson explained, there was absolutely no chance that the United States could be forced into war against its will, unless it was itself guilty of aggression, in which case it would be at war anyway.

These were, Wilson admitted, legal technicalities, and, he added, he would not base his case for American participation in the League of Nations upon them. The issue was not who had the power to make decisions for war, but whether the American people were prepared to go wholeheartedly into the

League, were determined to support a collective security system unreservedly, and were willing to make the sacrifices that were necessary to preserve peace. Wilson summarized all his pleading with unrivaled feeling at the Mormon capital:

> Instead of wishing to ask to stand aside, get the benefits of the League, but share none of its burdens or responsibilities, I for my part want to go in and accept what is offered to us, the leadership of the world. A leadership of what sort, my fellow citizens? Not a leadership that leads men along the lines by which great nations can profit out of weak nations. Not an exploiting power, but a liberating power—a power to show the world that when America was born it was indeed a finger pointed toward those lands into which men could deploy some of these days and live in happy freedom, look each other in the eyes as equals, see that no man was put upon, that no people were forced to accept authority which was not of their own choice, and that, out of the general generous impulse of the human genius and the human spirit, we were lifted along the levels of civilization to days when there should be wars no more, but men should govern themselves in peace and amity and quiet. That is the leadership we said we wanted, and now the world offers it to us. It is inconceivable that we should reject it.

We come now to the well-known tragic sequel. Following his address at Pueblo, Colorado, on September 25, 1919, Wilson showed such obvious signs of exhaustion that his physician canceled his remaining engagements and sped the presidential train to Washington. On October 2, Wilson suffered a severe stroke and paralysis of the left side of his face and body. For several days his life hung in the balance; then he gradually revived, and by the end of October he was clearly out of danger. But his recovery was only partial at best. His mind remained relatively clear; but he was physically enfeebled, and the disease had wrecked his emotional constitution and aggravated all his more unfortunate personal traits.

Meanwhile, the Senate was nearing the end of its long debate over the Treaty of Versailles. Senator Lodge presented his revised fourteen reservations on behalf of the Foreign Relations Committee to the upper house on November 6, 1919. Senator Gilbert M. Hitchcock of Nebraska, the Democratic minority leader, countered with five reservations, four of which Wilson had approved in substance before he embarked upon his western tour. They simply sought to make clear the American understanding of Article 10 and other provisions of the Treaty. The issue before the Senate, therefore, now seemed clear—whether to approve the Treaty with reservations that did not impair the American obligation to uphold the Covenant, or whether to approve the Treaty with reservations that permitted repudiation of all compelling obligations and promised American support for only a limited international system.

Lodge beat down the Hitchcock reservations with the help of the irreconcilables and then won adoption of his own. Now Wilson had to choose between acceptance of the Lodge reservations or run the risk of the outright defeat of the Treaty. He gave his decision to Hitchcock in a brief conference at the White House on November 17 and in a letter on the following day: Under no circumstances could he accept the Lodge reservation to Article 10, for it meant nullification of the Treaty. When the Senate voted on November 19, therefore, most of the Democrats joined the irreconcilables to defeat approval with the Lodge reservations by a count of thirty-nine ayes to fifty-five nays. The Democratic leaders, hoping to split the Republican ranks and win the support of the mythical mild reservationists then moved unconditional approval of the Treaty. This strategy, upon which Wilson had placed all his hopes, failed, as a firm Republican majority defeated the resolution with the help of the irreconcilables by a vote of thirty-eight ayes to fifty-three nays.

The great mystery is why Wilson rejected the Lodge reservation to Article 10. Before he left on his western tour, Wilson handed Hitchcock four "interpretive" reservations to the articles relating to the right of member nations to withdraw, Article 10, the nonjurisdiction of the League over domestic matters like immigration, and the Monroe Doctrine. Wilson's reservation to Article 10 said that the Senate understood that the advice of the League Council with regard to the use of armed force was to be "regarded only as advice and leaves each member free to exercise its own judgment as to whether it [were] wise or practicable to act upon that advice or not." Hitchcock's own reservation, which presumably Wilson had approved, went even further and said that Congress would have to approve the use of armed force if so requested by the Council.

Why, when the two sides were so close together, did Wilson reject the Lodge reservation to Article 10? Having built so grandly at Paris, having fought so magnificently at home for his creation, why did he remove by his own hand the cornerstone of his edifice of peace? Were there inner demons of pride and arrogance driving him to what Thomas A. Bailey has called "the supreme infanticide"?

Dr. Weinstein has described the effects of the devastating stroke on Wilson's personality and perceptions at this time. He is convinced that, had Wilson been in full health, he would have found the formula to reconcile the differences between the Lodge and Hitchcock reservations. There is a great deal of evidence to support this hypothesis. When Wilson made his decision, on November 17, to reject the Lodge reservation, he was still a very sick man. His mind could function well in certain circumstances, but his whole emotional balance had been shattered. He was sick, petulant, and rigid. He saw very few people between his stroke and November 17, and those who talked to him were careful not to upset him. From his lonely isolation in a sickroom, he saw the outside world from a limited and distorted view. A healthy Wilson certainly would have spent most of his time from his return to Washington from the West to mid-November conferring, cajoling, and doing everything possible to find an acceptable compromise on the reservation to Article 10. This was part of the genius of his leadership. He had displayed it many times before, most notably in negotiating the writing of the Federal Reserve Act and the Versailles Treaty.

Wilson's isolation and the unfortunate pathological effects of his stroke might well have caused him to give the most literal reading possible to the Lodge reservation to Article 10. Taken literally, this reservation could be read as an emphatic repudiation of American responsibilities under the Covenant. It read:

> The United States assumes no obligation to preserve the territorial integrity or political independence of any other country or to interfere in controversies between nations—whether members of the league or not—under the provisions of Article 10, or to employ the military or naval forces of the United States under any article of the treaty for any purpose, unless in any particular case the Congress, which, under the Constitution, has the sole power to declare war or authorize the employment of the military or naval forces of the United States, shall by act or joint resolution so provide.

Even a healthy Wilson might have concluded that this reservation amounted, as he put it, to nullification of the Treaty. And any strong President would have bridled at the closing phrases of the reservation, for they constituted the first important congressional constraints against the President as commander in chief to this point in American history and were probably unconstitutional.

Wilson, whether because of his illness or not, did read the reservation literally. He believed, very deeply, that the one issue now at stake was whether the United States would join the League of Nations and give leadership to it wholeheartedly and without reservations, or whether it would join the League grudgingly, with no promises to help maintain the peace of the world. To Wilson, the difference between what he stood for and what the Republicans would agree to was the difference between the success or failure and the life or death of mankind's best hope for peace.

The vote on November 19 was not the end of the struggle, for during the following months an overwhelming majority of the leaders of opinion in the United States refused to accept the vote as the final verdict. In the absence of any reliable indices, it is impossible to measure the division of public opinion as a whole; but there can be little doubt that an overwhelming majority of thoughtful people favored ratification with some kind of reservations, even with the Lodge reservations, if that was necessary to obtain the Senate's consent.

Consequently, there was enormous pressure upon the leaders in both parties for compromise during the last weeks of 1919 and the early months of 1920. Prominent Republicans who had taken leadership in a nonpartisan campaign for the League (including former President Taft), scores of editors, the spokesmen of various academic, religious, and labor organizations, and Democratic leaders who dared oppose the President (like William J. Bryan and Colonel House) begged Lodge and Wilson to find a common ground. Alarmed by the possibility of American rejection of the Treaty, spokesmen for the British government declared publicly that limited American participation in the League would be better than no participation at all.

Under this pressure, the moderate leaders in both camps set to work in late December and early January to find a basis for agreement. Even Lodge began to weaken and joined the bipartisan conferees who were attempting to work out an acceptable reservation to Article 10. But the Massachusetts Senator and his friends would not yield the essence of their reservation, and it was Wilson who had to make the final choice.

By January, Wilson had recovered sufficient strength to take personal leadership of the Democrats in the Senate. One effect of his stroke was a strong if not complete tendency to deny that he was ill. For example, he would refer to his paralyzed left arm as "it" and not as a part of his body. He was absolutely convinced that he had the great mass of the people behind him and that they would crush any senator or party who opposed him. Living as he did in a world of unreality, Wilson concocted two stratagems.

The first stratagem was to challenge the fifty-seven senators from thirty-eight states who opposed the Treaty altogether or supported the Lodge reservations to resign and then run for reelection in special elections. Should they be reelected, Wilson would appoint a leader of the opposition as Secretary of State and he, Wilson, and his Vice President would resign and the Republican leader would become President. This plan proved to be unfeasible because of variations in state election laws.

Then Wilson, ever innovative, turned to his second stratagem—to make the treaty the leading issue of the coming presidential campaign. Moreover, he would be the Democratic nominee; he would go once again to the people and win an overwhelming mandate for the League. He even drafted a Democratic platform and his speech of acceptance. He set this plan in motion in a letter to the Jackson Day Dinner in Washington, then the chief meeting of Democrats preliminary to a presidential campaign, on January 8, 1920. He repeated his principal arguments for ungrudging approval, declared that "the overwhelming majority" of the people desired ratification of the Treaty, and concluded:

> If there is any doubt as to what the people of the country think on this vital matter, the clear and single way out is to submit it for determination at the next election to the voters of the nation, to give the next election the form of a great and solemn referendum, a referendum as to the part the United States is to play in completing the settlements of the war and in the prevention in the future of such outrages as Germany attempted to perpetrate.

The Jackson Day letter spelled disaster for ratification of the Treaty in any form. Wilson committed the supreme error of converting what had really not been a partisan issue, except in the parliamentary sense, into a hostage of party loyalty and politics. Henceforth most Republican senators would have to vote as Republicans, most Democrats as Democrats, even though they might want to put the interests of the country above those of party and vote for ratification with reservations.

Secondly, in spite of his unshakable faith in the wisdom of the people, Wilson, an expert in the American constitutional and political systems, should have known that there is no way to convert a presidential election into a referendum upon a single issue. Bryan had tried to make the election of 1900 a referendum upon the question of imperialism and had failed utterly to do so. As it turned out in 1920, Warren G. Harding, the Republican nominee and a strong reservationist, had no trouble in muting and sidestepping the League issue. Indeed, a group of thirty-one prominent pro-League Republicans issued a statement during the campaign assuring their fellow Republicans that Harding's election would be the best assurance of ratification and American membership in the League of Nations!

Thirdly, and ironically, Wilson's Jackson Day letter destroyed Wilson's leadership among the various segments of elite opinion makers who had heretofore been his strongest supporters—religious leaders, educational leaders, publicists, editors, and politically active professionals. A reading of their correspondence, journals, editorials, and resolutions reveals a sharp and sudden turn in their opinion. In their view, Wilson was a petulant and sick man and now the principal obstacle to ratification. These leaders of opinion were in utter despair and confusion. Most of them simply gave up the fight. The effect would be devastating for Democratic fortunes during the presidential campaign.

However, Wilson continued to hope that he would lead the Democrats to victory as their presidential candidate. He made plans to have his name put in nomination at the Democratic national convention and to have himself nominated by acclamation. A group of his closest friends had to tell him that it was impossible.

Meanwhile, the parliamentary phase of the struggle moved to its inexorable conclusion when the Senate took its second and final vote on the Treaty on March 19, 1920. The only hope for approval lay in the chance that enough Democrats would defy Wilson, as many friends of the League were urging them to do, to obtain a two-thirds majority for the Lodge reservations. Twenty-one Democrats did follow their consciences rather than the command from the White House, but not enough of them defected to put the Treaty across. The Treaty with the Lodge reservations failed by seven votes.

In this, the last and greatest effort of his life, did Wilson spurn the role of statesman for that of prophet? It is easy enough from our vantage point to say that, in rejecting ratification on the only possible terms and in throwing the issue into the party arena, he did not act as a statesman. It is also clear that his illness gravely impaired his perceptions of political reality and was probably the principal cause of his strategic errors.

However, when we view the situation through Wilson's eyes, his behavior seems neither irrational nor quixotic. As has been said many times, he believed that he had the overwhelming support of the people. He had gone to them many times before, and, except in 1918, with resounding success. He was confident that he, or another pro-League Democrat, could do so again in 1920.

His friends feared that he would be devastated by Harding's victory. On the contrary, he was serene and confident on the morning after the election.

He told his private secretary, "The Republicans have committed suicide." To the end of his life he was confident of the ultimate outcome and of the rectitude of his own position. As he put it: "I would rather fail in a cause that will ultimately triumph than triumph in a cause that will ultimately fail."

Wilson was fundamentally right in the one great principle at stake in the Treaty fight. The most immoral thing that a nation (or individual) can do is to refuse to exercise power responsibly when it possesses it. The United States exercised the greatest economic and potentially the greatest military power in the world in 1920. At least for a time it spurned the responsibility that accompanied its power.

Moreover, Wilson was fundamentally right in the long run. As he put it in a speech on Armistice Day in 1923: "We shall inevitably be forced by the moral obligations of freedom and honor to retrieve that fatal error and assume once more the role of courage, self-respect, and helpfulness which every true American must wish to regard as our natural part in the affairs of the world."

The postwar version of collective security failed in the crucial tests of the 1930s, not because the Treaty of Versailles was responsible or the peace-keeping machinery of the League of Nations was defective, but because the people of Great Britain, France, and the United States were unwilling to confront aggressors with the threat of war. Consequently, a second and more terrible world conflict came in 1939, as Wilson had prophesied it would.

The American people, and other peoples, learned the lesson that Wilson taught in 1919 and 1920, but at a fearful cost. And it is Wilson the prophet and pivot of the twentieth century who survives in history, in the hopes and aspirations of mankind for a peaceful world, and in whatever ideals of international service that the American people still cherish. One thing is certain, now that nations have the power to sear virtually the entire face of the earth: The prophet of 1919–1920 was right in his vision; the challenge that he raised then is today no less real and no less urgent than it was in his own time.

Henry Cabot Lodge's Perspective

WILLIAM C. WIDENOR

Just as Wilson was heralding the formation of his "league for peace" Charles Evans Hughes warned that "it is not the part of wisdom to create expectations on the part of the people of the world which the Covenant cannot satisfy." On that point Wilson would have differed, for Hughes's advice ran counter to the President's conception of political leadership. Believing that in international relations idealism could be a self-fulfilling proposition, Wilson saw his duty in inspiring the people to believe that they need no longer be

From *Henry Cabot Lodge and the Search for an American Foreign Policy.* © 1980 The Regents of the University of California, reprinted by permission of the University of California Press.

content with human imperfection, that the war could be a war to end all wars and the league a means of ensuring perpetual peace. He first engaged and then ultimately commanded and personified the hopes and aspirations of millions both at home and abroad. Many Americans came to believe (no other word is as descriptive) in the League of Nations. Their acceptance of the League bore many of the marks of an act of faith rather than of careful analysis of the factors (other than faith) requisite for the successful operation of a collective security system. When their hopes did not materialize, when the Senate developed reservations with respect to American entry into the League and international relations returned to their normal desultory pattern, it was easier to believe that this state of affairs was the result of the machinations of "evil" men than to entertain the proposition that their own faith might have been misplaced. The corollary of the "self-righteous martyred saint attitude" adopted toward Wilson by his many disciples was the idea that the will of the American people had been frustrated by "a little group of powerful men" or, more specifically, by the "craft and acumen," "the consummate cunning" of Lodge, who almost single-handedly "beat back this enormous movement" and kept the United States out of the League. Hence, the prominent place in American demonology which Lodge has long occupied.

Such interpretations vary in their sophistication, but share a common quality: their defense of Wilson and of his conception of a league rests primarily on impugning the motives and character of those who opposed him. That alone should be sufficient to arouse suspicion. Moreover, such criticism has inhibited rational consideration of the problems involved in the enforcement of peace, and it is precisely on that point that American thinking has tended to imprecision. Apparently, as Lodge once suggested, we will always have with us "those who wish to have the world's peace assured by force, without using force to do it." The conclusions of those who have made the most thorough study of the issues involved (John Chalmers Vinson's work on Article X and Warren Kuehl's careful comparison of Wilson's conception of a league with that of other prominent American internationalists) indicate that ideas did play an important, even determinant, role in the struggle over the league. It served the interests of many of those involved to believe that the struggle was essentially one of partisan politics and personal hatred, but the real problem was that Americans could not agree upon the nature of the League they wanted or upon the arrangements necessary to make it work.

Both Wilson and Taft occupied an uncomfortable position. As Walter Lippmann later recognized, "in them the idealism which prompts Americans to make large and resounding commitments was combined with the pacifism which causes Americans to shrink from the measures of force that are needed to support the commitments." Wishing to minimize the exertions so important to the Europeans (the commitment to come to their aid with troops), hoping and often convincing himself that the United States would never in practice be called upon to fulfill its commitment to use force on behalf of the territorial integrity of other states, Wilson came to depict the League in a manner reflecting the isolationism to which it was the supposed antithesis. Trapped by the contradictions inherent in their own desires (a contradiction laid bare by Borah when he pointedly asked "What will your league amount to if it does not contain powers that no one dreams of giving it"), it is perhaps understandable that when it came their turn to write the nation's history Wilsonians found it profitable to argue personalities and motives rather than issues.

It also behooves us to be suspicious of those interpretations which depict Lodge as the villain of the fight over the League because that was the manner in which it pleased Wilson to view the struggle. Lodge was singled out by name in the 1920 Democratic platform for his alleged inconsistency on the League and peace issue, and "the Republican Senate" was condemned for "its refusal to ratify the treaty merely because it was the product of Democratic statesmanship, thus interposing partisan envy and personal hatred in the way of peace and renewed prosperity of the world." The objections to such an interpretation are manifold. Apart from the fact that it denigrates the role of ideas in the determination of human behavior, it remains a little too convenient. The Democrats found it politic to run against Lodge in 1918 and again in 1920, and Wilsonians have been doing so ever since. Lodge was never a popular figure on the American political scene. Indeed, he presented an inviting target and outside New England his very virtues were readily converted into liabilities. As even the admiring Barrett Wendell noted, Lodge was "not sympathetic in either temper or in address"; even when "really large and constructive in his purposes, he . . . managed to impress people as a rather cynical opportunist at best." It was Lodge's misfortune that his demeanor presented a standing invitation to opponents to disregard the issues he wanted to stress, but it would not seem unreasonable to expect historians to endeavor to surmount that obstacle.

Implicit in all "Wilsonian" interpretations is the assumption that Lodge would have supported a league such as Wilson advocated if a Republican had proposed it. Certainly Lodge hated Wilson and was intent on effecting his political demise, but that does not mean that his animosity was solely a function of personal or partisan feelings. He also hated what Wilson stood for and the way he did things, not least the manner in which he conducted the nation's foreign policy. It is one thing to claim that Lodge had a political and even personal interest in the defeat of the League, which is obvious, and yet quite another to say that interest so dominated his thinking that he would have supported a league such as Wilson fashioned if only its sponsorship had been different. That goes in the face of Lodge's course with respect to the Taft arbitration treaties and of everything which I have been able to discover about his foreign policy views. Lodge's views on Wilson's league were not only compatible with, but flowed directly out of, his perception of the type of foreign policy most appropriate under American conditions. . . .

Wilson preferred as in May of 1916 and January of 1917 to let the league be all things to all men. He made no attempt to educate public opinion on what Lodge considered the all important details of prospective world organization. Both personally and politically he found it convenient to ignore the problems inherent in the relationship between force and peace. The league as depicted in his Fourteen Points Address seemed to rest on an implied threat to use force against would-be violators of the new international order, and yet the pacifist impulse in his thinking and in that of many of his followers was so strong that it was tempting to picture a league so morally ascendant that force would never have to be employed. It was this particularly Wilsonian straddle that caused Roosevelt to focus on the problem of credibility, and to fear that Wilson would inevitably make the league a thing of words and do his best to substitute "some fake policy of permanent pacifism" for one based on permanent preparation.

While the war was in progress Lodge also had little to say on the subject of a league. To him all talk of a league still carried the connotation of a desire for a negotiated settlement, and he saw no reason to change the position detailed in his February 1, 1917 speech on "The President's Plan For World Peace." When the subject of the league again came to the fore he had only to reach back to that speech for his arguments. It continued to serve his purposes. He had emphasized the practical and political difficulties involved in the construction of a system to actually enforce peace, had warned against entangling the question of how to make peace permanent with the peace to end the present war, and had insisted that "a treaty which cannot or will not be scrupulously fulfilled is infinitely worse than no treaty at all." He recurred to the latter point during the war, characterizing the maintenance of the sanctity of treaties as "one of the war's great features and objects." But like most Congressmen he focused his attention on more immediate issues and left it to Roosevelt, the publicist in the partnership of parliamentarian and publicist, to carry on discussion of the league proposal.

To Roosevelt the spirit behind a league remained of more significance than its institutional arrangements. He thought it might be possible to limit future wars, but only "by wise action, based equally on observed good faith and on thoroughly prepared strength" and those, he insisted, were the precise characteristics in which his countrymen were wanting. Hence, he accorded a higher priority to the cultivation of those characteristics than to the formation of a league. "Sound nationalism" was still a necessary antecedent to "sound internationalism." Roosevelt was ready to see the United States join a league to enforce peace, but only on condition that "we do not promise what will not or ought not to be performed" and "do not surrender our right and duty to prepare our own strength for our own defense." Above all he wanted the country to be wary of those who thought it possible "to secure peace without effort and safety without service and sacrifice. . . ." His greatest problem with Wilson's version of a league was that the President seemed to be telling the American people that a league and preparedness need not go hand in hand, that if they accepted the league they could safely reject preparedness. Roosevelt, on the contrary, felt that only on the basis of the adoption of a policy of permanent national preparedness could the U.S. afford to try the league experiment. He and Taft were eventually able to get together on the league issue because Taft came out for universal military training, and this allowed Roosevelt to say that he backed the

League to Enforce Peace as an addition to, and not as a substitute for, national preparation.

The battle lines, drawn since the winter of 1916–17, became ever more taut as the war neared its conclusion. "Unanimity in approving a world organization," as Lansing later so aptly put it, "did not mean that opinion might not differ radically in working out its forms and functions." Just under the surface of support for the principle lay a plethora of qualifications. Roosevelt in conditioning his support for league membership on a prior commitment to national preparedness was engaged in something of a personal crusade, but there was also a widespread feeling (at least in Republican ranks) that the league was already a reality, that the Allies constituted a de facto league. Lodge thought the Allies a "good enough league for the present at least," and even Taft and Lowell felt the league might initially consist of only the major Allied powers—England, France, Italy, Japan, and the U.S. Other and predictable Republican concerns were the preservation of the Monroe Doctrine (with Roosevelt taking up Cosmos's idea and suggesting the reservation of specific spheres of influence under any league arrangement) and the revitalization of the Hague Tribunal, a way of expressing their continued interest in a juridically based internationalism. Most people were still talking about a league in general terms, but the magic phrase "league for peace" already masked many different and even contradictory ideas about how it ought to be constituted. Many people had already formulated distinct reservations with respect to a league. . . .

It was "easy to talk about a league of nations and the beauty and necessity of peace," he [Lodge] said, "but the hard practical demand is, are you ready to put your soldiers and your sailors at the disposition of other nations?" In public he left the answer open, but, aware of the strength of the pacifist and isolationist blocs in Congress, he never for a moment thought a plan for an international army could get through the Senate. There was an insuperable obstacle to the formation of an effective league. That obstacle lay deep in the American character and in the nature of the American political system. Hence Lodge could confidently state that "the strength of our position is to show up the impossibility of any of the methods proposed and invite them, when they desire our support, to produce their terms; they cannot do it." What was required for the construction of an effective collective security organization was never politically feasible at home. It was a dilemma from which Lodge determined that Wilson should not be permitted to escape.

Though he was already in close contact with people like Beveridge who were reassuming the traditional "isolationist" posture, Lodge's concerns were never theirs. True, their arguments were often the same and Lodge was as opposed as anyone to any derogation of national sovereignty. But Lodge cared about the peace settlement in Europe in a way that the "isolationists" never did (was concerned not only about its morality but about its viability), and many of the considerations which impelled him to oppose a league of Wilsonian design were "internationalist" reasons. During the war he often made the "internationalist" point that, the Monroe Doctrine notwithstanding, we *were* interfering in Europe and there was no longer any place for talk about the war being three thousand miles away and of no concern. Naturally, he still believed in Washington's injunction against permanent alliances, but, as he expressed it, "we must make up our minds that as we have shared in the war we must share in the settlement of peace." He also had a concern for the preservation of close relations with the Allies unknown among those who became isolationists. Though technically the U.S. had no treaty of alliance with those on whose side it fought, technicalities, he maintained, were of no consequence in the presence of facts. "To encourage or even to permit any serious differences to arise between the United States and Great Britain, or with France, or Italy, or Belgium, would be a world calamity of the worst kind." Carrying out the peace with Germany would be the work of a generation and would necessitate the closest cooperation among the Allies.

Another measure of Lodge's internationalism can be derived from the fact that on the eve of the Peace Conference he seemed willing to go considerably further than Wilson in making the United States a guarantor of the European settlement. He considered it imperative that the Slavic nationalities be helped in establishing themselves as independent states, and privately he even suggested the possibility of the United States becoming a mandatory for such trouble spots as Constantinople. At a time when Wilson was trying to distance himself from the Allied governments, Lodge wanted to tie the United States more closely to them.

> We cannot halt or turn back now. We must do our share to carry out the peace as we have done our share to win the war, of which the peace is an integral part. We must do our share in the occupation of German territory. ... We can not escape doing our part in aiding the peoples to whom we have helped to give freedom and independence in establishing themselves with ordered governments, for in no other way can we erect the barriers which are essential to prevent another outbreak by Germany upon the world. ...

Lodge's outlook, in short, was no more isolationist than Wilson's and, in its emphasis on sacrifice and on the responsibilities of the United States, perhaps less so. Even Taft was prompted to remark in response to Lodge's Senate speech on the 21st of December that it "was the best yet made on the aims of the Allies and the elements of a satisfactory treaty of peace. ... Its great merit is in its broad vision of the real purposes of the United States and her present obligation. ... He [Lodge] is not a little American."

Both Lodge and Wilson were internationalists interested in making the peace secure, but there the similarity ended. Their respective priorities were quite different. The President's mind, as Lodge suggested, was "fixed on general questions lying outside the making of a peace with Germany." Lodge could not have been too surprised that immediately upon reaching Paris Wilson announced that the foundation of a League of Nations would be the first and foremost task of the conference. The Senator believed, on the other hand, that "the first and controlling purpose of the peace must be to put Germany in such a position that it will be physically impossible for her to break out again upon other nations with a war for world conquest." Lodge saw no alternative.

Only by building on present conditions, only by the "existing and most efficient league" [the Allies], could the peace be effectively implemented. "The attempt to form now a league of nations—and I mean an effective league, with power to enforce its decrees—no other is worth discussing—can tend at this moment only to embarrass the peace that we ought to make at once with Germany." Both privately in a memorandum prepared to be shown to Balfour, Clemenceau, and Nitti, and publicly in the Senate he warned that the consequences of Wilson's persistence could be dire:

> ... under no circumstances must provisions for such a league be made a part of the peace treaty which concludes the war with Germany. Any attempt to do this would not only long delay the signature of the treaty of peace, which should not be unduly postponed, but it would make the adoption of the treaty, unamended, by the Senate of the United States and other ratifying bodies, extremely doubtful.

There developed out of this what Arno Mayer has described as a "transnational political confrontation." The patterns of allegiance and mistrust formed in the years of America's neutrality were too strong to be overcome. Lodge so distrusted the President that he was quite willing to undermine his position at the Peace Conference. In his affinity for the British Lodge was prepared to undercut Wilson as Hamilton had once undercut John Jay. His views had long been more in accord with those of the leaders of the Allies, and now he sought to encourage them to stand up to Wilson, particularly on the league issue and the exaction of physical guarantees. The memorandum he gave to Henry White might "in certain contingencies be very important to them [Balfour, Clemenceau, and Nitti] in strengthening their position." His December 21 Senate speech was "intended chiefly for the benefit of the Allies."

Wilson for his part distrusted not only Lodge but also the Allied leaders and told his advisers that the men with whom they were about to deal did not really represent their respective nations. Tragically, events had long since precluded even the possibility of Lodge and Wilson listening to one another. Lodge's warnings probably only increased Wilson's determination to put his own stamp on the Peace Conference. Perhaps even more unfortunate, their disdain for each other also precluded an appreciation of their respective abilities and strengths. As a result Wilson began to think in terms of arranging things so that the Senate would be forced to accept a league and Lodge, having confidence only in the sense of the Allies, determined to "force Wilson, as we forced him before, to do what ought to be done but which he is not planning to do." Thus did they underestimate one another and thus did a historic and (if there be any logic in history) well-nigh inevitable struggle begin. . . .

The initiative was entirely Wilson's. It was his League that was before the Peace Conference and his League that would eventually come before the Senate. Only if Lodge, Root, or Roosevelt had been in actual control of American foreign policy could they have constructed an alternative to the Wilsonian settlement. As it was, their ideas were little more than hypotheses.

The time *was* opportune; the United States *was* ripe for an abandonment of the isolation against which Lodge had long, and Wilson more recently, contended. But there remained the question of what kind of internationalism would take its place. Root was convinced that Wilson was on the wrong track and told Lodge that if his proposal is not materially amended "the world will before very long wake up to realize that a great opportunity has been wasted in the doing of a futile thing." Lodge also felt that a great opportunity was being wasted and urged Root to "show the public what ought to be done to accomplish as much as can practically be accomplished by a union of the nations to promote general peace and disarmament." This Root soon did in a March 29 letter to Republican National Chairman Will Hays, a letter which culminated in six far-reaching amendments to Wilson's draft. But their position was defensive by definition; they could try to amend Wilson's proposal but they had no power to put anything in its place. The President was in a position to force them to adopt a narrow, insular national-ism in order to prevent the construction of what they regarded as a dangerous, unstable form of internationalism. "In trying to do too much," Lodge feared (prophetically as it turned out) that "we might lose all." It might have been otherwise. As Root recounted, when the proposal had been laid before the Paris Conference, the French representative, Leon Bourgeois, emphasized that "we do not present it as something that is final, but only as the result of an honest effort to be discussed and to be examined not only by this con-ference but the public opinion of the world."

But this was not the manner in which Wilson presented the League to the American people. He offered a finished product, a *fait accompli*. On his return to Paris Wilson did try to meet some of Taft's suggestions for amend-ments, did try, for example, to secure some recognition of the Monroe Doc-trine and establish a category of domestic issues over which the League would have no jurisdiction, but one would be hard pressed to argue that the Covenant underwent any substantial revision between February 15 and April 28, 1919, when the final draft was published. Lodge called Root that night to say that he found the amendments unsatisfactory and thought the League in its new form "but slight improvement over the first draft." His complaints were essentially the same as in February. Still he was probably not too sur-prised. At the time of the Round Robin he still hoped to jolt the Peace Con-ference into a full reconsideration of the Covenant, but only two weeks later (after Wilson's uncompromising New York Opera speech) he had despaired of this happening and had suggested that it would have to be done elsewhere —plainly in the Senate. . . .

Never a universalist, Lodge early sought to differentiate between a "gen-eral, indefinite, unlimited scheme of always being called upon to meddle in European, Asian and African questions" and a policy designed to ensure that the strong barrier-states necessary to fetter Germany were erected. As he saw it, the future peace of the world depended, not on the universal prev-alence of American ideals, but rather on the strength of France, a fact which Wilson seemed not to appreciate.

Lodge's conception of America's world role was as idealistic as Wilson's, but there was a crucial difference. Lodge believed that America had evolved a special, historical individuality and a unique system of values which were as much the product of propitious circumstance as anything else. Though he was prepared to go to great lengths to defend and preserve that individuality, he did not, like Wilson, seek its preservation in an attempt to secure its universal acceptance. The United States, at least toward Europe, served best as an example; it would remain mankind's best hope only so long as it did not destroy itself by becoming involved in every broil that desolated the earth. Conservative in his assessment of the human condition and too particularist to believe it possible to universalize American values, he readily conceded that Europe had different interests and priorities and understood its own needs better than could any American. The United States, in his view, did have an interest in the European settlement, but he was quick to emphasize that "there is a wide difference between taking a suitable part and bearing due responsibility in world affairs and plunging the United States into every controversy and conflict on the face of the globe."

Lodge and Root would have done it differently:

> It seemed to me at the time and has seemed to me ever since so clear what the President ought to have done; that he should have said to the Powers associated with us in the war: "We want the world made safe against Germany and as long as that is done we are content. So far as European matters are concerned, you are the people to settle them. Settle them all among yourselves and we will back you up. When it comes to Asia and Africa, of course we expect to have a voice; and we ask to be let alone in our own hemisphere." If that had been done the situation today would have been wholly different. But Mr. Wilson has undertaken to be the final umpire in every European question, incurring hostility both for himself and for his country, and meddling with things in which the United States has no interest whatsoever.

But Wilson, having less appreciation of the factors that circumscribed the nation's ability to act wisely in foreign affairs, so influenced the Peace Conference that they "made omnipotence their province and occupied the entire sphere on national and international relations the world over." Policy divorced from the reality of interest produced such aberrations as the Conference's decisions respecting Fiume, Danzig, and Shantung. It probably would have turned out better, Lodge felt, had it all been in Clemenceau's hands. At any rate, the sooner a country that so mismanaged things got out of the business of meddling in other nations' affairs the better.

Shantung, like Fiume, had an importance which transcended the significance of the territory involved or the alleged "immorality" of the Conference's disposition of it. Lodge seems actually to have believed that "the taking of Shantung ... from an ally and handing it over to another ally as the price of a signature to the League is one of the blackest things in the history of diplomacy," equalling even the partition of Poland. This was probably not so much because he was a staunch defender of China as because he was

suspicious of "the Prussia of the East." It was the Shantung question that triggered massive attrition on the left flank of Wilson's support, and Lodge
used the issue to the hilt in the struggle for domestic political advantage.
But perhaps of even more significance to Lodge and Root was the fact that
Article X of the Covenant appeared to bind the United States to defend the
Shantung settlement, to sustain Japan against China should the latter rise
up and attack Japan in an effort to undo "the great wrong" of the cession
of control over Shantung. Public reaction to the Shantung arrangement convinced them that this was something the United States would never do, and
this in turn made them regard Article X with even greater suspicion. What
had a telling effect on public opinion in the short run, and put Wilson at a
political disadvantage, was also predictive of the form American public
opinion would take were the United States ever asked to support its pledge
under Article X. Therein lay a justification for exploiting the Shantung issue
and also proof that one can not readily draw a line between "political" and
"principled" opposition to the League. . . .

Another measure of the nature and extent of Lodge's internationalism
would follow if we could give a definite answer to Arthur Link's question
whether Lodge was himself "an irreconcilable who desired the defeat of the
treaty, or . . . merely a strong reservationist. . . ." Another way of putting it
would be to ask whether he sincerely advocated ratification with reservations
and made a sincere effort to effect the compromises that would have made
ratification possible. While some evidence supports the claim that Lodge was
just going through the motions and had no intention of compromising with
the Democrats, those who have emphasized Lodge's "willingness to accept
the treaty with reservations" and the fact that "he actually tried to get the
treaty through with his reservations" have slightly the better of the argument. Among the evidence they adduce is the negotiation Lodge undertook
with Colonel House through Stephen Bonsal in an effort to work out compromise language, Lodge's allowing the treaty to come to a second vote, his
willingness to enter into a bipartisan conference in January of 1920 which
sought to devise reservations language acceptable to most Senators, and
finally his support of changes in his own reservations that were designed to
meet Wilson's objections (as when he vainly tried to secure a provision
making American withdrawal dependent on a joint, rather than on a concurrent resolution of Congress).

Of more than passing interest are Lodge's relationships with other principals in the struggle over the League and their opinion of him and his position. Revealing, both in its praise of Lodge and in its foreclosure of any
other route to ratification, is a letter from Root to Lodge dated December
1, 1919, well after the vote in November. In Root's view Lodge's leadership
in the Senate had been "extraordinarily able"; he termed it "one of the greatest
examples of parliamentary leadership" he had ever known and expressed the
wish that all the friends of the Treaty could understand that it was Lodge
who had given the Treaty "its only chance for ratification. . . ." Another important figure, Viscount Grey, sent by the British Government as its Ambassador to the United States with the special mission of composing American

differences of opinion on the League, apparently came to the same conclusion as Root. He is said to have commented sympathetically on Lodge's handling of the treaty, and in a letter to the London *Times* he advocated British acceptance of the Lodge reservations as the best means of securing American participation.

The relationship between Lodge and the irreconcilables also deserves attention. Senator Knox thought that only pressure from the irreconcilables had kept Lodge in line, that "on one occasion he was on the point of surrendering to the mild reservationists. . . ." It is not an unreasonable construction of Borah's January 24, 1920, letter to Lodge (threatening to bolt the party unless Lodge dropped his backstage compromise negotiation with the Democrats) to say it demonstrated that Borah believed Lodge was doing his best to get the treaty ratified. The irreconcilables forced him to break off those negotiations, but in the following weeks he reasserted his independence and continued to modify his reservations, their views notwithstanding. He taunted the irreconcilables with the claim that his reservations had "acquired a sanctity with some of my friends which they did not have, I think, until after the 19th of November," announced his intention to support improvements in both substance and phraseology which might lead to securing a two-thirds vote for the treaty, and finally even suggested a substitute for that most sacrosanct of reservations, that to Article X. In addition he wrote a letter to Beveridge on February 16, 1920, which seemed to anticipate a favorable vote on ratification and which had the evident purpose of consoling Beveridge by telling him, first, that the reservations made the League safe for the United States and, second, that no one would be able to say it was a victory for Wilson since the reservations were "too clearly ours to allow such a charge to have any effect." Admittedly, the evidence cited here is selective. But it seems sufficient to make a fairly good case for the argument that Lodge was willing to acquiesce in ratification on the basis of strong and effective reservations. Nevertheless, that leaves much unsaid, for some of those reservations embodied principles which Lodge was not ready to compromise.

Many, however, have not been convinced of Lodge's willingness to accept ratification on the basis of his own reservations. A frequent charge has been that the reservations were a device to secure the treaty's defeat, and that if Wilson had shown any signs of accepting them Lodge would have come up with more drastic ones. These charges apparently had their origin in a 1928 Council on Foreign Relations publication alleging that Lodge had "declared privately" that he "had proposed reservations which he was confident the President would reject, and that he was prepared to add to them if it were necessary, his purpose being to have the League rejected." However, there is no hard evidence to support such an accusation. It has the markings of a rationalization employed by those seeking to defend Wilson's intransigence and is devoid of political logic. The Lodge who knew within what tight limits he had to operate would never have risked such an affront to the mild reservationists.

A better case has been made in support of the view that Lodge was really an irreconcilable and opposed to any league whatsoever. Some historians have argued against Lodge's sincerity by citing remarks and publications from a later date. However, all their damaging evidence postdates the final vote on the treaty. Lodge did gradually become more irreconcilable. Will Hays remarked on that and so did Root who, though he continued to believe that Lodge initially wanted to join the League with reservations, recognized that he had gradually fallen under the influence of Brandegee and the other irreconcilables. Lodge came eventually to feel that the Senate's rejection of the League had been "a fortunate result." He may even have thought so shortly after the vote. There is considerable psychological resonance in Alice Longworth's observation that though he "at one time persuaded himself to believe that he was in favor of the League of Nations if amply safeguarded by reservations, my opinion is that in his heart he was really as opposed to it in any shape as an irreconcilable. . . ." His views changed in response to the country's mood; as the country became more irreconcilable (not an unreasonable interpretation of the 1920 election results) he moved in the same direction, the more easily as the country's mood confirmed his view that America was not ready for such undertakings. But does that necessarily reflect on his sincerity in advocating ratification of the League before March 19, 1920, or on his willingness to compromise toward that end? It doesn't directly, but it seems to suggest that we may have been asking the wrong questions. Since Lodge appears to have abandoned his support for ratification rather readily after March 19, we might better ask whether he ever believed in the League and whether he thought the differences between his conception of a league and Wilson's—between his conception of the proper scope of American internationalism and the President's—could be compromised. . . .

Lodge was skeptical about the League from the outset and never entertained high hopes for it. In confidence he predicted its failure and to Lord Bryce he expressed the opinion that the League was "a mere ornament" since "the real force under the treaty with Germany is placed in the hands of the five great Powers." While sure that reservations would "do more for the chances of life to the League than anything else," he felt bound "to confess that this League is altogether too much like a political alliance to make me feel that it is likely to be either enduring or successful." Even worse from his point of view, the League arrangements sought to deny the power realities that underlay its existence and to that end made extravagant promises incapable of fulfillment. Lodge saw through to the heart of the dilemma confronting those trying to construct a workable universal collective security organization: "Really to fulfill the advertised intention of its framers, it would have been necessary to put force behind the League, . . ." and to have provided for an international army with an international command.

That being politically unacceptable, the result was the murky compromise known as Article X under which Member States pledged to defend one another's territorial integrity and political independence, it being left to the League Council to "advise upon the means by which this obligation shall be fulfilled." This uneasy compromise caused Wilson considerable difficulty at home; it permitted his opponents to attack the League from both sides in the manner of Borah's famous question: "What will your league amount to if it does not contain powers that no one dreams of giving it." This same uneasy compromise haunted the League throughout its history. Canada tried to have Article X suppressed in 1920, and the League Council could not in 1923 even decide whether its advice was binding.

Wilson, as John Chalmers Vinson has observed, never gave a compelling interpretation of American responsibilities under Article Ten. He was damned if he did and damned if he didn't. He could only equivocate. Though claiming that Article X was "the very backbone of the whole Covenant," he dared not claim that the Council's advice derogated from Congress's right "to exercise its independent judgment in all matters of peace and war." Consequently, he was left to resolve the contradictions inherent in American participation in the Covenant in the following unsatisfactory manner. The engagement under Article X, he claimed:

> . . . constitutes a very grave and solemn moral obligation. But it is a moral, not a legal obligation, and leaves our Congress absolutely free to put its own interpretation upon it in all cases that call for action. It is binding in conscience only, not in law.

At first glance it would appear that Wilson and Lodge were not far apart; Lodge wanted only a reservation saying that the United States "assumes no obligation" under Article X "unless in any particular case the Congress . . . shall by act or joint resolution so provide." But appearances were in this case particularly deceiving. To Wilson and his supporters the moral obligation was real (if only as a matter of faith), and their objection to Lodge's reservation to Article X was that it specifically removed that moral obligation. This was not a minor point, but rather *the* obstacle to ratification; the nature of the obligation assumed by Member States would determine what kind of organization the League would be. To Lodge and Root it appeared as if Wilson and the Democrats wanted to accept an obligation which the United States might thereafter refuse, while their position has been characterized as one of wanting to refuse an obligation which might thereafter be accepted. Believing that under American conditions it was important to make all commitments as definite as possible, they could never accept Wilson's attempt to distinguish between a moral and a legal obligation. It begged the question of whether the obligation was binding. Root denounced Wilson's "curious and childlike casuistry" and thought the attempted distinction "false, demoralizing and dishonest." Lodge, believing that such an obligation could only be moral, wanted to prevent there arising a situation where Congress could not exert its Constitutional rights without breaking that moral obligation. That was the purpose of his reservation to Article X; it "made us the judges of whether we should carry out the guarantees of Article 10 or not, and in case of our refusal this reservation prevented its being a breach of the treaty. . . ."

Since the success of a collective security organization would seem to rest on the absence of doubt as to the intentions of its members, that is, on the credibility of their commitments, Lodge's reservation stating that the United States assumed no obligation was a denial of the theory on which collective security was based. His reservations, though leaving the League a useful instrument of collaboration (which was the way he had conceived it in the first place), "would have transformed the League into a non-coercive or an intermediate type of international organization." That, of course, is essentially what it became.

But there remains the question of Lodge's intent and his understanding of what he was doing. Many of the irreconcilables were convinced that the reservations never amounted to anything, that once the League was set up they would influence its operation very little. Some historians in their eagerness to criticize Wilson's handling of the matter have also come to regard the Lodge reservations as innocuous. They claim that Lodge hardly hoped for more than party unity and face-saving reservations, and that therefore a "reasonably sagacious political approach" by Wilson would have assured ratification. Such arguments can, of course, be used to bolster either the case for Lodge's partisanship or the case for the "sincerity" of his internationalism, but they also carry the implication that Lodge was unfamiliar and unconcerned with the problems inherent in the application of force to ensure peace and neither appreciated Wilson's ploy nor understood how to meet it. Given what we now know about his thinking since the winter of 1916–17, that is difficult to accept. Despite the fact that he eventually became an irreconcilable, Lodge never wavered in the view that the reservations would have made the League safe for the United States. And making it safe for the United States could not help but change its structure. Lodge took his reservations seriously and so did Wilson; they both knew they had profound implications. They were so far apart in their views on Article X that it is reasonable to assume there was virtually no prospect for compromise. However, Americans have an abiding faith in their ability to compromise and that made Lodge's task more difficult. But Wilson at least would probably have understood and agreed with James Beck's observation that "the reservations would have driven a 'coach and four' through the League of Nations and made the obligations of the United States thereunder almost nominal. . . ."

Lodge was unyielding on two crucial points. In October of 1919 he told the Senate that "this treaty will never be ratified unless the Monroe Doctrine is finally and absolutely reserved from the jurisdiction of the League." In February of 1920 he declared that he could "never assent to any change in principle in the two reservations relating to the Monroe Doctrine and article 10." This could lead one to conclude that his efforts to reach a compromise in the context of the bipartisan committee were "an elaborate charade," but perhaps a fairer interpretation would be that, though he was convinced that compromise was impossible, he found it necessary to demonstrate that fact to others. Nothing short of an actual demonstration that nothing could be done by way of compromise would satisfy public opinion, he told Beveridge. Lodge attributed this to the press, which seemed "to overlook the fact that with the mass of the Senators this is not a question of personal fortune or party advantage but a great question of principle on which they cannot yield any essential point." To the end he complained that "the differences between what Hitchcock offers and what we are willing to accept are much deeper and broader than people generally understand." It was to counteract that situation that he agreed to the bipartisan conferences. "It was," he wrote to a confidant, "something we had to go through." It might also be described as the culmination of the educative process in which he had long been engaged. Viewed in that light the fact that he made up his mind "that if the conference was to break up without an agreement it should be on Article 10" appears less Machiavellian. Article 10 was "the crucial point throughout the contest over the covenant. . . ." What Lodge did was to arrange to break off the negotiations "on a question not only where I knew we could stand before the country but where, also, I could have my votes of more than one-third."

This suggests not necessarily the sincere advocate of ratification with reservations, nor yet the reasonable compromiser, but a man strongly opposed to the Wilsonian conception of a League and determined to reveal its faults and prevent the United States from getting deeply involved in it. As Lodge saw it, the League was grievously flawed and would not work. Thomas Bailey once observed that Lodge was a failure if he really wanted the Treaty, but he could scarcely have "really wanted" something in which he did not believe. Whether the United States joined the League was never of as much concern to him as were the conditions under which it joined. Those, as Wilson also understood, would determine the nature of the organization and involved "great principles." Lodge's detached view on the matter of American entry gave him a considerable tactical advantage and permitted him to maintain close working relations both with those who wanted and with those who did not want the United States in the League. He thereby maximized his control of the situation and ensured that no matter which way the final vote went his views would prevail. . . .

Wilson claimed not only that the United States had gone to war to establish a League of Nations, but that "the opinion of the whole world swung to our support and the support of the nations associated with us in the great struggle" because of that advocacy. Moreover, he insisted that any reservation to Article X would plunge the world back into imperialism and reaction, a clear invitation to the American people to attribute anything short of perfection in international relations to Lodge's reservations. Never willing to admit that there were serious problems involved in the formation of a league to enforce peace, Wilson sought to limit such discussion by the introduction of yet another myth, namely that the Republican Senate "interposing partisan envy and personal hatred in the way of the peace and prosperity of the world" had refused to ratify the treaty "merely because it was the product of Democratic statesmanship." Wilson knew something about lost causes and the manner in which they were romanticized. As a result, under the influence of another and even more horrible war, a new generation of Americans found it easy to believe that had the United States joined the League that war might not have occurred. In their devotion to atoning for the "mistake" of 1919–20 by constructing a new international organization for securing the world's peace, they were as blind to some of the other requisites of a lasting peace settlement as Wilson had been twenty-five years earlier. Instead of learning from their elders' mistakes, they only compounded their tragedy.

FURTHER READING

Thomas A. Bailey, *Woodrow Wilson and the Great Betrayal* (1945)
———, *Woodrow Wilson and the Lost Peace* (1944)
Paul Birdsall, *Versailles Twenty Years After* (1941)
Denna F. Fleming, *The United States and the League of Nations, 1918–1920* (1942)
Inga Floto, *Colonel House in Paris* (1973)
John A. Garraty, *Henry Cabot Lodge* (1953)
Lawrence E. Gelfand, *The Inquiry: American Preparations for Peace* (1963)
W. Stull Holt, *Treaties Defeated by the Senate* (1933)
Herbert Hoover, *The Ordeal of Woodrow Wilson* (1958)
Warren F. Kuehl, *Seeking World Order* (1969)
N. Gordon Levin, *Woodrow Wilson and World Politics* (1968)
Arno Mayer, *Politics and Diplomacy of Peacemaking* (1967)
Keith Nelson, *Victors Divided* (1973)
Robert E. Osgood, *Ideals and Self-Interest in American Foreign Relations* (1953)
Stuart I. Rochester, *American Liberal Disillusionment in the Wake of World War I* (1977)
Ralph A. Stone, *The Irreconcilables* (1970)
John Thompson, *Russia, Bolshevism, and the Versailles Peace* (1966)
Seth P. Tillman, *Anglo-American Relations at the Paris Peace Conference, 1919* (1961)

Diplomacy in the 1920s

4

Historians used to treat the 1920s as a backwater between the fast-moving streams of the First and Second World War eras. It was supposedly a time of "isolationism," when the American people, disillusioned over the souring experience of World War I and the League fight at home, pressed their government to reduce its international obligations, to return to unilateralism. New scholarship has revised that view. Historians now find a mix of unilateralism and internationalism, with the United States significantly involved in world affairs—helping Europe resolve its debts-reparations problem, for example. The United States remained a major trader; indeed, it was the economic giant of the world. A high degree of business-government cooperation helped advance the American economic frontier abroad. The United States participated in disarmament conferences and continued to count Latin America as its sphere of influence. In a world beset by economic dislocations, the challenging ideology of Bolshevism, and revolutionary nationalism like that in Mexico, the United States did not shrink from trying to influence international relations. American confusion there seemed to be, but not weakness, except perhaps in Asia. The characteristics of 1920s diplomacy are the subject of this chapter.

DOCUMENTS

At the Washington Conference of 1921–1922, Secretary of State Charles Evans Hughes insisted on substantial naval disarmament in a major opening address on November 12, 1921. The three conference treaties are reprinted as the second document. The third document, dated July 19, 1923, is a Hughes letter explaining why the United States still refused to recognize the government of Soviet Russia. Secretary of Commerce Herbert Hoover was an economic expansionist who mobilized his department to aid American business abroad. In a March 16, 1926, speech he explained foreign trade's place in the American economic system. In late 1926 the Coolidge administration ordered troops into Nicaragua when that Latin American country erupted in civil war, threatening the power of the American-backed Conservative Party. A leading anti-imperialist, Senator Burton K. Wheeler of Montana, in a speech of January 26, 1927, condemned this new United States intervention. The sixth document is the anti-war Kellogg-Briand Pact, signed by the United States and most of the world's nations in August of 1928. Finally, Edwin L. James, the chief European correspondent of the *New York Times,* wrote in October 1930 about shifts in American international power.

Charles Evans Hughes on Naval Disarmament, 1921

But if we are warned by the inadequacy of earlier endeavors for limitation of armament, we can not fail to recognize the extraordinary opportunity now presented. We not only have the lessons of the past to guide us, not only do we have the reaction from the disillusioning experiences of war, but we must meet the challenge of imperative economic demands. What was convenient or highly desirable before is now a matter of vital necessity. If there is to be economic rehabilitation, if the longings for reasonable progress are not to be denied, if we are to be spared the uprisings of peoples made desperate in the desire to shake off burdens no longer endurable, competition in armament must stop. The present opportunity not only derives its advantage from a general appreciation of this fact, but the power to deal with the exigency now rests with a small group of nations, represented here, who have every reason to desire peace and to promote amity. The astounding ambition which lay athwart the promise of the Second Hague Conference no longer menaces the world, and the great opportunity of liberty-loving and peace-preserving democracies has come. Is it not plain that the time has passed for mere resolutions that the responsible Powers should examine the question of limitation of armament? We can no longer content ourselves with investigations, with statistics, with reports, with the circumlocution of inquiry. The essential facts are sufficiently known. The time has come, and this Conference has been called, not for general resolutions or mutual advice, but for action. . . .

It is apparent that this can not be accomplished without serious sacrifices. Enormous sums have been expended upon ships under construction and building programs which are now under way can not be given up without heavy loss. Yet if the present construction of capital ships goes forward other ships will inevitably be built to rival them and this will lead to still others. Thus the race will continue so long as ability to continue lasts. The effort to escape sacrifices is futile. We must face them or yield our purpose. . . .

In making the present proposal the United States is most solicitous to deal with the question upon an entirely reasonable and practicable basis, to the end that the just interests of all shall be adequately guarded and that national security and defense shall be maintained. Four general principles have been applied:

(1) That all capital-ship building programs, either actual or projected, should be abandoned;

(2) That further reduction should be made through the scrapping of certain of the older ships;

(3) That in general regard should be had to the existing naval strength of the Powers concerned;

(4) That the capital ship tonnage should be used as the measurement of strength for navies and a proportionate allowance of auxiliary combatant craft prescribed.

The principal features of the proposed agreement are as follows:

Capital Ships

United States. The United States is now completing its program of 1916 calling for 10 new battleships and 6 battle cruisers. One battleship has been completed. The others are in various stages of construction; in some cases from 60 to over 80 per cent of the construction has been done. On these 15 capital ships now being built over $330,000,000 have been spent. Still, the United States is willing in the interest of an immediate limitation of naval armament to scrap all these ships.

The United States proposes, if this plan is accepted—

(1) To scrap all capital ships now under construction. This includes 6 battle cruisers and 7 battleships on the ways and in course of building, and 2 battleships launched.

The total number of new capital ships thus to be scrapped is 15. The total tonnage of the new capital ships when completed would be 618,000 tons.

(2) To scrap all of the older battleships up to, but not including, the *Delaware* and *North Dakota.* The number of these old battleships to be scrapped is 15. Their total tonnage is 227,740 tons.

Thus the number of capital ships to be scrapped by the United States, if this plan is accepted, is 30, with an aggregate tonnage (including that of ships in construction, if completed) of 845,740 tons.

Great Britain. The plan contemplates that Great Britain and Japan shall take action which is fairly commensurate with this action on the part of the United States.

It is proposed that Great Britain—

(1) Shall stop further construction of the 4 new Hoods, the new capital ships not laid down but upon which money has been spent. These 4 ships, if completed, would have tonnage displacement of 172,000 tons.

(2) Shall, in addition, scrap her pre-dreadnaughts, second line battleships, and first line battleships up to, but not including, the *King George V* class.

These, with certain pre-dreadnaughts which it is understood have already been scrapped, would amount to 19 capital ships and a tonnage reduction of 411,375 tons.

The total tonnage of ships thus to be scrapped by Great Britain (including the tonnage of the 4 Hoods, if completed) would be 583,375 tons.

Japan. It is proposed that Japan

(1) Shall abandon her program of ships not yet laid down, viz., the *Kii, Owari, No. 7* and *No. 8* battleships, and *Nos. 5, 6, 7,* and *8,* battle cruisers.

It should be observed that this does not involve the stopping of construction, as the construction of none of these ships has been begun.

(2) Shall scrap 3 capital ships (the *Mutsu* launched, the *Tosa,* and *Kago* in course of building) and 4 battle cruisers (the *Amagi* and *Akagi* in course of building, and the *Atoga* and *Takao* not yet laid down, but for which certain material has been assembled).

The total number of new capital ships to be scrapped under this paragraph is seven. The total tonnage of these new capital ships when completed would be 289,100 tons.

(3) Shall scrap all pre-dreadnaughts and battleships of the second line. This would include the scrapping of all ships up to but not including the *Settsu*; that is, the scrapping of 10 older ships, with a total tonnage of 159,828 tons.

The total reduction of tonnage on vessels existing, laid down, or for which material has been assembled (taking the tonnage of the new ships when completed), would be 448,928 tons.

Thus, under this plan there would be immediately destroyed, of the navies of the three Powers, 66 capital fighting ships, built and building, with a total tonnage of 1,878,043.

It is proposed that it should be agreed by the United States, Great Britain, and Japan that their navies, with respect to capital ships, within three months after the making of the agreement shall consist of certain ships designated in the proposal and numbering for the United States 18, for Great Britain 22, for Japan 10.

The tonnage of these ships would be as follows: Of the United States, 500,650; of Great Britain, 604,450; of Japan, 299,700. In reaching this result, the age factor in the case of the respective navies has received appropriate consideration. . . .

With the acceptance of this plan the burden of meeting the demands of competition in naval armament will be lifted. Enormous sums will be released to aid the progress of civilization. At the same time the proper demands of national defense will be adequately met and the nations will have ample opportunity during the naval holiday of 10 years to consider their future course. Preparation for offensive naval war will stop now. . . .

The Washington Conference Treaties, 1922

The Five-Power Treaty

Article III. Subject to the provisions of Article II, the Contracting Powers shall abandon their respective capital ship building programs, and no new capital ships shall be constructed or acquired by any of the Contracting Powers except replacement tonnage which may be constructed or acquired as specified in Chapter II, Part 3. . . .

Article IV. The total capital ship replacement tonnage of each of the Contracting Powers shall not exceed in standard displacement, for the United States, 525,000 tons (533,400 metric tons); for the British Empire 525,000 tons (533,400 metric tons); for France 175,000 tons (177,800 metric tons); for Italy 175,000 tons (177,800 metric tons); for Japan 315,000 tons (320,040 metric tons).

Article V. No capital ship exceeding 35,000 tons (35,560 metric tons) standard displacement shall be acquired by, or constructed by, for, or within the jurisdiction of, any of the Contracting Powers.

Article VI. No capital ship of any of the Contracting Powers shall carry a gun with a calibre in excess of 16 inches (406 millimetres).

Article VII. The total tonnage for aircraft carriers of each of the Contracting Powers shall not exceed in standard displacement, for the United States 135,000 tons (137,160 metric tons); for the British Empire 135,000 tons (137,160 metric tons); for France 60,000 tons (60,960 metric tons); for Italy 60,000 tons (60,960 metric tons); for Japan 81,000 tons (82,296 metric tons). . . .

Article XI. No vessel of war exceeding 10,000 tons (10,160 metric tons) standard displacement, other than a capital ship or aircraft carrier, shall be acquired by, or constructed by, for, or within the jurisdiction of, any of the Contracting Powers. Vessels not specifically built as fighting ships nor taken in time of peace under government control for fighting purposes, which are employed on fleet duties or as troop transports or in some other way for the purpose of assisting in the prosecution of hostilities otherwise than as fighting ships, shall not be within the limitations of this Article. . . .

Article XIX. The United States, the British Empire and Japan agree that the status quo at the time of the signing of the present Treaty, with regard to fortifications and naval bases, shall be maintained in their respective territories and possessions specified hereunder:

(1) The insular possessions which the United States now holds or may hereafter acquire in the Pacific Ocean, except (a) those adjacent to the coast of the United States, Alaska and the Panama Canal Zone, not including the Aleutian Islands, and (b) the Hawaiian Islands;

(2) Hongkong and the insular possessions which the British Empire now holds or may hereafter acquire in the Pacific Ocean, east of the meridian of 110° east longitude, except (a) those adjacent to the coast of Canada, (b) the Commonwealth of Australia and its Territories, and (c), New Zealand;

(3) The following insular territories and possessions of Japan in the Pacific Ocean, to wit: the Kurile Islands, the Bonin Islands, Anami-Oshima, the Loochoo Islands, Formosa and the Pescadores, and any insular territories or possessions in the Pacific Ocean which Japan may hereafter acquire.

The maintenance of the status quo under the foregoing provisions implies that no new fortifications or naval bases shall be established in the territories and possessions specified that no measures shall be taken to increase the existing naval facilities for the repair and maintenance of naval forces, and that no increase shall be made in the coast defenses of the territories and possessions above specified. This restriction, however, does not preclude such repair and replacement of worn-out weapons and equipment as is customary in naval and military establishments in time of peace. . . .

The Nine-Power Treaty

Article I. The Contracting Powers, other than China, agree:

(1) To respect the sovereignty, the independence, and the territorial and administrative integrity of China;

(2) To provide the fullest and most unembarrassed opportunity to China to develop and maintain for herself an effective and stable government;

(3) To use their influence for the purpose of effactually establishing and maintaining the principle of equal opportunity for the commerce and industry of all nations throughout the territory of China;

(4) To refrain from taking advantage of conditions in China in order to seek special rights or privileges which would abridge the rights of subjects or citizens of friendly States, and from countenancing action inimical to the security of such States.

Article II. The Contracting Powers agree not to enter into any treaty, agreement, arrangement or understanding, either with one another, or, individually or collectively, with any Power or Powers, which would infringe or impair the principles stated in Article I.

Article III. With a view to applying more effectually the principles of the Open Door or equality of opportunity in China for the trade and industry of all nations, the Contracting Powers, other than China, agree that they will not seek, nor support their respective nationals in seeking—

(a) any arrangement which might purport to establish in favor of their interests any general superiority of rights with respect to commercial or economic development in any designated region of China;

(b) any such monopoly or preference as would deprive the nationals of any other Power of the right of undertaking any legitimate trade or industry in China, or of participating with the Chinese Government, or with any local authority, in any category of public enterprise, or which by reason of its scope, duration or geographical extent is calculated to frustrate the practical application of the principle of equal opportunity.

It is understood that the foregoing stipulations of this Article are not to be so construed as to prohibit the acquisition of such properties or rights as may be necessary to the conduct of a particular commercial, industrial or financial undertaking or to the encouragement of invention and research.

China undertakes to be guided by the principles stated in the foregoing stipulations of this Article in dealing with applications for economic rights and privileges from Governments and nationals of all foreign countries, whether parties to the present Treaty or not.

Article IV. The Contracting Powers agree not to support any agreements by their respective nationals with each other designed to create Spheres of Influence or to provide for the enjoyment of mutually exclusive opportunities in designated parts of Chinese territory.

Article V. China agrees that, throughout the whole of the railways in China, she will not exercise or permit unfair discrimination of any kind. In particular there shall be no discrimination whatever, direct or indirect, in respect of charges or of facilities on the ground of the nationality of passengers or the countries from which or to which they are proceeding, or the origin or ownership of goods or the country from which or to which they are consigned, or the nationality or ownership of the ship or other means of conveying such passengers or goods before or after their transport on the Chinese Railways.

The Contracting Powers, other than China, assume a corresponding obligation in respect of any of the aforesaid railways over which they or their nationals are in a position to exercise any control in virtue of any concession, special agreement or otherwise.

Article VI. The Contracting Powers, other than China, agree fully to respect China's rights as a neutral in time of war to which China is not a party; and China declares that when she is a neutral she will observe the obligations of neutrality.

Article VII. The Contracting Powers agree that, whenever a situation arises which in the opinion of any one of them involves the application of the stipulations of the present Treaty, and renders desirable discussion of such application, there shall be full and frank communication between the Contracting Powers concerned. . . .

The Four-Power Treaty

I. The High Contracting Parties agree as between themselves to respect their rights in relation to their insular possessions and insular dominions in the region of the Pacific Ocean.

If there should develop between any of the High Contracting Parties a controversy arising out of any Pacific question and involving their said rights which is not satisfactorily settled by diplomacy and is likely to affect the harmonious accord now happily subsisting between them, they shall invite the other High Contracting Parties to a joint conference to which the whole subject will be referred for consideration and adjustment.

II. If the said rights are threatened by the aggressive action of any other Power, the High Contracting Parties shall communicate with one another fully and frankly in order to arrive at an understanding as to the most efficient measures to be taken, jointly or separately, to meet the exigencies of the particular situation.

Non-Recognition of Soviet Russia, 1923

You refer with just emphasis to the tyrannical exercise of power by this regime. The seizure of control by a minority in Russia came as a grievous disappointment to American democratic thought which had enthusiastically acclaimed the end of the despotism of the Czars and the entrance of free Russia into the family of democratic nations. Subsequent events were even more disturbing. The right of free speech and other civil liberties were denied. Even the advocacy of those rights which are usually considered to constitute the foundation of freedom was declared to be counter-revolutionary and punishable by death. Every form of political opposition was ruthlessly exterminated. There followed the deliberate destruction of the economic life of the country. Attacks were made not only upon property in its so-called capitalistic form, but recourse was had also to the requisitioning of labor. All voluntary organizations of workers were brought to an end. To unionize or strike was followed by the severest penalties. When labor retaliated by passive resistance, workmen were impressed into a huge labor army. The practical effect of this program was to plunge Russia once more into medievalism. Politically there was a ruthless despotism and economically the situation was equally disastrous.

It is true that, under the pressure of the calamitous consequences, the governing group in Russia has yielded certain concessions. The so-called new economic policy permitted a partial return to economic freedom. The termination of forcible requisitions of grain has induced the peasantry to endeavor to build up production once more and favorable weather conditions have combined to increase the agricultural output. How far the reported exports of Russian grain are justified by the general economy of the country is at least an open question. Manufacturing industry has to a great extent disappeared. The suffrage, so far as it may be exercised, continues to be limited to certain classes and even among them the votes of some categories count more than the votes of others. A new constitution has just now been promulgated providing in effect for the continuance of the regime of the 1917 *coup d'état* under a new title. The Constitution, it is understood, contains no bill of rights, and the civil liberties of the people remain insecure. There is no press except the press controlled by the regime, and the censorship is far-reaching and stringent. Labor is understood to be still at the mercy of the State. While membership in official unions is no longer obligatory, workmen may not organize or participate in voluntary unions. . . .

But while a foreign regime may have securely established itself through the exercise of control and the submission of the people to, or their acquiescence in, its exercise of authority, there still remain other questions to be considered. Recognition is an invitation to intercourse. It is accompanied on the part of the new government by the clearly implied or express promise to fulfill the obligations of intercourse. These obligations include, among other things, the protection of the persons and property of the citizens of one country lawfully pursuing their business in the territory of the other and abstention from hostile propaganda by one country in the territory of the other. In the case of the existing regime in Russia, there has not only been the tyrannical procedure to which you refer, and which has caused the question of the submission or acquiescence of the Russian people to remain an open one, but also a repudiation of the obligations inherent in international intercourse and a defiance of the principles upon which alone it can be conducted.

The persons of our citizens in Russia are for the moment free from harm. No assurance exists, however, against a repetition of the arbitrary detentions which some of them have suffered in the past. The situation with respect to property is even more palpable. The obligations of Russia to the taxpayers of the United States remain repudiated. The many American citizens who have suffered directly or indirectly by the confiscation of American property in Russia remain without the prospect of indemnification. We have had recent evidence, moreover, that the policy of confiscation is by no means at an end. The effective jurisdiction of Moscow was recently extended to Vladivostok and soon thereafter Moscow directed the carrying out in that city of confiscatory measures such as we saw in Western Russia during 1917 and 1918.

What is most serious is that there is conclusive evidence that those in control at Moscow have not given up their original purpose of destroying existing governments wherever they can do so throughout the world. Their efforts in this direction have recently been lessened in intensity only by the reduction of the cash resources at their disposal. You are well aware from the experiences of the American Federation of Labor of this aspect of the situation which must be kept constantly in view. I had occasion to refer to it last March in addressing the Women's Committee for the Recognition of Russia. It is worth while to repeat the quotations which I then gave from utterances of the leaders of the Bolshevik Government on the subject of world revolution, as the authenticity of these has not been denied by their authors. Last November Zinoviev said, "The eternal in the Russian revolution is the fact that it is the beginning of the world revolution." Lenin, before the last Congress of the Third Internationale, last fall, said that "the revolutionists of all countries must learn the organization, the planning, the method and the substance of revolutionary work." "Then, I am convinced," he said, "the outlook of the world revolution will not be good but excellent." And Trotsky, addressing the Fifth Congress of the Russian Communist Youths at Moscow last October,—not two years ago but last October,—said this: "That means, comrades, that revolution is coming in Europe as well as in America, systematically, step by step, stubbornly and with gnashing of teeth in both camps. It will be long protracted, cruel and sanguinary."

The only suggestion that I have seen in answer to this portrayal of a fixed policy is that these statements express the views of the individuals in control of the Moscow regime rather than of the regime itself. We are unable, however, to find any reason for separating the regime, and its purpose from those who animate it, and control it, and direct it so as to further their aims.

While this spirit of destruction at home and abroad remains unaltered the question of recognition by our Government of the authorities at Moscow cannot be determined by mere economic considerations or by the establishment in some degree of a more prosperous condition, which of course we should be glad to note, or simply by a consideration of the probable stability of the regime in question. There cannot be intercourse among nations any more than among individuals except upon a general assumption of good faith. We would welcome convincing evidence of a desire of the Russian authorities to observe the fundamental conditions of international intercourse and the abandonment by them of the persistent attempts to subvert the institutions of democracy as maintained in this country and in others. It may confidently be added that respect by the Moscow regime for the liberties of other peoples will most likely be accompanied by appropriate respect for the essential rights and liberties of the Russian people themselves. The sentiment of our people is not deemed to be favorable to the acceptance into political fellowship of this regime so long as it denies the essential bases of intercourse and cherishes, as an ultimate and definite aim, the destruction of the free institutions which we have laboriously built up, containing as they do the necessary assurances of the freedom of labor upon which our prosperity must depend.

Herbert Hoover on Foreign Trade, 1926

Foreign trade has become a vital part of the whole modern economic system. The war brought into high relief the utter dependence of the life of nations upon it. The major strategy of war is to crush the enemy by depriving him of it. In peace time our exports and imports are the margins upon which our well-being depends. The export of our surplus enables us to use in full our resources and energy. The creation of a wider range of customers to each production unit gives to that unit greater stability in production and greater security to the workers.

And we may quite well view our exports from the other side of the trade balance sheet. They enable us to purchase and import those goods and raw materials which we can not produce ourselves. We could probably get along as a nation if we had to suppress the 7 to 10 per cent of our production which goes to export, but our standard of living and much of the joy of living is absolutely dependent upon certain import commodities. We could not carry on our material civilization without some of the fibers, rubber, and some metals. Without diamonds we would not be able to get satisfactorily engaged to marry. The prosperity of our people in many ways can be measured by the volume of imports. . . .

The Government can chart the channels of foreign trade and keep them open. It can assist American firms in advancing their goods. In the improvement of all the foreign services the Department of Commerce has made great progress in the past five years, and it has been developed into organizing in internal cooperation and consultation with our industries and our merchants. I can refer to the success of that service without egotism, for it has been the work of Doctor Klein and his assistants. Some indication of the degree of their success is shown by the increased demand upon the services of the bureau they direct. The requests of merchants, manufacturers, and farm cooperatives for information and assistance have grown from some 15,000 inquiries per month four years ago to a total of 170,000 inquiries per month during the past year, a total of over 2,040,000 during the year.

I believe the effect of the efforts of the department in establishment of standards, elimination of waste, and the provision of wider information has been to expand the possibilities of foreign trade to many concerns not hitherto able to extend into this field. One of the interesting and encouraging facts is the rapid increase in the number of small concerns participating in export business. The surprisingly large number of inquiries now being received by the department from such firms amply proves that the virtues of high quality, specialized production, good service, precise export technique, and farsighted policy are by no means monopolized by big corporations. Literally thousands of small dealers and manufacturers, whose commodities have a strong specialty appeal and meet a definite need, are now successfully cultivating overseas markets. Foreign trade is thus becoming a national asset in the fullest sense of the word. . . .

We have the question propounded daily as to whether, with a stabilized Europe, we can continue successfully to hold our own share in the growth of the world's trade in competitive goods. It permits argument both ways, and we may recede on some particular commodities. I have the firm view, however, that the recovery of Europe will, by and large, help our foreign trade. Trade grows on prosperity, not on poverty. I believe that in most trades it has been more difficult to compete with Europe in neutral markets during the past few years against the underpaid labor and lower overhead costs of depreciating currencies than it will be when Europe is more stable and they have recovered their pre-war standards of living. Moreover, as Europe gains in stability and their living standards increase, they will become better customers for our goods in direct trade.

In a large sense the major proportion of foreign trade is a cooperative effort among nations to secure the greatest total output and total consumption. Foreign trade is too often visualized as a sort of battle. It is a misfortune that the terminology of trade has been so much infected by military terms. We speak of export trade as a matter of conquest, we talk of trade wars, trade strategy, of economic power—all carrying many implications of extermination. In larger vision our export trade does not grow by supplanting the other fellow but from the increased consuming power of the world.

I do not wish to be understood as saying that we are going to obtain our share of these increases without effort and without competition. What I wish to get clear is that, in the large view, our exports are not based on the destruction of our competitors but on insistence that we shall participate with them in the growth of world demand. . . .

Without entering upon any partisan discussion of the protective tariff, which I, of course, support, there is one phase of the tariff which I believe experience shows has less effect upon the volume of international movement of commodities than had at one time been assumed.

As a result of the hardships suffered by many people of both combatant and neutral nations during the war, there came to all nations a deep resolution, in so far as the resources of their countries permitted, to produce as far as possible their essential commodities. The struggle to overcome postwar unemployment has added to this impulse. The result is that 52 of the 70 nations of the world, including almost every important trading nation, increased their tariffs after the war. It might seem that these widespread protective policies would tend to localize industry and thus decrease the total volume of international trade. But it certainly appears that internal economic and social currents which make for prosperity or depression in a nation have a much larger effect upon the total volume of imports than the tariffs and thus more largely affect world trade as a whole. In our case, far from our present tariff diminishing our total imports, they have increased about 35 per cent since the higher tariff came into effect. This has also been the case with other nations which have progressed in internal economy. In any event our experience surely indicates that in considering the broad future of our trade we can dismiss the fear that our increased tariff would so diminish our total imports as to destroy the ability of other nations to buy from us.

The most commonly remarked revolution in our foreign economic relations is our shift from a debtor to a creditor nation upon a gigantic scale. It is the father of much speculative discussion as to its future effect upon our merchandise trade. Alarm has been repeatedly raised that repayment of the war debts must necessitate the increase of imports of competitive goods in order to provide for these payments—to the damage of our industry and workmen. These ideas are out of perspective. Our war debt when settled upon our own views of the capacity to pay will yield about $300,000,000 per annum, although as yet the actual payments are much less than this. The private foreign loans and investments to-day require repayments in principal and interest of about $600,000,000 annually, or nearly twice the war debt. I have heard of no suggestion that interest and repayment of these private debts will bring the disaster attributed to the war debt. The question is of importance, however, as to how this $800,000,000 or $900,000,000 of annual payments may affect our merchandise movement. There is a compensating factor in American trade relations unique to our country which has a large bearing upon this question—that is, the vast dimension of our invisible exports in the form of tourist expenditure, emigrants' remittances, and other forms of American expenditure abroad. These items in 1925 amounted to about $900,000,000, or about $100,000,000 more than our incoming payments on debts of all kinds. In other words, at this stage of calculation the balance of trade should be in our favor by about $100,000,000. But beyond this we are making, and shall long continue to make, loans abroad. For the last four years these loans have averaged nearly $700,000,000 a year, and in fact the merchandise balance in our favor has been running just about this amount.

Now the summation and purpose of all these words is the conclusion that there is no disastrous shift in our imports and exports of merchandise in prospect from debt causes.

The making of loans to foreign countries for reproductive purposes not only increases our direct exports but builds up the prosperity of foreign countries and is an economic blessing to both sides of the transaction. And I do not put this business of loans upon any sentimental footing, although the economic advantage to foreign countries of our great financial strength in these times can not be denied. Nor did we get this financial strength out of war profits. We lost enormously by the war. We created this reserve of capital, as any study of our economy will show, from our growth of efficiency, by hard work, and savings since the war. . . .

In conclusion, if we can keep in motion the social and economic forces which we have developed so greatly in the last decade, if we can multiply and improve education and skill, if we still further stimulate scientific research, if we continue to eliminate industrial waste, if we still continue to improve our business organization and maintain private initiative, we shall hold our own in our share in the world's trade.

By contributing to peace and economic stability, by the loan of our surplus savings abroad for productive purposes, by the spread of inventions over the world, we can contribute to the elevation of standards of living in foreign countries and the demand for all goods.

Senator Burton K. Wheeler
Condemns Intervention in Nicaragua, 1927

Mr. President, for days I have had in mind discussing the administration policy in Latin America. I confess I have found it a difficult task, owing to the fact that its policy has changed with every pressure that has been brought to bear upon it.

First we learned that the marines were sent to the little Republic to protect American lives and property; then they were sent there to protect the paper canal which we wrung from the people of Nicaragua by questionable means; at the end of the week we were there to protect the Americas from Bolshevism.

While men are tramping our streets with arms off, legs off, blind, deaf, and insane as a result of the last war, this administration begins preaching the hymn of hate, spreading false propaganda against a sister republic of Central America, all in the interest of those who seek to exploit and enslave other peoples. The American people are not fooled. They knew that this cry of Bolshevism and the protection of lives and property in Nicaragua is but an effort of this administration to justify war with Mexico. . . .

Why did not the President [Coolidge] frankly tell us why Vice President Sacasa left Nicaragua? Why did he not tell us that he was driven out by a usurper exercising dictatorial power at the head of the military forces of the country? Why did he not tell us that this usurper was aided and abetted by Diaz, whom we have recognized as President? Why did he not tell us why Doctor Sacasa did not return to the Corinto conference instead of suggesting that his absence meant that he had abandoned his claim to the Presidency? Why did not the President confide to Congress and through Congress to the country that Chamorro and Diaz, the two chief personages through whom our State Department has operated in Nicaragua, are professional revolutionists who have looted their country of millions of dollars, and are known and detested throughout Latin-speaking America as traitors of the meanest kind? Why did he not state fairly the character of the Congress that elected Diaz? Why, in a word, did he not candidly confess that Diaz was just as much a violator of the five-power treaty that was held to exclude Chamorro from the presidency as Chamorro himself, and that Diaz was thrust into power because he was known by experience to be the most perfect instrument available to enable the New York bankers to have their will of the defenseless people of Nicaragua? Why, oh why, did not President Coolidge frankly admit, what every person of average intelligence who looks into the matter can not fail to realize, that Dr. Juan B. Sacasa is the constitutional President of Nicaragua? . . .

It is impossible, in a speech of reasonable length, to follow in detail the rough-shod, antirepublican rule of our State Department in Nicaragua. To do so would be an arousing revelation to any American whose heart still beats in sympathy with the founders of our Republic.

The followers of Doctor Sacasa are to-day fighting for just those same principles of liberty and free government for which our forefathers fought in 1776. Indeed it is not too much to say that one would seek in vain in the history of our struggle for independence for a parallel to the brazen tyranny of our State Department in its dealings with the overwhelming majority of the people of Nicaragua. George III never dared to perpetrate upon the American Colonies such fiscal and political iniquities as our State Department has not hesitated to perpetrate upon the defenseless people of Nicaragua.

When it is generally known how our State Department, undeterred by the manifest disapproval of the United States Senate, has robbed the little State of Nicaragua of its every vestige of sovereignty, men and women of honor throughout our land will hang their heads in shame. The wretched instrument made use of by the State Department for the accomplishment of this great wrong was Adolfo Diaz. . . .

From the beginning of our active intervention in Nicaragua in the interest of profitable investments for bankers, to this moment—and never more than this very moment—Brown Bros. and J. & W. Seligman, New York, were and are the niggers in the Nicaraguan woodpile. Other American concession seekers and holders—notably the Knox group, La Luz & Los Angeles Mining Co.—have played a big bad part. But the State Department policy is built around the exploitation of Nicaragua by Brown Bros. and J. & W. Seligman. The big stake being played for at this moment and on which the future of Nicaragua absolutely depends is the control of 51 per cent of the stock of the National Bank of Nicaragua with the concessions.

Permit me to digress one moment to say that the concessions which go with that bank and which were in the possession of these people at one time, and which they are now seeking to get back, were the most unconscionable concessions that have ever been granted in the history of any country, I think, with the possible exception of the case of Haiti, when they turned over the rule of their country to one of the banks of the city of New York. . . .

Think of it; the railroads down there are incorporated in this country, and those people down there are paying income taxes to the United States upon their own railroads. The railroad and the bank have been absolutely the things that have dominated and controlled that country. They have had men in there collecting the taxes of that country, they have run the elections of the country, and they have absolutely taken away, as nearly as possibly could be taken away, the freedom of the people of that little country.

Wholesale graft has characterized the banker-State Department control of Nicaragua for the past 17 years. Patriotic Liberals and Conservatives agree on this. Behind the paper statements of prosperity the real conditions stick out plain to one who looks. Declared by the native business men and the populace to be intolerably bad. The operating expenses of the railroad increased from $30,000 to approximately $300,000, and no improvements were made. The railroads constantly deteriorated during the time they were under the charge of American business men, notwithstanding the fact that they promised to make certain improvements and extend the railroads. None were ever made. They violated not only their moral obligations, but their legal obligations as well. The customs duties were increased 100 per cent. . . .

Some people have been particularly severe in their criticism of Mr. Kellogg because of the fact that he gave out a statement charging that everybody and everything was caused in these countries by Bolshevism. But the people of this country should not be too harsh in their criticism of Mr. Kellogg. They should be reminded of the fact that a coup d'état took place out in Minnesota some years ago, when the Scandinavians took part in it, and ever since that coup d'état, which elevated Mr. Kellogg to the position of Secretary of State, he has been seeing Bolsheviks under every sagebrush throughout the entire length and breadth of this continent. . . .

Ever since the World War we have been manufacturing more goods than we can sell. We are looking for new markets. Latin America and South America afford these markets. And yet in order to allow a few bankers to exploit Nicaragua, our oil interests to exploit Mexico, we are willing to ruin the legitimate commercial business of this country. We are willing to let thousands of men remain out of employment who could be working in the manufacturing plants of this country if we by peaceful means sought the friendship and the trade of Central and South America.

It seems to me that the Senate's duty is clear. In view of these facts I think the time has come to assert ourselves, and I for one am no longer going to sit silent while the interests of this country are being compromised and the country's legitimate, material interests jeopardized by certain ruthless international bankers and their bureaucratic puppets in the State Department.

The Kellogg-Briand Pact, 1928

Article 1. The high contracting parties solemnly declare in the names of their respective peoples that they condemn recourse to war for the solution of international controversies, and renounce it as an instrument of national policy in their relations with one another.

Article 2. The high contracting parties agree that the settlement or solution of all disputes or conflicts of whatever nature or of whatever origin they may be, which may arise among them, shall never be sought except by pacific means. . . .

The Journalist Edwin L. James on America's World Power, 1930

The material situation of the United States of America is such that the resulting political influence is enormous, so enormous that a failure to place its true value on it may be explained by the circumstance that it has not yet made its real force felt to a degree that will surely materialize.

There is no country where the power of the dollar has not reached. There is no capital which does not take the United States into consideration at almost every turn. Conversely, there is no zone where our interests are not involved. Isolation is a myth. We are not isolated and cannot be isolated. The United States is ever present.

Officially, our government stays out of world organizations. We scorn the League of Nations; we continue to shy at the World Court. But such things count for less and less. We must deal with the world and the world must deal with us. Let there be an international conference, and the imponderable influences bring the United States there. A conference on reparations, we are there. The International Bank is set up, an American is made president. The World Court meets, an American is put on the bench. A naval conference gathers, and the whole business hangs largely on the American position. And so on, ad infinitum.

It is always the case that the American position is among the most important. Such is one of the prices of our power. Few world problems arise in which the influence of the United States will not swing the decision if we take a real interest. Opposition to the United States is a serious undertaking. Our dollars are powerful; there are so many of them.

Take the tariff. Such is the breadth of the trade of the United States that no nation ignores our markets. A higher duty voted in Washington affects work in countless cities abroad. Conversely, higher duties voted in foreign capitals may affect work in our cities from one seaboard to the other.

It is always a question of what the United States does or is going to do. No European nation plans peace without taking America into account. Nor will any European nation plan war without seeking to find out what is the attitude of Washington on the issues at stake. Supplies of credit, food and munitions from the United States mean one situation especially if our navy guarantees our shipments crossing the Atlantic successfully, and the lack of those supplies means quite another thing. Geneva can make no blockade which we do not recognize because there are no League members who will take a serious chance of antagonizing the United States.

Indeed, the position and power of this country is rapidly reaching the point when it will be said that we have gained the relative position which Great Britain held from the Battle of Waterloo up to 1914, which France held for approximately a century preceding and which through history belonged for varying periods to various nations. For all the indications point to this being our century.

To a large degree world greatness has been thrust upon us. It has come to us through the force of circumstances not all of our own making. That, by chance, may explain why nationally we have not come fully to realize where we are.

But there are signs in every direction that the situation which has been so mobile, with everything moving in our direction, is becoming stabilized. The current toward the United States is slackening. Things should tend to stabilize. In other words, in the next decade our progress will not be so great because it cannot bring the same increase in power as we enjoyed in the last ten years.

Furthermore, what we win in the next ten years we shall have to strive for to a much greater degree than since the war. The game of keeping our own markets for ourselves by shutting out foreign goods and at the same time enjoying the markets of other countries is going to be more and more difficult. Europe is back on its feet again and able to compete with us in the world markets.

But if the shake-up is largely over, it was surely to our advantage. The aftermath of the war has left the United States sitting on the top of the world. The predominance of our economic and financial position extends in every direction and is an example being used by the exponents of the movements for a Federated Europe and an economically united British Commonwealth of Nations.

It is generally realized in the United States how great the nation is economically. But there is not yet a realization of the great political power our material position has brought us. And whether we will use that power when we feel it as other nations have or whether we will use it in a new and different manner—there is the greatest question of world politics.

Just as an American observer who has been living in Europe gets the idea, on returning to the United States, that popularly there is an underestimation of the political power which America's material position has given us, he also finds what, looked upon from the other side, seems to be an exaggeration of the moral world influence of the United States.

America's great world political position is not due primarily to our moral leadership but primarily to our wealth and economic position. That is true because it is not to our moral teachings that the rest of the world responds, but to our material power. If we were a poor and weak nation the world would to-day care no more about what we thought than did the world before the Great War.

It is not difficult to understand why the Old World does not take our exhortations to heart any more. There is the old story of the League of Nations. There is the World Court. There are other things, like the International Bank—all of which seem to represent our advice to others as to how to do their business, while we do ours some other way.

Now those who still believe that "the moral sense" of America is a real factor in international affairs will surely cite the Kellogg pact as an example of how we do good and do it altruistically. But no one who has lived in Europe in recent years can believe in the dominant moral effect of the Kellogg pact as an active factor in world affairs. Almost the only attraction Europe ever saw in it was the line the United States signed on. No European nation promised anything in the anti-war pact that it had not already agreed to in the covenant of the League of Nations. But there was the signature of the United States, which seemed to promise the co-operation of our great material power in curbing the aggressor in another war. And that made a powerful appeal. But this appeal lay not in any new religion the Kellogg pact brought to a soul-hungry world. It was based on the great political power of America because of our enormous wealth and potential military and naval power.

Does any one believe seriously that the deference and respect Britain has shown for us in the past decade represent a belief in our moral superiority, a realization of a superior civilization on this side of the Atlantic or a better system of government and social order? Not at all. Britain is extremely practical in foreign affairs. There is no new approval of America and Americans, but there is a realization of our material power as something to be reckoned with seriously, and Britain does just that. . . .

Of course, there have been, in the past, indications pointing to a real influence of our moral advice. In the first five years after the World War the nations of Europe, on their backs and seeking American aid, took all pains to avoid offending us and therefore appeared to give careful and weighty consideration to our altruistic advice. The succeeding five years changed that. To-day, Europe, to a rapidly increasing degree, feels itself getting back to where it may treat with us on a plane of equality. And that puts Europe in a position to do what the Old World likes about our advice. More and more we shall hear that words unaccompanied by acts will not be taken as seriously as in the past.

But Europeans do know the importance of America in the world. Because they are more used to studying and judging world affairs than we are, they realize, perhaps better than we do, just how important is the United States. Their eyes are on us all the time. They must reckon with us; they must do business with us. And so they must know what we are doing and what we may be going to do. That gives us our great importance and out of that grows our influence. Although not exercised as actively as it will be later on, American world political power is interestingly important not only because of its might, but because of its present under-development.

ESSAYS

Both essays in this chapter reflect the recent scholarship that depicts the United States as a major power in the 1920s. In the first, Robert Freeman Smith of the University of Toledo argues that the United States was attempting to develop an "informal empire" through non-military—especially economic—tactics. America's search for world order to further its interests is the story of his essay. The second essay, by John Braeman of the University of Nebraska, takes a different approach to understanding the period. He questions the assumption that the United States was weak. After a survey of American military preparedness, Braeman concludes that United States power was adequate for its interests at the time.

American Expansion and World Order

ROBERT FREEMAN SMITH

For years too many academicians have treated the Republican era, 1921–1932, as a blighted period—a slough of corruption and isolationism separating the "brilliant" (and liberal) administrations of Woodrow Wilson and Franklin D. Roosevelt. New Deal-oriented historians blamed the policy makers of the interregnum for creating many of the foundations of World War II. The original sin was, of course, the rejection of League of Nations, but this guilt was compounded by disarmament conferences and a reliance on tactics colored by "legalistic rhetoric" and "naïve pacifism." When the facade is stripped away from the argument, the basic charge against the policy makers of the period 1921–1932 is that they did not rely to any extent on tactics of defensive alliances and military force; this in turn is supposedly related to the causes of German and Japanese "aggression" in the 1930s.

There is another way to view this period that gives the men of the 1920s

From "Republican Policy and Pax Americana, 1921–1932" by Robert Freeman Smith, in *From Colony to Empire*, William Appleman Williams, ed. (1972). Reprinted by permission of the author, Robert Freeman Smith. (Author's note, 1983: The Open Door concept held by American policymakers of this era was a generally accurate view of the international order and the legitimate place of U.S. interests in that order.)

due credit for what they did and did not do, without letting them off the hook of historical causality. They were deeply involved in the task of developing and refining the tactics of informal empire—the *Pax Americana* of Charles Evans Hughes. For the most part these officials were trying to utilize nonmilitary tactics. This general unwillingness and/or inability to mount large-scale military projects to defend and expand the American position in the world placed limitations on the extent of governmental involvement (or meddling). In turn, this forced officials to be more flexible and less militant in their dealings with other nations. They could retreat, change course, and even limit (or prohibit) United States involvement in situations where extensive military commitments in blood, money, and prestige could have resulted in ever deepening police operations. Disputes had to be limited and compromised when the military factor was not readily available. Conciliation and negotiation became necessities rather than occasional options.

On the other hand, the policy makers of the period did not really confront the basic dilemma involved in the continued economic-ideological expansion of the United States. This expansion contained the potential for conflict if other nations decided that the United States constituted a serious challenge to their own defined interests and rejected the rules-of-the-game promulgated by her. In such situations would the leaders of the United States eventually choose confrontation over loss of predominance? Or would they modify their definition of interests, which was based upon a belief in the vital connection between domestic prosperity and the control of external markets, sources of raw materials, and investment opportunities? Henry Cabot Lodge III pointed to this blind spot in his critique of the Kellogg-Briand Pact:

> They [United States leaders] might have pointed to the ever-increasing number of business houses, which since the war have been promoting American foreign trade at the expense of such nations as Great Britain, for instance, to whom foreign trade is far more essential than it is to us. They might have made it clear that there are certain business men who, by asking the Department of Commerce for aid in promoting the foreign sale of their product, are actually building up causes of war. These very business men, to be sure, would hotly deny such a charge. They would be perfectly sincere in so doing. But in some cases at least they are making for economic pressure, and their activities are, in fact, contributing causes of war. . . .
>
> If these and similar commercial activities were curtailed, real sacrifices in money, production, and employment would be the result. Perhaps this curtailment would not be worth doing; perhaps war is cheaper in the end. But why not face the real facts, and, after facing them, make the decision? An active, growing state collides with its neighbors.

Edwin Borchard, one of the leading experts on international law, pursued this criticism even further when he wrote; "The abolition of war will, therefore, have to be pursued along other lines. Possibly in the elimination of the economic causes of conflict, including the attempted monopoly of raw materials and markets, and in the entente of business interests across national boundaries, there lies more hope than in legal efforts to preserve by force the status quo." Officials and businessmen had been trying to devise the systems that would achieve these results. The onslaught of world depression undermined these efforts before they became firmly implanted as viable alternatives to intense rivalry and conflict. Also, such plans for world order excluded systems that were not based on private enterprise capitalism.

For the most part the officials of the period were not forced to confront this dilemma and make choices. The only important exception involved Japanese expansion into Manchuria in 1931. The Administration divided over the issue of United States predominance in eastern Asia, with Secretary of State Henry L. Stimson leading the confrontationists. President Herbert Hoover continued to follow the path of accommodation. But the deterioration of world economic conditions intensified economic nationalism and international rivalries during the subsequent years. These rivalries vastly exceeded those anticipated by Lodge in 1929. And it was no accident (and even symbolically fitting) when Stimson returned to the seats of power as Secretary of War in an Administration that—after some hesitancy—had chosen confrontation over loss of predominance. The result was United States involvement in a two-front war in Asia and in Europe.

In spite of disagreements within governmental and business ranks over policy tactics and the priority of various parts of the world, there still existed an underlying unity of basic socio-economic values (ideology) and foreign policy goals; for example, some officials and businessmen advocated the development of economic relations with the Soviet Union, and even governmental recognition. Others intensely disagreed and argued for little, if any, contact. Both tactics, however, were proposed as means to change the Soviet system and restore the country to the international ranks of capitalism. The basic goals of both groups were identical.

Intense and prolonged debate over tactics can alter or modify the objectives. It is possible that the tactics utilized by the Hoover Administration reflected the beginning of such a process. But, for the period 1921–1932, consistency and continuity in foreign policy were more evident than variation or random happenings; the "woods" had a definite contour and coloration in spite of some peculiar "trees" here and there. The influence and leadership of Herbert Hoover provided one of the more important elements of this continuity. According to one colleague he was, "Secretary of Commerce and Under-Secretary of all other departments."

Government and business leaders of the period were true believers in the marketplace ideology that defined prosperity and security as two sides of the same coin. According to this view the United States required an expanding frontier of markets, sources of cheap raw materials, and opportunities for profitable investment of capital. Secretary of State Stimson explained in 1932: "The investments of our farmers and industrialists, the wages of our labor upon both factory and farm, have all been geared to a scale to fit the development of our trade which has taken place. The prosperity of the American people and the standard of living of our workers is now closely related to the development and maintenance of this trade structure." Warren Harding had succinctly labeled this "struggle for commercial and industrial supremacy" as the basis for all foreign relations, and Secretary of State Charles Evans Hughes defined the "great object" of all departments (including State) as "American prosperity" based upon the "imperative demands of American business." National security consisted of protecting these frontiers and their links to the metropolis.

These policy makers believed that the basic goals could be achieved by building a world order based on the Open-Door concept, a belief that they shared with preceding administrations. In theory the "Open-Door World Order" would provide the industrial-creditor nations with equal access to the economic fruits of the world and would modify their conflicts of interests. In practice, the Open Door had been rather modified for Latin America (especially for the Caribbean area), and after the war United States leaders were prepared to push for primacy in some other parts of the world. World War I had demonstrated the vulnerability of the Open Door when the policy was confronted by conflicts intensified by modern technology. The objective was to promote the kind of political-economic stability that would permit the peaceful consolidation and expansion of a United States-led "Open Door World."

Two basic problems involved in promoting stability were preventing the spread of revolutionary nationalism in the underdeveloped areas and preventing conflict between the industrial-creditor nations. Secretaries Hughes, Kellogg, and Stimson tried to attain these objectives by developing a treaty system and utilizing various forms of dollar diplomacy, especially the promotion of coordinated efforts by private business to expand investments and trade and the utilization of loans to undergird economic (and political) stability. The goal was a "law-bound" world in which the industrial powers would agree to respect the Open-Door concept, refrain from conflict, and generally cooperate in policing the underdeveloped world. The latter involved the enforcement of the international-legal order of the developed nations to force underdeveloped nations to fulfill their "international obligations," which were considered "contracts" to protect foreign investors and traders. The promotion of such a legal order would, it was hoped, regulate the relations of the industrial powers with each other and with the underdeveloped countries; and would pressure the latter to conduct their affairs in such a way as to protect international capitalism.

The United States-installed treaty system was intended to establish general, regional arrangements that would, in effect, bind the nations in a legal contract to support the political status quo, maintain the economic Open Door, and promote arms control. The system may be labeled as a legalistic approach to world order, but it was not derived from abstract principles. Rather, it was a series of legalisms that were directly connected to (and symbolic of) specific interests and goals. The "law-bound world order" was a tactic to promote the defined interests of the United States by creating a semi-institutionalized middle ground between the League of Nations and purely unilateral imperial control. The United States would on occasion still resort to unilateral action (as in Nicaragua), but the main impulse of the period was toward the institutionalization and systemization of the Open-Door World.

The officials of the period were not being "unrealistic" in their attempts to maintain peace and order in the world by such legalistic mechanisms as treaty systems, conferences, arbitration-mediation proceedings, and the World Court. Edwin Borchard argued that the desired process was one of converting political issues to legal questions (which could then be resolved by legal procedures). He explained the heart of the problem:

> This tendency [lack of self restraint in national rivalries] is promoted . . . by the *unregulated competition* which prevails among the nations and by the fact that in the most important sphere of international activity, the commercial field, few if any rules of law have yet entered. Here international life is carried on under a sort of jungle law until the conflict of economical interests, which is continually generated, develops into an important national issue which is then called a conflict of political interest and a political question. It is not believed that such unregulated commercial competition for raw materials and markets, for transportation and communication facilities . . . is essential to the exchange of the world's goods, but the failure to realize how important a source of war is embodied in this economic activity accounts for the apparent indifference to its more sensible regulation. It is therefore of considerable importance that the domain of law be extended to new fields which, as a matter of self-interest, might persuade the nations thus to convert political issues into legal issues.

Calvin Coolidge outlined the economic and political activities of the United States government (in cooperation with business) and observed: "All of these efforts represent the process of reducing our domestic and foreign relations to a system of law. They consist of a determination of clear and definite rules of action. It is a civilizing and humanizing method adopted by means of conference, discussion, deliberation, and determination."

But, one might ask, why would the nations of the world voluntarily submit their vital interests to a "recognized rule of law"? Borchard explained: "Here then lies the only chance of an extension in the reign of law. In a period when nations still prefer to constitute themselves simultaneously plaintiffs, judge, and sheriff in their own causes, the conviction must be brought home that a nation has more to lose by war than a peaceful solution." Borchard, Coolidge, Hughes, Hoover, and many others believed that the horrors of World War I had convinced most of the nations of the self-evident necessity for regulating international competition through cooperative, legal means. As Coolidge noted about the nations, "A clearer vision has shown them not alone the horrors but the terrible futility of war." Based upon their beliefs and experiences, United States leaders were convinced that other nations would recognize the advantages and stability of a treaty-bound world order and that no one nation would want to disrupt it for fear of undermining all stability and peace. They realized that World War I had been at heart a world civil war between the industrial powers and their allies. They were convinced that another such struggle would destroy capitalism and the civilization associated with it, and assumed that other national leaders realized the necessity of creating a law-bound order. Secretary Stimson explained to the Japanese Ambassador in 1933 that his opposition to Japanese actions in Manchuria was not motivated by hostility but:

> ... by a desire to preserve and maintain certain peace treaties which I regarded as vital and important not only to the world at large but also to Japan.... I said I believed the Great War had demonstrated that we had developed both in Japan and in this country and in many parts of Europe and the rest of the world a complex industrial civilization which could not withstand modern war, and I explained to him in detail what I meant. I pointed out that we were developing into great congested populations of people who were not self-supporting, but were dependent upon trade and commerce for their supplies and food; that I believed that the Great War had shown that unless future wars could be checked and minimized this civilization would be destroyed.

In theory the treaty system was to provide for national equality, but in practice some nations were "more equal than others." As Secretary Stimson stated in regard to naval disarmament negotiations in 1932, "... that when it came to navies the guiding principle of our Delegation must be that the superiority on the seas of the Anglo-Saxon nations must not be imperiled." Yet the desire to maintain the system did cause United States officials to observe some limitations on governmental actions. During the Huerta Rebellion in Mexico (1924), the United States backed the government of Mexico. When urged by American investors to supply four torpedo boats to the Mexican Government, Hughes replied that such action was forbidden by United States obligations under the Washington Conference Treaties. He concluded: "It is not only an obligation on our part to comply with this provision [forbidding transfer of naval vessels] but it is our policy not to encourage any evasion of it here or elsewhere." Similarly, when the Firestones pressured the government to send a warship to Liberia in 1933 (the Liberian Government had passed legislation antagonistic to the interests of their rubber company), Secretary Stimson expressed bitter opposition. He explained that such action would be "... directly inconsistent with our entire policy in the Far East and even in Latin America." The Secretary was trying to uphold the legal principle that international disputes should be settled by nonmilitary means within the treaty systems of the regions.

An integral part of this belief in the inherent rationality of a treaty-bound world order was the idea that the root of most international rivalry was economic competition and pressures. United States leaders believed that these competitive forces were subject to rational control. The main focal point for this rivalry of the industrial-creditor nations was the underdeveloped areas. Borchard wrote: "It is out of the competition of national policies for the control of economic spheres of influence that the international relations of the immediate future will shape their new setting and alignments. It is upon the intelligent regulation of this competition that the peace of the future depends."

In actual practice United States officials and businessmen attempted by treaty and economic pressure to restrict certain competitive tactics, not to eliminate economic competition per se. Other nations must not compete against United States interests by using cartel arrangements (such as the German Potash Syndicate), treaties to exclude United States business (as the San Remo Agreement of 1920 through which Britain, France, and Holland divided the oil fields of the Near East), or armed force (Japanese invasion of Manchuria in 1931). By eliminating these forms of competition, United States officials hoped that American corporations would be able to gain a greater, or even predominant, share of the markets, raw materials, and investment opportunities of the underdeveloped areas. In China, for example, Ambassador Nelson Trusler Johnson recommended that financial assistance be given to an American controlled airline so that it could prevent the German airline Lufthansa from establishing a Nanking to Berlin service. Johnson hoped to direct Chinese air traffic towards the Philippines and concluded: "You can imagine what this will mean for business generally, and particularly the silk trade. The thing works both ways, and it means that mail and the influence that goes with it will flow from the Yangtsze Valley through the United States towards Europe, rather than in the opposite direction, as would be the case if the Germans win in this matter."

United States officials considered disarmament treaties a vital part of a treaty-bound world order. For one thing, such limitations would restrict one form of competition. In addition, they believed that expenditures for arms created financial instability that in turn aggravated economic competition. Secretary Stimson noted in 1932, "An armed camp is not a favorable breeding place for either trade or investment."

United States policy makers also considered the economic stability of the industrial nations to be a vital part of the regulation of international rivalry and the prevention of revolution. Utilizing the financial predominance of United States investment banks, Secretaries Hoover, Hughes, and Andrew Mellon (Treasury) set the pattern for a kind of United States regulation of the world economy. Among other things, they used dollar diplomacy (primarily loans) to open the economic door in the Near East and Europe, to obtain the readmittance of Germany to the world economy, to prevent the formation of several cartel arrangements, and to bolster the economies of several nations in Europe and Latin America. President Coolidge described the stabilizing aspect of dollar diplomacy:

> Everyone knows that it was our resources that saved Europe from a complete collapse immediately following the armistice. Without the benefit of our credit an appalling famine would have prevailed over great areas. In accordance with the light of all past history, disorder and revolution . . . would have rapidly followed. . . . When the work of restoring the fiscal condition of Europe began, it was accomplished again with our assistance. When Austria determined to put her financial house in order, we furnished a part of the capital. When Germany sought to establish a sound fiscal condition, we again contributed a large proportion of the necessary gold loan. . . . What we have done for France, Italy, Belgium, Czechoslovakia, Poland, and other

countries, is all a piece of the same endeavor. . . . no positive and constructive accomplishment of the past five years compares with the support which America has contributed to the financial stability of the world. . . . Peace, we know rests to a great extent upon justice, but it is very difficult for the public mind to divorce justice from economic opportunity.

Thus the treaty system would be undergirded by a United States-directed economic stabilization program based upon private loans, trade, and the expansion of branch factories. Under this *Pax Americana,* peace, prosperity, progress, and the Open Door would be protected; all the nations of the world (even those in outer darkness such as the Soviet Union) would be attracted to the light of this system: a subdued version of Manifest Destiny, to be sure, but one that relied more on the less volatile canons of business and law rather than on the hyperbolic litany of religion or nationalistic democracy.

The ideas and beliefs of the Republican policy makers reflected a firm faith in the ability of private enterprise capitalism to promote progress and prosperity and in the fundamental identity of interests of the industrial-creditor nations. These "self-evident truths," reinforced by the war, seemed to make a legal order a logical development in international evolution. One might call it a lawyer's view of the world, and indeed many policy makers were attorneys. In addition, their ideas were rooted in the works of such international legal authorities as Elihu Root, John Bassett Moore, Edwin Borchard, and William Howard Taft.

To these men, legal systems represented the most rational and acceptable method of reconciling conflict between groups. The recent experiences of the United States seemed to offer a model for such action. An important aspect of progressivism was the development of new legal mechanisms to regulate competition, to rationalize corporate activity, and to mediate group conflict. Hoover noted that "business organization is moving strongly toward cooperation," to reduce "overreckless competition." The country was moving by a "natural process" into a "period of associational activities." Julius Klein (head of the Bureau of Foreign and Domestic Commerce) stated that such activities were aimed at modifying the "destructive elements in our business life."

To Hoover, Klein, and Coolidge, the government was a partner with corporate business in the movement to reduce competition and conflict and to promote stability through cooperation. This form of corporate liberalism (stabilization of the social order through cooperative efforts on the part of corporate business and government) stressed voluntarism and noncompulsion. The Trade Association Movement promoted by Hoover represented the prime example of such voluntary cooperation for stability.

Believing in the success of corporate liberalism at home and in the fundamental similarity between domestic and international conflicts, the Republican leadership asserted the ideas and mechanisms of corporate liberalism to curb international competition. On another level, the same ideology was utilized for government-business cooperation to facilitate economic expansion abroad. In effect, the nations of the world were voluntarily to associate in a Trade Association for stability under the auspices of the United States. Calvin Coolidge pointed out this relationship between the foreign and domestic regulation of competition and stated that the policies of the government represented the "... processes of reducing our domestic and foreign relations to a system of law. ... It has sought to remove compulsion from the business life of the country and from our relationships with other nations."

The concept of a law-bound world as a substitute for the League of Nations (and Article X) was solidly based upon the corporate ideology and domestic experiences of the Republican policy makers. Rivalry and instability were to be controlled by corporate cooperation. In most symbolic editorials, the editor of the *Wall Street Journal* denounced Nikolai Lenin and Henry Ford as the greatest enemies of capitalism and stability; one had emerged as the prime competitor of an international capitalistic order and the other was regarded as the most disruptive, competitive force inside the United States. Either at home or abroad, corporate liberalism had no place for the competition of socialism or the independent capitalist who would not play by the "rules of the game."

The policy makers of the period also worked under a variety of domestic constraints that helped to shape and to limit policy tactics. For example, the growing disillusionment over World War I and the opposition to high taxes for military spending was reflected by the Congress. In turn, the policy makers were limited in their use of tactics that involved military force. The peace-time military force was not large enough to allow widespread deployment, even if officials had so desired. Budgetary factors made the Marine Corps quite willing to cooperate with State Department and remove the Marine garrison from Cuba in 1922.

Various peace and church groups went beyond this general antagonism to military spending and mounted attacks on the limited (or potential) military interventions of the period. During late 1926 and early 1927, the Coolidge Administration sent the marines back to Nicaragua and appeared to be heading for some type of military action against Mexico. A diverse assortment of churchmen, labor leaders, academicians, and congressmen vigorously opposed the Administration's policies. These pressures were felt by the policy makers. A State Department official noted privately that only two major newspapers supported the Administration: The *Washington Post* and the *Chicago Tribune*. Secretary Kellogg complained that on the Mexican issue, even the Ku Klux Klan was against the Administration.

The "red scare" argument that Kellogg raised in January 1927 failed to produce much support. Congressional denunciations were loud and clear. Senator George Norris of Nebraska was not in the minority when he poetically chided the administration:

> Once't there was a Bolshevik who wouldn't say his prayers,
> So Kellogg sent him off to bed, away upstairs;
> An' Kellogg heerd him holler, and Coolidge heerd him bawl,

But when they turn't the kivers down he wasn't there at all.
They seeked him down in Mexico, they cussed him in the press,
They seeked him round the Capitol, an' ever'where I guess.
But all they ever found of him was whiskers, hair and clout;
An' the Bolsheviks 'ill get you ef you don't watch out.

Considerable weight was added to the opposition when some leading businessmen and business publications attacked military intervention. Thomas W. Lamont (J. P. Morgan and Co.) declared:

The theory of collecting debts by gunboat is unrighteous, unworkable and obsolete. While I have, of course, no mandate to speak for my colleagues of the investment banking community, I think I may safely say that they share this view with Mr. [Dwight] Morrow and myself.

Paul Shoup (Southern Pacific Railroad), Lamont, and Morrow carried out private efforts to prevent the use of force against Mexico, and Morrow's appointment as Ambassador in 1927 was in part a reflection of these efforts.

Another limiting factor faced by the policy makers was the tariff policy enacted by the congressional representatives of commercial farmers and moderately small industrialists. The Farm Bureau Federation and the National Association of Manufacturers pushed for higher duties on their various products. Their efforts were reflected in the Fordney-McCumber Tariff of 1922, and even more in the Smoot-Hawley Act of 1930. Higher duties restricted the sales of foreign producers in domestic markets and encouraged tariff retaliation. In turn, these factors hampered the efforts of leaders to promote the export trade and develop the degree of international exchange that they believed was necessary for world economic stability.

The Republican leadership was limited, however, in what it could do with tariff legislation by the fact that the Republican Party was a coalition of the high-tariff groups and the export-oriented (low-tariff), major metropolitan industrialists. As a cross-regional coalition the GOP reflected the ongoing tariff conflict between the metropolitan and commercial agricultural interests. The Republican leaders were forced to compromise on the tariff question and the opening of domestic markets. Along with their business allies, they had to develop other tactics for market expansion, including ways to subsidize exports and to bypass foreign tariffs. Loans by American bankers to foreign governments and enterprises rapidly became the main form of subsidy by creating a kind of additional foreign purchasing power. "Trade follows investments," became one of the most important business slogans of the period. Foreign loans served the dual (and related) function of promoting stability and United States trade. After many of these loans were defaulted after 1929, Herbert Hoover would argue: "However if we assume the loss to U.S. investors was a billion, it certainly was a cheap method of unemployment and agricultural relief." Manufacturers also rapidly expanded the building of branch factories to promote exports and overcome tariff barriers.

Policy makers of the period manifested a diversity of views concerning the tactics of world order. None was truly isolationist, but an influential bloc of Republican congressmen did reject the tactics of membership in the League of Nations or the World Court. Officials wanted to utilize United States membership in the Court as a logical part of a world legal order, but the opposition prevented such action. The conflict over approaches to world order and membership in the Court reflected the tactical division between the metropolitan and agricultural groups. An influential leader of the latter group, Senator Gerald P. Nye of North Dakota, believed that the industrial and financial metropolis of the East (in conjunction with Great Britain) was hostile to agriculture. His views were shared by the Nonpartisan League of North Dakota, which in 1926 denounced the World Court as a "tool of the international bankers." This interrelated antagonism toward Great Britain, the international bankers, and the eastern metropolis was a part of the commercial farmers' view of the world that had developed during the latter half of the nineteenth century. Its survival in the twentieth century meant that the agricultural groups (especially in the West and Midwest) viewed any international political organization as a hostile alliance of these three groups.

Confronted with these various limitations, Republican policy makers tried to formulate foreign policy tactics that would overcome the divisions within the party and still work for a world order. The treaty system creating a law-bound order was, in part, a reflection of these internal divisions within the party. Although they were defeated on the World Court issue, officials did establish informal relations with the League and its various agencies. These arrangements enabled policy makers to utilize the League in the scheme of world order while maintaining freedom of action for the United States. In the general sense, this juggling of interests and tactics created contradictions in policy that produced practical difficulties in achieving objectives and subjected the Republican leadership to attacks on the grounds of inconsistency (or hypocrisy). The Democrats especially hammered at the dichotomy between expanding world trade and raising tariffs. They would face similar dilemmas in the 1930s.

Did these inconsistencies and contradictions justify the label "isolationism"? Only if one ignores the totality of foreign relations during the period. John Bassett Moore provided an excellent answer to the charges in a letter to Secretary Hughes. Moore sent the Secretary several editorials discussing the question of "isolation," and noted:

> These sentences may be considered partly as a passing but conciliatory tribute to a phantasm which has its victims in all countries. There never has been, for instance, a more shallow absurdity than the talk of the "isolation" of the United States. The policy of holding aloof from foreign and particularly from European political alliances and intrigues, while extending commercial and other nonpolitical activities, alone has rendered possible that political disinterestedness that has been the essential condition and the main spring of the immense influence which the United States has exerted in the development of international law and the spread of popular institutions.

The Oklahoma humorist Will Rogers recognized the extent of United States involvement in international affairs and in 1926 chided President Coolidge: "...if Argentina, Brazil, Peru, Chile or anybody else have any disputed territory and they want to populate it, or the Amazon, or the Andes, or Tacna Arica, or Tincture of Arnica, or anything else, with Peruvians, Chileans, Llamas, Boa Constrictors, Petrified Mummies or fertilizing Nitrates, why, let them go ahead and do it. What business is it of ours?" Whatever the merits of the foreign policy of the period, it can hardly be characterized as, "drifting aimlessly at the mercy of events. . . ."

United States officials and businessmen considered Latin America to be one of the most vital areas of national interest. Through generally nonmilitary policies they worked to extend United States hegemony, enforce the industrial-creditor version of stability and order, and at the same time improve the national image throughout Latin America. A United States-directed order for the hemisphere was clearly spelled out in the instructions to the delegates attending the Pan American Conference in 1928:

> "It may be observed that the United States is uninfluenced even by the willingness or desire of any American State to yield any transfer of its territory or to submit to any form of political control or influence of a non-American State. In maintaining its position, the United States has been governed primarily by its own interests, involving its conception of what was essential to its security and its distinctive position in this hemisphere."

Anti-Yankee sentiment seemed to be growing rapidly after the war, and leaders in the United States were increasingly concerned about its effect on trade and investments, especially with the renewal of European competition. This feeling continued throughout the 1920s and often cropped up in trade journals, conventions, and books about Latin America. The effect of Latin American feeling toward the United States on trade competition was fully realized. In 1921 an editorial in *Iron Age* stated:

> Confronted as American Steel exporters now are with unfavorable financial and trade conditions and with the possibility of competition from Germany, which before the war did a large business with South America, the need of the right attitude at Washington toward our customer nations on the South is evident.

Other factors were interpreted as evidence of the feeling of Latin Americans. Laws restricting economic activity were passed by several countries during the decade, and in others such laws were threatened. While Congress debated a measure to extend immigration quota restrictions to Latin America in 1928, the State Department received a number of letters from firms doing business in the region which cited the retaliatory legislation (such as higher taxes, restrictions on employment, and confiscation) that could result from the passage of such a bill. Boycotts of American goods were put into effect from time to time and a general boycott throughout Latin America was feared in 1927.

Various organizations composed primarily of businessmen were active during the 1920s in promoting a "business Pan-Americanism." The Chile-American Association (founded in 1918) was composed of members from Anaconda Copper, Bethlehem Chile Iron Mines, E. I. du Pont de Nemours Company, W. R. Grace and Company, International General Electric, Ingersoll-Rand Company, and Guggenheim Brothers and Co. The Pan-American Society (organized in 1912) had as officers in 1927 John L. Merrill, Robert H. Patchin, Sosthenes Behn, Charles A. Muchnic, and Minor C. Keith. These groups not only advocated better relations, but carried on active programs to influence Latin Americans (both in the United States and in Latin America). The Pan-American Information Service and the Pan-American Highway Commission differed from the others in scope of action, but their basic goals were the same. A number of leading businessmen were active in several of the above groups. In addition, some of these same men represented the United States at the Pan-American Commercial Conventions in 1919 and 1927. Several of them were also members of the Inter-American High Commission, that quasigovernment group headed by the Secretary of Commerce from 1921 to 1933.

The United States government followed a more cooperative policy with regard to other aspects of inter-American relations. Between 1921 and 1933 she participated in 41 out of 44 conferences involving nations of the Western Hemisphere, in contrast to her participation in 23 out of the 50 such conferences held between 1889 and 1921. The Inter-American High Commission was involved in several of these conferences and in addition carried on a general program of settling problems of a commercial nature. The actions of this group during a typical year included: organization of a visit of road engineers to the United States (out of which grew the Pan-American Highway Commission and the Pan-American Highway Conference of 1925), and negotiation of conventions concerning arbitration of commercial disputes, protection of trade marks, protection of commercial travelers, and uniform classification of merchandise. This lower-level, noncrisis diplomacy by a quasigovernmental body was indicative of the general trend of the policy—multilateral cooperation to clear the highways of commerce.

The United States government also made several not too costly concessions to nationalism in Latin America. The treaty with Colombia provided for a $25 million payment to compensate for the loss of Panama (but without apologies). In 1925 the Isle of Pines Treaty with Cuba was finally approved by the Senate, and the island became the property of Cuba. The Clark *Memorandum on the Monroe Doctrine* was another public relations item designed to change the image of the United States. Published in 1930, it argued that armed intervention was not part of the Doctrine. As Clark noted in the letter of introduction (not published), the memorandum was designed to strengthen the prestige of the Monroe Doctrine. He noted that intervention did not require a doctrine stated in advance, and the issue did not have to be flaunted "in the face" of Latin America.

The Republican leadership did try to restrict military activity in the area, even though it did not repudiate such action. Marines were removed from

Cuba in 1922, the Dominican Republic in 1924, and Nicaragua in 1925 (only to return in 1927). The Haitian occupation continued, but plans for withdrawal had been made by 1933. The use of temporary "landing parties" was also placed under restraints that had not existed previously. Moreover, during the numerous revolts that took place between 1929 and 1933, the State Department refused all requests for armed intervention. Several destroyers were sent to El Salvador during the unsuccessful "Communist-led" revolt in 1932; possibly, the United States would have intervened if the "Communists" had won. However, President Hoover stated frankly (and his actions accorded with his words) that he did not want the United States represented abroad by marines.

As in other parts of the world, United States leaders devised a treaty system to settle disputes peacefully and to promote political order. The Gondra Convention of 1923 called for a cooling-off period during international disputes; this was institutionalized at the Washington Conference on Conciliation and Arbitration, which met in late 1928. Charles Evans Hughes provided active leadership at this conference, and Coolidge and Kellogg supported his advocacy of American acceptance of the resulting treaties with reservation. The United States ratified the treaties and joined the Inter-American Court of Arbitration. In addition to these measures, the State Department acted as a kind of one-nation inter-American court by arbitrating numerous boundary disputes. By 1933 the United States had performed this role in regard to disputes involving almost three-quarters of the Latin American nations.

Most officials regarded Central America as the most unsettled part of the hemisphere and the one most requiring a system of order; almost all of the independent Caribbean states were already bound by individual treaty arrangements and loan agreements. In 1923, under the guidance of the United States, the Central American nations signed the Treaty of Peace and Amity. This revived the General Treaty of 1907, which had utilized the Tobar Doctrine of discouraging coups and revolts by nonrecognition of the resulting governments. The 1923 treaty added even more restrictive conditions for recognition. The system was intended to discourage revolutions of any kind and to preserve the status quo. During the 1920s many members of the conservative Central American elite groups eagerly supported such a treaty, especially since they feared the spread of revolutionary nationalism from Mexico.

Although the United States did not sign the treaty, it was nonetheless an instrument of American policy and she provided the leadership in enforcing the treaty. Writing in 1932, Francis White, Assistant Secretary for Latin American Affairs, cited the 1923 treaty as the basis of policy in Central America and asserted that this policy had either prevented revolution or forced a return to the status quo in at least four nations since 1927. "The rules," he observed, "were naturally set forth to discourage revolution and to encourage constitutional and orderly procedure."

Nicaragua provided the most important, and controversial, challenge to the treaty system. The decision to intervene in 1927 was based in part on the determination to enforce the rules even though the challenger, Emiliano Chamorro, was a conservative supported by some officials and by various business groups with Nicaraguan holdings. Coolidge and Kellogg decided, however, that the status quo throughout Central America could be best preserved by forcing Nicaragua to follow "constitutional procedures" for political change. There were other factors involved in the intervention. American properties were potentially threatened by the civil war between the political factions, and Mexico was giving aid to elements of the Liberal Party. The administration wanted to prevent any expansion of Mexican influence, with its possible implications for economic nationalism. Even if the Liberals won power they must do so under the auspices of the United States-enforced system. Assistant Secretary White later claimed that the intervention really established the force of the treaty system.

The Nicaraguan intervention, coupled as it was with the possibility of war with Mexico, provoked heated opposition. With mounting opposition from Congress, Administration leaders realized that they could not sustain any extensive military operation. Henry L. Stimson was sent as a mediator to arrange a "constitutional" settlement pleasing to all the old-line political factions. (With the exception of Augusto Sandino, most Nicaraguan political leaders were conservative and pro-United States anyway.) The marine corps was given the job of building a national guard rather than pacifying the country. Some marine officers wanted to wipe out the guerrilla forces of Sandino, but the administration had decided that United States forces were not to be involved in Nicaraguan politics. The idea was to construct a "legal" compromise as quickly as possible, provide a politically neutral national guard to sustain the treaty system, and then to remove the United States presence.

Actually, the adverse reaction (both in the United States and in Latin America) to the Nicaraguan venture, and the wave of successful revolts in Latin America after 1928, prompted Hoover and Stimson to further modify their tactics. The rules for recognition would be officially maintained, and "new governments" would be asked to furnish some "legal" proof of constitutional continuity. However, this would be interpreted rather broadly. Stimson also ruled out military actions and tried to curtail political meddling by diplomats and businessmen.

American Military Power and Security

JOHN BRAEMAN

Since Pearl Harbor, American foreign policy during the Harding-Coolidge-Hoover years has received a largely negative appraisal from historians. In the aftermath of World War II, the adherents of Wilsonian internationalism

From "Power and Diplomacy: The 1920s Reappraised," *The Review of Politics*, 44 (July 1982). Reprinted with the permission of the editor of *The Review of Politics*, Notre Dame, Indiana 46556.

dominated the writing of American diplomatic history. The crux of their indictment of the Republican administrations of the twenties was that this country's refusal to participate in collective-security arrangements for upholding the peace was responsible for the breakdown of international order in the years that followed. If the United States had joined the League of Nations, or at the minimum cooperated with the peace-loving nations, Britain, France, and, until the illusions of the wartime alliance collapsed, the Soviet Union, against would-be or actual aggressors, the Second World War could have been avoided. Although this view has continued to have its champions, the hardening of Cold War tensions—and the accompanying disillusionment with the efficacy of the United Nations—spurred a major counterattack upon what George F. Kennan has termed the "legalistic-moralistic approach to international problems." With the emergence of the so-called realist school came a different—though no more positive—evaluation of the role played by the United States during the age of normalcy.

The dominant intellectual figure in the post-World War II realist movement was University of Chicago political scientist Hans J. Morgenthau. Morgenthau's starting point was a complex of assumptions about the behavior of nations and, more fundamentally, about human nature, which were in striking contrast to the nineteenth-century liberal faith in the existence of an inherent harmony of interests that underlay the Wilsonian vision of collective security.

"The primordial social fact," he postulated in *Scientific Man vs. Power Politics*, "is conflict, actual or potential. . . ." Or as he put the matter more bluntly still in his now-classic *Politics Among Nations*, "the struggle for power is universal in time and space and is an undeniable fact of experience." Within most nations, he acknowledged, there existed a community of interests and values that tended to reduce the intensity of conflict. But the international arena was different. "The history of the nations active in international politics shows them continuously preparing for, actively involved in, or recovering from organized violence in the form of war." In such an anarchical world, force remained the ultimate arbiter. Thus, whatever the long-term goals of a nation, "power is always the immediate aim." And given this country's geopolitical situation, he defined as the American national interest "to preserve the unique position of the United States as a predominant power without rival" in the Western Hemisphere and "the maintenance of the balance of power" in Europe and Asia.

The trouble was, runs the realist indictment, few Americans in the age of normalcy grasped those truths. Robert E. Osgood lamented that the post-World War I revulsion against Wilsonian utopianism had fostered a no less dangerous set of illusions: a millennialist hope for "peace by incantation," "a blind aversion to war and the instruments of war as absolute evils abstracted from the conflicts of power and national self-interest which lead to war," and, thus, a refusal to accept "the uses of force and the threat of force as indispensable instruments of national policy." Robert H. Ferrell placed much of the responsibility for this situation upon the organized peace movement, which was in the 1920's at the zenith of its influence; more still upon an "immature" and "appallingly naive" public. But the elite was as much at fault as the man in the street. Betty Glad penned a damning portrait of Secretary of State Charles Evans Hughes, the chief architect of American foreign policies in the 1920's, belaboring his "evasion of the role of power in international politics." Herbert Feis blamed the ineffectiveness of American "dollar diplomacy" during the Harding-Coolidge-Hoover administrations upon "the hazy, lazy faith"—shared by the public, business leaders, and government policymakers—that trade, loans, and investments would automatically promote world peace without backing "the dollar with our diplomacy and, if essential, by arms." "Far from coordinating force and diplomacy," J. Chalmers Vinson summed up, "the American statesmen and people set the two up as incompatible." The dominant ethos was rather that peace could, and would, be maintained, "by persuasion and example rather than force."

Military historians deplored the lack of machinery for civilian-military consultation in formulating foreign policies, the resulting widening gap between goals and capabilities, and the flight from "reality" in the services' own strategic planning. The United States's refusal to assume a share of the burdens of economic reconstruction, its aloofness from foreign political involvements, and what Edward W. Bennett has stigmatized as its "indifference to, or even revulsion from, the principle of the balance of power" were blamed for undercutting the Versailles settlement in Europe. Even heavier fire was directed against this country's Far Eastern policies. A minority of the postwar realists questioned the wisdom of American hostility to Japanese ambitions; and the revulsion against the Vietnam war has given this line new popularity. But the preponderant view among the post-Pearl Harbor generation of historians was that the fault lay in this country's failure to maintan sufficient military strength to meet the Japanese challenge. Popular hostility to naval spending, congressional economizing, and the naval limitations agreements undercut the deterrent power of the navy. And when Japan in Manchuria launched the first major direct attack upon the world order, the United States responded with no more than words.

There is no question that the political and intellectual atmosphere in the United States during the twenties opposed large-scale military and naval expenditures. But a nation's military capability cannot be measured by any absolute standard. Even in the narrow sense of armed forces-in-being, what matters is their relative size and efficiency vis-à-vis those of potential enemies. And in the larger sense, a nation's "military potential" depends upon a number of factors: its geographical vulnerability; the kind of war to be fought; and most importantly, as World War I had demonstrated, its technological and economic capacity. Perhaps the most salient feature of the Republican era was this country's overwhelming superiority in the economic sphere. In the late 1920's, the United States produced an output of manufactures larger than that of the other six major powers—Great Britain, Germany, France, the Soviet Union, Italy, and Japan—combined. The extent to which a nation translates its available resources into mobilized strength is a political decision. That decision, as Klaus Knorr has pointed out, reflects a "cost-gain calculation" of the advantages and disadvantages anticipated from the maintenance of military strength at different levels. "The desirability of ready combat strength depends, first, on the importance of the prevailing goals for the achievement of which military power is a means and, secondly, on the prevailing assumptions about the amount of military resources necessary to achieve these goals." If such variables are taken into account, substantial evidence exists for a reappraisal of the conventional wisdom about American policies during the Harding-Coolidge-Hoover years.

In the first place, the extent of pacifist influence upon American policy during the 1920's should not be exaggerated. Although the organized peace groups mobilized impressive shows of public support on such issues as naval disarmament and outlawing war, the military services could, and did, rally the backing of veterans' organizations, patriotic societies, and special interest groups. Viewing the world as a competitive arena in which each nation pursued its self-interest, the increasingly influential professional careermen in the State Department had no illusions that moral force did, or could, regulate international relations. And their thinly veiled hostility toward those peace enthusiasts who hoped for a radical transformation of the international order was shared by their politically responsible superiors. Nor was there any lack of consultation with the services on matters involving national security; even Hoover, the most pacifist-minded of the chief executives of the era, took pains to do so. The crux of the services' grievance was that their advice was not always followed when purely military considerations conflicted with larger policy goals. Most important, the Republican administrations remained committed to the basic principles of military and naval policy that had been formulated during the preceding two decades: "a strong Navy and battle fleet, second to none, as a first line of defense capable of dominating the western Atlantic and the eastern Pacific"; "a small Regular Army devoted primarily to the preservation and increase of military knowledge, the training of civilian components, and the preparation of plans for future wars"; and "a strong civilian industrial economy capable of conversion to war production in an emergency."

Post-World War I army planning was based upon an "insurance" concept of preparedness resting upon a small professional force capable of emergency defense, while providing the nucleus for the mobilization and training of a mass "citizen" army. Funding limitations did keep the army's enlisted strength in the latter twenties and early thirties to 118,750 men—a far cry from the 280,000 maximum envisaged by the National Defense Act of 1920 and below the 165,000 figure estimated by the General Staff as required for carrying out the army's responsibilities. But even in the midst of the depression appropriations were more than double the pre-World War I level. And while during the years of prosperity recruiters found difficulty in attracting and retaining high-caliber enlistees, the impact of hard times allowed the army to upgrade its standards. The officer corps remained at approximately twice the prewar level, thus providing the cadre that was able to lead the vastly expanded army of World War II. This pool of potential leaders was reinforced by the continuation of Citizens' Military Training Camps and the expansion of the Reserve Officers' Training Corps in the colleges. Reflecting the World War I experience, Section 5A of the 1920 National Defense Act provided for a new assistant secretary of war responsible for procurement and industrial mobilization planning. At first, this office concentrated upon improving procurement procedures, but in the latter 1920's—drawing upon studies by the newly established Industrial War College and in cooperation with business leaders—formulated the landmark "Industrial Mobilization Plan" of 1930.

Far from a time of stagnation, the Republican years witnessed significant improvements in the army's effectiveness: the introduction of a more rational promotion system; expanded theoretical education for officers; and the establishment of a War Plans Division within the General Staff responsible for strategic planning. The General Staff's intelligence branch (G-2) displayed an impressive breadth of interest in foreign events, making a continuing effort to view military questions in their larger political, social, and economic context. Despite the handicaps of higher-echelon conservatism, financial stringency, and the fact that the theories of mechanized warfare advocates outran the existing technology, a group of younger officers pushed forward with the beginnings of a modern tank force. Under the stimulus of depression-inspired demand for economy, the pace of innovation to make the most efficient use of limited resources accelerated during the Hoover years. Up until 1929 the army had relied largely upon equipment left over from World War I. Although funds were not available for any large-scale reequipment, the War Department in late 1929 inaugurated a systematic program of research and development aimed at developing pilot models of new equipment that could be mass-produced when more monies became available, with the General Staff setting as its top priority work on what became the Garand semiautomatic rifle. In 1932, Chief of Staff General Douglas A. MacArthur put through a sweeping revamping of the army's organizational structure—the so-called four-army plan—for the more rapid deployment of combat units in the event of war.

Nor was there any threat on the European side warranting a larger American buildup. The military establishments of all the major European powers—except for the Soviet Union—suffered during the twenties from popular suspicion, stringent budgetary limitations, and a loss of self-confidence that bordered upon defeatism. From 1919 until its abrogation in 1932, British military policy was shaped by the "Ten Year Rule" that the Empire would not become involved in a major war during the next decade. Given this assumption, the strength of pacifist sentiment, and the country's near-desperate need for financial retrenchment, the British army was cut back to a level barely capable of handling its routine peacetime responsibilities. Although France as of 1933 had 450,000 officers and men under arms—with plans to mobilize within two weeks sufficient reserves to raise the total to a million

—Paris' anxiety over Germany's superior population and industry, and its potential military superiority, bred a state-of-siege mentality. The Treaty of Versailles had bound the German army by a network of restrictions down to the equipping and arming of units. Despite the growing evasion of these limitations after mid-decade, *Reichswehr* in the years before Hitler did not envisage the possibility of mobilizing more than a maximum 300,000-man force in the event of war and doubted their ability to equip even that many. The Soviet Union was probably the most formidable military power on the continent. In the late twenties, its regular army numbered 562,000 men, and starting in 1931 a large-scale program of expansion and reequipment was launched under a leadership committed to an offensive strategy based on mobility, maneuver, and mechanization. But the USSR's technological and industrial backwardness, its continuing internal problems, and its leaders' obsession with the threat of "capitalist encirclement" made the avoidance of war the keystone of Soviet policy.

Similarly exaggerated are the charges, made then and since, that American policymakers were blind to the revolutionary potentialities of air power. The Army Reorganization Act of 4 June 1920 provided formal recognition of the Air Service as a combatant arm, while the Air Force Act of 1926 provided for a new assistant secretary of war to deal with aviation matters, added an air section to each of the General Staff divisions, and authorized a five-year program of expansion in personnel and equipment. Insufficient money prevented achievement of the authorized 1800-plane force. But appropriations did rise sharply, with the result that by 1933 the Air Corps boasted 1619 planes, of which over 1100 were regarded as first-line craft. While balking at granting the air arm full autonomy as an independent service, the General Staff in its contingency war planning from 1923 on envisaged establishment of a consolidated air strike force under a single commander directly responsible to Army General Headquarters. By the early 1930's, army officialdom was gradually moving toward acceptance of this organizational setup for peacetime. Although the most vocal champion of the supremacy of air power, Brigadier General "Billy" Mitchell, was forced out of the service, his ideas about the airplane as primarily an offensive weapon whose function was to destroy the enemy's industrial base had come to permeate Air Corps' thinking. If the air power enthusiasts failed to achieve all their goals, the reasons were not simply old-guard obstructionism and congressional parsimony. The major obstacles were the limits of the existing technology, substantive differences over strategy and tactics, and the absence of any immediate threat. "Despite popular legend," World War II Air Corps chief H. H. "Hap" Arnold acknowledged, "we could not have had any real air power much sooner than we got it."

The same factors retarded air power development abroad. In structure and theory, Britain was in advance of the United States. An independent Royal Air Force and Air Ministry had been established in World War I, and the air staff's doctrine of the deterrent role of strategic bombing directed against an enemy's industrial base was accepted as official government policy. Yet financial stringency prevented full implementation of the 52-squadron Home Defence Force program authorized in 1923. Thus, in 1930, the RAF had 770 front-line aircraft compared to France's 1300, Italy's 1100, and the United States's 900. By the spring of 1932, Britain's first-line air strength had slipped to fifth place, behind France, the Soviet Union, the United States, and Italy. Although the world leader in number of aircraft, the French air force remained until 1933 a branch of the army, which envisaged for air power no more than a limited auxiliary role in support of ground forces. Notwithstanding an impressive short-run showing in the 1920's, Italy lacked the resource base to remain a major air power. Despite the increasing momentum of German secret air rearmament after 1926, the *Reichswehr* had by the spring of 1932 only 228 aircraft—with a goal of 274 for the following year—of which 192 were converted civilian planes. Probably no government of the time was more air conscious than the Soviet, which rapidly expanded the size of the Red Air Force to roughly 2200 planes by the end of 1932. But the Soviets continued to lag behind the Western powers in technology and training. And given the domination of the air force by the Red Army, major emphasis was placed upon providing tactical support for ground campaigns.

Most important, aviation technology still left the oceans as safe defenses. Even the head of the Air Service acknowledged in the fall of 1925 that the United States was not in any immediate danger of air attack. Eight years later, a board headed by Major General Hugh A. Drum, the army's deputy chief of staff—pointing to the difficulties attending the flight of the highly rated Italian bombers to the Chicago World Fair—reaffirmed that this country need not fear attack by land-based planes. As late as 1935, Britain's top heavy bomber, the Hawker "Hendon," could carry 1,500 pounds of bombs for no more than a thousand miles round trip. Despite the enthusiasm of *Reichswehr* air planners from the early twenties for a long-range strategic bomber, the first steps toward implementing its development were not undertaken until late 1933, and Germany would remain without an operational heavy bomber at the beginning of World War II. Rather than lagging behind, the United States was in the forefront of long-range bomber development. The landmark breakthrough came in 1931 with the appearance of the Martin B-10, an all-metal monoplane that was the first of the modern bombers. In July 1933 the Air Corps Materiel Division began work on the plans for what would become the B-17 Flying Fortress. And what would prove decisive in the long run, the growth of civilian aviation and the aircraft industry— stimulated by the Air Mail Act of 1925, the Air Commerce Act of 1926, Charles Lindbergh's 1927 transatlantic flight, and the Air Corps's policy of encouraging private manufacturers to build up their design and engineering staffs through placing orders for experimental prototypes—gave the United States an industrial and technological infrastructure in the aeronautics field that no rival could match.

The most controversial issue involved the state of the navy. Whereas the army command acquiesced without major protest in civilian decisions about funding and manpower levels, most naval officers made no secret of their unhappiness. Their anger was first roused by the restrictions placed upon capital ships by the Five Power Treaty of the Washington Conference of 1921–1922: a ten-year ban upon new construction; maximum tonnage quotas; and a 5:5:3 ratio for the United States, Britain, and Japan. Their anxieties about the navy's deterrent capability was heightened by the agreement reached at the London Conference of 1930. That pact continued the holiday in capital ship construction until 1936 and reduced further the tonnage allowances; fixed tonnage quotas for heavy cruisers, light cruisers, destroyers, and submarines; and provided for a 10:10:7 ratio in the first three categories with parity in submarines. Domestic political realities were an important factor in the American government's championship of naval limitation. The struggle over the naval appropriations bill of 1921 demonstrated the resistance to implementing the Wilson administration's planned building program. But the key point, and what made the agreements possible, was that similar forces were at work in this country's two major sea rivals. In Britain, the mood of pacificism and the demand for financial retrenchment joined to exert tremendous pressure for major cutbacks in naval expenditures. Similarly, the balance of political forces in Japan up until the Great Depression worked in favor of a policy of accommodation with the United States: the backlash against military interventionism spurred by the unsuccessful Siberian invasion; the growing influence of the political parties; the acceptance by the civilian decision-making elite that Japan's interests in China were primarily economic; the financial burdens of a naval arms race; Japan's dependence on this country for vital raw materials; and the sense of security given the existing favorable power balance in the western Pacific.

Qualitatively, the agreements were, as William R. Braisted has suggested, "a service to the Navy" by requiring the service to make the most efficient use of its available resources. The reduced capital ship tonnage required by the Five Power Treaty allowed the navy to eliminate overaged and obsoletely equipped vessels. With new construction halted, the navy concentrated upon an extensive program of modernization of its remaining battleships. The installation of new engines and the conversion from coal to oil increased speed and range; new electrical power systems were developed; improvements in the elevating mechanism of turreted guns resulted in increased firing power; and the substitution of plastics and aluminum for heavier materials allowed improved armor while keeping within the tonnage limitations. Naval researchers made important advances in radio communications, in radar, and in radio-controlled torpedoes. And despite their reputed obsession with the battleship, naval planners in the 1920's were committed to the construction and maintenance of a balanced fleet. Most of the eighteen of the 8-inch-gunned cruisers the navy had in 1941 were authorized between 1922 and 1933. As for light cruisers, the ten *Omaha* class commissioned between 1923 and 1925 were regarded by foreign sources as the finest of their type in the world. The large number of destroyers—349—built or building at the end of World War I precluded the construction of additional vessels until the existing ships reached overage classification twelve years after their commissioning. But starting in 1931–1932, Congress authorized the beginning of an extensive replacement program that would be continued by the Roosevelt administration. When the test came after Pearl Harbor, the American treaty-era ships proved "effective if not optimal military units, capable of performing their fundamentally defensive strategic function."

Similarly impressive were the innovations in strategy. In line with its assigned mission of capturing Japanese bases in Micronesia in support of the fleet in the western Pacific, the Marine Corps during the twenties worked out the basic principles of amphibious assault doctrine, gave increased emphasis in its training, course work, and maneuvers to landing operations, and worked out techniques of air support for such landings. The navy's most glaring weakness was in submarines. But the Naval Research Laboratory worked to improve submarine technology; submarine officers engaged in an ongoing study of design and tactics; and the London Conference's restrictions on tonnage forced a rethinking of submarine design to maximize cruising distance and torpedo power. Probably most significant for the future was the progress achieved in naval aviation. Despite its ponderousness and slowness, the airplane carrier *Langley*—a converted old fleet collier commissioned in 1922—proved invaluable for training and experimental purposes. When commissioned in 1927, the *Saratoga* and *Lexington* were the finest carriers afloat. Although the undersized *Ranger* proved a misstep, the navy in 1933 gained congressional authorization for the *Yorktown* and *Enterprise*. At the same time, a group of younger aviation-oriented officers pioneered in formulating the concept of the carrier as an independent striking force. By contrast, British carrier development lagged because of the Royal Air Force's preoccupation with long-range, land-based strategic bombers. And though more active than the British in this area, the Japanese continued to view the carrier as an auxiliary in support of the main battle fleet. This country's fleet aircraft, Rear Admiral Ernest J. King, chief of the Bureau of Aeronautics, reported in 1934, "have reached a degree of efficiency not equaled by any other power."

Even quantitatively, American negotiators struck a hard bargain. Memories of World War I disputes over neutral rights, the existence of a wide range of continuing frictions, and sensitivity to the possible threat to the Western Hemisphere from British bases in the West Indies made Washington adamant in its demand for naval parity with Britain. Despite angry protests from the Admiralty about the disparity in defensive responsibilities borne by the two fleets, Whitehall, hobbled by British financial weakness and anxious to conciliate the United States, yielded to the American position. What remained in dispute was the mix of different type vessels and the tonnage levels that would constitute parity. The differences about cruisers were sufficiently formidable to block agreement at Geneva in 1927. When a compromise was reached at London in 1930, the British made the larger concessions, accepting a future cruiser total far below what the Admiralty had deemed the minimum required. Whereas American naval planners were convinced in the aftermath of the Washington Conference that Britain's navy remained actually superior in fighting strength, they regarded the London treaty as leaving the British battle fleet inferior to this country's. After 1929, Britain ceased to appear as a possible enemy in the annual estimates drawn up by the navy's War Plans Division, and in 1932, the division's director reported optimistically that "as Britain's power wanes, the power of the United States should be increasingly effective, particularly in matters relating to the Western Pacific." In 1933, the British government formalized its long-standing assumption in practice when the Defense Requirements Subcommittee was instructed to exclude any consideration of preparations for war against the United States when drawing up its rearmament program.

In view of congressional and public attitudes toward large naval expenditures, the Five Power Treaty's 10:6 ratio for this country vis-à-vis Japan in capital ships was, as Ernest R. Andrade, Jr., has pointed out, "not a great sacrifice for the United States but instead a diplomatic achievement of major importance" since the Navy General Board's own figures showed "that without the treaty the ratio might have been even more unfavorable." Given this country's failure in the years that followed to keep pace with Japanese building in the unrestricted categories, the limitations adopted at London similarly gave the United States a more favorable balance than existed in practice. Japan would have to halt all new cruiser construction for five years to allow the United States to build up, while the tonnage allowed for submarines was below what the Japanese navy strategists viewed as a safe minimum. While American admirals fumed at the abandonment of the 10:6 ratio, Tokyo's Naval General Staff bitterly protested that the agreement jeopardized Japanese national security. The explanation for the outcry by naval officialdom on the two sides of the Pacific lies in the mirror-image complex of strategic principles that each side held. There was no question that the United States retained sufficient naval strength—except in what even American planners acknowledged was the highly unlikely circumstance of a joint Anglo-Japanese assault—to defend the Western Hemisphere and the eastern Pacific. The crux of the issue was the ability of the United States to undertake offensive operations in the western Pacific.

In their planning for possible war with Japan, so-called War Plan Orange, American naval planners assumed—as did their Japanese counterparts—that the outcome of a United States-Japanese war would be decided by a showdown battle between the two main battle fleets in the western Pacific. Given this country's lack of advanced bases in the area, the distance to be sailed from Hawaii, and the attrition the fleet would suffer en route from Japanese cruiser, destroyer, submarine, and air assaults, they estimated that the attacking fleet would require to start out with a 2:1 superiority to assure victory. Hence the grievance at the 10:6 ratio for capital ships; the much deeper alarm over the London Conference's 10:7 ratio; and, worse still, the failure by the administration and Congress even to build up to the allowed totals. Reversing these assumptions, the Japanese Naval General Staff postulated a 10:7 ratio as the minimum to guarantee Japanese victory. Its dissatisfaction with the Washington Conference's 10:6 ratio for capital ships was mitigated by the absence of any restrictions on building in the other categories. But that advantage was lost at London. The net result was a balance of strategic power that left neither side confident of winning. That men convinced of the likelihood of war would be unhappy over this situation is understandable. But why should the two countries come to blows? Although American big-navy advocates talked much about the threat of a possible attack on the Philippines, their underlying assumption—again shared by Japanese strategists—was that hostilities would result from a clash over Japanese expansionism in China. Thus, the question of the adequacy of the American navy—and of American military capability generally—rests in the final analysis upon what were this country's foreign policy objectives.

Generally, the more ambitious a nation's foreign policy objectives, the larger its armed forces will be. Or to put the matter in different terms, a nation's mobilized strength is a function of what its decision-makers—and to the extent that their policies require popular support, what its public opinion —regards as the "national interest." Given the multiplicity of definitions that have been advanced, many political scientists deny that there is, in any objective sense, such a thing as "the national interest." But what counts is how men at any given time view the situation of their nation vis-à-vis other nations. To take over Donald E. Nuechterlein's definition, *"the national interest is the perceived needs and desires of one sovereign state in relation to other sovereign states comprising the external environment."* In this broad sense, national interests may be strategic, economic, or ideological. All interests do not weigh in the balance the same. The stakes involved are felt, on an ascending scale of "intensity," as "peripheral," "major," "vital," and "survival." The most crucial question is what makes an interest "vital." As a rule of thumb, a "vital" interest exists when "serious harm will very likely result to the state unless strong measures"—including military force—are taken to deter or counter "an adverse action by another state."

The most important single factor shaping, and delimiting, United States foreign policymaking in the Republican era was this country's overwhelming sense of security. While favoring the expansion of overseas trade and investment, American officials were not willing to incur excessive costs and risk in their pursuit. Washington was most activist in backing American business abroad when such action coincided with its larger strategic and political goals: the World War I-inspired desire for American control over petroleum reserves, cables, and banking facilities in Latin America; defense of the traditional Open Door policy in China; and access to the oil of the Middle East and Dutch East Indies because of the feared depletion of American reserves. Where such political and strategic objectives were not at stake, State Department support for private interests was limited to routine calls for equal opportunities for American firms. Exports and overseas investments represented no more than a minor factor in the total national economy. The country remained self-sufficient in most mineral resources; by the latter 1920's even the anxieties over oil supplies had largely faded. The third world, as we now call it, remained under colonial rule; most of the underdeveloped countries that were independent, far from resisting, welcomed American investment from a wish to play this country off against more immediately threatening powers to tap new sources of revenue, or to promote economic growth.

American strategic planning for Latin America up to the late thirties envisaged United States interests almost exclusively in terms of the Caribbean region as this country's "soft underbelly." Although plans were drawn up for intervention in each of the South American countries, these were more conceptual and intellectual exercises than operational realities. Even with regard to the Caribbean area, the absence of any meaningful danger from Europe after World War I led American policymakers to inaugurate a shift away from military intervention in favor of other methods of promoting order and stability. When temporary intervention was required to safeguard American lives and property, the forces at the disposal of the navy's Special Squadron were sufficient for the purpose. Only in Nicaragua was there significant resistance—and the *Sandinistas* were more a political embarrassment than a military threat. Nor was there—except for Mexico—any effective challenge to American primacy south of the border from the larger Latin American countries. Developments during and after World War I had strengthened the bonds of Latin American economic dependency upon this country. Notwithstanding the strain of anti-Americanism among Latin American intellectuals, most local elites welcomed the Yankee dollar. Apart from Argentina, the South American republics deferred to American leadership in political matters. The 1920's did witness major frictions with Mexico, partly because of the threat to American property rights from Mexican revolutionary nationalism, partly because of the Mexican government's anti-clerical campaign. But, despite rumors to the contrary, American officials never seriously contemplated using force. And a judicious mixture of pragmatic official and unofficial diplomacy with economic pressure brought a resolution of the differences on terms satisfactory to Washington.

Despite the popular distrust of Old World entanglements, the Republican administrations of the age of normalcy were not indifferent to, nor aloof from, European problems. On the contrary, the establishment of a peaceful and prosperous Europe ranked high upon their list of priorities. American negotiators disregarded congressional guidelines to scale down substantially the Allied war debts. Convinced of the adverse political and economic effects of excessive reparations, Washington simultaneously labored to work out a "realistic" solution based upon Germany's capacity to pay. After the failure of his efforts to forestall the French occupation of the Ruhr, Secretary of State Charles Evans Hughes took the lead in arranging for the Dawes Plan settlement of the deadlock. The Federal Reserve—encouraged and supported by the Treasury—cooperated with the European central banks to achieve currency stabilization. Although the United States took no formal part in the security arrangements reached at Locarno, American officials exerted behind-the-scenes pressure in favor of the accord by warning that continued American loans depended upon the return of political stability. In contrast with the later ridicule of the naiveté of outlawing war, the Kellogg-Briand treaty was hailed by contemporaries as the harbinger of a larger role by the United States in world affairs, while influential elements in this country saw in the pact an opening wedge for American cooperation with collective action against aggressors.

The question is not the fact of United States involvement in European affairs, but its extent. The promotion of European recovery did take a secondary place in the calculations of American officialdom to what was regarded as more important priorities, such as tariff protection for the home market and reducing the burden on American taxpayers. Nor did support for European political stability extend to a willingness to make binding diplomatic or military commitments. Yet, even leaving aside the domestic political constraints upon American decision-makers, what more *should* the United States have done? American political and business leaders remained confident—and here Herbert Hoover was simply the most articulate spokesman of a widely shared optimism—that the United States could prosper economically, regardless of what happened in Europe. Diplomatic and military commitments meant in the context of the time support for France against Germany. Although regarding a strong France as indispensable for a European balance of power, Washington did not accept Paris' definition of what constituted French security. American officials were convinced that the French hard line on reparations, their refusal to meet Germany's legitimate grievances, and their efforts to keep Germany down were self-defeating by undermining the possibility of a prosperous, satisfied, republican Germany. Thus, they worried that any commitments on this country's part would strengthen French intransigence. Nor were they alone in this view. Their British counterparts were no more willing to underwrite the *status quo*.

If from the vantage point of the Second World War, the failure to back up France appears misguided, was that the wisest course in the 1920's? Despite the Treaty of Versailles, Germany remained potentially the most powerful nation in Europe. Nothing short of the massing of overwhelming military force could have kept Germany in a permanently inferior status. The disastrous results of Hitler's rise to power showed the validity of the American view that future European peace depended upon the success of the Weimar Republic. More immediately relevant, American policies appeared to have been successful. The influx of American loans that followed adoption of the Dawes Plan, and the achievement of currency stabilization, led to a spurt of economic growth and a new mood of optimism in Europe. The resulting prosperity contributed to muting the social conflicts that had wracked the domestic politics of the European nations in the first half of the decade. American leaders shared the contemporary optimism about the Locarno settlement as the dawn of a new era of cooperation and peace. With the benefit of hindsight, historians have emphasized the fragility of the "spirit of Locarno." While the historian can only speculate about what might have been, there is no difficulty in imagining a better Europe in the 1930's were it not for the devastating impact of the Great Depression. In the context of the time, the pact did establish, as William J. Newman has persuasively argued, "a viable and stable balance . . . which held considerable promise of diplomatic and international stability in Europe."

When this structure began to crumble under the impact of the Great Depression, the Hoover administration was not blind to the dangers. In the face of the German financial crisis in the spring of 1931, the president moved boldly to forestall the threatened collapse of the Central European banking and financial structure with his moratorium, while simultaneously working behind the scenes to promote a new debt-reparations settlement. By 1932, he had become sufficiently alarmed at the deadlock at the Geneva Disarmament Conference to take new initiatives that went far toward meeting the French demand for security guarantees. Reversing its long-standing position, Washington endorsed a system of international supervision and control as part of any new arms limitation agreement. Although Hoover continued to balk at making commitments in advance—even if no more than a formal consultative pact—American officials repeatedly assured the Western Europeans that this country would not interfere with collective action against aggressors. That Hoover's efforts to unravel the debt-reparations tangle proved a failure was due as much to the intransigence of the European powers as to domestic political impediments. The administration's decision not to go further in meeting French security anxieties reflected in part popular and congressional hostility to involvement in European power rivalries, partly the chief executive's own fear that such involvement might entangle the United States in responsibilities and dangers, such as in Eastern Europe, not commensurate with its interests.

Limited interest similarly shaped United States policy in the Far East. Although firms with a large economic stake in China, such as Standard Oil, were not without political muscle, this country's trade with and investment in China were relatively minor—and substantially below trade with and investment in Japan. Nor did American bankers, despite State Department urgings, show any enthusiasm for loans to China. American interests in China were primarily ideological, or, to put the matter more bluntly, sentimental. Captivated by the image of this country as the protector and friend of China, a vocal body of American opinion spearheaded by the missionary lobby indulged in fanciful visions of the United States as the mentor to China's evolution into a modern liberal democracy. Responsible government officials had a more realistic grasp of the rampant confusion and chaos in China, and were painfully aware of this country's limited ability to shape events in the Celestial Empire to its liking. Taking as axiomatic their duty to protect the lives, property, and rights of American citizens abroad, American diplomats kept up a drumfire of protests when those were threatened. Wishing to maintain a show of the flag, the State Department overruled the army's wish to withdraw the tiny force stationed in China. But the major thrust of American policy toward China during the twenties was toward accommodation with Chinese nationalism. The Hoover administration even accepted in principle, and entered into negotiations for, the gradual relinquishment of the keystone of the so-called unequal treaty system, the right of extraterritoriality.

Those historians who fault American policymakers for failing to take a firmer stand against Japan fail to ask what was the alternative to the attempt at a *modus vivendi* inaugurated by Secretary of State Charles Evans Hughes. China was a weak reed; Russia in the aftermath of the war was in temporary eclipse as a Far Eastern power; and Britain, painfully aware of its vulnerability in Asia, was anxious to avoid provoking the Japanese. American efforts first under Taft and then under Wilson to resist Japanese ambitions in China had antagonized the Japanese without any substantive gain for the United States. Most importantly, Hughes did not think the Open Door a sufficiently vital interest for the United States to be worth fighting for. Even if he had, the public and their representatives in Congress were not willing to make the military and naval expenditures required to deter Japan if she determined to close the door. Given this situation, Hughes achieved at the Washington Conference a diplomatic triumph that gained for the United States the abrogation of the long-suspect Anglo-Japanese Alliance, Japan's formal withdrawal of Group V of the Twenty-One Demands, and its pledge to respect the Open Door and China's independence and territorial integrity. And until 1931, Tokyo remained committed to the "Washington system" of peaceful economic expansion in China and cooperation with the Anglo-American powers.

The United States was not without blame for the breakdown of Japanese adherence to the "Washington system." The Japanese exclusion provision of the 1924 immigration act contributed to undercutting the pro-Western moderates, as did this country's unilateral support for Chinese nationalism. But more important were forces beyond Washington's control: the continued strength of traditional attitudes and values antagonistic to the new "cooperative diplomacy"; the shifting balance of power on the Asiatic mainland with the rise of Chinese nationalism and the reemergence of Russia as a Far Eastern power; and Japan's worsening economic difficulties. Would a stronger United States navy have deterred the invasion of Manchuria? The militants who precipitated the crisis were not moved by a feeling of strength but rather by a sense of weakness: by anxieties about Japan's isolation in the world; by fear that the London naval agreement of 1930 jeopardized Japanese supremacy in the western Pacific; and by alarm over Chiang Kai-shek's growing pressure on the Japanese position in Manchuria. When a broad cross section of Japanese opinion forced the government in Tokyo to sanction the actions taken by the soldiers in the field, what could the United States do? As Christopher Thorne has brilliantly shown, given the Japanese domestic political situation and Japan's preponderant military power in the area, "there was little that the United States, Britain and France, singly or even together, could do to make the Japanese surrender over Manchuria . . . without accepting a high risk of extensive costs."

Was the risk worth taking? The answer to that question depends upon an estimate of if, and how much, Japanese ambitions menaced American national interests. Throughout the interwar period, naval planners predicated their strategic thinking upon the probability, if not inevitability, of war with Japan. In part, naval officers exploited the supposed Japanese menace as a stratagem to win larger appropriations; in part, they continued to hew to the Mahan thesis that United States prosperity depended upon access to the China market. But there were dissenting voices even within the naval establishment. Admiral William V. Pratt, chief of Naval Operations from 1930 to 1933, never shared his colleagues' belief in the inevitability of a United States-Japanese war. Admiral Montgomery Taylor, commander of the Asiatic fleet during the Manchurian crisis, dismissed the possibility of saving China as a hopeless proposition; his successor, Admiral F. B. Upham, questioned the importance of trade with China given the costs of maintaining an American position there. Although paying lip service to War Plan Orange, army planners had grown increasingly dubious about the possibility of its successful execution, doubts that would culminate in 1935 in their calling for writing off the Philippines as a military liability and adopting the Alaska-Hawaii-Panama triangle as this country's strategic perimeter. Army officials downgraded—at least until the late thirties—the likelihood of war with Japan in the foreseeable future. In contrast to their naval counterparts, they did not regard Japanese expansionism on the Asiatic continent as a threat to any vital American interests.

That view was shared by the public at large, Congress, and administration leaders. Although popular and congressional sentiment was strongly anti-Japanese and there was a widespread feeling that the United States should do something, the near-universal opinion was against any action that carried the danger of war. The support that existed for economic sanctions rested upon the assumption that such pressure would suffice to force Tokyo to retreat without further escalation of the crisis. But Hoover was convinced that the result would be war. And while he believed that the United States could not allow Japan's treaty violation to pass without protest, he regarded this country's vital interests as limited to the defense of the Western Hemisphere. His secretary of state, Henry L. Stimson, was more enamored of the importance of the China market, more disposed by temperament to trying to bluff Japan into backing down, and more optimistic about the success of economic sanctions. At the same time, he was no more willing than his chief to risk a showdown with Japan. Nor were his top advisers. No one was more committed to the importance of maintaining the Open Door or more imbued with the sense of America's special responsibility to China than was Stanley K. Hornbeck, chief of the State Department's Division of Far Eastern Affairs. Yet when faced with the Japanese challenge in Manchuria, Hornbeck was torn between militancy and caution—with caution gaining the upper hand. Even when the Japanese in the spring of 1933 advanced into Northern China, he acknowledged that the "United States has not much to lose . . . there is nothing there that is vital to us."

The post-Pearl Harbor argument to the contrary rests, in the final analysis, upon the assumption—at times made explicit, but more generally implicitly accepted—that there was a direct line of planned aggression from Manchuria culminating in Pearl Harbor. But perhaps the most striking feature of Japanese policymaking after 1931 was its ambivalence, confusion, and *ad hoc* quality. Recent Japanese scholarship indicates that the general staff blundered into, rather than plotted, the war with China that began in 1937 and thereafter was unable to find a way out of that deepening morass. And the Japanese decision to move southward—which, rather than the war in China, would be the major precipitating factor bringing on conflict with the United States—was not the result of any long-hatched master plan, but was rather a response to what appeared to be the opportunities made possible by the European war. Japanese army planners did not seriously envisage the possibility of war with the United States until mid-1940. Up to then, the army had looked first upon the Soviet Union, then upon Britain as Japan's most likely antagonist. Even the navy, which had long viewed the United States as Japan's most probable foe, drifted into the "determination" to go to war without much thought about what that involved. Not until mid-1941 did Japanese decision-makers come to accept—more fatalistically than optimistically—that the decision to advance south would inevitably bring war with the United States.

The basic flaw in the realist indictment of American foreign and military policies during the so-called age of normalcy is a case of confusing the 1920's with the 1930's. The years after 1933 did witness an extraordinarily rapid shift in the world balance of power. That shift was due partly to the accelerating pace of technological innovation, but more to the differing willingness by the major powers to allocate resources to arms. If the United States was ill-prepared to meet the resulting challenges, the fault lay with the men in charge when those changes took place. In the context of 1921–1933, however, American policies were neither naive nor unwise. Perhaps at no time in its history —before or since—has the United States been more secure. Nor did his Republican successors have Wilson's messianic zeal to create a new global order. "The foreign policy of small nations is often determined for them," the British scholar A. E. Campbell has pointed out, "but in a nation complex, powerful, and unusually secure the assessment of the national interest can only rest on a general conception of the world situation. . . . Politically conscious men will have such a conception at the back of their minds, if not always at the forefront, and against that conception they will test the importance or unimportance for their nation of specific world events, and so the need for government action." Thus, what must be kept in mind about the years after World War I is that "the United States possessed a unique combination of great power and an isolated position."

FURTHER READING

Derek H. Aldcroft, *From Versailles to Wall Street, 1919–1929* (1977)

John Braeman, "American Foreign Policy in the Age of Normalcy: Three Historiographical Traditions," *Amerikastudian/American Studies,* 26 (1981), 125–158

Thomas Buckley, *The United States and the Washington Conference, 1921–1922* (1970)

Frank Costigliola, "The United States and the Reconstruction of Germany in the 1920s," *Business History Review,* 50 (1976), 477–502

Charles DeBenedetti, *Origins of the Modern American Peace Movement, 1915–1929* (1978)

Roger Dingman, *Power in the Pacific: The Origins of Naval Arms Limitations, 1914–1922* (1976)

L. Ethan Ellis, *Republican Foreign Policy, 1921–1933* (1968)

Robert H. Ferrell, *American Diplomacy in the Great Depression* (1957)

———, *Frank B. Kellogg and Henry L. Stimson* (1963)

———, *Peace in Their Time* (1952)

Peter Filene, *Americans and the Soviet Experiment, 1917–1933* (1967)

Betty Glad, *Charles Evans Hughes and the Illusions of Innocence* (1966)

Kenneth J. Grieb, *The Latin American Policy of Warren G. Harding* (1976)

Ellis W. Hawley, ed., *Herbert Hoover, Secretary of Commerce, 1921–1928* (1981)

Michael J. Hogan, *Informal Entente: The Private Structure of Cooperation in Anglo-American Economic Diplomacy* (1977)

Harold Josephson, *James T. Shotwell and the Rise of Internationalism in America* (1976)

Melvyn P. Leffler, *The Elusive Quest: America's Pursuit of European Stability and French Security, 1919–1933* (1979)

———, "Political Isolationism, Economic Expansionism, or Diplomatic Realism? American Policy toward Western Europe, 1921–1933," *Perspectives in American History,* 8 (1974), 413–461

Richard Lowitt, *George W. Norris: The Persistence of a Progressive, 1913–1933* (1971)

Sally Marks, *The Illusion of Peace: International Relations, 1918–1933* (1976)

Elting E. Morison, *Turmoil and Tradition* (1960)

Robert K. Murray, *The Harding Era* (1969)

Carl Parrini, *Heir to Empire* (1969)

Robert D. Schulzinger, *The Making of the Diplomatic Mind: The Training, Outlook, and Style of United States Foreign Service Officers, 1908–1931* (1975)

George Soule, *Prosperity Decade* (1947)

Anthony Sutton, *Western Technology and Soviet Economic Development, 1917–1930* (1968)

Joan Hoff Wilson, *Herbert Hoover* (1975)

———, *Ideology and Economics: U.S. Relations with the Soviet Union, 1918–1933* (1974)

———, "A Reevaluation of Herbert Hoover's Foreign Policy," in Martin L. Fausold and George T. Mazuzan, eds., *The Hoover Presidency: A Reappraisal* (1974), 164–186

William A. Williams, "Latin America: Laboratory of American Foreign Policy in the Nineteen Twenties," *Inter-American Economic Affairs,* 11 (1957), 3–30

———, "The Legend of Isolationism in the 1920s," *Science and Society,* 18 (1954), 1–20

Franklin D. Roosevelt,
Isolationism, and World War II

5

*The rise of European aggression in the 1930s presented Americans once
again with questions of war or peace, neutrality or alliance. Congress passed
Neutrality Acts to isolate the nation from the crises in Europe, and
President Franklin D. Roosevelt publicly concurred with the neutral position
of the United States. Remembering World War I with distaste and beset
by a terrible depression at home, many Americans endorsed what was
popularly known as isolationism. They wanted no part of European troubles,
especially because it appeared that the Europeans themselves could not
solve their own problems.*

*After the outbreak of full-scale war in October 1939, Roosevelt and the
nation gradually moved toward an interventionist posture, repealing the
arms embargo and agreeing to supply Britain with valuable military supplies
in the form of Lend-Lease.*

*The study of American foreign policy in the 1930s up to the American
entry into World War II in December 1941, and especially the diplomacy of
Franklin D. Roosevelt, has generated controversial questions: Was Roosevelt
an isolationist? Why was he so cautious in acting to assist Britain? What
role did politics play in his decisions? Was he a leader or follower of public
opinion? How did he treat his critics?*

DOCUMENTS

In the first selection, Senator Gerald P. Nye explains the result of the investigation
he led into alleged business pressure on the Wilson administration to enter World
War I. His speech on May 28, 1935, reflected ideas that helped to pass the Neu-

trality Acts. In the third selection, a speech on August 14, 1936, at Chautauqua, President Franklin D. Roosevelt passionately condemns war. His abhorrence of war matched that of many isolationists. The next document is the President's address to the nation in a "fireside chat" on December 29, 1939, in which he announced that he would make the United States the "arsenal of democracy." The Lend-Lease Act was passed the following March.

In the fifth document, distinguished historian and isolationist Charles A. Beard testifies in 1941 before a Senate committee against the Lend-Lease measure, which he views as a step toward war. The final document is the Atlantic Charter penned by Roosevelt and British Prime Minister Winston Churchill on August 14, 1941, after their summit meeting off the coast of Newfoundland. These principles were popularly considered the war objectives of the Allies.

Senator Gerald P. Nye on the Causes of War, 1935

This past year has witnessed the most intensive inquiry into the questions of arms traffic, munitions, war profits, and profits from preparedness for war that the world ever saw undertaken. It has been my privilege to work with six other Members of the United States Senate in this study. I am happy tonight to say that it grows increasingly evident that our labors have not been in vain and that truly worth-while legislation will be forthcoming to meet the frightful challenge which the inquiry disclosures have been. Largely because the people have shown tremendous interest in the subject, I am sure that substantial legislation is on the way to restrain those racketeers who find large profit in breeding hate, fear, and suspicion as a base for large preparedness programs, and who have learned that while there is large profit in preparing for war, there is larger profit for them in war itself.

But out of this year of study has come tremendous conviction that our American welfare requires that great importance be given the subject of our neutrality when others are at war.

Tonight I think we will do well to give some thought to causes behind our entry into the Great War. Those causes as well as the results which have since followed are an experience we should not soon forget.

Nineteen hundred and fourteen found America just as determined, just as anxious for peace as it is now. But less than 3 years later we were in the greatest of all wars, creating obligations and burdens which even to this day bend our backs. What was it that took us into that war in spite of our high contrary resolve?

To me there is something sinister involved in using the language of 1914 in this present pre-war year of 1935. There is, I fear, danger that the soft, evasive, unrealistic, untrue language of 21 years ago will again take root and then rise up and slay its millions as it did then, both during and after a war.

Let me make this clear. If the people of the world are told again that the next war is a political war for the noblest possible ideals, those same people will be the ones to suffer not only during the war, but also when the war is over and the peace signed on the basis of the crude, economic struggle.

Did the English or the Germans or the French in 1914 know that they were fighting the battle of commercial rivalries? No. Did the American people know that they were fighting to save the skins of the bankers who had coaxed the people into loaning $2,000,000,000 to the Allies? No. They all thought that they were fighting for national honor, for democracy, for the end of war. . . .

Let us be as frank before the next war comes as Wilson was frank after the last war was over. Let us know that it is sales and shipments of munitions and contraband, and the lure of the profits in them, that will get us into another war, and that when the proper time comes and we talk about national honor, let us know that simply means the right to go on making money out of a war.

Let us have done with all the fraud, and we will have done with all the post-war friction.

There are many who have tried to keep us from being involved in entangling foreign political alliances. But since wars are for economic causes basically, it is as important to avoid becoming involved in entangling foreign economic alliances. That is the crux of the matter. It is useless to pretend that our isolation from foreign political entanglements means anything if we open wide the gates to foreign loans and credits for munitions and spread out a network of munition ships that will be ignition points of another war.

What are the facts behind these conclusions of men familiar with the real causes of our entering the war?

From the year ending June 30, 1914, to the year ending June 30, 1916, our exports to the Allies increased almost 300 percent, or from $825,000,000 to $3,214,000,000. During the same period our exports to the Central Powers fell from $169,000,000 to $1,000,000. Long before we declared war on Germany we had ceased to have any economic interests in her fate in the war, because she was buying nothing from us.

The bulk of our sales during this pre-war period were in munitions and war materials. It must be remembered that the World War inaugurated war on the scale of whole nations pitted against nations—not simply of armies, however large, against armies. Consequently, foodstuffs and raw materials for the manufacture of items essential to modern war were declared contraband by one belligerent or another. In the year 1914 more than half of our total exports to all countries were munitions and war materials of this kind. In 1915 our sales of such materials were 179 percent greater than they had been in the preceding year and constituted 86 percent of our total exports to all countries. In 1916 our sales of these articles were 287 percent greater than in 1914 and totaled $3,700,000,000, which was 88 percent of our total exports. The growth of our sales of explosives may be taken as a single example. In the year ending June 30, 1914, we exported only $10,000,000 worth of explosives. In the year ending June 30, 1915, this figure had grown to $189,000,000, and in the next year it reached $715,000,000.

America officially regarded the right to engage in this trade as part of our neutral rights and no attempt was made to discourage it. . . .

Now, we must not forget that this enormous trade required financing also on an enormous scale. Our State Department at the outset of the war announced that "in the judgment of this Government loans by American bankers to any foreign nation which is at war are inconsistent with the true spirit of neutrality." But once we had recognized and encouraged the trade in war materials as a neutral right, it proved impossible to deny the demands for normal financing of that trade.

While the State Department was officially opposed to loans, our bankers were not. Mr. Lamont has written that J. P. Morgan & Co. was whole-heartedly in back of the Allies from the start. Mr. Davison was sent to England to place the firm's services at England's disposal. As early as February 1915 Morgan signed his first contract with the Du Pont Co. as agent for an allied power. Of the total sales by Du Pont to France and England, totalling practically half a billion dollars, over 70 percent were made through Morgan & Co., although Morgan & Co. acted as agents for the Allies only from the spring of 1915 until shortly after we entered the war—a little over 2 years.

From the early days of the war the State Department did not object to bank credits being extended to belligerents as distinguished from loans. In November 1914 France received $10,000,000 on 1-year treasury notes from the National City Bank, and in May 1915 Russia received $10,200,000 for a year from the same source. In April 1915 France received short-term credit of about $30,000,000 arranged by J. P. Morgan. Brown Bros. opened a commercial line of credit of $25,000,000 for French merchants in the summer of 1915.

In October 1915 America's bankers ceased distinguishing between credits and loans and the Government was helpless to prevent this. American investors began to finance the Allies in earnest with the flotation of the great Anglo-French loan of $500,000,000 through a huge banking syndicate headed by J. P. Morgan & Co. Similar loans followed fast, and by 1917 total loans and credits to the Allies of well over $2,000,000,000 were outstanding. Morgan & Co. had a demand loan or overdraft due from Great Britain of approximately $400,000,000, which obviously could not be paid at that time. Instead Great Britain desperately needed enormous new credits.

By this time the history of the bank credits up to October 1915 had been repeated—on a far larger scale. In the early part of 1917 it was clear that our private financial and banking resources were exhausted. Unless the great credit of the American Nation could itself be pledged, the flow of goods to Europe would end and the claims of our banks, who had made possible this flow of goods in the past, would not be paid. No one stopped to inquire whether new funds would not similarly be burned up in the holocaust of European war and would be used in the natural course of events to bail out the American banks. The facts are that by November 11, 1918, $7,000,000,000 were lent to Europe by our Government and, though most of this is still unpaid, the private loans were redeemed and the securities behind them have disappeared.

We are now discussing things that have heretofore been whispered only—things that most of us felt couldn't be true because they shouldn't be true.

But if a recognition of ugly facts will help us prevent another disaster we must discuss them openly. . . .

The experience of the last war includes the lesson that neutral rights are not a matter for national protection unless we are prepared to protect them by force. Senator Clark and I, and, I believe, Representative Maverick and other colleagues in Congress, believe that the only hope of our staying out of war is through our people recognizing and declaring as a matter of considered and fervently held national policy, that we will not ship munitions to aid combatants and that those of our citizens who ship other materials to belligerent nations must do so at their own risk and without any hope of protection from our Government. If our financiers and industrialists wish to speculate for war profits, let them be warned in advance that they are to be limited to speculation with their own capital and not with the lives of their countrymen and the fabric of their whole nation.

We must, however, frankly face the cost which this kind of decision demands. We must be realists. It requires the giving up of part at least of our present trade balance. It will mean a loss of part of our present revenue from our merchant marine and from banking. More important still, it will mean the abandonment of really vast new profits held temptingly before us.

If we cannot give up these things we cannot hope for peace. I for one believe that great though this cost is, it is insignificant compared to the catastrophe of war.

The Neutrality Acts, 1935–1939

The 1935 Act

Resolved by the Senate and House of Representatives of the United States of America in Congress assembled, That upon the outbreak or during the progress of war between, or among, two or more foreign states, the President shall proclaim such fact, and it shall thereafter be unlawful to export arms, ammunition, or implements of war from any place in the United States, or possessions of the United States, to any port of such belligerent states, or to any neutral port for transshipment to, or for the use of, a belligerent country.

The President, by proclamation, shall definitely enumerate the arms, ammunition, or implements of war, the export of which is prohibited by this Act.

The President may, from time to time, by proclamation, extend such embargo upon the export of arms, ammunition, or implements of war to other states as and when they may become involved in such war. . . .

The 1936 Act

Resolved by the Senate and House of Representatives of the United States of America in Congress assembled, That section 1 of the joint resolution . . . approved August 31, 1935, be, and the same hereby is, amended by striking out in the first section, on the second line, after the word "assembled" the following words: "That upon the outbreak or during the progress of war between", and inserting therefor the words: "Whenever the President shall find that there exists a state of war between"; and by striking out the word "may" after the word "President" and before the word "from" in the twelfth line, and inserting in lieu thereof the word "shall". . . .

Sec. 2. There are hereby added to said joint resolution two new sections, to be known as sections 1a and 1b, reading as follows:

"*Sec. 1a.* Whenever the President shall have issued his proclamation as provided for in section 1 of this Act, it shall thereafter during the period of the war be unlawful for any person within the United States to purchase, sell, or exchange bonds, securities, or other obligations of the government of any belligerent country, or of any political subdivision thereof, or of any person acting for or on behalf of such government, issued after the date of such proclamation, or to make any loan or extend any credit to any such government or person. . . ."

The 1937 Act

Whenever the President shall have issued a proclamation under the authority of section 1 of this Act it shall thereafter be unlawful for any citizen of the United States to travel on any vessel of the state or states named in such proclamation, except in accordance with such rules and regulations as the President shall prescribe . . .

The 1939 Act

Section 1. (a) That whenever the President, or the Congress by concurrent resolution, shall find that there exists a state of war between foreign states, and that it is necessary to promote the security or preserve the peace of the United States or to protect the lives of citizens of the United States, the President shall issue a proclamation naming the states involved; and he shall, from time to time, by proclamation, name other states as and when they may become involved in the war. . . .

Sec. 2. (a) Whenever the President shall have issued a proclamation under the authority of section 1 (a) it shall thereafter be unlawful for any American vessel to carry any passengers or any articles or materials to any state named in such proclamation. . . .

(c) Whenever the President shall have issued a proclamation under the authority of section 1 (a) it shall thereafter be unlawful to export or transport, or attempt to export or transport, or cause to be exported or transported, from the United States to any state named in such proclamation, any articles or materials (except copyrighted articles or materials) until all right, title, and interest therein shall have been transferred to some foreign government, agency, institution, association, partnership, corporation, or national. . . .

Franklin D. Roosevelt on
War, at Chautauqua, 1936

Many who have visited me in Washington in the past few months may have been surprised when I have told them personally and because of my own daily contacts with all manner of difficult situations I am more concerned and less cheerful about international world conditions than about our immediate domestic prospects.

I say this to you not as a confirmed pessimist but as one who still hopes that envy, hatred, and malice among nations have reached their peak and will be succeeded by a new tide of peace and good will. I say this as one who has participated in many of the decisions of peace and war before, during, and after the World War; one who has traveled much, and one who has spent a goodly portion of every 24 hours in the study of foreign relations.

Long before I returned to Washington as President of the United States I had made up my mind that, pending what might be called a more opportune moment on other continents, the United States could best serve the cause of a peaceful humanity by setting an example. That was why on the 4th of March, 1933, I made the following declaration:

"In the field of world policy I would dedicate this nation to the policy of the good neighbor—the neighbor who resolutely respects himself and, because he does so, respects the rights of others—the neighbor who respects his obligations and respects the sanctity of his agreements in and with a world of neighbors."

This declaration represents my purpose; but it represents more than a purpose, for it stands for a practice. To a measurable degree it has succeeded; the whole world now knows that the United States cherishes no predatory ambitions. We are strong; but less powerful nations know that they need not fear our strength. We seek no conquest: we stand for peace. . . .

But, of necessity, we are deeply concerned about tendencies of recent years among many of the nations of other continents. It is a bitter experience to us when the spirit of agreements to which we are a party is not lived up to. It is an even more bitter experience for the whole company of nations to witness not only the spirit but the letter of international agreements violated with impunity and without regard to the simple principles of honor. Permanent friendships between nations as between men can be sustained only by scrupulous respect for the pledged word.

In spite of all this we have sought steadfastly to assist international movements to prevent war. We cooperated to the bitter end—and it was a bitter end—in the work of the General Disarmament Conference. When it failed we sought a separate treaty to deal with the manufacture of arms and the international traffic in arms. That proposal also came to nothing. We participated—again to the bitter end—in a conference to continue naval limitations, and, when it became evident that no general treaty could be signed because of the objections of other nations, we concluded with Great Britain and France a conditional treaty of qualitative limitations which, much to my regret, already shows signs of ineffectiveness.

We shun political commitments which might entangle us in foreign wars; we avoid connection with the political activities of the League of Nations; but I am glad to say that we have cooperated wholeheartedly in the social and humanitarian work at Geneva. Thus we are a part of the world effort to control traffic in narcotics, to improve international health, to help child welfare, to eliminate double taxation, and to better working conditions and laboring hours throughout the world.

We are not isolationists except insofar as we seek to isolate ourselves completely from war. Yet we must remember that so long as war exists on earth there will be some danger that even the nation which most ardently desires peace may be drawn into war.

I have seen war. I have seen war on land and sea. I have seen blood running from the wounded. I have seen men coughing out their gassed lungs. I have seen the dead in the mud. I have seen cities destroyed. I have seen 200 limping, exhausted men come out of line—the survivors of a regiment of 1,000 that went forward 48 hours before. I have seen children starving. I have seen the agony of mothers and wives. I hate war.

I have passed unnumbered hours, I shall pass unnumbered hours thinking and planning how war may be kept from this nation.

I wish I could keep war from all nations, but that is beyond my power. I can at least make certain that no act of the United States helps to produce or to promote war. I can at least make clear that the conscience of America revolts against war and that any nation which provokes war forfeits the sympathy of the people of the United States. . . .

The Congress of the United States has given me certain authority to provide safeguards of American neutrality in case of war.

The President of the United States, who, under our Constitution, is vested with primary authority to conduct our international relations, thus has been given new weapons with which to maintain our neutrality.

Nevertheless—and I speak from a long experience—the effective maintenance of American neutrality depends today, as in the past, on the wisdom and determination of whoever at the moment occupy the offices of President and Secretary of State.

It is clear that our present policy and the measures passed by the Congress would, in the event of a war on some other continent, reduce war profits which would otherwise accrue to American citizens. Industrial and agricultural production for a war market may give immense fortunes to a few men; for the nation as a whole it produces disaster. It was the prospect of war profits that made our farmers in the west plow up prairie land that should never have been plowed but should have been left for grazing cattle. Today we are reaping the harvest of those war profits in the dust storms which have devastated those war-plowed areas.

It was the prospect of war profits that caused the extension of monopoly and unjustified expansion of industry and a price level so high that the normal relationship between debtor and creditor was destroyed.

Nevertheless, if war should break out again in another continent, let us not blink the fact that we would find in this country thousands of Americans who, seeking immediate riches—fools' gold—would attempt to break down or evade our neutrality.

They would tell you—and, unfortunately, their views would get wide publicity—that if they could produce and ship this and that and the other article to belligerent nations the unemployed of America would all find work. They would tell you that if they could extend credit to warring nations that credit would be used in the United States to build homes and factories and pay our debts. They would tell you that America once more would capture the trade of the world.

It would be hard to resist that clamor. It would be hard for many Americans, I fear, to look beyond, to realize the inevitable penalties, the inevitable day of reckoning that comes from a false prosperity. To resist the clamor of that greed, if war should come, would require the unswerving support of all Americans who love peace.

If we face the choice of profits or peace, the Nation will answer—must answer—"we choose peace." It is the duty of all of us to encourage such a body of public opinion in this country that the answer will be clear and for all practical purposes unanimous. . . .

We can keep out of war if those who watch and decide have a sufficiently detailed understanding of international affairs to make certain that the small decisions of each day do not lead toward war, and if, at the same time, they possess the courage to say "no" to those who selfishly or unwisely would let us go to war.

Of all the nations of the world today we are in many ways most singularly blessed. Our closest neighbors are good neighbors. If there are remoter nations that wish us not good but ill, they know that we are strong; they know that we can and will defend ourselves and defend our neighborhood.

We seek to dominate no other nation. We ask no territorial expansion. We oppose imperialism. We desire reduction in world armaments.

We believe in democracy; we believe in freedom; we believe in peace. We offer to every nation of the world the handclasp of the good neighbor. Let those who wish our friendship look us in the eye and take our hand.

Roosevelt on the "Arsenal of Democracy," 1940

Never before since Jamestown and Plymouth Rock has our American civilization been in such danger as now.

For, on September 27, 1940, by an agreement signed in Berlin, three powerful nations, two in Europe and one in Asia, joined themselves together in the threat that if the United States of America interfered with or blocked the expansion program of these three nations—a program aimed at world control —they would unite in ultimate action against the United States.

The Nazi masters of Germany have made it clear that they intend not only to dominate all life and thought in their own country, but also to enslave the whole of Europe, and then to use the resources of Europe to dominate the rest of the world. . . .

Does anyone seriously believe that we need to fear attack anywhere in the Americas while a free Britain remains our most powerful naval neighbor in the Atlantic? Does anyone seriously believe, on the other hand, that we could rest easy if the Axis powers were our neighbors there?

If Great Britain goes down, the Axis powers will control the continents of Europe, Asia, Africa, Australasia, and the high seas—and they will be in a position to bring enormous military and naval resources against this hemisphere. It is no exaggeration to say that all of us, in all the Americas, would be living at the point of a gun—a gun loaded with explosive bullets, economic as well as military.

We should enter upon a new and terrible era in which the whole world, our hemisphere included, would be run by threats of brute force. To survive in such a world, we would have to convert ourselves permanently into a militaristic power on the basis of war economy.

Some of us like to believe that even if Great Britain falls, we are still safe, because of the broad expanse of the Atlantic and of the Pacific.

But the width of those oceans is not what it was in the days of clipper ships. At one point between Africa and Brazil the distance is less than from Washington to Denver, Colorado—five hours for the latest type of bomber. And at the North end of the Pacific Ocean America and Asia almost touch each other.

Even today we have planes that could fly from the British Isles to New England and back again without refueling. And remember that the range of the modern bomber is ever being increased. . . .

Analyze for yourselves the future of two other places even nearer to Germany if the Nazis won. Could Ireland hold out? Would Irish freedom be permitted as an amazing pet exception in an unfree world? Or the Islands of the Azores which still fly the flag of Portugal after five centuries? You and I think of Hawaii as an outpost of defense in the Pacific. And yet, the Azores are closer to our shores in the Atlantic than Hawaii is on the other side.

There are those who say that the Axis powers would never have any desire to attack the Western Hemisphere. That is the same dangerous form of wishful thinking which has destroyed the powers of resistance of so many conquered peoples. The plain facts are that the Nazis have proclaimed, time and again, that all other races are their inferiors and therefore subject to their orders. And most important of all, the vast resources and wealth of this American Hemisphere constitute the most tempting loot in all the round world. . . .

The experience of the past two years has proven beyond doubt that no nation can appease the Nazis. No man can tame a tiger into a kitten by stroking it. There can be no appeasement with ruthlessness. There can be no reasoning with an incendiary bomb. We know now that a nation can have peace with the Nazis only at the price of total surrender. . . .

The history of recent years proves that shootings and chains and concentration camps are not simply the transient tools but the very altars of modern dictatorships. They may talk of a "new order" in the world, but what they have in mind is only a revival of the oldest and the worst tyranny. In that there is no liberty, no religion, no hope.

The proposed "new order" is the very opposite of a United States of Europe or a United States of Asia. It is not a Government based upon the consent of the governed. It is not a union of ordinary, self-respecting men and women to protect themselves and their freedom and their dignity from oppression. It is an unholy alliance of power and pelf to dominate and enslave the human race.

The British people and their allies today are conducting an active war against this unholy alliance. Our own future security is greatly dependent on the outcome of that fight. Our ability to "keep out of war" is going to be affected by that outcome.

Thinking in terms of today and tomorrow, I make the direct statement to the American people that there is far less chance of the United States getting into war, if we do all we can now to support the nations defending themselves against attack by the Axis than if we acquiesce in their defeat, submit tamely to an Axis victory, and wait our turn to be the object of attack in another war later on.

If we are to be completely honest with ourselves, we must admit that there is risk in any course we may take. But I deeply believe that the great majority of our people agree that the course that I advocate involves the least risk now and the greatest hope for world peace in the future.

The people of Europe who are defending themselves do not ask us to do their fighting. They ask us for the implements of war, the planes, the tanks, the guns, the freighters which will enable them to fight for their liberty and for our security. Emphatically we must get these weapons to them in sufficient volume and quickly enough, so that we and our children will be saved the agony and suffering of war which others have had to endure.

Let not the defeatists tell us that it is too late. It will never be earlier. Tomorrow will be later than today.

Certain facts are self-evident.

In a military sense Great Britain and the British Empire are today the spearhead of resistance to world conquest. They are putting up a fight which will live forever in the story of human gallantry.

There is no demand for sending an American Expeditionary Force outside our own borders. There is no intention by any member of your Government to send such a force. You can, therefore, nail any talk about sending armies to Europe as deliberate untruth.

Our national policy is not directed toward war. Its sole purpose is to keep war away from our country and our people.

Democracy's fight against world conquest is being greatly aided, and must be more greatly aided, by the rearmament of the United States and by sending every ounce and every ton of munitions and supplies that we can possibly spare to help the defenders who are in the front lines. It is no more unneutral for us to do that than it is for Sweden, Russia and other nations near Germany, to send steel and ore and oil and other war materials into Germany every day in the week.

We are planning our own defense with the utmost urgency; and in its vast scale we must integrate the war needs of Britain and the other free nations which are resisting aggression.

This is not a matter of sentiment or of controversial personal opinion. It is a matter of realistic, practical military policy, based on the advice of our military experts who are in close touch with existing warfare. These military and naval experts and the members of the Congress and the Administration have a single-minded purpose—the defense of the United States.

This nation is making a great effort to produce everything that is necessary in this emergency—and with all possible speed. This great effort requires great sacrifice. . . .

We must be the great arsenal of democracy. For us this is an emergency as serious as war itself. We must apply ourselves to our task with the same resolution, the same sense of urgency, the same spirit of patriotism and sacrifice as we would show were we at war.

We have furnished the British great material support and we will furnish far more in the future.

There will be no "bottlenecks" in our determination to aid Great Britain. No dictator, no combination of dictators, will weaken that determination by threats of how they will construe that determination.

The British have received invaluable military support from the heroic Greek army, and from the forces of all the governments in exile. Their strength is growing. It is the strength of men and women who value their freedom more highly than they value their lives.

I believe that the Axis powers are not going to win this war. I base that belief on the latest and best information.

We have no excuse for defeatism. We have every good reason for hope— hope for peace, hope for the defense of our civilization and for the building of a better civilization in the future.

I have the profound conviction that the American people are now determined to put forth a mightier effort than they have ever yet made to increase our production of all the implements of defense, to meet the threat to our democratic faith.

As President of the United States I call for that national effort. I call for it in the name of this nation which we love and honor and which we are privileged and proud to serve. I call upon our people with absolute confidence that our common cause will greatly succeed.

Charles A. Beard Criticizes
Lend-Lease, 1941

There is no question here of sympathy for Britain; this nation is almost unanimous in its sympathy. There is no question here of aid to Britain; the Nation is agreed on that. Our immediate task is to analyze the meaning of the language employed in this bill, and to calculate as far as may be humanly possible the consequences for our country that are likely to flow from its enactment into law—to rend, if we can, some corner of the dark veil that hides the future from our vision. . . .

Unless this bill is to be regarded as a mere rhetorical flourish—and respect for its authors precludes the thought of such frivolity—then, I submit, it is a bill for waging an undeclared war. We should entertain no delusions on this point. We should now face frankly and with such knowledge and intelligence as we may have the nature and probable consequences of that war. Without indulging in recriminations, we are bound to consider that fateful prospect.

The contention that this is a war measure has been, I know, hotly denied. The bill has been called a bill to keep the United States out of war. It has been said that we are "buying peace" for ourselves, while others are fighting our war for democracy and defense. I invite your special attention to this line of argument. I confess, gentlemen of the committee, an utter inability to understand the reasoning and morals of those who use this formula. My code of honor may be antiquated, but under it I am bound to say that if this is our war for democracy and if foreign soldiers are now fighting and dying for the defense of the United States, then it is shameful for us to be buying peace with gold, when we should be offering our bodies as living sacrifices. As I am given to see things, buying peace for ourselves, if this is our war, buying it with money renders us contemptible in the eyes of the world and, if I understand the spirit of America, contemptible in our own eyes. However, that may be, there is no guaranty that this bill will buy peace and keep us out of war, despite professions to that effect.

If the bill is enacted into law and efficiently carried into execution, it will engage our government in war activities, involve us officially in the conflicts of Europe and Asia, and place in jeopardy everything we cherish in the United States. It is true that some Americans doubt this risk. They appear to be confident that they can divine the future in Europe and Asia infallibly. They seem to believe that the United States can determine the destiny of those continents without incurring the peril of war and ruin for the American people. But I am not one of those astrologers. My knowledge of Europe and Asia is less extensive than theirs. I am merely certain that Europe is old, that Asia is old; that the peoples and nations of Europe and Asia have their respective traditions, institutions, forms of government, and systems of economy; and that Europe and Asia have been torn by wars, waged under various symbols and slogans, since the dawn of recorded history.

The history of Europe and Asia is long and violent. Tenacious emotions and habits are associated with it. Can the American people, great and ingenious though they be, transform those traditions, institutions, systems, emotions, and habits by employing treasure, arms, propaganda, and diplomatic lectures? Can they, by any means at their disposal, make over Europe and Asia, provide democracy, a bill of rights, and economic security for everybody, everywhere, in the world? With all due respect for those Americans who clamor that this is the mission of the United States, I am compelled to say that, in my opinion, their exuberance is on a par with the childish exuberance of the Bolshevik internationalists who preach the gospel of one model for the whole world. And I am bound to say, furthermore, that it is an exuberance more likely to bring disasters upon our own country than to carry happiness and security to the earth's weary multitudes.

Against embarking on such a crusade, surely we are put on our guard by the history of the last World War. For public consumption and partly with a view to influencing American public opinion, several European belligerents put forth numerous formulations of war origins and war aims. Later, unexpected revolutions in Russia, Germany, and Austria ripped open the diplomatic archives of those countries. Then were revealed to us the maneuvers, negotiations, and secret treaties spread over many years, which preceded and accompanied that World War. I have spent many weary months studying these documents, and I will say, gentlemen of the committee, that these documents do not show that the European conflict was, in the aims of the great powers, a war for democracy, or for the defense of the United States, or had anything to do with protecting the interests of the United States.

And to state the case mildly, those secret agreements among the powers do not exactly square with the public statements of the belligerents respecting the origins and aims of that war. Nor indeed did the so-called settlement at Paris, in 1919, exactly square with the declared war aims of President Wilson.

This is not to say that the present war is identical with the last war or to recite that false phrase, "History repeats itself"—for it never does. Yet we do know that the present war did not spring out of a vacuum, nor merely out of the Versailles Treaty. Its origins, nature, and course are rooted in the long history of the Old World and the long conflicts of the great powers. In the light of that long history and those long conflicts, a discussion of their mere war aims shrivels into futility.

We, however, poised now on the brink of the fateful decision respecting ourselves, are under positive obligation to discuss the aims of the government of the United States in the activities which would be let loose under this bill, if enacted. Indeed it becomes the solemn duty of all members of Congress to do this. If they are not to vote thoughtlessly and recklessly, they will ask themselves certain grave questions before they vote. And I may say, gentlemen of the committee, I do not envy you that solemn task that falls upon you. Congress cannot in truth escape these questions, for it will be answering them if it passes this bill—answering them conceivably in a manner fraught with infinite tragedy for the United States.

Here are the questions:

Does Congress intend to guarantee the present extent, economic resources, and economic methods of the British Empire forever to the government of Great Britain by placing the unlimited resources of the United States forever at the disposal of the British government, however constituted?

Does Congress intend to supply money, ships, and commodities of war until the French Republic is restored? Until the integrity of its empire is assured? Until all the lands run over by Hitler are once more vested with full sovereignty? Until Russia has returned to Finland and Poland the territories wrested from them? Until democracy is reestablished in Greece? Until the King of Albania has recovered his throne?

Is Congress prepared to pour out American wealth until the Chungking government in China has conquered the Nanking government? Until Japan is expelled from the continent? Until Chinese Communists are finally suppressed? And until Soviet Russia is pushed back within the old Russian borders?

And if European or Asiatic powers should propose to make settlements without providing democracy, a bill of rights, and economic security for everybody, everywhere, will Congress insist that they keep on fighting until the President of the United States is satisfied with the results? If none of the countries deemed under the terms of this bill to be defending the United States succeeds in defeating its enemy with the material aid rendered by the United States, will Congress throw millions of boys after the billions of dollars?

Two more crucial questions are before our Nation in council. After Europe has been turned into flaming shambles, with resolutions exploding right and left, will this Congress be able to supply the men, money, and talents necessary to reestablish and maintain order and security there? Are the members of Congress absolutely sure, as they think about this bill, that the flames of war and civil commotion will not spread to our country? That when the war boom of fools' gold has burst with terrific force, Congress will be able to cope at home with the problems of unemployment and debts with which it had wrestled for years prior to this present false prosperity by borrowing money to meet the needs of distressed farmers, distressed industries, the distressed third of the nation?

As a nation in council, we should not mislead ourselves by phrases and phantoms. The present business of our Congress, it seems to me, is not to split hairs over the mere language of this bill or to try to restrict its consequences to one or two years of presidential experimentation. The present business of Congress is to decide now, in voting on this bill, whether it is prepared on a showdown to carry our country into the war in Europe and Asia, and thus set the whole world on fire, or whether it is resolved, on a showdown, to stay out to the last ditch and preserve one stronghold of order and sanity even against the gates of hell. Here, on this continent, I believe we may be secure and should make ourselves secure from the kind of conflict and terrorism in which the old worlds have indulged for such long ages of time.

The Atlantic Charter, 1941

Joint declaration of the President of the United States of America and the Prime Minister, Mr. Churchill, representing His Majesty's Government in the United Kingdom, being met together, deem it right to make known certain common principles in the national policies of their respective countries on which they base their hopes for a better future for the world.

First, their countries seek no aggrandizement, territorial or other;

Second, they desire to see no territorial changes that do not accord with the freely expressed wishes of the peoples concerned;

Third, they respect the right of all peoples to choose the form of government under which they will live; and they wish to see sovereign rights and self-government restored to those who have been forcibly deprived of them;

Fourth, they will endeavor, with due respect for their existing obligations, to further the enjoyment by all states, great or small, victor or vanquished, of access, on equal terms, to the trade and to the raw materials of the world which are needed for their economic prosperity;

Fifth, they desire to bring about the fullest collaboration between all nations in the economic field with the object of securing, for all improved labor standards, economic advancement, and social security;

Sixth, after the final destruction of the Nazi tyranny, they hope to see established a peace which will afford to all nations the means of dwelling in safety within their own boundaries, and which will afford assurance that all the men in all the lands may live out their lives in freedom from fear and want;

Seventh, such a peace should enable all men to traverse the high seas and oceans without hindrance;

Eighth, they believe that all of the nations of the world, for realistic as well as spiritual reasons, must come to the abandonment of the use of force. Since no future peace can be maintained if land, sea, or air armaments continue to be employed by nations which threaten, or may threaten, aggression outside of their frontiers, they believe, pending the establishment of a wider and permanent system of general security, that the disarmament of such nations is essential. They will likewise aid and encourage all other practicable measures which will lighten for peace-loving peoples the crushing burden of armaments.

ESSAYS

Robert A. Divine of the University of Texas argues that Franklin D. Roosevelt was a sincere isolationist who shared the views of a majority of Americans against involvement in another war. Divine surveys Roosevelt's reactions to the crises of the 1930s. On the other hand, James MacGregor Burns of Williams College, a Roosevelt biographer, thinks that Roosevelt's foreign policy was governed by the President's political ambitions, making him cautious in challenging isolationism and therefore timid as a leader. In the final essay, Richard W. Steele of San Diego State University reports in his essay that Roosevelt became an active leader in 1940–1941, going as far as trying to discredit his isolationist critics by associating them in the public mind with the Nazi threat.

Roosevelt the Isolationist

ROBERT A. DIVINE

Roosevelt's foreign policy in the 1930's toward the totalitarian threat of Germany, Italy, and Japan would seem to offer little room for historical contro-

Robert A. Divine, *Roosevelt and World War II* (Baltimore: Johns Hopkins University Press, 1969), pp. 5–11, 20–30, 30–37, 38–40, 43–48. Copyright © 1969 by The Johns Hopkins University Press. Reprinted by permission of The Johns Hopkins University Press.

versy. The record is clear—Roosevelt pursued an isolationist policy, refusing to commit the United States to the defense of the existing international order. He accepted a series of isolationist neutrality laws passed by Congress, objecting only to those provisions which infringed on his freedom of action as President; he acquiesced in Italy's seizure of Ethiopia, Japan's invasion of China, and Germany's takeover of Austria and the Sudetenland in Czechoslovakia. The sole exception that can be cited is the Quarantine speech in 1937, and even this apparently bold statement was so ambiguous that historians have never been able to agree on the President's precise intention.

Yet this isolationist policy does not square with the usual image of Franklin Roosevelt as a perceptive world leader who recognized the danger to the United States from Axis aggression and who eventually led his nation into war to preserve American security. Troubled by this contradiction, historians have argued that Roosevelt subordinated his own internationalist preferences and gave in to the isolationist mood of the American people. As a shrewd politician, he knew that the electorate would not tolerate an active foreign policy in the midst of the depression, and so he wisely surrendered to the public will. His major desires in the mid-thirties were to achieve recovery and carry out sweeping domestic reforms; he could not jeopardize these vital goals with an unpopular foreign policy. Implicit in this interpretation is the belief that Roosevelt was an internationalist at heart. Thus Basil Rauch argues that the President acted wisely in drifting with the current in the 1930's; later in the decade, when the totalitarian threat became more intense, he was finally able to win the people over to an active policy. James MacGregor Burns is less charitable. He accuses Roosevelt of floating helplessly on a flood tide of isolationism and thus failing to fulfill his obligation of leadership. "As a foreign policy maker," Burns concludes, "Roosevelt during his first term was more pussyfooting politician than political leader."

Charles A. Beard, in his book *American Foreign Policy in the Making, 1932–1940,* offers a simpler and more convincing explanation of Roosevelt's behavior. In the 1930's, Beard contends, Roosevelt *was* an isolationist. Though Beard in a later book accuses the President of lying the nation into war, his earlier study provides a sound interpretation of Roosevelt's foreign policy. If we accept Roosevelt's own public statements at their face value, then we can dismiss the concept of two Roosevelts, one the public figure saying what the people wanted to hear, the other the private man with an entirely different set of beliefs. Equally important, we no longer have to explain Roosevelt's conduct on the basis of a devious political expediency. Instead, we can state simply that Roosevelt pursued an isolationist policy out of genuine conviction.

It is not surprising that F.D.R. shared in the isolationist temper of his times. The mood was deep and pervasive in the 1930's. The First World War had led to a profound sense of disillusion that found expression in an overwhelming national desire to abstain from future world conflicts. The generation of the thirties embraced pacifism as a noble and workable ideal—students demonstrated on college campuses every spring in massive antiwar strikes; religious and pacifist societies waged a campaign to remove ROTC units from colleges and universities; millions of Americans applauded the limited naval disarmament of the 1920's and followed with intense interest the futile disarmament conference that went on at Geneva through the early years of the decade. Feeding this pacifism was the belief that the same wicked businessmen who had destroyed the economic health of the nation were responsible for fomenting war. The Nye investigation struck a responsive chord with the airing of charges that it was merchants of death like Pierre Du Pont and J. P. Morgan who had brought the United States into the First World War. And many Americans accepted the argument that the depression was the final legacy of that war.

Roosevelt, in his speeches and letters, constantly reiterated his belief that the United States should avoid all future conflicts. In his first two years in office, he tended to ignore foreign policy as he concentrated on the problems of economic recovery at home. But in 1935, as the world crisis unfolded with Hitler's rearmament of Germany and Mussolini's attack on Ethiopia, the President began to speak out on international issues. In an Armistice Day address in 1935, after commenting on the rising danger in Europe, he said, "the primary purpose of the United States of America is to avoid being drawn into war." The nation's youth, he continued, "know that the elation and prosperity which may come from a new war must lead—for those who survive it—to economic and social collapse more sweeping than any we have experienced in the past." He concluded by stating that the proper American role was to provide an example to all mankind of the virtues of peace and democracy. In a letter to William Dodd, the American ambassador to Germany, a few weeks later, he repeated this advice, writing, "I do not know that the United States can save civilization but at least by our example we can make people think and give them the opportunity of saving themselves."

Roosevelt's initial response to the rising totalitarian threat was thus in the classic tradition of American isolationism. The United States was to play a passive role as the beacon of liberty to mankind, providing a model for the world to follow, but avoiding any active participation in a foreign conflict. In his annual message to Congress in January, 1936, for the first time he dwelt at some length on foreign policy, warning the congressmen and senators of the dangers to peace that were developing in Europe. If war came, he declared, the only course the United States could follow was neutrality, "and through example and all legitimate encouragement and assistance to persuade other Nations to return to the ways of peace and good-will." In a Dallas speech in mid-1936, he spoke again of the troubles plaguing the European nations and expressed his sympathy for their plight. "We want to help them all that we can," he stated, "but they have understood very well in these latter years that help is going to be confined to moral help, and that we are not going to get tangled up with their troubles in the days to come."

Roosevelt voiced his isolationist convictions most forthrightly in his famous Chautauqua address in August, 1936. This speech came after he had been renominated for the presidency by the Democratic Party, and it was the only speech he made in the 1936 campaign that dealt with foreign policy. Once again he concentrated on the perilous world situation, and again he reaffirmed his determination to keep the nation out of any conflict that might arise. He played on the merchants of death theme, warning that the lure of "fool's gold" in the form of trade with belligerents would lead many greedy Americans to attempt to evade the neutrality laws. "If we face the choice of profit or peace," Roosevelt demanded, "the Nation will answer—must answer—'we choose peace.' " He went on to point out how hard it would be to keep out of a major war and said that only careful day-by-day conduct of foreign policy by the Secretary of State and the President could keep the nation at peace.

The most striking passage came when Roosevelt revealed his own emotional distaste for war:

> I have seen war. I have seen war on land and sea. I have seen blood running from the wounded. I have seen men coughing out their gassed lungs. I have seen the dead in the mud. I have seen cities destroyed. I have seen two hundred limping, exhausted men come out of line—the survivors of a regiment of one thousand that went forward forty-eight hours before. I have seen children starving. I have seen the agony of mothers and wives. I hate war.
>
> I have passed unnumbered hours, I shall pass unnumbered hours, thinking and planning how war may be kept from this nation.

Here Roosevelt laid bare the source of his isolationism. Some commentators dismissed his words as campaign rhetoric, empty phrases designed simply to win votes in the coming election. But the words carry a sense of conviction and honesty that belies such hypocrisy. Samuel Rosenman testifies to Roosevelt's sincerity, stating that the President considered the Chautauqua address one of his most important speeches. The following Christmas, after he had been safely re-elected, Roosevelt sent close friends a specially printed and inscribed copy of the speech as a holiday gift. For Roosevelt, the Chautauqua address was more than a campaign speech; it was a clear and precise statement of his innermost beliefs. He shared fully in the hatred of war that was at the root of American isolationism in the depression decade, and he was determined to insure that the United States would remain a beacon of peace and sanity in a world going mad.

Roosevelt's fundamental aversion to war determined his responses to the hostile acts committed by Italy, Japan, and Germany in the 1930's. As these totalitarian powers expanded into Ethiopia, China, and Central Europe, Roosevelt was torn between his strong distaste for their aggression and his conviction that the United States should stay out of war at any cost. In subtle ways, he tried to throw the weight of American influence against the totalitarian states, but never at the risk of American involvement.

The Italian invasion of Ethiopia in early October of 1935 touched off the first major foreign crisis that Roosevelt faced as President. The Ethiopian war had been developing for over a year, and the imminence of this conflict had goaded Congress into passing the first Neutrality Act in late August. This legislation instructed the President to apply an embargo on the export of arms to nations at war and permitted him, at his discretion, to warn American citizens against traveling on belligerent ships. The idea of preventing munitions-makers from selling weapons to countries at war appealed to Roosevelt, but he was distressed at the mandatory nature of the arms embargo, preferring discretionary power that would enable him to decide when and against whom such embargoes should be levied. Nevertheless, he decided not to veto the Neutrality Act when Congress limited it to a six-month trial period. Roosevelt realized that this legislation would not hamper him if war broke out in Africa. Italy, which had the money and ships to import arms from the United States, would be adversely affected, while Ethiopia would be no worse off.

Thus, when reporters asked him his opinion of the Neutrality Act on August 28, he could reply candidly that he found it "entirely satisfactory." "The question of embargoes as against two belligerents meets the need of the existing situation," he explained. "What more can one ask?" . . .

When Hitler announced plans for German rearmament in 1935 and then marched into the Rhineland the next year, the Roosevelt administration remained silent. In both cases, Germany was violating the Treaty of Versailles, but the fact that the United States was not a party to this agreement meant that there were no grounds for an American protest. Privately, Roosevelt did speak out, commenting to his associates that Hitler was an international gangster, a bandit who someday would have to be halted. After the German seizure of Austria in March, 1938, Cordell Hull issued a cautious statement expressing American concern over the effect of this German act on world peace. Roosevelt was also disturbed, but he was not ready to alter his policy. In a letter to the American ambassador in Ireland in April, 1938, he commented that the only hopeful sign about the world situation was "that we in the United States are still better off than the people or the governments of any other great country."

The real test of Roosevelt's policy came with the Czech crisis in September of 1938 which culminated in the Munich Conference. Moving inexorably toward his goal of uniting all German people in Europe into a Greater Third Reich, Hitler began demanding the cession of the Sudeten provinces of Czechoslovakia. The Czechs refused and turned to England and France for help. Neville Chamberlain, the British Prime Minister, flew to Germany on September 15 to confer with Hitler. A week later, England and France announced that Czechoslovakia would turn over to Hitler the districts in which Germans were in the majority. But the German dictator refused to be content with these concessions. Instead, he stepped up his demands to include areas in which the Germans were in the minority and insisted that the transfer be accomplished by October 1. British and French public opinion stiffened, and by September 25 it seemed likely that Chamberlain and Edouard Daladier, the French Premier, would fight rather than surrender completely to Hitler.

As the deadline approached, William Bullitt, the American ambassador in Paris, sent a series of urgent cables asking Roosevelt to call for an international conference to head off a major war. At one point, Bullitt even suggested that Roosevelt offer his services as a neutral arbitrator. The idea of personal diplomatic intervention appealed to the President, but Hull and other State Department advisers cautioned him against any dramatic step. Finally, on September 26, Roosevelt issued a public appeal to Hitler, Chamberlain, Daladier, and Eduard Beneš, the Czech leader, calling for a resumption of the negotiations.

When Hitler sent back a negative reply, Roosevelt dispatched a personal appeal to Mussolini, asking him to do everything possible to continue the diplomatic negotiations. Then, late on September 27, the President sent a telegram to Hitler appealing once again for a peaceful solution and suggesting an international conference at some neutral spot in Europe. The next afternoon, the British and French leaders announced that they would meet with Hitler and Mussolini at Munich on September 29 to continue the quest for peace. When Roosevelt heard the news, he immediately cabled Chamberlain the brief but enthusiastic message, "Good man."

Historians still debate Roosevelt's responsibility for the Munich Conference. Basil Rauch, in a tortuous reading of the sequence of events, interprets Roosevelt's actions as an effort to bolster the willingness of Chamberlain and Daladier to stand up to Hitler! In a more carefully reasoned article, John McVickar Haight argues that Roosevelt was indeed trying to stand behind England and France, but that the French in particular misinterpreted his actions. "The president's messages," Haight concluded, "were couched in such cautious terms they were misread." William L. Langer and S. Everett Gleason deal with the Munich Conference briefly at the outset of *The Challenge to Isolation*, where they flatly state that "there is no reason to suppose that the President's appeal influenced Hitler in his decision to call the Munich Conference." James MacGregor Burns is even harsher, charging that Roosevelt pursued "a policy of pinpricks and righteous protest." "No risks, no commitments," writes Burns, "was the motto of the White House."

A careful reading of the texts of the messages Roosevelt sent on September 26 and 27 indicates that the President was genuinely perplexed by the Czech crisis. He realized that war impended; he hoped desperately to use American influence to prevent it; but he was still paralyzed by his fear of war. "Should hostilities break out, the lives of millions of men, women, and children in every country involved will most certainly be lost under circumstances of unspeakable horror," he wrote. He recognized that the United States would inevitably be affected by such a conflict, stating that "no nation can escape some measure of the consequences of such a world catastrophe." But while he urged the European leaders to come together again and seek a peaceful solution, he refrained from making any specific American commitments. Thus, in his appeal to Hitler on September 27 in which he proposed a major international conference, he made it clear that the United States would not attend. "The Government of the United States has no political involvements in Europe," Roosevelt informed Hitler, "and will assume no obligations in the conduct of the present negotiations." Nothing he might have said could have been more damaging. In effect, he gave Hitler a green light, saying that the United States would not concern itself in any meaningful way with the settlement of the gravest international crisis since the end of World War I. In that limited and indirect way, he must bear some of the responsibility for the Munich debacle.

But what is most significant is Roosevelt's inner turmoil. In a letter on September 15 to William Phillips, the American ambassador to Italy, he confessed his fear that negotiations with Hitler might only postpone "what looks to me like an inevitable conflict within the next five years." "Perhaps when it comes," he commented, "the United States will be in a position to pick up the pieces of European civilization and help them to save what remains of the wreck—not a cheerful prospect." Yet in the same letter he goes on to say, "if we get the idea that the future of our form of government is threatened by a coalition of European dictators, we might wade in with everything we have to give." A month later, after Munich, he revealed the same contradiction in his thought in a note to Canadian Prime Minister Mackenzie King. He began by saying that he rejoiced in the peaceful solution of the Czech crisis, claiming that it proved that the people of the world had a clear perception of how terrible a general European war would be. Yet, he continued, "I am still concerned, as I know you are, when we consider prospects for the future." He concluded with the fatalistic estimate that world peace depended on Hitler's continued willingness to co-operate.

It does seem clear that by the end of 1938, Roosevelt was no longer the confirmed isolationist he had been earlier in the decade. The brutal conquests by Italy, Japan, and Germany had aroused him to their ultimate threat to the United States. But he was still haunted by the fear of war that he voiced so often and so eloquently. His political opponents and subsequent historians have too readily dismissed his constant reiteration of the horrors of war as a politician's gesture toward public opinion. I contend that he was acting out of a deep and sincere belief when he declared that he hated war, and it was precisely this intense conviction that prevented him from embracing an interventionist foreign policy in the late 1930's. In the Munich crisis, he reveals himself in painful transition from the isolationist of the mid-1930's who wanted peace at almost any price to the reluctant internationalist of the early 1940's who leads his country into war in order to preserve its security.

No aspect of Roosevelt's foreign policy has been more controversial than his role in American entry into World War II. Although much of the discussion centers on the events leading to Pearl Harbor, I do not intend to enter into that labyrinth. The careful and well-researched studies by Herbert Feis, Roberta Wohlstetter, and Paul Schroeder demonstrate that while the administration made many errors in judgment, Roosevelt did not deliberately expose the fleet to a Japanese attack at Pearl Harbor in order to enter the war in Europe by a back door in the Pacific. This revisionist charge has already received far more attention than it deserves and has distracted historians from more significant issues.

What is more intriguing is the nature of Roosevelt's policy toward the war in Europe. There are a number of tantalizing questions that historians have not answered satisfactorily. Why was Roosevelt so devious and indirect in his policy toward the European conflict? When, if ever, did F.D.R. decide that the United States would have to enter the war in Europe to protect its own security? And finally, would Roosevelt have asked Congress for a declaration of war against Germany if Japan had not attacked Pearl Harbor?

In the months that followed the Munich Conference, President Roosevelt gradually realized that appeasement had served only to postpone, not to prevent, a major European war. In January, 1939, he sought to impart this fact in his annual message to Congress. He warned the representatives and senators that "philosophies of force" were loose in the world that threatened "the tenets of faith and humanity" on which the American way of life was founded. "The world has grown so small and weapons of attack so swift," the President declared, "that no nation can be safe" when aggression occurs anywhere on earth. He went on to say that the United States had "rightly" decided not to intervene militarily to prevent acts of aggression abroad and then added, somewhat cryptically, "There are many methods short of war, but stronger and more effective than mere words, of bringing home to aggressor governments the aggregate sentiments of our own people." Roosevelt did not spell out these "methods short of war," but he did criticize the existing neutrality legislation, which he suggested had the effect of encouraging aggressor nations. "We have learned," he continued, "that when we deliberately try to legislate neutrality, our neutrality laws may operate unevenly and unfairly—may actually give aid to an aggressor and deny it to the victim. The instinct of self-preservation should warn us that we ought not to let that happen any more."

Most commentators interpreted the President's speech as a call to Congress to revise the existing neutrality legislation, and in particular the arms embargo. Yet for the next two months, Roosevelt procrastinated. Finally, after Hitler's armies overran the remainder of Czechoslovakia in mid-March, Senator Key Pittman came forward with an administration proposal to repeal the arms embargo and permit American citizens to trade with nations at war on a cash-and-carry basis. The Pittman bill obviously favored England and France, since if these nations were at war with Nazi Germany, they alone would possess the sea power and financial resources to secure arms and supplies from a neutral United States. At the same time, the cash-and-carry restrictions would guard against the loss of American lives and property on the high seas and thus minimize the risk of American involvement.

Although the Pittman bill seemed to be a perfect expression of Roosevelt's desire to bolster the European democracies yet not commit the United States, the President scrupulously avoided any public endorsement in the spring of 1939. His own political stock was at an all-time low as a result of the court-packing dispute, a sharp economic recession, and an unsuccessful effort to purge dissident Democrats in the 1938 primaries. By May, Roosevelt's silence and Pittman's inept handling had led to a deadlock in the Senate. The President then turned to the House of Representatives, meeting with the leaders of the lower chamber on May 19 and telling them that passage of the cash-and-carry measure was necessary to prevent the outbreak of war in Europe. Yet despite this display of concern, Roosevelt refused to take the issue to the people, asking instead that Cordell Hull champion neutrality revision. The presidential silence proved fatal. In late June, a rebellious House of Representatives voted to retain the arms embargo and thus sabotage the administration's effort to align the United States with Britain and France.

Belatedly, Roosevelt decided to intervene. He asked the Senate Foreign Relations Committee to reconsider the Pittman bill, but in early July the Committee rebuffed the President by voting 12 to 11 to postpone action until the next session of Congress. Roosevelt was furious. He prepared a draft of a public statement in which he denounced congressional isolationists "who scream from the housetops that this nation is being led into a world war" as individuals who "deserve only the utmost contempt and pity of the American people." Hull finally persuaded him not to release this inflammatory statement. Instead, Roosevelt invited a small bipartisan group of senators to meet with him and Cordell Hull at the White House. The senators listened politely while the President and Secretary of State warned of the imminence of war in Europe and the urgent need of the United States to do something to prevent it. Senator William Borah, a leading Republican isolationist, then stunned Roosevelt and Hull by announcing categorically that there would be no war in Europe in the near future, that he had access to information from abroad that was far more reliable than the cables arriving daily at the State Department. When the other senators expressed their belief that Congress was not in the mood to revise the Neutrality Act, the meeting broke up. In a press release the next day, Roosevelt stated that the administration would accept the verdict of Congress, but he made it clear that he and Hull still believed that its failure to revise the neutrality legislation "would weaken the leadership of the United States . . . in the event of a new crisis in Europe." In a press conference three days later, Roosevelt was even blunter, accusing the Republicans of depriving him of the only chance he had to prevent the outbreak of war in Europe.

When the German invasion of Poland on September 1, 1939, touched off World War II, Roosevelt immediately proclaimed American neutrality and put the arms embargo and other restrictions into effect. In a radio talk to the American people on the evening of September 3, he voiced his determination to keep the country out of the conflict. "We seek to keep war from our firesides," he declared, "by keeping war from coming to the Americas." Though he deliberately refrained from asking the people to remain neutral in thought as Wilson had done in 1914, he closed by reiterating his personal hatred of war and pledging that, "as long as it remains within my power to prevent, there will be no blackout of peace in the United States."

President Roosevelt did not give up his quest for revision of the Neutrality Act, however. After a careful telephone canvass indicated that a majority of the Senate would now support repeal of the arms embargo, the President called Congress into special session. On September 21, Roosevelt urged the senators and representatives to repeal the arms embargo and thereby return to the traditional American adherence to international law. Calling Jefferson's embargo and the neutrality legislation of the 1930's the sole exceptions to this historic policy, he argued that the removal of the arms embargo was a way to insure that the United States would not be involved in the European conflict, and he promised that the government would also insist that American citizens and American ships be barred from entering the war zones. Denying that repeal was a step toward war, Roosevelt asserted that his proposal "offers far greater safeguards than we now possess or have ever possessed to protect American lives and property from danger . . . . There lies the road to peace." He then closed by declaring that America must stand aloof from the conflict so that it could preserve the culture of Western Europe. "Fate seems now to compel us to assume the task of helping to maintain in the western world a citadel wherein that civilization may be kept alive," he concluded.

It was an amazing speech. No less than four times the President declared that his policy was aimed at keeping the United States out of the war. Yet the whole intent of arms embargo repeal was to permit England and France to purchase arms and munitions from the United States. By basing his appeal on a return to international law and a desire to keep out of the war, Roosevelt was deliberately misleading the American people. The result was a long and essentially irrelevant debate in Congress over the administration bill to repeal the arms embargo and to place all trade with belligerents on a cash-and-carry basis. Advocates of the bill followed the President's cue, repeatedly denying that the legislation was aimed at helping Britain and France and insisting that the sole motive was to preserve American neutrality. Isolationist opponents quite logically asked, if the purpose was to insure neutrality, why did not the administration simply retain the arms embargo and add cash-and-carry for all other trade with countries at war. With heavy majorities already lined up in both houses, administration spokesmen refused to answer this query. They infuriated the isolationists by repeating with parrot-like precision the party line that the substitution of cash-and-carry for the arms embargo would keep the nation out of war.

The result was an overwhelming victory for Roosevelt. In late October the Senate, thought to be the center of isolationist strength, voted for the administration bill by more than two to one; in early November the House concurred after a closer ballot. Now Britain and France could purchase from the United States anything they needed for their war effort, including guns, tanks, and airplanes, provided only that they paid cash and carried away these supplies in their own ships.

Roosevelt expressed his thoughts most clearly in a letter to William Allen White a month later. "Things move with such terrific speed, these days," he wrote, "that it really is essential to us to think in broader terms and, in effect, to warn the American people that they, too, should think of possible ultimate results in Europe. . . . Therefore, my sage old friend, my problem is to get the American people to think of conceivable consequences without scaring the American people into thinking that they are going to be dragged into this war." In 1939, Roosevelt evidently decided that candor was still too risky, and thus he chose to pursue devious tactics in aligning the United States indirectly on the side of England and France.

The blitzkrieg that Adolf Hitler launched in Europe in the spring of 1940 aroused Americans to their danger in a way that Roosevelt never could. Norway and Denmark fell in April, and then on May 10 Germany launched an offensive thrust through the low countries into northern France that drove Holland and Belgium out of the war in less than a week and forced the British into a humiliating retreat from the continent at Dunkirk before the month was over. The sense of physical security from foreign danger that the United States had enjoyed for over a century was shattered in a matter of days. The debate over policy would continue, but from May, 1940, on, virtually all Americans recognized that the German victories in Europe imperiled the United States. . . .

In early June, the news from Europe became even worse. As he sat in his White House study one evening reading the latest dispatches, Roosevelt remarked to his wife, "All bad, all bad." He realized that a vigorous defense program was not enough—that American security depended on the successful resistance of England and France to German aggression. As Hitler's armies swept toward Paris and Mussolini moved his troops toward the exposed French frontier on the Mediterranean, Roosevelt sought to throw American influence into the balance. On June 10, he was scheduled to deliver a commencement speech at the University of Virginia in Charlottesville. Going over the State Department draft, he stiffened the language, telling a diplomat who called at the White House that morning that his speech would be a " 'tough' one—one in which the issue between the democracies and the Fascist powers would be drawn as never before." News that Italy had attacked France reached the President just before he boarded the train to Charlottesville and reinforced his determination to speak out boldly.

Addressing the graduates that evening, President Roosevelt condemned the concept of isolationism that he himself had held so strongly only a few years before. He termed the idea that the United States could exist as a lone island of peace in a world of brute force "a delusion." "Such an island," he declared, "represents to me and to the overwhelming majority of Americans today a helpless nightmare of a people without freedom—the nightmare of a people lodged in prison, handcuffed, hungry, and fed through the bars from day to day by the contemptuous, unpitying masters of other continents." In clear and unambiguous words, he declared that his sympathies lay wholly on the side of "those nations that are giving their life blood in combat" against Fascist aggression. Then, in his most significant policy statement, he announced that his administration would follow a twofold course of increasing the American defense effort and extending to England and France "the material resources of this nation."

The Charlottesville speech marks a decisive turn in Roosevelt's policy. At the time, most commentators focused on one dramatic sentence, written in at the last moment, in which he condemned the Italian attack on France by saying, "the hand that held the dagger has struck it into the back of its neighbor." But far more important was the President's pledge to defend American security by giving all-out aid to England and France. By promising to share American supplies with these two belligerents, Roosevelt was gambling that they could successfully contain Germany on the European continent and thus end the threat to American security. Given the German military advantages, the risks were enormous. If Roosevelt diverted a large portion of the nation's limited supply of weapons to England and France and then they surrendered to Hitler, the President would be responsible for leaving this country unprepared to meet a future German onslaught.

At the same time, the President's admirers have read too much into the Charlottesville speech. Basil Rauch argues that the speech ended America's status as a neutral. Robert Sherwood goes even further, claiming that at Charlottesville Roosevelt committed the United States "to the assumption of responsibility for nothing less than the leadership of the world." Samuel Rosenman is more moderate, labeling this address as "the beginning of all-out aid to the democracies," but noting that it stopped short of war. But is it even accurate to say that the speech signified all-out aid short of war? An examination of Roosevelt's subsequent steps to help France and England reveals that the President was still extremely reluctant to do anything that would directly involve the United States in the European conflict.

The French quickly discovered the limitations of the President's new policy. Heartened by Roosevelt's words at Charlottesville, Paul Reynaud, the French Premier, immediately tried to secure American military intervention to save his country. In a personal appeal to Roosevelt on June 14, Reynaud asked him to send American troops as well as American supplies in France's hour of greatest need. The next day, the President replied. The United States admired the stubborn and heroic French resistance to German aggression, Roosevelt wrote, and he promised to do all he could to increase the flow of arms and munitions to France. But there he drew the line. "I know that you will understand that these statements carry with them no implication of military commitments," the President concluded. "Only the Congress can make such commitments." On June 17, the French, now fully aware that American military involvement was out of the question, surrendered to Germany.

The British, left waging the fight alone against Germany, also discovered that Roosevelt's actions failed to live up to the promise of his words. On May 15, five days after he replaced Neville Chamberlain as Prime Minister, Winston Churchill sent an urgent message to President Roosevelt. Churchill eloquently expressed his determination to fight Hitler to the bitter end, but he warned that Britain had to have extensive aid from the United States. Above all else, England needed forty or fifty American destroyers to protect the Atlantic supply line from German submarine attacks. Churchill pointed out that England had lost thirty-two destroyers since the war began, and she needed most of her remaining sixty-eight in home waters to guard against a German invasion. "We must ask, therefore," Churchill concluded, "as a matter of life or death, to be reinforced with these destroyers."

Despite the urgency of the British request, Roosevelt procrastinated. On June 5, the President told Secretary of the Interior Harold Ickes that it would require an act of Congress to transfer the destroyers to Great Britain. Even pressure from several other cabinet members, including Henry Morgenthau and the two new Republicans Roosevelt appointed in June, Secretary of War Henry Stimson and Secretary of the Navy Frank Knox, failed to move Roosevelt. His reluctance was increased when Congress decreed on June 28 that the President could not transfer any warships to a belligerent until the Chief of Naval Operations certified that they were "not essential to the defense of the United States."

Roosevelt's inaction caused deep concern among members of the Committee to Defend America by Aiding the Allies, the pro-British pressure group headed by William Allen White. A few of the more interventionist members of White's committee developed the idea in mid-July of arranging a trade whereby the United States would give Britain the needed destroyers in return for the right to build naval and air bases on British islands in the Western Hemisphere. On August 1, a three-man delegation called at the White House to present this idea to the President, who received it noncommittally. Lord Lothian, the British ambassador, had suggested as far back as May 24 that England grant the United States the rights for bases on Newfoundland, Bermuda, and Trinidad, and in July, in talks with Secretary of the Navy Frank Knox, Lothian linked the possibility of these bases with the transfer of destroyers. Knox liked the idea, but he could not act without the President's consent. And Roosevelt remained deaf to all pleas, including one by Churchill on July 21 in which the British Prime Minister said, "Mr. President, with great respect I must tell you that in the long history of the world this is a thing to do NOW."

Churchill's appeal and the possibility of justifying the transfer of the destroyers as a trade for bases evidently persuaded Roosevelt to act. On August 2, when Frank Knox raised the issue in a cabinet meeting, Roosevelt approved the idea of giving Britain the destroyers in return for the right to build bases on British islands in the Atlantic and Caribbean, and, in addition, in return for a British pledge to send its fleet to the New World if Germany defeated England. Roosevelt still believed that the destroyer transfer would require an act of Congress, and the cabinet advised him to secure the support of Wendell Willkie, the Republican candidate for the presidency in the forthcoming campaign, to insure favorable Congressional action. Through William Allen White, who acted as an intermediary, Roosevelt received word that while Willkie refused to work actively to line up Republican support in Congress, he did agree not to make the destroyer deal a campaign issue.

Roosevelt called his advisers together on August 13 to make a final decision. With the help of Morgenthau, Knox, Stimson, and Undersecretary of State Sumner Welles, Roosevelt drafted a cable to Churchill proposing the transfer of fifty destroyers in return for eight bases and a private pledge in regard to the British fleet. The next day a joyous Churchill cabled back his acceptance of these terms, saying that "each destroyer you can spare to us is measured in rubies." But Churchill realized that the deal meant more than just help at sea. "The moral value of this fresh aid from your Government and your people at this critical time," he cabled the President, "will be very great and widely felt."

It took two more weeks to work out the details of the transaction, and during that period a group of distinguished international lawyers convinced the Attorney General that the administration could transfer the destroyers without the approval of Congress. One final hitch developed when Churchill insisted that the bases be considered free gifts from the British; Roosevelt finally agreed that two of the sites would be gifts, but that the remaining six would have to be considered a *quid pro quo* for the destroyers. On September 3, the President made the transaction public in a message to Congress in which he bore down heavily on the advantages to be gained by the United States. Barely mentioning the transfer of the destroyers, the President called the acquisition of eight naval and air bases stretching in an arc from Newfoundland to British

Guiana "an epochal and far-reaching act of preparation for continental defense in the face of grave danger." Searching desperately for a historical precedent, Roosevelt described the trade as "the most important action in the reinforcement of our national defense that has been taken since the Louisiana Purchase."

What is most striking about the destroyer-for-bases deal is the caution and reluctance with which the President acted. In June he announced a policy of all-out aid to Britain, yet he delayed for nearly four months after receiving Churchill's desperate plea for destroyers. He acted only after interventionists had created strong public support, only after the transfer could be disguised as an act in support of the American defense program, only after the leader of the opposition party had agreed not to challenge him politically on this issue, and only after his legal advisers found a way to bypass Congress. What may have appeared on the surface to be a bold and courageous act by the President was in reality a carefully calculated and virtually foolproof maneuver.

It would be easy to dismiss the destroyer-for-bases deal as just another example of Roosevelt's tendency to permit political expediency to dictate his foreign policy. Certainly Roosevelt acted in this case with a careful eye on the political realities. This was an election year, and he was not going to hand Wendell Willkie and the Republicans a ready-made issue. But I believe that Roosevelt's hesitation and caution stem as much from his own uncertainty as from political calculation. He realized that the gift of vessels of war to a belligerent was a serious departure from traditional neutrality, and one that might well give Germany the grounds on which to declare war against the United States. He wanted to give England all-out aid short of war, but he was not at all sure that this step would not be an act of war. Only when he convinced himself that the destroyer-for-bases deal could be construed as a step to defend the nation's security did he give his consent. Thus his rather extravagant public defense of his action was not just a political move to quiet isolationist critics; rather it was his own deeply felt rationalization for a policy step of great importance that undoubtedly moved the United States closer to participation in the European conflict.

Perhaps even more significant is the pattern that emerges from this review of Roosevelt's policy in the spring and summer of 1940, for it is one that recurs again and again in his conduct of foreign policy. Confronted by a major crisis, he makes a bold and forthright call at Charlottesville for a policy of all-out aid short of war. But then, having pleased the interventionists with his rhetoric, he immediately retreats, turning down the French appeal for intervention and delaying on the British plea for destroyers, thus reassuring his isolationist critics. Then, as a consensus begins to form, he finally enters into the destroyer-for-bases deal and thus redeems the pledge he had made months before at Charlottesville. Like a child playing a game of giant steps, Roosevelt moved two steps forward and one back before he took the giant step ahead. Movement in a straight and unbroken line seems to have been alien to his nature—he could not go forward until he had tested the ground, studied all the reactions, and weighed all the risks. . . .

After his triumphant election to a third term, Roosevelt relaxed on a Caribbean cruise. But after only a week, a navy seaplane arrived with an urgent dispatch from Winston Churchill. The Prime Minister gave a lengthy and bleak description of the situation in Europe and then informed the President that England was rapidly running out of money for continued purchases of American goods. "The moment approaches when we shall no longer be able to pay cash for shipping and other supplies," Churchill wrote, concluding with the confident assertion that Roosevelt would find "ways and means" to continue the flow of munitions and goods across the Atlantic.

When the President returned to Washington in mid-December, he called in the press, and in his breeziest and most informal manner began to outline the British dilemma and his solution to it. His advisers were working on several plans, he said, but the one that interested him most was simply to lend or lease to England the supplies she needed, in the belief that "the best defense of Great Britain is the best defense of the United States." Saying that he wanted to get rid of the dollar sign, Roosevelt compared his scheme to the idea of lending a garden hose to a neighbor whose house was on fire. When the fire is out, the neighbor either returns the hose or, if it is damaged, replaces it with a new one. So it would be, Roosevelt concluded, with the munitions the United States would provide Britain in the war against Nazi Germany.

In a fireside chat to the American people a few days later, Roosevelt justified this lend-lease concept on grounds of national security. Asserting that Hitler aimed not just at victory in Europe but at world domination, Roosevelt repeated his belief that the United States was in grave peril. If England fell, he declared, "all of us in the Americas would be living at the point of a gun." He admitted that the transfer of arms and munitions to Britain risked American involvement in the conflict, but he argued that "there is far less chance of the United States getting into war if we do all we can now to support the nations defending themselves against attack by the Axis than if we acquiesce in their defeat, submit tamely to an Axis victory, and wait our turn to be the object of attack in another war later on." He declared that he had no intention of sending American troops to Europe; his sole purpose was to "keep war away from our country and our people." Then, in a famous phrase, he called upon the United States to become "the great arsenal of democracy."

Congress deliberated over the lend-lease bill for the next two months, and a strong consensus soon emerged in favor of the measure. Leading Republicans, including Wendell Willkie, endorsed the bill, and most opponents objected only to the leasing provision, suggesting instead an outright loan to Britain. The House acted quickly, approving lend-lease by nearly 100 votes in February; the Senate took longer but finally gave its approval by a margin of almost two to one in early March. After the President signed the legislation into law, Congress granted an initial appropriation of seven billion dollars to guarantee the continued flow of vital war supplies to Great Britain.

Roosevelt had thus taken another giant step forward, and this time without any hesitation. His election victory made him bolder than usual, and Churchill's candid plea had convinced him that speed was essential. The granting of lend-lease aid was very nearly an act of war, for it gave Britain unrestricted access to America's enormous industrial resources. But the President felt with great sincerity that this policy would lead not to American involvement but to a British victory that alone could keep the nation out of war. . . .

In the six months preceding Pearl Harbor, Franklin Roosevelt moved slowly but steadily toward war with Germany. On July 7, he announced that he had sent 4,000 American marines to Iceland to prevent that strategic island from falling into German hands. Secretary of War Stimson, though pleased with this action, expressed disappointment over the President's insistence on describing it solely as a measure of hemispheric self-defense. Iceland was the key to defending the supply route across the Atlantic, and Stimson believed that the President should have frankly told Congress that the United States was occupying the island to insure the delivery of goods to Britain.

Once American forces landed in Iceland, Roosevelt authorized the Navy to convoy American ships supplying the marines on the island. In addition, he at first approved a naval operations plan which permitted British ships to join these convoys and thus receive an American escort halfway across the Atlantic, but in late July he reversed himself, ordering the Navy to restrict its convoys to American and Icelandic vessels. In August, at the famous Atlantic Conference with Churchill, Roosevelt once again committed himself to the principle of convoying British ships halfway across the Atlantic, but he failed to give the necessary order to the Navy after his return to Washington.

Roosevelt's hesitancy and indecision finally ended in early September when a German submarine fired a torpedo at the American destroyer *Greer*. Though subsequent reports revealed that the *Greer* had been following the U-boat for more than three hours and had been broadcasting its position to nearby British naval units, Roosevelt interpreted this incident as a clear-cut case of German aggression. In a press release on September 5, he called the attack on the *Greer* deliberate, and on the same day he told Samuel Rosenman to begin drafting a statement that would express his determination "to use any means necessary to get the goods to England." Rosenman and Harry Hopkins prepared a strongly worded speech, and after a few revisions the President delivered it over a worldwide radio network on the evening of September 11.

In biting phrases, Roosevelt lashed out against Hitler and Nazi Germany. He described the attack on the *Greer* as part of a concerted German effort to "acquire absolute control and domination of the seas for themselves." Such control, he warned, would lead inevitably to a Nazi effort to dominate the Western Hemisphere and "create a permanent world system based on force, terror, and murder." The attack on the *Greer* was an act of piracy, Roosevelt declared; German submarines had become the "rattlesnakes of the Atlantic." Then, implying but never openly saying that American ships would shoot German submarines on sight, Roosevelt declared that henceforth the United States Navy would escort "all merchant ships—not only American ships but ships of any flag—engaged in commerce in our defensive waters."

Contemporary observers and many historians labeled this the "shoot-on-sight" speech, seeing its significance primarily in the orders to American naval officers to fire at German submarines in the western Atlantic. "The undeclared war" speech would be a better label, for its real importance was that Roosevelt had finally made a firm decision on the convoy issue on which he had been hedging ever since the passage of lend-lease by Congress. Branding the Germans as "pirates" and their U-boats as "rattlesnakes" distracted the American people from the fact that the President was now putting into practice the policy of convoying British ships halfway across the ocean, and thereby assuming a significant share of the responsibility for the Battle of the Atlantic. The immediate effect was to permit the British to transfer forty destroyers from the western Atlantic to the submarine-infested waters surrounding the British Isles. In the long run, the President's decision meant war with Germany, since from this time forward there would inevitably be more and more U-boat attacks on American destroyers, increasingly heavy loss of life, and a direct challenge to the nation's honor and prestige. Only Hitler's reluctance to engage in war with the United States while he was still absorbed in the assault on Russia prevented an immediate outbreak of hostilities.

With the convoy issue now resolved, Roosevelt moved to revise the Neutrality Act. In mid-October he asked the House to permit the arming of American merchant ships with deck guns, and then later in the month he urged the Senate to remove the "carry" provision of the law so that American merchantmen could take supplies all the way across the Atlantic to British ports. When a German submarine torpedoed the destroyer *Kearney* near Iceland, Roosevelt seized on the incident to speed up action in Congress.

"America has been attacked," the President declared in a speech on October 27. "The U.S.S. *Kearney* is not just a Navy ship. She belongs to every man, woman, and child in this Nation." Describing Nazi efforts at infiltration in South America, the President bluntly charged that Germany was bent on the conquest of "the United States itself." Then, coming very close to a call for war, he asserted, "The forward march of Hitlerism can be stopped—and it will be stopped. Very simply and very bluntly—we are pledged to pull our own oar in the destruction of Hitlerism." Although he called only for the revision of the Neutrality Act, the tone of the entire address was one of unrelieved belligerency, culminating in the following peroration: "Today in the face of this newest and greatest challenge, we Americans have cleared our decks and taken our battle stations. We stand ready in the defense of our Nation and the faith of our fathers to do what God has given us the power to see as our full duty."

Two weeks later, by quite slim majorities, Congress removed nearly all restrictions on American commerce from the Neutrality Act. For the first time since the war began in 1939, American merchant vessels could carry supplies all the way across the Atlantic to British ports. The significance of this action was obscured by the Japanese attack on Pearl Harbor which triggered American entry into the war in December and gave rise to the subsequent charge that Roosevelt led the nation into the conflict via the back door. Revision of the Neutrality Act was bound to lead to war with Germany within a matter of months. Hitler could be forbearing when it was only a question of American escort vessels operating in the western Atlantic. He could not have permitted American ships to carry a major portion of lend-lease supplies to Britain without giving up the Battle of the Atlantic. With the German offensive halting before Leningrad and Moscow in December, Hitler would have been compelled to order his submarine commanders to torpedo American ships as the only effective way to hold Britain in check. And once Germany began sinking American ships regularly, Roosevelt would have had to ask Congress for a declaration of war.

The crucial question, of course, is why Roosevelt chose such an oblique policy which left the decision for peace or war in the hands of Hitler. His apologists, notably Robert Sherwood and Basil Rauch, insist that he had no choice. The isolationists were so powerful that the President could not lay the issue squarely before Congress and ask for a declaration of war. If he had, writes Basil Rauch, he would have "invited a prolonged, bitter, and divisive debate" and thereby have risked a defeat which would have discredited the administration and turned the nation back to isolationism. Sherwood sadly agrees, saying, "He had no more tricks left. The hat from which he had pulled so many rabbits was empty. The President of the United States was now the creature of circumstance which must be shaped not by his own will or his own ingenuity but by the unpredictable determination of his enemies."

In part this was true, but these sympathetic historians fail to point out that Roosevelt was the prisoner of his own policies. He had told the nation time and time again that it was not necessary for the United States to enter the war. He had propounded the doctrine that America could achieve Hitler's downfall simply by giving all-out aid to England. He had repeatedly denied that his measures would lead the nation to war. In essence, he had foreclosed to himself the possibility of going directly to the people and bluntly stating that the United States must enter the war as the only way to guarantee the nation's security. All he could do was edge the country closer and closer, leaving the ultimate decision to Germany and Japan.

We will never know at what point Roosevelt decided in his own mind that it was essential that the United States enter the war. His own personal hatred of war was deep and genuine, and it was this conviction that set him apart from men like Stimson and Morgenthau, who decided that American participation was necessary as early as the spring of 1941. William Langer and Everett Gleason believe that Roosevelt realized by the fall of 1941 that there was no other way to defeat Hitler, but they conclude that, even so, he thought the American military contribution could be limited to naval and air support and not include the dispatch of an American army to the European battlefields.

It is quite possible that Roosevelt never fully committed himself to American involvement prior to Pearl Harbor. His hesitancy was not just a catering to isolationist strength but a reflection of his own inner uncertainty. Recognizing that Hitler threatened the security of the United States, he took a series of steps which brought the nation to the brink of war, but his own revulsion at the thought of plunging his country into the most devastating conflict in history held him back until the Japanese attack left him no choice.

The Cautious Politician as
Foreign Policy Maker

JAMES MACGREGOR BURNS

The record is clear. As a foreign policy maker, Roosevelt during his first term was more pussyfooting politician than political leader. He seemed to float almost helplessly on the flood tide of isolationism, rather than to seek to change both the popular attitudes and the apathy that buttressed the isolationists' strength.

He hoped that people would be educated by events; the error of this policy was that the dire events in Europe and Asia confirmed the American suspicion and fear of foreign involvement rather than prodding them into awareness of the need for collective action by the democracies. In short, a decisive act of interpretation was required, but Roosevelt did not interpret. At a minimum he might have avoided the isolationist line about keeping clear of joint action with other nations. Yet at a crucial moment—when he approved the Neutrality Act shortly before Italy's attack on Ethiopia—he talked about co-operating with other nations "without entanglement."

The awful implications of this policy of drift would become clear later on when Roosevelt sought to regain control of foreign policy making at home as the forces of aggression mounted abroad. But the immediate question is: Why did Roosevelt allow himself to be virtually immobilized by isolationist feeling? Why did he not, through words or action, seek to change popular attitudes and thus rechannel the pressures working on him?

The enigma deepens when Roosevelt's private views are considered. In his private role he was an internationalist. He believed, that is, in the proposition that America's security lay essentially in removing the economic and social causes of war and, if war threatened, in uniting the democracies, America included, against aggressive nations. But in his public role he talked about keeping America disentangled from the political affairs of other nations; he often talked, in short, like an isolationist.

The mystery deepens still further when one considers that the President had emphatic, though perhaps ill-defined, ideas about the need for leadership in a democracy. He must have recognized the potential in leadership when, in addressing the Woodrow Wilson Foundation at the end of 1933, he asserted roundly that the "blame for the danger to world peace lies not in the world population but in the political leaders of the population." At the same time he was concerned about the perennially weak leadership that the politicians gave France. He was perhaps aware, too, that simply following a line of policy lying at the mean between two extremes would not necessarily lead to the wisest course. In the case of Ethiopia, for instance, the British and French through their indecisive maneuverings succeeded neither in keeping Mussolini out of Germany's orbit nor in vindicating the ideals of collective security. Washington's foreign policies were equally muddled.

Excerpted from *Roosevelt: The Lion and the Fox* © 1956 by James MacGregor Burns. Reprinted by permission of Harcourt Brace Jovanovich, Inc.

The reasons for the sharp divergence between Roosevelt's private and public roles in foreign policy making were several. In the first place, the President's party was cleft through the middle on international issues. The internationalist wing centered in the southern and border states was balanced by isolationists rooted in the West and Midwest. To win the nomination Roosevelt had given hostages to both groups. Part of the price of success in 1932 had been categorical opposition to United States co-operation with the collective security efforts of the League, and a cautious policy of neutrality based on nonentanglement. In the second place, Roosevelt in his campaign had so ignored foreign policy, or fuzzed the issue over when he did touch on it, that he had failed to establish popular attitudes on foreign policy that he could later evoke in support of internationalism. Moreover, during his first term the President gave first priority to domestic policies; a strong line on foreign affairs might have alienated the large number of isolationist congressmen who were supporting the New Deal. Indeed, many isolationists seemed to believe that any marked interest in foreign affairs by the President was virtually a betrayal of progressivism.

In addition, the President had surrounded himself with men from both sides. Men like Hull and Howe and Morgenthau were generally on the international end of the spectrum, but others like Moley and Hopkins and Hugh Johnson and Ickes were at the opposite end. Ickes had been so pleased by the Senate action on the World Court that he had telephoned and congratulated Hiram Johnson, whom he found "as happy as a boy." The development of the New Deal's policies of economic nationalism, tinged with the rhetoric of international good will and economic co-operation, resulted from and reinforced this division.

But the main reason for Roosevelt's caution involved the future rather than the past. The election of 1936 was approaching, and at this point he was not willing to take needless risks. It was significant that after he and Mackenzie King had signed a trade agreement in Washington—and a rather moderate one at that—Roosevelt wrote to King in April 1936 that "in a sense, we both took our political lives in our hands. . . ." The immediate goal of re-election was the supreme goal; the tasks of leadership, he hoped, could be picked up later. . . .

What was the matter? In the gravest international situation the nation had ever faced, where was the leadership of the man whose very name since 1933 had become the symbol of candor and courage?

When a leader fails to live up to the symbolic role he has come to occupy, his admirers cling to the image they love by imputing mistakes to the leader's advisers. Stories went the rounds in 1939 that Roosevelt's trouble really lay in Hull's timidity and in Kennedy's belief in appeasement. The stories were not true. Hull, to be sure, did seem to move slowly, but he was working against the embargo law before Roosevelt took a definite stand, and he was calling existing legislation "a wretched little bob-tailed, sawed-off" substitute for the established rules on international law while the President was using far softer words. As for Kennedy, Roosevelt knew that he had sympathized with the appeasement policies of Chamberlain and the so-called "Cliveden set" and to an extent valued him for this. But he would not let his ambassador get out of hand. When Kennedy submitted a draft of a talk he was to give in London, the President and Hull went over it line by line to adjust it to administration policy.

The President's tactics were his own. Another explanation for his caution lay in the nature of the opposition in Congress and among the people. Certainly the opposition to an internationalist or collective security program was not to be dismissed lightly. In a 1937 poll nineteen out of twenty people answered a flat "No" to the query whether the United States should enter another world war. Most of the people trusted Congress rather than the President to keep America out of war. They were powerfully drawn by the symbols of Peace and Neutrality—and they tended to equate the two. To be sure, these attitudes somewhat lacked stability and durability. But they had a terrible intensity. The late 1930's was the period when the famous aviatrix Laura Ingalls showered the White House with "peace" leaflets from her plane, when Father Coughlin and John L. Lewis were whipping up isolationist feeling, when to some fascism constituted the "wave of the future." Two decades of bitterness over World War I and its aftermath had left a hard, smarting scar tissue.

Any attempt by Roosevelt to override this feeling clearly would have been disastrous. His real mission as a political leader was to modify and guide this opinion in a direction closer to American interests as he saw them. To raise this question is again to confront the paradox of Roosevelt's leadership.

For under the impact of shattering events abroad, people's attitudes were slowly shifting. Most Americans, of course, clung to their "Keep-Out-of-War" position. But between Munich and the outbreak of war a great majority of the people swung over to the position of all help to Britain and France short of war. By September 1939 about 37 per cent of the people favored positive help to Britain, France, and Poland; less than half of these wanted to dispatch military help then or at any later time, while most favored sending food and materials. This 37 per cent interventionist element confronted a hard-core isolationist bloc that opposed any aid at all to either side. In the middle was a group of about 30 per cent that would refuse to sell to either side except on a cash-and-carry basis.

It was this vast middle group that offered the President his supreme opportunity. For this group was clinging to the symbol of nonentanglement while grasping the need of American help to nations under attack. This group, combined with the interventionists, would have given heavy backing to Roosevelt's all aid-short-of-war policies. Was it possible that these millions of middle-of-the-roaders thought that cash and carry in 1939 meant material help to *neither* side? No; a later poll showed that 90 per cent favored cash and carry even if in practice only Britain and France got the supplies. Without question these middle attitudes were shot through with confusions and uncertainties. But this made a real leader's opportunity all the greater, for opinions that are superficial and volatile are the most subject to influence. A situation that was an opportunity for Napoleon, A. N. Whitehead has observed, would appear as an unmanageable disorder to most of us.

Roosevelt felt that events and facts themselves would educate the public. So they did—but not quickly enough. Each time in the race between aggression and American opinion victory went to the former. The early months of 1939 were the supreme test. Roosevelt's great hope was that he could demonstrate to Hitler that America would give material aid to nations the Nazis planned to attack. The President's tactic was based on a sound proposition—the best way to keep America out of war would be to keep war out of the world. But he did not lead opinion toward a position of all aid short of war. He tagged along with opinion. Sometimes, indeed—most notably when he was frightened by the reaction to the "quarantine" speech and later by the furore over America's frontier being "on the Rhine"—he lagged behind the drift of opinion favoring more commitment by the United States to joint efforts against aggression.

The President's immediate problem was not, of course, isolationist feeling in general but the mighty isolationist phalanxes in Congress. Doubtless he feared that defeat of a crucial bill on the Hill might mean a permanent setback for his hopes to aid the democracies and might so dishearten friends of America abroad as to encourage more appeasement. If such was Roosevelt's tactic with Congress, the fate of embargo repeal in the spring of 1939 suggests that he failed. Perhaps if he had taken a position against the embargo much sooner and much more openly and consistently, he could have won repeal in the spring of 1939. But the fact is that only when he knew he had the votes on the Hill did he utter the clarion call that resulted in repeal in October of that year. Once again events, not the President, had done the job of educating —and once again the time was tragically late.

Roosevelt's Campaign Against His Isolationist Critics

RICHARD W. STEELE

From the spring of 1940 until the Japanese attack on Pearl Harbor and the German declaration of war in early December 1941, President Franklin D. Roosevelt confronted a situation as frightening for the nation as any since the Civil War. By the end of 1940, Adolf Hitler had convincingly demonstrated to the world his ambitions and the awesome power of his military force. The British, ineffectual in their efforts to halt Hitler's advance on the Continent, stood alone awaiting an assault they appeared ill-prepared to repel. But the German air attack failed; the invasion did not come. Hitler's opponents, actual and potential, thus were given an opportunity to look to their defenses and consider the next moves, both theirs and his.

From "Franklin D. Roosevelt and His Foreign Policy Critics." Reprinted with permission from the *Political Science Quarterly*, 94 (Spring 1979), 15–23, 24–28, 31–32.

In the United States, the administration's efforts to make the most of the opportunity were limited by widespread cynicism about the origins of the European war and well-organized resistance to direct American involvement. The situation was troubling and potentially dangerous, and the rapid conversion of public attitudes became an important part of Roosevelt's foreign policy. Isolationism, with its strong emotional appeal and the sanction of American tradition, might be challenged by words, but only Hitler's final, and perhaps fatal, offensive could conclusively disprove its value. Rather than wait for the "Great Debate" to bring the American people to its senses, FDR resolved to supplement the persuasive effects of world events and the arguments of the interventionist forces by seeking to silence or discredit the critics of his administration's foreign policy.

The chief objects of Roosevelt's concern were not spies, saboteurs, enemy propagandists, or even those whose activities could be construed as violating the 1940 peacetime sedition law. The very few who fit these categories had almost no impact on American foreign policy and were effectively dealt with by federal authorities under existing law. Roosevelt's problem was with those whose obstructive advocacy skirted the borders of constitutionally protected free speech. Dealing with these people was a frustrating task that sent the president on a wide-ranging search for effective means. Although his efforts were neither systematic nor entirely fruitful, the persistence and energy he devoted to the attempt provide insights into Roosevelt's attitudes toward free expression and the limits of presidential authority.

The source of much of FDR's concern was the seemingly special nature of the Nazi threat. In the common-sense view of the period, Nazi Germany was not an ordinary state but the instrument of a madman. From this perspective, Nazi actions were not simply a series of aggressions, but a worldwide conspiracy directed ultimately against free people everywhere. This idea was sustained in part by Nazi propaganda, the rantings of Hitler, and by the existence of Nazi groups outside Germany that subscribed to Hitler's racial concepts and supported the ambitions of the "new" Germany. The capacity of the German army to exceed the expectations of military experts also argued the unprecedented and unconventional nature of the Nazi threat. The battles that unfolded in 1940 seemed only the opening phase of the war of the future—a war that appeared revolutionary in strategy and equipment. Since the Nazis, and the war they waged, were unique, the administration plausibly concluded that the nation could no longer rest secure behind its traditional defenses.

The changes in the nature of war were so apparent that they raised for FDR the question of how loyal Americans could continue to talk as if these changes had not occurred. If isolationism was so obviously obsolete, how could one account for the stubborn dissidence of a willful minority? Events in Europe suggested an explanation. Press reports created the widely held belief that Nazi agents and sympathizers, a fifth column, prepared the way for German armies, sealing the fate of Hitler's victims even before the first plane or tank crossed their frontiers. This "boring from within," undermining the will and capacity of the democracies to resist, was thought to hold the key to Germany's success. The strength and pervasiveness of this myth understandably suggested to Roosevelt that those who opposed his foreign policies constituted an American equivalent of the fifth column. The idea thrived on information, some of it originating with British intelligence, "documenting" the link between Berlin and the administration's opponents.

While the circumstances of the European war made an American fifth column plausible, they did not dictate that Roosevelt act upon the idea. What transformed an appealing rationale into a course of conduct was the president's disposition to see dissidence as disloyalty and the proper subject of government action. This attitude was in evidence long before, and in circumstances far removed from, the threat to national security manifest in 1940. As early as 1934 President Roosevelt had directed the Federal Bureau of Investigation to investigate the "Nazi movement in the United States." The object of this investigation was an obnoxious conglomeration of groups dedicated to building and preserving cultural ties with Germany. Despite their anti-Semitism and the efforts of the German government to use the "movement," they posed little threat to American security. Their sometimes frightening, sometimes comic, antics helped, in fact, to intensify American awareness of the Nazi menace.

The systematic investigation of dissidents begun in 1934 soon expanded, pursuant to the president's instructions, to include *all* suspected subversives. It is clear that from the outset, at least some of the individual investigations ordered by the president were politically inspired and only remotely related to the commission of a crime or "subversion." In 1940, FBI Director J. Edgar Hoover suggested privately that the administration, as well as the bureau, would be seriously embarrassed if the nature and scope of FBI operations came to light. Thus, for example, in 1935 Roosevelt referred a pamphlet accusing the president of being a "Socialist Pure and Simple" to the attorney general with the injunction to "find out who is paying for this"; also, in late 1940, FDR directed Hoover to investigate George Seldes, the publisher of the left-wing *In Fact* which had been critical of the president.

John L. Lewis, head of the United Mine Workers, was among those subjected to FBI inquiry. Although Roosevelt denied it at a White House confrontation in 1940, since 1938 the FBI, with FDR's knowledge, and probably on his initiative, had been tapping the phones at Mine Workers' headquarters. The reason is not entirely clear. It is true that Lewis was engaged in negotiations involving Mexican officials and the sale of oil to Germany, and these activities, although not illegal, invited FDR's suspicion. On the other hand, the friction between Lewis and the White House since 1936 suggests a political motive. Whatever the rationale, only a strained concept of national security would appear to justify the action.

In dealing with his isolationist critics, Roosevelt was guided by the same intolerant, conspiratorial outlook that had characterized his attitude toward earlier critics. As a result, the president too readily concluded that his long-standing political opponents had now aligned themselves with the nation's enemies, either to hurt him or to promote their own interests. "A small group of selfish men," he publicly described the isolationist leaders, "who would clip the wings of the American eagle to feather their own nests. . . . Partisan groups . . . who wrap themselves in a false mantle of Americanism to promote their own economic, financial, or political advantage." On the eve of the 1940 election, Roosevelt warned that "something evil is happening in this country," citing what he called the "unholy alliance" between Republican leaders and the forces of both communism and nazism. Such statements may have overstated the president's feelings, but not by much. Following the election, he told an associate that he thought "too many" in the Republican hierarchy, moved by their materialistic outlook, had come to think "in terms of appeasement of Hitler." Actually, although the motives of his critics varied, isolationism, as one scholar has noted, was not only "devoid of political, economic, or social content," but also "neither liberal nor conservative, capitalist nor socialist, Fascist nor Communist, Democratic nor Republican." Isolationists may have been mistaken, but they were not preeminently greedy, necessarily cynical or stupid, nor, as Roosevelt would also suggest, "soft" on nazism.

Although Roosevelt was inclined to see his isolationist critics as opportunists, when this did not suffice to explain their actions he questioned their loyalty. This predilection is apparent in his dealings with Charles A. Lindbergh. When Lindbergh first emerged as a leading advocate of isolationism, Roosevelt assumed that the one-time national hero was merely power hungry. But when Lindbergh refused FDR's offer of a cabinet post and continued his attacks, Roosevelt confided to an associate that he was "absolutely" convinced that his adversary was a "Nazi." The president's inclination to see his opponents as enemies is reflected in that label; Lucky Lindy was now indeed a racist, an admirer of the "new" Germany, and disenchanted with aspects of American society, but his obnoxious ideas made him neither disloyal nor a Nazi. By thinking of his opponents in this manner, Roosevelt denied the legitimacy of their claims and hence their right to be heard.

On the outbreak of hostilities in September 1939, the White House learned that the German government had ordered its agents in the United States to work for the retention of the Neutrality Law. Press Secretary Stephen Early quickly informed the press of Berlin's instructions to "its friends in the United States," thus implying from the outset of the struggle over foreign policy that opponents of the administration were ultimately guided from abroad. Although Early publicly eschewed administration propaganda on the neutrality issue, he and Assistant Secretary of State Adolf Berle immediately arranged to have the alleged "Berlin connection" made widely known through various unofficial spokesmen.

In the months that followed, FDR led an education campaign that portrayed his domestic critics as part of the Nazi conspiracy. His efforts gained credibility from the fifth column myth that, due in part to the propaganda efforts of the administration and its interventionist supporters, had established a firm grip on the American imagination. Probably the single most influential administration endeavor along this line was the widely circulated exposé written by William J. Donovan and Edgar Mowrer. The four-part series of articles, sponsored and endorsed by Secretary of the Navy Frank Knox, purportedly derived from Donovan's observations on a trip through Europe. In fact it was based on material supplied by British intelligence. The story, which appeared in virtually every newspaper in the nation in August 1940, authoritatively informed the American public that Hitler's success could be explained by the democracies' susceptibility to internal subversion. More frightening was Donovan's assertion that the same conspiracy that had undermined the free nations of Europe was now at work in the United States, breaking down national morale and enlisting traitors. In fact, according to Donovan, "as matters now stand the United States possesses the finest Nazi-schooled fifth column in the world." Although no less an authority than J. Edgar Hoover privately minimized the alleged fifth column, the Donovan reports were subsequently broadcasted on a nationwide hookup, issued in pamphlet form with a preface by Knox, and elaborated in a State Department publication. Hundreds of books, articles, and movies on the subject followed, and thousands of private citizens alerted the FBI to various suspected fifth column activities.

The president himself contributed to public anxiety by repeatedly warning Americans during 1940–41 that it could happen, indeed was happening, here. The struggle in Europe, he declared, was not an "ordinary war," but a "revolution" that had unleashed forces in the United States that were dividing and weakening the nation. "Let us no longer blind ourselves," he told the American people, "evil forces . . . are already within our own gates." And on another occasion he warned that "great numbers" of "secret agents and their dupes" were already in the United States and Latin America, doing their subversive work. In making these statements FDR repeatedly linked his critics to foreign-inspired subversion, labeling those who stubbornly fought American involvement in the war as "apologists for foreign aggression," "appeaser fifth columnists," and "conscious disorganizers or unwitting dupes."

Even as he sought to convince the public that isolationism was subversion, Roosevelt proceeded against dissidents and critics as if his allegations were fact. In the aftermath of the 1940 election, Roosevelt warned his critics: "No one can tell the exact character of the emergency situations that we may be called upon to meet, [and] the Nation's hands must not be tied when the Nation's life is in danger. . . . The best way of dealing with the few slackers or troublemakers in our midst is first, to shame them by patriotic example, and if that fails, to use the sovereignty of Government to save Government."

Roosevelt's interpretation of sovereignty was apparently broad enough to sanction official interest in anyone who openly dissented from administration policy. Thus, the names of those who wrote to the White House in the spring of 1940 protesting American foreign policy were forwarded to the Justice Department. Although the government defended this action as merely routine, the covering note from Stephen Early to Hoover accompanying a batch of these referrals suggests otherwise: "As the telegrams all were more or less in opposition to national defense, the President thought you might like to look them over, noting the names and addresses of the senders." In spite of public protest, the practice continued.

Immediately following his reelection in 1940, Roosevelt sought to expand his capacity to deal with his critics. He assigned responsibility for devising a program to a group of cabinet officers led by Harold Ickes, the administration's chief anti-Nazi and, second only to Roosevelt himself, its most effective spokesman. Ickes was a civil libertarian of sorts, but his commitment to personal freedom extended most readily to those of whom he approved— dissidents on the left, persecuted racial minorities, labor organizers, and the like. His contempt for isolationist dissenters left him unmoved by any claim to free expression they might have.

FDR commissioned the Ickes group to act as a kind of command staff to mobilize the full resources of the government for the struggle against isolationism. The group, which included the secretaries of war and navy and the attorney general, agreed that the task would require the complete cooperation of existing government intelligence agencies to monitor "subversive" propaganda and to expose its financial backers. But when Solicitor General Francis Biddle was consulted, he argued that "vigorously expressed" isolationism, not a foreign conspiracy, was at the heart of the administration's difficulties, and that since "such opposition was not illegal," he could not sanction any government action that "would tend to smother and suppress this opposition." Attorney General Robert Jackson, worried by criticism raised by the White House referral of telegrams to the Justice Department, agreed, and the endeavor collapsed. Much to Ickes's disappointment, the president refused to pursue the plan. His desire to combat dissidence was real, but not without bounds. Isolationist critics were only one of many political concerns confronting FDR, and he did not allow them (as well he might have) to become an all-consuming preoccupation. If he could hurt them readily, he welcomed the opportunity. He was not, however, disposed to act recklessly, without regard to the difficulties or political risks entailed.

Biddle's concern for the constitutional rights of the government's "enemies" troubled the president, and when Biddle was mentioned as a possible successor to Jackson as attorney general, Roosevelt confided to an associate that he thought the aristocratic Philadelphia lawyer "too strict at a time like this when . . . we ought to have an attorney general who can close his eyes on occasion." Further inquiries, however, convinced him that Biddle would be "tough enough," and neither "too liberal" nor "too conscientious." Roosevelt correctly gauged his ability to handle Biddle. In a number of instances, including the forced relocation of West Coast Japanese-Americans in 1942, Biddle, although expressing doubts about the justice of the proposed actions, loyally did his duty. Nevertheless, Biddle served as the administration's conscience, reminding Roosevelt of the purist view of civil liberties.

The collapse of the Ickes committee's efforts left Roosevelt still without an effective way of exposing the roots of isolationism. British intelligence, which included among its varied activities in the United States manipulating public opinion and discrediting opponents of intervention, was a continuous source of inspiration and help. But in February 1941, feeling the need for additional investigative resources, Roosevelt created a secret White House intelligence unit responsible only to himself. Its varied and undefined functions were directed by John Franklin Carter, whose qualifications for secret agency were a modestly successful career as a journalist and radio commentator; a short tour in the diplomatic service; and, above all, a strong interest in foreign intrigue—a passion reflected in the several novels he wrote on that theme. "Special emergency" State Department monies financed the operation, which by the end of 1941 employed a staff of eleven.

Some of Carter's assignments served the president's interest in his critics' motives and associations; among his earliest projects was Burton K. Wheeler, the leader of Senate isolationists. Carter's efforts to get something on the Montana Democrat produced only some allegations of "crookedness" in Wheeler's office, and the preposterous suggestion that Wheeler's isolationism was tied to the Great Northern Railway's commercial stake in trade with Japan. Roosevelt, forever hopeful, forwarded these charges to Ickes, apparently hoping he would succeed in encouraging a reluctant J. Edgar Hoover to investigate further.

Roosevelt's search for the men behind the most formidable isolationist group, the America First Committee, followed a somewhat different course. It began in February 1941 when Roosevelt sent the FBI an America First flyer and requested that the bureau find out "who is paying for this." Hoover promptly responded with a short history of the organization, together with biographical data on its founders and leaders—information readily available from public sources. Follow-up reports contained basically the same unsensational information: the organization was well run and well financed; its activities effective and legal; and its backers (otherwise) upstanding citizens, many of them wealthy, and some known for their support of right-wing causes.

The FBI assessment of America First was confirmed by Carter who in July 1941 forwarded a report to the president that concluded there was no evidence of Nazi influence in the organization. Indeed, according to the report, America First National Committee Chairman Robert Wood "had no use for the Nazis or their doctrines, and would not tolerate any dealings with them if he knew of such dealings." The president, however, did not abandon his search for the Nazi-isolationist link. In September he asked Federal Communications Commission Chairman James L. Fly to confirm his suspicion that former President Herbert Hoover was supplying Axis propagandists with material. Fly could not, but promised to keep on trying. Meanwhile, federal agents monitored America First operations and meetings, and FDR pressed for congressional and grand jury investigations. The voluntary dissolution of the organization following the Japanese attack at Pearl Harbor destroyed the rationale for such actions. . . .

Roosevelt's campaign against isolationism led him to challenge the ideal of an informed public and a free press. FDR's "management" of the news during 1940–41 has long proven embarrassing to even his staunchest defenders. However, given the Nazi menace and the stubborn obtuseness of the American public, a little lying has usually been judged a tolerable thing. As one recent commentator has it, "the cause justified the dubious means employed." Any favorable judgment on this score must rest ultimately on the assumption that the nation's security, not the administration's sensibility, was the intended beneficiary of the information policy adopted. An examination of Roosevelt's attitudes and actions toward his critics in the press suggests that these were needlessly restrictive and stemmed as much from personal preference and political expedience as from a realistic appraisal of national interests.

Although Roosevelt prided himself on his thick skin, he was in fact annoyed and sensitized by the hostile, and sometimes unfair, press coverage he received during his first two terms. He attributed this, correctly in many instances, to the selfish biases of wealthy publishers. Journalists who consistently criticized his administration, he believed, were the tools of his ideological enemies. For example, in 1937 FDR described his critics as a "small minority" that sought "by every means within its power to thwart the will of the majority." More important, he suggested that the news media might somehow be held accountable for their "truth, justice, and fair play." This theme was to resurface after the outbreak of war in Europe.

A major factor determining the public's attitude toward isolationism was its perception of events. Insofar as events suggested the inevitability of conflict and the capacity of the United States to deal with it successfully, Americans were apt to rally behind the president. But events did not always speak for themselves. The meaning they conveyed reflected largely the manner in which they were presented. Thus, what was reported and how it was interpreted were critical elements in determining whether events argued for or against the administration's policy. In this situation Roosevelt concluded that dispensing information about international affairs and national policy was too important to be left entirely to the judgment of journalists. Nevertheless, outright censorship was a politically volatile issue, especially in the absence of a declared state of war; thus the president had to proceed carefully in his dealings with the press. In early 1941 Roosevelt rejected an overly ambitious Army-Navy censorship plan; and when an Office of Censorship was created following American involvement in the war, its controls were modest and voluntary. Rather than invoke a potentially disruptive rigid censorship, he chose to rely on the government's ability to limit public access to information bearing on military and diplomatic events, and on the newsmen's acceptance of these controls. At a press conference the morning after the German attack on Poland he told reporters that they had an obligation to confine their reporting to "straight facts," that is, to information supplied or verified by the appropriate government official. During the next several months the military and State Department, and ultimately other defense agencies, adopted policies designed to curtail severely the kinds of war information made public. The president made it clear that he expected press cooperation with this restrictive policy and publicly questioned the ethics and patriotism of newspapermen whose stories contained information the government wanted withheld.

In FDR's view, no story that in any way hurt the administration was justified; neither the accuracy of the account nor its remoteness from military affairs vitiated the rule. Thus, in April 1941 FDR condemned a story about the destroyer *Niblack*'s attack on a German submarine and another on confusion and conflict within the cabinet over the creation of the Office of Civilian Defense. Without denying the reliability of either account, Roosevelt told an associate that "no decent columnist ought to print stories which would hurt the prosecution of our defense program." Since the president sought to control the release of news, and on several occasions distorted the news he released, newsmen who complied with his appeals to patriotism and responsibility, as most did, became little more than semiofficial propagandists. Those who refused to "cooperate" found their motives impugned.

White House press conferences reflected these views. While Roosevelt urged citizens to withhold judgment on newspaper accounts until they had determined whether they were truthful, that is, officially sanctioned, he proceeded to undermine the value of the major source of authoritative information on his administration's actions and intent. During 1940, presidential press conferences, once the pride of the administration and the joy of reporters, became a pale reflection of Roosevelt's earlier performances; FDR deliberately avoided serious comment on current issues and ridiculed those reporters with the temerity to challenge his policy.

Roosevelt found in radio an effective and more malleable alternative to the press. As he told one publisher in June 1940, his problems in getting "factual" news to the American people had obliged him "to resort to other media in order to give the people of the country the facts they are entitled to." Broadcasters, already acutely aware of the government's regulatory authority, readily accepted the role the government had cast for them. Asked immediately after the outbreak of hostilities in September 1939 to comment on speculation that the president was contemplating radio censorship, Press Secretary Stephen Early in effect confirmed the suspicion. The administration was listening carefully, he said, to see how the youthful industry would respond to its first major test of maturity. "If we find that a child is well mannered it will be left to move along on its own. If it proves to be a bad child, there would be a disposition to teach it some manners, correct it, and make it behave itself." In ensuing months the White House had reason to be well satisfied with radio's performance, which the president's chief adviser on media relations attributed, at least in part, to the constant threat of adverse administration action.

The threatening tone of much of the president's discourse on press relations was inconsistent with the reality of the "problem." Only a relatively small number of journalists resisted the accelerating drift toward intervention. Radio broadcasters, acting out of sympathy or fear, bent over backward to present the administration's case; the majority of newspapers supported the administration's foreign policy and cooperated with its efforts to promote public awareness of the Axis threat. Far from wishing to challenge the administration's view of international developments, influential papers solicited the White House for ways in which they might be more helpful. Nevertheless, the dissenting minority seemed to dominate Roosevelt's thinking. How much this criticism disrupted or interfered with national purposes, and how much it simply irritated FDR is not certain. Both elements were probably present, but the president apparently made no attempt to distinguish between them. . . .

Isolationism confronted the president with serious problems of public leadership, but his response in many instances bore no close relationship to the "threat." FDR's "enemies" did not constitute a fifth column—a conclusion verified by the FBI, the Justice Department, and even his own personal investigator. FDR's decision to disregard this information and to act instead on the necessarily suspect suggestions of British intelligence suggests that his judgment was strongly conditioned by the hopes of using the loyalty issue to smear his critics and to set the stage for public acceptance of the globalism toward which his policies were moving.

It is true (although hardly to his credit) that Roosevelt's campaign against dissent victimized relatively few people. Moreover, had a fifth column actually threatened national security his actions might be viewed as reasonable, indeed restrained. What the president battled, however, was not disloyalty but the doubts of a minority of Americans concerning the origins and purposes of the war. Instead of tackling these misgivings head on, admittedly a difficult task of education, FDR chose to discredit and dismiss them. In dealing with opposition by managing the news and by the systematic use of unfounded accusations and innuendo, Roosevelt limited, rather than expanded, the public's understanding of national issues. More importantly, he tended to cultivate the American disposition to view dissent on foreign policy matters as subversion.

FURTHER READING

Frederick Adams, *Economic Diplomacy: The Export-Import Bank and American Foreign Policy, 1934–1939* (1976)

Selig Adler, *The Isolationist Impulse* (1957)

——, *The Uncertain Giant* (1965)

Mark Chadwin, *The Hawks of World War II* (1968)

Wayne S. Cole, *America First: The Battle Against Intervention, 1940–1941* (1953)

——, *Charles A. Lindbergh and the Battle Against American Intervention in World War II* (1974)

——, *Roosevelt and the Isolationists, 1932–1945* (1983)

——, *Senator Gerald P. Nye and American Foreign Relations* (1962)

James V. Compton, *The Swastika and the Eagle* (1967)

David H. Culbert, *News for Everyman: Radio and Foreign Affairs in Thirties America* (1976)

Robert Dallek, *Franklin D. Roosevelt and American Foreign Policy, 1933–1945* (1979)

Robert A. Divine, *The Illusion of Neutrality* (1962)
———, *The Reluctant Belligerent* (1979)
Justus Doenecke, "Beyond Polemics: An Historiographical Re-appraisal of American Entry into World War II," *History Teacher*, 12 (1979), 217–251
Jean-Baptiste Duroselle, *From Wilson to Roosevelt* (1963)
Lloyd Gardner, *Economic Aspects of New Deal Diplomacy* (1964)
Thomas N. Guinsburg, *The Pursuit of Isolationism in the United States Senate from Versailles to Pearl Harbor* (1981)
John M. Haight, Jr., *American Aid to France, 1938–1940* (1970)
Manfred Jonas, *Isolationism in America* (1966)
Kenneth P. Jones, *U.S. Diplomats in Europe, 1919–1941* (1981)
Thomas C. Kennedy, *Charles A. Beard and American Foreign Policy* (1975)
Warren F. Kimball, *The Most Unsordid Act: Lend-Lease, 1939–1941* (1969)
———, ed., *Franklin Roosevelt and the World Crisis, 1937–1945* (1973)
Charles P. Kindleberger, *The World in Depression, 1929–1939* (1973)
William E. Kinsella, Jr., *Leadership in Isolation* (1978)
William L. Langer and S. E. Gleason, *The Challenge to Isolation, 1937–1940* (1952)
———, *The Undeclared War, 1940–1941* (1953)
William E. Leuchtenburg, *Franklin D. Roosevelt and the New Deal* (1963)
Leonard P. Liggio and James J. Martin, eds., *Watershed of Empire: Essays on New Deal Foreign Policy* (1976)
Thomas R. Maddux, *Years of Estrangement: American Relations with the Soviet Union, 1933–1941* (1980)
Arnold Offner, *American Appeasement* (1969)
———, *The Origins of the Second World War* (1975)
Thomas G. Paterson, "Isolationism Revisited," *The Nation*, 209 (1969), 166–169
Julius Pratt, *Cordell Hull* (1964)
Willard Range, *Franklin D. Roosevelt's World Order* (1959)
David Reynolds, *The Creation of the Anglo-American Alliance, 1937–41* (1982)
Robert Freeman Smith, "American Foreign Relations, 1920–1942," in Barton J. Bernstein, ed., *Towards a New Past* (1968)
Raymond Sontag, *A Broken World, 1919–1939* (1971)
John Wiltz, *From Isolation to War, 1919–1939* (1971)
———, *In Search of Peace: The Senate Munitions Inquiry* (1963)

Japanese-American Relations and Pearl Harbor

6

When war came to the United States, it struck not in Europe but in the Pacific at an American naval base in the Hawaiian Islands—Pearl Harbor. For a decade before that surprise attack, the United States had protested the steady Japanese military movement through China. In 1931 Japanese forces seized Manchuria and, in 1937, after the outbreak of the "China Incident," marched through much of China. The United States began to expand its navy and did not invoke the Neutrality Acts (thereby permitting China to buy armaments in America); however, lacking adequate power in Asia, it could do little more at first than protest the aggression.

In September 1940, after Japan gained air bases in French Indochina and signed a Tripartite Pact with Germany and Italy, the United States embargoed shipments of scrap iron and steel to the island nation. In July 1941, after Japanese troops occupied French Indochina, Washington froze Japanese assets in the United States, thereby crippling Japanese-American trade and denying Japan vital petroleum imports. Proposals and counterproposals were exchanged by Tokyo and Washington for the rest of the year, all to no avail. On December 7 Japanese pilots boldly bombed Pearl Harbor.

Historians have grappled with controversial questions in explaining the coming of World War II: Was Japan on an inexorable path of aggression? Did the United States push Japan into war? Was Pearl Harbor deliberately set up for disaster by a Roosevelt administration that wanted to get into war through the Asian "back door"? Were there alternatives to war? Should Roosevelt have met with Prince Konoye? Were American proposals realistic?

DOCUMENTS

On January 7, 1932, after the Japanese overran Manchuria, Secretary of State Henry L. Stimson issued what has become known as the "Stimson Doctrine," a policy of non-recognition that guided the United States for the rest of the decade. On October 5, 1937, President Franklin D. Roosevelt told a crowd in Chicago that aggressors should be "quarantined." Although he obviously directed his words at Japan, he offered no concrete plans.

The final American proposals before the outbreak of Japanese-American war were dated November 29, 1941; they sought to roll back Japanese expansion and to revive the emasculated principles of the Open Door Policy. The Japanese position is evident in Tokyo's counterproposals of December 7, 1941, which charged that the United States was uncompromising and unreasonable. Finally, President Roosevelt addressed Congress on December 8, after the "infamy" at Pearl Harbor, asking for a declaration of war.

The Stimson Doctrine, 1932

With the recent military operations about Chinchow, the last remaining administrative authority of the Government of the Chinese Republic in South Manchuria, as it existed prior to September 18th, 1931, has been destroyed. The American Government continues confident that the work of the neutral commission recently authorized by the Council of the League of Nations will facilitate an ultimate solution of the difficulties now existing between China and Japan. But in view of the present situation and of its own rights and obligations therein, the American Government deems it to be its duty to notify both the Imperial Japanese Government and the Government of the Chinese Republic that it cannot admit the legality of any situation *de facto* nor does it intend to recognize any treaty or agreement entered into between those Governments, or agents thereof, which may impair the treaty rights of the United States or its citizens in China, including those which relate to the sovereignty, the independence, or the territorial and administrative integrity of the Republic of China, or to the international policy relative to China, commonly known as the open door policy; and that it does not intend to recognize any situation, treaty or agreement which may be brought about by means contrary to the covenants and obligations of the Pact of Paris of August 27, 1928, to which Treaty both China and Japan, as well as the United States, are parties.

Roosevelt's "Quarantine" Speech, 1937

Some fifteen years ago the hopes of mankind for a continuing era of international peace were raised to great heights when more than sixty nations solemnly pledged themselves not to resort to arms in furtherance of their national aims and policies. The high aspirations expressed in the Briand-Kellogg Peace Pact and the hopes for peace thus raised have of late given way to a haunting fear of calamity. The present reign of terror and international lawlessness began a few years ago.

It began through unjustified interference in the internal affairs of other nations or the invasion of alien territory in violation of treaties; and has now reached a stage where the very foundations of civilization are seriously threatened. The landmarks and traditions which have marked the progress of civilization toward a condition of law, order and justice are being wiped away.

Without a declaration of war and without warning or justification of any kind, civilians, including vast numbers of women and children, are being ruthlessly murdered with bombs from the air. In times of so-called peace, ships are being attacked and sunk by submarines without cause or notice. Nations are fomenting and taking sides in civil warfare in nations that have never done them any harm. Nations claiming freedom for themselves deny it to others.

Innocent peoples, innocent nations, are being cruelly sacrificed to a greed for power and supremacy which is devoid of all sense of justice and humane considerations.

To paraphrase a recent author "perhaps we foresee a time when men, exultant in the technique of homicide, will rage so hotly over the world that every precious thing will be in danger, every book and picture and harmony, every treasure garnered through two millenniums, the small, the delicate, the defenseless—all will be lost or wrecked or utterly destroyed."

If those things come to pass in other parts of the world, let no one imagine that America will escape, that America may expect mercy, that this Western Hemisphere will not be attacked and that it will continue tranquilly and peacefully to carry on the ethics and the arts of civilization.

If those days come "there will be no safety by arms, no help from authority, no answer in science. The storm will rage till every flower of culture is trampled and all human beings are leveled in a vast chaos."

If those days are not to come to pass—if we are to have a world in which we can breathe freely and live in amity without fear—the peace-loving nations must make a concerted effort to uphold laws and principles on which alone peace can rest secure.

The peace-loving nations must make a concerted effort in opposition to those violations of treaties and those ignorings of humane instincts which today are creating a state of international anarchy and instability from which there is no escape through mere isolation or neutrality.

Those who cherish their freedom and recognize and respect the equal right of their neighbors to be free and live in peace, must work together for the triumph of law and moral principles in order that peace, justice and confidence may prevail in the world. There must be a return to a belief in the pledged word, in the value of a signed treaty. There must be recognition of the fact that national morality is as vital as private morality.

A bishop wrote me the other day: "It seems to me that something greatly needs to be said in behalf of ordinary humanity against the present practice of carrying the horrors of war to helpless civilians, especially women and children. It may be that such a protest might be regarded by many, who claim to be realists, as futile, but may it not be that the heart of mankind is so filled with horror at the present needless suffering that that force could be mobilized in sufficient volume to lessen such cruelty in the days ahead. Even though it may take twenty years, which God forbid, for civilization to make effective its corporate protest against this barbarism, surely strong voices may hasten the day."

There is a solidarity and interdependence about the modern world, both technically and morally, which makes it impossible for any nation completely to isolate itself from economic and political upheavals in the rest of the world, especially when such upheavals appear to be spreading and not declining. There can be no stability or peace either within nations or between nations except under laws and moral standards adhered to by all. International anarchy destroys every foundation for peace. It jeopardizes either the immediate or the future security of every nation, large or small. It is, therefore, a matter of vital interest and concern to the people of the United States that the sanctity of international treaties and the maintenance of international morality be restored.

The overwhelming majority of the peoples and nations of the world today want to live in peace. They seek the removal of barriers against trade. They want to exert themselves in industry, in agriculture and in business, that they may increase their wealth through the production of wealth-producing goods rather than striving to produce military planes and bombs and machine guns and cannon for the destruction of human lives and useful property.

In those nations of the world which seem to be piling armament on armament for purposes of aggression, and those other nations which fear acts of aggression against them and their security, a very high proportion of their national income is being spent directly for armaments. It runs from thirty to as high as fifty percent. We are fortunate. The proportion that we in the United States spend is far less—eleven or twelve percent.

How happy we are that the circumstances of the moment permit us to put our money into bridges and boulevards, dams and reforestation, the conservation of our soil and many other kinds of useful works rather than into huge standing armies and vast supplies of implements of war.

I am compelled and you are compelled, nevertheless, to look ahead. The peace, the freedom and the security of ninety percent of the population of the world is being jeopardized by the remaining ten percent who are threatening a breakdown of all international order and law. Surely the ninety percent who want to live in peace under law and in accordance with moral standards that have received almost universal acceptance through the centuries, can and must find some way to make their will prevail.

The situation is definitely of universal concern. The questions involved relate not merely to violations of specific provisions of particular treaties; they are questions of war and of peace, of international law and especially of principles of humanity. It is true that they involve definite violations of agreements, and especially of the Covenant of the League of Nations, the Briand-Kellogg Pact and the Nine Power Treaty. But they also involve problems of world economy, world security and world humanity.

It is true that the moral consciousness of the world must recognize the importance of removing injustices and well-founded grievances; but at the same time it must be aroused to the cardinal necessity of honoring sanctity of treaties, of respecting the rights and liberties of others and of putting an end to acts of international aggression.

It seems to be unfortunately true that the epidemic of world lawlessness is spreading.

When an epidemic of physical disease starts to spread, the community approves and joins in a quarantine of the patients in order to protect the health of the community against the spread of the disease.

It is my determination to pursue a policy of peace. It is my determination to adopt every practicable measure to avoid involvement in war. It ought to be inconceivable that in this modern era, and in the face of experience, any nation could be so foolish and ruthless as to run the risk of plunging the whole world into war by invading and violating, in contravention of solemn treaties, the territory of other nations that have done them no real harm and are too weak to protect themselves adequately. Yet the peace of the world and the welfare and security of every nation, including our own, is today being threatened by that very thing.

No nation which refuses to exercise forbearance and to respect the freedom and rights of others can long remain strong and retain the confidence and respect of other nations. No nation ever loses its dignity or its good standing by conciliating its differences, and by exercising great patience with, and consideration for, the rights of other nations.

War is a contagion, whether it be declared or undeclared. It can engulf states and peoples remote from the original scene of hostilities. We are determined to keep out of war, yet we cannot insure ourselves against the disastrous effects of war and the dangers of involvement. We are adopting such measures as will minimize our risk of involvement, but we cannot have complete protection in a world of disorder in which confidence and security have broken down.

If civilization is to survive, the principles of the Prince of Peace must be restored. Trust between nations must be revived.

Most important of all, the will for peace on the part of peace-loving nations must express itself to the end that nations that may be tempted to violate their agreements and the rights of others will desist from such a course. There must be positive endeavors to preserve peace.

America hates war. America hopes for peace. Therefore, America actively engages in the search for peace.

American Proposals to Japan, November 1941

SECTION I *Draft Mutual Declaration of Policy*

The Government of the United States and the Government of Japan both being solicitous for the peace of the Pacific affirm that their national policies are directed toward lasting and extensive peace throughout the Pacific area, that they have no territorial designs in that area, that they have no intention of threatening other countries or of using military force aggressively against any neighboring nation, and that, accordingly, in their national policies they will actively support and give practical application to the following fundamental principles upon which their relations with each other and with all other governments are based:

1. The principle of inviolability of territorial integrity and sovereignty of each and all nations.
2. The principle of non-interference in the internal affairs of other countries.
3. The principle of equality, including equality of commercial opportunity and treatment.
4. The principle of reliance upon international cooperation and conciliation for the prevention and pacific settlement of controversies and for improvement of international conditions by peaceful methods and processes.

The Government of Japan and the Government of the United States have agreed that toward eliminating chronic political instability, preventing recurrent economic collapse, and providing a basis for peace, they will actively support and practically apply the following principles in their economic relations with each other and with other nations and peoples:

1. The principle of non-discrimination in international commercial relations.
2. The principle of international economic cooperation and abolition of extreme nationalism as expressed in excessive trade restrictions.
3. The principle of non-discriminatory access by all nations to raw material supplies.
4. The principle of full protection of the interests of consuming countries and populations as regards the operation of international commodity agreements.
5. The principle of establishment of such institutions and arrangements of international finance as may lend aid to the essential enterprises and the continuous development of all countries and may permit payments through processes of trade consonant with the welfare of all countries.

SECTION II *Steps To Be Taken by the Government of the United States and by the Government of Japan*

The Government of the United States and the Government of Japan propose to take steps as follows:

1. The Government of the United States and the Government of Japan will endeavor to conclude a multilateral non-aggression pact among the British Empire, China, Japan, the Netherlands, the Soviet Union, Thailand and the United States.

2. Both Governments will endeavor to conclude among the American, British, Chinese, Japanese, the Netherland and Thai Governments an agreement whereunder each of the Governments would pledge itself to respect the territorial integrity of French Indochina and, in the event that there should develop a threat to the territorial integrity of Indochina, to enter into immediate consultation with a view to taking such measures as may be deemed necessary and advisable to meet the threat in question. Such agreement would provide also that each of the Governments party to the agreement would not seek or accept preferential treatment in its trade or economic relations with Indochina and would use its influence to obtain for each of the signatories equality of treatment in trade and commerce with French Indochina.

3. The Government of Japan will withdraw all military, naval, air and police forces from China and from Indochina.

4. The Government of the United States and the Government of Japan will not support—militarily, politically, economically—any government or regime in China other than the National Government of the Republic of China with capital temporarily at Chungking.

5. Both Governments will give up all extraterritorial rights in China, including rights and interests in and with regard to international settlements and concessions, and rights under the Boxer Protocol of 1901.

Both Governments will endeavor to obtain the agreement of the British and other governments to give up extraterritorial rights in China, including rights in international settlements and in concessions and under the Boxer Protocol of 1901.

6. The Government of the United States and the Government of Japan will enter into negotiations for the conclusion between the United States and Japan of a trade agreement, based upon reciprocal most-favored-nation treatment and reduction of trade barriers by both countries, including an undertaking by the United States to bind raw silk on the free list.

7. The Government of the United States and the Government of Japan will, respectively, remove the freezing restrictions on Japanese funds in the United States and on American funds in Japan.

8. Both Governments will agree upon a plan for the stabilization of the dollar-yen rate, with the allocation of funds adequate for this purpose, half to be supplied by Japan and half by the United States.

9. Both Governments will agree that no agreement which either has concluded with any third power or powers shall be interpreted by it in such a way as to conflict with the fundamental purpose of this agreement, the establishment and preservation of peace throughout the Pacific area.

10. Both Governments will use their influence to cause other governments to adhere to and to give practical application to the basic political and economic principles set forth in this agreement.

The Japanese Position, 1941

Ever since the China Affair broke out owing to the failure on the part of China to comprehend Japan's true intentions, the Japanese Government has striven for the restoration of peace and it has consistently exerted its best efforts to prevent the extension of war-like disturbances. It was also to that end that in September last year Japan concluded the Tripartite Pact with Germany and Italy.

However, both the United States and Great Britain have resorted to every possible measure to assist the Chungking regime so as to obstruct the establishment of a general peace between Japan and China, interfering with Japan's constructive endeavours toward the stabilization of East Asia. Exerting pressure on the Netherlands East Indies, or menacing French Indo-China, they have attempted to frustrate Japan's aspiration to the ideal of common prosperity in cooperation with these regions. Furthermore, when Japan in accordance with its protocol with France took measures of joint defence of French Indo-China, both American and British Governments, willfully misinterpreting it as a threat to their own possessions, and inducing the Netherlands Government to follow suit, they enforced the assets freezing order, thus severing economic relations with Japan. While manifesting thus an obviously hostile attitude, these countries have strengthened their military preparations perfecting an encirclement of Japan, and have brought about a situation which endangers the very existence of the Empire. . . .

From the beginning of the present negotiation the Japanese Government has always maintained an attitude of fairness and moderation, and did its best to reach a settlement, for which it made all possible concessions often in spite of great difficulties. As for the China question which constituted an important subject of the negotiation, the Japanese Government showed a most conciliatory attitude. As for the principle of non-discrimination in international commerce, advocated by the American Government, the Japanese Government expressed its desire to see the said principle applied throughout the world, and declared that along with the actual practice of this principle in the world, the Japanese Government would endeavour to apply the same in the Pacific Area including China, and made it clear that Japan had no intention of excluding from China economic activities of third powers pursued on an equitable basis. Furthermore, as regards the question of withdrawing troops from French Indo-China, the Japanese Government even volunteered, as mentioned above, to carry out an immediate evacuation of troops from Southern French Indo-China as a measure of easing the situation.

It is presumed that the spirit of conciliation exhibited to the utmost degree by the Japanese Government in all these matters is fully appreciated by the American Government.

On the other hand, the American Government, always holding fast to theories in disregard of realities, and refusing to yield an inch on its impractical principles, caused undue delay in the negotiation. It is difficult to understand this attitude of the American Government and the Japanese Government desires to call the attention of the American Government especially to the following points:

1. The American Government advocates in the name of world peace those principles favorable to it and urges upon the Japanese Government the acceptance thereof. The peace of the world may be brought about only by discovering a mutually acceptable formula through recognition of the reality of the situation and mutual appreciation of one another's position. An attitude such as ignores realities and imposes one's selfish views upon others will scarcely serve the purpose of facilitating the consummation of negotiations.

Of the various principles put forward by the American Government as a basis of the Japanese-American Agreement, there are some which the Japanese Government is ready to accept in principle, but in view of the world's actual conditions, it seems only a utopian ideal on the part of the American Government to attempt to force their immediate adoption.

Again, the proposal to conclude a multilateral non-aggression pact between Japan, United States, Great Britain, China, the Soviet Union, the Netherlands and Thailand, which is patterned after the old concept of collective security, is far removed from the realities of East Asia.

2. The American proposal contained a stipulation which states—"Both Governments will agree that no agreement, which either has concluded with any third power or powers, shall be interpreted by it in such a way as to conflict with the fundamental purpose of this agreement, the establishment and preservation of peace throughout the Pacific area." It is presumed that the above provision has been proposed with a view to restrain Japan from fulfilling its obligations under the Tripartite Pact when the United States participates in the War in Europe, and, as such, it cannot be accepted by the Japanese Government.

The American Government, obsessed with its own views and opinions, may be said to be scheming for the extension of the war. While it seeks, on the one hand, to secure its rear by stabilizing the Pacific Area, it is engaged, on the other hand, in aiding Great Britain and preparing to attack, in the name of self-defense, Germany and Italy, two Powers that are striving to establish a new order in Europe. Such a policy is totally at variance with the many principles upon which the American Government proposes to found the stability of the Pacific Area through peaceful means.

3. Whereas the American Government, under the principles it rigidly upholds, objects to settle international issues through military pressure, it is exercising in conjunction with Great Britain and other nations pressure by economic power. Recourse to such pressure as a means of dealing with international relations should be condemned as it is at times more inhumane than military pressure.

4. It is impossible not to reach the conclusion that the American Government desires to maintain and strengthen, in coalition with Great Britain and other Powers, its dominant position it has hitherto occupied not only in China but in other areas of East Asia. It is a fact of history that the countries of East Asia for the past hundred years or more have been compelled to observe the

status quo under the Anglo-American policy of imperialistic exploitation and to sacrifice themselves to the prosperity of the two nations. The Japanese Government cannot tolerate the perpetuation of such a situation since it directly runs counter to Japan's fundamental policy to enable all nations to enjoy each its proper place in the world.

The stipulation proposed by the American Government relative to French Indo-China is a good exemplification of the above-mentioned American policy. Thus the six countries,—Japan, the United States, Great Britain, the Netherlands, China and Thailand,—excepting France, should undertake among themselves to respect the territorial integrity and sovereignty of French Indo-China and equality of treatment in trade and commerce would be tantamount to placing that territory under the joint guarantee of the Governments of those six countries. Apart from the fact that such a proposal totally ignores the position of France, it is unacceptable to the Japanese Government in that such an arrangement cannot but be considered as an extension to French Indo-China of a system similar to the Nine Power Treaty structure which is the chief factor responsible for the present predicament of East Asia.

5. All the items demanded of Japan by the American Government regarding China such as wholesale evacuation of troops or unconditional application of the principle of non-discrimination in international commerce ignored the actual conditions of China, and are calculated to destroy Japan's position as the stabilizing factor of East Asia. The attitude of the American Government in demanding Japan not to support militarily, politically or economically any regime other than the regime at Chungking, disregarding thereby the existence of the Nanking Government, shatters the very basis of the present negotiation. This demand of the American Government falling, as it does, in line with its above-mentioned refusal to cease from aiding the Chungking regime, demonstrates clearly the intention of the American Government to obstruct the restoration of normal relations between Japan and China and the return of peace to East Asia.

In brief, the American proposal contains certain acceptable items such as those concerning commerce, including the conclusion of a trade agreement, mutual removal of the freezing restrictions and stabilization of yen and dollar exchange, or the abolition of extra-territorial rights in China. On the other hand, however, the proposal in question ignores Japan's sacrifices in the four years of the China Affair, menaces the Empire's existence itself and disparages its honour and prestige. Therefore, viewed in its entirety, the Japanese Government regrets that it cannot accept the proposal as a basis of negotiation.

Roosevelt's War Message, 1941

Yesterday, December 7, 1941—a date which will live in infamy—the United States of America was suddenly and deliberately attacked by naval and air forces of the Empire of Japan.

The United States was at peace with that Nation and, at the solicitation of

Japan, was still in conversation with its Government and its Emperor looking toward the maintenance of peace in the Pacific. Indeed, one hour after Japanese air squadrons had commenced bombing in Oahu, the Japanese Ambassador to the United States and his colleague delivered to the Secretary of State a formal reply to a recent American message. While this reply stated that it seemed useless to continue the existing diplomatic negotiations, it contained no threat or hint of war or armed attack.

It will be recorded that the distance of Hawaii from Japan makes it obvious that the attack was deliberately planned many days or even weeks ago. During the intervening time the Japanese Government has deliberately sought to deceive the United States by false statements and expressions of hope for continued peace.

The attack yesterday on the Hawaiian Islands has caused severe damage to American naval and military forces. Very many American lives have been lost. In addition American ships have been reported torpedoed on the high seas between San Francisco and Honolulu.

Yesterday the Japanese Government also launched an attack against Malaya.

Last night Japanese forces attacked Hong Kong.

Last night Japanese forces attacked Guam.

Last night Japanese forces attacked the Philippine Islands.

Last night the Japanese attacked Wake Island.

This morning the Japanese attacked Midway Island.

Japan has, therefore, undertaken a surprise offensive extending throughout the Pacific area. The facts of yesterday speak for themselves. The people of the United States have already formed their opinions and well understand the implications to the very life and safety of our Nation.

As Commander-in-Chief of the Army and Navy I have directed that all measures be taken for our defense.

Always will we remember the character of the onslaught against us.

No matter how long it may take us to overcome this premeditated invasion, the American people in their righteous might will win through to absolute victory.

I believe I interpret the will of the Congress and of the people when I assert that we will not only defend ourselves to the uttermost but will make very certain that this form of treachery shall never endanger us again.

Hostilities exist. There is no blinking at the fact that our people, our territory, and our interests are in grave danger.

With confidence in our armed forces—with the unbounded determination of our people—we will gain the inevitable triumph—so help us God.

I ask that the Congress declare that since the unprovoked and dastardly attack by Japan on Sunday, December seventh, a state of war has existed between the United States and the Japanese Empire.

ESSAYS

In his essay, Herbert Feis, historian and long-time State Department official, reacts to criticism of the Roosevelt administration's handling of Asian affairs and defends Washington's policies as necessary in the face of Japanese aggression. In particular, he responds to charges made by historian Charles C. Tansill in the early 1950s that Roosevelt plotted to get the United States into war.

Writing in 1972 at a time when American intervention in the Vietnam War spurred a good deal of questioning about the causes of wars, past and present, political scientist Bruce M. Russett of Yale University wrote a "skeptical view" of the United States entry into World War II, titled *No Clear and Present Danger*. His thesis: war was avoidable and unnecessary. The United States, he argues, placed demands on Japan—such as full withdrawal from China—that were impossible to achieve and wrongly interpreted Japanese actions as unlimited aggression.

The Challenge from Japanese Aggression

HERBERT FEIS

Ten years after victory, we look ruefully at the way the world has gone. It is right and natural to search out any errors of judgment or faults of character that have led us to our present pass. But such self-scrutiny can go awry if governed by a wish to revile rather than a wish to understand. Unless we are alert, that could happen as a result of the suspicions that have come to cluster around the way in which the United States became engaged in the Second World War—torch-lit by the Pearl Harbor disaster.

The more recently available sources have added but little to our knowledge of the events that led to our entry into the war. The books of memoirs written by Japanese witnesses have told us something more, especially about the struggle within the Japanese Government. But in my reading, while they may improve our knowledge of details, they do not change the fundamental view of this experience or its main features. In American and British records still kept secret there may be information or explanations that would do so. But even this I doubt. With no new great revealing facts to display, and no great new insights to impart, the most useful service would seem to be to act as caretaker of what is known, and in particular to deal with certain warped comments and inferences that seasonally must feel the straightening edge of evidence.

Of all the accusations made, the one most shocking to me is that Roosevelt and his chief advisers deliberately left the Pacific Fleet and base at Pearl Harbor exposed as a lure to bring about a direct Japanese attack upon us.

This has been diffused in the face of the fact that the Japanese High Military

Herbert Feis, "War Came at Pearl Harbor: Suspicions Considered," *The Yale Review,* 45 (1956), 378–390. Copyright © Yale University.

Command conference before the Imperial Throne on September 6, 1941, resolved that "If by the early part of October there is no reasonable hope of having our demands agreed to in the diplomatic negotiations mentioned above, we
will immediately make up our minds to get ready for war against America (and
England and Holland)." This is September 6. The plan for the attack on Pearl
Harbor was not approved and adopted until October; and Secret Operation
Order #1, the execution of the plan, was not issued until November 5. The
presence of the Pacific Fleet at Pearl Harbor was not a lure but an obstacle.

The literature of accusation ignores or rejects the real reasons why the Pacific Fleet was kept in Hawaii. It must do so, since one of the main reasons was
the hope that its presence there would deter the Japanese from making so
threatening a move south or north that American armed forces might have to
join in the war. It scorns the fact that the American military plans—to be executed in the event that we became engaged in war—assigned vital tasks to this
Pacific Fleet. A mind must indeed be distracted if it can believe that the American Government could, at one and the same time, use the Pacific Fleet as a
target and count on having it as part of its main defending force.

A variant of this accusation, which at least does not require such a willingness to believe the worst, might also be noted—that despite ample knowledge
that Pearl Harbor was about to be attacked, the American Government purposefully left it exposed and allowed the event to happen.

Those who do not find such an idea at odds with their view of the sense of
duty and regard for human life of President Roosevelt and his chief advisers
can find striking points about the occurrence that may be construed to cor-
respond with this conception. How they glare out of the record in hindsight:
Ambassador Grew's warnings; Secretary Hull's acute gleam put into words
at least three times in Cabinet Councils in November that the Japanese attack
might come "at any moment, anywhere"; the intercepted Japanese messages
telling of the Japanese effort to secure minute information as to the location
of the ships of our Pacific Fleet in the Harbor; carelessness in checking up on
the protective measures taken by the local commanders; failure to use the
chance to give an effective last-minute warning to Hawaii. How else, it is asked,
can these be explained except in terms of secret and conscious purpose?

However, just as hindsight makes the failure of perception plain, so it also
makes it understandable—but only by bringing back to mind the total circumstances. That can be done here only in the barest way. Up to then Japanese
strategy had been wary, one small creeping step after another, from Manchuria
to North China into China and down into Indo-China. American military circles
came to take it for granted that it would go on that way. Then there was the fact
that Japan's basic objectives lay to the south and southeast; there and there only
it could get what it needed—raw materials, oil, and island bases to withstand the
attack from the West. Expectation already set in that direction was kept there
by impressive and accurate intelligence reports of movements under way.
Against this flow of preconception, the signs pointing to Pearl Harbor were not
heeded.

Such features of contemporary thinking within the American Government explain, though they do not excuse, the failure to discern that Pearl Harbor was going to be attacked. To think the contrary is to believe that the President and the heads of the American Army, Navy, and Air Force were given to deep deception, and in order to have us enter the war were ready to sacrifice not only the Pacific Fleet but the whole war plan for the Pacific. This, I think, is the difference between history and police court history.

I have taken note of these accusations that have been built about the disaster at Pearl Harbor because they appeal to the sense of the sinister which is so lively in our times. But I am glad to turn to ideas and interpretations of broader historical import.

The first of these is that Roosevelt and the Joint Chiefs of Staff were obligated by secret agreements with Churchill and their British colleagues to enter the war at some time or other, in one way or other. Therefore, it is further supposed, the American authors of this agreement had to cause either Germany or Japan, or both, to attack us.

This view derives encouragement from the fact that the American Government *did* enter into a secret agreement about strategy with the British. The accord, known as ABC-1 Staff Agreement, adopted at Washington in March, 1941, set down the respective missions of the British and American elements in the event that the United States should be at war with Germany or Japan, or both; and subsequently the American basic joint war plan, Rainbow-5, was adjusted to fit this combined plan of operations. An attempt was made at a similar conference in Singapore soon after to work out a more detailed United States-British-Dutch operating plan for the Pacific. This attempt failed; but the discussion that took place there left a lasting mark on American official thinking, for the conferees defined the limits on land and sea beyond which Japanese forces could not be permitted to go without great risk to the defenders.

The ABC-1 agreement did not place the Roosevelt Administration under *political* obligation to enter the war against either Germany or Japan, not even if Japan attacked British or Dutch areas in the Far East. Nor did Roosevelt give a promise to this effect to Churchill when they met at Newfoundland in August, 1941. Up to the very eve of the Japanese assault the President refused to tell the British or Dutch what we would do. In short, the Government kept itself officially free from any obligation to enter the war, certainly free of any obligation to thrust itself into the war.

But I do think this accord conveyed responsibilities of a moral sort. After ABC-1 was adopted, production of weapons in the United States and the British Commonwealth took it into account; and the allocation of weapons, troops, ships, and planes as between threatened areas was based on the expectation that the United States would carry out the assignments set down in the plan.

Thus, it may be fairly thought, Roosevelt and his administration were obligated to try to gain the consent of Congress and the American people to play the part designated in the joint plans if Japanese assaults crossed the land and sea boundaries of resistance that were defined at these joint staff conferences. In the last November weeks when the end of the diplomatic talks with Japan came into sight, and General Marshall and Admiral Stark were asked what measures should be taken in face of the threatened Japanese advances, they advised the President to declare the limits defined at Singapore, and to warn the Japanese that we would fight if these were crossed. There is much reason to think this would have been done even had the Japanese not struck at Pearl Harbor and the Philippines, and this boundary would have been the line between peace and war. But this reaffirmation was made not as a measure required to carry out a secret accord, but because it was believed to be the best course.

A variant explanation of the way we dealt with Japan runs somewhat as follows: that Roosevelt was determined to get into the war against Germany; that he had to find a release from his public promises that the United States would not enter "foreign wars" unless attacked; that his efforts to do so by unneutral aid to Britain and the Soviet Union had failed because Hitler had refused to accept the challenge; and so he sought another door into war, a back door, by inviting or compelling the Japanese attack.

This interpretation, with its kick at the end, twists the record around its own preconception. The actions taken did not flow from a settled wish to get us into war. They trailed along the rim of necessity of the true purpose—which was to sustain resistance against the Axis. How many times the American Government refused to do what the British, French, Chinese, Russians, Dutch asked it to do, because it might involve us in actual combat!

This slant of reasoning about American action passes by the course of Japanese conduct which aroused our fears and stimulated our opposition: the way in which, despite all our pleas and warnings, Japan pressed on. By not recognizing that these Japanese actions called for American counteraction, it excuses them. Thus our resistance is made to appear as nothing else but a deceitful plot to plunge us into war. Furthermore, it dismisses as insincere the patient attempt to calm Japan by diplomatic talks, by offers to join in safeguarding its security.

There were influential individuals in the Roosevelt Administration who wanted to get into the war and indifferent as to how we got into it. Of these, Secretary of the Interior Ickes was, I believe, the most candid, at any rate in his diary entries. Secretary of the Treasury Morgenthau and his staff also had a positive wish that we should engage in war—but against Germany, not against Japan, for that might have brought a diversion of forces to the Pacific. Secretary of War Stimson thought that it would not be possible for Great Britain to sustain the fight unless we entered it; but toward the very end, particularly as it was becoming plain that the Soviet Union was going to survive the Nazi assault, he began to wish for delay. However, time and time again the memoirs and diaries record the impatience of these officials, and those who thought like them, with Hull's caution and Roosevelt's watchful indirection.

The most genuine point made by those who dissent, one that merits thorough analysis, is that the American Government, in conjunction with the British and Dutch, refused to continue to supply Japan with machines and materials vital to it—especially oil. It is contended that they thereby compelled Japan to resort to war, or at least fixed a time period in which Japan was faced with the need of deciding to yield to our terms or go to war.

In reflecting upon this action, the reasons for it must not be confused with the Japanese response to it. Japan showed no signs of curbing its aggressive course. It paid no heed to repeated and friendly warnings that unless it did, the threatened countries would have to take counter-measures. As when on February 14, 1941, while the Lend-Lease Act was being argued in Congress, Dooman, Counsellor of the American Embassy in Japan and known to be a firm and straightforward friend of that country, carried back from Washington the message for the Vice-Minister for Foreign Affairs: that the American people were determined to support Britain even at the risk of war; that if Japan or any other country menaced that effort "it would have to expect to come in conflict with the United States"; and that the United States had abstained from an oil embargo in order not to impel Japan to create a situation that could only lead to the most serious outcome. Japan's answer over the following months had been to force its way further into Indo-China and threaten the Dutch East Indies.

This sustained proof that Japan was going on with its effort to dominate Asia, and the alliance pledging it to stand by Germany if that country got into war with the United States, made a continuation of trade with Japan an act of meekness on our part. Japan was concentrating its foreign purchases on products needed for war, while reducing civilian use by every means, and was thus accumulating great reserve stocks. These were enabling it to maintain its invasion of China without much strain, while continuing to expand its war-making power. Had *effective* restraints—note that I do not say *total* restraints—not been imposed, the American Government would have been in the strange position of having declared an unlimited national emergency, of calling upon the American people to strengthen their army, navy, and air force in great urgency, while at the same time nourishing the opponent that might have to be met in battle. This was a grave, if not intolerable, responsibility.

It is hard to tell how squarely the American and British Governments faced the possible consequence of their restrictive measures. My impression is that they knew the danger of war with Japan was being increased; that Japan might try to get by force the means denied it. The Japanese Government served plain warnings that this game of thrust and counterthrust might so end. These were soberly regarded, but did not weaken the will that Japan was not to have its way by threat.

Mingled with the anxiety lest these restrictive measures would make war more likely, there was a real hope that they might be a deterrent to war. Conceivably they would bring home to the Japanese people that if it came to war, they might soon run out of the means for combat, while the rapid growth of American military strength would make it clear that they could not in the end win. And, as evidence of these probabilities became plain, the conciliatory elements in the Japanese Government would prevail over the more militant ones.

This almost happened. But the reckless ones, those who would rather court fatality than accept frustration, managed to retain control of Japanese decision. The pressure applied by us did not prevent war, and may have brought the time of decision for war closer. The valid question, however, is not whether the American Government resorted to these restrictions *in order* to drive Japan to attack; it is whether the American Government failed to grasp a real chance, after the restraints had begun to leave their mark in Japanese official circles, to arrive at a satisfactory understanding that would have averted war. Twice, in the opinion of some qualified students of the subject, such a chance emerged, or at least appeared on the horizon of diplomacy. Were they real opportunities or merely mirages or decoys?

The first of these was the occasion when in the autumn of 1941, the Japanese Prime Minister, Prince Konoye, sought a personal meeting with the President. It is averred that the President's failure to respond lost a chance to avert the war without yielding any American principle or purpose. Some think the reason was that American diplomacy was inflexible, dull in its insight, and too soaked in mistrust. Others, more accusatory, explain the decision by a lack of desire for an agreement that would have thwarted the design for war.

Since there is no conclusive evidence of what Konoye intended to propose or could have achieved, comment on this subject must enter into "the boggy ground of what-might-have-been." Some observers, including Ambassador Grew, believe that Konoye could have made a real, and an irreversible, start toward meeting American terms. It will always be possible to think that this is so. But to the Americans in authority, the chance seemed small. Konoye was a man who in every past crisis had allowed himself to flounder between criss-crossed promises; hence there was good reason to fear an attempt at deception. Such glimpses as we have of what he might have proposed do not support the view that he could have offered a suspension or end of the fight against China. His freedom to negotiate would have been subject to the conditions stated by those who had controlled Japan's course up to then—their price for allowing him to go to meet the President.

Even so, to repeat, it is possible that skilled and more daring American diplomacy might have handled the meeting so as to get a satisfactory accord; or, failing that—and this is the more likely chance—to bring about so deep a division within the Japanese circle of decision as to have prevented warlike action. These alluring historical queries will continue to roam in the land of might-have-been.

But the risks were great. The echoes of Munich and its aftermath were still loud. The American Government might have found itself forced to make a miserable choice: either to accept an accord which would have left Japan free to complete its conquest of China and menace the rest of Asia, or to face a deep division among the American people. Any understanding with Japan that was not clear and decisive would have had unpredictable consequences. The Chinese Government might have felt justified in making a deal following our own. The Soviet Union, at this time just managing with the greatest effort and agony to prevent German victory, might also have chosen to compromise with Hitler rather than to fight it out. Speculations such as these must leave the subject unsettled. But in any case I think it clear that the American decision was one of judgment, not of secret intent. Konoye was not told that the President would not meet with him; he was told that he would not do so until more progress had been made toward defining what the Japanese Government was prepared to propose.

The same basic question had to be faced in the final crisis of negotiation in November, 1941: whether to relax restraints on Japan and leave it in a position to keep on trying to control much of Asia in return for a promise not to press on farther for the time being.

The opinion that the Japanese truce offer made at this last juncture accepted the main purposes and principles for which the American Government had been standing may be summarily dismissed. It was ambiguously worded, it was silent about the alliance with Germany, and it would have required the American Government to end its support of China—for the last of its numbered five points read: "The Government of the United States undertakes to refrain from such measures and actions as will be prejudicial to the endeavors for the restoration of general peace between Japan and China." This scant and unclear proposal was at once deemed "entirely unacceptable." Furthermore, there seemed little use and much possible damage in making a counter truce-offer of the same variety. The intercepted Japanese messages stated flatly that this was Japan's last and best offer. They told of the swift dismissal of a much more nearly acceptable one that Nomura and Kurusu asked their superiors in Tokyo to consider. A deadline had been set. Thus it was all but sure that the reduced counteroffer which had been patched together in Washington would be unheeded. But it might shake the coalition to which by then the opponents of the Axis had pledged their lives and national destinies.

This seems to have been the thought uppermost in Hull's mind in recommending to the President that the counter truce-offer be withheld. As set down in his historic memo of November 26, he had been led to this conclusion by the opposition of the Chinese, the half-hearted support or actual opposition of the British, Dutch, and Australian governments, and the further excited opposition to be expected because of lack of appreciation of the importance and value of a truce. This I believe to have been the true determining reason for a decision reluctantly taken. Even if by then Japan was genuinely ready for reform, the repentance had come too late. The situation had grown too entangled by then for minor measures, its momentum too great. Germany-Italy-Japan had forced the creation of a defensive coalition more vast than the empire of the Pacific for which Japan plotted. This was not now to be quieted or endangered by a temporary halt along the fringe of the Japanese advance.

Even though these reasons for dropping the idea of a truce may seem sufficient, they leave the question why the American Government could not have given a softer and less declaratory answer. Why had it to give one so "bleakly uncompromising"? It could have said simply that the Japanese offer did not convey the assurances that would warrant us and the alliance for which we spoke to resume the shipment of war materials to Japan and end our aid to China. Why was it deemed advisable or essential at this juncture to state fully and forcibly our maximum terms for a settlement in the Pacific? Was it foreseen that, scanned with mistrust as it would almost surely be, this would be construed as a demand for the swift abandonment of Japan's whole program? Was it done, as the accusation runs, with the deliberate intent of banning any last chance for an accord? Of propelling the Japanese attack?

That this was not the reason I am as sure as anyone can be on a matter of this sort; but I can offer only conjecture as to what the inspiring purposes were. Perhaps to vindicate past actions and decisions. Perhaps a wish to use the dramatic chance to put in the record a statement of the aims for which the risk of war was being accepted, and of the basis on which the Americans would found the peace when the time came. Such an idea was in accord with the usual mode of thought of the men in charge of the Executive Branch of the Government and of most of the American people. It gave vent to the propensity exemplified in Hull to find a base in general principles meant to be at once political standards and moral ideals. After long caution, it appealed as a defiant contradiction of the Axis program. All this, however, is surmise rather than evidenced history.

But I think it is well within the realm of evidenced history that the memo of November 26 was not in any usual sense of the word an ultimatum. It did not threaten the Japanese with war or any other form of forceful punishment if our terms were not accepted. It simply left them in the state of distress in which they were, with the prospect that they might later have to submit to our requirements. The Japanese Government could have, as Konoye and Nomura pleaded with it to do, allowed the situation to drag along, with or without resuming talks with the American Government. Its power to make war would have been depleted, but neither quickly nor crucially. The armed forces and even the position in China could have been maintained.

Notably, the final Japanese answer which ended negotiations on December 7, 1941, does not accuse the American Government of confronting it with an ultimatum, but only of thwarting the larger Japanese aims. Part 14—the clinching part of this note—reads: "Obviously it is the intention of the American Government to conspire with Great Britain and other countries to obstruct Japan's efforts toward the establishment of peace through the creation of a New Order in East Asia, and especially to preserve Anglo-American rights and interests by keeping Japan and China at war. This intention has been revealed clearly during the course of the present negotiations. Thus, the earnest hope of the Japanese Government to adjust Japanese-American relations and to preserve and promote the peace of the Pacific through coöperation with the American Government has finally been lost."

This is a more nearly accurate description of the purposes of the American Government under Roosevelt than those attributed to it by hostile and suspicious American critics. Our Government did obstruct Japanese efforts, believing them to be unjust, cruel, and a threat to our national security, especially after Japan became a partner with Hitler's Germany and Mussolini's Italy and bent its efforts toward bringing the world under their combined control.

This determination stood on the proposition that it was better to take the risks of having to share in the suffering of the war than of finding ourselves moved or compelled to fight a more desperate battle against the Axis later on. The American Government, I believe, knew how serious a risk of war was being taken. But in its addresses to the American people it chose to put in the forefront the perils we would face if the Axis won, and to leave in the background, even to camouflage, the risks of finding ourselves plunged into wars which during the election campaign it had promised would not occur. Whether any large number of Americans were fooled by this, or whether most of them, in reality, were content to have the prospect presented that way rather than in a more blunt and candid way, I do not know.

No Clear and Present Danger

BRUCE M. RUSSETT

Whatever criticisms of twentieth-century American foreign policy are put forth, United States participation in World War II remains almost entirely immune. According to our national mythology, that was a "good war," one of the few for which the benefits clearly outweighed the costs. Except for a few books published shortly after the war and quickly forgotten, this orthodoxy has been essentially unchallenged. The isolationists stand discredited, and "isolationist" remains a useful pejorative with which to tar the opponents of American intervention in foreign lands.

Such virtual unanimity on major policy matters is rare. World War I long ago came under the revisionists' scrutiny. The origins of the cold war have been challenged more recently, with many people asking whether the Soviet-American conflict was primarily the result of Russian aggressiveness or even whether it was the inevitable consequence of throwing together "two scorpions in a bottle." But all orthodoxy ought to be confronted occasionally, whether the result be to destroy, revise, or reincarnate old beliefs. Furthermore, this does seem an auspicious time to reexamine the standard credo about participation in World War II. Interventionism is again being questioned and Americans are groping toward a new set of principles to guide their foreign policy. Where should we intervene and where withdraw; where actively to support a "balance of power" and where husband our resources? A reexamination of the World War II experience is deliberately a look at a limiting case—an effort to decide whether, in the instance where the value of intervention is most widely accepted, the interventionist argument really is so persuasive. We should consider the World War II experience not because intervention was obvious folly, but indeed because the case for American action there is strong.

I do *not*, of course, argue that one can readily generalize from the choices of 1941 to those of 1950 or 1970. The world has changed, and many of the favorable conditions that once made isolationism or "continentalism" a plausible policy to some have vanished, perhaps forever. I feel ambivalent about the contemporary meaning of the theme developed here, in view of the mani-

From *No Clear and Present Danger: A Skeptical View of the U.S. Entry into World War II* by Bruce M. Russett, pp. 17–23, 44–62. Copyright © 1972 by Bruce M. Russett. Reprinted by permission of Harper & Row, Publishers, Inc.

fest changes of the past 30 years and the more or less "internationalist" policy preferences that I have shared with most Americans for many years. But almost all of us do on occasion invoke the "lessons" of Manchuria, Munich, the Spanish Civil War, or Pearl Harbor; or for that matter Rome and Carthage or the Peloponnesian Wars. We therefore owe it to ourselves to look critically at this historical experience, too. I think the theme of this essay needs stating even at the risk that some people may apply it inappropriately.

Furthermore, a new look at World War II is in some real sense merely an extension of arguments that have been raised against contemporary American intervention in Southeast Asia. The intervention has been justified both on moral grounds—the need to save a small country from communist dictatorship, and on strategic grounds of American self-interest—the need to prop up dominoes and prevent the extension of a hostile power's sphere of influence.

And the opponents of that intervention have included among their arguments some that recall the debates of 1941: America cannot be the world's policeman stepping in to halt everything we might consider to be aggression or to resist governments whose philosophies or policies we consider repugnant. Nor from a pure self-interest viewpoint would such critics accept our action in South Vietnam. It is a small country, far away. Its entire national income is equivalent only to the normal *growth* of the United States national income in a single month. Communist rule in that state, or even in its immediate neighbors as well, would make but an insignificant difference to the global balance of power. In any case, the forces of nationalism render very dubious an assumption that a Communist government would represent a dependable long-term gain for China or Russia.

Thus, in an important way the record of discussion in 1940 and 1941 is being replayed now. Opponents of contemporary intervention may well find ammunition by pointing out the inflated nature of the interventionists' rhetoric preceding World War II. If in the cold light of the seventies the original arguments seem excessive, then how much more misleading must be the recent versions? Or on the contrary, if a man is sure that the Southeast Asian operation was a mistake, can he still justify the World War II experience? Perhaps his continued acceptance of the latter should cause him to rethink his extreme opposition to the American interventions of the last decade.

The theme of this brief book should already be apparent, but I will state it explicitly here before going further: American participation in World War II had very little effect on the essential *structure* of international politics thereafter, and probably did little either to advance the material welfare of most Americans or to make the nation secure from foreign military threats (the presumed goals of advocates of a "realist" foreign policy). (By structure I mean the basic balance of forces in the world, regardless of which particular nations are powerful vis-à-vis the United States.) In fact, most Americans probably would have been no worse off, and possibly a little better, if the United States had never become a belligerent. Russia replaced Germany as the great threat to European security, and Japan, despite its territorial losses, is once more a major power. The war was not clearly a mistake as most of us now consider the Vietnam War to have been. Yet it may well have been an unnecessary war that did little for us and that we need not have fought. Moreover, it set some precedents for our thinking that led too easily to later interventions—interventions that might have been challenged more quickly and more effectively in the absence of such vivid memories of World War II. . . .

Many readers surely will be uncomfortable with the book's theme, and even offended by it. For example, it can hardly be easy for a man who spent two or three of his prime years fighting World War II to think that his sacrifice had little point. Moreover, the moral outrage against Nazism that we all share makes it difficult to separate ethics from an objective assessment of the threat Germany and Japan actually posed to American national security. To suggest that the two must be kept *analytically* distinct—even if in the end one sees the former as justifying intervention after all—is to risk being considered at least a first cousin of the Beast of Belsen.

Yet it is precisely moral considerations that demand a reexamination of our World War II myths. Social scientists have accepted too many assumptions uncritically. Too few Americans, especially government officials, really looked very hard at their beliefs about the origins of the cold war before about five years ago, or seriously considered "economic" interpretations of foreign policy. Recently, however, we have been illuminated as well as blinded by an occasion we could not ignore. On watching the fireball at Alamogordo in 1945 Robert Oppenheimer mused, "I am become death, destroyer of worlds." Vietnam has been to social scientists what Alamogordo was to the physicists. Few of those who have observed it can easily return to their comfortable presumptions about America's duty, or right, to fight in distant lands.

One serious problem in reevaluating American foreign policy before World War II stems from its distance in time. How do we treat the knowledge we gain from actually observing the intervening thirty years? Is it fair to judge the friends and opponents of Franklin Roosevelt with the advantages of 20-20 hindsight? Certainly we must keep separate what they knew or could have known, and what was unavoidably hidden from them. From captured documents we now see more clearly the motivations of some Axis leaders than contemporaries could have; we know with just what strength the Soviet Union emerged in Central Europe after the elimination of German power. If they exaggerated the then-present danger how can we be too condemning?

Nevertheless, the purpose in reconsidering World War II is not to judge, but to learn. In retaining our own humility it is fair to insist on a degree of humility in our leaders of all eras. Many of those who advocated war against Germany and Japan were very sure of themselves and their visions; the same could be said of many "cold warriors." They supported acts which left millions dead and changed all our lives. Some considered Hitler not only a devil, but to have near God-like powers enabling him to walk across the water to North America. The "yellow horde" was ready to invade from the other side; I remember being told how the Japanese coveted California. Both recall more recent images of the Russians as ten feet tall. In fact, our alleged vulnerability to the Axis threat was often used to justify continued involvement and active opposition to apparent Soviet expansionism in the post-war world. Without seeking judgment or scapegoats, perhaps we still can learn by identifying even the most excusable errors of others.

My intention here is to be provocative and not to set forth revealed truth. The argument is not one subject to the principles of measurement and the strict canons of hypothesis-testing—the mode of inquiry with which I feel most comfortable. Nevertheless the subject is too important to leave untouched simply because the whole battery of modern social science cannot be brought to bear on it. Similarly, there is an intellectual dialectic, driven by the need of most thinkers to relate their ideas to established thought patterns, that requires a new view to be stated forcefully and one-sidedly. Hamlets do not make revolutions. Hence we shall proceed to the argument, though the reader—and sometimes the writer too—will doubtless have reservations.

Although I have tried to give some evidence to support the more controversial statements of fact, full documentation would be out of place in such an essay. The need is not to uncover new facts from the archives, but to look again at the old facts from a different perspective. Some of my interpretations will be challengeable, and many readers may decide that despite my arguments the war still was worthwhile. Any retrospective analysis of "might-have-beens" is subject to all the perils of conjecture. We more or less know what *did* happen as a result of American participation in the war, and can only speculate on what would otherwise have happened. But that reservation cuts two ways, since those who will disagree with this book's interpretations are also forced into speculation.

In any case, I think defenders of American intervention will find that their case ultimately rests on other, and less confident, grounds than most have previously accepted. I suspect that no reader will ever again view World War II in quite the same way as before. A new look should at least clear aside many previous exaggerations of the kind of threat foreign powers could then and now present to the United States.

If one rejects the purely moral justification of American entry into the war against Hitler, no very effective moral brief can then be made for the war in the Pacific. True, the Japanese were often unkind conquerors, though this can easily be exaggerated by American memories of the Bataan death march and other horrors in the treatment of prisoners. Japanese occupation was often welcomed in the former European colonies of Southeast Asia, and Japan retains some reservoir of good will for its assistance, late in the war, of indigenous liberation movements. In any case it is Hitler, not Tojo, who is customarily presented as the personification of evil. Possibly Americans did have some vague obligation to defend Chinese independence, but more clearly than in Europe the basis for American participation has to be *realpolitik*. The case has to be founded on a conviction that Japan was too powerful, too dangerously expansionist without any apparent restraint, to have been left alone. An extreme but widely accepted version is given by an early chronicler of the war:

Japan in the spring and summer of 1941 would accept no diplomatic arrangement which did not give it everything that it might win in the Far East by aggression, without the trouble and expense of military campaigns.

The evidence, however, shows quite a different picture both of intent and capability. Nor is it enough simply to assert that, because Japan attacked the United States at Pearl Harbor, America took no action to begin hostilities. This is formally true, but very deceptive. The Japanese attack would not have come but for the American, British, and Dutch embargo on shipment of strategic raw materials to Japan. Japan's strike against the American naval base merely climaxed a long series of mutually antagonistic acts. In initiating economic sanctions against Japan the United States undertook actions that were widely recognized in Washington as carrying grave risk of war. To understand this requires a retracing of the events of the preceding years.

By the beginning of the 1940s Japan was involved in an exhausting and seemingly endless war on the Asian mainland. The "China incident" dated back to the Japanese seizure of Manchuria in 1931, and was greatly escalated by the clash at the Marco Polo Bridge which expanded into severe open warfare with China in 1937. Although the Army did willfully create an incident at Mukden in 1931, the Marco Polo Bridge affair seems not to have been a deliberate provocation by Tokyo. Nevertheless most Japanese military and political leaders did seek a "Co-Prosperity Sphere" of economic and political predominance. They apparently believed that their Empire's status as an independent world power depended on military equality with Russia and the United States in the Far East; that in turn depended on a hegemonial position, preferably economic but achieved by force if necessary, in the area of China. Though this seems strange now, an adequate view of Japanese policy in its contemporary context has to remember Tokyo's position as a latecomer to colonialism, in a world where France, Britain, and the United States all had their own spheres of influence.

Japanese forces made important initial gains by occupying most of the Chinese coast and most of China's industrial capacity, but with a trickle of American aid the nationalist armies hung on in the interior. By 1941 the Japanese armies were bogged down, and their progress greatly impeded by raw material shortages. In 1940 Congress placed fuel oil and scrap iron under the new National Defense Act as goods which could not be shipped out of the Western Hemisphere without an export license. Although commerce in these products was not actually cut off for another year, the threat to Japan of a raw material scarcity was obvious, and deliberately invoked by an American government seeking to apply pressure against the Japanese campaign in China. This strategy was exercised in a series of dozens of gradually tightening economic measures—an escalation that was to drive Japan not to capitulation, as it was intended to do, but to war with the United States.

Following the July 1941 freeze on Japanese assets in America, and the consequent cessation of shipment of oil, scrap iron, and other goods from the United States, Japan's economy was in most severe straits and her power to wage war directly threatened. Her military leaders estimated that her reserves of oil, painfully accumulated in the late 1930s when the risk of just such a squeeze became evident, would last at most two years. She was also short of rice, tin, bauxite, nickel, rubber and other raw materials normally imported from the Dutch East Indies and Malaya. Negotiations with the Dutch authorities to supply these goods, plus extraordinary amounts of oil from the wells of Sumatra, had failed, ostensibly on the grounds that the Dutch feared the material would be reexported to the Axis in Europe. The United States, and the British and Dutch, made it quite clear that the embargo would be relaxed only in exchange for Japanese withdrawal from air and naval bases in Indochina (seized in order to prosecute better the war against China) and an agreement which would have meant the end of the Japanese involvement in China and the *abandonment* of any right to station troops in that country, not just a halt to the fighting. The purpose of the Western economic blockade was to force a favorable solution to the "China incident."

Under these conditions, the High Command of the Japanese navy demanded a "settlement" of one sort or another that would restore Japan's access to essential raw materials, most particularly oil. Without restored imports of fuel the fleet could not very long remain an effective fighting force. While the navy might have been willing to abandon the China campaign, it was utterly opposed to indefinite continuation of the status quo. Either raw material supplies had to be restored by a peaceful settlement with the Western powers, or access to the resources in Thailand, Malaya, and the Indies would have to be secured by force while Japan still retained the capabilities to do so.

If the navy demanded either settlement or war, most members of the Japanese elite were opposed to any settlement which would in effect have meant withdrawal from China. No serious thought was given to the possibility of peace with Chiang's government, for it would have meant the end of all hopes of empire in East Asia and even, it was thought, of influence on the continent of Asia. Moderate Foreign Minister Shigenori Togo reacted to the most forceful statement of American demands, on November 27, 1941, "Japan was asked not only to abandon all the gains of her years of sacrifice, but to surrender her international position as a power in the Far East." In his view, that surrender would have been equivalent to national suicide.

In any case, the Army High Command simply would not have tolerated any abandonment of its position in China. Its own prestige and influence had been built up step by step during the war there, and its position in China became its power base in Japanese domestic politics. General Hideki Tojo, by no means the most violent of the Army war hawks, feared that any concession on the China issue would risk an actual revolt by extremist elements in the Army. In fact, on the resignation of Prince Konoye's government in October 1941 Tojo had urged the appointment of Prince Higashi-Kuni as Premier, on the principle that, should a compromise with the United States be decided upon, only a member of the royal family would have a chance to control the Army and make peace. In the context of Japanese politics of the 1930s, when there had been several plotted coups and when one after another of the political leaders thought to be too conciliatory toward foreign elements were assassinated by extreme nationalists, this was hardly a far-fetched fear. Togo once characterized the Japanese internal political situation in these terms to Joseph C. Grew, American Ambassador to Tokyo, "If Japan were forced to give up suddenly all the fruits of the long war in China, collapse would follow." Before we judge the Japanese too harshly Americans must remember their own difficulties in terminating a stalemated war 30 years later.

Thus, for the various elements in the Japanese government, and for somewhat different reasons, a peaceful settlement ultimately become unacceptable. They could not accede to the American demands, and they could not even continue to drag out the negotiations because of the increasingly precarious nature of the war economy and especially the Navy's fuel supplies. On rejecting this unpalatable alternative they were again thrown back on the other; the necessary raw material could be obtained only by seizing Thailand, where there was rice; Malaya, with its sources of tin, nickel, and rubber; and the Dutch East Indies, with their oil. But, according to the Japanese calculations, the United States was certain to fight if British or Dutch territory in the Far East were attacked. Japanese analysts reached the latter conclusion despite the absence of any American threat or promise. At the Atlantic Conference, Roosevelt had acceded to Churchill's plea that he issue a "war warning" with regard to any further conquests by Japan in the Far East. After he returned to Washington, however, the State Department dissuaded him and no such warning was ever issued. The nearest equivalents were two statements by President Roosevelt to Ambassador Nomura in July and August of 1941. The first declared:

> If Japan attempted to seize oil supplies by force in the Netherlands East Indies, the Dutch would, without the shadow of doubt, resist, the British would immediately come to their assistance, and, in view of our policy of assisting Great Britain, an exceedingly serious situation would immediately result.

On the second occasion Roosevelt stated:

> If the Japanese Government takes any further steps in pursuance of a policy of program of military domination by force or threat of force of neighboring countries the government of the United States will be compelled to take immediately any and all steps which it may deem necessary toward safeguarding the legitimate rights and interests of the United States and American nationals and toward insuring the safety and security of the United States.

Despite its firm language, this was not an unequivocal warning. On presentation to Nomura it was, as Langer and Gleason point out, not given the status of a "written statement" or even of an "oral statement." It was merely private "reference material," for Nomura's use in communicating with his own government. No unequivocal warning could be given, simply because President Roosevelt could not be sure of American reaction in the actual event of crisis. He was fully aware of the need to secure congressional approval for war, of the strength of isolationist sentiment in the United States, of the difficulties involved in demonstrating that an attack on British and Dutch colonies was a direct threat to American interests, and of the dangers inherent in going to war with the country deeply divided.

By autumn 1941, however, opinion was crystalizing in the highest levels of the American decision-making system. In November, Roosevelt informally polled his cabinet on the question of whether the country would support war against Japan in the event of attack on Malaya or the Indies. All members responded in the affirmative. General Marshall and Admiral Stark, the Chiefs of Staff, concluded that the United States should fight if Japan attacked British or Dutch territory, or Siam west of 100 degrees East or south of 10 degrees North. In two conversations on December 1 and 3 Roosevelt assured Lord Halifax, British Ambassador to Washington, that the United States would give Britain armed support if the Japanese attacked British or Dutch territories, or if Britain went to war as a result of a Japanese landing in Siam. This assurance was communicated to London, and from there to Sir Robert Brooke-Popham, British commander in the Far East. On the morning of December 7 in Washington (before the Pearl Harbor raid, which took place at dawn, Hawaii time) Secretaries Hull (State), Knox (Navy), and Stimson (War) discussed the anticipated Japanese attack on Siam or Malaya. They agreed the United States should go to war if the British did. Roosevelt then expected to go before Congress the next day to explain why a Japanese invasion of Siam threatened the security of the United States.

These decisions came too late, however, to affect directly the Japanese deliberations. By the beginning of December their attack was irrevocably set in motion. The Japanese conviction that war could not be limited to the British and Dutch had to be based wholly on inference. Yet it was a correct analysis and a solid conviction, as shown by the otherwise inexplicable risk they took at Pearl Harbor.

Rather close links had been forged between the United States and the colonies in Malaya and the East Indies, bonds that were known to the Japanese and considered to be of great importance. The Southwest Pacific area was of undeniable economic importance to the United States—at the time most of America's tin and rubber came from there, as did substantial quantities of other raw materials. American political involvement in the area was also heavy. The United States was cooperating closely with the British and Dutch governments, and according to the Japanese evaluation, if the United States failed to defend the Indies it would lose its influence in China and endanger the Philippines. Premier Tojo even referred in this context to the approval given Pan American World Airways to establish an air route between Singapore and Manila.

Unilateral American actions to build up their military forces, both generally and in the Pacific in particular, were seen as evidence of aggressive intent. But most convincing of all were the military ties apparently being established among the ABCD (American-British-Chinese-Dutch) powers. The United States was known to be supplying munitions and arms, including aircraft, not just to China but to British and Dutch forces in the Pacific. In cooperation with the British, Dutch, Australians, New Zealanders, and the Free French (at New Caledonia), the United States had begun construction of a string of airfields to the Philippines. Furthermore, the United States had participated in staff conversations with British and Dutch military personnel at Singapore. The Japanese came to associate these conversations with an "Anglo-American policy of encirclement against Japan in the Southern Pacific Ocean." This notion of encirclement appears time and again in Japanese official documents and memoirs. The freezing of Japanese assets by the United States, British, and Netherlands East Indies governments occurred on the same day: July 26, 1941. Although that act was in direct response to Japan's occupation of southern Indo-China, her leaders nevertheless saw it as the final link in their bondage.

As early as spring 1941, in fact, the Japanese army and navy general staffs had agreed among themselves that military action in the Southwest Pacific meant war with the United States. As we have seen, no definite decision by the United States had been reached, due largely to the state of American public opinion. But President Roosevelt and Secretary Hull were quite willing to have the Japanese believe that a joint American-British-Dutch plan of defense of the Indies existed. The conviction only grew stronger with time, and was reinforced by the intelligence received from the Japanese embassy in Washington. On December 3, 1941, for example, the Washington embassy cabled Tokyo: "Judging from all indications, we feel that some joint military action between Great Britain and the United States, with or without a declaration of war, is a definite certainty in the event of an occupation of Thailand."

The American fleet in the Pacific, while inferior to the Japanese in many respects, was strong enough to endanger seriously a sustained offensive and quite possibly strong enough to postpone Japan's effective occupation of the Indies until her raw materials ran out. The oil fields might be put out of operation for many months, and in any case the shipment of these supplies to Japan under the threat of American air and naval attack would be too risky. Japan simply dared not undertake such operations while the American fleet remained intact.

Having decided against withdrawal from China, failed to negotiate a settlement with America, and decided on the necessity of seizing supplies from Southeast Asia, they were faced with the need to blunt what they regarded as the inevitable American response. Thus they launched a surprise attack on Pearl Harbor to destroy any American capability for immediate naval offensive. For all the audacity of the strike at Hawaii, its aims were limited: to destroy existing United States offensive capabilities in the Pacific by tactical surprise. The Japanese High Command hoped only to give its forces time to occupy the islands of the Southwest Pacific, to extract those islands' raw materials, and to turn the whole area into a virtually impregnable line of defense which could long delay an American counteroffensive and mete out heavy casualties when the counterattack did come. As a result of their early success the Japanese naval and military chiefs extended this line a little farther than they had first meant to do, but their original intentions were not grandiose.

In deciding to attack Pearl Harbor the Japanese took what they fully recognized to be a great risk. There is no doubt but that the Imperial government realized it could not win a long war with the United States if the Americans chose to fight such a war. Japanese strategists calculated that America's war potential was seven to eight times greater than their own; they knew that Japan could not hope to carry the war to the continental United States. General Suzuki, chairman of the Planning Board, had reported that Japan's stockpile of resources was not adequate to support a long war. Admiral Yamamoto, the brilliant inventor of the Pearl Harbor attack plan, warned: "In the first six months to a year of war against the U.S. and England I will run wild, and I will show you an uninterrupted succession of victories; I must also tell you that, should the war be prolonged for two or three years, I have no confidence in our ultimate victory."

Because the proposed attack seemed an escape from the dilemma it was grasped with more enthusiasm than it deserved. The Japanese never seriously considered exactly what would cause the United States to forego crushing Japan, or how Japan might best create the proper conditions for a negotiated peace. Certain key elements, such as the probable effect of the Pearl Harbor attack on the American will to win, were left completely unanalyzed. Japan's sole strategy involved dealing maximum losses to the United States at the outset, making the prospects of a prolonged war as grim as possible, and counting, in an extremely vague and ill-defined way, on the American people's "softness" to end the war.

Nor, certainly, can the Japanese decision be explained simply as an act of "irrationality," an impulsive act by an unstable leader. Such explanations depend either upon a situation of great stress, which would warp the actions of all or most of the participants in the decision process, or really apply only to circumstances where a single individual in fact makes the decision. Some of Hitler's most costly mistakes in World War II, for example, were highly individualistic decisions for which he alone was responsible. Typical of the pattern was his order to stand and fight at Stalingrad rather than allow his army to retreat and regroup. High stress plus the peculiarities of the Fuehrer's personality produced a command different from what other men would have given.

The Japanese decision to attack Pearl Harbor, however, was neither the decision of a single individual, where much of his behavior could be explained by his own personality, nor a decision arrived at under time pressures. It was reached incrementally and reinforced at several steps along the line. On July 2, 1941, it was decided to press ahead with expansion in Southeast Asia even though this meant a high risk of war with the United States. After deep consideration by high Japanese military and naval officials for months, a formal commitment was made at the Imperial Conference of September 6 that either negotiations must result in lifting the United States embargo on strategic raw materials, or Japan would have to fight the Americans. October 15 was set as the deadline for success in negotiation. But even though the strategic commitment (in the sense of a decision for the next move dependent upon the opponent's reaction to this one) had seemingly been made, it was the subject of a great deal of reexamination over the subsequent three months. Prince Konoye's government resigned following the expiration of the deadline, but the new cabinet formed under General Tojo took office not as a regime determined to take the nation into war, but rather as one still seeking a way out. Serious negotiation with the United States continued through November. A new secret deadline of November 25 was once set, "after which things are going to happen automatically," but it too was extended until November 30.

Whatever the nature of the decision to go to war, it was arrived at and re-inforced over a long period of time, and was not the result of anyone's possibly "irrational" impulse. In any case, the decision was in no important sense the act of a single man whose peculiar traits can be used to explain it. Rather, it was a carefully—if incompletely—considered collective attempt to break out of a dilemma that no man would relish.

This analysis is meant to establish an important proposition: that the Japanese attack on Pearl Harbor, and for that matter on Southeast Asia, is not evidence of any unlimited expansionist policy or capability by the Japanese government. It was the consequence only of a much less ambitious goal, centering on an unwillingness to surrender the position that the Japanese had fought for years to establish in China. When that refusal met an equal American determination that Japan should give up many of her gains in China, the result was war. Japanese expansion into Southeast Asia originated less in strength than in weakness; it was predominantly instrumental to the China campaign, not a reach for another slice of global salami. Of course there were Japanese political and military leaders with wider ambitions, but they were not predominant in policy-making.

Throughout the 1930s the United States government had done little to resist the Japanese advance on the Asian continent. There were verbal protests, but little more. Even in early 1941 Washington apparently would have settled for a *halt* in China, and saw little danger of a much wider move into Southeast Asia. But the application of economic sanctions against Tokyo was very successful; it was obviously hurting, and the moderate Premier Prince Konoye proposed a direct meeting with Roosevelt to try to reach an understanding. At about that point the American Government seems to have been so impressed with its success that it rebuffed Konoye's approach, demanding that he agree in advance on terms of a settlement. Konoye's cabinet fell, and American observers concluded—on the basis of untestable evidence that sounded a bit like sour grapes—that he could not have enforced a "reasonable" settlement in Japanese politics anyway. Washington then raised the ante, calling for a Japanese *withdrawal* from all occupied territory in China. Several officials in the State Department proposed settling for a halt, giving China a breathing spell that would have served it better for several more years of war while America made its main effort in the Atlantic. Hull considered and then rejected their plan for such a *modus vivendi,* which rather closely resembled the second of two Japanese proposals ("Plan B") that represented Tokyo's last efforts. Economic sanctions continued to provide a warm moral glow for those who disapproved of trading with an aggressor, but they then served to make inevitable an otherwise avoidable war which was peripheral to American vital interests and for which the country was ill-prepared.

It was widely understood in Washington that the next move would probably be some sort of Japanese attack in Southeast Asia. Ambassador Grew in Tokyo had long been warning of the limited nature of Japanese goals and the consequences of resisting them. As early as 1940, Under-secretary of State Sumner

Welles had cautioned that an embargo would bring Japanese occupation of the Dutch East Indies.

Why then did President Roosevelt and his advisers embark on a series of incremental pressures that had the effect of pushing the Japanese into war? In large part, of course, they decided that Japanese ambitions in China posed a long-term threat to American interests, and so they forced a confrontation. A sentimental American attitude toward China as a "ward" also must not be forgotten. From missionary days they had been a people "we had always helped," to whom there was a sense of obligation. Roosevelt had a long-time emotional attachment to China, and from his days as Assistant Secretary of the Navy had allegedly "become imbued with the Navy's conviction that Japan was America's Number One enemy."

Nor should economic, as opposed to strategic, motives be ignored as they have been in most conventional histories of the period. Beginning with Dr. Sun Yat-Sen's idea that Chinese reconstruction would have to be brought about in collaboration with other countries, the nationalist government sought foreign economic and technical assistance. Some interest was expressed in the United States, with a few loans forthcoming. Nondiscrimination in East Asian trade was almost always included in American demands on Japan. According to one analyst with a revisionist perspective:

> Although the Great China Market never materialized, many American leaders in the New Deal period . . . acted upon the assumption that it would, and this gave them reason to oppose Japan's forward movement in Asia.

Another demonstrates the importance of perceived commercial possibilities in China in the first American extension of economic assistance to belligerent China. Yet another, commenting on policy toward all the Axis states, says:

> The actual defense of the United States was one factor involved in the move to an "all-out aid short of war" policy, but the restoration of the Open Door world order was of at least equal importance to the Roosevelt administration.

Such considerations surely applied, and probably in greater strength, to continental Europe, where Nazi plans for autarchy threatened an American market that was quantitatively very much more important. The economic prospect of a German-Soviet dominated Europe must have seemed unattractive— though, objectively, the threat to the national interest as a whole amounted to less than two percent of American GNP for those exports and imports combined. There also was some fear of German economic penetration into South America. But as for the Far East, by embargoing Japan in 1941 the United States was giving up an export trade at least four times that with China. While one must not equate dollar volume perfectly with relative political influence, the impact of China traders can easily be exaggerated.

It is of course impossible to separate and weigh the relative importance of the various influences. Strategic considerations, however muddled, were in the forefront. Certainly the above evaluation implies no conspiracy by Roosevelt against the general welfare of the United States, but it does require us again to evaluate the military and political situation of the day, in light of what was known then and of what we know now.

On purely strategic grounds some observers might argue that the danger was not from Germany, Italy, or Japan alone, but rather from their combination in an aggressive alliance encircling the Western Hemisphere. The rhetoric of the time could suggest such a threat, but in fact the Tripartite Pact of Germany and Italy with Japan had become quite fragile. As explained in the preceding chapter, it was designed to deter United States entry into either of the then still-separate conflicts. The Japanese foreign minister in early 1941, Yosuke Matsuoka, had negotiated the Pact and was by far its strongest supporter in the cabinet. He tried to persuade his colleagues to follow the German attack on Russia with a similar act by Japan, but failed and was deposed. Thereafter the Pact faded in importance to the Tokyo government. In considering their subsequent negotiations with the United States the Japanese leaders were fully willing to sacrifice the Pact in return for the necessary economic concessions. Had Hitler managed to get himself into war with America in the Atlantic he could not successfully have invoked the Pact unless the Japanese clearly had seen war to be in their own interests.

Moreover, this drift away from Germany was, it has been well argued, adequately known to American and British officials—Ambassadors Grew and Craigie, Cordell Hull, Roosevelt and Churchill—thanks in part to American ability to crack the codes used in all Japanese secret cables. "After Matsuoka's fall . . . no Axis leader was able even to keep up the pretense of expecting Japanese intervention in behalf of Germany and Italy." In the context of late 1941, therefore, the prospects of close cooperation among Germany, Italy and Japan were not very menacing. Given their very diverse long-run interests, and Hitler's racial notions, a "permanent" alliance surely does not seem very plausible. A special irony of the situation is that Roosevelt was particularly anxious to see Hitler beaten first, and that British and Dutch colonial possessions in Southeast Asia, which seemed essential to the European war, be unmolested. His belated insistence on Japanese evacuation from China then pushed the Axis back together and endangered his other goals.

Would Japanese success in China alone, without reference to their allies, have posed such a long-term threat as has sometimes been imagined? It is easy subconsciously to invoke old Western fears that still plague American China policy. Even limited to the home islands, after two decades of spectacular growth Japan today has the world's third largest GNP. Yet it is only about one-sixth as large as that of the United States, and a third of Russia's. This third-ranking power is still manifestly weaker than the United States, as it was in 1941. From a thirty year perspective it is hard to argue that the great war made much ultimate difference either way in Japan's potential power in the world.

Firm Japanese control of all China would of course be a different matter, and would indeed have put at Tokyo's disposal an empire of awesome size.

Still, really what are the prospects that Imperial Japan could effectively have ruled a population seven times larger than her own? Herbert Hoover at the time urged:

> We must remember some essentials of Asiatic life . . . that while Japan has the military ascendancy today and no doubt could take over parts or all of China, yet the Chinese people possess transcendent cultural resistance; that the mores of the race have carried through a dozen foreign dynasties over the 3,000 years . . . No matter what Japan does . . . they will not Japanify China and if they stay long enough they will be absorbed or expelled by the Chinese. For America to undertake this on behalf of China might expedite it, but would not make it more inevitable.

The Japanese War in China was going so badly in 1941 that it seems rather far-fetched to imagine firm domination ever being established. Japan was already bogged down on the Asian mainland, as other powers have done since. The Chinese nationalists, and the Communists, probably could have continued to resist for years with continuing American and Russian military assistance short of war. Maybe not, but even so it would seem that there would have been substantial warning, still allowing the United States to institute a tough policy against the Japanese later on when the evidence was clear.

FURTHER READING

Patrick Abbazia, *Mr. Roosevelt's Navy* (1975)

Irvine H. Anderson, *The Standard-Vacuum Oil Company and United States East Asia Policy* (1975)

Harry Elmer Barnes, ed., *Perpetual War for Perpetual Peace* (1953)

Charles A. Beard, *President Roosevelt and the Coming of the War, 1941* (1948)

Dorothy Borg, *The United States and the Far Eastern Crisis of 1933–1938* (1964)

———— and Shumpei Okamoto, eds., *Pearl Harbor as History* (1973)

Russell D. Buhite, *Nelson T. Johnson and American Policy Toward China, 1925–1941* (1968)

Richard Dean Burns and Edward M. Bennett, eds., *Diplomats in Crisis* (1974)

Robert J. C. Butow, *The John Doe Associates: Backdoor Diplomacy for Peace, 1941* (1974)

————, *Tojo and the Coming of the War* (1961)

Warren I. Cohen, *America's Response to China* (1980)

James Crowley, *Japan's Quest for Autonomy* (1966)

Roger Dingman, *Power in the Pacific* (1976)

Herbert Feis, *The Road to Pearl Harbor* (1950)

Waldo H. Heinrichs, Jr., *American Ambassador: Joseph C. Grew and the Development of the United States Diplomatic Tradition* (1966)

James H. Herzog, *Closing the Open Door* (1973)

Saburō Ienaga, *The Pacific War* (1978)

Akira Iriye, *Across the Pacific* (1967)

————, *After Imperialism* (1969)

Peter Lowe, *Great Britain and the Origins of the Pacific War* (1977)

Martin V. Melosi, *The Shadow of Pearl Harbor* (1977)

James W. Morley, ed., *Deterrent Diplomacy* (1976)

————, ed., *The Fateful Choice: Japan's Advance into Southeast Asia, 1939–1941* (1979)

Charles Neu, *The Troubled Encounter* (1975)

William L. Neumann, *America Encounters Japan* (1963)

Stephen Pelz, *Race to Pearl Harbor* (1974)

Gordon W. Prange, *At Dawn We Slept: The Untold Story of Pearl Harbor* (1981)

Armin Rappaport, *Henry L. Stimson and Japan, 1931–1933* (1963)

Paul W. Schroeder, *The Axis Alliance and the Japanese-American Relations, 1941* (1958)

Charles C. Tansill, *Back Door to War* (1952)

James C. Thomson, Jr., Peter W. Stanley, and John C. Perry, *Sentimental Imperialists* (1981)

John Toland, *Infamy: Pearl Harbor and Its Aftermath* (1982)

Paul A. Varg, *The Closing of the Door* (1973)

Gerald E. Wheeler, *Prelude to Pearl Harbor: The United States Navy and the Far East, 1921–1931* (1963)

Robert Wohlstetter, *Pearl Harbor: Warning and Decision* (1962)

The Grand Alliance
of the Second World War

7

The Grand Alliance of Great Britain, the United States, and the Soviet
Union won the Second World War. In the process of hurling defeat
at Germany and Japan, and in the final triumph itself, the structure of
international relations was transformed. World War II was a true watershed
in world history, a time when power shifted from some states to others,
when decolonization ate into traditional empires, when war-ravaged economic
and political institutions took new shapes. The major objective of Allied
leaders Winston S. Churchill, Franklin D. Roosevelt, and Josef Stalin was,
of course, to win the war. But they did not always agree on military strategy,
and because military decisions carried postwar political consequences, they
debated the principles that might guide them in the transition to peace. As
they gradually ground down the Axis powers, the Allies negotiated among
themselves. They exchanged strong views on the opening of a second, or
western, front; they differed over the location for new military campaigns;
they suspected each other of flirting with separate peaces; they jockeyed
for political position in the countries liberated from Nazi control, such as
Poland; they struggled to define the configuration of world power in the
postwar era. When Germany and Japan were crushed, the Grand Alliance
came apart.

    The politics of the Grand Alliance and the linkage between World War
II and the Cold War have sparked considerable historical debate. Some
critics have faulted President Roosevelt for making military choices without
adequately considering their long-term diplomatic impact. Some have held
him responsible for the Russian domination of Eastern Europe, a divided
Germany, and the onset of the Cold War. The wartime conferences, such as

the Yalta Conference, have stirred controversy because they produced plans for winning the war and fashioning the peace that generated Allied tensions and failed to supply postwar stability. The most common charge against Roosevelt after the war was that, naive and unrealistic, he gave into the Russians, encouraging their expansionist ambitions. Other commentators treat Roosevelt's wartime diplomacy more favorably, emphasizing the unique complexities of conducting a global war, American dependency upon Soviet military forces in Europe, and Roosevelt's grasp of power realities. After all, the Allies did achieve the impressive feat of smashing powerful enemies, and if the peace plans did not hold, Roosevelt's successors must share some responsibility. Some scholars have argued, moreover, that the United States used the opportunity of war to weaken the British Empire, expand American interests, including new overseas bases, and thwart a rising political left. The United States under Roosevelt's leadership, then, self-consciously developed and protected a larger American sphere of influence while offering to honor the spheres of the other great powers. Many of these interpretations are expressed in the selections for this chapter.

DOCUMENTS

When to open a second or western front was a major Allied issue until June 6, 1944, when British and American troops crossed the channel into France. Until that time, the Russians pressed hard for action. In a Washington meeting between Franklin D. Roosevelt and Soviet Commissar for Foreign Affairs V. M. Molotov on May 30, 1942, the President promised such an operation before year's end. But delays set in, and Soviet Premier Josef Stalin grew impatient. His letter of June 24, 1943, to Roosevelt, the second document, demonstrates his concern. At an Allied conference held in Teheran, Iran, during late November and early December 1943, Roosevelt and Stalin exchanged ideas about having "Four Policemen" govern the postwar world.

The interest in spheres of influence is illustrated by the fourth document: a Churchill-Roosevelt agreement of October 1944, delineating the British and Russian roles in the liberated countries. This account is drawn from Churchill's memoirs. The next two documents emerged from the important Yalta Conference of February 4–11, 1945, when the Allied leaders were near victory over Germany. In a letter dated April 5, 1945, Roosevelt chided Stalin for suggesting that the United States was negotiating with the Germans in Switzerland behind Russian backs. Just before his death, in response to Churchill's growing irritation over Soviet manipulation of Poland, Roosevelt wrote the British Prime Minister. His letter of April 11, 1945, is reprinted here as the eighth document. The last document is the transcript of some comments Dwight D. Eisenhower, Supreme Allied Commander in Europe, made on March 3, 1949, about whether American troops should have raced to Berlin to beat the Russians there.

Franklin D. Roosevelt's Promise of a
Second Front, 1942

Opening the general discussion, the President remarked to Admiral King and General Marshall that he first wished to place them *au courant* with the questions Mr. Molotov had raised, and he hoped that Mr. Molotov himself would then put the situation before them in detail. Mr. Molotov, the President continued, had just come from London, where he had been discussing with the British authorities the problem of a second (invasion) front in Western Europe. He had, the President added, been politely received, but had as yet obtained no positive commitment from the British. There was no doubt that on the Russian front the Germans had enough superiority in aircraft and mechanized equipment to make the situation precarious. The Soviets wished the Anglo-American combination to land sufficient combat troops on the continent to draw off 40 German divisions from the Soviet front. We appreciated, he continued, the difficulties of the situation and viewed the outlook as serious. We regarded it as our obligation to help the Soviets to the best of our ability, even if the extent of this aid was for the moment doubtful. That brought up the question, what we can do even if the prospects for permanent success might not be especially rosy. Most of our difficulties lay in the realm of ocean transport, and he would in this connection merely remark that getting any one convoy through to Murmansk was already a major naval operation. The President then suggested that Mr. Molotov should treat the subject in such detail as suited his convenience.

Mr. Molotov thereupon remarked that, though the problem of the second front was both military and political, it was predominantly political. There was an essential difference between the situation in 1942 and what it might be in 1943. In 1942 Hitler was the master of all Europe save a few minor countries. He was the chief enemy of everyone. To be sure, as was devoutly to be hoped, the Russians might hold and fight on all through 1942. But it was only right to look at the darker side of the picture. On the basis of his continental dominance, Hitler might throw in such reinforcements in manpower and material that the Red Army might *not* be able to hold out against the Nazis. Such a development would produce a serious situation which we must face. The Soviet front would become secondary, the Red Army would be weakened, and Hitler's strength would be correspondingly greater, since he would have at his disposal not only more troops, but also the foodstuffs and raw materials of the Ukraine and the oil-wells of the Caucasus. In such circumstances the outlook would be much less favorable for all hands, and he would not pretend that such developments were all outside the range of possibility. The war would thus become tougher and longer. The merit of a new front in 1942 depended on the prospects of Hitler's further advantage, hence the establishment of such a front should not be postponed. The decisive element in the whole problem lay in the question, when are the prospects better for the United Nations: in 1942 or in 1943.

Amplifying his remarks, Mr. Molotov observed that the forces on the Soviet front were large, and, objectively speaking, the balance in quantity of men, aviation, and mechanized equipment was slightly in Hitler's favor. Nevertheless, the Russians were reasonably certain they could hold out. This was the most optimistic prospect, and the Soviet morale was as yet unimpaired. But the main danger lay in the probability that Hitler would try to deal the Soviet Union a mighty crushing blow. If, then, Great Britain and the United States, as allies, were to create a new front and to draw off 40 German divisions from the Soviet front, the ratio of strength would be so altered that the Soviets could either beat Hitler this year or insure beyond question his ultimate defeat.

Mr. Molotov therefore put this question frankly: could we undertake such offensive action as would draw off 40 German divisions which would be, to tell the truth, distinctly second-rate outfits? If the answer should be in the affirmative, the war would be decided in 1942. If negative, the Soviets would fight on alone, doing their best, and no man would expect more from them than that. He had not, Mr. Molotov added, received any positive answer in London. Mr. Churchill had proposed that he should return through London on his homeward journey from Washington, and had promised Mr. Molotov a more concrete answer on his second visit. Mr. Molotov admitted he realized that the British would have to bear the brunt of the action if a second front were created, but he also was cognizant of the role the United States plays and what influence this country exerts in questions of major strategy. Without in any way minimizing the risks entailed by a second front action this summer, Mr. Molotov declared his government wanted to know in frank terms what position we take on the question of a second front, and whether we were prepared to establish one. He requested a straight answer.

The difficulties, Mr. Molotov urged, would not be any less in 1943. The chances of success were actually better at present while the Russians still have a solid front. "If you postpone your decision," he said, "you will have eventually to bear the brunt of the war, and if Hitler becomes the undisputed master of the continent, next year will unquestionably be tougher than this one."

The President then put to General Marshall the query whether developments were clear enough so that we could say to Mr. Stalin that we are preparing a second front. "Yes," replied the General. The President then authorized Mr. Molotov to inform Mr. Stalin that we expect the formation of a second front this year.

Josef Stalin's Impatience over a Second Front, 1943

I fully realise the difficulty of organising an Anglo-American invasion of Western Europe, in particular, of transferring troops across the Channel. The difficulty could also be discerned in your communications.

From your messages of last year and this I gained the conviction that you and the President were fully aware of the difficulties of organising such an operation and were preparing the invasion accordingly, with due regard to the difficulties and the necessary exertion of forces and means. Even last year you told me that a large-scale invasion of Europe by Anglo-American troops would be effected in 1943. In the Aide-Mémoire handed to V. M. Molotov on June 10, 1942, you wrote:

"Finally, and most important of all, we are concentrating our maximum effort on the organisation and preparation of a large-scale invasion of the Continent of Europe by British and American forces in 1943. We are setting no limit to the scope and objectives of this campaign, which will be carried out in the first instance by over a million men, British and American, with air forces of appropriate strength."

Early this year you twice informed me, on your own behalf and on behalf of the President, of decisions concerning an Anglo-American invasion of Western Europe intended to "divert strong German land and air forces from the Russian front." You had set yourself the task of bringing Germany to her knees as early as 1943, and named September as the latest date for the invasion.

In your message of January 26 you wrote:

"We have been in conference with our military advisers and have decided on the operations which are to be undertaken by the American and British forces in the first nine months of 1943. We wish to inform you of our intentions at once. We believe that these operations together with your powerful offensive, may well bring Germany to her knees in 1943."

In your next message, which I received on February 12, you wrote, specifying the date of the invasion of Western Europe, decided on by you and the President:

"We are also pushing preparations to the limit of our resources for a cross-Channel operation in August, in which British and United States units would participate. Here again, shipping and assault-landing craft will be the limiting factors. If the operation is delayed by the weather or other reasons, it will be prepared with stronger forces for September."

Last February, when you wrote to me about those plans and the date for invading Western Europe, the difficulties of that operation were greater than they are now. Since then the Germans have suffered more than one defeat: they were pushed back by our troops in the South, where they suffered appreciable loss; they were beaten in North Africa and expelled by the Anglo-American troops; in submarine warfare, too, the Germans found themselves in a bigger predicament than ever, while Anglo-American superiority increased substantially; it is also known that the Americans and British have won air superiority in Europe and that their navies and mercantile marines have grown in power.

It follows that the conditions for opening a second front in Western Europe during 1943, far from deteriorating, have, indeed, greatly improved.

That being so, the Soviet Government could not have imagined that the British and U.S. Governments would revise the decision to invade Western Europe, which they had adopted early this year. In fact, the Soviet Government was fully entitled to expect that the Anglo-American decision would be carried out, that appropriate preparations were under way and that the second front in Western Europe would at last be opened in 1943.

That is why, when you now write that "it would be no help to Russia if we threw away a hundred thousand men in a disastrous cross-Channel attack," all I can do is remind you of the following:

First, your own Aide-Mémoire of June 1942 in which you declared that preparations were under way for an invasion, not by a hundred thousand, but by an Anglo-American force exceeding one million men at the very start of the operation.

Second, your February message, which mentioned extensive measures preparatory to the invasion of Western Europe in August or September 1943, which, apparently, envisaged an operation, not by a hundred thousand men, but by an adequate force.

So when you now declare: "I cannot see how a great British defeat and slaughter would aid the Soviet armies," is it not clear that a statement of this kind in relation to the Soviet Union is utterly groundless and directly contradicts your previous and responsible decisions, listed above, about extensive and vigorous measures by the British and Americans to organise the invasion this year, measures on which the complete success of the operation should hinge.

I shall not enlarge on the fact that this responsible decision, revoking your previous decisions on the invasion of Western Europe, was reached by you and the President without Soviet participation and without inviting its representatives to the Washington conference, although you cannot but be aware that the Soviet Union's role in the war against Germany and its interest in the problems of the second front are great enough.

There is no need to say that the Soviet Government cannot become reconciled to this disregard of vital Soviet interests in the war against the common enemy.

You say that you "quite understand" my disappointment. I must tell you that the point here is not just the disappointment of the Soviet Government, but the preservation of its confidence in its Allies, a confidence which is being subjected to severe stress. One should not forget that it is a question of saving millions of lives in the occupied areas of Western Europe and Russia and of reducing the enormous sacrifices of the Soviet armies, compared with which the sacrifices of the Anglo-American armies are insignificant.

Roosevelt and Stalin on the "Four Policemen," at Teheran, 1943

The President then said the question of a post-war organization to preserve peace had not been fully explained and dealt with and he would like to discuss with the Marshal the prospect of some organization based on the United Nations.

The President then outlined the following general plan:

(1) There would be a large organization composed of some 35 members of the United Nations which would meet periodically at different places, discuss and make recommendations to a smaller body.

Marshal Stalin inquired whether this organization was to be world-wide or European, to which the President replied, world-wide.

The President continued that there would be set up an executive committee composed of the Soviet Union, the United States, United Kingdom and China, together with two additional European states, one South American, one Near East, one Far Eastern country, and one British Dominion. He mentioned that Mr. Churchill did not like this proposal for the reason that the British Empire only had two votes. This Executive Committee would deal with all non-military questions such as agriculture, food, health, and economic questions, as well as the setting up of an International Committee. This Committee would likewise meet in various places.

Marshal Stalin inquired whether this body would have the right to make decisions binding on the nations of the world.

The President replied, yes and no. It could make recommendations for settling disputes with the hope that the nations concerned would be guided thereby, but that, for example, he did not believe the Congress of the United States would accept as binding a decision of such a body. The President then turned to the third organization which he termed "The Four Policemen," namely, the Soviet Union, United States, Great Britain, and China. This organization would have the power to deal immediately with any threat to the peace and any sudden emergency which requires this action. He went on to say that in 1935, when Italy attacked Ethiopia, the only machinery in existence was the League of Nations. He personally had begged France to close the Suez Canal, but they instead referred it to the League which disputed the question and in the end did nothing. The result was that the Italian Armies went through the Suez Canal and destroyed Ethiopia. The President pointed out that had the machinery of the Four Policemen, which he had in mind, been in existence, it would have been possible to close the Suez Canal. The President then summarized briefly the idea that he had in mind.

Marshal Stalin said that he did not think that the small nations of Europe would like the organization composed of the Four Policemen. He said, for example, that a European state would probably resent China having the right to apply certain machinery to it. And in any event, he did not think China would be very powerful at the end of the war. He suggested as a possible alternative, the creation of a European or a Far Eastern Committee and a European or a Worldwide organization. He said that in the European Commission there would be the United States, Great Britain, the Soviet Union and possibly one other European state.

The President said that the idea just expressed by Marshal Stalin was somewhat similar to Mr. Churchill's idea of a Regional Committee, one for Europe, one for the Far East, and one for the Americas. Mr. Churchill had also suggested that the United States be a member of the European Commission, but he doubted if the United States Congress would agree to the United States' participation in an exclusively European Committee which might be able to force the dispatch of American troops to Europe.

The President added that it would take a terrible crisis such as at present before Congress would ever agree to that step.

Marshal Stalin pointed out that the world organization suggested by the President, and in particular the Four Policemen, might also require the sending of American troops to Europe.

The President pointed out that he had only envisaged the sending of American planes and ships to Europe, and that England and the Soviet Union would have to handle the land armies in the event of any future threat to the peace. He went on to say that if the Japanese had not attacked the United States he doubted very much if it would have been possible to send any American forces to Europe. The President added that he saw two methods of dealing with possible threats to the peace. In one case if the threat arose from a revolution or developments in a small country, it might be possible to apply the quarantine method, closing the frontiers of the countries in question and imposing embargoes. In the second case, if the threat was more serious, the four powers, acting as policemen, would send an ultimatum to the nation in question and if refused, [it] would result in the immediate bombardment and possible invasion of that country. . . .

Marshal Stalin then stated he still was dubious about the question of Chinese participation.

The President replied that he had insisted on the participation of China in the 4 Power Declaration at Moscow not because he did not realize the weakness of China at present, but he was thinking farther into the future and that after all China was a nation of 400 million people, and it was better to have them as friends rather than as a potential source of trouble.

The President, reverting to Marshal Stalin's statements as to the ease of converting factories, said that a strong and effective world organization of the 4 Powers could move swiftly when the first signs arose of the beginning of the conversion of such factories for warlike purposes.

Marshal Stalin replied that the Germans had shown great ability to conceal such beginnings.

The President accepted Marshal Stalin's remark. He again expressed his agreement with Marshal Stalin that strategic positions in the world should be at the disposal of some world organization to prevent a revival of German and Japanese aggression.

The Churchill-Stalin Percentage Deal, 1944

The moment was apt for business, so I said, "Let us settle about our affairs in the Balkans. Your armies are in Rumania and Bulgaria. We have inter-

From *Triumph and Tragedy* by Winston S. Churchill. Copyright 1953 by Houghton Mifflin Company. Copyright © renewed 1981 by the Honourable Lady Sarah Audley and the Honourable Lady Soames. Reprinted by permission of Houghton Mifflin Company.

ests, missions, and agents there. Don't let us get at cross-purposes in small ways. So far as Britain and Russia are concerned, how would it do for you to have ninety per cent predominance in Rumania, for us to have ninety per cent of the say in Greece, and go fifty-fifty about Yugoslavia?" While this was being translated I wrote out on a half-sheet of paper:

Rumania	
Russia	90%
The others	10%
Greece	
Great Britain	90%
(in accord with U.S.A.)	
Russia	10%
Yugoslavia	50-50%
Hungary	50-50%
Bulgaria	
Russia	75%
The others	25%

I pushed this across to Stalin, who had by then heard the translation. There was a slight pause. Then he took his blue pencil and made a large tick upon it, and passed it back to us. It was all settled in no more time than it takes to set down.

Of course we had long and anxiously considered our point, and were only dealing with immediate war-time arrangements. All larger questions were reserved on both sides for what we then hoped would be a peace table when the war was won.

After this there was a long silence. The pencilled paper lay in the centre of the table. At length I said, "Might it not be thought rather cynical if it seemed we had disposed of these issues, so fateful to millions of people, in such an offhand manner? Let us burn the paper." "No, you keep it," said Stalin.

The Yalta Protocol of Proceedings, 1945

The Crimea Conference of the Heads of the Governments of the United States of America, the United Kingdom, and the Union of Soviet Socialist Republics which took place from February 4th to 11th came to the following conclusions:

I. World Organization

It was decided:

1. that a United Nations Conference on the proposed world organization should be summoned for Wednesday, 25th April, 1945, and should be held in the United States of America.

2. the Nations to be invited to this Conference should be:

a. the United Nations as they existed on the 8th February, 1945; and

b. such of the Associated Nations as have declared war on the common enemy by 1st March, 1945. (For this purpose by the term "Associated Nations" was meant the eight Associated Nations and Turkey). When the Conference on World Organization is held, the delegates of the United Kingdom and United States of America will support a proposal to admit to original membership two Soviet Socialist Republics, i.e. the Ukraine and White Russia.

3. that the United States Government on behalf of the Three Powers should consult the Government of China and the French Provisional Government in regard to decisions taken at the present Conference concerning the proposed World Organization.

4. that the text of the invitation to be issued to all the nations which would take part in the United Nations Conference should be as follows:

Invitation

The Government of the United States of America, on behalf of itself and of the Governments of the United Kingdom, the Union of Soviet Socialist Republics, and the Republic of China and the Provisional Government of the French Republic, invite the Government of ——— to send representatives to a Conference of the United Nations to be held on 25th April, 1945, or soon thereafter, at San Francisco in the United States of America to prepare a Charter for a General International Organization for the maintenance of international peace and security.

The above named governments suggest that the Conference consider as affording a basis for such a Charter the Proposals for the Establishment of a General International Organization, which were made public last October as a result of the Dumbarton Oaks Conference, and which have now been supplemented by the following provisions for Section C of Chapter VI:

"C. Voting

"1. Each member of the Security Council should have one vote.

"2. Decisions of the Security Council on procedural matters should be made by an affirmative vote of seven members.

"3. Decisions of the Security Council on all other matters should be made by an affirmative vote of seven members including the concurring votes of the permanent members; provided that, in decisions under Chapter VIII, Section A and under the second sentence of paragraph 1 of Chapter VIII, Section C, a party to a dispute should abstain from voting."

Further information as to arrangements will be transmitted subsequently.

In the event that the Government of ——— desires in advance of the Conference to present views or comments concerning the proposals, the Government of the United States of America will be pleased to transmit such views and comments to the other participating Governments.

Territorial Trusteeship. It was agreed that the five Nations which will have permanent seats on the Security Council should consult each other prior to the United Nations Conference on the question of territorial trusteeship.

The acceptance of this recommendation is subject to its being made clear that territorial trusteeship will only apply to (a) existing mandates of the League of Nations; (b) territories detached from the enemy as a result of the present war;

(c) any other territory which might voluntarily be placed under trusteeship; and (d) no discussion of actual territories is contemplated at the forthcoming United Nations Conference or in the preliminary consultations, and it will be a matter for subsequent agreement which territories within the above categories will be placed under trusteeship.

II. Declaration on Liberated Europe

The following declaration has been approved:

The Premier of the Union of Soviet Socialist Republics, the Prime Minister of the United Kingdom and the President of the United States of America have consulted with each other in the common interests of the peoples of their countries and those of liberated Europe. They jointly declare their mutual agreement to concert during the temporary period of instability in liberated Europe the policies of their three governments in assisting the peoples of the former Axis satellite states of Europe to solve by democratic means their pressing political and economic problems.

The establishment of order in Europe and the rebuilding of national economic life must be achieved by processes which will enable the liberated peoples to destroy the last vestiges of Nazism and Fascism and to create democratic institutions of their own choice. This is a principle of the Atlantic Charter— the right of all peoples to choose the form of government under which they will live—the restoration of sovereign rights and self-government to those peoples who have been forcibly deprived of them by the aggressor nations.

To foster the conditions in which the liberated peoples may exercise these rights, the three governments will jointly assist the people in any European liberated state or former Axis satellite state in Europe where in their judgment conditions require (a) to establish conditions of internal peace; (b) to carry out emergency measures for the relief of distressed peoples; (c) to form interim governmental authorities broadly representative of all democratic elements in the population and pledged to the earliest possible establishment through free elections of governments responsive to the will of the people; and (d) to facilitate where necessary the holding of such elections.

The three governments will consult the other United Nations and provisional authorities or other governments in Europe when matters of direct interest to them are under consideration.

When, in the opinion of the three governments, conditions in any European liberated state or any former Axis satellite state in Europe make such action necessary, they will immediately consult together on the measures necessary to discharge the joint responsibilities set forth in this declaration.

By this declaration we reaffirm our faith in the principles of the Atlantic Charter, our pledges in the Declaration by the United Nations, and our determination to build in cooperation with other peace-loving nations world order under law, dedicated to peace, security, freedom and general well-being of all mankind.

In issuing this declaration, the Three Powers express the hope that the Provisional Government of the French Republic may be associated with them in the procedure suggested.

III. Dismemberment of Germany

It was agreed that Article 12 (a) of the Surrender Terms for Germany should be amended to read as follows:

> The United Kingdom, the United States of America and the Union of Soviet Socialist Republics shall possess supreme authority with respect to Germany. In the exercise of such authority they will take such steps, including the complete disarmament, demilitarization and dismemberment of Germany as they deem requisite for future peace and security.

The study of the procedure for the dismemberment of Germany was referred to a Committee, consisting of Mr. Eden (Chairman), Mr. Winant and Mr. Gousev. This body would consider the desirability of associating with it a French representative.

IV. Zone of Occupation for the French and Control Council for Germany

It was agreed that a zone in Germany, to be occupied by the French Forces, should be allocated to France. This zone would be formed out of the British and American zones and its extent would be settled by the British and Americans in consultation with the French Provisional Government.

It was also agreed that the French Provisional Government should be invited to become a member of the Allied Control Council of Germany.

V. Reparation

The heads of the three governments agreed as follows:

1. Germany must pay in kind for the losses caused by her to the Allied nations in the course of the war. Reparations are to be received in the first instance by those countries which have borne the main burden of the war, have suffered the heaviest losses and have organized victory over the enemy.

2. Reparation in kind to be exacted from Germany in three following forms:

   a. Removals within 2 years from the surrender of Germany or the cessation of organized resistance from the national wealth of Germany located on the territory of Germany herself as well as outside her territory (equipment, machine-tools, ships, rolling stock, German investments abroad, shares of industrial, transport and other enterprises in Germany etc.), these removals to be carried out chiefly for purpose of destroying the war potential of Germany.

   b. Annual deliveries of goods from current production for a period to be fixed.

   c. Use of German labor.

3. For the working out on the above principles of a detailed plan for exaction of reparation from Germany an Allied Reparation Commission will be set up in Moscow. It will consist of three representatives—one from the Union of

Soviet Socialist Republics, one from the United Kingdom and one from the United States of America.

4. With regard to the fixing of the total sum of the reparation as well as the distribution of it among the countries which suffered from the German aggression the Soviet and American delegations agreed as follows:

> The Moscow Reparation Commission should take in its initial studies as a basis for discussion the suggestion of the Soviet Government that the total sum of the reparation in accordance with the points (a) and (b) of the paragraph 2 should be 20 billion dollars and that 50% of it should go to the Union of Soviet Socialist Republics.

The British delegation was of the opinion that pending consideration of the reparation question by the Moscow Reparation Commission no figures of reparation should be mentioned.

The above Soviet-American proposal has been passed to the Moscow Reparation Commission as one of the proposals to be considered by the Commission.

VI. Major War Criminals

The Conference agreed that the question of the major war criminals should be the subject of enquiry by the three Foreign Secretaries for report in due course after the close of the Conference.

VII. Poland

The following Declaration on Poland was agreed by the Conference:

> A new situation has been created in Poland as a result of her complete liberation by the Red Army. This calls for the establishment of a Polish Provisional Government which can be more broadly based than was possible before the recent liberation of Western part of Poland. The Provisional Government which is now functioning in Poland should therefore be recognized on a broader democratic basis with the inclusion of democratic leaders from Poland itself and from Poles abroad. This new Government should then be called the Polish Provisional Government of National Unity.
>
> M. Molotov, Mr. Harriman and Sir. A. Clark Kerr are authorized as a commission to consult in the first instance in Moscow with members of the present Provisional Government and with other Polish democratic leaders from within Poland and from abroad, with a view to the reorganization of the present Government along the above lines. This Polish Provisional Government of National Unity shall be pledged to the holding of free and unfettered elections as soon as possible on the basis of universal suffrage and secret ballot. In these elections all democratic and anti-Nazi parties shall have the right to take part and to put forward candidates.
>
> When a Polish Provisional Government of National Unity has been properly formed in conformity with the above, the Government of the U.S.S.R., which now maintains diplomatic relations with the present Provisional Government of Poland, and the Government of the United Kingdom and the Government

of the United States of America will establish diplomatic relations with the new Polish Provisional Government of National Unity, and will exchange Ambassadors by whose reports the respective Governments will be kept informed about the situation in Poland.

The three Heads of Government consider that the Eastern frontier of Poland should follow the Curzon Line with digressions from it in some regions of five to eight kilometers in favor of Poland. They recognize that Poland must receive substantial accession of territory in the North and West. They feel that the opinion of the new Polish Provisional Government of National Unity should be sought in due course on the extent of these accessions and that the final delimitation of the Western frontier of Poland should therefore await the Peace Conference.

[Following this declaration, but omitted here, are brief statements on Yugoslavia, the Italo-Yugoslav frontier and Italo-Austrian frontier, Yugoslav-Bulgarian relations, Southeastern Europe, Iran, meetings of the three Foreign Secretaries, and the Montreux Convention and the Straits.]

Agreement on Soviet Entry into the War Against Japan, 1945

The leaders of the three Great Powers—the Soviet Union, the United States of America and Great Britain—have agreed that in two or three months after Germany has surrendered and the war in Europe has terminated the Soviet Union shall enter into the war against Japan on the side of the Allies on condition that:

1. The *status quo* in Outer-Mongolia (The Mongolian People's Republic) shall be preserved;
2. The former rights of Russia violated by the treacherous attack of Japan in 1904 shall be restored, viz:

    a. the southern part of Sakhalin as well as all the islands adjacent to it shall be returned to the Soviet Union,

    b. the commercial port of Dairen shall be internationalized, the preeminent interests of the Soviet Union in this port being safeguarded and the lease of Port Arthur as a naval base of the USSR restored,

    c. the Chinese-Eastern Railroad and the South-Manchurian Railroad which provides an outlet to Dairen shall be jointly operated by the establishment of a joint Soviet-Chinese Company it being understood that the preeminent interests of the Soviet Union shall be safeguarded and that China shall retain full sovereignty in Manchuria;
3. The Kuril islands shall be handed over to the Soviet Union.

It is understood, that the agreement concerning Outer-Mongolia and the ports and railroads referred to above will require concurrence of Generalissimo Chiang Kai-Shek. The President will take measures in order to obtain this concurrence on advice from Marshal Stalin.

The Heads of the three Great Powers have agreed that these claims of the Soviet Union shall be unquestionably fulfilled after Japan has been defeated.

For its part the Soviet Union expresses its readiness to conclude with the National Government of China a pact of friendship and alliance between the USSR and China in order to render assistance to China with its armed forces for the purpose of liberating China from the Japanese yoke.

Roosevelt's Anger with Stalin, 1945

I have received with astonishment your message of April 3 containing an allegation that arrangements which were made between Field Marshals Alexander and Kesselring at Berne "permitted the Anglo-American troops to advance to the East and the Anglo-Americans promised in return to ease for the Germans the peace terms."

In my previous messages to you in regard to the attempts made in Berne to arrange a conference to discuss a surrender of the German army in Italy I have told you that: (1) No negotiations were held in Berne, (2) The meeting had no political implications whatever, (3) In any surrender of the enemy army in Italy there would be no violation of our agreed principle of unconditional surrender, (4) Soviet officers would be welcomed at any meeting that might be arranged to discuss surrender.

For the advantage of our common war effort against Germany, which today gives excellent promise of an early success in a disintegration of the German armies, I must continue to assume that you have the same high confidence in my truthfulness and reliability that I have always had in yours.

I have also a full appreciation of the effect your gallant army has had in making possible a crossing of the Rhine by the forces under General Eisenhower and the effect that your forces will have hereafter on the eventual collapse of the German resistance to our combined attacks.

I have complete confidence in General Eisenhower and know that he certainly would inform me before entering into any agreement with the Germans. He is instructed to demand and will demand unconditional surrender of enemy troops that may be defeated on his front. Our advances on the Western Front are due to military action. Their speed has been attributable mainly to the terrific impact of our air power resulting in destruction of German communications, and to the fact that Eisenhower was able to cripple the bulk of the German forces on the Western Front while they were still west of the Rhine.

I am certain that there were no negotiations in Berne at any time and I feel that your information to that effect must have come from German sources which have made persistent efforts to create dissension between us in order to escape in some measure responsibility for their war crimes. If that was Wolff's purpose in Berne, your message proves that he has had some success.

With a confidence in your belief in my personal reliability and in my determination to bring about, together with you, an unconditional surrender of the Nazis, it is astonishing that a belief seems to have reached the Soviet Government that I have entered into an agreement with the enemy without first obtaining your full agreement.

Finally I would say this, it would be one of the great tragedies of history if at the very moment of the victory, now within our grasp, such distrust, such lack of faith should prejudice the entire undertaking after the colossal losses of life, material and treasure involved.

Frankly I cannot avoid a feeling of bitter resentment toward your informers, whoever they are, for such vile misrepresentations of my actions or those of my trusted subordinates.

Roosevelt's Last Letter to Churchill, 1945

I would minimize the general Soviet problem as much as possible because these problems, in one form or another, seem to arise every day and most of them straighten out as in the case of the Berne meeting.

We must be firm, however, and our course thus far is correct.

General Dwight D. Eisenhower on Beating the Russians to Berlin in 1945, 1949

QUESTION: General, the general feeling is that if our army had marched into Berlin and if General Patton's army had occupied Prague, the picture in the post-war period might have been different.

May I ask you whether, in your opinion, had our political leaders taken for granted at face value the declarations of Joseph Stalin and the others of what their ultimate objectives in the world were, might they not have been restrained from interfering with you in going through your regular military procedure of taking as much as our armies might take, and if it had not been interfered with, don't you think the post-war picture might have been different?

GENERAL EISENHOWER: I must, sir, make one thing clear: Your question seems to imply that the decision not to march into Berlin was a political decision. On the contrary, there is only one person in the world responsible for that decision. That was I. There was no one who interfered with me in the slightest way.

Until the day I die, there is one thing that I will testify to in favor of or on the side of Mr. Roosevelt's skill in handling a country at war. When he put his men into the field, he did not interfere with them as long as he left them there.

The War Department, the President, the Chief of Staff, the support from them was absolutely unique, almost, in the annals of warfare.

Now, I will give you a short outline of the situation, and then I will make you this amateur judge I was telling about a while ago, and let us see whether you would have tried to capture Berlin.

When the final campaign plan was made up, it was before we had completed our crossings of the Rhine, or just about at the time we were crossing. We were lying 300 miles from Berlin.

The Russians had attacked on January 12th, and that attack, you will recall, had carried them clear across the Oder. They had a bridgehead west of the Oder, and strong forces within thirty miles of Berlin. They told us that coincident with our leaping forward from the Rhine they were ready to attack again. So I sent around to Moscow the details of my plan. I saw no possible chance of going 300 miles, crossing the Elbe at the end of 250 miles, a big river, getting in and surrounding Berlin, with the Russians having to attack from thirty miles off.

Now, another great problem arose: When two friendly forces are moving toward each other directly to crush like a nutcracker an enemy in between, you get a very serious problem, far more serious than it was in the days of Napoleon, because the danger zone, or the risk zone, you might say, in Napoleon's time was limited by the length of a musket shot or a cannon that could shoot 800 yards. Today your fighter bombers range out 200 miles ahead of you. They are whipping and knocking down everything they see in your path.

As these two friendly forces come together, and, remember, your big guns shoot twenty-five miles, as you come toward each other the danger of lunging into a battle between friends is very, very great, and that is multiplied when you realize that you cannot speak the other's language at all. All you can do is switch your radio on to talk to each other and tell them where to stop and what to do, "And, for goodness' sake, Joe, stop shooting. This is Ike!"

So you have to work out extremely simple, easily-understood methods of recognition in what you are going to do.

Now, in eastern Germany, I figured we could go as far as the Elbe, the great Elbe lying along there. There was a natural line for us to go up to and line up against, from all of our calculations, which would be just about the place we would meet the Russians, and then the Elbe was extended on into western Czechoslovakia, with the great mountains, so that looked like a perfect line, and with us having to march 275 miles to the other fellow's forty-five, it looked like a good deal to us.

And then, remember this, although it was not allowed to influence the military decision: The political heads of our government had already agreed that our line of occupation would be way back, starting at the north at Denmark, with Linz on the south, so what good would it have done us to capture Berlin? There might have been a bit of prestige, but we had to leave right away and go back 150 miles anyway. The American forces had to retreat 125 miles to get into the zone already decided by the European Advisory Commission, approved by our leaders at Yalta, so where would there have been any difference in the post-war situation?

We had to be close enough to the Russian general there so we could have told him where we were and, at the same time, go forward without risk. We did, as far as Pilsen, and then we said, "We are in Pilsen; shall we come any further? Where are you?" He said, "No. We are just outside of Prague and about to enter," so we did not go, but, remember, in those days we were certainly trying to trust people that we hoped were our friends.

But the thing is, you see, it is a terrific problem and you have to keep your men from getting killed through your own blunders and errors, and that is what we were trying to do, work out a plan.

ESSAYS

In his essay on Allied diplomacy, John Lewis Gaddis of Ohio University studies Soviet-American problems, the second front controversy, Soviet intentions, and the difficulties Roosevelt faced in trying to thwart the expansion of Soviet power. Roosevelt was a realist, but he failed to prepare the American people for the postwar world. The second essay, written in 1950 by *New York Times* military correspondent Hanson W. Baldwin, presents a common indictment of Roosevelt's diplomacy. He thinks Roosevelt blundered by being too trusting of the Russians and too lax in exercising American power, especially as it related to the future status of Eastern Europe. Stephen E. Ambrose of the University of New Orleans addresses one of Baldwin's specific points: the capture of Berlin. Ambrose, a specialist on Dwight D. Eisenhower, argues that the decision about Berlin was wisely made on necessary military grounds and that a different decision might have produced a sharp break with Russia.

Roosevelt, Realism, and the Russians

JOHN LEWIS GADDIS

Churchill claims to have worried that, in view of all that had transpired between 1939 and 1941, the Russians might be shy about requesting help from the West in their fight against Hitler. Such proved not to be the case. As early as July 1941, Stalin asked the British, who were in no position to comply, to invade northern France. Later that month, he told Harry Hopkins that he would welcome American troops, under American command, anywhere on the Russian front. In September, he argued that Churchill could "without risk" send "twenty-five or thirty" British divisions to Archangel or the Caucasus—this at a time when London was straining shipping capabilities to the limit just to put two additional divisions into the Middle East. "By her passive attitude Britain is helping the Nazis," Stalin complained to the Soviet ambassador in London: "Do the British realise this? I think they do. What is it then that they want? It seems they want us to be weakened."

From *Russia, The Soviet Union, and the United States: An Interpretive History,* by John Lewis Gaddis. Copyright © 1978 by John Wiley & Sons. Reprinted by permission of John Wiley & Sons, Inc.

This was an unjust accusation, but it did reflect the frustrations the Russians felt over a fundamental strategic fact of life in World War II: neither Great Britain nor the United States had come under direct ground attack. Both enjoyed, as a result, a certain flexibility in deciding how and when to strike back at the enemy. For the Russians, there could be no such choice: reeling from invasion on a broad front, their only option, short of capitulation, was all-out resistance. Obtaining relief from this pressure, whether through the dispatch of American and British troops to the Soviet Union or the creation of a second front against the Germans in Europe, accordingly became Stalin's chief diplomatic priority.

Roosevelt was not, at first, averse to creating an early second front. His military advisers, trained in the tradition of striking the enemy in the most direct manner and concerned about the strategic implications of a Soviet defeat, pushed strongly for an attack across the English Channel as soon as possible. Roosevelt, too, favored such an operation, partly out of a desire to stave off growing pressures inside the United States for an all-out offensive against Japan, partly out of fear that delay in confronting the Germans might lead Stalin to seek a separate peace, partly as an inducement to the Soviet leader to postpone discussion of postwar territorial claims in Europe, which Roosevelt feared might disrupt the common war effort. (That Stalin would not have been thinking about postwar territorial claims had he not expected to win does not seem to have occurred to the president, whose ability to see the interconnection of military and diplomatic problems was sometimes limited.) Accordingly, in June 1942, Roosevelt publicly promised Soviet Foreign Minister Molotov that a second front would be established somewhere in Europe before the end of the year.

In the end, however, Roosevelt had to break this promise. The slow pace of American mobilization and training ensured that any 1942 attack would be primarily a British operation, and Churchill, haunted by memories of World War I trench warfare, was not inclined to launch costly attacks to relieve an ally whose concern over Britain's plight between 1939 and 1941 had been minimal. And even if the British had been willing, it would not have been possible in 1942 to accumulate sufficient transports to launch an invasion of Europe with any prospect of success. As a result, Roosevelt and Churchill agreed on a substitute plan involving joint Anglo-American landings in Vichy-occupied North Africa in November 1942. This operation met Roosevelt's desire to get American troops into action against the Germans before the end of the year, but it did little to take pressure off the Red Army. Delays in clearing the Germans out of Africa in turn made it impossible to launch a cross-Channel attack in 1943—the invasion of Italy, and that state's forced withdrawal from the Axis coalition, was, for the Russians, small comfort. The true second front would not come until June 1944, a year and a half later than Roosevelt had promised.

The Russians believed at the time, and have charged since, that the delay in constituting the second front was deliberate. Roosevelt and Churchill, the argument runs, resolved to let the Soviet Union bear the brunt of the fighting, leaving the British and Americans to step in at the last moment to shape the peace settlement. There can be no doubt that it was the Russians who, as Churchill put it, "tore the guts" out of the German army. Total German losses, including killed, wounded, and missing, came to over six million on the eastern front, as compared to just over one million in Western Europe and the Mediterranean. Throughout most of the war the Red Army was confronting, on the eastern front, more than 200 enemy divisions. Prior to the Normandy landings in June 1944, the British and Americans rarely faced more than 10 German divisions at any one time. A recent Soviet account has noted pointedly but accurately that for every American killed in the war against the Axis, fifty Russians died.

It is frequently forgotten, though, that the British and the Americans had their own second front problem in the Far East, where the Soviet Union had refrained from declaring war on the Japanese. Roosevelt and Churchill appreciated the Russians' unwillingness to take on an additional enemy at a time when the German army was just outside Moscow. At no point did they ask Stalin to enter the Far Eastern war until after Germany's defeat. But requirements of the war against Japan did significantly restrict the United States' ability to amass the troops and equipment—particularly landing craft —necessary to launch an early cross-Channel attack in Europe. The delayed second front was, thus, part of the price the Russians paid for neutrality in the Far East.

It is also not often taken into account what impact the recruitment of additional manpower would have had on American war production, much of which went to Great Britain and the Soviet Union in the form of Lend-Lease. Some $43.6 billion, or 14% of total American defense expenditures in World War II, was allocated for Lend-Lease; of this, approximately $11 billion, or 3.5% of total expenditures, went to the Soviet Union. As it was, the United States mobilized almost as high a percentage of its population as did the USSR (12% versus 13%); its factories produced 35% of all the combat munitions used against Germany and its allies and 85% of those used against the Japanese. The United States might have been able to collect enough men in Britain in 1943 to launch a second front, but only by taking pressure off Japan in the Far East (thereby increasing the Soviet Union's security problems in that part of the world) and cutting back on the industrial production which played such a vital role in shaping the outcome of the war.

Anglo-American reluctance to incur casualties also worked to delay the second front. Churchill's preoccupation with this matter has been well documented; less well known is the extent to which Roosevelt shared this concern. The Russians, denied the luxury of deciding how to use their manpower, naturally resented this situation. But the fact that the British and Americans refused to launch suicide attacks to take pressure off the Red Army does not necessarily imply a determination on their part to deny Stalin the legitimate fruits of victory. Had such been their intent, the best strategy would have been to invade Europe at once regardless of casualties, so as to keep the Russians out of as much of it as possible. Rather, Anglo-American strategy reflected the rational balancing of objectives and resources which any wise statesman will engage in, *if he has the choice*. Stalin, in part as a result of his own bungling diplomacy between 1939 and 1941, was simply unfortunate enough not to have had that choice.

Anglo-American military strategy was not without its price, though. The caution Roosevelt and Churchill demonstrated in planning military operations gave the Russians a credible basis for claiming that, having borne a disproportionate share of the costs of fighting the war, they should in turn enjoy disproportionate influence in determining the postwar settlement. There is, to be sure, nothing automatic about the proposition that investments in blood necessarily produce equivalent dividends in political influence; if anything, the World War I experience had demonstrated precisely the opposite. Stalin's great fear was that Roosevelt and Churchill might try to repeat Wilson's performance in that earlier conflict—let the major belligerents bleed each other white, then demand, at a decisive moment, the right to shape the peace settlement. But for a variety of reasons, London and Washington failed to take advantage of their strategic flexibility to secure for themselves a decisive role at the peace table. Much to his surprise, Stalin found himself being petitioned to grant concessions to the West, rather than the other way around.

Stalin probably had no precise blueprint for the kind of settlement he wanted, but he did have a set of operating assumptions which had consistently governed his foreign policy. These included the convictions: (1) that the outside world would, for the foreseeable future, remain hostile to the Soviet Union; (2) that, despite this circumstance, the security of the USSR should not be risked to promote world revolution; (3) that such security could best be obtained (a) by taking advantage of conflicts between potential adversaries to keep them divided, and (b) by dominating spheres of influence along Russia's periphery, in order to place as much controlled territory between the Soviet Union and its enemies as possible. These principles had governed Stalin's diplomacy during his abortive period of collaboration with Hitler; given the opportunity, he could be expected to apply them as well in his dealings with his Western allies.

The Soviet leader had sought as early as December 1941 to have the British confirm the territorial gains Russia had made from the Nazi-Soviet Pact—eastern Poland, the Baltic states, and parts of Finland and Rumania. "All we ask for," he told Anthony Eden, "is to restore our country to its former frontiers." Stalin advanced these claims cautiously, however, and when the Americans objected, agreed not to press them, for fear of destroying chances for an early second front. By 1943, however, Soviet military fortunes had decidedly improved, even without a cross-Channel attack. Gradually Stalin let it be known that he would insist, not just on a return to his 1939–1941 frontiers, but on the installation as well of governments "friendly" to the Soviet Union throughout Eastern Europe and the Balkans. The result promised to be an intrusion of Russian power into Europe unprecedented since the days of Alexander I.

Such a development would pose great problems for Britain and the United States, whose policies, both in World Wars I and II, had been based on the proposition that a balance of power on the European continent was crucial to their security. Complicating the issue was the fact that Roosevelt had chosen to justify American entry into the war, not solely in terms of the considerations of power politics which weighed most heavily in his own mind, but in idealistic terms as well. Thus the president, with Churchill, had pledged himself in the Atlantic Charter to oppose "territorial changes that do not accord with the freely expressed wishes of the peoples concerned," and to seek to have "sovereign rights and self government restored to those who have been forcibly deprived of them." Whether on grounds of *realpolitik* or Wilsonian ideals, therefore, the massive expansion of Soviet power in Europe was not a prospect Anglo-American leaders could view with equanimity.

Options for avoiding this prospect, however, were decidedly limited. One would have been to negotiate a separate peace with Germany before the Soviet Union had moved into a position of dominance. Certainly Stalin feared this possibility—his suspicious mind could never completely free itself from the fear that his capitalist allies might make common cause with his capitalist foes. In fact, though, such an arrangement was never seriously considered. Roosevelt and Churchill stuck strictly to the view that Hitler was more dangerous than Stalin, and even if they had not, public opinion in neither Britain nor the United States would have tolerated dealings with the Germans. The furor set off by General Dwight Eisenhower's relatively innocent discussions with Admiral Darlan of Vichy France in November 1942, gives some clue to what the reaction would have been had Roosevelt and Churchill tried to deal with the Germans at Soviet expense.

Furthermore, there was always the danger that the Russians might play the same game. Not having public opinion to worry about, Stalin could have carried off such an arrangement far more easily than could his Western colleagues, as indeed his 1939 actions had demonstrated. In an effort to guard against this possibility and to reassure public opinion, Roosevelt and Churchill proclaimed the doctrine of unconditional surrender at Casablanca in January 1943. Despite this, the evidence indicates that Stalin did authorize tentative contacts with the Germans the following summer, a low point in Russian relations with the West because of the delay in creating the second front. It was his own increasingly frequent military successes, not his allies' assurances, which kept him from pursuing these initiatives.

Another way of avoiding the expansion of Soviet power into central Europe would have been to organize military operations in such a way as to interpose British and American forces between the Russians and the Germans. An Anglo-American invasion of the Balkans was the most frequently mentioned possibility, but one which carried with it overwhelming difficulties. Logistical and topographical obstacles were so great there could be no assurance of reaching Germany ahead of the Russians. And, although Stalin from time to time suggested such a plan, it seems unlikely that he would have welcomed large-scale Western military operations in the Balkans, an area he regarded as within his postwar sphere of influence. Such an operation also would have encountered stiff opposition from the American military, already impatient with Churchill's "indirect" strategy of attrition, suspicious of him (unjustly, as it turned out) for seeking to substitute in place of the cross-Channel attack operations which would promote British political objectives in the eastern Mediterranean.

Still another way of attempting to ensure Russian postwar cooperation might have been to impose political conditions on the Lend-Lease aid which the United States was sending, in increasing quantities, to the USSR. By the spring of 1943, several of Roosevelt's top advisers were recommending such a course of action. But there were problems with this strategy too. Although aid to Russia did speed military operations against the Germans, the tide of battle on the eastern front had largely been reversed before aid had begun to arrive in quantity. The Russians at no point were so dependent on Lend-Lease that they would have been willing to compromise, in any significant way, their postwar plans. Then, too, even if promises had been made, there was no way of ensuring that the Russians would keep them, as American officials had learned to their dismay during the years following the Roosevelt-Litvinov agreements of 1933.

Other problems as well inhibited direct opposition to Stalin's program. Washington officials attached great importance to securing Soviet participation in the war against Japan, which projections indicated would last at least a year and a half after Germany's defeat and would cost at least as many casualties. Similarly, Moscow's cooperation was deemed essential in the organization of the United Nations, which many Americans expected to be the major instrument for maintaining world order after the war. It is significant that when Ambassador Harriman proposed raising the question of Poland at the Moscow Foreign Ministers' Conference in October 1943, Secretary of State Cordell Hull rejected the idea: "I don't want to deal with these piddling little things," he complained. "We must deal with the main issues." As it turned out, the USSR probably would have entered both the Far Eastern war and the United Nations without inducements from the United States, simply because Stalin considered both moves advantageous to the Soviet Union's position as a great power. The Kremlin autocrat was shrewd enough to appear reluctant, though, thereby further limiting his allies' ability to contest his postwar claims.

This complex of considerations convinced Roosevelt that there was no feasible way to employ Anglo-American strategic flexibility to block Soviet expansion. Instead, he concluded that the only way to achieve both military victory and a favorable postwar settlement would be to try to integrate Stalin's war aims with those of his Western allies. This would not be, Roosevelt thought, an impossible task. Proceeding on the assumption that insecurity, not ideology, drove Stalin's expansionism, the president reasoned that if the Soviet dictator's fears could be relieved, his motives for seeking to project influence beyond his borders would disappear and a settlement agreeable to all might be reached. Roosevelt sought to accomplish this end: (1) by ensuring the total destruction of German and Japanese power; (2) by meeting, where possible, Stalin's legitimate security needs in Europe and the Far East; and (3) by seeking to build an atmosphere of mutual trust between the Soviet leader and his Western allies which would assure him that he had nothing to fear.

Unconditional surrender had been part of that strategy; so too had been the president's insistence, over the objections of the State Department, on the postwar partition of Germany. On Eastern Europe, Roosevelt had at first opposed Stalin's proposed boundary changes, on grounds that they would have violated the spirit of the Atlantic Charter. But by the spring of 1943 he had come to the conclusion that the West lacked the means of denying Stalin the gains he wanted, and that his own efforts should be directed toward arranging the best possible compromise. Accordingly, he worked to restore relations between Moscow and the staunchly anti-Soviet Polish government-in-exile, located in London. He also hoped to convince Stalin to hold plebiscites in the Baltic states in order to make their incorporation into the USSR palatable to American and world opinion. But Roosevelt's chief priority was to arrange a personal meeting with the Soviet dictator, in the expectation that the feeling of trust which had come to characterize the Roosevelt-Churchill relationship could be expanded to include Stalin as well. After several delays, occasioned by the president's unsuccessful attempts to exclude Churchill and by Stalin's reluctance to leave Moscow, the Big Three finally agreed to meet in Teheran at the end of November 1943.

The conference was, to all appearances, a great success. Roosevelt and Churchill made the final commitment to Stalin to launch a second front in the spring of 1944, and the Soviet leader promised in turn to enter the war against Japan three months after Germany's surrender. The president also indicated to Stalin that he would not oppose territorial changes in Eastern Europe, although the Russians must not expect public acknowledgment until after the 1944 election. Roosevelt appealed to Stalin to handle Eastern European issues in such a way as not to offend world opinion and urged upon him, without success, the idea of a plebiscite for the Baltic states. Stalin enthusiastically seconded Roosevelt's advocacy of harsh treatment for Germany, though no final agreements were reached on specifics. Most important, the conference took place in the atmosphere of hearty good-fellowship which Roosevelt considered essential if his goal of integrating Stalin's war aims with those of the Western allies was to be achieved.

It seems likely that the Big Three left Teheran with differing ideas of what had been accomplished. To Stalin, the fact that his Anglo-American colleagues had not objected to the Eastern European boundary changes he wanted probably suggested that they viewed the Atlantic Charter as window dressing; Roosevelt and Churchill, he believed, had tacitly recognized the Soviet Union's right to have subservient governments along its borders. After all, the British prime minister himself had proclaimed that in the postwar world the big powers must be satisfied, like rich, happy men. Roosevelt, on the other hand, believed that by demonstrating that he had found Stalin's requests reasonable, he had thereby won the Soviet leader's trust. Stalin, he thought, would not presume upon this relationship to press extreme demands. Provided the Poles could be made to see the futility of their anti-Russian position, there was no reason why free elections could not be held throughout Eastern Europe which would, in turn, produce governments friendly to the Soviet Union.

That there was a considerable gap between these perceptions quickly became apparent, most obviously with regard to Poland. While Roosevelt and Churchill had reluctantly accepted Stalin's position on boundaries, they were not prepared to see the independence of what remained of that country compromised. Britain had gone to war in 1939 on Poland's behalf, and, in the United States, a large and vociferous Polish-American community ensured that any East European settlement would be strictly tested against the principles of the Atlantic Charter. Stalin, however, took advantage of the Red Army's entry onto Polish soil to establish the nucleus of a new government, subservient to the Soviet Union, independent of the Polish government-in-exile in London, unrecognized by either the British or the Americans. George Kennan noted the significance of these developments in his diary on August 1: "The jealous and intolerant eye of the Kremlin can distinguish, in the end, only vassals and enemies; and the neighbors of Russia, if they do not wish to be the one, must reconcile themselves to being the other."

The same day Kennan wrote those lines, the Polish underground organization in Warsaw, knowing that the Red Army was approaching the city and encouraged by Soviet broadcasts to take action, launched an uprising against the Germans. To the horror of Western observers, Stalin refused to order an advance to help the Poles, or to allow British and American planes to land at Soviet airfields after dropping supplies. It is to this day unclear whether Stalin's behavior was based solely on military considerations or was a calculated move to decimate the pro-Western Polish underground. The latter was clearly the effect, however, and from this point many of Roosevelt's advisers came strongly to doubt Soviet willingness to allow anything but satellite governments in Eastern Europe. Kennan himself thought that the time had come to cut off all aid to the Soviet Union until Moscow became more cooperative. Ambassador Harriman was not willing to go that far, but he did warn Washington that "unless we take issue with the present policy there is every indication the Soviet Union will become a world bully wherever their interests are involved."

By this time, problems had developed in other areas as well. Citing the Anglo-American occupation of Italy as a precedent, Stalin refused to allow his allies anything more than a token role in the occupation of Rumania, Bulgaria, and Hungary, into which the Red Army also marched in 1944. Attempts to arrange the exchange of military information for the coming joint effort against Japan produced little fruit, while the Russians insisted on terminating a plan for the shuttle-bombing of Germany, using Ukrainian air bases, after only a few missions. The Russians had, by the fall, expressed reservations about voting procedures in the United Nations; they also persistently refused, despite repeated requests, to distinguish between Lend-Lease aid intended for military purposes and that to be used for postwar reconstruction. Wartime collaboration brought no change in the policies of harassment to which Westerners in Moscow had long been subject. And, finally, Roosevelt and his principal military advisers had evidence, by this time, of a sustained effort by Soviet intelligence to penetrate the security of the top-secret Anglo-American project to develop the atomic bomb.

Roosevelt refused, however, to interpret these events as evidence that his policy of winning Stalin's trust had failed. Himself a realist when it came to international affairs, the president saw little surprising or reprehensible in the Soviet leader's desire to have friendly governments in Eastern Europe. He still nursed the hope that, with Germany's defeat and demilitarization, Stalin's demands would become less severe—such sentiments may well have influenced his brief support for the punitive Morgenthau Plan in the fall of 1944. At the same time, though, as a realist in domestic politics, Roosevelt could not allow Stalin a completely free hand. Eastern Europe had the potential of becoming a major campaign issue in the 1944 election; it might also generate sufficient opposition within the Senate to block American participation in the United Nations. Accordingly, the president tried throughout 1944 to keep the issue as quiet as possible, in the hope of achieving some kind of compromise between the legitimate security interests of the USSR and the principles of the Atlantic Charter.

Roosevelt was not wholly without resources in seeking such a compromise. The president rejected his advisers' recommendation that he impose political conditions on future Lend-Lease aid, but he did make clear his intention not to grant postwar credits to the Russians "until we get what we want." In a reversal from his previous support for the Morgenthau Plan, Roosevelt had also come, by the end of 1944, to accept the State Department's argument that United States and Great Britain should retain as much control as possible over the flow of reparations from Germany to the Soviet Union. He had further decided, by this time, not to inform the Russians of the atomic bomb project, even though he knew they were aware, through espionage, of the program's existence. While the president's motives in making these decisions are not entirely clear, there is reason to believe that he may have anticipated the possibility, at some point in the future, of trading reconstruction aid and information about the bomb for political concessions. His chief resource in winning Stalin's cooperation, however, remained his own belief in his ability to "get through" to the Soviet leader in face-to-face negotiations. To this end, he attached great importance to arranging another meeting of the Big Three, which took place at Yalta, in the Crimea, in February 1945.

Like Teheran, Yalta produced surface conviviality and surface agreements. The Big Three agreed that the Lublin Polish government, which Stalin had recognized the month before, would "be reorganized on a broader democratic basis with the inclusion of democratic leaders from Poland itself and from Poles abroad." Elections for a permanent government, Stalin promised, would be held soon, possibly within a month. Roosevelt, Churchill, and Stalin also signed a "Declaration on Liberated Europe," calling for the creation of governments in Eastern Europe "broadly representative of all democratic elements in the population and pledged to the earliest possible establishment through free elections of governments responsible to the will of the people." No final agreements were reached on Germany, other than to accept, "as a basis for negotiations," a Soviet request for reparations in the amount of $10 billion. In the Far East, Roosevelt and Churchill promised Stalin, in return for his agreement to enter the war against Japan after Germany's defeat, the Kurile Islands, lower Sakhalin, leases at Port Arthur and Dairen, control of the Chinese Eastern and South Manchurian railroads, and recognition of the independence from China of Outer Mongolia.

Contrary to charges made in later years, Roosevelt gave up nothing at Yalta not already under Stalin's actual or potential control. His chief concern was cosmetic: to put the best possible face on a bad situation in order to make palatable to the American people the postwar expansion of Soviet influence. Otherwise, he feared, the gap between the ideals for which the war had been fought and its very realistic outcome would be so great as to render peacetime Soviet-American cooperation impossible. The president relied heavily on Stalin's cooperation in this process: the Soviet leader, he hoped, would be discreet in projecting power beyond his borders, operating behind the facade of democratic procedures wherever possible. Perhaps, in time, Soviet insecurity might decline to the point that illusion might approach reality. Yalta, Roosevelt told the Congress in his final appearance before that body, was not a perfect peace. "But it can be a peace—and it will be a peace—based on the sound and just principles of the Atlantic Charter."

Stalin would not cooperate, however, in conveying even the appearance of action consistent with Western ideals. Within two weeks of signing the Declaration on Liberated Europe, he violated it by forcing a subservient government on Rumania. Tedious negotiations to broaden the Soviet-sponsored government of Poland got nowhere. In March, reports began reaching Washington that the Russians were mistreating American prisoners-of-war liberated from the Germans; that same month, Moscow announced that Foreign Minister Molotov would be too busy to attend the San Francisco Conference on the organization of the United Nations. "Our gallant allies," Ambassador Harriman's daughter noted in a letter from Moscow, "are being most bastard-like." Worst of all, Stalin chose to interpret an abortive Anglo-American effort to arrange the surrender of German forces in Italy as a plot, coordinated with Berlin, to keep the Red Army out of Central Europe. "I cannot avoid a feeling of bitter resentment," Roosevelt fumed, "toward your informers, whoever they are, for such vile misrepresentations of my actions and those of my trusted subordinates."

There are indications that Roosevelt was reassessing his policy toward the Soviet Union at the time of his death. "Averell [Harriman] is right," he told a friend on March 23. "We can't do business with Stalin. He has broken every one of the promises he made at Yalta." Roosevelt remained firm in his refusal to consider a postwar loan until Russian intentions had become clearer, nor did he object when Congress that month prohibited the use of Lend-Lease for reconstruction purposes. Nor did the president alter his policy of withholding information about the atomic bomb. "We must not permit anybody to entertain a false impression that we are afraid," he wrote to Churchill on April 6. "Our armies will in a very few days be in a position that will permit us to become 'tougher' than has heretofore appeared advantageous to the war effort."

None of this means that Roosevelt had abandoned his hope of cooperating with the Russians to build a new postwar order. "I would minimize the general Soviet problem as much as possible," he observed in his last cable to Churchill, "because these problems, in one form or another, seem to arise every day and most of them straighten out." It does seem likely, however, that events since Yalta had convinced Roosevelt of the futility of trying to win Stalin's trust and of the need to place dealings with the Russians henceforth on the strict *quid-pro-quo* basis that Harriman and the other Soviet specialists had been recommending for more than a year.

Critics would charge, in retrospect, that Roosevelt had been naive to the point of irresponsibility by persisting in the belief that he could win Stalin's trust through personal cordiality, political appeasement, and unconditional aid. In fact, however, his approach was more realistic than that. A policy which withheld the second front for two years, tied reconstruction aid to political concessions, and rejected the sharing of atomic bomb information can hardly be regarded as one of timid acquiescence. When Roosevelt did make concessions, it was generally in areas where Anglo-American power could not feasibly be brought to bear to deny the Russians what they wanted. The president saw more clearly than most observers that insecurity, not world revolutionary ambitions, drove Soviet expansionism; he was also correct in his perception that only Stalin was in a position to modify the tradition of institutionalized suspicion which separated Russia from the West.

Roosevelt's mistakes, it would appear, were three: (1) He underestimated the depth of Stalin's paranoia—not until after Yalta did he see that the Soviet dictator's distrust of his allies had been just as great as his fear of the Germans. (2) He overestimated the intensity of American isolationism, thus discounting the United States' capacity to project political influence in the postwar world—it is significant that he told Stalin at Yalta that public opinion would not tolerate the retention of American troops overseas for more than two years after the war. (3) He failed, whether because of want of insight or energy, to use his own considerable persuasive powers to prepare the American people for the kind of realistic postwar settlement his own instincts told him would be inevitable. It was Roosevelt's fate to live just long enough to see that these mistakes had been made; devising strategies to correct them would be up to his diligent but ill-informed and inexperienced successor.

America's Wartime Blunders

HANSON W. BALDWIN

In February, 1945, at Yalta and on June 6, 1944, the date of the Allied invasion of Normandy, it might be said that we lost the peace. American political and strategic mistakes during the war possibly lengthened it, certainly made it more difficult, and are largely responsible for the difficulties and crises through which we have been passing since the war.

It is, of course, easy to be wise in retrospect and to look back with the benefit of hindsight at the greatest war in history and to point to errors and confusion. They were inevitable, for war is conducted by men and men are fallible. A historian's judgments, moreover, are something like those of a global Monday morning quarterback. Yet if we are ever to learn from our mistakes we must identify them.

The major American wartime errors were all part and parcel of our political immaturity. We fought to win, period. We did not remember that wars are merely an extension of politics by other means; that wars have objectives; that wars without objectives represent particularly senseless slaughters; that unless a nation is to engage in an unlimited holocaust those objectives must be attainable by the available strength and are limited by the victor's capacity to enforce them and by the willingness of the vanquished state to accept them; and that the general objective of war is a more stable peace. We forgot that, in the words of Colonel the Honorable E. H. Wyndham, "the unity of outlook between allies in war never extends to the subsequent discussion of peace terms." We forgot that "while the attainment of military objectives brings victory in war, it is the attainment of political objectives which wins the subsequent peace." The United States, in other words, had no peace aims; we had only the vaguest kind of idea, expressed in the vaguest kind of general principles (the Atlantic Charter; the United Nations), of the kind of post-war world we wanted.

Our judgments were emotionally clouded by the perennial American hope for the millennium, the Russian military accomplishments, the warm sense of comradeship with our allies which the common purpose of victory induced, and by the very singlemindedness of our military-industrial effort. Wartime propaganda added to illusion; all our enemies were knaves, all our allies friends and comrades—military victory our only purpose. We were, in other words, idealists but not pragmatists. We embarked upon total war with all the zeal and energy and courage for which Americans are famous, but we fought to win; in the broader sense of an objective, we did not know what we were fighting for.

The political mistakes we made sprang, therefore, from the receptive soil of this immaturity, but they were fertilized, too, by a lack of knowledge or

Hanson W. Baldwin, "Our Worst Blunders in the War," *Atlantic Monthly* (January 1950). Reprinted by permission of Curtis Brown, Ltd. Copyright © 1950 by Hanson W. Baldwin.

a lack of adequate interpretation of that knowledge. This was particularly true of our wartime relationship with Russia. Our policy was founded basically on four great and *false* premises—certainly false in retrospect, and seen by some to be false at the time. These were:

1. That the Politburo had abandoned (with the ostensible end of the Communist International) its policy of a world Communist revolution and was honestly interested in the maintenance of friendly relations with capitalist governments.
2. That "Joe" Stalin was a good fellow and that we could "get along with him." This was primarily a personal Rooseveltian policy and was based in part upon the judgments formed by Roosevelt as a result of his direct and indirect contacts with Stalin during the war. This belief was shaken in the last months of Roosevelt's life, partly by the Soviet stand on Poland.
3. That Russia might make a separate peace with Germany. Fear of this dominated the waking thoughts of our politico-strategists throughout the early phase of the war, and some anticipated such an eventuality even after our landing in Normandy.
4. That Russian entry into the war against Japan was either (*a*) essential to victory, or (*b*) necessary to save thousands of American lives. Some of our military men clung to this concept even after the capture of the Marianas and Okinawa.

All these basic misconceptions except the second had one common denominator: lack of adequate knowledge about Russian strengths, purposes, and motivations and inadequate evaluation and interpretation of the knowledge we did possess.

The second mistaken premise could not have been avoided by any amount of knowledge or by the best possible interpretation. The Presidential office with its vast powers can, under an executive who is so inclined, formulate a personal foreign policy. This is particularly true in wartime. President Roosevelt liked to transact business—even international business—on a man-to-man basis; he depended heavily upon personal emissaries like Harry Hopkins and upon his own judgment, and was confident that his estimate of the other fellow was correct. "I just have a hunch," William C. Bullitt quotes Roosevelt as telling him, "that Stalin . . . doesn't want anything but security for his country, and I think that if I give him everything I possibly can and ask nothing from him in return, *noblesse oblige,* he won't try to annex anything and will work with me for a world of democracy and peace."

It was in the character of the President to administer and to govern and to bargain on a "first-name" basis; he relied heavily upon his great persuasive powers and charm, as well as upon his political ego.

A graphic instance of this tendency toward snap decisions and casual dependence upon Stalin's good intentions was provided at Teheran. At that conference, in late 1943, Roosevelt, in one of his tête-à-têtes with Stalin and Churchill, casually agreed, unknown to virtually all his advisers, that the

Russians ought to have one third of the surrendered Italian Fleet. This agreement was put in the form of an oral promise and Stalin was not one to forget promises.

Our Navy and the British Navy, which were then trying to utilize the surrendered Italian ships—manned by their own crews—to best advantage in Mediterranean convoy and antisubmarine work, knew nothing of this agreement until Russian representatives in Washington asked early in 1944 when they could expect "their share of the Italian Fleet." Navy, State Department, and Joint Chiefs of Staff were dumfounded. All our efforts had been directed toward enlisting Italian support in the war against Germany; assignment of one third of the Italian fleet to the Russians as spoils of war would have been a political bombshell which would have handicapped the war effort in the Mediterranean. Accordingly, and to repair the damages of a casual promise made cavalierly without benefit of advice, the Russians were persuaded to accept, in lieu of the Italian vessels, some American and British men-of-war.

This is but one example of Roosevelt's personalized foreign policy—a foreign policy marked more, perhaps, by idealism and altruism than by realism. This Rooseveltian tendency toward international altruism, too often unmoderated by practical politics, seems a strange manifestation in one who domestically was a pragmatic and consummate politician. But it must be remembered that the vision of a "brave new world" was strong in Roosevelt's mind, and his optimistic nature and the great inner wellspring of his faith in man sometimes affected his judgment.

As William L. Langer notes, Roosevelt regarded Russia as the lesser of two evils, and he "shared an idea common at the time that the cult of world revolution was already receding in the minds of the Soviet leaders and they were becoming more and more engrossed in purely national problems." As a result he turned away from the only practical policy that should have governed our actions, opposition to all dictatorships and reliance upon the time-tested balance-of-power policy, to the chimera of so many Americans —a brave, new world.

The Presidential ego unavoidably became stronger in Roosevelt's closing years. His great wartime power, the record of victory, the high esteem in which he was held by the world, and the weakness of the State Department all combined to reinforce the President's tendency to depend upon himself.

One of our greatest weaknesses in the policy field during the war was the failure to equate, evaluate, and integrate military and political policy; there was then no adequate government mechanism, save in the person of the President himself, for such integration.

Former Secretary of War Stimson points out in his book *On Active Service* that the formal organization of the Joint Chiefs of Staff had "a most salutary effect [in the military field] on the President's weakness for snap decisions; it thus offset a characteristic which might otherwise have been a serious handicap to his basically sound strategic instincts." But there was no political counterpart of the Joint Chiefs of Staff; and even if there had been, it is difficult to conceive that such an organization could have tempered materially the personal views which Roosevelt formed about Stalin.

The other fallacious premises upon which our wartime Russian policy was based could, however, have been avoided. We became victims of our own propaganda: Russian aims were good and noble, Communism had changed its stripes. A study of Marxian literature and of the speeches and writings of its high apostles, Lenin and Stalin, coupled with the expert knowledge of numerous American specialists, should have convinced an unbiased mind that international Communism had not altered its ultimate aim; the wolf had merely donned a sheep's skin. Had we recognized this—and all past experience indicates we should have recognized it—our wartime alliance with Russia would have been understood for what it clearly was: a temporary marriage of expediency. In the same manner a careful study of strategical facts and available military information should have indicated clearly the impossibility, *from the Russian point of view,* of a separate peace with Germany. Such a peace could only have been bought in the opening years of the war by major territorial concessions on Russia's part—concessions which might well have imperiled the Stalin regime, and which, in any case, would have left the Russo-German conflict in the category of "unfinished business." In the closing years of the war when Russia had everything to gain and nothing to lose by continuing the struggle to complete victory, a separate peace would have been politically ludicrous.

There is no doubt whatsoever that it would have been to the interest of Britain, the United States, and the world to have allowed—and indeed encouraged—the world's two great dictatorships to fight each other to a frazzle. Such a struggle, with its resultant weakening of both Communism and Nazism, could only have aided in the establishment of a more stable peace. It would have placed the democracies in supreme power in the world, instead of elevating one totalitarianism at the expense of another and *of the democracies.*

The great opportunity of the democracies for establishing a stable peace came on June 22, 1941, when Germany invaded Russia, but we muffed the chance. Instead of aiding Russia with supplies and munitions, but not too much; instead of bombing and blockading Germany, but not too much, Britain—joined after Pearl Harbor by the United States—went all out for "unconditional surrender." We should, in other words, have occupied the bargaining position during the war, vis-à-vis Russia. Russia was the invaded power; Russia, fighting a desperate battle on her own soil, was in a death grapple with Germany. We were not similarly threatened. Russia *had* to have our help; we did not, to the same extent, require hers. This misjudgment put us in the role—at times a disgraceful role—of fearful suppliant and propitiating ally, anxious at nearly any cost to keep Russia fighting. As William C. Bullitt put it, "this topsy-turvy world turned upside down, Alice Through the Looking Glass attitude toward the Soviet Union, which our government adopted in the latter part of 1941 was our first step down the road to our present danger."

In retrospect, how stupid we were! A man being strangled to death struggles with all that's in him; Russia could not quit.

In the same manner and for much the same reasons we reversed the policy we should have followed in the Pacific War. Instead of recognizing that Russia, at nearly all costs, would have to participate in that war if she was to serve her own interests, we "bribed" her to enter it. Port Arthur is written upon the Russian heart; Manchuria has been the locale of Russian expansionist ambitions for nearly a century. Russia had everything to gain and nothing to lose by entering the Pacific War, particularly in 1944 and 1945 when the power of Germany was broken and Japan was beleaguered and in a strategically hopeless position. Yet again we begged and induced, though we, not Russia, occupied the commanding position. We should have tried to keep Russia out of the war against Japan instead of inviting her entry.

Such were the mistakes of basic policy and principle—most of them stemming from a political immaturity and an international naïveté—which influenced most of our wartime decisions and dominated the nature of the peace. They form the psychological background for many of the mistakes of detail here recounted. But a cautionary and qualifying caveat must immediately be entered. Some of these itemized errors were purely fortuitous, the illegitimate offspring of peculiar personalities or specialized circumstance; others were powerfully influenced by American humanitarianism—a desire to save lives; still others were military mistakes, with political connotations—what Bullitt has called "military imagination functioning in political ignorance." But, regardless of their psychological origins, they have one thing in common: they were mistakes.

I am not presenting here a comprehensive catalogue of error, nor am I concerned with tactical mistakes or with those military decisions which had no political consequence. I have selected a few of the broad and far-reaching errors which influenced the course of the war or affected the peace.

Unconditional Surrender—Casablanca

The insistence on unconditional surrender was perhaps the biggest political mistake of the war. In the First World War, Wilson took care to distinguish between the Kaiser and the militaristic Junker class and the German people; in the Second, Stalin drew a clear line between Hitler and the Nazis, and the German people and even the German Army. The opportunity of driving a wedge between rulers and ruled, so clearly seized by Wilson and by Stalin, was muffed by Roosevelt and Churchill. Unconditional surrender was an open invitation to unconditional resistance; it discouraged opposition to Hitler, probably lengthened the war, cost us lives, and helped to lead to the present abortive peace.

This policy grew in part out of the need for a psychological war cry; in part it was intended, as William L. Langer points out, as a reassurance to "the Bolshevik leaders that there would be no compromise with Hitler and that the Allies would fight on to total victory." The haunting fear that motivated so many of our actions during the war—the fear of a separate Russian peace with Germany—and Russia's growing suspicions of the Western

Allies because of their inability until that time (January, 1943) to open a "second front" on land in Western Europe dictated the famous declaration of Casablanca. It is noteworthy that Stalin was never associated with formulating "unconditional surrender" as a doctrine; he refused the invitation to the Casablanca conference and later specifically criticized this doctrine. Some historians point to the Four-Power declaration at Moscow in October, 1943, as an indication of Soviet acceptance of the unconditional surrender policy.

Actually, however, this is an oversimplified and inaccurate assessment of the Russian reaction. Prior to and after the Casablanca-Moscow conferences Stalin took peculiar care to differentiate between the unconditional surrender of Hitlerism and the unconditional surrender of Germany. Obviously the more complete the German defeat, the greater the extension of Russian power, but Stalin understood well the political advantages of strengthening the anti-Hitler opposition in Germany. In one pronouncement (November 6, 1942) he even promised that a German defeat would not mean the end of "all military force in Germany," and the Soviets took active measures through the Free Germany Committee, the Union of German Officers, and the high-ranking Germans captured at Stalingrad and elsewhere (Field Marshal von Paulus, Major General Seydlitz, and others) to back up words with deeds and to build up an active opposition to Hitler.

"This 'soft line' was developed to Germany [by Russia] all through the Summer and Autumn of 1943," Wallace Carroll, who did so much to form our psychological warfare policy during the war, comments. ". . . in November, Stalin challenged the use of the 'hard line' of unconditional surrender at the Teheran Conference." Even as late as May, 1945, when Harry Hopkins was conferring with Stalin in Moscow, Stalin balked at unconditional surrender for Japan, since "if we stick to [it] . . . the Japs will not give up and we will have to destroy them as we did Germany." President Roosevelt ignored these challenges to his "hard line" at Teheran, in December, 1943, after the conference, when he was asked by the British in Washington what he was going to do to meet Stalin's objections, and again on later occasions.

Unconditional surrender was a policy of political bankruptcy which delayed our military objective—victory—and confirmed our lack of a reasoned program for peace. It cost us dearly in lives and time, and its essentially negative concept has handicapped the development of a positive peace program. By endorsing the policy, we abandoned any pragmatic political aims; victory, as defined in these terms, could not possibly mean a more stable peace, for "unconditional surrender" meant, as Liddell Hart has noted, the "complete disappearance of any European balance. War to the bitter end was bound to make Russia 'top dog' on the Continent, to leave the countries of Western Europe gravely weakened and to destroy any buffer."

Invasion of Western Europe—Loss of Eastern Europe

The long wartime history of strategic differences between Britain and the United States started soon after Pearl Harbor. From then until just before the invasion of Southern France in August, 1944—when the British finally

failed in their last effort to persuade us to undertake a Balkan invasion—
we steadily championed an invasion of Western Europe and the British consistently proposed an invasion of the "underbelly."

The two differing strategic concepts were separated not only by geography
and terrain but by centuries of experience. We sought only military victory,
the quickest possible victory. The British looked toward the peace; victory
to them had little meaning if it resulted in political losses. We saw in the
British insistence upon Southern European "adventures" all sorts of male-
volent motives; some of our brash young strategists even claimed the British
did not want to fight.

It is true that Churchill and his advisers were concerned about saving
lives; the blood bath of World War I had weakened Britain dangerously.
Churchill was determined to avoid the holocaust of great casualties and long
stalemate. As Stimson put it, "the shadows of Passchendaele and Dunkerque
still hang too heavily over the imagination of the British." It is also true
that to Churchill, victim of the Dardanelles fiasco in World War I, the
Balkans were a psychological magnet; victory there in World War II would
justify the ill-executed plans of World War I. The great war leader believed
in "eccentric" strategy: the utilization of the Allies' superior naval and air
power to conduct attrition attacks against the enemy's coastlines. The pattern of England's strategy in the Napoleonic wars was in his mind.

These, perhaps, were contributory reasons behind the British strategy. But
fundamentally the British evaluation was politico-military; we ignored the
first part of that compound word. The British wanted to invade Southern
Europe because its lands abut upon the Mediterranean and are contiguous
to the Near East, important to Britain's power position in the world. For
centuries Britain had had major politico-economic interests in Greece, other
Balkan states, and Turkey; for centuries her traditional policy had been to
check the expansionism of Russia, to support Turkish control of the Dardanelles, to participate in Danubian riparian rights. In 1942 and 1943, with
the Russians in deep retreat and the Germans almost at the Caspian, the
British may not have foreseen 1944 and 1945, with the Russians entering
the Balkans, but they perceived clearly the political importance of this area,
and they saw that an invasion there would preserve it—in the best possible
manner, by soldiers on the ground—against either Russian or German interests, and in so doing would safeguard the British "lifeline" through the Mediterranean. Thus the British believed Germany could be beaten and the
peace won by a series of attritions in Northern Italy, in the Eastern Mediterranean, in Greece, in the Balkans, in Rumania and other satellite countries. They believed an invasion through the "soft underbelly" would catch
the German Army in the rear, would find a recruitment of strength from
the doughty Slavs of the occupied countries, and would provide via the
Danube a broad highway into Germany.

These proposals were advanced not only by the British generals, but
chiefly and most vigorously by British statesmen—Churchill, Eden, and
Smuts. Stimson noted their insistence, yet in his book *On Active Service,*

after citing the factual history of our strategic divergences, he describes as "wholly erroneous" the view that "the British opposition to Overlord [invasion of Western France] was guided by a desire to block Soviet Russia by an invasion further east.

"Never in any of his [Stimson's] long and frank discussions with the British leaders was any such argument advanced, and he saw no need whatever to assume any such grounds for the British position. Not only did the British have many good grounds to fear a cross-Channel undertaking, but Mr. Churchill had been for nearly thirty years a believer in what he called the 'right hook.' In 1943 he retained all his long-held strategic convictions, combined with a natural British concern for the Mediterranean theatre," and in Stimson's view that was all there was to it.

But there was more behind the British position than military logic, Stimson notwithstanding. It is true that the British in general, and except in their most intimate conversations with lower-level Americans than Stimson, utilized military rather than political arguments to bolster their case. But this was natural; Mr. Roosevelt at some of the conferences sided with the Russians rather than with Churchill. Moreover, many of our strategic discussions were three-cornered; the British could not very well utilize political arguments—the hope of blocking Russia—in conferences which Russian representatives attended; an effort had to be made to maintain the stability of the unnatural "Big Three" alliance that had been created. It must be remembered that during the latter part of the war it was Britain that filled the role the United States now occupies, of chief protagonist vis-à-vis Russia, in the battle for Europe. Roosevelt was the "mediator," Stalin and Churchill the polite but definite antagonists of the conference tables.

Thus, soon after we entered the war, the British proposed Operation Gymnast (later called Super-Gymnast and finally Torch)—an invasion of North Africa, at Dakar, Casablanca, the Cape Verdes, or Oran. The original date mentioned was March, 1942! By January 2, 1942, when General Joseph W. Stilwell, then slated to command Gymnast, attended one of his early conferences in Washington, the lines had been drawn: "Gerow, Somervell, Arnold, Clark, Chief of Staff, and I. All against it. Limeys claim Spain would 'bitterly oppose' Germans. What rot."

The dispute roared on down the roads of time, exploding now and again at conferences—never settled, always recurrent. The British won the first round; they got the North African invasion, then Sicily and Italy. But they lost in the end; the growing military power of the United States and the self-assurance of our strategists—sound militarily but weak politically—overbalanced them.

From the time of our entry into the war, and even prior to it, our strategists—Eisenhower, Wedemeyer, Marshall, and Stimson particularly—advocated the defeat of Germany by an invasion of Western France. This proposal, as Stimson puts it, was the "brain child of the United States Army." This invasion was to be timed for 1943; if necessary, to save the Russian front from utter collapse, a small diversionary landing was to be made in

France in 1942. The British were distinctly lukewarm about the plan; Churchill was particularly horrified at the thought of the projected 1942 "sacrifice" landing, and from the beginning championed the invasion of North Africa. The President initially lent tacit support to the 1943 invasion and, if necessary, to the 1942 diversionary landing, but he was never fully persuaded, and in June, 1942, the whole subject was reopened.

Then, in a famous meeting at the White House, described by Martin Sommers in the *Saturday Evening Post* (February 8, 1947—"Why Russia Got the Drop on Us"), Churchill and the American strategists, with Wedemeyer as our spokesman, debated strategy. In this meeting Churchill was eloquent in favor of a "surge from the Mediterranean along the historic Belgrade-Warsaw axis"; Wedemeyer, without the benefit of the Churchillian rhetoric, spoke logically in favor of the 1943 cross-Channel operation. According to Sommers, "Churchill, because of his influence on President Roosevelt, won his fight to avoid a cross-Channel operation in 1943. He lost on his determination to force an offensive via Belgrade to Warsaw—*to an extent because when the Russians heard about this plan, they raised shrill objections*" (italics mine).

The President, moved in part by his impatience for action, in part by domestic political considerations, insisted upon some American operation in the European-North African theater in 1942; and, as Stimson puts it, Gymnast, the North African invasion, was the "President's great secret baby." The President's insistence upon action, plus the course of events—the Russians in July, 1942, were fighting with their backs to the wall at Stalingrad and in the Caucasus—led to a conference in London in late July, 1942. At this conference, as Admiral Ernest J. King, wartime commander of the U.S. Fleet, puts it, "the British Chiefs of Staff were adamant in their view that the invasion of northern France [Sledgehammer] could not be undertaken. This view was initially opposed by the United States Chiefs of Staff and the United States Government. The conference decided, however, that invasion of French Northwest Africa could and should be undertaken. . . ."

At Casablanca in January, 1943, after the successful invasion of North Africa, the British—to the ill-concealed fury of our strategists—insisted that the cross-Channel operation tentatively scheduled for the spring of 1943 could not possibly be undertaken before the fall, if then.

In retrospect it is now obvious that our concept of invading Western Europe in 1942 was fantastic; our deficiencies in North Africa, which was a much needed training school for our troops, proved that. The British objection to a 1943 cross-Channel operation was also soundly taken militarily; we would have had in that year neither the trained divisions, the equipment, the planes, the experience, nor (particularly) the landing craft to have invaded the most strongly held part of the Continent against an enemy whose strength was far greater than it was a year later.

Sicily inevitably led to an invasion of Italy, an operation envisaged first as a limited one against the heel and toe of the boot of the Italian peninsula, then later aimed at the seizure of air bases at Foggia, the quick capture of

Rome, and the consequent political-psychological advantage. Churchill saw Italy and Sicily as bases for a jump eastward into the Balkans and he continued, with the aid of his military leaders, to push this project.

Admiral King points out that although the British specifically agreed to limit the Italian operations and the Mediterranean effort, "they nevertheless as time went on and succeeding conferences took place, continued to press more and more for operations in the Mediterranean and to oppose final and firm commitments for the cross-channel operation. Indeed at ANFA [Casablanca] a number of the British delegation were confident that Germany would accept defeat by January 1, 1944."

But American strength had now been mobilized; Roosevelt was firm for Overlord (formerly called Roundup), the invasion of Normandy, and the British were forced to agree at Quebec in August, 1943, that Overlord should have the "inside track." While planning and preparations for the cross-Channel operation in late spring of 1944 were being made, the indefatigable "P.M."—never one to surrender easily once he had sunk his teeth into an argument—tried in various ways to modify or postpone Overlord, or at least to parallel it by an invasion of the Balkans. He was persistent and insistent, and so were his advisers. Churchill returned to the charge at the Moscow Conference of Foreign Ministers in October, and at Cairo on November 24 he made a long and eloquent talk to the American and British staff and to Roosevelt about the advantages of operations in the Aegean Sea and against the island of Rhodes.

At Teheran in late 1943 the British again advocated the Balkan invasion, but Roosevelt, stressing the geographical advantages of the cross-Channel assault and the terrain difficulties of the Balkans, said that only an invasion of Western France could be considered, from the Russian point of view, a "second front." Stalin naturally sided with Roosevelt; indeed, the two "got along" not only at Teheran but at Yalta. The personality of each attracted the other; the language barrier helped rather than handicapped the process; Stalin's flattery, but not Stalin's subtle manipulations, reached the President. And so it was that on November 30, 1943, the invasion of Normandy was finally decided at Teheran, and *Stalin strongly supported the Southern France invasion,* rather than a trans-Adriatic operation into the Balkans, which was mentioned by Roosevelt and backed strongly by Churchill.

Major General John R. Deane in his book *The Strange Alliance* says of Teheran: "Stalin appeared to know exactly what he wanted at the Conference. This was also true of Churchill, but not so of Roosevelt. This is not said as a reflection on our President, but his apparent indecision was probably the *direct result of our obscure foreign policy.* President Roosevelt was thinking of *winning the war;* the others were thinking of their *relative positions when the war was won.* Stalin wanted the Anglo-American forces in Western, not Southern Europe; Churchill thought our postwar position would be improved and British interests best served if the Anglo-Americans as well as the Russians participated in the occupation of the Balkans" (*italics mine*).

Even after the definitive decisions of Teheran, Churchill was not quite done; although the Normandy operation was now certain, a companion invasion of the Balkans might be possible.

In Italy the Allies had been halted in the tangled mountain country south of Rome; the Rapido ran red with blood. Churchill conceived, pushed, and all but executed an amphibious end run. Operation Shingle, the Anzio beachhead landing, was intended to expedite the taking of Rome. But Anzio, too, bogged down and major American energies were now concentrated on Overlord and Normandy.

Rome fell, and Normandy was invaded, and in the summer of 1944—a summer of Allied triumphs, with the Russian armies still in Russia—Churchill made his final efforts to influence the future fate of the world. The British tried repeatedly to have the forces that were to be used in the invasion of Southern France committed instead to a cross-Adriatic operation—the objective a landing in the Trieste-Fiume area to take the German armies in Italy on the flank, a push through the Ljubljana gap into Austria, and a fanning out into the Austro-Hungarian plain with its ideal sites for air bases.

By then Churchill, as he has revealed in private discussions since the war, had no illusions about saving the Balkans from Russian domination; he knew possession, in the Russian lexicon, was nine tenths of the law, but he did hope that Central Europe could be liberated first by the Western Allies. At a meeting at the headquarters of Field Marshal Sir Henry Maitland Wilson, British supreme commander in the Mediterranean, General Marshall tried to sound out the British and American Mediterranean commanders about the project, which in view of strong British backing was assuming formidable dimensions. General Ira Eaker, then commanding the Mediterranean Air Forces, had not been briefed about General Marshall's antipathy for what he considered an unsound (militarily) diversion, and when asked his opinion in the meeting Eaker said that from the air point of view it would be easier to support a trans-Adriatic operation than the invasion of Southern France. The bases, he pointed out, already had been established in Italy and our planes could operate in support of the Trieste move from these bases. But the Southern France operation would have to be supported from new bases in Corsica.

After the meeting was over, General Marshall commented wryly and somewhat bitterly to General Eaker: "You've been too damned long with the British."

In furtherance of their final effort to put Allied troops into Central Europe before the Red Armies occupied those countries, the British "worked" on General Mark W. Clark, then commanding our army in Italy. The King of England, on a visit to the Italian front in July, 1944, about a month before the Southern France invasion, is said to have suggested to Clark the advantages of such a Balkan operation and reportedly tried to enlist his support of the project with the Joint Chiefs of Staff.

General Clark, in a letter to me dated October 15, 1948, recalls the King's visit "when we were approaching the Apennines," but adds: "I do not recall that he discussed with me the advisability of pushing our principal effort into the Balkans.

". . . it was common knowledge that the British were desirous of carrying the war into the Balkans. This subject was discussed with me on several occasions by various Britishers in high places, commencing early in 1944. I recall General Alexander [later Field Marshal Viscount Alexander, then in command of all land forces in Italy] presenting his views on this subject. . . . I must say that I agreed with the wisdom of pushing our main effort to the East rather than continue to buck straight ahead against the mountains and the overwhelming resistance of the Germans. To have taken advantage of Tito's situation with the opportunity of landing a part of our forces across the Adriatic, behind protected beachheads which Tito could have provided, with the bulk of our forces in Italy attacking through the Ljubljana Gap would, if successful, have placed the Western Allies in a much stronger position at the end of the war to meet the ever-increasing challenge of Soviet world domination."

In all these discussions of a trans-Adriatic operation, the Ljubljana gap and the Istrian peninsula were usually favored, but landings further south along the Dalmatian coast near Zara or Split were also mentioned. The British were persistent; the project was pushed even as late as September, 1944, after the forces that invaded Southern France had formed a junction with Patton's rampaging army that had broken out of the Normandy beachhead.

Much has been made, since the war, of the strategic importance of the Southern France invasion; without it, it has been said, most of the German forces south of Brittany would have escaped. But we now know that most of the German forces did escape. The Southern France invasion was originally timed to coincide with the invasion of Normandy in June, 1944, and simultaneous invasions in West and South would have divided the German forces in France. But lack of landing craft forced a postponement of the Southern France operation until August 15, and we now know from German records that a Nazi withdrawal from France already had started even before the Anvil-Dragoon (Southern France) landings. Many German troops were cut up and captured by the junction of Patton's forces with those that landed on the Côte d'Azur, but many of the enemy combat units completed successfully their withdrawal to the German frontier. Much of the strategic meaning of the Southern France invasion undoubtedly was lost when the two-month postponement became necessary; when this decision was reached, the arguments for the trans-Adriatic invasion became overwhelming.

Despite these arguments it was not to be; the British, notwithstanding the great eloquence of Churchill and the reasoned logic of his staff, had failed; the American strategy—heartily endorsed by the Russians—was the pattern of conquest.

It was, of course, a successful pattern, for it was a sound plan militarily and it led to unconditional surrender. But it also led to the domination of Eastern and Central Europe by Russia and to the post-war upset in the European balance of power which has been so obvious since the war.

American strategy was not, of course, the only factor in this political defeat. Churchill made his share of mistakes. His—and our—abandonment of Mikhailovitch in Yugoslavia and his endorsement of Tito (formalized at Teheran), whom he thought he could control with British gold; and the tacit acceptance of Russia's claims to Poland's eastern territories and the division of Europe into spheres of influence, with predominant control in the Balkans—except for Greece and Yugoslavia—allotted to Russia, also contributed to our loss of the peace. The latter was a particularly heinous mistake. Churchill was its principal architect. He recognized—apparently as early as 1942—Russia's "predominant interest" in Eastern Europe. Secretary Hull opposed this concept but the President, without Hull's knowledge, agreed to the initial arrangement. Further agreements between London and Moscow in 1944, *coupled with the concentration of Western military strength in France, instead of Southern Europe,* further fortified the Russian position.

But the dominant factor in the political complexion of Europe after the war was the presence of Red Army soldiers in all the countries east of the Trieste-Stettin line. The eruption of the Russians into the Danube basin gave them control over one of Europe's greatest waterways, access to Central Europe's granaries and great cities, and a strategical position of tremendous power at the center of Europe.

All of this Churchill and the British had clearly foreseen; none of this, so far as the record goes, did we foresee. Yet, so great was our physical strength, so impeccable our military logic, that rationalization triumphed over foresight. Today the principal architects of our policy understand their mistakes; many of the great military figures of the war admit freely that the British were right and we were wrong. For we forgot that all wars have objectives and all victories conditions; we forgot that winning the peace is fully as important as winning the war; we forgot that politico-military is a compound word.

Loss of Central Europe

In March and April, 1945, as the war against Germany was drawing to an end, Eastern Europe had gone irretrievably; our earlier failure to invade the Balkans had cost us dearly. But important parts of Central Europe—Berlin, the Bohemian bastion and Prague, and possibly Vienna—were still at stake.

As early as March 28, with the Allied armies on the Rhine 300 miles from Berlin and the Russians on the Oder 30 miles from Berlin, General Eisenhower sent a personal message to Stalin via the U.S. Military Mission in Moscow. This message outlined his plans for a strong push in the center by General Omar Bradley's American forces to a junction with the Russians on the Elbe, to be followed by flank drives by the British in the north to cut off the Danish peninsula and seize the North German ports, and by the Americans and French in the south into Austria to eliminate the possibility of a last-ditch stand by the Nazis in the so-called "National Redoubt." Churchill protested this communication by Eisenhower to Stalin as an intrusion by the military into political matters, and was vehemently critical of the plan; in Eisenhower's words, "he was greatly disappointed and disturbed because my plan did not first throw Montgomery forward with all the strength I could give him from the American forces in the desperate attempt to capture Berlin before the Russians could do so." But Churchill's protest to Washington was overruled.

Eisenhower's defense against this protest has some merits. There is no doubt that he was perfectly within his rights in communicating his plans to Stalin; he had been previously authorized to do so. But his dismissal of the Berlin plan as militarily unwise, and his fear that an attempt to take the city would force diversion of forces from other parts of the front to that sole task—a "stupid" diversion—and his overemphasis upon the "National Redoubt" were, it is now clear, mistaken. Intelligence failures again played a part in this mistake. The "National Redoubt" (fortifications and supplies supposed to have been prepared by the Nazi SS formations in the German-Austrian Alps for a last stand) was grossly overrated in our estimates; we learned later that relatively little work on the "Redoubt" had been done; the scheme was more an idea than an accomplishment. Churchill, in other words, again emerges in the Berlin matter a wily old fox of international politics; his vision was not obscured by the needs of the moment.

Our troops after crossing the Rhine swept eastward with relatively little opposition. Agreements had been reached with the Russians that when contact between the two armies seemed imminent, a line of demarcation should be arranged beyond which each army should not move. This boundary was "temporarily fixed"—in the words of General Eisenhower's final report— "in the central sector" along the easily identified line of the Elbe and Mulde Rivers; the Russians were so notified in Eisenhower's message to Stalin of March 28 (which evoked the Churchill protest). By April 12, the first American bridgehead across the Elbe had been established; we were 100 miles from Berlin and the Russians, 30 miles from that city on the Oder, were just starting their final offensive. It was not until April 25 that the Russians reached the Elbe; in other words, for about three weeks our forces remained virtually static on that line of demarcation, and not until early May was the Russian battle for Berlin finally won.

Further south our troops moved into Czechoslovakia on April 18, and then on to Pilsen. Prague lay virtually defenseless near at hand; reconnaissance elements of the Third Army were in its outskirts. The Soviet High Command, when informed by General Eisenhower that our troops would move on toward Prague if (in former Secretary of State Byrnes's words) "the situation required it," requested that our forces "should not advance beyond the Budejovice-Pilsen-Karlsbad line." So again our troops marked time, and the political prestige of taking Prague went to the Russians.

So, too, in the south, where the agreed demarcation line ran down the Budejovice-Linz railroad and along the valley of the Enns, Vienna, a possible prize, was voluntarily relinquished.

There was some military reason for this restraint. Two armies surging forward toward each other—a desperate enemy in between—are difficult to control; Eisenhower was concerned about accidental collisions. Moreover, it would not have been easy for us to take Berlin first. The Russians were only 30 miles from that city when we were 100 miles away on the Elbe.

Furthermore, General Omar N. Bradley had estimated that though we could take the city, it would be at the cost of perhaps 100,000 casualties. Our troops had been moving fast and hard; the supply problem was difficult—and in any case the Western Allies had advanced far beyond the zonal boundaries agreed upon by the Allied governments and further advance would only have meant eventual evacuation of additional territory east of the Elbe.

Eisenhower felt moreover (in his own words in his final report) that "Berlin no longer represented a military objective of major importance" and that "military factors, when the enemy was on the brink of final defeat, were more important . . . than the political considerations involved in an Allied capture of the capital."

Both political and military decisions, therefore, halted our armies along the Elbe, the Mulde, and the Enns in the closing days of the Third Reich. There *were* military reasons, which seemed good at the time, for not pressing the advance to the utmost, but they were not decisive. The boundaries marked out by the European Advisory Commission and approved at Quebec and Yalta colored the thinking of our commanders. We *could* have moved further eastward. But the political die had been cast; there was not much point in military sacrifice for a political lost cause.

The effect of all these decisions was to make Berlin an island in a Russian sea and to give Soviet troops firm control of Central Europe.

Military Decisions and Diplomatic Dilemmas

STEPHEN E. AMBROSE

There has been much confusion about Churchill's advocacy of Berlin as a target. It is commonly asserted that he wanted to keep the Russians out of eastern Germany, to retain a united Germany, and to maintain Berlin's status as the capital, and that if only the Allies had captured the city there would be no Berlin problem today. This is nonsense. Aside from the military factors (it is probable that Eisenhower's men could never have taken Berlin ahead of the Red Army), these views do not remotely reflect the policies Churchill was advocating. He never thought in terms of denying to the Russians their position in East Europe generally or eastern Germany specifically, a position that had been agreed to much earlier. Once the 1943 cross-Channel attack had been scuttled, there never was the slightest chance that the Russians could be kept out of East Europe. Churchill realized this: His famous agreement with Stalin during their Moscow meetings in the fall of 1944 signified his recognition that Russian domination of East Europe was inevitable.

What Churchill did want from the capture of Berlin was much less grandiose. His major concern was prestige. He told Roosevelt that the Russians were going to liberate Vienna. "If they also take Berlin, will not their impression that they have been the overwhelming contributor to our common victory be unduly imprinted in their minds?" The idea that an Allied capture of Berlin could eradicate the Russians' feeling that they had done the most to defeat Hitler was really rather absurd, but it had great appeal to Churchill.

Roosevelt would have none of it. His own major concerns, in the weeks before his death on April 12, were to create the United Nations (the San Francisco Conference to draw up the Charter began its sessions shortly thereafter), to insure the participation of the U.S.S.R. in the United Nations, and to maintain cordial relations with Stalin. He refused to take a hard line with Stalin on the Russian occupation of Poland or on Stalin's suspicions about the surrender of the German forces in Italy to the Western Allies. The President was not an experienced diplomat, and right to the end he had no clear goals for the postwar world. His sponsorship of the United Nations indicated that he had adopted Woodrow Wilson's belief in collective security, but the nature of the United Nations Roosevelt wanted, dominated as it was by the great nations on the Security Council, indicated that he retained a belief in spheres of influence for the great powers. So did his frequent remarks about the "Four Policemen" (China, Russia, Britain, and the United States).

But if much of Roosevelt's policy was cloudy, mystifying even his closest advisers, one thing was clear. To the exasperation of some members of the State Department, not to mention the Ambassador to Russia, W. Averell Harriman, the President refused to become a staunch anti-Soviet. Harriman, Churchill, and later Truman assumed that Russia would be unreasonable, grasping, probing, power hungry, and impossible to deal with except from a position of great strength and unrelenting firmness. F.D.R. rejected such assumptions. Furthermore, he seems to have felt it was only reasonable for the Russians to be uneasy about the nature of the governments on Russia's western frontier, and therefore was willing to consider Stalin's demands in East Europe. There was also an assumption, shared even by Churchill, that Stalin was stating the obvious when he remarked in early 1945 that "whoever occupies a territory also imposes on it his own social system." Churchill, who had taken the lead in establishing this principle in Italy and Greece, later denounced Stalin for practicing it in East Europe, but the evidence indicates that Roosevelt was realistic enough to accept the quid pro quo.

The nature of the alliance with Russia was generally confusing. After the Nazi invasion the Red Army became heroic, and Stalin appeared as a wise and generous leader in the American press. Whether this had a deep or lasting effect on a people who mistrusted and feared Communism as much as they did Fascism is doubtful. Behind the scenes, meanwhile, and especially in the State Department, anti-Soviet feeling kept bubbling up. George Kennan, though a rather minor functionary in the State Department at the time, best expressed the mood two days after the Nazis invaded Russia in 1941: "We should do nothing at home to make it appear that we are following the course Churchill seems to have entered upon in extending moral support to the Russian cause. It seems to me that to welcome Russia as an associate in the defense of democracy would invite misunderstanding." Kennan felt that throughout Europe "Russia is generally more feared than Germany," and he implied that he agreed with this estimate of the relative dangers of Communism and Fascism.

The sentiment that Kennan expressed in 1941 may have been dominant in the State Department, but the Department was not setting policy. Roosevelt extended lend-lease to the Russians and gave moral support to Stalin. Bending to State Department pressure, he did refuse Stalin's request in 1941 for an agreement that would recognize Russian territorial gains under the Nazi-Soviet Pact, remarking that territorial questions could be settled at the end of the war. But beyond that issue Roosevelt concentrated on working together with Stalin against the common enemy. Kennan continued to protest. In 1944, when the Red Army had driven the Germans out of Russia and was preparing for the final offensive, Kennan argued that the time had come for a "full-fledged and realistic political showdown with the Soviet leaders." He wanted to confront them with "the choice between changing their policy completely and agreeing to collaborate in the establishment of truly independent countries in Eastern Europe or of forfeiting Western Allied support and sponsorship for the remaining phases of their war effort."

By this time Kennan was the chief adviser to the American Ambassador in Moscow, Harriman, who accepted Kennan's views. Harriman advised F.D.R. to cut back on or even eliminate lend-lease shipments to Russia. Roosevelt refused and the aid continued to flow, providing Russia with essential equipment, especially trucks. The West needed the Red Army at least as badly as the Russians needed lend-lease. Although Kennan had failed to see this, Marshall and Roosevelt were clear enough about who needed whom the most. Their greatest fear was precisely Kennan's greatest hope—that once the Red Army reached Russian borders, it would stop. The Germans could then have turned and marched west, confronting the Western Allies with the bulk of the Wehrmacht. Britain and America had not mobilized nearly enough ground troops to batter their way into Berlin against such opposition.

Further, there was the frightening possibility of new secret weapons. Germany had made rapid strides in military technology during the war, German propaganda continued to urge the people to hold on just a little longer until the new weapons were ready, and F.D.R. knew that the Germans were working on an atomic bomb. The V-weapons, jet-propelled aircraft, and snorkel submarines were bad enough. To halt lend-lease to the Russians would slow the Red Army advance, giving the Germans more time to perfect their weapons, if it did not cause Stalin to withdraw from the war altogether.

The central dilemma of the war was embodied in these considerations. Until the end almost no one in power wanted Russia to stop its advance, but few Americans or British wanted Russia to dominate East Europe. It had to be one or the other. Roosevelt decided that the greater danger lay in an end to Russian offensives, and he continued to give Stalin aid and encouragement for the Russian drive to the west.

At his own level Eisenhower made his decision about Berlin on military grounds. He thought it was madness to send his forces dashing toward Berlin when there was little, if any, chance that they would arrive before the Red Army. He also needed a clearly recognizable demarcation line, so that when his forces met the Russians there would be no unfortunate incidents of the two allies mistakenly shooting at each other. He therefore informed Stalin that he would halt when he reached the Elbe River. Churchill kept pestering him to push on eastward; finally Eisenhower wired the Combined Chiefs of Staff: "I am the first to admit that a war is waged in pursuance of political aims, and if the Combined Chiefs of Staff should decide that the Allied effort to take Berlin outweighs purely military considerations in this theater, I would cheerfully readjust my plans and my thinking so as to carry out such an operation." He was not, in other words, willing to risk the lives of a hundred thousand or more men for no military gain. The Combined Chiefs made no reply, and for Eisenhower, military considerations remained paramount.

While Eisenhower's forces occupied southern Germany, the Russians battered their way into Berlin, suffering heavy casualties, probably in excess of a hundred thousand. Herbert Feis points out that they gained "the first somber sense of triumph, the first awesome sight of the ruins, the first parades under the pall of smoke." Two months later they gave up to the West over half the city they had captured at such an enormous price. At the cost of not a single life, Great Britain and the United States had their sectors in Berlin, and they have been there ever since.

More important, the war ended without any sharp break with the Russians. There had been innumerable strains in the strange alliance, but the United States and Russia were still allies, and in May 1945 the possibility of continued cooperation was, if frail, alive. Much would depend on the attitude of the United States toward Soviet actions in East Europe. It was as certain as the sun's rising that Stalin would insist on "friendly" governments there, which, translated, meant Communist dictatorships controlled by Moscow. The economic and political leaders of the old regimes, landlords and factory owners, generals and aristocrats, would be thrown out, along with religious leaders and editors. With them would go some of the most cherished concepts in the West—freedom of speech, free elections, freedom of religion, and free enterprise. The men who ran the American government could not look with any approval on the suppression of precisely those liberties they had fought Hitler to uphold. President Harry S Truman (F.D.R. had died in April 1945), his advisers, and the American people would never be able to accept the forced communization of Eastern Europe without protest.

But the experience of World War II indicated that the United States still had alternatives, that hostility was not the only possible reaction to Stalin's probable moves. The United States had demonstrated an ability to make realistic, pragmatic responses to developing situations. America had aided Tito and supported the French Resistance, had refused to get tough with the Russians, had made major decisions solely for the purpose of bringing about the fall of Nazi Germany.

In the spring of 1945 America had enormously more power, both absolutely and in relation to the rest of the world, than she had possessed in 1941. To a lesser degree that had also been the situation in 1918, and after World War I America had disarmed and for the most part refused to intervene in affairs outside the North American continent. She could do so again, and indeed Roosevelt had privately confessed to Churchill that he doubted if he could keep American troops in Europe for more than a year or so after the conclusion of hostilities.

America was the victor. Her decisions would go far toward shaping the postwar world. In May 1945, as had been the case throughout the war, she did not have a firm idea of what those decisions would be. It was still possible for the United States to travel down any one of several roads.

FURTHER READING

Stephen E. Ambrose, *Eisenhower and Berlin, 1945* (1967)
Robert Beitzell, *The Uneasy Alliance* (1972)
A. Russell Buchanan, *The United States and World War II* (1964)
James M. Burns, *Roosevelt: The Soldier of Freedom* (1970)
Thomas M. Campbell, *Masquerade Peace: America's UN Policy, 1944–1945* (1973)
Diane Shaver Clemens, *Yalta* (1970)
Robert Dallek, *Franklin D. Roosevelt and American Foreign Policy, 1933–1945* (1979)
Robert A. Divine, *Roosevelt and World War II* (1969)
———, *Second Chance* (1967)
Herbert Feis, *Between War and Peace* (1960)
———, *Churchill, Roosevelt, Stalin* (1957)
Louis Fischer, *The Road to Yalta: Soviet Foreign Relations, 1941–1945* (1972)
Kent R. Greenfield, *American Strategy in World War II* (1963)
Victor Israelian, *The Anti-Hitler Coalition* (1971)
Warren Kimball, "Churchill and Roosevelt: The Personal Equation," *Prologue*, 6 (1974), 169–182
Gabriel Kolko, *The Politics of War* (1968)
William Langer, *Our Vichy Gamble* (1947)
Michael Leigh, *Mobilizing Consent: Public Opinion and American Foreign Policy, 1937–1947* (1976)
Ralph B. Levering, *American Opinion and the Russian Alliance* (1976)
William R. Louis, *Imperialism at Bay: The United States and the Decolonization of the British Empire* (1978)
Richard Lukas, *The Strange Alliance: The United States and Poland, 1941–1945* (1978)
William H. McNeill, *America, Britain, and Russia* (1953)
Vojtech Mastny, *Russia's Road to the Cold War* (1979)
Samuel Eliot Morison, *Strategy and Compromise* (1958)
William L. Neumann, *After Victory* (1967)
Raymond G. O'Connor, *Diplomacy for Victory: FDR and Unconditional Surrender* (1971)
Michael S. Sherry, *Preparing for the Next War* (1977)

Robert E. Sherwood, *Roosevelt and Hopkins* (1948)
Gaddis Smith, *American Diplomacy During the Second World War* (1965)
John L. Snell, *Illusion or Necessity* (1963)
Richard W. Steele, *The First Offensive, 1942* (1973)
Mark A. Stoler, *The Politics of the Second Front* (1977)
Kenneth W. Thompson, *Winston Churchill's World View* (1983)
Christopher Thorne, *Allies of a Kind* (1978)
Adam Ulam, *Expansion and Coexistence: The History of Soviet Foreign Policy, 1917–1973* (1974)
Brian L. Villa, "The Atomic Bomb and the Normandy Invasion," *Perspectives in American History,* II (1977–1978), 461–502
Llewellyn Woodward, *British Foreign Policy in the Second World War* (1970–71)

The Origins of the Cold War

8

The Big Three alliance of World War II, often strained during the war
itself, quickly splintered as the victors began to plan the peace. Questions of
territorial boundaries, spheres of influence, atomic weaponry, trade, economic
reconstruction, political principles, and international organizations divided
Britain, the United States, and the Soviet Union. In Germany, Iran, Eastern
Europe, China—indeed, on a global scale—the major powers, especially
America and Russia, competed for postwar influence, using the economic,
political, military, and ideological means available to them. The result was
the Cold War.

   Why the Cold War developed with such divisiveness is a topic of spirited
debate among scholars and surviving participants of this postwar antagonism.
Were the causes to be found in the flawed and broken international system
itself? Or in a totalitarian Communist Russia bent on aggression? Or in a
powerful, expansionist United States? Or in the particular decisions of
such strong personalities as Harry S. Truman and Josef Stalin? Recent
scholarship makes clear that there is no single explanation for the origins
of the Cold War and that the historian's task is not to pin blame on one
antagonist or the other, but to probe for the complex national and international tensions and drives that pitted nation against nation.

DOCUMENTS

The first three documents speak to the American decision to use the atomic
bomb against Japan and its impact on international relations. In early May 1945,

Secretary of War Henry L. Stimson appointed an Interim Committee, with himself as chairman, to advise on atomic energy and the uranium bombs the Manhattan Engineering District project was about to produce. In the committee's meeting of May 31, 1945, the conferees agreed to keep the bomb project a secret from the Russians and to use the atomic bomb against the Japanese. On June 11, 1945, a group of atomic scientists in Chicago, headed by Jerome Franck, futilely petitioned Stimson for a non-combat demonstration of the bomb in order to improve the chances for postwar international control. On September 11, 1945, Stimson himself sent President Harry S. Truman a memorandum in which he argued that Russian-American relations were being "dominated by the problem of the atomic bomb." He now urged that the United States approach Russia to discuss controls.

In May 1945 President Truman sent a special representative to Moscow to speak with Josef Stalin, but not about the atomic bomb. Harry Hopkins, who for years had advised Franklin D. Roosevelt, already knew the Soviet Premier. On May 27, as the fourth document reveals, they talked frankly about a host of issues, including the abrupt American termination of Lend-Lease aid to Russia and the repressive Soviet presence in Poland. The next document, from the gifted pen of George F. Kennan, is his influential "long telegram" of February 22, 1946, which Kennan, then attaché in the American Embassy in Moscow, sent to Washington to spell out what he thought were the underlying sources of Soviet behavior. Former British Prime Minister Winston S. Churchill's "iron curtain" speech of March 5, 1946, delivered in Fulton, Missouri, stirred debate. The next document, a July 1946 memorandum given the President by Secretary of Commerce Henry A. Wallace, criticized Truman's "get tough" policies. Truman forced Wallace to resign in September. On March 12, 1947, the President addressed Congress to outline the "Truman Doctrine" or containment doctrine, at least as it applied to Greece and Turkey. The final document is a small portion of National Security Council Paper No. 68 (NSC-68), dated April 7, 1950. This important report was alarmist in its depiction of a world beset by Soviet expansionism that only the United States could halt.

The Interim Committee on Military Use of the Atomic Bomb, 1945

Secretary Stimson explained that the Interim Committee had been appointed by him, with the approval of the President, to make recommendations on temporary war-time controls, public announcement, legislation and post-war organization. . . . He expressed the hope that the [four] scientists would feel completely free to express their views on any phase of the subject. . . .

The Secretary explained that General Marshall shared responsibility with him for making recommendations to the President on this project with particular reference to its military aspects; therefore, it was considered highly desirable that General Marshall be present at this meeting to secure at first hand the views of the scientists.

The Secretary expressed the view, a view shared by General Marshall, that this project should not be considered simply in terms of military weapons, but as a new relationship of man to the universe. This discovery might be compared to the discoveries of the Copernican theory and of the laws of gravity, but far more important than these in its effect on the lives of men. While the advances in the field to date had been fostered by the needs of war, it was important to realize that the implications of the project went far beyond the needs of the present war. It must be controlled if possible to make it an assurance of future peace rather than a menace to civilization.

The Secretary suggested that he hoped to have the following questions discussed during the course of the meeting:

1. Future military weapons
2. Future international competition
3. Future research
4. Future controls
5. Future developments, particularly non-military.

At this point *General Marshall* discussed at some length the story of charges and counter-charges that have been typical of our relations with the Russians, pointing out that most of these allegations have proven unfounded. The seemingly uncooperative attitude of Russia in military matters stemmed from the necessity of maintaining security. He said that he had accepted this reason for their attitude in his dealings with the Russians and had acted accordingly. As to the post-war situation and in matters other than purely military, he felt that he was in no position to express a view. With regard to this field he was inclined to favor the building up of a combination among like-minded powers, thereby forcing Russia to fall in line by the very force of this coalition. General Marshall was certain that we need have no fear that the Russians, if they had knowledge of our project, would disclose this information to the Japanese. He raised the question whether it might be desirable to invite two prominent Russian scientists to witness the test.

Mr. Byrnes expressed a fear that if information were given to the Russians, even in general terms, Stalin would ask to be brought into the partnership. He felt this to be particularly likely in view of our commitments and pledges of cooperation with the British. In this connection *Dr. Bush* pointed out that even the British do not have any of our blue prints on plants. *Mr. Byrnes* expressed the view, *which was generally agreed to by all present,* that the most desirable program would be to push ahead as fast as possible in production and research to make certain that we stay ahead and at the same time make every effort to better our political relations with Russia.

It was pointed out that one atomic bomb on an arsenal would not be much different from the effect caused by any Air Corps strike of present dimensions. However, *Dr. Oppenheimer* stated that the visual effect of an atomic bombing would be tremendous. It would be accompanied by a brilliant luminescence which would rise to a height of 10,000 to 20,000 feet. The neutron effect of the explosion would be dangerous to life for a radius of at least two-thirds of a mile.

After much discussion concerning various types of targets and the effects to be produced, *the Secretary expressed the conclusion, on which there was general agreement, that we could not give the Japanese any warning; that we could not concentrate on a civilian area; but that we should seek to make a profound psychological impression on as many of the inhabitants as possible. At the suggestion of Dr. Conant the Secretary agreed that the most desirable target would be a vital war plant employing a large number of workers and closely surrounded by workers' houses.*

There was some discussion of the desirability of attempting several strikes at the same time. *Dr. Oppenheimer's* judgment was that several strikes would be feasible. *General Groves,* however, expressed doubt about this proposal and pointed out the following objections: (1) We would lose the advantage of gaining additional knowledge concerning the weapon at each successive bombing; (2) such a program would require a rush job on the part of those assembling the bombs and might, therefore, be ineffective; (3) the effect would not be sufficiently distinct from our regular Air Force bombing program.

The Franck Committee on a Non-Combat Atomic Demonstration, 1945

The way in which the nuclear weapons, now secretly developed in this country, will first be revealed to the world appears of great, perhaps fateful importance.

One possible way—which may particularly appeal to those who consider the nuclear bombs primarily as a secret weapon developed to help win the present war—is to use it without warning on an appropriately selected object in Japan. It is doubtful whether the first available bombs, of comparatively low efficiency and small size, will be sufficient to break the will or ability of Japan to resist, especially given the fact that the major cities like Tokyo, Nagoya, Osaka and Kobe already will largely be reduced to ashes by the slower process of ordinary aerial bombing. Certain and perhaps important tactical results undoubtedly can be achieved, but we nevertheless think that the question of the use of the very first available atomic bombs in the Japanese war should be weighed very carefully, not only by military authority, but by the highest political leadership of this country. If we consider international agreement on total prevention of nuclear warfare as the paramount objective, and believe that it can be achieved, this kind of introduction of atomic weapons to the world may easily destroy all our chances of success. Russia, and even allied countries which bear less mistrust of our ways and intentions, as well as neutral countries, will be deeply shocked. It will be very difficult to persuade the world that a nation which was capable of secretly preparing and suddenly releasing a weapon, as indiscriminate as the rocket bomb and a thousand times more destructive, is to be trusted in its proclaimed desire of having such weapons abolished by international agreement. We have large accumulations of poison gas, but do not use them, and recent polls have shown that public opinion in this country would disapprove of such a use even if it would accelerate the winning of the Far Eastern war. It is true, that some irrational element in mass psychology makes gas poisoning more revolting than blasting by explosives, even though gas warfare is in no way more "inhuman" than the war of bombs and bullets. Nevertheless, it is not at all certain that the American public opinion, if it could be enlightened as to the effect of atomic explosives, would support the first introduction by our own country of such an indiscriminate method of wholesale destruction of civilian life.

Thus, from the "optimistic" point of view—looking forward to an international agreement on prevention of nuclear warfare—the military advantages and the saving of American lives, achieved by the sudden use of atomic bombs against Japan, may be outweighed by the ensuing loss of confidence and wave of horror and repulsion, sweeping over the rest of the world, and perhaps dividing even the public opinion at home.

From this point of view a demonstration of the new weapon may best be made before the eyes of representatives of all United Nations, on the desert or a barren island. The best possible atmosphere for the achievement of an international agreement could be achieved if America would be able to say to the world, "You see what weapon we had but did not use. We are ready to renounce its use in the future and to join other nations in working out adequate supervision of the use of this nuclear weapon."

This may sound fantastic, but then in nuclear weapons we have something entirely new in the order of magnitude of destructive power, and if we want to capitalize fully on the advantage which its possession gives us, we must use new and imaginative methods. After such a demonstration the weapon could be used against Japan if a sanction of the United Nations (and of the public opinion at home) could be obtained, perhaps after a preliminary ultimatum to Japan to surrender or at least to evacuate a certain region as an alternative to the total destruction of this target.

It must be stressed that if one takes a pessimistic point of view and discounts the possibilities of an effective international control of nuclear weapons, then the advisability of an early use of nuclear bombs against Japan becomes even more doubtful—quite independently of any humanitarian considerations. If no international agreement is concluded immediately after the first demonstration, this will mean a flying start of an unlimited armaments race. If this race is inevitable, we have all reason to delay its beginning as long as possible in order to increase our headstart still further. . . . The benefit to the nation, and the saving of American lives in the future, achieved by renouncing an early demonstration of nuclear bombs and letting the other nations come into the race only reluctantly, on the basis of guesswork and without definite knowledge that the "thing does work," may far outweigh the advantages to be gained by the immediate use of the first and comparatively inefficient bombs in the war against Japan. At the least, pros and cons of this use must be carefully weighed by the supreme political and military leadership of the country, and the decision should not be left to considerations, merely, of military tactics.

One may point out that scientists themselves have initiated the development of this "secret weapon" and it is therefore strange that they should be reluctant to try it out on the enemy as soon as it is available. The answer to this question was given above—the compelling reason for creating this weapon with such speed was our fear that Germany had the technical skill necessary to develop such a weapon without any moral restraints regarding its use.

Another argument which could be quoted in favor of using atomic bombs as soon as they are available is that so much taxpayers' money has been invested in those projects that the Congress and the American public will require a return for their money. The above-mentioned attitude of the American public opinion in the question of the use of poison gas against Japan shows that one can expect it to understand that a weapon can sometimes be made ready only for use in extreme emergency; and as soon as the potentialities of nuclear weapons will be revealed to the American people, one can be certain that it will support all attempts to make the use of such weapons impossible.

Henry L. Stimson's Appeal for Atomic Talks with Russia, 1945

The advent of the atomic bomb has stimulated great military and probably even greater political interest throughout the civilized world. In a world atmosphere already extremely sensitive to power, the introduction of this weapon has profoundly affected political considerations in all sections of the globe.

In many quarters it has been interpreted as a substantial offset to the growth of Russian influence on the continent. We can be certain that the Soviet Government has sensed this tendency and the temptation will be strong for the Soviet political and military leaders to acquire this weapon in the shortest possible time. Britain in effect already has the status of a partner with us in the development of this weapon. Accordingly, unless the Soviets are voluntarily invited into the partnership upon a basis of co-operation and trust, we are going to maintain the Anglo-Saxon bloc over against the Soviet in the possession of this weapon. Such a condition will almost certainly stimulate feverish activity on the part of the Soviet toward the development of this bomb in what will in effect be a secret armament race of a rather desperate character. There is evidence to indicate that such activity may have already commenced.

If we feel, as I assume we must, that civilization demands that some day we shall arrive at a satisfactory international arrangement respecting the control of this new force, the question then is how long we can afford to enjoy our momentary superiority in the hope of achieving our immediate peace council objectives.

Whether Russia gets control of the necessary secrets of production in a minimum of say four years or a maximum of twenty years is not nearly as important to the world and civilization as to make sure that when they do get it they are willing and co-operative partners among the peace-loving nations of the world. It is true if we approach them now, as I would propose, we may be gambling on their good faith and risk their getting into production of bombs a little sooner than they would otherwise.

To put the matter concisely, I consider the problem of our satisfactory relations with Russia as not merely connected with but as virtually dominated by the problem of the atomic bomb. Except for the problem of the control of that bomb, those relations, while vitally important, might not be immediately pressing. The establishment of relations of mutual confidence between her and us could afford to await the slow progress of time. But with the discovery of the bomb, they became immediately emergent. Those relations may be perhaps irretrievably embittered by the way in which we approach the solution of the bomb with Russia. For if we fail to approach them now and merely continue to negotiate with them, having this weapon rather ostentatiously on our hip, their suspicions and their distrust of our purposes and motives will increase. It will inspire them to greater efforts in an all-out effort to solve the problem. If the solution is achieved in that spirit, it is much less likely that we will ever get the kind of covenant we may desperately need in the future. This risk is, I believe, greater than the other, inasmuch as our objective must be to get the best kind of international bargain we can—one that has some chance of being kept and saving civilization not for five or for twenty years, but forever.

The chief lesson I have learned in a long life is that the only way you can make a man trustworthy is to trust him; and the surest way to make him untrustworthy is to distrust him and show your distrust.

If the atomic bomb were merely another though more devastating military weapon to be assimilated into our pattern of international relations, it would be one thing. We could then follow the old custom of secrecy and nationalistic military superiority relying on international caution to prescribe the future use of the weapon as we did with gas. But I think the bomb instead constitutes merely a first step in a new control by man over the forces of nature too revolutionary and dangerous to fit into the old concepts. I think it really caps the climax of the race between man's growing technical power for destructiveness and his psychological power of self-control and group control—his moral power. If so, our method of approach to the Russians is a question of the most vital importance in the evolution of human progress.

Since the crux of the problem is Russia, any contemplated action leading to the control of this weapon should be primarily directed *to* Russia. It is my judgment that the Soviet would be more apt to respond sincerely to a direct and forthright approach made by the United States on this subject than would be the case if the approach were made as a part of a general international scheme, or if the approach were made after a succession of express or implied threats or near threats in our peace negotiations.

My idea of an approach to the Soviets would be a direct proposal after discussion with the British that we would be prepared in effect to enter an arrangement with the Russians, the general purpose of which would be to control and limit the use of the atomic bomb as an instrument of war and so far as possible to direct and encourage the development of atomic power for peaceful and humanitarian purposes. Such an approach might more specifically lead to the proposal that we would stop work on the further improvement in, or manufacture of, the bomb as a military weapon, provided the Russians and the British would agree to do likewise. It might also provide that we would be willing to impound what bombs we now have in the United States provided the Russians and the British would agree with us that in no event will they or we use a bomb as an instrument of war unless all three Governments agree to that use. We might also consider including in the arrangement a covenant with the U. K. and the Soviets providing for the exchange of benefits of future developments whereby atomic energy may be applied on a mutually satisfactory basis for commercial or humanitarian purposes.

I would make such an approach just as soon as our immediate political considerations make it appropriate.

I emphasize perhaps beyond all other considerations the importance of taking this action with Russia as a proposal of the United States—backed by Great Britain but peculiarly the proposal of the United States. Action of any international group of nations, including many small nations who have not demonstrated their potential power or responsibility in this war would not, in my opinion, be taken seriously by the Soviets. The loose debates which would surround such proposal, if put before a conference of nations, would provoke but scant favor from the Soviet. As I say, I think this is the most important point in the program.

After the nations which have won this war have agreed to it, there will be ample time to introduce France and China into the covenants and finally to incorporate the agreement into the scheme of the United Nations. The use of this bomb has been accepted by the world as the result of the initiative and productive capacity of the United States, and I think this factor is a most potent lever toward having our proposals accepted by the Soviets, whereas I am most skeptical of obtaining any tangible results by way of any international debate. I urge this method as the most realistic means of accomplishing this vitally important step in the history of the world.

Harry Hopkins and Josef Stalin
Discuss Lend-Lease and Poland, 1945

Mr. Hopkins said that last night the Marshal had indicated that there were a number of questions concerning the United States which were worrying him. He asked Marshal Stalin if he would perhaps care to begin with these questions.

Marshal Stalin said he would not attempt to use Soviet public opinion as a screen but would speak of the feeling that had been created in Soviet governmental circles as a result of recent moves on the part of the United States Government. He said these circles felt a certain alarm in regard to the attitude of the United States Government. It was their impression that the American attitude towards the Soviet Union had perceptibly cooled once it became obvious that Germany was defeated, and that it was as though the Americans were saying that the Russians were no longer needed. He said he would give the following examples: . . .

[1] 3. The attitude of the United States Government towards the Polish question. He said that at Yalta it had been agreed that the existing government was to be reconstructed and that anyone with common sense could see that this meant that the present government was to form the basis of the new. He said no other understanding of the Yalta Agreement was possible. Despite the fact that they were simple people the Russians should not be regarded as fools which was a mistake the West frequently made, nor were they blind and could quite well see what was going on before their eyes. It is true that the Russians are patient in the interests of a common cause but that their patience has its limits.

[2] 4. The manner in which Lend Lease had been curtailed. He said that if the United States was unable to supply the Soviet Union further under Lend Lease that was one thing but that the manner in which it had been done had been unfortunate and even brutal. For example, certain ships had been unloaded and while it was true that this order had been cancelled the whole manner in which it had been done had caused concern to the Soviet Government. If the refusal to continue Lend Lease was designed as pressure on the Russians in order to soften them up then it was a fundamental mistake. He said he must tell Mr. Hopkins frankly that [if] the Russians were approached frankly on a friendly basis much could be done but that reprisals in any form would bring about the exact opposite effect. . . .

Mr. Hopkins said he first of all wished to express his appreciation of the frankness with which Marshal Stalin had exposed his worries. He said that insofar as he and Ambassador Harriman were able they would answer equally frankly and if on certain points they did not have full information they would endeavor to obtain it. . . .

Mr. Hopkins then said on the subject of Lend Lease he thought it had been clear to the Soviet Union that the end of the war with Germany would necessitate a reconsideration of the old program of Lend Lease to the Soviet Union.

Marshal Stalin said that was entirely understandable.

Mr. Hopkins continued that the history of Lend Lease showed that although in certain cases we had not always been able to meet every Soviet request we had nonetheless freely accepted commitments which we had done our best to carry out in spirit as well as in fact.

Marshal Stalin said that was undoubtedly true.

Mr. Hopkins stated that even prior to the end of the war in Europe we had made an agreement with the Soviet Union known as Annex 3 to Protocol 1 [*IV*], which involved delivery of supplies which might be of use in the Far

East. He said that this grew out of recent conferences in which Far Eastern matters had been discussed. He emphasized that this commitment was accepted in full by the United States and we were in the process of carrying it out. In regard to the unloading of the ships he said that that was a technical misunderstanding and did not in any sense represent a decision of policy on the part of the United States. That it had been the action of one government agency involved in Lend Lease and that it had been countermanded promptly within twenty-four hours. He said that no one who was responsible for Lend Lease policy or American Government policy had had anything to do with that mistaken order. The only question which had to be reconsidered was the program of deliveries to the Soviet Union which had been based on the needs of the war against Germany and that it had been made clear that on the basis of this reconsideration we would be glad to reconsider any Soviet requests and that he thought some were now being considered. He said he wished to emphasize that he had seen no tendency on the part of those responsible for American policy to handle the question of future Lend Lease to the Soviet Union in an arbitrary fashion. It was in fact a question of law, since the basic Lend Lease Act made it clear that materials could only be delivered which would be useful in the process of the war. The United States Government, however, had interpreted this in its broadest sense and had included in addition to munitions of war foodstuffs and other non-military items.

Marshal Stalin said this was true.

Mr. Hopkins concluded by saying that there had naturally been considerable confusion in the United States Government as to the status of Lend Lease towards Russia at the end of the war and that there had been varying legal interpretations but that he wished to emphasize that the incident to which Marshal Stalin referred did not have any fundamental policy significance.

Marshal Stalin said he wished to make it clear that he fully understood the right of the United States to curtail Lend Lease shipments to the Soviet Union under present conditions since our commitments in this respect had been freely entered into. Even two months ago it would have been quite correct for the United States to have begun to curtail shipments but what he had in mind was the manner and form in which it was done. He felt that what was after all an agreement between the two Governments had been ended in a scornful and abrupt manner. He said that if proper warning had been given to the Soviet Government there would have been no feeling of the kind he had spoken of; that this warning was important to them since their economy was based on plans. He added that they had intended to make a suitable expression of gratitude to the United States for the Lend Lease assistance during the war but the way in which this program had been halted now made that impossible to do.

Mr. Hopkins replied that what disturbed him most about the Marshal's statement was the revelation that he believed that the United States would use Lend Lease as a means of showing our displeasure with the Soviet Union. He wished to assure the Marshal that however unfortunate an impression this question had caused in the mind of the Soviet Government he must believe that there was no attempt or desire on the part of the United States to use it as a pressure weapon. He said the United States is a strong power and does not go in for those methods. Furthermore, we have no conflict of immediate interests with the Soviet Union and would have no reason to adopt such practices.

Marshal Stalin said he believed Mr. Hopkins and was fully satisfied with his statement in regard to Lend Lease but said he hoped Mr. Hopkins would consider how it had looked from their side.

Ambassador Harriman then suggested that he and Mr. Molotov might go into the details of the whole Lend Lease matter together with Mr. Mikoyan the following day.

Mr. Hopkins concluded the discussions of Lend Lease by stating that he thought it would be a great tragedy if the greatest achievement in cooperation which the Soviet Union and the United States had on the whole worked out together on the basis of Lend Lease were to end on an unsatisfactory note. He said he wished to add that we had never believed that our Lend Lease help had been the chief factor in the Soviet defeat of Hitler on the eastern front. That this had been done by the heroism and blood of the Russian Army. . . .

Mr. Hopkins then said with the Marshal's permission he would like to review the position of the United States in regard to Poland. He said first of all he wished to assure the Marshal that he had no thought or indeed any right to attempt to settle the Polish problem during his visit here in Moscow, nor was he intending to hide behind American public opinion in presenting the position of the United States.

Marshal Stalin said he was afraid that his remark concerning Soviet public opinion has cut Mr. Hopkins to the quick and that he had not meant to imply that Mr. Hopkins was hiding behind the screen of American public opinion. In fact he knew Mr. Hopkins to be an honest and frank man.

Mr. Hopkins said that he wished to state this position as clearly and as forcibly as he knew how. He said the question of Poland per se was not so important as the fact that it had become a symbol of our ability to work out problems with the Soviet Union. He said that we had no special interests in Poland and no special desire to see any particular kind of government. That we would accept any government in Poland which was desired by the Polish people and was at the same time friendly to the Soviet Government. He said that the people and Government of the United States felt that this was a problem which should be worked out jointly between the United States, the Soviet Union and Great Britain and that we felt that the Polish people should be given the right to free elections to choose their own government and their own system and that Poland should genuinely be independent. The Government and people of the United States were disturbed because the preliminary steps towards the reestablishment of Poland appeared to have been taken unilaterally by the Soviet Union together with the present Warsaw Government and that in fact the United States was completely excluded. He said he hoped that Stalin would believe him when he said that this feeling was a fact. Mr. Hopkins said he urged that Marshal Stalin would judge American policy by the actions of the United States Government itself and not by the attitudes and public expressions of the Hearst newspapers and the *Chicago Tribune*. He hoped that the Marshal would put his mind to the task of thinking up what diplomatic methods could be used to settle this question keeping in mind the feeling of the American people. He said he himself was not prepared to say how it could be done but that he felt it must be done. Poland had become a symbol in the sense that it bore a direct relation to the willingness of the United States to participate in international affairs on a world-wide basis and that our people must believe that they are joining their power with that of the Soviet Union and Great Britain in the promotion of international peace and the well being of humanity. Mr. Hopkins went on to say that he felt the overwhelming majority of the people of the United States felt that the relations between the United States and the U.S.S.R. could be worked out in a spirit of cooperation despite the differences in ideology and that with all these factors in its favor he wished to appeal to the Marshal to help find a way to the solution of the Polish problem.

Marshal Stalin replied that he wished Mr. Hopkins would take into consideration the following factors: He said it may seem strange although it appeared to be recognized in United States circles and Churchill in his speeches also recognized it, that the Soviet Government should wish for a friendly Poland. In the course of twenty-five years the Germans had twice invaded Russia via Poland. Neither the British nor American people had experienced such German invasions which were a horrible thing to endure and the results of which were not easily forgotten. He said these German invasions were not warfare but were like the incursions of the Huns. He said that Germany had been able to do this because Poland had been regarded as a part of the *cordon sanitaire* around the Soviet Union and that previous European policy had been that Polish Governments must be hostile to Russia. In these circumstances either Poland had been too weak to oppose Germany or had let the Germans come through. Thus Poland had served as a corridor for the German attacks on Russia. He said Poland's weakness and hostility had been a great source of weakness to the Soviet Union and had permitted the Germans to do what they wished in the East and also in the West since the two were mixed together. It is therefore in Russia's vital interest that Poland should be both strong and friendly. He said there was no intention on the part of the Soviet Union to interfere in Poland's internal affairs, that Poland would live under the parliamentary system which is like Czechoslovakia, Belgium and Holland and that any talk of an intention to Sovietize Poland was stupid. He said even the Polish leaders, some of whom were communists, were against the Soviet system since the Polish people did not desire collective farms or other aspects of the Soviet system. In this the Polish leaders were right since the Soviet system was not exportable—it must develop from within on the basis of a set of conditions which were not present in Poland. He said all the Soviet Union wanted was that Poland should not be in a position to open the gates to Germany and in order to prevent this Poland must be strong and democratic. Stalin then said that before he came to his suggestion as to the practical solution of the question he would like to comment on Mr. Hopkins's remarks concerning future United States interests in the world. He said that whether the United States wished it or not it was a world power and would have to accept world-wide interests. Not only this war but the previous war had shown that without United States intervention Germany could not have been defeated and that all the events and developments of the last thirty years had confirmed this. In fact the United States had more reason to be a world power than any other state. For this reason he fully recognized the right of the United States as a world [power] to participate in the Polish question and that the Soviet interest in Poland does not in any way exclude those of England and the United States. Mr. Hopkins had spoken of Russian unilateral action in Poland and United States public opinion concerning it. It was true that Russia had taken such unilateral action but they had been compelled to. He said the Soviet Government had recognized the Warsaw Government and concluded a treaty with it at a time when their Allies did not recognize this government. These were admittedly unilateral acts which would have been much better left undone but the fact was they had not met with any understanding on the part of their Allies. The need for these actions had arisen out of the presence of Soviet troops in Poland and it would have been impossible to have waited until such time as the Allies had come to an agreement on Poland. The logic of the war against Germany demanded that the Soviet rear be assured and the Lublin Committee had been of great assistance to the Red Army at all times and it was for this reason that these actions had been taken by the Soviet Government. He said it was contrary to the Soviet policy to set up [a] Soviet administration on foreign soil since this would look like occupation and be resented by the local inhabitants. It was for this reason that some Polish administration had to be established in Poland and this could be done only with those who had helped the Red Army. He said he wished to emphasize that these steps had not been taken with any desire to eliminate or exclude Russia's Allies. He must point out however that Soviet action in Poland had been more successful than British action in Greece and at no time had they been compelled to undertake the measures which they had done in Greece. Stalin then turned to his suggestion for the solution of the Polish problem.

Marshal Stalin said that he felt that we should examine the composition of the future Government of National Unity. He said there were eighteen or twenty ministries in the present Polish Government and that four or five of these portfolios could be given representatives of other Polish groups taken from the list submitted by Great Britain and the United States (Molotov whispered to Stalin who then said he meant four and not five posts in the government). He said he thought the Warsaw Poles would not accept more than four ministers from other democratic groups. He added that if this appears a suitable basis we could then proceed to consider what persons should be selected for these posts. He said of course that they would have to be friendly to the U.S.S.R. and to the Allies. He added that Mikolajczyk had been suggested and he thought he was acceptable and that the question was now who else. He inquired of Mr. Hopkins whether possibly Professor Lange might be willing to join the government.

Mr. Hopkins said he doubted whether Professor Lange, who was an American citizen could be induced to give up his American citizenship for this purpose but that of course was only a private opinion.

Marshal Stalin then said it might be wise to ask some of the Warsaw leaders to come to Moscow now and to hear what they had to say and to learn more of what had been decided. He added that if we are able to settle the composition of the new government he felt that no differences remained since we were all agreed on the free and unfettered elections and that no one intended to interfere with the Polish people.

Mr. Hopkins said he would like to have some time to consider the Marshal's suggestion.

George F. Kennan's "Long Telegram," 1946

At bottom of Kremlin's neurotic view of world affairs is traditional and instinctive Russian sense of insecurity. Originally, this was insecurity of a peaceful agricultural people trying to live on vast exposed plain in neighborhood of fierce nomadic peoples. To this was added, as Russia came into contact with economically advanced West, fear of more competent, more powerful, more highly organized societies in that area. But this latter type of insecurity was one which afflicted rather Russian rulers than Russian people; for Russian rulers have invariably sensed that their rule was relatively archaic in form, fragile and artificial in its psychological foundation, unable to stand comparison or contact with political systems of Western countries. For this reason they have always feared foreign penetration, feared direct contact between Western world and their own, feared what would happen if Russians learned truth about world without or if foreigners learned truth about world within. And they have learned to seek security only in patient but deadly struggle for total destruction of rival power, never in compacts and compromises with it.

It was no coincidence that Marxism, which had smouldered ineffectively for half a century in Western Europe, caught hold and blazed for first time in Russia. Only in this land which had never known a friendly neighbor or indeed any tolerant equilibrium of separate powers, either internal or international, could a doctrine thrive which viewed economic conflicts of society as insoluble by peaceful means. After establishment of Bolshevist regime, Marxist dogma, rendered even more truculent and intolerant by Lenin's interpretation, became a perfect vehicle for sense of insecurity with which Bolsheviks, even more than previous Russian rulers, were afflicted. In this dogma, with its basic altruism of purpose, they found justification for their instinctive fear of outside world, for the dictatorship without which they did not know how to rule, for cruelties they did not dare not to inflict, for sacrifices they felt bound to demand. In the name of Marxism they sacrificed every single ethical value in their methods and tactics. Today they cannot dispense with it. It is fig leaf of their moral and intellectual respectability. Without it they would stand before history, at best, as only the last of that long succession of cruel and wasteful Russian rulers who have relentlessly forced country on to ever new heights of military power in order to guarantee external security of their internally weak regimes. This is why Soviet purposes must always be solemnly clothed in trappings of Marxism, and why no one should underrate importance of dogma in Soviet affairs. Thus Soviet leaders are driven [by?] necessities of their own past and present position to put forward a dogma which [apparent omission] outside world as evil, hostile and menacing, but as bearing within itself germs of creeping disease and destined to be wracked with growing internal convulsions until it is given final *coup de grace* by rising power of socialism and yields to new and better world. This thesis provides justification for that increase of military and police power of Russian state, for that isolation of Russian population from outside world, and for that fluid and constant pressure to extend limits of Russian police power which are together the natural and instinctive urges of Russian rulers. Basically this is only the steady advance of uneasy Russian nationalism, a centuries old movement in which conceptions of offense and defense are inextricably confused. But in new guise of international Marxism, with its honeyed promises to a desperate and war torn outside world, it is more dangerous and insidious than ever before.

It should not be thought from above that Soviet party line is necessarily disingenuous and insincere on part of all those who put it forward. Many of them are too ignorant of outside world and mentally too dependent to question [apparent omission] self-hypnotism, and who have no difficulty making themselves believe what they find it comforting and convenient to believe. Finally we have the unsolved mystery as to who, if anyone, in this great land actually receives accurate and unbiased information about outside world. In atmosphere of oriental secretiveness and conspiracy which pervades this Government, possibilities for distorting or poisoning sources and currents of information are infinite. The very disrespect of Russians for objective truth—indeed, their disbelief in its existence—leads them to view all stated facts as instruments for furtherance of one ulterior purpose or another. There is good reason to suspect that this Government is actually a conspiracy within a conspiracy; and I for one am reluctant to believe that Stalin himself receives anything like an objective picture of outside world. Here there is ample scope for the type of subtle intrigue at which Russians are past masters. Inability of foreign governments to place their case squarely before Russian policy makers—extent to which they are delivered up in their relations with Russia to good graces of obscure and unknown advisers whom they never see and cannot influence—this to my mind is most disquieting feature of diplomacy in Moscow, and one which Western statesmen would do well to keep in mind if they would understand nature of difficulties encountered here. . . .

In summary, we have here a political force committed fanatically to the belief that with US there can be no permanent *modus vivendi,* that it is desirable and necessary that the internal harmony of our society be disrupted, our traditional way of life be destroyed, the international authority of our state be broken, if Soviet power is to be secure. This political force has complete power of disposition over energies of one of world's greatest peoples and resources of world's richest national territory, and is borne along by deep and powerful currents of Russian nationalism. In addition, it has an elaborate and far flung apparatus for exertion of its influence in other countries, an apparatus of amazing flexibility and versatility, managed by people whose experience and skill in underground methods are presumably without parallel in history. Finally, it is seemingly inaccessible to considerations of reality in its basic reactions. For it, the vast fund of objective fact about human society is not, as with us, the measure against which outlook is constantly being tested and re-formed, but a grab bag from which individual items are selected arbitrarily and tendenciously to bolster an outlook already preconceived. This is admittedly not a pleasant picture. Problem of how to cope with this force in [is] undoubtedly greatest task our diplomacy has ever faced and probably greatest it will ever have to face. It should be point of departure from which our political general staff work at present juncture should proceed. It should be approached with same thoroughness and care as solution of major strategic problem in war, and if necessary, with no smaller outlay in planning effort. I cannot attempt to suggest all answers here. But I would like to record my conviction that problem is within our power to solve—and that without recourse to any general military conflict. And in support of this conviction there are certain observations of a more encouraging nature I should like to make:

1. Soviet power, unlike that of Hitlerite Germany, is neither schematic nor adventuristic. It does not work by fixed plans. It does not take unnecessary risks. Impervious to logic of reason, and it is highly sensitive to logic of force. For this reason it can easily withdraw—and usually does—when strong resistance is encountered at any point. Thus, if the adversary has sufficient force and makes clear his readiness to use it, he rarely has to do so. If situations are properly handled there need be no prestige-engaging showdowns.

2. Gauged against Western World as a whole, Soviets are still by far the weaker force. Thus, their success will really depend on degree of cohesion, firmness and vigor which Western World can muster. And this is factor which it is within our power to influence.

3. Success of Soviet system, as form of internal power, is not yet finally proven. It has yet to be demonstrated that it can survive supreme test of successive transfer of power from one individual or group to another. Lenin's death was first such transfer, and its effects wracked Soviet state for 15 years. After Stalin's death or retirement will be second. But even this will not be final test. Soviet internal system will now be subjected, by virtue of recent territorial expansions, to series of additional strains which once proved severe tax on Tsardom. We here are convinced that never since termination of civil war have mass of Russian people been emotionally farther removed from doctrines of Communist Party than they are today. In Russia, party has now become a great and—for the moment—highly successful apparatus of dictatorial administration, but it has ceased to be a source of emotional inspiration.

Thus, internal soundness and permanence of movement need not yet be regarded as assured.

4. All Soviet propaganda beyond Soviet security sphere is basically negative and destructive. It should therefore be relatively easy to combat it by any intelligent and really constructive program.

For these reasons I think we may approach calmly and with good heart problem of how to deal with Russia. As to how this approach should be made, I only wish to advance, by way of conclusion, following comments:

1. Our first step must be to apprehend, and recognize for what it is, the nature of the movement with which we are dealing. We must study it with same courage, detachment, objectivity, and same determination not to be emotionally provoked or unseated by it, with which doctor studies unruly and unreasonable individual.

2. We must see that our public is educated to realities of Russian situation. I cannot over-emphasize importance of this. Press cannot do this alone. It must be done mainly by Government, which is necessarily more experienced and better informed on practical problems involved. In this we need not be deterred by [ugliness?] of picture. I am convinced that there would be far less hysterical anti-Sovietism in our country today if realities of this situation were better understood by our people. There is nothing as dangerous or as terrifying as the unknown. It may also be argued that to reveal more information on our difficulties with Russia would reflect unfavorably on Russian-American relations. I feel that if there is any real risk here involved, it is one which we should have courage to face, and sooner the better. But I cannot see what we would be risking. Our stake in this country, even coming on heels of tremendous demonstrations of our friendship for Russian people, is remarkably small. We have here no investments to guard, no actual trade to lose, virtually no citizens to protect, few cultural contacts to preserve. Our only stake lies in what we hope rather than what we have; and I am convinced we have better chance of realizing those hopes if our public is enlightened and if our dealings with Russians are placed entirely on realistic and matter-of-fact basis.

3. Much depends on health and vigor of our own society. World communism is like malignant parasite which feeds only on diseased tissue. This is point at which domestic and foreign policies meet. Every courageous and incisive measure to solve internal problems of our own society, to improve self-confidence, discipline, morale and community spirit of our own people, is a diplomatic victory over Moscow worth a thousand diplomatic notes and joint communiqués. If we cannot abandon fatalism and indifference in face of deficiencies of our own society, Moscow will profit—Moscow cannot help profiting by them in its foreign policies.

4. We must formulate and put forward for other nations a much more positive and constructive picture of sort of world we would like to see than we have put forward in past. It is not enough to urge people to develop political processes similar to our own. Many foreign peoples, in Europe at least, are tired and frightened by experiences of past, and are less interested in ab-

stract freedom than in security. They are seeking guidance rather than responsibilities. We should be better able than Russians to give them this. And unless we do, Russians certainly will.

5. Finally we must have courage and self-confidence to cling to our own methods and conceptions of human society. After all, the greatest danger that can befall us in coping with this problem of Soviet communism, is that we shall allow ourselves to become like those with whom we are coping.

Winston S. Churchill's "Iron Curtain" Speech, 1946

The United States stands at this time at the pinnacle of world power. It is a solemn moment for the American democracy. With primacy in power is also joined an awe-inspiring accountability to the future. As you look around you, you feel not only the sense of duty done but also feel anxiety lest you fall below the level of achievement. Opportunity is here now, clear and shining, for both our countries. To reject it or ignore it or fritter it away will bring upon us all the long reproaches of the after-time. It is necessary that constancy of mind, persistency of purpose, and the grand simplicity of decision shall guide and rule the conduct of the English-speaking peoples in peace as they did in war. We must and I believe we shall prove ourselves equal to this severe requirement. . . .

Before we cast away the solid assurances of national armaments for self-preservation, we must be certain that our temple is built, not upon shifting sands or quagmires, but upon the rock. Anyone with his eyes open can see that our path will be difficult and also long, but if we persevere together as we did in the two World Wars—though not, alas, in the interval between them—I cannot doubt that we shall achieve our common purpose in the end.

I have, however, a definite and practical proposal to make for action. Courts and magistrates cannot function without sheriffs and constables. The United Nations Organization must immediately begin to be equipped with an international armed force. In such a matter we can only go step by step; but we must begin now. I propose that each of the powers and states should be invited to dedicate a certain number of air squadrons to the service of the world organization. These squadrons would be trained and prepared in their own countries but would move around in rotation from one country to another. They would wear the uniform of their own countries with different badges. They would not be required to act against their own nation but in other respects they would be directed by the world organization. This might be started on a modest scale and a grow [sic] as confidence grew. I wished to see this done after the First World War and trust it may be done forthwith.

It would nevertheless be wrong and imprudent to entrust the secret knowledge or experience of the atomic bomb, which the United States, Great Britain, and Canada now share, to the world organization, while it is still in its infancy.

It would be criminal madness to cast it adrift in this still agitated and un-united world. No one in any country has slept less well in their beds because this knowledge and the method and the raw materials to apply it are at present largely retained in American hands. I do not believe we should all have slept so soundly had the positions been reversed and some Communist or neo-Fascist state monopolized, for the time being, these dread agencies. The fear of them alone might easily have been used to enforce totalitarian systems upon the free democratic world, with consequences appalling to human imagination.

God has willed that this shall not be, and we have at least a breathing space before this peril has to be encountered, and even then, if no effort is spared, we should still possess so formidable a superiority as to impose effective deterrents upon its employment or threat of employment by others. Ultimately when the essential brother of man is truly embodied and expressed in a world organization, these powers may be confided to it. . . .

There is . . . an important question we must ask ourselves. Would a special relationship between the United States and the British Commonwealth be inconsistent with our overriding loyalties to the world organization? I reply that on the contrary, it is probably the only means by which that organization will achieve its full stature and strength. There are already the special United States relations with Canada and between the United States and the South American republics. We also have our twenty years' treaty of collaboration and mutual assistance with Soviet Russia. I agree with Mr. Bevin that it might well be a fifty-year treaty. We have an alliance with Portugal unbroken since 1384. None of these clash with the general interest of a world agreement. On the contrary they help it. "In my Father's house are many mansions." Special associations between members of the United Nations which have no aggressive point against any other country, which harbor no design incompatible with the charter of the United Nations, far from being harmful, are beneficial and, as I believe, indispensable. . . .

A shadow has fallen upon the scenes so lately lighted by the Allied victory. Nobody knows what Soviet Russia and its Communist international organization intends to do in the immediate future, or what are the limits, if any, to their expansive and proselytizing tendencies. I have a strong admiration and regard for the valiant Russian people and for my wartime comrade, Marshal Stalin. There is sympathy and good will in Britain—and I doubt not here also —toward the peoples of all the Russias and a resolve to persevere through many differences and rebuffs in establishing lasting friendships.

We understand the Russian need to be secure on her western frontiers from all renewal of German aggression. We welcome her to her rightful place among the leading nations of the world. Above all, we welcome constant, frequent, and growing contacts between the Russian people and our own people on both sides of the Atlantic. It is my duty, however, to place before you certain facts about the present position in Europe.

From Stettin in the Baltic to Trieste in the Adriatic, an iron curtain has descended across the continent. Behind that line lie all the capitals of the ancient states of Central and Eastern Europe. Warsaw, Berlin, Prague, Vienna,

Budapest, Belgrade, Bucharest, and Sofia, all these famous cities and the populations around them lie in the Soviet sphere and all are subject, in one form or another, not only to Soviet influence but to a very high and increasing measure of control from Moscow. Athens alone, with its immortal glories, is free to decide its future at an election under British, American, and French observation.

The Russian-dominated Polish government has been encouraged to make enormous and wrongful inroads upon Germany, and mass expulsions of millions of Germans on a scale grievous and undreamed of are now taking place. The Communist parties, which were very small in all these eastern states of Europe, have been raised to preeminence and power far beyond their numbers and are seeking everywhere to obtain totalitarian control. Police governments are prevailing in nearly every case, and so far, except in Czechoslovakia, there is no true democracy.

Turkey and Persia are both profoundly alarmed and disturbed at the claims which are made upon them and at the pressure being exerted by the Moscow government. An attempt is being made by the Russians in Berlin to build up a quasi-Communist party in their zone of occupied Germany by showing special favors to groups of left-wing German leaders. At the end of the fighting last June, the American and British Armies withdrew westward, in accordance with an earlier agreement, to a depth at some points of 150 miles on a front of nearly 400 miles, to allow the Russians to occupy this vast expanse of territory which the Western democracies had conquered.

If now the Soviet government tries, by separate action, to build up a pro-Communist Germany in their areas, this will cause new serious difficulties in the British and American zones, and will give the defeated Germans the power of putting themselves up to auction between the Soviets and the Western democracies. Whatever conclusions may be drawn from these facts—and facts they are—this is certainly not the liberated Europe we fought to build up. Nor is it one which contains the essentials of permanent peace.

In front of the iron curtain which lies across Europe are other causes for anxiety. In Italy the Communist party is seriously hampered by having to support the Communist-trained Marshall Tito's claims to former Italian territory at the head of the Adriatic. Nevertheless, the future of Italy hangs in the balance. Again, one cannot imagine a regenerated Europe without a strong France. . . .

However, in a great number of countries, far from the Russian frontiers and throughout the world, Communist fifth columns are established and work in complete unity and absolute obedience to the directions they receive from the Communist center. Except in the British Commonwealth, and in the United States, where communism is in its infancy, the Communist parties or fifth columns constitute a growing challenge and peril to Christian civilization. These are somber facts for anyone to have to recite on the morrow of a victory gained by so much splendid comradeship in arms and in the cause of freedom and democracy, and we should be most unwise not to face them squarely while time remains.

The outlook is also anxious in the Far East and especially in Manchuria.

The agreement which was made at Yalta, to which I was a party, was extremely favorable to Soviet Russia, but it was made at a time when no one could say that the German war might not extend all through the summer and autumn of 1945 and when the Japanese war was expected to last for a further eighteen months from the end of the German war. In this country you are all so well informed about the Far East and such devoted friends of China that I do not need to expatiate on the situation there. . . .

Our difficulties and dangers will not be removed by closing our eyes to them; they will not be removed by mere waiting to see what happens; nor will they be relieved by a policy of appeasement. What is needed is a settlement, and the longer this is delayed, the more difficult it will be and the greater our dangers will become. From what I have seen of our Russian friends and allies during the war, I am convinced that there is nothing they admire so much as strength, and there is nothing for which they have less respect than for military weakness. For that reason the old doctrine of a balance of power is unsound. We cannot afford, if we can help it, to work on narrow margins, offering temptations to a trial of strength. If the Western democracies stand together in strict adherence to the principles of the United Nations Charter, their influence for furthering these principles will be immense and no one is likely to molest them. If, however, they become divided or falter in their duty, and if these all-important years are allowed to slip away, then indeed catastrophe may overwhelm us all.

Last time I saw it all coming, and cried aloud to my own fellow countrymen and to the world, but no one paid any attention. Up till the year 1933 or even 1935, Germany might have been saved from the awful fate which has overtaken her and we might all have been spared the miseries Hitler let loose upon mankind.

There never was a war in all history easier to prevent by timely action than the one which has just desolated such great areas of the globe. It could have been prevented without the firing of a single shot, and Germany might be powerful, prosperous, and honored today, but no one would listen and one by one we were all sucked into the awful whirlpool.

We surely must not let that happen again. This can only be achieved by reaching now, in 1946, a good understanding on all points with Russia under the general authority of the United Nations and by the maintenance of that good understanding through many peaceful years, by the world instrument, supported by the whole strength of the English-speaking world and all its connections.

Henry A. Wallace Questions the "Get Tough" Policy, 1946

How do American actions since V-J Day appear to other nations? I mean by actions the concrete things like $13 billion for the War and Navy Depart-

Henry A. Wallace, "The Path to Peace with Russia," *New Republic,* 115 (1946), 401–406.

ments, the Bikini tests of the atomic bomb and continued production of bombs, the plan to arm Latin America with our weapons, production of B-29s and planned production of B-36s, and the effort to secure air bases spread over half the globe from which the other half of the globe can be bombed. I cannot but feel that these actions must make it look to the rest of the world as if we were only paying lip service to peace at the conference table. These facts rather make it appear either (1) that we are preparing ourselves to win the war which we regard as inevitable or (2) that we are trying to build up a predominance of force to intimidate the rest of mankind. How would it look to us if Russia had the atomic bomb and we did not, if Russia had ten thousand-mile bombers and air bases within a thousand miles of our coast lines and we did not?

Some of the military men and self-styled "realists" are saying: "What's wrong with trying to build up a predominance of force? The only way to preserve peace is for this country to be so well armed that no one will dare attack us. We know that America will never start a war."

The flaw in this policy is simply that it will not work. In a world of atomic bombs and other revolutionary new weapons, such as radioactive poison gases and biological warfare, a peace maintained by a predominance of force is no longer possible.

Why is this so? The reasons are clear:

First. Atomic warfare is cheap and easy compared with old-fashioned war. Within a very few years several countries can have atomic bombs and other atomic weapons. Compared with the cost of large armies and the manufacture of old-fashioned weapons, atomic bombs cost very little and require only a relatively small part of a nation's production plant and labor force.

Second. So far as winning a war is concerned, having more bombs—even many more bombs—than the other fellow is no longer a decisive advantage. If another nation had enough bombs to eliminate all of our principal cities and our heavy industry, it wouldn't help us very much if we had ten times as many bombs as we needed to do the same to them.

Third. The most important, the very fact that several nations have atomic bombs will inevitably result in a neurotic, fear-ridden, itching-trigger psychology in all the peoples of the world, and because of our wealth and vulnerability we would be among the most seriously affected. Atomic war will not require vast and time-consuming preparations, the mobilization of large armies, the conversion of a large proportion of a country's industrial plants to the manufacture of weapons. In a world armed with atomic weapons, some incident will lead to the use of those weapons.

There is a school of military thinking which recognizes these facts, recognizes that when several nations have atomic bombs, a war which will destroy modern civilization will result and that no nation or combination of nations can win such a war. This school of thought therefore advocates a "preventative war," an attack on Russia now, before Russia has atomic bombs. This scheme is not only immoral but stupid. If we should attempt to destroy all the principal Russian cities and her heavy industry, we might well succeed. But the immediate countermeasure which such an attack would call forth is the prompt occupation of all continental Europe by the Red Army. Would we be prepared to destroy the cities of all Europe in trying to finish what we had started? This idea is so contrary to all the basic instincts and principles of the American people that any such action would be possible only under a dictatorship at home.

Thus the "predominance of force" idea and the notion of a "defensive attack" are both unworkable. The only solution is the one which you have so wisely advanced and which forms the basis of the Moscow statement on atomic energy. That solution consists of mutual trust and confidence among nations, atomic disarmament and an effective system of enforcing that disarmament.

There is, however, a fatal defect in the Moscow statement, in the Acheson report, and in the American plan recently presented to the United Nations Atomic Energy Commission. That defect is the scheme, as it is generally understood, of arriving at international agreements by "easy stages," of requiring other nations to enter into binding commitments not to conduct research into the military uses of atomic energy and to disclose their uranium and thorium resources while the United States retains the right to withhold its technical knowledge of atomic energy until the international control and inspection system is working to our satisfaction. In other words, we are telling the Russians that if they are "good boys" we may eventually turn over our knowledge of atomic energy to them and to the other nations. But there is no objective standard of what will qualify them as being "good" nor any specified time for sharing our knowledge.

Is it any wonder that the Russians did not show any great enthusiasm for our plan? Would we have been enthusiastic if the Russians had a monopoly of atomic energy, and offered to share the information with us at some indefinite time in the future at their discretion if we agreed now not to try to make a bomb and give them information on our secret resources of uranium and thorium? I think we should react as the Russians appear to have done. We would have put up counterproposal for the record, but our real effort would go into trying to make a bomb so that our bargaining position would be equalized. . . .

Insistence on our part that the game must be played our way will only lead to a deadlock. The Russians will redouble their efforts to manufacture bombs, and they may also decide to expand their "security zone" in a serious way. Up to now, despite all our outcries against it, their efforts to develop a security zone in Eastern Europe and in the Middle East are small change from the point of view of military power as compared with our air bases in Greenland, Okinawa and many other places thousands of miles from our shores. We may feel very self-righteous if we refuse to budge on our plan and the Russians refuse to accept it, but that means only one thing—the atomic armament race is on in deadly earnest.

I am convinced therefore that if we are to achieve our hopes of negotiating a treaty which will result in effective international atomic disarmament we must abandon the impractical form of the "step-by-step" idea which was presented to the United Nations Atomic Energy Commission. We must be prepared to reach an agreement which will commit us to disclosing information and destroying our bombs at a specific time or on terms of specified actions by other countries, rather than at our unfettered discretion. If we are willing to negotiate on this basis, I believe the Russians will also negotiate seriously with a view to reaching an agreement.

There can be, of course, no absolute assurance the Russians will finally agree to a workable plan if we adopt this view. They may prefer to stall until they also have bombs and can negotiate on a more equal basis, not realizing the danger to themselves as well as the rest of the world in a situation in which several nations have atomic bombs. But we must make the effort to head off the atomic bomb race. We have everything to gain by doing so, and do not give up anything by adopting this policy as the fundamental basis for our negotiation. During the transition period toward full-scale international control we retain our technical know-how, and the only existing production plants for fissionable materials and bombs remain within our borders. . . .

Our basic distrust of the Russians, which has been greatly intensified in recent months by the playing up of conflict in the press, stems from differences in political and economic organizations. For the first time in our history defeatists among us have raised the fear of another system as a successful rival to democracy and free enterprise in other countries and perhaps even our own. I am convinced that we can meet that challenge as we have in the past by demonstrating that economic abundance can be achieved without sacrificing personal, political and religious liberties. We cannot meet it, as Hitler tried to, by an anti-Comintern alliance.

It is perhaps too easy to forget that despite the deep-seated differences in our culture and intensive anti-Russian propaganda of some twenty-five years' standing, the American people reversed their attitudes during the crisis of war. Today, under the pressure of seemingly insoluble international problems and continuing deadlocks, the tide of American public opinion is again turning against Russia. In this reaction lies one of the dangers to which this letter is addressed.

I should list the factors which make for Russian distrust of the United States and of the Western world as follows: The first is Russian history, which we must take into account because it is the setting in which Russians see all actions and policies of the rest of the world. Russian history for over a thousand years has been a succession of attempts, often unsuccessful, to resist invasion and conquest—by the Mongols, the Turks, the Swedes, the Germans and the Poles. The scant thirty years of the existence of the Soviet government has in Russian eyes been a continuation of their historical struggle for national existence. The first four years of the new regime, from 1917 through 1921, were spent in resisting attempts at destruction by the Japanese, British and French, with some American assistance, and by the several White Russian armies encouraged and financed by the Western powers. Then, in 1941, the Soviet state was almost conquered by the Germans after a period during which the Western European powers had apparently acquiesced in the rearming of Germany in the belief that the Nazis would seek to expand eastward rather than westward.

The Russians, therefore, obviously see themselves as fighting for their existence in a hostile world.

Second, it follows that to the Russians all of the defense and security measures of the Western powers seem to have an aggressive intent. Our actions to expand our military security system—such steps as extending the Monroe Doctrine to include the arming of the Western Hemisphere nations, our present monopoly of the atomic bomb, our interest in outlying bases and our general support of the British Empire—appear to them as going far beyond the requirements of defense. I think we might feel the same if the United States were the only capitalistic country in the world and the principal socialistic countries were creating a level of armed strength far exceeding anything in their previous history. From the Russian point of view, also, the granting of a loan to Britain and the lack of tangible results on their request to borrow for rehabilitation purposes may be regarded as another evidence of strengthening of an anti-Soviet bloc.

Finally, our resistance to her attempts to obtain warm water ports and her own security system in the form of "friendly" neighboring states seems, from the Russian point of view, to clinch the case. After twenty-five years of isolation and after having achieved the status of a major power, Russia believes that she is entitled to recognition of her new status. Our interest in establishing democracy in Eastern Europe, where democracy by and large has never existed, seems to her an attempt to reestablish the encirclement of unfriendly neighbors which was created after the last war and which might serve as a springboard of still another effort to destroy her.

If this analysis is correct, and there is ample evidence to support it, the action to improve the situation is clearly indicated. The fundamental objective of such action should be to allay any reasonable Russian grounds for fear, suspicions and distrust. We must recognize that the world has changed and that today there can be no "one world" unless the United States and Russia can find some way of living together. For example, most of us are firmly convinced of the soundness of our position when we suggest the internationalization and defortification of the Danube or of the Dardanelles, but we would be horrified and angered by any Russian counterproposal that would involve also the internationalizing and disarming of Suez or Panama. We must recognize that to the Russians these seem to be identical situations.

We should ascertain from a fresh point of view what Russia believes to be essential to her own security as a prerequisite to the writing of the peace and to cooperation in the construction of a world order. We should be prepared to judge her requirements against the background of what we ourselves and the British have insisted upon as essential to our respective security. We should be prepared, even at the expense of risking epithets of appeasement to agree to reasonable Russian guarantees of security. . . .

We should also be prepared to enter into economic discussions without demanding that the Russians agree in advance to discussion of a series of what are to them difficult and somewhat unrelated political and economic concessions. Although this is the field in which my department is most directly concerned, I must say that in my opinion this aspect of the problem is not as critical as some of the others, and certainly is far less important than the question of atomic energy control. But successful negotiation in this field might help considerably to bridge the chasm that separates us. The question of a loan should be approached on economic and commercial grounds and should be dissociated as much as possible from the current misunderstandings which flow from the basic differences between their system and ours. You have already clearly dissociated yourself and the American people from the expressions of anti-Soviet support for the British loan. If we could have followed up your statement on signing the British loan bill with a loan to the USSR on a commercial basis and on similar financial terms, I believe that it would have clearly demonstrated that this country is not attempting to use its economic resources in the game of power politics. In the light of the present Export-Import Bank situation it is now of the greatest importance that we undertake general economic discussions at an early date.

It is of the greatest importance that we should discuss with the Russians in a friendly way their long-range economic problems and the future of our co-operation in matters of trade. The reconstruction program of the USSR and the plans for the full development of the Soviet Union offers tremendous opportunities for American goods and American technicians.

American products, especially machines of all kinds, are well established in the Soviet Union. For example, American equipment, practices and methods are standard in coal mining, iron and steel, oil and nonferrous metals.

Nor would this trade be one-sided. Although the Soviet Union has been an excellent credit risk in the past, eventually the goods and services exported from this country must be paid for by the Russians by exports to us and to other countries. Russian products which are either definitely needed or which are noncompetitive in this country are various nonferrous metal ores, furs, linen products, lumber products, vegetable drugs, paper and pulp and native handicrafts. . . .

Many of the problems relating to the countries bordering on Russia could more readily be solved once an atmosphere of mutual trust and confidence is established and some form of economic arrangements is worked out with Russia. These problems also might be helped by discussions of an economic nature. Russian economic penetration of the Danube area, for example, might be countered by concrete proposals for economic collaboration in the development of the resources of this area, rather than by insisting that the Russians should cease their unilateral penetration and offering no solution to the present economic chaos there.

This proposal admittedly calls for a shift in some of our thinking about international matters. It is imperative that we make this shift. We have little time to lose. Our postwar actions have not yet been adjusted to the lessons to be gained from experience of Allied cooperation during the war and the facts of the atomic age.

It is certainly desirable that, as far as possible, we achieve unity on the home front with respect to our international relations; but unity on the basis of building up conflict abroad would prove to be not only unsound but disastrous. I think there is some reason to fear that in our earnest efforts to achieve bipartisan unity in this country we may have given away too much to isolationism masquerading as tough realism in international affairs.

The Truman Doctrine, 1947

The gravity of the situation which confronts the world today necessitates my appearance before a joint session of the Congress.

The foreign policy and the national security of this country are involved.

One aspect of the present situation, which I present to you at this time for your consideration and decision, concerns Greece and Turkey.

The United States has received from the Greek Government an urgent appeal for financial and economic assistance. Preliminary reports from the American Economic Mission now in Greece and reports from the American Ambassador in Greece corroborate the statement of the Greek Government that assistance is imperative if Greece is to survive as a free nation. . . .

The British Government has informed us that, owing to its own difficulties, it can no longer extend financial or economic aid to Turkey.

As in the case of Greece, if Turkey is to have the assistance it needs, the United States must supply it. We are the only country able to provide that help.

I am fully aware of the broad implications involved if the United States extends assistance to Greece and Turkey, and I shall discuss these implications with you at this time.

One of the primary objectives of the foreign policy of the United States is the creation of conditions in which we and other nations will be able to work out a way of life free from coercion. This was a fundamental issue in the war with Germany and Japan. Our victory was won over countries which sought to impose their will, and their way of life, upon other nations.

To ensure the peaceful development of nations, free from coercion, the United States has taken a leading part in establishing the United Nations. The United Nations is designed to make possible lasting freedom and independence for all its members. We shall not realize our objectives, however, unless we are willing to help free peoples to maintain their free institutions and their national integrity against aggressive movements that seek to impose upon them totalitarian regimes. This is no more than a frank recognition that totalitarian regimes imposed upon free peoples, by direct or indirect aggression, undermine the foundations of international peace and hence the security of the United States.

The peoples of a number of countries of the world have recently had totalitarian regimes forced upon them against their will. The Government of the United States has made frequent protests against coercion and intimidation, in violation of the Yalta agreement, in Poland, Rumania, and Bulgaria. I must also state that in a number of other countries there have been similar developments.

At the present moment in world history nearly every nation must choose between alternative ways of life. The choice is too often not a free one.

One way of life is based upon the will of the majority, and is distinguished by free institutions, representative government, free elections, guarantees of individual liberty, freedom of speech and religion, and freedom from political oppression.

The second way of life is based upon the will of a minority forcibly imposed upon the majority. It relies upon terror and oppression, a controlled press and radio, fixed elections, and the suppression of personal freedoms.

I believe that it must be the policy of the United States to support free peoples who are resisting attempted subjugation by armed minorities or by outside pressures.

I believe that we must assist free peoples to work out their own destinies in their own way.

I believe that our help should be primarily through economic and financial aid which is essential to economic stability and orderly political processes.

The world is not static, and the *status quo* is not sacred. But we cannot allow changes in the *status quo* in violation of the Charter of the United Nations by such methods as coercion, or by such subterfuges as political infiltration. In helping free and independent nations to maintain their freedom, the United States will be giving effect to the principles of the Charter of the United Nations.

It is necessary only to glance at a map to realize that the survival and integrity of the Greek nation are of grave importance in a much wider situation. If Greece should fall under the control of an armed minority, the effect upon its neighbor, Turkey, would be immediate and serious. Confusion and disorder might well spread throughout the entire Middle East.

Moreover, the disappearance of Greece as an independent state would have a profound effect upon those countries in Europe whose peoples are struggling against great difficulties to maintain their freedoms and their independence while they repair the damages of war.

It would be an unspeakable tragedy if these countries, which have struggled so long against overwhelming odds, should lose that victory for which they sacrificed so much. Collapse of free institutions and loss of independence would be disastrous not only for them but for the world. Discouragement and possibly failure would quickly be the lot of neighboring peoples striving to maintain their freedom and independence.

Should we fail to aid Greece and Turkey in this fateful hour, the effect will be far reaching to the West as well as to the East.

We must take immediate and resolute action.

I therefore ask the Congress to provide authority for assistance to Greece and Turkey in the amount of $400,000,000 for the period ending June 30, 1948. In requesting these funds, I have taken into consideration the maximum amount of relief assistance which would be furnished to Greece out of the $350,000,000 which I recently requested that the Congress authorize for the prevention of starvation and suffering in countries devastated by the war.

In addition to funds, I ask the Congress to authorize the detail of American civilian and military personnel to Greece and Turkey, at the request of those countries, to assist in the tasks of reconstruction, and for the purpose of supervising the use of such financial and material assistance as may be furnished. I recommend that authority also be provided for the instruction and training of selected Greek and Turkish personnel.

Finally, I ask that the Congress provide authority which will permit the speediest and most effective use, in terms of needed commodities, supplies, and equipment, of such funds as may be authorized.

If further funds, or further authority, should be needed for the purposes indicated in this message, I shall not hesitate to bring the situation before the Congress. On this subject the Executive and Legislative branches of the Government must work together.

This is a serious course upon which we embark.

I would not recommend it except that the alternative is much more serious.

The United States contributed $341,000,000,000 toward winning World War II. This is an investment in world freedom and world peace.

The assistance that I am recommending for Greece and Turkey amounts to little more than $\frac{1}{10}$ of 1 percent of this investment. It is only common sense that we should safeguard this investment and make sure that it was not in vain.

The seeds of totalitarian regimes are nurtured by misery and want. They spread and grow in the evil soil of poverty and strife. They reach their full growth when the hope of a people for a better life has died.

We must keep that hope alive.

The free peoples of the world look to us for support in maintaining their freedoms.

If we falter in our leadership, we may endanger the peace of the world—and we shall surely endanger the welfare of this Nation.

Great responsibilities have been placed upon us by the swift movement of events.

I am confident that the Congress will face these responsibilities squarely.

National Security Council
Paper No. 68 (NSC-68), 1950

Within the past thirty-five years the world has experienced two global wars of tremendous violence. It has witnessed two revolutions—the Russian and the Chinese—of extreme scope and intensity. It has also seen the collapse of five empires—the Ottoman, the Austro-Hungarian, German, Italian and Japanese—and the drastic decline of two major imperial systems, the British and the French. During the span of one generation, the international distribution of power has been fundamentally altered. For several centuries it had proved impossible for any one nation to gain such preponderant strength that a coalition of other nations could not in time face it with greater strength.

The international scene was marked by recurring periods of violence and war, but a system of sovereign and independent states was maintained, over which no state was able to achieve hegemony.

Two complex sets of factors have now basically altered this historical distribution of power. First, the defeat of Germany and Japan and the decline of the British and French Empires have interacted with the development of the United States and the Soviet Union in such a way that power has increasingly gravitated to these two centers. Second, the Soviet Union, unlike previous aspirants to hegemony, is animated by a new fanatic faith, antithetical to our own, and seeks to impose its absolute authority over the rest of the world. Conflict has, therefore, become endemic and is waged, on the part of the Soviet Union, by violent or non-violent methods in accordance with the dictates of expediency. With the development of increasingly terrifying weapons of mass destruction, every individual faces the ever-present possibility of annihilation should the conflict enter the phase of total war.

On the one hand, the people of the world yearn for relief from the anxiety arising from the risk of atomic war. On the other hand, any substantial further extension of the area under the domination of the Kremlin would raise the possibility that no coalition adequate to confront the Kremlin with greater strength could be assembled. It is in this context that this Republic and its citizens in the ascendancy of their strength stand in their deepest peril.

The issues that face us are momentous, involving the fulfillment or destruction not only of this Republic but of civilization itself. They are issues which will not await our deliberations. With conscience and resolution this Government and the people it represents must now take new and fateful decisions. . . .

Our overall policy at the present time may be described as one designed to foster a world environment in which the American system can survive and flourish. It therefore rejects the concept of isolation and affirms the necessity of our positive participation in the world community.

This broad intention embraces two subsidiary policies. One is a policy which we would probably pursue even if there were no Soviet threat. It is a policy of attempting to develop a healthy international community. The other is the policy of "containing" the Soviet system. These two policies are closely interrelated and interact on one another. Nevertheless, the distinction between them is basically valid and contributes to a clearer understanding of what we are trying to do.

The policy of striving to develop a healthy international community is the long-term constructive effort which we are engaged in. It was this policy which gave rise to our vigorous sponsorship of the United Nations. It is of course the principal reason for our long continuing endeavors to create and now develop the Inter-American system. It, as much as containment, underlay our efforts to rehabilitate Western Europe. Most of our international economic activities can likewise be explained in terms of this policy.

In a world of polarized power, the policies designed to develop a healthy international community are more than ever necessary to our own strength.

As for the policy of "containment," it is one which seeks by all means short of war to (1) block further expansion of Soviet power, (2) expose the falsities of Soviet pretensions, (3) induce a retraction of the Kremlin's control and influence and (4) in general, so foster the seeds of destruction within the Soviet system that the Kremlin is brought at least to the point of modifying its behavior to conform to generally accepted international standards.

It was and continues to be cardinal in this policy that we possess superior overall power in ourselves or in dependable combination with other like-minded nations. One of the most important ingredients of power is military strength. In the concept of "containment," the maintenance of a strong military posture is deemed to be essential for two reasons: (1) as an ultimate guarantee of our national security and (2) as an indispensable backdrop to the conduct of the policy of "containment." Without superior aggregate military strength, in being and readily mobilizable, a policy of "containment"—which is in effect a policy of calculated and gradual coercion—is no more than a policy of bluff.

At the same time, it is essential to the successful conduct of a policy of "containment" that we always leave open the possibility of negotiation with the U.S.S.R. A diplomatic freeze—and we are in one now—tends to defeat the very purposes of "containment" because it raises tensions at the same time that it makes Soviet retractions and adjustments in the direction of moderated behavior more difficult. It also tends to inhibit our initiative and deprives us of opportunities for maintaining a moral ascendency in our struggle with the Soviet system.

In "containment" it is desirable to exert pressure in a fashion which will avoid so far as possible directly challenging Soviet prestige, to keep open the possibility for the U.S.S.R. to retreat before pressure with a minimum loss of face and to secure political advantage from the failure of the Kremlin to yield or take advantage of the openings we leave it.

We have failed to implement adequately these two fundamental aspects of "containment." In the face of obviously mounting Soviet military strength ours has declined relatively. Partly as a byproduct of this, but also for other reasons, we now find ourselves at a diplomatic impasse with the Soviet Union, with the Kremlin growing bolder, with both of us holding on grimly to what we have and with ourselves facing difficult decisions. . . .

It is apparent from the preceding sections that the integrity and vitality of our system is in greater jeopardy than ever before in our history. Even if there were no Soviet Union we would face the great problem of the free society, accentuated many fold in this industrial age, of reconciling order, security, the need for participation, with the requirements of freedom. . . .

It is quite clear from Soviet theory and practice that the Kremlin seeks to bring the free world under its dominion by the methods of the cold war. The preferred technique is to subvert by infiltration and intimidation. Every institution of our society is an instrument which it is sought to stultify and turn against our purposes. Those that touch most closely our material and moral strength are obviously the prime targets, labor unions, civic enterprises, schools, churches, and all media for influencing opinion. The effort is not so much to make them serve obvious Soviet ends as to prevent them from serving our ends, and thus to make them sources of confusion in our economy, our culture and our body politic. The doubts and diversities that in terms of our values are part of the merit of a free system, the weaknesses and the problems that are peculiar to it, the rights and privileges that free men enjoy, and the disorganization and destruction left in the wake of the last attack on our freedoms, all are but opportunities for the Kremlin to do its evil work. Every advantage is taken of the fact that our means of prevention and retaliation are limited by those principles and scruples which are precisely the ones that give our freedom and democracy its meaning for us. None of our scruples deter those whose only code is, "morality is that which serves the revolution."

Since everything that gives us or others respect for our institutions is a suitable object for attack, it also fits the Kremlin's design that where, with impunity, we can be insulted and made to suffer indignity the opportunity shall not be missed, particularly in any context which can be used to cast dishonor on our country, our system, our motives, or our methods. Thus the means by which we sought to restore our own economic health in the '30's, and now seek to restore that of the free world, come equally under attack. The military aid by which we sought to help the free world was frantically denounced by the Communists in the early days of the last war, and of course our present efforts to develop adequate military strength for ourselves and our allies are equally denounced.

At the same time the Soviet Union is seeking to create overwhelming military force, in order to back up infiltration with intimidation. In the only terms in which it understands strength, it is seeking to demonstrate to the free world that force and the will to use it are on the side of the Kremlin, that those who lack it are decadent and doomed. In local incidents it threatens and encroaches both for the sake of local gains and to increase anxiety and defeatism in all the free world.

The possession of atomic weapons at each of the opposite poles of power, and the inability (for different reasons) of either side to place any trust in the other, puts a premium on a surprise attack against us. It equally puts a premium on a more violent and ruthless prosecution of its design by cold war, especially if the Kremlin is sufficiently objective to realize the improbability of our prosecuting a preventive war. It also puts a premium on piece-meal aggression against others, counting on our unwillingness to engage in atomic war unless we are directly attacked. We run all these risks and the added risk of being confused and immobilized by our inability to weigh and choose, and pursue a firm course based on a rational assessment of each.

The risk that we may thereby be prevented or too long delayed in taking all needful measures to maintain the integrity and vitality of our system is great. The risk that our allies will lose their determination is greater. And the risk that in this manner a descending spiral of too little and too late, of doubt and recrimination, may present us with ever narrower and more desperate alternatives, is the greatest risk of all. For example, it is clear that our present weakness would prevent us from offering effective resistance at any of several vital pressure points. The only deterrent we can present to the Kremlin is the evidence we give that we may make any of the critical points which we cannot hold the occasion for a global war of annihilation.

The risk of having no better choice than to capitulate or precipitate a global war at any of a number of pressure points is bad enough in itself, but it is multiplied by the weakness it imparts to our position in the cold war. Instead of appearing strong and resolute we are continually at the verge of appearing and being alternately irresolute and desperate; yet it is the cold war which we must win, because both the Kremlin design, and our fundamental purpose give it the first priority. . . .

A more rapid build-up of political, economic, and military strength and thereby of confidence in the free world than is now contemplated is the only course which is consistent with progress toward achieving our fundamental purpose. The frustration of the Kremlin design requires the free world to develop a successfully functioning political and economic system and a vigorous political offensive against the Soviet Union. These, in turn, require an adequate military shield under which they can develop. It is necessary to have the military power to deter, if possible, Soviet expansion, and to defeat, if necessary, aggressive Soviet or Soviet-directed actions of a limited or total character. The potential strength of the free world is great; its ability to develop these military capabilities and its will to resist Soviet expansion will be determined by the wisdom and will with which it undertakes to meet its political and economic problems. . . .

Our position as the center of power in the free world places a heavy responsibility upon the United States for leadership. We must organize and enlist the energies and resources of the free world in a positive program for peace which will frustrate the Kremlin design for world domination by creating a situation in the free world to which the Kremlin will be compelled to adjust. Without such a cooperative effort, led by the United States, we will have to make gradual withdrawals under pressure until we discover one day that we have sacrificed positions of vital interest.

It is imperative that this trend be reversed by a much more rapid and concerted build-up of the actual strength of both the United States and the other nations of the free world. The analysis shows that this will be costly and will involve significant domestic financial and economic adjustments. . . .

In summary, we must, by means of a rapid and sustained build-up of the political, economic, and military strength of the free world, and by means of an affirmative program intended to wrest the initiative from the Soviet Union, confront it with convincing evidence of the determination and ability of the free world to frustrate the Kremlin to the new situation. Failing that, the unwillingness of the determination and ability of the free world to frustrate the Kremlin design of a world dominated by its will. Such evidence is the only means short of war which eventually may force the Kremlin to abandon its present course of action and to negotiate acceptable agreements on issues of major importance.

The whole success of the proposed program hangs ultimately on recognition by this Government, the American people, and all free peoples, that the cold war is in fact a real war in which the survival of the free world is at stake. Essential prerequisites to success are consultations with Congressional leaders designed to make the program the object of non-partisan legislative support, and a presentation to the public of a full explanation of the facts and implications of the present international situation. The prosecution of the program will require of us all the ingenuity, sacrifice, and unity demanded by the vital importance of the issue and the tenacity to persevere until our national objectives have been attained.

ESSAYS

J. Samuel Walker, an historian of the United States Nuclear Regulatory Commission, identifies the key questions in the debate over the origins of the Cold War in his review of the historical literature. He finds that a once-acrimonious debate between "traditionalists" and "revisionists" has given way to a new "consensus." The second essay, by Thomas G. Paterson of the University of Connecticut, concludes that the Cold War had three related sources: the international system, the different needs and ideas of the two major antagonists, and the styles and personalities of Russia's and America's leaders. In the last essay, Barton J. Bernstein of Stanford University surveys in detail the thinking of the Roosevelt and Truman administrations about the atomic bomb and its role in diplomacy. Although he agrees that Truman hoped to end the war quickly to save American lives, he argues that the bomb provided the United States with a "diplomatic bonus"—an opportunity to bargain more forcefully with the Russians to gain concessions from them.

Historians and Cold War Origins

J. SAMUEL WALKER

No topic in American diplomatic history in the past decade has inspired as much literature or provoked as much acrimony as the origins of the cold war. The revisionist challenge to traditional interpretations shattered the consensus that had dominated historical writing on the cold war in the 1950s and early 1960s. The ensuing controversy often resembled a political debate more than an academic one as partisans on opposing sides of the issue exchanged polemics. But it also aroused interest and generated research on a wide variety of questions. In recent years, a vast body of writing, based on extensive research in newly opened sources, has produced a new cold war

Reprinted from "Historians and Cold War Origins: The New Consensus," by J. Samuel Walker, from *American Foreign Relations: A Historiographical Review,* Edited by Gerald K. Haines and J. Samuel Walker. Used with the permission of the Editors and Greenwood Press, Westport, Connecticut.

consensus. The new consensus draws from both traditional and revisionist interpretations to present a more balanced explanation of the beginning of the cold war. The defusing of the passions of the debate and the emergence of broad agreement on many key issues need not consign cold war scholarship to bland, bloodless eclecticism, however, because important questions remain unanswered.

The prevailing consensus in cold war literature of the 1950s and early 1960s cited Soviet aggression and expansion as the fundamental cause of postwar tensions. But within that general traditionalist framework, scholars offered divergent opinions about the nature of the Soviet threat and the appropriateness of the American response. A single "orthodox" explanation of the cold war never existed in the period; writing divided among three different schools of interpretation. One group consisted of conservatives who condemned Presidents Roosevelt and Truman for failing to recognize and take decisive action to stop the Soviet drive for world conquest. Roosevelt, they alleged, surrendered eastern Europe and China to Joseph Stalin at Yalta, while Truman was too conciliatory and irresolute in dealing subsequently with the communist menace. The conservative interpretation of the cold war received little support in academic circles, but it seemed a plausible explanation to large numbers of Americans who believed that the United States was losing its struggle with international communism. In that sense, it was an accurate reflection of widespread frustration with United States foreign policy in the early 1950s.

In contrast to the right-wing critics, a liberal school of interpreters defended and applauded America's cold war policies. The liberals, like the conservatives, viewed the Soviet Union as driven by communist ideology to seek unlimited expansion. They denied, however, that Roosevelt had sold out at Yalta and praised Truman for a firm but restrained manner of dealing with Russia. The liberals identified Soviet aggression and residual isolationism in the United States as the two major problems confronting American policymakers. They hailed the Truman Doctrine, therefore, as a bold initiative that not only thwarted Soviet expansion but also marked the final triumph over isolationism. The liberal interpretation, though not simply a product of "court historians," coincided with official versions of the origins of the cold war. It contained little that Harry Truman or Dean Acheson could have found objectionable.

A much more critical perspective on United States cold war policies was provided by a group of writers known as realists. They also attributed the origins of the cold war to Soviet transgressions, but they strongly disapproved of the way the United States responded. Realists argued that the basic flaw in twentieth-century American foreign policy was the tendency to act according to moralistic and idealistic precepts that ignored the realities of power. Excessive moralism and vacuous universalism led the United States to make commitments that transcended its capabilities and disregarded its national interest. The Truman Doctrine offered a prime example of the worst aspects of America's diplomatic tradition. Although the realists believed that aid to Greece was necessary to preserve the European balance of power and protect legitimate American interests in the Mediterranean, they condemned Truman for undertaking an ideological crusade to uphold freedom throughout the world. "Thus the Truman Doctrine," wrote Hans J. Morgenthau, "transformed a concrete interest of the United States in a geographically defined part of the world into a moral principle of worldwide validity, to be applied regardless of the limits of American interest and American power."

Many realists, unlike the conservatives and liberals, deemphasized communist ideology as the basis of Soviet expansion. Morgenthau and Louis J. Halle, for example, contended that Stalin's foreign policy was an effort to carry out traditional Russian objectives rather than an attempt to incite world revolution. Stalin sought limited goals, and the challenge he posed was an outgrowth of Russian imperialism, not Marxist ideology. George F. Kennan partially dissented from that view by stressing ideology as the fundamental reason for intense Soviet hostility toward the West and by asserting that a "complete sweep of dominant Soviet influence over Europe and Asia . . . was Stalin's initial postwar hope." But he too argued that Soviet foreign policy was flexible and that its power, not its ideology, threatened American national interests.

The realists shared a sense of fatalism about the origins of the cold war. Halle articulated that tendency most clearly by comparing America and Russia to a scorpion and tarantula in a bottle, locked "in a situation of irreducible dilemma." A historical tradition of insecurity and suspicion of the West compelled the Soviets to expand, and the Wilsonian legacy caused the United States to react as it did. The result was a tragic but inevitable conflict. Kennan considered the cold war unavoidable because of the implacable hostility of Soviet leaders and their need to cite foreign enemies as the reason for perpetuating their absolute authority over the Russian people. In general, the realists concurred in depicting the cold war as an inevitable result of World War II. Although they suggested that tensions could have been reduced significantly if the United States had recognized a Soviet sphere of influence in eastern Europe, they believed that American diplomatic tradition precluded that possibility.

The realist view, which was probably the most influential and certainly the most sophisticated of the traditional interpretations of the cold war, was highly critical of many American policies, but it did not question the conventional idea that Soviet actions triggered the cold war. A few writers in the 1950s and early 1960s did argue that the United States at least shared responsibility for postwar tensions, but their efforts made little impression on the prevailing consensus. Not until the mid-1960s did revisionist studies begin to generate serious debate about the origins of the cold war. The most consequential challenge to traditional interpretations was Gar Alperovitz's contention that the United States had dropped atomic bombs on Japan not because of military necessity but to impress the Russians and make them more tractable in eastern Europe. Although it received far less attention than Alperovitz's book, David Horowitz published at about the same time a general indictment of United States policies throughout the cold war era. Horowitz, like Alperovitz, argued that Truman reversed Roosevelt's conciliatory position toward Russia immediately after taking office. The United States severed the wartime alliance, initiated the cold war, and failed to recognize that much of Stalin's expansionist drive was an effort to secure his borders.

Much of the Alperovitz and Horowitz critiques was not particularly new. Others had previously asserted that the United States had used the atomic bomb more for political than military reasons, and Horowitz's analysis followed along the same basic lines as D. F. Fleming's 1961 book, *The Cold War and Its Origins.* The timing as much as the content of their books explained why Alperovitz and eventually Horowitz had more impact on cold war historiography than earlier revisionists. A new generation of scholars came of age in the mid-1960s. It was natural that younger writers whose memories of brinksmanship and bomb shelters were more vivid than of World War II and its aftermath would have a new perspective on the cold war. Although neither the Alperovitz nor the Horowitz book approached being definitive—Alperovitz admitted that his conclusions were tentative and Horowitz based his polemic on sparse research—both raised questions that older scholars had not seriously considered. It was inevitable that a body of revisionist writing on the cold war would appear, as had occurred in interpretations of other major events in American diplomatic history.

The Vietnam conflict gave additional impetus to cold war revisionism. The war did not precipitate the rise of revisionism, which was underway before Southeast Asia became a major issue. But Vietnam made the beginning of the cold war a much more urgent and controversial subject than it might otherwise have been and enhanced the credibility of revisionist arguments. As Ronald Steel observed in 1971: "To reject the war in Vietnam is to question the basic assumptions on which American foreign policy rests. It is to ask not only whether the prevalent conception of the cold war might now be wrong, but whether it was ever right." The passions aroused by the war and its impact on college campuses intensified the debate over that question to a point where scholarly restraint and tolerance for opposing opinions were often conspicuously lacking.

In a remark that foreshadowed the tone of the emerging controversy, Arthur M. Schlesinger, Jr., wrote in October 1966: "Surely the time has come to blow the whistle before the current outburst of revisionism regarding the origins of the cold war goes much further." A year later, in an article published in *Foreign Affairs,* he regretted that he had remonstrated "somewhat intemperately" and affirmed that revisionism remained "an essential part of the process by which history . . . enlarges its perspectives and enriches its insights." Schlesinger then offered an analysis of the cold war that combined elements of the liberal and realist views while countering revisionist opinions. He submitted that a fundamental conflict between the American commitment to universalism (which he regarded more sympathetically than the realists) and Stalin's insistence on a Soviet sphere of influence in eastern Europe led to the cold war. Stalin misinterpreted American protests against his policies in eastern Europe as an effort to undermine Russian security, and the United States misread Stalin's intentions by assuming he planned to expand into western Europe. Schlesinger further argued that communist ideology, Soviet totalitarianism, and Stalin's personal paranoia made postwar cooperation between the United States and the Soviet Union impossible. Like Kennan, he contended that American acts of friendship and generosity could not have overcome Stalin's suspicion or changed Soviet policy, and that revisionists erred in believing otherwise.

Schlesinger's article, if such were his intention, was no more effective than his earlier appeal in whistling revisionism to a halt. Revisionist scholars rejected his assumption that a more conciliatory American posture would not have reduced postwar tensions and questioned his premise that Stalin's personality and communist ideology guaranteed Soviet intransigence in the early cold war period. They claimed that American actions, at least as much as Soviet ones, provoked the cold war. Yet for the most part the early revisionists had not provided an adequate explanation of why the United States took a hostile position toward Russia. Only William Appleman Williams in *The Tragedy of American Diplomacy* had offered a comprehensive view that placed American cold war policies in a broad historical context. He contended that the driving force behind twentieth-century United States foreign policy was overseas economic expansion. Business and political leaders agreed that American domestic prosperity depended on the availability of foreign markets and they focused their attention on maintaining an Open Door for trade opportunities throughout the world. American insistence on preserving the Open Door clashed with Stalin's primary objectives after World War II, because he did not welcome the prospect of United States economic penetration in areas he regarded as vital to Soviet security. Thus, in Williams's opinion, America's aggressive economic expansion, supported by its predominant power, initiated postwar tensions. When *The Tragedy of American Diplomacy* first appeared in 1959, it exerted little perceptible influence on cold war historiography. By the end of the 1960s, however, Williams's analysis had emerged as the nucleus of a burgeoning body of revisionist literature. Stressing foreign economic expansion as the central impulse in American diplomacy, Walter LaFeber, Lloyd C. Gardner, Barton J. Bernstein, Stephen E. Ambrose, and Joyce and Gabriel Kolko published major studies that advanced what was by then referred to as the new left interpretation of the cold war.

Despite disagreements among themselves on some issues and variations in tone and emphasis, new left scholars concurred on many key points that contrasted with the realist and liberal interpretations. The most fundamental and obvious distinction was the revisionist contention that the United States, not Russia, was primarily responsible for the cold war. They argued that America's overwhelming power and its concerted effort to shape the postwar world created friction with the Soviet Union. Few new left historians —the Kolkos were a notable exception—found the United States solely to blame for postwar tensions. But their analyses of American policies differed sharply from the traditional view that the country had responded defensively to Soviet thrusts. According to Gardner, for example, the United States determined "the *way* in which the Cold War developed, at least," because "it had much greater opportunity and far more options to influence the course of events than the Soviet Union."

New left writers also departed from traditional interpretations by emphasizing economic factors as the basis of American diplomacy. Some revisionists, such as Diane Shaver Clemens and Athan Theoharis, focused on the personalities and visceral anticommunism of American leaders rather than on economic considerations in explaining United States hostility toward Russia. But most, dissenting from the realist argument that moralistic and legalistic precepts were the fundamental motivating forces in American foreign policy, stressed America's commitment to Open Door expansion as the key to its cold war position. New left scholars, as Barton J. Bernstein and Robert W. Tucker pointed out, disagreed among themselves on the relationship between America's economy and its foreign policy. The most extreme revisionists, represented by the Kolkos, considered overseas economic expansion as essential for the functioning of the capitalist system and, therefore, unalterable as long as capitalism survived. The more moderate position, most clearly outlined by Williams, held that American leaders mistakenly believed that foreign markets were critical for domestic prosperity and, therefore, a change in attitudes could modify the Open Door ideology. A similar dichotomy existed in how the new left viewed American idealism. Williams and most other revisionists regretted that United States economic activity abroad subverted the nation's ideal of self-determination and genuine concern for the well-being of other peoples. The Kolkos, on the other hand, refused to take idealistic pronouncements of American policymakers seriously. Those differences, however, were less striking than the contrast between the broad agreement among new left historians on the primacy of economic concerns and traditional interpretations that largely ignored economic aspects of American foreign policy.

The new left interpretation presented an image of American leaders that markedly diverged from that provided by the realists. Realists credited Truman and his chief advisors with good intentions, but portrayed United States policies as drifting, misguided, and innocent of the realities of power politics. Revisionists, however, depicted American policymakers as purposeful, calculating, and effective in promoting Open Door expansion. They credited United States leaders with being competent in carrying out lamentable objectives. Revisionists played down the importance of chance and accident in determining national actions. "Whereas a conventional historiography emphasizes the role of the unforeseen, the contingent, and the inadvertent," commented Robert Tucker, "a radical historiography leaves very little scope to these factors."

New left writers viewed Stalin's leadership in quite different terms than liberals and some realists. They described him as tentative, cautious, and flexible and agreed with realists such as Morgenthau and Halle that his goals were limited. Revisionists denied the assertion that Stalin was paranoid; Williams, for example, argued that American policymakers did not deal with him as though he were demented and that Stalin had ample rational reasons for suspecting United States hostility. In new left analyses, American policies after the war shattered Stalin's hope for cooperation with the West, prompting him to consolidate his hold on eastern Europe and reluctantly adopt an antagonistic position toward the United States.

Unlike the realists, most revisionists did not regard the cold war as inevitable. "To see the Cold War as a struggle between two scorpions in a bottle," commented Gardner, "reduces history to a cast of witless characters." New left historians generally maintained that a more conciliatory position on a number of crucial issues could have significantly altered the course of postwar events. If the United States had been more accommodating by sharing information on atomic energy, offering the Soviets economic assistance for reconstruction, accepting a Russian sphere of influence in eastern Europe, and recognizing legitimate Soviet security concerns, the cold war, or at least the worst aspects of it, could have been averted. From the new left frame of reference, those policies would have required the United States to compromise substantially its commitment to worldwide economic expansion. Therefore, only those revisionists who thought that American capitalism was flexible enough to modify its adherence to the Open Door system could argue that the cold war was preventable. As Christopher Lasch pointed out, scholars who believed that the imperatives of capitalism required American leaders to act as they did to protect the nation's economic interests necessarily affirmed the inevitability of the cold war. "According to a certain type of revisionism," he wrote, "American policy has all the rigidity the orthodox historians attribute to the U.S.S.R., and this inflexibility made the cold war inevitable." Most revisionists eschewed such a stance, however, and insisted that the Truman administration had the means and the opportunity, but lacked the will or the wisdom, to get along with Russia after the war.

The growing volume and impact of revisionist literature provoked a spirited reaction from traditionalist-minded scholars. Some dismissed the new left interpretation as thoroughly deficient. John W. Spanier thought it made the cold war "into a fairy tale," Adam B. Ulam declared that "as history this revisionism is fallacious," and Robert H. Ferrell asserted in 1972 "that the revisionists have not proved a single one of their points." Others compared cold war critics to revisionists of previous conflicts in American history and suggested that the new left would have no more lasting influence than their predecessors. Some writers, however, while questioning revisionist assumptions and conclusions, took their arguments seriously. For example, Robert Tucker, who published an extended and sophisticated commentary on "radical left" historians, was sharply critical of their emphasis on economic expansion as the determinant of U.S. diplomacy and their supposition that a socialist United States would carry out a more benign foreign policy than capitalist America. But he also maintained that revisionism was more than a passing fad and had made important contributions to understanding the conduct of American foreign policy.

There were no such concessions in the most controversial assessment of the revisionist interpretation, Robert James Maddox's *The New Left and the Origins of the Cold War*. Rather than contesting the revisionists on the basis of their arguments, Maddox attacked them on their use of sources. After checking the footnotes of books by seven leading revisionists—Williams, Fleming, Horowitz, Kolko, Alperovitz, Clemens, and Gardner—he accused all of deliberately distorting the evidence. "Perhaps," he wrote, "the New Left view of American foreign policy during and after World War II can *only* be sustained by doing violence to the historical record?" Maddox left little doubt that his answer to that question was affirmative. His book and the response to it highlighted the choleric tone that was so typical of the cold war controversy. The authors of the books examined retorted angrily. Many traditionalists felt gratified and vindicated while many revisionists attacked Maddox with the same harshness that infused his book. Those who stood somewhere between the two positions often were saddened by the spectacle. Warren F. Kimball, for example, found the bitterness of the debate more disturbing than the charges in Maddox's book. "It is not hypocritical to disagree with someone in a gentle, courteous manner," he observed. "Granted, it is far easier and much more fun to be vitriolic and sarcastic, but such writing hardly qualifies as a dispassionate search for truth; rather it merely polarizes the argument."

The vituperative tone of the dispute over cold war origins obscured the fact that the revisionist and realist (though not the liberal) positions were not totally irreconcilable. Although a balanced synthesis drawing on both interpretations was theoretically possible, the pattern of mutual recrimination made it difficult for scholars on one side of the debate to recognize virtues in the opposing view. A dearth of sources also contributed to polarization. Before the early 1970s, only a relatively few official records and personal papers were available to cold war historians, who had to rely on scattered sources that failed even to approach giving a full account of the early postwar period. It was easy for scholars to interpret the limited evidence according to their own predilections and difficult for others to refute their arguments convincingly. Therefore, much of the cold war debate was an intemperate exchange of biases for which there seemed no middle ground. The opening of new sources did not eliminate that problem, of course, but it did provide a more complete picture of American policies and allowed for a more sophisticated and judicious explanation of the historical context in which they were formulated. It was no accident that the beginning of a new phase of cold war scholarship, characterized by a more restrained tone and more balanced interpretation, coincided with the availability of a growing body of fresh evidence. In fact, Maddox's book was something of an atavism the day it was published, because a trend toward moderation and eclecticism was already under way.

The most prominent example of the emerging trend was John Lewis Gaddis's 1972 study, *The United States and the Origins of the Cold War, 1941–1947*. Drawing on many recently opened sources, Gaddis stressed the fundamental continuity of Roosevelt's and Truman's foreign-policy aims and their incompatibility with Stalin's primary objectives. Truman sincerely wanted to continue his predecessor's conciliatory policies toward Russia, but by the early months of 1946 he and his advisors had reluctantly concluded that the only way to preserve world peace and American security was to adopt a posture of firmness. Gaddis agreed with the revisionists that domestic factors significantly influenced the Truman administration's diplomatic stance and that the United States had attempted to use economic pressure to extract political concessions from the Soviets. But he contended that other domestic concerns, particularly public opinion and congressional attitudes, played a much more important role in shaping Truman's decisions than did economic considerations.

In assessing responsibility for the development of the cold war, Gaddis took a moderate position that was slightly right of center. He denied the new left argument that more accommodating American policies toward eastern Europe, economic assistance for Russia, or sharing atomic information were feasible options for United States leaders because of adamant public and congressional opposition. He concurred, however, with revisionists who viewed the cold war as avoidable, though he did so on abstract philosophical grounds rather than citing specific actions that might have changed the course of postwar events. Gaddis maintained that neither the United States nor the Soviet Union was solely at fault for the cold war, but he concluded that Stalin was more to blame because he was free of the domestic constraints that so limited the alternatives available to Truman. Many traditionalists hailed Gaddis's book as an effective antidote to revisionism. But his measured tone, balanced interpretation, and emphasis on the complexities of postwar issues were more an indication of the direction in which cold war scholarship was moving than a vindication of rigid traditionalism.

The trend toward eclecticism so apparent in Gaddis's book was also evident in major studies published in 1973 by George C. Herring, Jr., and Thomas G. Paterson. Both provided richly detailed and thoroughly researched examinations of the central question raised by new left scholars—the role of economic motives in American cold war policies. Herring [in *Aid to Russia, 1941–1946*] investigated American lend-lease assistance to Russia during and after World War II. He agreed with many revisionists that Truman's abrupt termination of lend-lease in May 1945 and later failure to extend credit to Russia contributed to the onset of the cold war by reinforcing Soviet suspicion of the West. But Herring attributed those policies to bureaucratic ineptness, bad planning, and domestic pressures rather than a deliberate attempt to extort concessions from the Soviet Union. He denied that more generous American actions would have significantly allayed Stalin's distrust or won his gratitude. The cold war, he believed, evolved from "the depth of the issues that divided the two allies," and was to some degree and in some form, unavoidable. Herring, like Gaddis, took a moderately right-of-center position and assigned the United States partial responsibility for the cold war. He incorporated some revisionist arguments in his book but rejected their overall view of an aggressive United States using its economic power to coerce the Soviet Union.

Paterson [in *Soviet-American Confrontation*] was much more critical of American actions than was Herring, but he too offered an evenhanded analysis that affirmed some elements of the new left interpretation while questioning others. He echoed a revisionist theme by asserting that American policy was "not accidental or aimless: rather it was self-consciously expansionist." A crucial part of that expansionism was economic, and, in contrast to Herring, Paterson argued that premeditated American efforts to use economic power to pressure the Soviets were an important cause of the cold war. Unlike many new left scholars, however, he emphasized that factors other than economic considerations also played a key role in United States cold war diplomacy. He did not depict American economic concerns as inherently pernicious, and viewed United States economic pressure as a tactical effort to influence Soviet behavior in eastern Europe rather than an attempt to secure markets and guarantee an open world for trade opportunities. Paterson contended that the Soviets did not adamantly oppose American trade expansion and that the Truman administration undercut its own economic objectives by sharply reducing commerce with and withholding economic assistance from Russia and eastern Europe. He denied that the cold war was inevitable, because "Washington was free to make different choices or, at the very least, to pursue its reconstruction plans less coercively." Paterson's left-of-center interpretation condemned American cold war policies much more severely than Gaddis or Herring, but his tone and perspective were in keeping with the trend toward moderation and recognition of the complexities of the cold war.

The availability of new sources and the continuing debate over cold war origins inspired investigations of a broad range of specific issues. Most of them necessarily concentrated on American policies and perceptions because that was what the documents revealed. But within the constraints imposed by the evidence, a vast body of literature provided new insights and deeper understanding into the Truman administration's response to postwar crises. Those studies, though frequently disagreeing with one another on particulars, generally conformed with the trend toward eclecticism that narrowed the cleavage between the realist and new left views. Many offered fresh ideas and original analyses, but most fell within the broad perimeters defined by the basic interpretations.

Considerable attention focused on American policies toward eastern Europe. Although realists and revisionists had agreed that the Truman administration should have conceded Stalin a sphere of influence in eastern Europe, they sharply differed on other points. Realists regarded Stalin's violation of the Yalta accords in eastern Europe as the basic cause of the cold war, and maintained that American opposition, which was largely rhetorical, stemmed from its commitment to the ideal of self-determination. Revisionists argued that the United States attempted to undermine Soviet control of eastern Europe through economic coercion and atomic diplomacy to promote Open Door expansion. They stressed that Stalin had no preconceived plan for dealing with eastern Europe and gradually tightened his hold on all the countries in that area in response to American pressure.

Studies of the United States stance in eastern Europe that appeared in the mid-1970s did not accept either realist or new left arguments in their pure form but stood somewhere between the two positions. Lynn Etheridge Davis supported much of the realist view by emphasizing the principles of the Atlantic Charter rather than economic concerns as the guiding force in American policies. But she suggested that the United States shared responsibility for the beginning of the cold war because its protests against Soviet behavior aroused Stalin's fears and prompted him to extend his domination of eastern Europe. Geir Lundestad agreed with revisionists that Stalin took a flexible position toward eastern Europe and that the United States did apply some pressure on him. But like the realists, he deemphasized economic motives as the basis of American diplomacy and regarded postwar tensions as unavoidable. In an examination of United States policies toward Czechoslovakia, Mark S. Steinitz contended that America's fundamental goal of self-determination was undermined by its own "inflexible economic diplomacy" as well as by Soviet machinations. Without discounting Russian accountability, Stephen A. Garrett cited misperceptions by American policymakers of the situation in eastern Europe as contributing to cold war tensions. Hugh De Santis considered psychological and bureaucratic factors in describing divergent American responses to the situation in eastern Europe. He asserted that American diplomats stationed there concluded that America and Russia were locked in an ideological struggle long before desk officers at the State Department, who continued to hope for cooperation between the two nations until early 1946, reached that conclusion.

There was wide agreement among postrevisionist studies of the American stance toward eastern Europe that the United States lacked a coherent policy, and that other than lodging verbal protests, did little to challenge Soviet domination of the region. Bennett Kovrig and Walter Ullmann, taking a conservative position that seemed curiously anachronistic in the 1970s, asserted that more decisive American actions might have prevented Soviet subjugation of eastern European nations. Lundestad maintained that American leaders did not view eastern Europe as an area of vital concern and vacillated between promoting universalist principles and accepting a Soviet sphere of influence. The result was a "non-policy" in eastern Europe. Hugh B. Hammett claimed that Roosevelt's failure to define his goals and make them clear to Stalin and the American people led to misunderstandings after the war. Davis indicted American officials for neglecting to give much thought to how Atlantic Charter principles could be implemented and how efforts to do so might affect United States relations with Russia. Eduard M. Mark found American policies more calculated than other postrevisionist scholars. He maintained that the Truman administration was willing to accept a Soviet sphere of influence in eastern Europe as long as it was "open" but objected to the "exclusive" spheres that Stalin established.

If the Truman administration largely acquiesced in Soviet control of eastern

Europe, then the explanation of why the United States adopted a firm posture toward Russia must be found elsewhere. A number of scholars stressed United States-Soviet conflict in the Near East as the key to the origins of America's containment policies. In the realist view, Stalin's thrusts into Iran, Turkey, and Greece were aggressive and provocative, and, unlike eastern Europe, could not be justified as defensive measures. The United States took decisive action to protect legitimate national interests. Revisionists argued that American economic expansion in the Near East was a basic source of tension. They depicted Stalin's aims in Iran and Turkey as limited and reasonable and his role in the Greek revolution as virtually nonexistent. Therefore, a strong American reaction was necessary only to uphold economic interests.

In recent writing on the United States and the Near East, some scholars adhered closely to one or the other side of the debate. Eduard M. Mark followed the new left interpretation by describing Russian intervention in Iran as a response to American economic activities that seemed to endanger Soviet oil supplies. David S. McLellan affirmed the realist position by contending that Soviet pressure in Iran and Turkey demonstrated its lack of respect for the sovereignty of its neighbors and imperiled the world balance of power. American leaders interpreted Soviet actions as an indication of unlimited ambitions and reacted accordingly.

Other writers combined elements of the realist and revisionist views. Gary R. Hess attributed Soviet activities in Iran to their concern for national security and prestige. Although their methods were heavy-handed, the United States overreacted and unnecessarily intensified cold war tensions and mutual misunderstandings. In studies of the civil war in Greece, John O. Iatrides and D. George Kousoulas characterized the Greek Communists as acting independently of Stalin, who abided by his promise to Winston Churchill not to interfere in that country. Iatrides, however, concluded that if the Greek Communists had triumphed, they probably would have become "Stalin's helpless wards." Kousoulas asserted that the situation in Greece suggested that Stalin put national interests ahead of revolutionary ones, and that he did not direct a coordinated international communist movement. But he also argued that the United States reacted responsibly to what appeared to be serious provocation. In a comprehensive and thoroughly researched study of the internal situations in and American policies toward Iran, Turkey, and Greece, Bruce R. Kuniholm elaborated on previous scholarship. He maintained that before the Truman Doctrine, "containment in the Near East was a realistic and pragmatic" response to Soviet activities. But he agreed with Iatrides and Kousoulas in their description of Stalin's role in the Greek revolution. He also suggested that the "public rationalization" of containment and the universalization of policies that appeared to succeed in the Near East seriously impaired the vision and restricted the alternatives of American policymakers in dealing with subsequent crises.

Another flashpoint of the cold war, Germany, has been the subject of several comprehensive studies reflecting various perspectives. Bruce Kuklick took a revisionist position by asserting that the American commitment to economic expansion caused conflict with the Soviet Union and led to the division of Germany. The United States was determined to ensure German recovery because it was essential to the economic revival of Europe and, therefore, vital to American economic interests. In Kuklick's opinion, the Truman administration's resistance to Soviet claims for reparations that would impede German recovery and its efforts to unify Germany under American control played a major role in generating postwar tensions. John Gimbel dissented from both the new left interpretation and the traditionalist view that Soviet ambitions and intransigence destroyed four-power cooperation in occupied Germany. Unlike traditionalists, he insisted that French rather than Russian obstructions undermined the Potsdam agreements and that the Soviet stance toward Germany was flexible and pragmatic. The State Department, however, "leveled its guns on the Russians" and ignored French obstinance to secure congressional approval of the Marshall Plan. In contrast to revisionists, Gimbel denied that American policies in Germany were either consistent or carefully planned. He attributed them instead to a "series of pragmatic bureaucratic decisions and compromises" that attempted to reconcile the views and demands of the State Department, United States Army occupation authorities, the nations of western Europe, Congress, and the American people.

John H. Backer agreed with Gimbel that the United States lacked a single-minded approach in Germany and described United States actions as a series of incremental decisions that eventually defined the American position. Although he rejected the revisionists' emphasis on economic expansion as the basis of American policies, he accepted their view that Soviet demands were reasonable and negotiable. In an analysis of the origins of the Marshall Plan, Scott Jackson maintained that Gimbel's emphasis on bureaucratic rivalries and American concern over German questions as the basic catalysts for the plan provided only a partial explanation. He contended that strategic and security interests and economic considerations played a more central role in the formulation of the European recovery program. Although Gimbel, Backer, and Jackson all took eclectic positions, their studies illustrated that within that general framework, there was ample allowance for differing emphases and viewpoints.

Much cold war scholarship focused more on the domestic roots of United States foreign policy than on interactions between America and Russia. The role of public opinion inspired considerable debate but remained an elusive subject. Several writers disputed the argument, most clearly set forth by John Lewis Gaddis, that public and congressional attitudes sharply limited the foreign-policy options available to American leaders. In a theoretical analysis published before Gaddis's book, Bernard C. Cohen suggested that the public was generally uninformed about foreign affairs and usually could be persuaded to endorse the government's course of action without great difficulty. Walter LaFeber and Thomas Paterson accepted that line of reasoning and asserted that the Truman administration molded, not followed, public and congressional opinion in the early cold war period. Peter H. Irons concluded that

Polish-Americans, despite strenuous lobbying, exerted little effective influence on Roosevelt's and Truman's policies toward Poland. Michael Leigh took a middle position on the issue by agreeing that Truman manipulated public opinion to an extent. But he added that "the need to mobilize consent is itself witness to the constraint that national leaders perceive as inhering in the mass public."

Scholars also differed on how the American people regarded Russia immediately after World War II. Richard M. Freeland and Athan Theoharis, for example, maintained that most Americans were kindly disposed toward their wartime ally and hopeful of continuing cooperation between the United States and the Soviet Union. Ralph B. Levering and Gary J. Buckley, on the other hand, contended that a legacy of suspicion and animosity toward the Soviets lingered throughout the war and that public gratitude for Russian contributions to defeating Germany quickly dissipated. Despite their disagreements on other matters, many writers concurred in depicting the enunciation of the Truman Doctrine as a public relations effort that backfired. Gaddis, for example, argued that the effect of Truman's speech was "to imprison American diplomacy in an ideological straitjacket." Freeland and Theoharis condemned it even more harshly. Both viewed the Truman Doctrine as a crucial element in a series of anticommunist activities that destroyed public goodwill toward Russia and laid the foundations for McCarthyism.

Other domestic influences, related to but separate from public opinion, received less attention. Although scholars frequently cited the impact of Congress on the administration's diplomatic position, they did not undertake detailed examinations of the pressures, impulses, and traditions that defined its role in the cold war era. In a brief look at the subject, John T. Rourke concluded that Congressmen's views on foreign policy were parochial and their impact was unconstructive. The need remains for closer scrutiny of the institutional functions of Congress and the ideas and influence of its individual members. A number of writers investigated the societal roots of American diplomacy. They denied that the public or the Congress had any significant input and attributed United States foreign policy to the decisions of a group of elites. They did not, however, fully agree on who the elites were or where they came from. G. William Domhoff emphasized their social and educational background while Gabriel Kolko argued that they represented "dominant business circles and their law firms." Richard J. Barnet denounced the power of the "national security bureaucracy" and John C. Donovan identified a "policy elite" drawn from leading financial institutions, law firms, corporations, and universities. All of those studies reflected a revisionist perspective and none was definitive, but they raised intriguing questions that deserve careful examination. A few scholars focused on the intellectual foundations of American cold war diplomacy. Donovan stressed the "mind-set" of the policy elite, based largely on its "obsessive fear of communist expansion" and "voracious hunger for foreign markets." Les K. Adler and Thomas G. Paterson traced the transfer of fear and hatred of Nazi Germany to the Soviet Union by American leaders and the public. Ernest R. May described how the Truman administration applied the "lessons" of the 1930s in adopting a policy of firmness toward Russia after the war. Biographies of individuals also shed light on intellectual trends, but the subject requires further study.

The relationship between military considerations and foreign policy has generated growing interest among cold war scholars. The controversy over the use of the atomic bomb inspired several detailed studies that have achieved a broad consensus. Martin J. Sherwin, Barton J. Bernstein, and Lisle A. Rose agreed that the United States dropped the bomb primarily to hasten the war's end. Sherwin and Bernstein argued that American leaders viewed the weapon as a means of winning concessions from Stalin, though that was a distinctly secondary goal. Rose, Bernstein, and Gregg F. Herken also concurred that the Truman administration attempted to take advantage of its atomic monopoly to secure diplomatic objectives. Atomic diplomacy not only proved futile, but it escalated cold war tensions and diminished the already slight possibility of United States-Soviet cooperation on international control of atomic energy. The consensus on the role of the bomb in the cold war combined the traditional view that the United States had no ulterior motives in using it against Japan with the revisionist assertion that its inclusion in America's diplomatic arsenal helped cause the cold war.

The increasing availability of military documents stimulated research on the role of the armed services in the cold war. Historians approached the subject in a variety of ways. In a study of the Joint Chiefs of Staff, Walter S. Poole asserted that aggressive Soviet expansion transformed the chiefs' position from conciliation to a conviction that Stalin sought world domination and that peaceful coexistence was impossible. Lawrence S. Wittner, by contrast, contended that the Office of Strategic Services in the spring of 1945 expressed deep concern about Soviet activities and formulated an early rationale for a policy of containment. Other writers emphasized that a systematic attempt to coordinate strategy and diplomacy occurred for the first time in the cold war period. Jonathan Knight demonstrated how Secretary of the Navy Forrestal promoted "casual" visits by American ships to Mediterranean ports to uphold United States interests and guarantee an important role for the navy in combating communism. Thomas H. Etzold and John Lewis Gaddis compiled a volume of original documents to show that containment was a product of the effort "to integrate political and military considerations in national security planning." In an introductory essay, Etzold described the origins and functions of the agencies created to carry out that task. He concluded that the National Security Council and the Policy Planning Staff of the State Department performed more effectively than the Joint Chiefs or the Central Intelligence Agency. Alfred D. Sander, however, maintained that Truman made little use of the National Security Council until after the Korean War began. Although many key documents have opened too recently to be incorporated into cold war studies, the prospects are promising that they will add an exciting new dimension to the historiography of the period.

Many important contributions to cold war scholarship have appeared in biographies of major, and in some cases, minor figures. The rise of revisionism inspired many scholars to examine the careers of critics of American cold war policies. The most prominent opponent of Truman's diplomacy, Henry A. Wallace, commanded considerable attention. Although Edward L. and Frederick H. Schapsmeier took a traditional view by depicting Wallace's stand as naive and misguided, others regarded him more sympathetically. Norman D. Markowitz compared him favorably with cold war liberals, though he criticized Wallace for failing to recognize the defects inherent in American capitalism. Richard J. Walton hailed Wallace as a remarkably prescient observer whose ideas, had they been followed, could have prevented the cold war. J. Samuel Walker argued that Wallace offered a restrained and sensible critique of United States foreign policy in the early cold war period, and despite flaws in his position, deserved better treatment and a fairer hearing than he received.

Other less conspicuous dissenters often fared better in the hands of historians than they had with their contemporaries. Wallace's running mate in his 1948 presidential campaign, Glen H. Taylor, Senator from Idaho, was the subject of an admiring biography by F. Ross Peterson. A number of critics who attacked United States foreign policy from various perspectives, including Wallace, Taylor, Walter Lippmann, James Paul Warburg, Claude Pepper, Robert A. Taft, and I. F. Stone, were portrayed favorably in a collection of essays edited by Thomas G. Paterson. Ronald Radosh sought to rehabilitate a group of conservative spokesmen by stressing their opposition to American globalism. James T. Patterson provided a sympathetic portrait of Robert A. Taft, though he was less impressed with Taft's views than was Radosh. Two obscure conservatives, Lawrence Dennis, an avowed fascist, and James P. Kem, Senator from Missouri, also won praise from scholars for the objections they voiced to American cold war policies.

Key figures in the Truman administration also were the subjects of biographies. Although a full scholarly treatment of Truman's career has yet to appear, John Lewis Gaddis and Richard S. Kirkendall contributed brief, appreciative accounts. Wilson D. Miscamble, in a study of Truman's prepresidential views on foreign policy, emphasized his fear that the country would retreat to isolationism and his guarded hope for cooperation with the Soviet Union after the war. David S. McLellan and Gaddis Smith provided sympathetic portraits of Dean Acheson that described his concern that Soviet expansion would undermine the world balance of power and threaten American strategic interests. George T. Mazuzan traced the American ambassador to the United Nations Warren R. Austin's gradual disillusionment with the Soviet Union and showed how little his appeals for collective security through the United Nations influenced the administration.

Scholars studied and debated the ideas of George F. Kennan more than any other administration official. C. Ben Wright disputed Kennan's claims that his original concept of containment had been distorted and militarized. Wright contended that Kennan made a substantial contribution "to the Cold

War mentality" because his writings envisioned the use of military power in many parts of the world to stop communism. Kennan angrily denied Wright's assertions. He received support from John L. Gaddis, who argued that Kennan's containment theory had always stressed the limits of American power and deemphasized the value of military intervention. Gaddis's article, in turn, brought sharp rejoinders from Eduard Mark, Michael H. Hunt, and John W. Coogan. The exchange of opinions about Kennan's views left the question unresolved and in need of further investigation. . . .

Although analyses of Stalin's foreign policy are inherently precarious, a few recent books on the topic made notable contributions to cold war historiography. In an examination of the major components of Soviet diplomacy, Morton Schwartz argued that Stalin's weakness relative to the United States made him cautious, though he launched a rhetorical offensive in hopes that harsh words would disguise his vulnerability. In general, Stalin acted "tough but restrained, belligerent but cautious, assertive but not adventurous." Schwartz also insisted, however, that ideology was an important motivating factor in Soviet diplomacy and a major cause of the outbreak of the cold war. Like Schwartz, Adam B. Ulam regarded Stalin's political power as absolute. In most ways, Ulam's portrait of Stalin conformed with the traditionalist image. He depicted the Soviet leader as cunning, ruthless, suspicious, and unapproachable. In return for giving in on minor points at Teheran and Yalta, the wily dictator secured major concessions from the West. Ulam maintained that winning Stalin's respect, not trying to allay his distrust, was the proper way to deal with him. In certain respects, however, Ulam's analysis was compatible with revisionist arguments. He viewed Stalin's primary goal in eastern Europe as being the establishment of friendly governments, though not necessarily communist ones. He contended that Stalin asserted complete control over Russia's neighbors in response to American policies, particularly the Marshall Plan. Ulam denied that Stalin was paranoid, at least until about 1947.

In a study of Stalin's wartime diplomacy, Vojtech Mastny disputed revisionist views even more sharply than Ulam. He argued that during the war Stalin planned to expand into eastern Europe and beyond and that his ambitions were tempered only by his fear of inciting a strong reaction from the West by going too far. The United States and Britain blundered by not firmly opposing Stalin's actions much earlier than they did. William O. McCagg provided a different picture of Stalin's foreign policy by emphasizing how domestic concerns shaped it. He contended that during the war, Stalin lost some of his political control to military leaders and industrial managers. In an effort to regain that power, he moved to revive the Communist party, which necessitated a renewed rhetorical emphasis on ideology. Stalin realized that this would cause misunderstandings with the West, but he declined to make his limited foreign-policy ambitions clear in order to carry out his domestic priorities. Both the Mastny and McCagg books were scrupulously researched and richly documented. Their focus and analysis were dissimilar; McCagg, for example, regarded Stalin as less belligerent and ambitious than did Mastny. Both were important works, though at present their impact on cold war historiography is difficult to predict.

In the late 1970s, three major comprehensive studies of the early cold war were published. Each was balanced and moderate in interpretation and drew on the work of scholars during the previous decade. Robert J. Donovan's *Conflict and Crisis: The Presidency of Harry S. Truman, 1945–1948* was more anecdotal than analytical and reflected the author's journalistic background. But it was a serious book that indicated that revisionist arguments had influenced even quasi-popular writing on the cold war. Though clearly sympathetic to Truman, Donovan was neither reverential nor uncritical. He chided Truman, for example, for failing to consider that Soviet expansion in eastern Europe might have been an outgrowth of national insecurity and for "his tendency to exaggerate Soviet motives." He agreed with scholars who contended that administration officials hoped that increased diplomatic leverage would be a valuable by-product of using the atomic bomb. In discussing the 1946 Iranian crisis, Donovan faulted Truman and Byrnes for not "allowing for the possibility that Stalin's actions may have been essentially defensive." Those and other reproachful comments hardly qualified Donovan's book as a revisionist tract. But it was much more evenhanded than fellow reporter Cabell Phillips's 1966 acclamatory account of the Truman administration, which also had been directed at a general audience.

Donovan's book, despite its lively style and considerable merit, failed to provide much original analysis and arrived at conclusions that carried eclecticism to the point of blandness. A more creative and stimulating examination of Truman's diplomacy was Daniel Yergin's *Shattered Peace*. Yergin described a fundamental dichotomy in how American leaders viewed the Soviet Union. State Department officials, including William Bullitt, Loy Henderson, George Kennan, Charles Bohlen, and others, adhered to the "Riga axioms," which held that Soviet foreign policy followed ideological dictates and plotted world revolution and unlimited expansion. The United States could deal with the Soviets only by being firm and wary. Other American leaders, including Roosevelt and Harry Hopkins, espoused the "Yalta axioms," which assumed that Stalin sought traditional Russian diplomatic goals and could be approached as a "realistic, rational statesman." They believed that the United States could and must win Stalin's trust and lay the foundations for civil if not harmonious relations after the war. After Truman took office, he took a position between the two axioms. Gradually, however, he lost patience with Russia, partly because of his own convictions and partly because of the influence of his advisors, Congress, and public opinion. By the summer of 1946, the Riga axioms had clearly triumphed as government officials and most Americans came to view the Soviet Union as an ideological foe with unlimited ambitions. At that point, the United States ceased trying to resolve its differences with the Soviets through diplomacy and began building a formidable military arsenal.

Yergin synthesized much existing scholarship and contributed new insights of his own, such as his emphasis on the competing axioms, his discussion of how bureaucratic rivalries within the military added to the growing fear of Russia, and his explanation of the rise of the "gospel of national security." On issues that divided traditionalists and revisionists, his analysis was thoroughly eclectic. He criticized many American policies and perceptions, for example, but also depicted them as understandable, though unfortunate, responses to Soviet activities. Yergin acknowledged the presence of economic considerations in United States foreign policy, but found other motives, such as Wilsonian principles and strategic concerns, more important. He suggested that a cold war in some form was inevitable, but argued that by not following the Yalta axioms, the United States "not only helped to make the division sharper than it might otherwise have been, but also made the Soviet-American confrontation more highly militarized and much more costly and dangerous." *Shattered Peace* received many rave notices, but it also inspired some sharp attacks. Carolyn Eisenberg thought its basic premises were flawed because they rested "upon the indefensible refusal to acknowledge the American stake in the maintenance of a liberal capitalist international order." Daniel F. Harrington denied that either Kennan or Bohlen believed in the Riga axioms as outlined by Yergin, since neither viewed the Soviets as primarily motivated by ideology or a quest for world domination.

In the most recent general study of the origins of the cold war [*On Every Front*], Thomas G. Paterson attributed the growth of Soviet-American tensions to the frictions inherent in the postwar situation, the varying needs and ideologies of the two countries, and the diplomatic tactics employed by their leaders. While pointing out that any international system is "conflict-ridden," he argued that the power vacuums, economic dislocations, and political upheavals caused by the war intensified differences between the United States and Russia. Paterson cited both American and Soviet policies as responsible for creating dissension. Each nation sought to establish spheres of influence, and viewed the activities of the other as an effort to threaten its own sphere and undermine its interests. The vital concerns of both nations, he maintained, derived from a complex mixture of ideological, political, economic, strategic, and historical factors that generated tensions and escalated mutual misapprehensions. In addition, the personalities and tactics of American and Soviet officials contributed to an atmosphere of distrust and discord. Although Truman sought the same fundamental goals as Roosevelt, his brash, abrasive, and impatient manner of conducting diplomacy offended the Soviets. On the other hand, Americans generally found Soviet leaders to be "rude, untrustworthy, excessively suspicious, devious, unreceptive to gestures of kindness, and too dependent upon direct instructions from the Kremlin." Paterson's book, like Yergin's, incorporated the opinions and perspectives of a wide range of previous studies to produce an original analysis. Both works featured an eclectic approach and a balanced interpretation that was characteristic of postrevisionist cold war scholarship.

By the late 1970s a broad consensus, amalgamating elements of the realist and revisionist interpretations, had emerged on the basic questions that had divided the two viewpoints. First and most obviously, nearly all cold war scholars agreed that America and Russia shared responsibility for the onset of the cold war in approximately equal proportions. Some found the United States slightly more culpable while others allocated a somewhat greater share of the blame to the Soviet Union. But the idea that either the United States or Russia was exclusively or chiefly accountable for the development of tensions gave way to a middle position. Assigning responsibility was a central focus of writing on the cold war, and the shift to an even-handed assessment was a major historiographical milestone that testified to the impact of the new left. Furthermore, recent studies generally regarded a cold war in some form as inevitable, but also maintained that United States policies exacerbated the situation and made the American-Soviet rivalry more intense than it otherwise would have been. The argument that even if the postwar conflict were unavoidable it could have been less bitter blended the fatalism of the realists with the new left conviction that the cold war was largely preventable.

Revisionists and many realists had always concurred in viewing Stalin's foreign-policy objectives as limited and motivated more by Soviet national concerns than by ideological commitments. That premise remained prevalent in postrevisionist literature, along with a number of corollaries that followed from it. Most scholars, without depicting Stalin's aims as perfectly benign, contended that the United States misperceived and overreacted to the Soviet threat. As a result, the Truman administration took actions that it saw as defensive, but that appeared aggressive to the Soviets. Growing misunderstanding and failure to communicate effectively escalated tensions and exaggerated differences. One consequence was that Stalin consolidated his hold on eastern Europe by assuming control in nations where he had permitted some autonomy immediately after the war. For the most part, recent writing on the cold war has described a pattern of challenge and response, action and reaction by both countries rather than a case of one side responding to the aggressive expansion of the other.

The trend toward eclecticism was also evident in the partial acceptance in recent works of two major components of the new left position. Few postrevisionist scholars endorsed the thesis that economic considerations were the fundamental motivating forces in United States diplomacy or the basic cause of conflict with the Soviet Union. Many did agree, however, that the United States tried to use economic pressure to modify Soviet behavior and that economic concerns were a part of the complex mixture of factors that activated American foreign policy. Similarly, most recent studies of the cold war did not confirm the new left image of United States policymakers implementing coherent, well-planned diplomatic objectives. They have, on the other hand, generally shown that American leaders, in dealing with day-to-day pressures and problems, were neither naive nor overly idealistic in their responses.

Within the consensus that has materialized on the origins of the cold war, differences still exist on many specific issues. All of the points on which scholars generally, though not unanimously, agree are subject to further reassessment and reinterpretation, especially as more sources become available.

The new cold war consensus, though based on a much larger body of evidence than the old one, remains provisional. . . .

The Sources of the Cold War

THOMAS G. PATERSON

The Cold War derived from three closely intertwined sources: the conflict-ridden *international system,* the divergent *fundamental needs and ideas* of the major antagonists, America and Russia, and the diplomatic conduct or *tactics* of American and Soviet leaders. To reduce the conflict inherent in the postwar structure, to satisfy their strategic and economic needs and ideologies, and to conduct diplomacy true to their individual personalities and domestic political environments, officials in Washington and Moscow abandoned any quest for a community of nations and instead built competing spheres of influence. They thereby expanded and protected what they respectively perceived to be their interests, divided the world, and stimulated more conflict, which took the form of a "prolonged armed truce," to use the words of Soviet diplomat Maxim Litvinov. . . .

In the rubble-strewn postwar world, international relations changed markedly from prewar interactions. Any historical period, such as the Cold War, is identified by a particular structure of relationships among the world's leading nations—by, in short, the international "system." Thus, the Napoleonic era of the late eighteenth and early nineteenth centuries was characterized by bipolarism, wherein France and Britain vied for world mastery, established alliances with lesser powers, frequently clashed in war, and managed far-flung empires. The period between the Congress of Vienna in 1815 and the outbreak of World War I in 1914, often called the era of Pax Britannica, was multipolar, with a number of leading actors on the international stage who preferred diplomatic negotiations to military combat and who deliberately set about to create a balance of power for the maintenance of a conservative, imperial, antirevolutionary world.

Any international system is conflict-ridden. "Peace," after all, is a very abstract term, difficult to employ as a description of any era. "Anarchy" probably more aptly approximates historical reality. The attempts nations make to reduce the anarchy constitute our diplomatic history. Conflict is inherent in any international system simply because countries seldom share common goals, interests, or ideologies. Some nations are more powerful or influential than others and flaunt their superiority. Others may resist. Some countries are dependent upon others. Some have what others want—territory, food, water, minerals, labor, and a multitude of things over which peoples have squabbled for centuries. Great nations are always looking for friends who will join them in formal or informal alliances to check the

From *On Every Front: The Making of the Cold War* by Thomas G. Paterson (New York: W. W. Norton & Company, 1979).

growth of those states they consider unfriendly or potentially so. Small nations have to be wary of the major actors, who may cast longing eyes on them and exploit their vulnerability. Nations which may wish to remain "neutral" or unaligned are wooed or cajoled.

The leading powers, whether aligned or at loggerheads, watch one another suspiciously, on the assumption that in international politics, as in business, one can supposedly trust friends seldom, enemies never. Slight shifts in the distribution of power—of resources—arouse concern. What one government considers "defense," another labels "offense." The construction of a military base, the testing of a new weapon, a request to alter a boundary, the signing of a treaty—all can be defined as both defensive or offensive, depending upon one's point of view. A rifle is a defensive weapon if seen from the butt, but it is a weapon of attack if one is staring into the muzzle. Suspicion and fear, those ancient diseases, undermine trust and prompt countermeasures. Leaders may assume evil intentions on the part of other nations and plan for the worst. Governments feel compelled to match the decisions of those whom they assume to be adversaries. Failure to develop a new weapon, for example, might entail extreme risk, for an enemy might gain advantage by producing it. Hence, leaders often escalate the level of conflict and chances for war through exaggerated perceptions of danger. In short, there is always an expanding nation, and there are countries reacting to that expansion. Differences in goals among the several parties of the international system feed instability. The degree of conflict may vary, but there is always conflict. "This is a lawless world," University of Chicago Professor Herman Finer told a radio audience in 1947, "because it is a world without a common morality or a common superior. Nationalisms and moralities collide."

Higher degrees of conflict are reached when the international system undergoes significant change, when it metamorphoses into a new or revised system. Such was the case after World War II. Change, by definition, is destabilizing. Some postwar leaders, even though immersed in day-to-day decisionmaking, pondered the general characteristics of the international system. They knew that significant changes had altered the configuration of power. As participants in and shapers of a new age, they were "present at the creation." But the outline of the new system was only vaguely evident. With the historian's advantage of hindsight, however, we can delineate the peculiar properties of the postwar world and suggest that the process of creating a new system out of the ashes of the discredited prewar system intensified the conflict inherent in any international structure.

Yet this view of systemic conflict cannot serve as a comprehensive explanation for the origins of the Cold War. For if the Soviet–American confrontation was simply the inevitable product of the conflict-ridden international system, there would be little purpose in studying the leaders, ideas, policies, or needs of individual nations, because events would be largely beyond their control. Under this interpretation the system would dictate antagonistic relations. It would not matter whether different personalities or different national policies existed. Few scholars, however, subscribe to this restricted analysis of history. We know that leaders made choices, even if they only dimly understood their consequences. Harry S. Truman, Winston Churchill, and Josef Stalin helped to create the international system to which they had to react. A complete history of the beginnings of the Cold War, then, must include not only the traits of the international system but also the dynamics of particular nations and individuals. In this chapter a macro-analytic view will enable us to identify the opportunities and constraints which faced the major actors. Or, as Professor Bruce M. Russett has suggested, this level of analysis outlines the "menu" of world affairs—the choices available, as well as the limits of choice. It sketches the "big picture," so that the disparate components of the postwar system can be examined in proper relationship. It helps us to determine which nations held real or potential power and why, ultimately, they moved toward restrictive spheres of influence and away from a community of interest and international cooperation.

Conflict in the postwar years was accentuated by wrenching changes in the international system—a redistribution of power and a departure from a Europe-centered world. Two nations emerged from the rubble of World War II to claim first rank. The competitive interaction between the United States and the Soviet Union—"like two big dogs chewing on a bone," said Senator J. William Fulbright—contributed to the bipolarism of the immediate postwar years. "Not since Rome and Carthage," Dean Acheson observed, "had there been such a polarization of power on this earth." This new bipolar structure replaced the multipolar system of the 1930s, wherein at least six nations were active, influential participants. By the late 1940s, decisions made in Washington, D.C. and Moscow often determined whether people in other nations voted, where they lived, and how much they ate. The nations which had tried to wield such authority in the 1930s had fallen from their elevated status. Japan, Italy, and Germany were defeated and occupied; England, nearly bankrupt, dependent, and unable to police its empire, was reduced to a resentful second-rate power; France, much of whose territory had been held by the Germans during the war, was still suffering from unstable politics and no longer mustered international respect.

The abrupt removal of Germany and Japan from positions of high authority in international relations created power vacuums in Europe and Asia. The United States and Soviet Russia, eager to fulfill their visions of the postwar world and to seize opportunities for extending their respective influence, were attracted to these vacuums. With the old barriers to American and Soviet expansion gone, Russia and America clashed over occupation policies in Germany, Italy, Japan, Austria, and Korea. They squabbled over which political groups should replace the Nazi regimes in Eastern Europe. The filling of gaps or vacuums in any system is a natural process. In the postwar period the gaps were huge and worldwide, inviting a high degree of competition and conflict.

Another change wrought by World War II was the destruction of the economic world. The war cut an ugly scar across Europe and Asia, but bypassed one major nation, the United States. "If Hitler succeeds in nothing else," mused OSS officer Allen Dulles, "like Samson, he may pull down the pillars of the temple and leave a long and hard road of reconstruction." The postwar task was forbidding. Not only did cities have to be rebuilt, factories opened, people put back to work, rails repaired, rivers and roads made passable, and crop yields increased, but the flow of international commerce and finance had to be reestablished if nations were to raise through exports the revenue needed to buy the imports required for recovery. Many old commercial and financial patterns had been broken and, given the obstacle of economic wreckage, new exchanges were difficult to establish. Where would Germany's vital coal and steel go? Would industrial Western Europe and agricultural Eastern Europe recreate old commercial ties? Would the restrictive trade practices of the 1930s, especially the tariff barriers, continue into the 1940s? Would subservient colonies continue to serve as sources of rich raw materials? Could international agreements and organizations curb economic nationalism? Would trade be conducted on a multilateral, "open door" basis, as the United States preferred, or by bilateral or preferential methods, as many others, such as Britain and Russia, practiced? The answers helped to define the international system of the post-1945 era. These issues held more importance than simple economics, for leaders recognized that the economic disorders of the 1930s and the far-reaching impact of the Great Depression contributed to political chaos, aggression, and war. The new international system, it was hoped, would create stable economic conditions which would facilitate the development of pacific international relations. Yet the very efforts to realize these hopes engendered conflict.

World War II also bequeathed domestic political turmoil to its survivors. The regimes of the 1930s, now discredited, vied with insurgent groups for the governing power in many states. Socialists, Communists, and other varieties of the political left, many of whom had fought in the underground resistance movements and had thus earned some popular respect, challenged the more entrenched, conservative elites, many of whom had escaped into exile when the German armies rolled into their countries. In Poland, the Communist, Soviet-endorsed Lublin Poles challenged the political standing of the Poles who had fled to London. The conservative Dutch government-in-exile watched warily as leftist resistance groups gradually built a popular following. Political confusion in the Netherlands was heightened by the wartime loss of voting lists. In Greece a coalition of leftists in the National Liberation Front (EAM) vigorously resisted the return to power of a British-created government and the unpopular Greek monarchy of King George. In France Charles de Gaulle vied for power with the Communists. In China the civil war, which had raged for years between the Communists of Mao Tse-tung and the Nationalists of Chiang Kai-shek, flared up again at the close of the war. Yugoslavia was the scene of political battle between Josip Broz Tito's Partisans and a group headed by Dr. Ivan Subasic of the London emigré government, which in turn suffered strained ties with King Peter. Moreover, in the occupied nations of Germany, Austria, and Korea, the victors created competitive zones, postponing the creation of central governments. In the defeated countries of Japan and Italy, American officials decided who would rule, whereas in parts of Eastern Europe, Soviet officials placed Communists in positions of authority.

The major powers, in short, intervened abroad to exploit the political opportunities created by the destructive scythe of World War II. The stakes seemed high. A change in a nation's political orientation might presage a change in its international alignment. The great powers tended to ignore local conditions which might mitigate against alignment with an outside power. Americans feared that a leftist or Communist Greece would look to the East and permit menacing Soviet bases on Greek territory or open the door to a Soviet naval presence in the Mediterranean. The Russians dreaded a conservative anti-Soviet Polish government led by the London faction, for it might prove so weak and so hostile to Moscow as to permit a revived Germany to send stormtroopers once again through the Polish corridor into the heart of Russia. A Communist China, thought Americans, might align with Russia; a Nationalist China would remain in the American camp. All in all, the rearranging of political structures *within* nations drew the major powers into competition, accentuating the conflict inherent in the postwar international system.

If the war threw politics into chaos, it also hastened the disintegration of colonial and informal empires. The Japanese movement into French Indochina and their drive for Dutch East Indies oil had led to Pearl Harbor in 1941. The initially successful Japanese expansion had the effect of demonstrating to many Asian nationalists that their white imperial masters could be defeated. Some nationalists collaborated during the war with their Asian brethren from Tokyo, and the Japanese, in need of administrators to manage occupied areas, trained and armed some native leaders. Japan granted Burma considerable autonomy in 1942, for example, and after the war the Burmese were determined not to return to a position of subservience to Great Britain. At the end of the war, the European powers, exhausted and financially hobbled, had to struggle to reestablish mastery over rebellious colonies. The appeal of the principle of self-determination, still echoing from the days of Woodrow Wilson and given new emphasis by the Atlantic Charter of 1941, was far-reaching.

No empire seemed immune to disintegration. The United States granted the Philippines independence in 1946. The British, worn low by the war and by the challenges of nationalist groups demanding independence, retreated from India (and Pakistan) in 1947 and from Burma and Ceylon in 1948. Israel, carved out of British-governed Palestine, became a new independent state in 1948. The British also found it difficult to maintain their sphere of influence in Iran, Greece, and Egypt and began retreats from those politically unsteady states. The French attempted to hold on to Indochina, where nationalist forces led by Ho Chi Minh had declared an independent Vietnam. Bloody battle ensued, leading ultimately to French withdrawal in 1954. The Dutch also decided to fight, but after four debilitating years of combat, they pulled out of Indonesia in 1949. The defeated Japanese were forced to give up their claims to Formosa and Korea, as well as Pacific island groups. Italy departed from Ethiopia and lost its African colonies of Tripolitania (Libya) and Eritrea. Lebanon, Syria, and Jordan, areas once managed by Europeans, gained independence in 1943, 1944, and 1946, respectively.

The world map, as after World War I, was redrawn. The emergence of so many new states, and the instability associated with the transfer of authority, shook the very foundations of the international system. Power was being redistributed. In varying degrees, Russia and America competed for the allegiance of the new governments, meddled in colonial rebellions, and generally sought to exploit opportunities for an extension of their influence. Again, the stakes seemed high. The new nations could serve as strategic bases, markets for exports, sources of vital raw materials, sites for investments, and votes in international organizations. States such as India, which chose nonalignment in the developing Cold War, were wooed with foreign aid and ideological appeals. In the case of Indochina, the powers supported different sides: Washington backed the ruling French, and Moscow endorsed Ho and his insurgents.

As one United States government study noted, the disintegration of empires, especially the withdrawal of the British from their once vast domain, created an "over-all situation of near chaos" in the international system. In some areas, such as Southeast Asia, it meant a "new balance of power." The upheaval was fundamental: "Old values are being changed and new ones sought. New friendships are being formed." The international system creaked and swayed under this unsettled burden.

Conflict also sprang from efforts to launch a new international organization to replace the defunct League of Nations. At the Dumbarton Oaks Conference in 1944, the Allies initiated plans for a United Nations Organization. The United States, Britain, and Russia were its chief architects, and the institution they created at the San Francisco Conference from April to June of 1945 reflected their insistence on big-power domination. They agreed upon a veto power for the five "permanent members" of the Security Council (Britain, Russia, United States, France, and China) and assigned the General Assembly, the forum for smaller nations, a subordinate status. Nevertheless, because each of the Allies recognized that the new international body was potentially an instrument, through bloc voting, of one nation's foreign policy, they argued. Churchill crudely complained that China, hardly a "great" power, would be a "faggot vote on the side of the United States," and Russia protested that France would simply represent a British vote. "China was a joke," remarked State Department veteran John Hickerson, "a FDR joke." Because Britain could marshall the votes of several of its Commonwealth countries and the United States could count on most of the Latin American nations in the General Assembly, the conferees at the Yalta Conference of early 1945 granted Russia three votes, in order to alter somewhat the glaring imbalance.

Such compromise, however, broke down at the San Francisco Conference.

Membership applications from Argentina and Poland produced heated differences. Against vehement Soviet objections Argentina, which had declared war against Germany at the last minute and which some critics considered a "fascist" nation, gained membership after the United States backed its application and the nations of the Western Hemisphere voted "yes" as a bloc. Yet when Lublin-led Poland, not yet reorganized according to the American interpretation of the Yalta accords, applied for entry, the United States voted "no," and the conference denied Poland a seat. Moscow railed at this, charging a double standard. The United Nations Organization, which held its first session in January of 1946, thus began amidst controversy. Rather than serving as a stabilizing force in the postwar international system, the United Nations early became a source of conflict, a verbal battleground for the allegiance of world opinion, a vehicle for condemnatory resolutions, a largely United States–dominated institution, and a graveyard for idealistic hopes— in short, part of a "masquerade peace."

The postwar international system suffered, too, from the destabilizing effect of the new atomic bomb. The "most terrible weapon ever known in human history," Secretary of War Henry L. Stimson quietly told the President, unsettled the world community, for it was an agent of massive human destruction, and "in a world atmosphere already extremely sensitive to power, the introduction of this weapon has profoundly affected political considerations in all sections of the globe." Nations which possessed "the bomb" seemed to hold an advantage in international politics, for it could serve as a deterrent against an adversary as well as a means to annihilate an enemy. When combined with air power and a long-range delivery capability, it also hurdled geographical boundaries, rendering them useless as protective elements in a nation's security shield. With the perfecting of air war in World War II, "the roof blew off the territorial state." As General Douglas MacArthur remarked after the atomic explosions: "Well, this changes warfare!" The prospect of nuclear annihilation bothered everybody, but the United States was especially concerned about nuclear proliferation, which meant the loss of its atomic monopoly.

A question dogged the peacemakers: How were they to control the development, spread, and use of atomic energy? There had been arms races before, and ineffective disarmament conferences in the 1920s and 1930s, but the postwar nuclear race was conducted at a far different and more dangerous level. The atomic bomb was the "absolute weapon," not only more violent but also capable of speedy delivery, rapid retaliation, and immediate cataclysm. Challenging the American monopoly, the Soviet Union successfully produced its own bomb in 1949. As the two bickering major powers groped for ways in which to deal with "the bomb" and undertook their atomic development programs, others held their breath. One observer suggested that a Soviet–American war "might not end with *one* Rome but with *two* Carthages." The atomic bomb, uncontrolled, envied, copied, and brandished, became a major obstacle to a peaceful, orderly postwar international system.

The shrinkage of the world and the growth of a global outlook must be included in any estimation of the impact of World War II on the international system. Geography had not changed, but ways of moving across it and of thinking about it had. Improvements in transportation, especially in aviation, brought nations closer to one another. The world seemed more compact and accessible. People had to think now not only in traditional land miles but also in flying hours. In a popularization for school children, N. L. Englehardt, Jr. urged his young readers to think "air thoughts" and titled one of his chapters "How the World Has Shrunk." Because the Atlantic Ocean could be traversed easily and quickly, that once-prominent barrier between the Old and New Worlds disappeared. As America was brought closer to Europe and the world, American strategic thinking expanded as well. In the world contracted by science, events in Greece or Iran or China held greater significance than ever before for American security. The Japanese attack upon Pearl Harbor, accomplished after crossing 3,500 miles of the Pacific Ocean, had proved that great distances no longer served as protectors of security. "If you imagine two or three hundred Pearl Harbors occurring all over the United States," prophesied Assistant Secretary of State A. A. Berle, "you will have a rough picture of what the next war might look like. . . ." Observers began to speak not only of an "atomic age," but of an "air age" and a "global age." The global war of 1939–45 had helped spawn a postwar globalism—an international interdependence. "The entire relations of the United States with the world," declared Dean Acheson, "are a seamless web. . . ." Geographical isolation was gone with the past. Stimson perceived that the United States could never again "be an island to herself. No private program and no public policy, in any sector of our national life can now escape from the compelling fact that if it is not framed with reference to the world, it is framed with perfect futility."

United States Chief of Staff General George C. Marshall typified strategic reconsiderations. "For probably the last time in the history of warfare those ocean distances were a vital factor in our defense. We may elect again to depend on others and the whim and error of potential enemies, but if we do we will be carrying the treasure and freedom of this great Nation in a paper bag." Because frontiers had been extended, because nations were brought nearer one another, and because the world had shrunk, the major powers coveted bases far from home, much as the United States had sought and acquired bases in the Caribbean in the early twentieth century to protect the Panama Canal. "We are now concerned with the peace of the entire world," said Marshall. Two years later President Truman described a "much smaller earth—an earth whose broad oceans have shrunk and whose national protections have been taken away by new weapons of destruction." In a similar vein, a joint Chiefs of Staff report of late 1947 looked ten years into the future and predicted a "continuing shrinkage of the world from the accelerated pace of technological progress." In short, a new aspect of the postwar international system was the interdependence or intertwining of events in all parts of the world, thereby drawing great powers into confrontations as never before. Globalism insured conflict.

Such was the postwar international system—with its opportunities and constraints, with its characteristics insuring conflict. The makers of the peace sought to reduce the conflict, but their decisions exacerbated it. . . .

The postwar international system, lacking stability and rife with tension, provided its two most prominent members with numerous opportunities to clash and to build spheres of influence. The United States and the Soviet Union, groping toward their different definitions of the new world order, did just that. "Something new had to be created," recalled Dean Acheson, and the role for the United States "was one of fashioning, trying to help fashion what would come after the destruction of the old world."

Clearly, systemic conditions drew the major powers into conflict, yet the United States and Russia themselves, for their own reasons, had to decide whether or not to exploit opportunities, struggle against the profound problems bequeathed by the Second World War, and undertake an activist, inevitably globalist, foreign policy. Nations do not simply react to the international environment or to the foreign policies of other countries. They also act purposefully to expand and protect what in general they consider to be their national well-being or, in the case of the United States, to shape an "environment in which the American experiment of life can prosper." Internal stimuli, then, helped to prompt the American and Soviet governments to "fashion" a new postwar international system of spheres of influence.

The focus [now] is on the internal factors that propelled the United States to center stage. What American "fundamentals"—ideas, economic and strategic needs, power—explain why the United States wanted to and had to become a central participant in the making of the postwar world. The fundamentals transcended personalities or changes in administration; both Franklin D. Roosevelt and Harry S. Truman were guided by them. Foreign policy, diplomat Charles Bohlen reminded Americans, was not rooted in particular leaders but "in our American traditions and in the requirements of the national interest." The *fundamentals* or *whys* of American foreign relations, therefore, were distinct from the *tactics* or *hows* of diplomacy. Policymakers . . . determined not the fundamental factors themselves, but how they were to be satisfied and exercised.

Ideology, economic-strategic needs, and elements of national power comprised America's fundamentals, generating an activist, expansionist diplomacy. Among the components of the American ideology, we can discover American dreams about the new world order—what they wanted to avoid, sought to create, and hoped to enjoy. American economic and political ideals and principles from the past pointed the way: an "open door" world of equal trade and investment opportunity; private enterprise, as opposed to government ownership of the means of production; multilateralism or cooperation in foreign commerce; freedom of the seas; the right of self-determination and self-government; democratic, constitutional procedures; the limitation of force in international relations; "good neighborism"; and freedom of religion and speech. Woodrow Wilson immortalized many of these ideas in his famous Fourteen Points, Roosevelt implanted some of them in the Atlantic Charter, and Truman listed many of them as the "fundamentals" of American foreign policy in his Navy Day speech of October, 1945. All in all, Americans believed in an "open world," free from barriers to political democracy and economic opportunity.

Americans in the postwar years, remembering the tragedies wrought by economic depression, aggression, and war in the 1930s, constantly spoke of the interlocking connection between peace and prosperity. Just before his death, President Roosevelt told Congress that "we cannot succeed in building a peaceful world unless we build an economically healthy world." Congressman Carl T. Durham of North Carolina informed columnist Marquis Childs in 1945 that "starvation, illness, and the coming cold winter are foregone conclusions in many countries, and we are all aware of what this will breed." Indeed, "hungry people are not reasonable people," concluded a State Department official. Americans believed that economic instability and poverty bred political chaos, revolutionary behavior, totalitarianism, violence, aggression, and war. It was assumed that these conditions were attractive to political extremists like Communists who always preyed on weaknesses and dislocations. George F. Kennan expressed the prevailing sentiment starkly: "World communism is like a malignant parasite which feeds only on diseased tissue." Economic reconstruction and the revival of free-flowing world trade and finance offered one route to prosperity and, in turn, peace. "Nations which act as enemies in the marketplace," Under-Secretary of State Will Clayton mused, "cannot long be friends at the council table." President Truman stated that "in fact the three—peace, freedom, and world trade—are inseparable."

Because the postwar world economy was interdependent, Americans understood that economic catastrophes did not respect national boundaries. Secretary of the Interior Julius Krug remarked that "depressions are as catching as the common cold," and W. Averell Harriman, describing the United States as the "financial and economic pivot of the world," feared that "economic stagnation in the United States would drag the rest of the world down with us." To prevent contagious depressions, to insure that the world did not plummet again into the depths of depression, the United States had to restore and maintain its primacy in the international economy. In 1947 the United States accounted for one-third of the world's total exports and about half of the world's industrial output. Secretary of State George C. Marshall told a Harvard University audience, in advocating the "plan" for economic recovery that eventually bore his name, that "it is logical that the United States should do whatever it is able to do to assist in the return of normal economic health in the world, without which there can be no political stability and no assured peace." Acheson summarized the question earlier when he explained that the "great difference in our second attempt to establish a peaceful world is the wide recognition that peace is possible only if countries work together and prosper together. That is why the economic aspects are no less important than the political aspects of peace."

The political world Americans envisioned was very much like their own. They rightfully prided themselves on their Bill of Rights, their enduring

Constitution, and their stable, representative form of government. What is more, they assumed that other peoples would want the same and should be shown the way. Roosevelt's special aide Harry Hopkins said in 1945:

> I have often been asked what interests we have in Poland, Greece, Iran, or Korea. Well I think we have the most important business in the world—and indeed, the only business worthy of our traditions. And that is this—to do everything within our diplomatic power to foster and encourage democratic government throughout the world. We should not be timid about blazoning to the world our desire for the right of all peoples to have a genuine civil liberty. We believe our dynamic democracy is the best in the world....

As Hopkins's impassioned words attest, embedded in the American ideology was the belief that the United States was blessed with superior principles and institutions which others should adopt. Call it missionary zeal, a sense of manifest destiny, conceit, arrogance, or chauvinism, Americans had it: a self-image which obscured blatant violations (such as racial segregation at home)—a self-satisfaction that Americans were an exceptional people. The Puritan fathers thought so when they delivered their lofty sermons against the perfidies of the Old World; American rebels in 1776 echoed the belief in casting off the British yoke; President James Monroe espoused his "doctrine" in 1823 to emphasize the uniqueness of the Western Hemisphere; Woodrow Wilson had insisted in the era of World War I that America was a beacon of sanity for mankind; and during the Second World War, the United States became the "arsenal of democracy." "All nations succumb to fantasies of innate superiority," historian Arthur M. Schlesinger, Jr., has written. "When they act on these fantasies, as the Spanish did in the sixteenth century, the French in the seventeenth, the English in the eighteenth, the Germans and Japanese and Russians and Americans in the twentieth, they tend to become international menaces." Certainly postwar Americans never classified themselves as such. Rather, they were benefactors, celebrants of the American success story, spreading their economic and political riches to the less fortunate through world leadership.

Lessons from the past also held a place in the American ideology. Biographer Gaddis Smith has noted that Dean Acheson believed that "only the United States had the power to grab hold of history and make it conform." What history? The history of depression, political extremism, aggression, and war in the twentieth century. Americans recalled that they had jilted the League of Nations and had courted isolationism and an appeasement policy in the dreadful 1930s. Many Americans blamed themselves for permitting Japanese militarists, German stormtroopers, and Italian fascists to march and plunder. "History has bestowed on us a solemn responsibility," Truman remarked in 1944. "We shall, we must, be a mighty force at the peace conference. We failed before to give a genuine peace—we dare not fail this time." It was America's second chance—the opportunity to throw off the mistakes of the past and claim its rightful first ranking among nations. The United States would permit no more Munichs, no more appeasement, no more compromise with aggressive totalitarianism, no more depression, and no more Pearl Harbors. The new bywords were leadership and preparedness. "We must continue to be a military nation if we are to maintain leadership among other nations," Truman told his Cabinet in his worry about the dangers of demobilizing too rapidly. Secretary Byrnes added that "we must not make the mistake made after the last war."

As an avid reader of historical works, President Truman believed that history "has some extremely valuable lessons to teach." Indeed, he wrote, "we must know how to apply the lessons of history in a practical way." The lessons he drew from history often reached as far back as the days of ancient Greece, but his immediate instruction came from the tumultuous events of the decade of the Great Depression. He and other Americans feared that the 1940s would be an ugly replay of the 1930s, and they came to believe that the Soviets were seizing the staff of aggressive totalitarianism wrested from the Nazis in World War II. NBC news analyst Clifton Utley expressed a popular postwar assumption: "If we run out again we will create a vacuum." The experience of pre-1945 American–Russian relations helped to conjure up the image of a self-interested, recalcitrant, revolutionary, untrustworthy nation bent on destroying Western capitalism—a burly, bewhiskered Bolshevik whacking away at the foundations of world order. The iconoclastic Bolshevik Revolution, the seizure of foreign-owned property, the refusal to honor Czarist debt obligations, antagonism between Americans and Communists during the Allied intervention in the Russian civil war, anticapitalist propaganda, the ineffectiveness of American diplomatic recognition in 1933 in smoothing relations, and the gruesome Stalinist purges all served to sear this image on the American mind. The Nazi-Soviet pact of 1939, furthermore, convinced Americans that Nazi Germany and Soviet Russia were really two of a kind, that, as the *Wall Street Journal* put it, "the principal difference between Mr. Hitler and Mr. Stalin is the size of their respective mustaches."

FBI Director J. Edgar Hoover, among others, coined a phrase for this simple Communist/Nazi analogy: "Red Fascism." "There isn't any difference in totalitarian states," asserted Truman. "I don't care what you call them, Nazi, Communist or Fascist. . . ." As Moscow spread its influence over Eastern Europe after the war, Americans warned against another system of "satellites." "It looks like the same pattern that Hitler adopted in 1936 when he began to take over the small countries around him," brooded one Congressman. General John R. Deane, head of the American military mission to Russia during the war, wrote in his 1947 memoir that even the marching style of Russian soldiers "closely resembled the [German] goose-step, with arms rigid and legs kicked stiffly to the front. . . ." New Deal "Brain Truster" A. A. Berle also drew heavily on the stereotyped "Red-Fascist" analogy when he recorded the following comments in his 1945 diary: "Same tactics are used: violent propaganda, smear accusations, portrayal of other people's patriotism as criminal or reactionary, financing of fifth columns, stimulated disorders, street terrorism, ultimately direct territorial and occupation demands." Thus, thought Americans, aggressive Nazism cloaked as aggressive

Communism (or vice-versa) linked the 1930s and 1940s, and menacing totalitarianism was once again roaming—this time as a Russian bear—far beyond its own habitat. "The image of a Stalinist Russia," Kennan argued a decade after popularization of the analogy," "poised and yearning to attack the West, and deterred only by our possession of atomic weapons, was largely a creation of the Western imagination." Imagination or not, distortion or not, Americans imbibed and nourished this component of their postwar ideology, one of the fundamental forces making an activist American foreign policy seem imperative.

Another well-spring of American foreign policy was the fundamental factor of economic-strategic needs—those requirements of the domestic economy and national security which had to be met in order to maintain American well-being. Throughout their history Americans had been a proud, successful trading people. Foreign commerce had always constituted a profitable segment of their economy, and in the War of 1812 and World War I, the United States was willing to fight to uphold the principle of freedom of the seas for its merchants. In the 1930s Secretary of State Cordell Hull, through the Reciprocal Trade Agreements Program and the Export-Import Bank, had attempted to maintain America's prominent position in the global economy. Foreign trade was more than a pocketbook issue; from the American perspective foreign trade contributed to economic health which permitted them, and other countries as well, to enjoy stable, democratic government. As David Potter illustrated in his book *People of Plenty,* Americans had long considered themselves democratic because they were prosperous and prosperous because they were democratic. Foreign trade was significant in strategic terms too, helping the United States to acquire vital raw materials essential to the production of defense goods. Moreover, it was assumed in the peace and prosperity idiom, that foreign trade created bonds of understanding among nations, reducing chances for breaches of peace.

In the postwar era, the United States was the largest supplier of goods to world markets, with exports valued at $10 billion in both 1945 and 1946 and $14 billion a year later. "Any serious failure to maintain this flow," declared an assistant secretary of state, "would put millions of American businessmen, farmers, and workers out of business." American leaders, fearing a postwar recession, believed that successful and expanding foreign trade spelled the difference between depression and prosperity. Statistics buttressed such an assumption. Although the value of exports seldom climbed above 10 percent of the Gross National Product, that seemingly low figure could be misleading. Key industries such as automobiles, trucks, coal, machine tools, and steel relied upon foreign outlets for their economic health. One-eighth of Monsanto Chemical's sales were to customers abroad, and General Motors shipped about 10 percent of its products overseas. Nearly 20 percent of American steel workers owed their jobs to steel exports; the figure for coal miners was 18 percent. In 1947 about half of America's wheat was shipped abroad, and surpluses of citrus fruits, eggs, cotton, rice, and tobacco also needed foreign markets. Secretary of the Treasury John Snyder persuasively pointed up the significance of foreign trade: "The importance of U.S. exports to the American economy is evidenced by the fact that they exceed in volume such important single elements of the national product as expenditures on producers' durable equipment, consumers' expenditures on durable goods, the net changes in business inventories, the total expenditures by State and local governments or even private construction."

Dire consequences were predicted should economic dislocations abroad, especially in Europe, make it difficult for foreign buyers to purchase American products. The Committee for Economic Development, a group of businessmen running America's largest corporations, anticipated "great readjustment, much inefficient production and a lower standard of living," and the president of the Chamber of Commerce, Eric Johnston, warned that a sharp drop in foreign trade "would mean vast population shifts, and . . . new ways of subsistence would have to be found for entire geographic regions." Truman himself joined the "peace and prosperity" ideology with economic-strategic needs in a 1946 statement: "A large volume of soundly based international trade is essential if we are to achieve prosperity in the United States, build a durable structure of world economy and attain our goal of world peace and prosperity."

American leaders also emphasized that exports paid for imports that were vital to American industry and to the military establishment. In many categories of raw materials, the United States was a "have-not" nation. The director of the Bureau of Mines reported domestic deficiencies in zinc, tin, mercury, manganese, lead, cobalt, tungsten, chromite, industrial diamonds, nickel, bauxite, and copper—or a total of more than fifty materials. Imported materials from fifty-seven different countries were necessary to American steel production. Truman noted that strategic raw materials from abroad contributed to a major new weapon in the American arsenal: "Without foreign trade . . . it would be difficult, if not impossible, for us to develop atomic energy." Oil also held both economic and strategic importance. A Senate committee concluded that "the United States, accounting for about two-thirds of the entire world's petroleum consumption, is compelled to control an adequate share of foreign oil production and reserves to insure high living standards in its domestic economy," and Petroleum Administrator for War Harold Ickes worried whether the United States would be able to "oil another war in the future." Petroleum, as World Wars I and II demonstrated and as the Japanese knew before Pearl Harbor, moved tanks, ships, and airplanes alike. American leaders feared that the Second World War, in its insatiable thirst for oil, had depleted American resources and that postwar consumption would outstrip supply. "Oil, enough oil, within our certain grasp seemed ardently necessary to greatness and independence in the twentieth century" was Herbert Feis' summary of American thinking, although he considered the fears exaggerated.

America's security needs demanded not only economic expansion in order to satisfy raw-materials requirements but also a global military watch. With the two vast oceans no longer providing natural defensive barriers, with the advent of atomic weapons, the air age, and wide-ranging naval fleets, Americans believed it necessary to secure outlying bases to protect approaches to the United States and to permit the American military to police or deter disorders far from home. "Experience in the recent war demonstrated conclusively," a Joint Chiefs of Staff (JCS) report noted in 1946, "that the defense of a nation, if it is to be effective, must begin beyond its frontiers." In early 1946 the JCS approved a list of twenty foreign locations where American military air transit rights were desired. Sites as far-flung as Algiers (Algeria), Cairo (Egypt), Dhahran (Saudi Arabia), Karachi (India), Saigon (French Indochina), Acapulco (Mexico), San Jose (Guatemala), and the Cook Islands (New Zealand) came within JCS's definition of needs. The State Department itself formulated an extensive list of foreign bases considered "essential" or "required" for national security. Burma, Canada, the Fiji Islands, New Zealand, Cuba, Greenland, Ecuador, French Morocco, Senegal, Iceland, Liberia, Panama, Peru, and the Azores, among others, earned spots in this impressive example of the postwar American global perspective. Many of these areas in fact became sites for the American military. Admiral Chester W. Nimitz reasoned that "the ultimate security of the United States depends in major part on our ability to control the Pacific Ocean," and he joined Truman Administration officials in a policy of retaining under American control the Pacific islands (Carolines, Marshalls, and Marianas) captured from the Japanese. "You mean to put them [American naval forces] everywhere?" Senator Claude Pepper of Florida asked Navy Secretary Forrestal on the telephone. "Wherever there is a sea," Forrestal crisply replied.

Nations seek to fulfill their ideological preferences and to realize their economic-strategic needs. They also strive to enlarge and protect their national power, another fundamental of American foreign policy. "International politics, like all politics," Hans J. Morgenthau has written, "is a struggle for power." Power is the facilitator, the enforcer, the symbol of greatness, and the ability to modify the conduct of other states or to prevent them from influencing you. Power, of course, is not absolute, and it never reaches as far as the nation possessing it would like it to reach because of obstacles thrown up by the international system and the hostility of other nations. No nation possessing power is willing to give it up. The very existence of power thrusts a nation into the maelstrom of world politics. "Evasion of major international issues is a real possibility for Costa Rica," concluded a National Security Council paper. "For the U.S. it is an illusion. Our silence is as loud as our words."

Foreign commentators sensed America's flush of power and wondered how it would be used. *The Economist* (London) editorialized in 1947 that World War II "has enormously increased the scale upon which the United States now towers above its fellows. Like mice in the cage of an elephant, they follow with apprehension the movements of the mammoth. What chance would they stand if it were to begin to throw its weight about, they who are in danger even if it only decides to sit down?" From the perspective of official

London, historian Christopher Thorne has written, the United States' quest for strategic predominance "began to take on some of the less endearing characteristics of a runaway rhinoceros." Indeed, the British ambassador to Washington drew London's attention to "America's consciousness of superior power, or as one columnist puts it, 'her capacity for Promethean rule,' " and remarked, with a touch of ridicule, that Americans were "accustomed enough at home to the idea of bigger and better elephants. . . ."

Because they seemed uneasy about wielding their power too conspicuously, Americans, quipped an Asian diplomat, were like the "virgin who wanted to do it, but didn't know how." Churchill was more frank, annoyed with American criticism of British practice of "power politics": "Is having a Navy twice as strong as any other 'power politics'? Is having an overwhelming Air Force, with bases all over the world, 'power politics'? Is having all the gold in the world buried in a cavern 'power politics'?" Actually, Americans had always known how to exercise power, their self-effacing confessions to the contrary notwithstanding, and their expansionist record in the nineteenth and twentieth centuries stood as salient testimony. In the postwar world, the foundations of their national power insured that they would want to and had to advance that record.

Economic power, political power, and military power were the elements of national strength for Americans. Their vast economic power gave them a heady place in the world economy and influence over war-torn nations eager for relief and reconstruction funds. Harriman assumed in 1944 that "economic assistance is one of the most effective weapons" with which the United States could affect events in Russia's developing sphere in Eastern Europe. British Prime Minister Clement Attlee recognized the impact of this economic power when his government asked Washington for a postwar loan. "We weren't in a position to bargain," he said. "We had to have the loan." Soviet official Andrei Zhdanov summarized an assumption common to both Communists and non-Communists: "Of all the capitalist powers, only one—the United States—emerged from the war not only unweakened, but even considerably stronger economically and militarily." America was the "workshop of the world." This prominent economic status carried responsibility. "The United States is the only country in the world today," Secretary Marshall announced in 1948, "which has the economic power and productivity to furnish the needed assistance." President Truman minced no words: "We are the giant of the economic world."

Americans were proud that they had more airplanes, more automobiles, more refrigerators, and more bathtubs than anybody else. They produced and used more coal and steel than any other people. Their corporations controlled 42 percent of the proved oil reserves in the Middle East. By 1948 Americans produced about 41 percent of the world's goods and services. Their abundant fields yielded an agricultural surplus to feed a hungry world. The president boasted that the United States had "fifty percent of the world's industrial machine and produces two-thirds of the world's combined industrial output. We are richly endowed with natural resources. We possess the mobility, the friends, and the good-will . . . that enable us to supplement our supply of raw materials with purchases throughout the world." In short, Truman asserted in 1947, "we have it in our power today either to make the world economy work or, simply by failing to take the proper action, to allow it to collapse."

The United States also enjoyed enviable international political power. As Truman said, America possessed "friends." The members of the American sphere of influence, in Asia, Latin America, the Middle East, and Europe, voted with the United States within international organizations. In the Security Council of the United Nations, the United States did not have to exercise its veto power until 1970. Its friends and clients in the Council provided American positions with majority votes, therein bestowing a "hidden veto" power upon the United States. Russia, on the other hand, had to resort conspicuously to the veto—105 times between 1946 and 1969. As it was, a large percentage of the Soviet vetoes were rendered impotent by American political power exerted somewhere else in the United Nations. For example, with the help of the usually loyal votes of some twenty Latin American governments, the United States commanded results in the General Assembly. In the period 1945–66, the United States repeatedly received a two-thirds majority vote for its positions on Cold War issues. . . .

In both the International Bank for Reconstruction and Development (World Bank) and the International Monetary Fund, the United States flexed its political (and economic) muscle. Created in 1944 at the Bretton Woods Conference, these institutions were nominally "international." Actually they became instruments of American diplomacy, because the Bank and Fund were located in Washington, D.C., Americans sat as key officials (the president of the World Bank has always been an American), the dollar was in great demand and all dollar loans from these organizations had to be approved by the United States, and especially because the United States, as the largest subscriber, held one-third of the votes. In the early years of the World Bank, loans went to American friends like France and Denmark and were denied to countries closely linked to the Soviet Union such as Poland and Czechoslovakia. A Bretton Woods negotiator recognized that the Bank and Fund came to resemble "the operation of power politics rather than of international cooperation—except that the power employed is financial instead of military and political." As the piper, the United States called the tune.

"The surest guaranty that no nation will dare again to attack us," Truman stated shortly after World War II, "is to remain strong in the only kind of strength an aggressor can understand—military power." Military power, he knew, meant more than soldiers and armaments. He pointed to the productive power of American farms, mines, and factories and the abundance of natural resources as important parts of the totality of American military power. Indeed, the "United States now has a fighting strength greater than at any time in our history. It is greater than that of any other nation in the world." The administration suffered public pressure to "bring the boys home" hurriedly after the war, but despite demobilization, the United States still maintained the world's largest navy, an unmatched air force of long-range capabilities, a peacetime army far larger than ever before, and a monopoly of the deadliest weapon of all, the atomic bomb. National security was insured and America's adversaries were at bay. Still, Americans sometimes felt insecure, uncertain as they were about Soviet intentions, usually believing the worst could happen and on occasion underestimating their own military might.

With its two-ocean navy, America was the postwar mistress of the seas. As Secretary Forrestal, who had enthusiastically read Alfred T. Mahan's *The Influence of Sea Power Upon History,* observed, "no enemy can reach us without crossing the sea. We cannot reach an aggressor without crossing the sea." The President waxed proud in October, 1945, when he detailed American naval superiority at the end of the war: "The fleet, on V-J Day, consisted of twelve hundred warships, more than fifty thousand supporting and landing craft, and over forty thousand navy planes. By that day, ours was a seapower never before equalled in the history of the world." Even after demobilization, he went on, "the United States will still be the greatest naval power on earth."

Truman also applauded America's air force. In the "air age," Americans flew supreme, able to defend American skies, to deliver destruction to others, and to frighten would-be aggressors. In 1943 Hollywood producer Walt Disney released a film, *Victory Through Air Power,* which helped herald the new era and to popularize the crippling capabilities of air power. According to one film critic, Disney impressed the "lay mind with the seemingly limitless potential of the airplane as an offensive instrument of war." Viewers of the dramatic film—including Roosevelt and Churchill, who viewed it one evening at the 1944 Quebec Conference—saw in "a roaring blaze of technicolor" the leveling of Japan by tons of air-delivered bombs. Aware of their air superiority, American officials could agree with Harriman's statement in 1947 that American air power served to deter the Soviet military, because "there is only one thing which the leaders of the Soviet Union fear, and that is the American air force."

American armed forces joined naval and air power to enhance the impressive military standing of the United States. Total American military personnel numbered 3 million in 1946 (down from the wartime peak of 12 million), 1.6 million in 1947, 1.4 million in 1948, and 1.6 million in 1949. The Army, which had major occupation responsibilities in Germany and Japan, accounted for much of this total. Civilian and military officials often complained that the Army was undersized and unready for combat, but an annoyed President trimmed the budget requests of all three armed services and lectured them that they exaggerated their needs. Even so, the federal budget reflected the new sense of military preparedness. In fiscal year 1947 defense expenditures represented one-third of the budget, "fabulously large compared to the prewar defense budgets." Secretary Forrestal was one who repeatedly warned about military inadequacies but, at the same time, boasted of American sea and atomic supremacy. Like Truman he knew that America's industrial strength also counted in judgments of military power, and he believed that large foreign aid programs—even though they might divert funds from the military —should receive priority. "As long as we can outproduce the world, can control the sea and can strike inland with the atomic bomb," Forrestal reasoned, "we can assume certain risks [spending less than the desired military appropriations so that funds could be spent instead in foreign aid programs] otherwise unacceptable in an effort to restore world trade, to restore the balance of power—military power—and to eliminate some of the conditions which breed war." Military strength, then, lay not just in arms and men but in an economically healthy, politically stable world.

The atomic bomb: Everyone mentioned it and stood in awe of it. This novel weapon had proven its deadly power over Hiroshima and Nagasaki, but it appears that in the postwar era its power was more symbolic than real, more diplomatic than military. Truman was not sure that "it can ever be used," and, of course, it never was used again in combat. Still, American leaders thought their monopoly of the atomic device, which prevailed until the Soviets exploded their own in 1949, bestowed advantages on the United States. The bomb, they hoped, would serve to restrain the Soviets and might prompt them to make diplomatic concessions, especially over Eastern Europe. The Joint Chiefs of Staff and General Dwight D. Eisenhower agreed that the "existence of the atomic bomb in our hands is a deterrent, in fact, to aggression in the world." Harriman reported from Moscow in the Fall of 1945 that the Soviets themselves "recognized it was an offset to the power of the Red Army. This must have revived their old feeling of insecurity."

Secretary Byrnes articulated more fully than most the potential diplomatic power of the atomic bomb. He "looks to having the presence of the bomb in his pocket" as an "implied threat" at the London Foreign Ministers Conference (1945), Secretary of War Henry L. Stimson grimly recorded in his diary. At that stormy conference itself, V. M. Molotov, as if he had been reading Stimson's private diary, asked Byrnes if he had an atomic bomb in his side pocket. Byrnes quipped that Southerners "carry our artillery in our hip pocket. If you don't cut out all this stalling and let us get down to work, I am going to pull an atomic bomb out of my hip pocket and let you have it." This apparently light moment carried diplomatic meaning: The United States was thinking about the marvels of its atomic power, a point that had to put other nations on edge.

The atomic bomb, then, was an implied threat. By the spring of 1946, however, it appears that Byrnes had learned that atomic power, rather than bearing diplomatic fruit, actually interfered with his attempt to negotiate peace treaties with Hitler's defeated satellites in Eastern Europe. At the March 22, 1946, Cabinet meeting, Byrnes said he believed that the forthcoming Bikini atomic test was "ill-advised" and should be postponed—or abandoned altogether. The reason: The dramatic explosion in the Pacific would disrupt the Paris Peace Conference. He remarked further that the operation had "developed into a big show on the strength of the atomic dictator"—the United States. Holstered or unholstered, the atomic bomb had

become a spectatcular symbol of American technological ingenuity and supremacy—of American power. The United States understandably would not
turn the weapon over to an international control authority. "When we get
down to cases," Truman remarked, "is any one of the Big Powers—are we?
—going to give up these locks and bolts which are necessary to protect our
house . . . against possible outlaw attack . . . until the community is sufficiently
stable? Clearly we are not. Nor are the Soviets."

Americans celebrated the elements of their national power and were cognizant of the weight they carried in international affairs, but not necessarily
of the reactions that power might trigger. They believed themselves to be
exceptional, and foreign observers frequently reminded them of their rare
status. American diplomats knew, too, that the prominent and activist international position of the United States spawned the envy and resentment of
others. Byrnes mentioned that Americans appeared to others to "hog leadership," and John Foster Dulles came back from Europe in mid-1947 to report
that "even in countries like Britain and France there is rising apprehension
at our alleged 'aggressive imperialism.' " Americans were generally and genuinely surprised that their power and intentions evoked hostility and suspicion
in others.

In the Fall of 1945, Truman's Cabinet discussed the need for universal
military training. One of the participants questioned why the United States
had to "police the world." The President declared emphatically that it must,
for "in order to carry out a just decision the courts must have marshals" and
"in order to collect monies for county governments it has been found necessary to employ a sheriff." Joseph Jones, who later helped write the momentous Truman Doctrine, captured the popular, postwar American mood: "The
moment is ours." Exuberant, self-confident, proud of their heritage and ideals,
instructed by lessons from the past, needing foreign trade, having a global
strategic outlook, and flushed with power, Americans wanted to, and felt
they had to, seize the moment—"to grab hold of history and make it conform." They ultimately failed to do so because their power was not omnip-
otent but relative—with its effectiveness dependent upon local and international conditions—and because a bold and hostile Soviet Russia, with another
vision of history, arose as a challenger. . . .

By whom and how diplomacy is made and conducted constitute part of a
comprehensive view of the Cold War. Conduct, or tactics, directly influence
foreign leaders and hence help to shape the chances for success or failure
in negotiations. Harriman believed that "personal relationships could influence—even if they could not determine—the affairs of nations. . . ." In the
last days of the 1944 presidential campaign, Harriman, as a Democrat and
ambassador to the Soviet Union, blended his political and diplomatic preferences when he publicly told the American people that Roosevelt had earned
the confidence of foreign leaders, "an invaluable asset in obtaining decisions
which will further our interests and build the kind of world in which we
want to live. This confidence we can ill afford to lose at this critical and
formative time." No doubt, Harriman had in mind the working relationship

between Roosevelt and Stalin and Stalin's own earnest hope that the president would be reelected.

Harriman's essential point, and the premise [here], is that how we behave affects how others react to us and hence influences the outcome of negotiations. If we shout or lecture, we may not be listened to. If we are rude, others may take offense. If we do not explain ourselves well, we may be misunderstood. If we dress in a particular way, we may be stereotyped. If we take off a shoe and pound it on the table, we may be considered emotionally unstable and unreliable. If we stalk out of a meeting in protest, we may be thought intemperate or lacking interest in serious talks. If we strut in a haughty manner, others may be put off. If we are self-righteously rigid, others may decide not to talk with us. How we express ourselves—the words we use—may determine how persuasive we are. For example, when a government report on United States relations with nations rich in raw materials used the expression "exploit" rather than "develop" to describe American purposes, a State Department official objected, for "the flavor of a word can make a great deal of difference in the effect of the document on sensitive readers in other countries." George F. Kennan, who probably exaggerated the significance of diplomatic style but who nevertheless knew its place, has written in his memoirs that "it is axiomatic in the world of diplomacy that methodology and tactics assume an importance by no means inferior to concept and strategy." How something is done, and who does it, matters. Many diplomatic leaders, who like others nurture their personal likes and dislikes, have thought so themselves.

Throughout the Cold War American and Soviet leaders have frequently disparaged the style and personnel of the other, bemoaning the apparent negative impact upon negotiations. "If Roosevelt lived," Molotov mused in late April of 1945, there would be much less chance of "complications" arising in Soviet-American relations. Several months later he complained that Truman, unlike Roosevelt, did not hold a "friendly" attitude toward the Soviet Union. In May, to allay such Soviet wariness about his administration, Truman sent the ailing Harry Hopkins—Roosevelt's trusted adviser and close friend—rather than Harriman to meet with Premier Josef Stalin. Stalin held Hopkins in high esteem because the American had made an exhausting trip to Russia in 1941 to demonstrate United States support for Russia after Germany's military attack of that June. The Soviet leader remembered that gesture, and as a result the Hopkins-Stalin talks of 1945 proceeded in an amiable and constructive manner, providing one of the few positive moments in the emerging Cold War. The American assumption had been that the outcome of this special assignment might be affected by whom the president chose to be his emissary.

Two years later Dean Acheson revealed how much he himself was affected by style. This polished, aristocratic public servant found the Soviets insulting, coarse, and offensive. "Senator," he remarked at a Congressional hearing, "I think it is a mistake to believe that you can, at any time, sit down with the Russians and solve questions." He pressed the point: "You cannot sit down with them." Out of office he was more outspoken: "I got along with everybody who was housebroken. But I was never very close to the Russians. They were abusive; they were rude. I just didn't like them." It is not surprising, then, that Acheson was one among a growing number of top American officials who presided over a gradual abandonment of diplomacy itself in the Cold War.

Acheson's contemporaries thought that tactics were important, and they spent considerable energy in scrutinizing the personalities, methods, and styles of their adversaries and commenting at length about personal likes and dislikes. The international system was inherently conflict-ridden, and the fundamental characteristics of the United States and the Soviet Union determined basic interests and policies, but had different individuals and styles been present, perhaps the sharper edges of the Soviet-American confrontation might have been blunted. At least we know that both Americans and Russians thought so. Systemic disorders and fundamental needs and beliefs foment profound diplomatic crises, but key individuals, operating with their particular traits, interpret the crises and determine whether they are kept manageable and defused quickly or are prolonged and escalated to the brink of war. Top diplomats decide whether negotiations are to serve as an avenue to tension-reducing solutions.

Decisionmaking in both the Roosevelt and Truman administrations was concentrated in the hands of the president and a small circle of advisers around him. Roosevelt was a devoted practitioner of personal diplomacy, often neglecting to inform the Department of State about his plans and decisions. Roosevelt believed that through his magnetic personality and contagious charm he could establish, as Harriman recalled, "a close personal relationship with Stalin in wartime, to build confidence among the Kremlin leaders that Russia, now an acknowledged major power, could trust the West." As Roosevelt told Churchill, "I think I can personally handle Stalin better than either your Foreign Office or my State Department." Roosevelt may not have been wrong. Stalin often deferred to Roosevelt but did not hesitate to "stick a knife into Churchill whenever he had the chance." Roosevelt's death in 1945 denies us a true testing of his firm belief in the magic of his personalized diplomacy, but we do know that the Soviets sensed a serious change in style and attitude with the entrance of Harry S. Truman into the White House.

V. M. Molotov witnessed the difference between the two presidents first-hand and early. On April 23, 1945, just over a week after FDR's death, Truman held a momentous meeting with the Soviet commissar. The new president sharply scolded the Soviet diplomat and demanded compliance with the Yalta agreement providing for the reorganization of the Polish government. Molotov insisted that the Soviets were working toward that goal. Truman pressed again, charging Moscow with failing to honor its side of the bargain. The usually blunt and irascible Molotov turned "a little ashy." According to Truman, the Soviet diplomat said, "I have never been talked to like that in my life." Truman shot back in Dutch-uncle style: "Carry out your agreements and you won't get talked to like that." Molotov stormed out of the White House. Harriman regretted that the President had gone "at it so hard," and Henry L. Stimson commented on Truman's "rather brutal frankness," but Truman himself gloated over what he called his "tough method": "I gave it to him straight 'one-two to the jaw.' I let him have it straight." Truman's dressing-down of Russia's foreign secretary suggested to officials in both Washington and Moscow that the new president was his own man, with his own ideas and ways of conducting diplomacy—certainly not a replica of Franklin D. Roosevelt. A British diplomat at the Potsdam Conference noted a difference. "Roosevelt's death changed everything," Lord Moran recorded in his diary. "Truman is very blunt; he means business" and "can hand out the rough stuff."

Truman was, of course, strikingly different from Roosevelt in background, personality, and style. Whereas the latter was a compromiser, the former usually made up his mind quickly, or at least gave this impression, and stuck steadfastly to his convictions. Blacks and whites, with few gray areas, characterized his thinking. Whereas Roosevelt was ingratiating, patient, and evasive, using a variety of techniques from jokes, to rambling storytelling, to "discursive flashes," to hard-nosed politicking to win his point, Truman was brash, abrupt, decisive, impatient, and quick-tempered—characterized by "promptness and snappiness," said Stimson. A man of simple dignity and personal integrity, Truman prided himself on blunt, tart, unadorned language; Roosevelt was a master of dissembling and used disarming, vague phrases. "The buck stops here," read a sign on Truman's desk. "Give 'em hell, Harry" his political aides recommended, and the President usually did. Truman was "best when he's been mad," noted one of his assistants. Churchill, long an unabashed commentator on human behavior, remarked favorably after meeting Truman at Potsdam that the Missourian was "a man of exceptional character and ability . . . , simple and direct methods of speech, and a great deal of self-confidence and resolution." Indeed, he "takes no notice of delicate ground, he just plants his foot down firmly on it." Truman himself wrote to his mother about his chairmanship at Potsdam: "They all say I took 'em for a ride when I got down to presiding." Indeed, he usually demonstrated simplicity, bravado, and verbal sparring but little low-key patience or understanding of subtleties that are usually essential to constructive diplomatic talks. A self-conscious, bumptious style of toughness came to stand as a trademark of the Truman administration and ultimately became an impediment to diplomacy. . . .

The president, in short, was and is the master of American foreign policy. When the Soviets insisted that they would not be "intimidated" by American and British "methods"—which they thought were designed to "impose their will upon other countries, and on the Soviet Union particularly"—they meant the activities of Truman and his subordinates, who, the Soviets believed, had deviated from both the style and policy of the Roosevelt administration. Roosevelt had been "a farsighted statesman of the first rank," and his death "was a veritable gift to the gods" of American reaction and expansion, concluded one Soviet analyst. Whereas Roosevelt and Stalin had "clicked," Truman and the Russian leader never warmed to one another. Stalin was "an S.O.B.," concluded Truman after Potsdam. "I guess he thinks I'm one too."

Stalin may have privately commented on Truman's parentage, but we do not know. In any case, it seems reasonable to suggest that the Soviet leader exaggerated the difference between Truman and Roosevelt by contrasting the two Presidents' starkly different styles and personalities. As different as Roosevelt and Truman were as individuals, it does not appear that their basic policies clashed to the extreme extent that Henry A. Wallace and the Soviets thought. FDR had to deal with the problems of war, of course, whereas Truman grappled with the issues of peace, so the question cannot be dealt with conclusively. Nevertheless, both presidents saw diplomatic bargaining power in the American monopoly of the atomic bomb; both sought to use America's economic power as leverage in diplomacy; both held to the essential tenets of the American ideology, with its emphasis on political and economic democracy; both wanted a United Nations Organization that would be dominated by the big powers, and especially the United States; both envisioned a strong United States as the major actor in the postwar world. John D. Hickerson, director of the Office of European Affairs, recalled that FDR's death did not alter ongoing negotiations and programs conducted by the State Department: "We went right ahead; really we weren't conscious of any change."

Still, the two presidents went about the business of diplomacy differently. Roosevelt was more patient with the Russians, more willing to settle issues at the conference table, more tame and less abusive in his language, less abrupt in his decisions, and more solicitous of Soviet opinion and fears than was Truman. Postwar conflict would have been present no matter which man was president. The characteristics of the international system and the clashing fundamental needs and ideas of the United States and the Soviet Union insured tension; but because the tactics and mechanics of policymaking in their administrations differed, the two men impressed the Soviets and others quite differently, as the record makes evident. Tactics joined system and fundamentals to cause the Cold War.

The Atomic Bomb and Diplomacy

BARTON J. BERNSTEIN

Ever since the publication in 1965 of Gar Alperovitz's *Atomic Diplomacy*, scholars and laymen have developed a new interest in the relationship of the atomic bomb to wartime and postwar diplomacy and to the origins of the Cold War. This bold book revived and sometimes recast old themes and

From "Roosevelt, Truman and the Atomic Bomb, 1941–1945: A Reinterpretation." Reprinted with permission from the *Political Science Quarterly*, 90 (Spring 1975), 23–24, 30–32, 34–62.

thereby sparked renewed interest in questions that once seemed settled: Why was the atomic bomb dropped on Japan? Why weren't other alternatives vigorously pursued? How did the bomb influence American policy before and after Hiroshima? Did the dropping of the bomb and postwar American atomic policies contribute to the cold war?

Unfortunately many studies of these questions have focused exclusively on the Truman period and thereby neglected the Roosevelt administration, which bequeathed to Truman a legacy of assumptions, options, and fears. Acting on the assumption that the bomb was a legitimate weapon, Roosevelt initially defined the relationship of American diplomacy and the atomic bomb. He decided to build the bomb, to establish a partnership on atomic energy with Britain, to bar the Soviet Union from knowledge of the project, and to block any effort at international control of atomic energy. These policies constituted Truman's inheritance—one he neither wished to abandon nor could easily escape. He was restricted politically, psychologically, and institutionally from critically reassessing this legacy.

Like Roosevelt, Truman assumed that the bomb was a legitimate weapon and also understood that it could serve as a bargaining lever, a military counter-weight, a threat, or a combat weapon in dealing with the Soviet Union in the postwar world. In addition to speeding the end of the war, the combat use of the bomb, the Truman administration understood, offered the United States great advantages in the postwar world. Policy makers assumed that use of the bomb would help shape the world in a desirable mold: The bomb would im-press the Soviets and make them more tractable. Contrary to some contentions, this consideration about the postwar world was not the controlling reason why the United States used the bomb. Rather, it was an additional reason reinforcing an earlier analysis. Ending the war speedily was the primary pur-pose; impressing the Soviet Union was secondary. This secondary aim did constitute a subtle deterrent to reconsidering combat use of the bomb and to searching for alternative means of ending the war. Had the use of the bomb threatened to impair, rather than advance, American aims for the postwar peace, policy makers would have been likely to reassess their assumptions and perhaps to choose other alternatives. . . .

Running through the tangled skein of America's wartime policy on atomic energy is the persistent evidence of concern about the Soviet Union. Roosevelt knew that the Soviets were gathering information about the bomb project, and on September 9, 1943, Henry L. Stimson, the secretary of war, informed the president that spies "are already getting information about vital secrets and sending them to Russia." In late December 1944, at two sessions, they again discussed these issues. On December 31, Roosevelt told Stimson that he, too, was worried about how much the Soviets might know about the project, and they briefly discussed trading information for substantial Soviet concessions. As Stimson later summarized the conversation in his diary:

> I told him . . . that I knew they [Russia] were spying on our work but that they had not yet gotten any real knowledge of it and that, while I was troubled by the possible effect of keeping from them even now that work, I believed that it

was essential not to take them into our confidence until we were sure to get a real quid pro quo from our frankness. I said I had no illusions as to the possibility of keeping permanently such a secret but that I did think that it was not yet time to share it with Russia. He said he thought he agreed with me.

They did not discuss the specific nature of the concessions, and perhaps Stimson and the president would not have agreed on how to use the bomb as a bargaining lever and what to demand from the Soviet Union. Whatever their unexplored differences on these issues, they did agree to continue for a period the same policy: exclusion of the Soviets. "It was quite clear," recorded General Leslie Groves, commanding general of the Manhattan Project, "that no one present was interested in bringing Russia into the picture, at least at this time." It is less clear why Roosevelt and Stimson, faced with the realization that the Soviet Union knew about the American research, still did not want formally to notify the Soviets about the bomb project. There is no direct evidence on this subject, but probably they feared that formal disclosure would lead to explicit Soviet inquiries and then to demands for participation that American leaders were not prepared to handle. As long as the United States technically kept the project secret, the Soviets could never raise issues about the bomb without admitting their espionage.

On March 15, 1945, at their last meeting together, Stimson and Roosevelt again discussed atomic energy. Roosevelt acknowledged that he would have to choose between (1) continuing the policy of secrecy and the Anglo-American partnership that barred the Soviets or (2) moving to international control with a sharing of information. Under Roosevelt, there was no further resolution of these issues. When he died in April, American policy had not advanced beyond the point where it had been in December.

Had Roosevelt lived, perhaps he would ultimately have reversed the policy of secrecy and decided to move toward international control in return for a *quid pro quo*—perhaps on Eastern Europe which he had "ceded" at Yalta to the Soviet Union. Any consideration of what "might have happened" is, of course, a matter of speculation, since the evidence is skimpy and oblique on what Roosevelt might have done. What is clear is that he had maintained the strategy of excluding the Soviets from knowledge of the bomb and of reserving the options of using it in the future as a bargaining lever, threat, military counterweight, or even a weapon against the Soviets.

It was not that he lacked opportunities to reverse his policy. He did not want to change policy—at least not up to April. At Yalta, in February, for example, Roosevelt might have approached Stalin on the bomb, but the president neither discussed this subject nor the loan that the Soviets wanted, and thereby he simply kept open the options for the future of using economic leverage and the bomb to secure concessions. His position, then, made possible the future strategy of "atomic diplomacy"—of using the bomb as an implied or explicit threat to influence negotiations and to compel concessions from the Soviets. Would he have practiced "atomic diplomacy"? Probably. But that answer is speculative and rests principally upon the theory that he would not have wasted the options he was jealously guarding.

Roosevelt and his advisers had more clearly defined another issue: the combat use of the bomb. From the inception of the project, when it was directed primarily against Germany, they usually assumed, and most policy makers never questioned, that the bomb was a legitimate weapon to be used in combat. This assumption was phrased as policy on a number of occasions. In October 1942, for example, Stimson had directed Groves that the mission is "to produce [the bomb] at the earliest possible date so as to bring the war to a conclusion." Any time "that a single day could be saved," the general should save that day. In 1944, policy makers were also talking comfortably about *"after* S–1 [the bomb] is used." "At no time," Stimson later wrote, "did I ever hear it suggested by the President, or by any other responsible member of the government, that atomic energy should not be used in war." . . .

When Harry S. Truman became president on April 12, 1945, he was only dimly aware of the existence of the Manhattan Project and unaware that it was an atomic-bomb project. Left uninformed of foreign affairs and generally ignored by Roosevelt in the three months since the inaugural, the new president inherited a set of policies and a group of advisers from his predecessor. While Truman was legally free to reverse Roosevelt's foreign policies and to choose new advisers on foreign policy, in fact he was quite restricted for personal and political reasons. Because Truman was following a very prestigious president whom he, like a great many Americans, loved and admired, the new president was not free psychologically or politically to strike out on a clearly new course. Only a bolder man, with more self-confidence, might have tried critically to assess the legacy and to act independently. But Truman lacked the confidence and the incentive. When, in fact, he did modify policy—for example, on Eastern Europe—he still believed sincerely, as some advisers told him, that he was adhering to his predecessor's agreements and wishes. When seeking counsel on foreign affairs, he usually did not choose new advisers but simply drew more heavily upon those members of Roosevelt's staff who were more anti-Soviet and relied less upon those who were more friendly to the Soviet Union. Even in this strategy, he believed that he was adhering to the policies of his predecessor, who, in his last weeks, Truman stressed, had become more suspicious of Stalin, more distressed by Soviet action in Eastern Europe, and more committed to resisting Soviet encroachments.

In the case of the international-diplomatic policy on the bomb, Truman was even more restricted by Roosevelt's decisions, for the new president inherited a set of reasonably clear wartime policies. Because Roosevelt had already decided to exclude the Soviets from a partnership on the bomb, his successor could not *comfortably* reverse this policy during the war—unless the late president's advisers pleaded for such a reversal or claimed that he had been about to change his policy. They did neither. Consider, then, the massive personal and political deterrents that blocked Truman from even reassessing this legacy. What price might he have paid at home if Americans learned later that he had reversed Roosevelt's policy and had launched a bold new departure of sharing with the Soviets a great weapon that cost the United States $2 billion? Truman, in fact, was careful to follow Roosevelt's strategy of concealing from Congress even the dimensions of the secret partnership on atomic energy with Britain.

Truman, depending as he did upon Roosevelt's advisers, could not easily reassess the prevailing assumption that the bomb was a legitimate weapon to be used in combat against Japan. Truman lacked the will and the incentive to reexamine this assumption, and his dependence upon Roosevelt's advisers and the momentum of the project confirmed this tendency. Only one close adviser, Admiral William Leahy, may have later challenged the use of the bomb, but he was an old "war horse," an expert on explosives of another era, who had often proclaimed that the bomb would not work, that the scientists were duping the administration, and that they were squandering $2 billion. His counsel could not outweigh the continuing legacy of assumptions and commitments, of advisers and advice, that Truman had inherited from Roosevelt. It was a subtle legacy, one that infiltrated decisions and shaped actions, so that Truman accepted it as part of his unquestioned inheritance. For Truman, the question would never be how openly to challenge this legacy, only how to fulfill it, how to remain true to it.

During his first weeks in office, Truman learned about the project from Stimson and from James F. Byrnes, Roosevelt's former director of the Office of War Mobilization and Reconversion who was to become Truman's secretary of state. Byrnes, despite his recent suspicions that the project might be a scientific boondoggle, told Truman, in the president's words, that "the bomb might well put us in a position to dictate our own terms at the end of the war." On April 25, Stimson discussed issues about the bomb more fully with Truman, especially the "political aspects of the S–1 [atomic bomb's] performance." The bomb, the secretary of war explained in a substantial memorandum, would probably be ready in four months and "would be the most terrible weapon ever known in human history [for it] . . . could destroy a whole city." In the future, he warned, other nations would be able to make atomic bombs, thereby endangering the peace and threatening the world. The bomb could be either a threat to or a guarantor of peace. "[I]n the light of our present position with reference to this weapon, the question of sharing it with other nations and, if so shared, upon what terms, becomes a primary question of our foreign relations," Stimson lectured the president. If "the problem of the proper use of this weapon can be solved, we would have the opportunity to bring the world into a pattern in which the peace of the world and our civilization can be saved."

The entire discussion, judging from Stimson's diary record and Groves's memorandum, assumed that the bomb was a legitimate weapon and that it would be used against Japan. The questions they discussed were not *whether* to use the bomb, but its relationship to the Soviet Union and the need to establish postwar atomic policies. Neither Stimson nor Truman sought then to resolve these outstanding issues, and Truman agreed to his secretary's proposal for the establishment of a high-level committee to recommend "action to the executive and legislative branches of our government when secrecy is no longer in full effect." At no time did they conclude that the committee would also consider the issue of whether to use the bomb as a combat weapon. For policy makers, that was not a question; it was an operating assumption.

Nor did Stimson, in his own charge to the Interim Committee, ever *raise* this issue. Throughout the committee's meetings, as various members later noted, all operated on the assumption that the bomb would be used against Japan. They talked, for example, about drafting public statements that would be issued after the bomb's use. They did not discuss *whether* but how to use it. Only one member ultimately endorsed an explicit advance warning to Japan, and none was prepared to suggest that the administration should take any serious risks to avoid using the bomb. At lunch between the two formal meetings on May 31, some members, perhaps only at one table, briefly discussed the possibility of a noncombat demonstration as a warning to Japan but rejected the tactic on the grounds that the bomb might not explode and the failure might stiffen Japanese resistance, or that Japan might move prisoners of war to the target area.

What impact would the bomb have on Japan? At the May 31 meeting, the Interim Committee, joined by its four-member scientific advisory panel, discussed this question. Some felt, according to the minutes, that "an atomic bomb on an arsenal would not be much different in effect" from present bombing attacks. J. Robert Oppenheimer, the eminent physicist and member of the scientific panel, expecting that the bomb would have an explosive force of between 2,000 and 20,000 tons of TNT, stressed its visual effects ("a brilliant luminescence which would run to a height of 10,000 to 20,000 feet") and its deadly power ("dangerous to life for a radius of at least two-thirds of a mile"). Oppenheimer's predictions did not answer the question. There were too many unknowns—about the bomb and Japan. According to the official minutes, Stimson concluded, with unanimous support: "that we could not concentrate on a civilian area; but we should seek to make a profound psychological impression on as many of the inhabitants as possible." At Conant's suggestion, "the Secretary agreed that the most desirable target would be a vital war plant employing a large number of workers and closely surrounded by workers' houses." ("I felt," Stimson later explained, "that to extract a genuine surrender from the Emperor and his military advisers, they must be administered a tremendous shock . . . proof of our power to destroy the empire.") The Interim Committee ruled out the strategy of several atomic strikes at one time, for, according to Groves, the United States would lose the benefit of additional knowledge from each successive bombing, would have to rush in assembling bombs and court error, and also would risk the possibility that multiple nuclear attacks "would not be sufficiently distinct from our regular Air Force bombing program."

Two weeks later, after the Franck Committee recommended a noncombat demonstration, Stimson's assistant submitted this proposal to the four-member scientific advisory panel for advice. The panel promptly rejected the Franck Committee proposal: "we can propose no technical demonstration likely to bring an end to the war; we see no acceptable alternative to direct military use." Had the four scientists known that an invasion was not scheduled until

November, or had they even offered their judgment after the unexpectedly impressive Alamogordo test on July 16, perhaps they would have given different counsel. But in June, they were not sure that the bomb explosion would be so dramatic, and, like many others in government, they were wary of pushing for a change in tactics if they might be held responsible for the failure of those tactics—especially if that failure could mean the loss of American lives.

A few days after the panel's report, the issue of giving Japan an advance warning about the bomb was raised at a White House meeting with the president, the military chiefs, and the civilian secretaries. On June 18, after they agreed upon a two-stage invasion of Japan, beginning on about November 1, Assistant Secretary of War John J. McCloy became clearly troubled by the omission of the bomb from the discussion and planning. When Truman invited him to speak, the assistant secretary argued that the bomb would make the invasion unnecessary. Why not warn the emperor that the United States had the bomb and would use it unless Japan surrendered? "McCloy's suggestion had appeal," the official history of the AEC later recorded, "but a strong objection developed" to warning Japan in advance, "which no one could refute—there was no assurance the bomb would work." Presumably, like the Interim Committee, they too feared that a warning, followed by a "dud," might stiffen Japan's morale. There was no reason, policy makers concluded, to take this risk.

Though the Interim Committee and high administration officials found no reason not to use the bomb against Japan, many were concerned about the bomb's impact, and its later value, in Soviet-American relations. "[I]t was already apparent," Stimson later wrote, "that the critical questions in American policy toward atomic energy would be directly connected with Soviet Russia." At a few meetings of the Interim Committee, for example, members discussed informing the Soviets of the bomb before its use against Japan. When the issue first arose, Bush and Conant estimated that the Soviet Union could develop the bomb in about four years and argued for informing the Soviets before combat use as a preliminary to moving toward international control and thereby avoiding a postwar nuclear arms race. Conant and Bush had been promoting this strategy since the preceding September. Even though Roosevelt had cast them to the side in 1943, when he cemented the Anglo-American alliance, the two scientist-administrators had not abandoned hope for their notions. They even circulated to the Interim Committee one of their memoranda on the subject. But at the meetings of May 18 and 31 they again met defeat. General Groves, assuming that America was far more advanced technologically and scientifically and also that the Soviet Union lacked uranium, argued that the Soviets could not build a bomb for about twenty years. He contributed to the appealing "myth" of the atomic secret—that there was a secret and it would long remain America's monopoly. James Byrnes, with special authority as secretary of state-designate and Truman's representative on the committee, accepted Groves's analysis and argued for maintaining the policy of secrecy—which the committee endorsed. Byrnes was apparently very pleased, and Stimson agreed, as he told Truman on June 6, "There should be no revelation to Russia or anyone else of our work on S–1 [the atomic bomb] until the first bomb has been laid successfully on Japan."

At a later meeting on June 21, the Interim Committee, including Byrnes, reversed itself. Yielding to the pleas of Bush and Conant, who were strengthened by the scientific panel's recommendations, the Interim Committee advised Truman to inform the Soviets about the bomb before using it in combat. Like the Franck Committee, the Interim Committee concluded (as the minutes record):

> In the hope of securing effective future control and in view of the fact that general information concerning the project would be made public shortly after the [Potsdam] conference, the Committee *agreed* that there would be considerable advantage, if suitable opportunity arose, in having the President advise the Russians that we were working on this weapon with every prospect of success and that we expected to use it against Japan.
>
> The President might say further that he hoped this matter might be discussed some time in the future in terms of insuring that the weapon would become an aid to peace.

Because of this recommendation, and perhaps also because of the continuing prodding of Bush and Conant, Stimson reversed his own position. He concluded that if the United States dropped the bomb on Japan without first informing the Soviet Union, that act might gravely strain Soviet-American relations. Explaining the committee's position to Truman, Stimson proposed that if the president "thought that Stalin was on good terms with him" at the forthcoming Potsdam conference, he would inform Stalin that the United States had developed the bomb, planned to use it against Japan, knew the Soviets were working on the bomb, and looked forward to discussing international control later. This approach left open the option of "atomic diplomacy."

The issues of the bomb and the Soviet Union had already intruded in other ways upon policy and planning. Awaiting the bomb, Truman had postponed the Potsdam conference, delayed negotiations with Russia, and hoped that atomic energy would pry some concessions from Russia. Truman explained in late May to Joseph Davies, an advocate of Soviet-American friendship, and in early June to Stimson that he was delaying the forthcoming Potsdam conference until the Alamogordo test, when he would know whether the United States had a workable atomic bomb—what Stimson repeatedly called the "master card." Truman also told some associates that he was delaying because he wanted to work out budget matters, but it is unlikely that the budget was the controlling reason. Certainly, there was no reason that he should have told Davies, who, unlike Stimson, was not counseling delay of the conference, that he was waiting for the bomb. Stimson's counsel of caution, offered on May 15, had apparently triumphed: it would be "a terrible thing to gamble with such high stakes in diplomacy without having your master card in your hand. . . . Over [the] tangled wave of problems the S–1 secret would be dominant." This was not the counsel for a "delayed showdown," as some have wrongly argued, but for no showdown and for delaying some negotiations until the bomb test so that policy makers could determine whether they would have to make concessions to the Soviet Union.

For the administration, the atomic bomb, if it worked, had great potential value. It could reduce the importance of early Soviet entry into the war and make American concessions unnecessary. It could also be a lever for extracting concessions from the Soviet Union. On June 6, for example, Stimson discussed with Truman "quid pro quos which should be established for our taking them [Russia] into [a nuclear] partnership. He [Truman] said that he had been thinking of the same things that I was thinking of, namely the settlement of the Polish, Rumanian, Yugoslavian, and Manchurian problems." There is no evidence that they were planning explicitly to threaten the Soviets to gain these concessions, but, obviously, they realized that the Soviets would regard an American nuclear monopoly as threatening and would yield on some issues in order to terminate that monopoly and thereby reduce, or eliminate, the threat. Neither Stimson nor Truman discussed brandishing the bomb or using it explicitly as a threat to compel concessions. "Atomic diplomacy," as a conception, advanced no further than the notion of possibly trading in the future an atomic partnership, which was still undefined, for Soviet concessions.

For policy makers, the atomic weapons scheduled for combat use against Japan were intimately connected with the problem of Russia. In recent years some historians have focused on this relationship and raised troubling questions: Did the bomb, for policy makers, constitute an alternative to Soviet intervention in the Pacific war? Did they delay or even try to prevent Soviet entry because the bomb made it unnecessary? If so, did they do this in order to use the bomb? Was the bomb dropped on Japan primarily to influence Russia? Did the bomb influence American policy at Potsdam?

At Yalta, Roosevelt had granted the Soviet Union concessions in China in order to secure Soviet entry into the Pacific war, which Stalin promised, within two to three months after V-E Day (May 8). Stalin made it clear that Soviet entry would await a Sino-Soviet pact ratifying these concessions. At the time of Yalta, American military planners were counting on a Soviet attack in Manchuria to pin down the Kwantung army there and hence stop Japan from shifting these forces to her homeland to meet an American invasion.

But by April, war conditions changed and military planners revised their analysis: Japan no longer controlled the seas and therefore could not shift her army, so Soviet entry was not essential. In May, the State Department asked Stimson whether Soviet participation "at the earliest possible moment" was so necessary that the United States should abide by the Far East section of the Yalta agreement. Stimson concluded that the Soviets would enter the war for their own reasons, at their schedule, and with little regard to any American action, that the Yalta concessions would be largely within the grasp of Soviet military power, and that Soviet assistance would be useful, but not essential, if an American invasion was necessary. If there is an invasion, "Russian entry," he wrote, "will have a profound military effect in that almost certainly it will materially shorten the war and thus save American lives." But if the bomb worked, he implied in other discussions, then an invasion would probably not be necessary and Soviet help would be less important. As a result, he urged a delay in settling matters with Russia on the Far East until after the Alamogordo test, and the president apparently followed this counsel.

On June 18, when the joint chiefs of staff, the civilian secretaries, and the president discussed plans for an American invasion of Kyushu on about November 1 and of Honshu during the following March, the issue of Soviet intervention again received attention. General George Marshall, the army chief of staff and the military leader Truman most admired, presented as his own views a JCS memorandum:

> It seems that if the Japanese are ever willing to capitulate short of complete military defeat in the field they will do it when faced by the completely hopeless prospect occasioned by (1) destruction already wrought by air bombardment and sea blockade, coupled with (2) a landing on Japan indicating the firmness of our resolution, and also perhaps coupled with (3) the entry or threat of Russian entry into the war.
>
> With reference to clean-up of the Asiatic mainland, our objective should be to get the Russians to deal with the Japs [sic] in Manchuria (and Korea)....
>
> An important point about Russian participation in the war is that the impact of Russian entry on the already hopeless Japanese *may well be the decisive action* levering them into capitulation at that time or shortly thereafter *if* we land in Japan. [Emphasis added.]

Marshall's counsel was ambiguous and should have raised questions at this meeting. In one place, he said that Soviet entry, when combined with an invasion and other continued destruction, might lead to Japan's capitulation. In another place, he suggested that Soviet entry alone, or followed by an American invasion, might lead to Japan's capitulation. And he was unclear whether Russia's "clean-up of the Asiatic mainland" was necessary if Japan surrendered without an invasion.

None apparently noted the ambiguities or raised questions about Marshall's meaning. After the group approved plans for an invasion of Kyushu on about November 1, with possibly 30,000 casualties in the first thirty days, Truman indicated that one of his "objectives [at Potsdam] . . . would be to get from Russia all the assistance in the war that was possible." Admiral Ernest L. King, chief of Naval Operations, pointed out, according to the minutes, that the Soviets "were not indispensable and he did not think we should go as far as to beg them to come in. While the cost of defeating Japan would be greater, there was no question in his mind but that we should handle it alone. . . . [R]ealization of this fact should greatly strengthen the President's hand" at Potsdam. Admiral Leahy also expressed a "jaundiced view" of the need for Soviet participation.

Truman claimed that he went to Potsdam to secure Soviet entry and that he never changed his position. The first part of that claim is correct, but the second part is dubious, for Truman did nothing substantive at Potsdam to encourage Soviet intervention and much to delay or prevent it. The successful test at Alamogordo emphasized to policy makers that prompt Soviet entry was no longer necessary and that the United States might even be able to end the war without Soviet entry. After the unexpectedly glowing report of the test, Truman wanted to know whether Marshall considered Soviet entry necessary. "Marshall felt," Stimson recorded, "that now with our new weapon we would not need the assistance of the Russians to conquer Japan." "The bomb as a merely probable weapon had seemed a weak reed on which to rely, but the bomb as a colossal reality was very different," Stimson later explained. From Potsdam on July 23, Churchill cabled London: "It is quite clear that the United States do not at the present time desire Russian participation in the war against Japan." The bomb had eliminated the importance of Russia's prompt entry, since the planned American invasion no longer seemed necessary. Invasion and the bomb were the likely alternatives. As a result, Truman had no reason to offer concessions to secure early Soviet entry.

Could the United States keep the Soviet Union out of the war? Did policy makers try to do this? In mid-July Soviet troops were stationed on the Manchurian border and would soon be ready to intervene. Marshall concluded that even if Japan surrendered on American terms before Soviet entry, Russia could still march into Manchuria and take virtually whatever she wanted there in the surrender terms. Truman, if he believed Marshall's analysis, had nothing to gain politically from deterring Soviet entry, unless he feared, as did Stimson, that the Soviets might try to reach the Japanese homeland and put in a "claim to occupy and help rule it." Perhaps Truman followed the counsel of Stimson and Byrnes, who, for slightly different reasons, were eager to restrain the Soviets.

Byrnes, unlike Stimson, was sometimes naively optimistic. Part of the time he hoped to keep the Soviet Union out of the war, and not simply delay her entry, in order to protect China. On July 28, he explained to Secretary of the Navy James Forrestal (in Forrestal's words): "Byrnes said he was most anxious to get the Japanese affair over with before the Russians got in, with particular reference to Dairen and Port Arthur." These were the areas that both Stimson and Marshall acknowledged the Soviets could seize. Walter Brown, the friend who accompanied the secretary to Potsdam, recorded in his diary notes for July 20 Byrnes's strategy: "JFB determined to outmaneuver Stalin on China. Hopes Soong [the Chinese foreign minister] will stand firm and then Russians will not go in war. Then he feels Japan will surrender before Russia goes to war and this will save China." On July 24, four days later, Brown noted that Byrnes was linking the bomb and Japan's surrender but was less optimistic about excluding Russia: "JFB still hoping for time, believing after atomic bombing Japan will surrender and Russia will not get in so much on the kill, thereby [not] being in a position to press for claims against China."

Byrnes purposely impeded Sino-Soviet negotiations in order to *prevent* the Soviets from entering the war. Did Truman support Byrnes for the *same* reasons?—as Byrnes claimed later and as Truman obliquely denied. Perhaps. But, more likely, Truman supported his secretary's strategy for a different reason: the early entry of the Soviets was no longer important and, therefore, Truman did not want Chiang to make the required concessions, which could later weaken Chiang's government. In addition, Truman *may* have concluded that Russia's delayed entry would weaken her possible claims for a role in the postwar occupation government in Japan.

Why didn't Truman invite Stalin to sign the Potsdam Proclamation of July 26 calling for Japan's surrender? Some analysts argued later that this omission was part of a devious strategy: that Truman wanted to use the bomb and feared that

Stalin's signature, tantamount to a declaration of war, might catapult Japan to surrender, thereby making a nuclear attack impossible. The major difficulty with this interpretation is that it exaggerates occasional, sometimes ambiguous, statements about the *possible* impact of Soviet entry and ignores the fact that this possible shock was not a persistent or important theme in American planning. Truman did not exclude the Soviets from the Proclamation in order to use the bomb. The skimpy, often oblique evidence *suggests* a different, more plausible explanation and a less devious pattern: he wanted to avoid requesting favors from the Soviets. As a result, he did not try this one possible, but not very likely, way of ending the war without using atomic weapons.

At Potsdam, on July 24, Truman told Stalin casually that the United States had developed "a new weapon of unusual destructive force" for use against Japan but did not specify an atomic weapon. Why didn't Truman explicitly inform Stalin about the atomic bomb? Was Truman, as some have suggested, afraid that the news would prompt Stalin to hasten Soviet intervention and therefore end the war and make combat use of the bomb impossible? Did Truman simply want to delay Soviet entry and did he, like Byrnes, fear that his news would have the opposite effect? Did Truman think that the destruction wrought by the bomb would not impress the Soviets as forcefully if they were informed in advance? Why did Truman reject the counsel of the Interim Committee, of Stimson, and even of Churchill, who, after the flowing news of the Alamogordo test, "was not worried about giving the Russians information on the matter but was rather inclined to use it as an argument in our favor in the negotiations"?

Many of these questions cannot be definitively answered on the basis of the presently available evidence, but there is enough evidence to refute one popular interpretation: that Truman's tactic was part of an elaborate strategy to prevent or retard Soviet entry *in order* to delay Japan's surrender and *thereby* make combat use of the bomb possible. That interpretation claims too much. Only the first part can be supported by some, albeit indirect, evidence: that he was probably seeking to delay or prevent Soviet entry. Byrnes later said that he feared that Stalin would order an immediate Soviet declaration of war if he realized the importance of this "new weapon"—advice Truman dubiously claimed he never received. Truman was not trying to postpone Japan's surrender *in order* to use the bomb. In addition to the reasonable theory that he was seeking to prevent or retard Soviet entry, there are two other plausible, complementary interpretations of Truman's behavior. First, he believed, as had some of his advisers earlier, that a combat demonstration would be more impressive to Russia without an advance warning and therefore he concealed the news. Second, he was also ill-prepared to discuss atomic energy with Stalin, for the president had not made a decision about postwar atomic policy and how to exploit the bomb, and probably did not want to be pressed by Stalin about sharing nuclear secrets. Perhaps all three theories collectively explain Truman's evasive tactics.

Even without explicit disclosure, the bomb strengthened American policy at Potsdam. The Alamogordo test stiffened Truman's resolve, as Churchill told Stimson after the meeting of the Big Three on July 22: "Truman was evidently much fortified . . . and . . . he stood up to the Russians in a most emphatic and decisive manner, telling them as to certain demands that they absolutely could not have." Probably, also, the bomb explains why Truman pushed more forcefully at Potsdam for the Soviets to open up Eastern Europe. It is less clear whether the bomb changed the substance of American policy at Potsdam. Probably Byrnes endorsed a reparations policy allowing the division of Germany because the bomb replaced Germany as a potential counterweight to possible Soviet expansion.

Not only did the bomb strengthen American resolve in dealing with the Soviets, but Stimson and Truman linked the bomb and the Soviet Union in another way: the selection of targets for atomic attacks. Kyoto, a city of religious shrines, was originally on the list, but Stimson removed it, with Truman's approval. Truman "was particularly emphatic in agreeing with my suggestion," Stimson wrote, because

> the bitterness . . . caused by such a wanton act might make it impossible during the long post war period to reconcile the Japanese to us in that area rather than to the Russians. It might thus, I pointed out, be the means of preventing what our policy demanded, namely, a sympathetic Japan to the United States in case there should be any aggression by Russia in Manchuria.

Scholars and laymen have criticized the combat use of the atomic bomb. They have contended, among other points, that the bombs were not necessary to end the war, that the administration knew or should have known this, that the administration knew that Japan was on the verge of defeat and *therefore* close to surrender, and that the administration was either short-sighted or had other controlling international-political motives (besides ending the war) for using the bomb. These varying contentions usually focus on the alleged failure of the United States to pursue five alternatives, individually or in combination, in order to achieve Japanese surrender before using the bomb: (1) awaiting Soviet entry, a declaration of war, or a public statement of intent (already discussed); (2) providing a warning and/or a noncombat demonstration (already discussed); (3) redefining unconditional surrender to guarantee the Imperial institution; (4) pursuing Japan's "peace feelers"; or (5) relying upon conventional warfare for a longer period. These contentions assume that policy makers were trying, or should have tried, to avoid using atomic bombs—precisely what they were not trying to do.

In examining these contentions, analysts must carefully distinguish between those writers (like Alperovitz) who maintain that there were ulterior motives for rejecting alternatives and those (like Hanson Baldwin) who regard policy makers as dangerously short sighted but without ulterior motives. It is logically possible to agree with Alperovitz and not Baldwin, or vice versa; but it is impossible logically to endorse both positions.

There were powerful reasons why the fifth alternative—the use of conventional weapons for a longer period *before* using atomic bombs—seemed undesirable to policy makers. The loss of American lives, while perhaps not great, would have been unconscionable and politically risky. How could policy makers have justified to themselves or to other Americans delaying the use of this great weapon and squandering American lives? Consider the potential political cost at home. In contrast, few Americans were then troubled by the mass killing of enemy citizens, especially if they were yellow. The firebombings of Tokyo, of other Japanese cities, and even of Dresden had produced few cries of outrage in the United States. There was no evidence that most citizens would care that the atomic bomb was as lethal as the raids on Dresden or Tokyo. It was unlikely that there would be popular support for relying upon conventional warfare and not using the atomic bomb. For citizens and policy makers, there were few, if any, moral restraints on what weapons were acceptable in war.

Nor were there any powerful advocates within the high councils of the administration who wanted to delay or not use the bomb and rely instead upon conventional warfare—a naval blockade, continued aerial bombings, or both. The advocates of conventional warfare were not powerful, and they did not directly oppose the use of the bomb. Admiral Ernest L. King, chief of Naval Operations, did believe that the invasion and the atomic bomb were not the only alternative tactics likely to achieve unconditional surrender. A naval blockade, he insisted, would be successful. The army, however, he complained, had little faith in sea power and, hence, Truman did not accept his proposal. Leahy had serious doubts about using the bomb, but as an old explosives expert who had long claimed that the bomb would never work, he carried little weight on this matter. Surprisingly, perhaps, he did not forcefully press his doubts on the president. Had Marshall plumped for the strategy of stepping up conventional warfare and delaying or not using the bomb, he might have been able to compel a reassessment. He had the respect and admiration of the president and could command attention for his views. But Marshall had no incentive to avoid the use of the bomb, prolong the war, and expend American lives. For him, nuclear weapons and invasion were likely alternatives, and he wanted to avoid invasion. If the bomb was used as quickly as possible, the invasion might be unnecessary and American lives would be saved.

For policy makers, the danger was not simply the loss of a few hundred American lives *prior* to the slightly delayed use of the bombs if the United States relied upon conventional warfare for a few more weeks. Rather the risk was that, if the nuclear attacks were even slightly delayed, the scheduled invasion of Kyushu, with perhaps 30,000 casualties in the first month, would be necessary. After the war, it became fashionable to assume that policy makers clearly foresaw and comfortably expected that an atomic bomb or two would shock Japan into a speedy surrender. But the evidence does not support this view. "The abrupt surrender of Japan came more or less as a surprise," Henry H. Arnold, commanding general of the air force, later explained. Policy makers were planning, if necessary, to drop at least three atomic bombs in August, with the last on about August 24, and more in September. Before Hiroshima, only occasionally did some policy makers imply (but never state explicitly) that one bomb or a few bombs might shock Japan into a prompt surrender: capitulation within a few days or weeks. Usually they were less optimistic, sometimes even pessimistic. They often assumed that the war might drag on after the nuclear attacks. Faced with this prospect, policy makers were unprepared to take risks and delay using the bombs. So unsure was Truman of the likelihood of a speedy surrender after the first atomic attack that he left domestic officials unprepared for the surrender and thereby seriously weakened his stabilization program and lost political support at home. Because policy makers feared that the attack on Hiroshima might not speedily end the war, they continued conventional bombing and also dropped the second bomb. Their aim was to end the war without a costly invasion of Kyushu. According to their analysis, atomic weapons, if employed promptly and combined with conventional attacks, were likely to achieve that goal. Delay was unconscionable, as Stimson later explained.

There have also been criticisms of the administration for failing to pursue two other alleged opportunities: (1) redefining the unconditional surrender demands before Hiroshima to guarantee the Imperial institution; and (2) responding to Japan's "peace feelers," which stressed the need for this guarantee. Byrnes and apparently Truman, however, were fearful at times that concessions might strengthen, not weaken, the Japanese military and thereby prolong, not shorten, the war. Some critics imply that Byrnes and Truman were not sincere in presenting this analysis and that they rejected concessions consciously in order to use the bomb. That is incorrect. Other critics believe that these policy makers were sincere but disagree with their assessment—especially since some intelligence studies implied the need for concessions on peace terms to shorten the war. Probably the administration was wrong, and these latter critics right, but either policy involved risks and some were very unattractive to Truman.

Truman, as a new president, was not comfortable in openly challenging Roosevelt's policy of unconditional surrender and modifying the terms. That was risky. It could fail and politically injure him at home. Demanding unconditional surrender meant fewer risks at home and, according to his most trusted advisers at times, fewer risks in ending the war speedily. Had his most powerful and trusted advisers pushed for a change in policy, perhaps he might have found reason and will to modify Roosevelt's policy well before Hiroshima. But most of Truman's closest advisers first counseled delay and then some moved into opposition. As a result, he too shifted from delay to opposition. At Potsdam, when Stimson pushed unsuccessfully for providing the guarantee in the Proclamation, Truman refused but told Stimson that he would carefully watch Japan's reactions on this issue and implied that he would yield if it seemed to be the only impediment to surrender. After August 10, when Japan made the guarantee the only additional condition, Truman yielded on the issue. He deemed it a tactical problem, not a substantive one. But even then, Byrnes was wary of offering this concession, despite evidence that it would probably end the war promptly —precisely what he wanted in order to forestall Soviet gains in the Far East.

Within the administration, the issue of redefining the terms of surrender was a subject of discussion for some months before Hiroshima. Since at least April, Joseph Grew, undersecretary of state and at times acting secretary of state, urged the administration to redefine unconditional surrender to permit a guarantee of the Imperial institution. He argued that these moderate terms would speed Japan's surrender and perhaps make an invasion unnecessary. Within the

Department of State, he met opposition from some high-ranking officials, including Dean Acheson and Archibald MacLeish, both assistant secretaries, who regarded the emperor as the bulwark of Japan's feudal-military tradition, which all wanted to destroy, and who feared that the American press and public opinion would be enraged by Grew's proposed concession. Hirohito, Japan's emperor, like Hitler and Mussolini, had become a wartime symbol of a hated enemy, of depravity, of tyranny, and of inhumanity.

On May 28, President Truman, perhaps then sympathetic to Grew's proposal, told him to discuss it with Stimson, Forrestal, Marshall, and King. Unlike Acheson and MacLeish, these military leaders approved the principle but apparently agreed with Marshall that publication of softened terms at that time would be premature. Grew later explained, "for certain military reasons, not divulged, it was considered inadvisable for the President to make such a statement just now. The question of timing was the nub of the whole matter according to the views of those present." Though Grew knew about the atomic bomb, its connection with the delay never seemed to occur to him, and he thought that Marshall and others were concerned *only* about the impact of the announcement on the fighting on Okinawa. In his diary, Stimson explained the opposition more fully: "It was an awkward meeting because there were people present . . . [before] whom I could not discuss the real features which would govern the whole situation, namely S–1 [the atomic bomb]." Stimson never revealed this to Grew, who reported to Truman that they decided to postpone the statement—a position that the president endorsed.

Some analysts have argued, wrongly, that this evidence indicates that Stimson and the others blocked the statement *because* they wanted to use the bomb and did not want to risk a peace before the bomb could be used. That is incorrect. In view of Stimson's frequent judgments that the United States would issue a warning *after* the atomic bombing but before the scheduled attack on Kyushu, his objection was what Grew reported—an issue of timing. On July 2, for example, when Stimson proposed as part of the warning a guarantee of the Imperial institution, he was apparently assuming, as he stated explicitly a week earlier, that he hoped "to get Japan to surrender by giving her a warning after she had been sufficiently *pounded possibly with S–1.*" Not until July 16, when Stimson learned of "the recent news of attempted approaches" by Japan for peace did he shift and call for a prompt warning *before* the atomic attacks.

"There was a pretty strong feeling" by mid-June, Stimson wrote in his diary, "that it would be deplorable if we have to go through [with] the military program with all its stubborn fighting to a finish." On June 18, Grew again went to Truman with his proposal, and the president told him, in Grew's words, that he "liked the idea [but] he had decided to hold this up until it could be discussed at the Big Three meeting" starting on July 16. Grew properly lamented that the government was missing an opportunity but did not speculate on whether the president had ulterior motives. Truman did not. A few hours later, he uneasily told associates that he, too, thought the requirement of unconditional surrender might drag out the war; that with "that thought in mind . . . [he] had left the door open for Congress to take appropriate action . . . [but] he did not feel that he could take any action at this time to change public opinion on the matter." Truman, apparently uneasy about departing from Roosevelt's policy, later explained that he delayed the guarantee until what he regarded as a more propitious time—the Potsdam conference, when the allies, by signing the proclamation, could forcefully demonstrate their "united purpose."

Had Cordell Hull, former secretary of state, Byrnes, and the JCS not intervened, Truman probably would have included in the Potsdam Proclamation a provision guaranteeing the Imperial institution. The provision was in early drafts. But Byrnes deleted it when Hull warned that it might stiffen Japan's resistance, and, if it failed, it could create serious political problems for the administration at home. The military chiefs, perhaps independently, also moved to delete the provision. Unlike Hull, they feared, among other problems, that the "guarantee would make it difficult or impossible to utilize the authority of the Emperor to direct a surrender of the Japanese forces in the outlying areas as well as in Japan proper." The guarantee, then, was not removed for ulterior purposes (because the administration wanted to use the bomb) but because advisers, with more power than Stimson and Grew, triumphed. Neither of these older men was close to Truman. Grew was headed for a quick retirement and was left behind in Washington when the president and top policy makers journeyed to Potsdam. Stimson, also headed for retirement, had so little influence by July that he was compelled to beg and scheme to attend the Potsdam conference and, while there, he was shunted to the side and seldom informed of negotiations.

Grew long maintained that America could have achieved peace without using atomic bombs if the United States had modified its demands and guaranteed the Imperial institution. In 1948, Stimson provided some support for this position: "It is possible, in the light of the final surrender, that a clearer and earlier exposition of American willingness to retain the Emperor would have produced an earlier ending to the war. Only on this question did [Stimson] . . . later believe," he wrote in his "autobiography," "that history might find that the United States, by its delay in stating its position, had prolonged the war." By implication, he was also criticizing the wartime fear—that he sometimes shared with Byrnes and most military advisers—that conciliatory offers would be interpreted in Japan "as an indication of [American] weakness" and thereby prolong the war. Probably policy makers were wrong in not acting earlier.

Let us look at the remaining, but connected, alternative—pursuing Japan's "peace feelers." Japan's so-called peace feelers were primarily a series of messages from the foreign minister to his nation's ambassador in Moscow, who was asked to investigate the possibility of having the Soviets serve as intermediaries in negotiating a peace. American intelligence intercepted and decoded all the messages. Most, if not all, were sent on to Potsdam, where Truman and Byrnes had access to them. Both men showed little interest in them, and may not even have read all of them, apparently because the proposed concessions were insufficient to meet American demands and because Truman and Byrnes had already decided that the peace party in Japan could not succeed until American attacks—including atomic bombs—crushed the military's hopes. The intercepted and decoded messages fell short of American expectations. Not only did Japan's foreign minister want to retain the Imperial institution, which was acceptable to some policy makers, but he also wanted a peace that would maintain his nation's "honor and existence," a phrase that remained vague. As late as July 27, the day after the Potsdam Proclamation, when Japan's foreign minister was planning a special peace mission to Russia, he was still unwilling or unable to present a "concrete proposal" for negotiations. What emerges from his decoded correspondence is a willingness by some elements in Japan's government to move toward peace, their fear of opposition from the military, and their inability to be specific about terms. Strangely, perhaps, though they feared that Stalin might be on the verge of entering the war, they never approached the United States directly to negotiate a peace settlement. For Truman and Byrnes, Japan was near defeat but not near surrender when the three powers issued the Potsdam Proclamation on July 26. When Japan's premier seemed to reject it, the president and secretary of state could find confirmation for their belief that the peace party could not triumph in Japan without more American "aid"—including nuclear attacks.

Given the later difficulties of Japan's peace party, even after the atomic bombings, after Soviet entry, and after more large-scale conventional bombings, top American policy makers could find evidence in the ambiguous record for their assessment that Japan's leaders were not ready to surrender before Hiroshima. More troubling were American policy makers' wartime convictions that any concessions or pursuit of unsure "peace feelers" might stiffen resistance. Most American leaders were fearful of softening demands. War had bred an attitude that any efforts at compromise might indicate to the enemy America's flaccidity of spirit and weakness of will. Toughness, for most policy makers, seemed to promise success.

Looking back upon these years, Americans may well lament the unwillingness of their leaders to make some concessions at this time and to rely upon negotiations before using the bombs. That lament, however, is logically separable from the unfounded charges that policy makers consciously avoided the "peace feelers" *because* they wanted to drop the bombs in order to intimidate the Soviets. It is true that American leaders did not cast policy in order to avoid using the atomic bombs. Given their analysis, they had no reason to avoid using these weapons. As a result, their analysis provokes ethical revulsion among many critics, who believe that policy makers should have been reluctant to use atomic weapons and should have sought, perhaps even at some cost in American lives, to avoid using them.

Truman inherited the assumption that the bomb was a legitimate weapon to use to end the war. No policy maker ever effectively challenged this conception. If the combat use of the bomb deeply troubled policy makers morally or politically, they might have been likely to reconsider their assumption and to search ardently for other alternatives. But they were generally inured to the mass killing of civilians and much preferred to sacrifice the lives of Japanese civilians to those of American soldiers. As a result, they were committed to using the bomb *as soon as possible* to end the war. "The dominant objective was victory," Stimson later explained. "If victory could be speeded by using the bomb, it should be used; if victory must be delayed in order to use the bomb, it should *not* be used. So far as . . . [I] knew, this general view was fully shared by the President and his associates." The morality of war confirmed the dictates of policy and reinforced the legacy that Truman had inherited. Bureaucratic momentum added weight to that legacy, and the relatively closed structure of decision making served also to inhibit dissent and to ratify the dominant assumption.

Had policy makers concluded that the use of the bomb would impair Soviet-American relations and make the Soviets intransigent, they might have reconsidered their assumption. But their analysis indicated that the use of the bomb would aid, not injure, their efforts to secure concessions from the Soviets. The bomb offered a bonus. The promise of these likely advantages probably constituted a subtle deterrent to any reconsideration of the use of the atomic bomb. Policy makers rejected the competing analysis advanced by the Franck Committee:

> Russia, and even allied countries which bear less mistrust of our ways and intentions, as well as neutral countries, will be deeply shocked. It will be very difficult to persuade the world that a nation which was capable of secretly preparing and suddenly releasing . . . [the bomb] is to be trusted in its proclaimed desire of having such weapons abolished by international agreement.

Instead, policy makers had come to assume that a combat demonstration would advance, not impair, the interests of peace—a position shared by Conant, Oppenheimer, Arthur H. Compton, Nobel laureate and director of the Chicago Metallurgical Laboratory, and Edward Teller, the physicist and future father of the hydrogen bomb. In explaining the thinking of the scientific advisory panel in recommending combat use of the bomb, Oppenheimer later said that one of the two "overriding considerations . . . [was] the effect of our actions on the stability . . . of the postwar world." Stimson's assistant, Harvey H. Bundy, wrote in 1946, that some thought "that unless the bomb were used it would be impossible to persuade the world that the saving of civilization in the future would depend on a proper international control of atomic energy." The bomb, in short, would impress the Soviets.

In addition, there was another possible advantage to using the bomb: retribution against Japan. A few days after Nagasaki, Truman hinted at this theme in a private letter justifying the combat use of the bombs:

> Nobody is more disturbed over the use of Atomic bombs than I am but I was greatly disturbed over the unwarranted attack by the Japanese on Pearl Harbor. The only language they seem to understand is the one that we have been using to bombard them. When you have to deal with a beast you have to treat him as a beast. It is most regrettable but nevertheless true.

In this letter, one can detect strains of the quest for retribution (the reference to Pearl Harbor), and some might even find subtle strains of racism (Japan was "a beast"). The enemy was a beast and deserved to be destroyed. War, as some critics would stress, dehumanized victors and vanquished, and justified inhumanity in the name of nationalism, of justice, and even of humanity.

In assessing the administration's failure to challenge the assumption that the bomb was a legitimate weapon to be used against Japan, we may conclude that Truman found no reason to reconsider, that it would have been difficult for him to challenge the assumption, and that there were also various likely benefits deterring a reassessment. For the administration, in short, there was no reason to avoid using the bomb and many reasons making it feasible and even attractive. The bomb was used primarily to end the war *promptly* and thereby to save American lives. There were other ways to end the war, but none of them seemed as effective. They would not produce victory as promptly and seemed to have greater risks. Even if Russia had not existed, the bombs would have been used in the same way. How could Truman, in the absence of overriding contrary reasons, justify not using the bombs, or even delaying their use, and thereby prolonging the war and sacrificing American lives?

Some who have searched for the causes of Truman's decision to use atomic weapons have made the error of assuming that the question was ever open, that the administration ever carefully faced the problem of *whether* to use the bombs. It was not a carefully weighed decision but the implementation of an assumption. The administration devoted thought to how, not whether, to use them. As Churchill later wrote, "the decision whether or not to use the atomic bomb to compel the surrender of Japan was never even an issue."

FURTHER READING

Les K. Adler and Thomas G. Paterson, "Red Fascism," *American Historical Review,* 75 (1970), 1046–1064

Gar Alperovitz, *Atomic Diplomacy* (1965)

Stephen Ambrose, *Rise to Globalism* (1976)

Terry H. Anderson, *The United States, Great Britain, and the Cold War, 1944–1947* (1981)

Paul R. Baker, ed., *The Atomic Bomb* (1976)

Barton J. Bernstein, ed., *The Atomic Bomb* (1975)

———, *Politics and Policies of the Truman Administration* (1970)

Robert J. C. Butow, *Japan's Decision to Surrender* (1954)

Committee for the Compilation of Materials on Damage Caused by the Atomic Bombs in Hiroshima and Nagasaki, *Hiroshima and Nagasaki* (1981)

Lynn Etheridge Davis, *The Cold War Begins* (1974)

Hugh DeSantis, *The Diplomacy of Silence: The American Foreign Service, the Soviet Union, and the Cold War, 1933–1947* (1980)

Robert J. Donovan, *Conflict and Crisis: The Presidency of Harry S. Truman, 1954–1948* (1977)

———, *Tumultuous Years: The Presidency of Harry S. Truman, 1949–1953* (1982)

Herbert Feis, *The Atomic Bomb and the End of World War II* (1966)

———, *From Trust to Terror* (1970)

Denna F. Fleming, *The Cold War and Its Origins* (1961)

Richard Freeland, *The Truman Doctrine and the Origins of McCarthyism* (1971)

John Lewis Gaddis, *Russia, the Soviet Union, and the United States* (1978)
——, *Strategies of Containment* (1982)
——, *The United States and the Origins of the Cold War* (1972)
Charles Gati, ed., *Caging the Bear: Containment and the Cold War* (1974)
Lloyd C. Gardner, *Architects of Illusion* (1970)
——, Arthur M. Schlesinger, Jr., and Hans J. Morgenthau, *Origins of the Cold War* (1970)
John Gimbel, *The American Occupation of Germany* (1968)
——, *The Origins of the Marshall Plan* (1976)
Louis Halle, *The Cold War as History* (1967)
Robert M. Hathaway, *Ambiguous Partnership: Britain and America, 1944–1947* (1981)
Gregg Herken, *The Winning Weapon* (1981)
George Herring, *Aid to Russia, 1941–1946* (1973)
Richard Hewlett and Oscar Anderson, *The New World* (1962)
Richard Kirkendall, ed., *The Truman Period as a Research Field* (1974)
Gabriel Kolko and Joyce Kolko, *The Limits of Power* (1972)
Bruce Kuklick, *American Policy and the Division of Germany* (1972)
Bruce Kuniholm, *The Origins of the Cold War in the Near East* (1980)
Walter LaFeber, *America, Russia, and the Cold War* (1980)
Ralph Levering, *The Cold War, 1945–1972* (1982)
Walter Lippmann, *The Cold War* (1947)
Geir Lundestad, *The American Non-Policy Towards Eastern Europe, 1943–1947* (1975)
Richard Mayne, *Recovery of Europe* (1973)
Robert L. Messer, *The End of an Alliance* (1982)
Lynn H. Miller and Ronald W. Pruessen, eds., *Reflections on the Cold War* (1974)
Thomas G. Paterson, ed., *Cold War Critics* (1971)
——, *The Origins of the Cold War* (1974)
——, *Soviet-American Confrontation* (1973)
Lisle Rose, *After Yalta* (1973)
Arthur M. Schlesinger, Jr., "Origins of the Cold War," *Foreign Affairs,* 46 (1967), 22–52
Martin Sherwin, *A World Destroyed* (1975)
Avi Shlaim, *The United States and the Berlin Blockade, 1948–1949* (1983)
Nikolai V. Sivachev and Nikolai N. Yakovlev, *Russia and the United States* (1979)
Gaddis Smith, *Dean Acheson* (1972)
John Spanier, *American Foreign Policy Since World War II* (1983)
Kenneth W. Thompson, *Cold War Theories* (1981)
William Taubman, *Stalin's American Policy* (1982)
Athan G. Theoharis, *The Yalta Myths* (1970)
Robert W. Tucker, *The Radical Left and American Foreign Policy* (1971)
Adam Ulam, *The Rivals* (1971)
Walter Ullmann, *The United States in Prague, 1945–1948* (1978)
J. Samuel Walker, *Henry A. Wallace and American Foreign Policy* (1976)
Piotr S. Wandycz, *The United States and Poland* (1980)
Richard Walton, *Henry Wallace, Harry Truman and the Cold War* (1976)
Patricia D. Ward, *The Threat of Peace* (1979)
Samuel F. Wells, Jr., "Sounding the Tocsin: NSC-68 and the Soviet Threat," *International Security,* 4 (1979), 116–158
Imanuel Wexler, *The Marshall Plan Revisited* (1983)
Lawrence S. Wittner, *American Intervention in Greece, 1943–1949* (1982)
Daniel Yergin, *Shattered Peace* (1977)

Mao's China and the Chances for Sino-American Accommodation

9

From 1945 to the victory of Mao Tse-tung's (Mao Zedong's) Communists in 1949, the United States was deeply involved in the Chinese civil war. About three billion dollars flowed to the regime of Chiang Kai-shek (Jiang Jieshi), leader of the Kuomintang (Guomindang), or Nationalists. American officials also urged reforms upon Chiang, gave his army military advisers, and tried to mediate between the warring parties. Although Americans recognized the indigenous roots of the civil war, they feared the international consequences of a Communist triumph—especially a Sino-Soviet alliance. The failure to draw successfully the containment line in China aroused President Harry S. Truman's critics, who believed he, Secretary of State Dean Acheson, and the China experts in the Foreign Service had "lost" China. The extreme anti-Communism called McCarthyism relentlessly pushed this charge, even accusing American leaders of Communist sympathies.

In this politically electric environment, the Truman administration considered whether to offer diplomatic recognition to the new People's Republic of China (PRC), or to back Chiang's exiled government on the island of Formosa, or Taiwan. Whether Truman and Acheson withheld recognition from Mao because of their fear of the domestic political consequences is a point of debate among historians. Some scholars suggest instead that the Truman administration was so inveterately anti-Communist that it interpreted the Communist victory as a Soviet thrust into Asia and hence passed up Chinese overtures for negotiations. Others have argued that the chances for Sino-American accommodation were minimal because of strong Chinese anti-Americanism. Historians agree, however, that the Korean War killed all chances. The origins of American non-recognition policy, which lasted until 1979, is the subject of this chapter.

DOCUMENTS

In May and June of 1949, the American Ambassador in China, John Leighton Stuart, was approached by Huang Hua, a Communist official. Stuart's two telegrams to Washington reported on the conversations and the tender of an "invitation from Mao and Chou to talk with them. . . ." In late May, Chou En-lai (Zhou Enlai), a high-ranking Chinese leader, made an indirect approach to the American Consulate General in Peking. This demarche was reported to Washington by Consul General O. Edmund Clubb in a June 1 telegram, reprinted here. The State Department's initial response to the Chou overture is the next document, followed by President Truman's attitude toward the demarche.

On July 30, 1949, the Department of State issued a "White Paper"—a huge volume of documents and analysis that defended pre-1949 American policies toward China against charges that the United States had "lost" the nation. Secretary Dean Acheson's public letter transmitting the book to the President is included below. The next document is a speech of August 18 by Mao Tse-tung. Several weeks earlier he had announced that China was "leaning to one side"— the Soviet side in the Cold War. In his August speech he revealed strong anti-American views, accusing the United States of aggression. In the last document, Senator William Knowland of California, known as a McCarthyite and member of the "China lobby," argued against recognition of the People's Republic. His speech was delivered to the Senate on January 5, 1950.

Ambassador Stuart Reports on Mao's
Overture, 1949

Telegram of May 14, 1949

Huang [Hua] called my residence last evening remaining almost 2 hours. Our conversation was friendly and informal. I refrained from political remarks until he opened way which he did after few personal exchanges. I then spoke earnestly of great desire that peoples of all countries had for peace, including, emphatically, my own, of dangerous situation developing despite this universal popular will; of indescribable horrors of next war; of my conviction that much, but not all, present tension due to misunderstandings, fears, suspicions which could be cleared away by mutual frankness; of fears Americans and other non-Communists had of Marxist-Leninist doctrine, subscribed to by CCP [Chinese Communist Party], that world revolution and overthrow of capitalistic governments necessary, thus proclaiming subversive interference or armed invasion as fixed policy. Huang spoke of Chinese people's resentment at American aid to Kmt [Kuomintang, or Nationalist Party] and other "mistakes" of US policy to which I briefly replied.

Huang asked about my plans and I told him of my instructions, adding that I was glad to stay long enough for symbolic purpose of demonstrating American people's interest in welfare of Chinese people as whole; that I wished to maintain friendly relations of past; that being near end of my active life I hoped to be able somewhat to help restore these relations as I knew my Government and people desired; that my aim was unity, peace, truly democratic government and international good will for which Huang knew I had worked all my life in China.

Huang expressed much interest in recognition of Communist China by USA on terms of equality and mutual benefit. I replied that such terms together with accepted international practice with respect to treaties would be only proper basis. He was greatly surprised at my explanation of status of armed forces in China particularly Marines in Shanghai. Our side of story, that is desire to protect American lives during civil disturbances and chaotic conditions brought on by war, appeared never to have occurred to him. He was obviously impressed. I explained question of national government was internal; that Communists themselves at present had none; that it was customary to recognize whatever government clearly had support of people of country and was able and willing to perform its international obligations; that therefore USA and other countries could do nothing but await developments in China. I hinted that most other nations would tend to follow our lead. I explained functions of foreign consulates in maintaining informal relations with *de facto* regional authorities.

Huang expounded upon needs of China for commercial and other relations with foreign countries. He said instructions had been issued to all military units to protect safety and interests of foreigners. Intrusion into my bedroom was discussed and he promised to do his best in constantly shifting military situation to trace offenders. He explained that first Communist troops in city had not been prepared or properly instructed on treatment of foreigners. . . .

Telegram of June 30, 1949

Huang Hua called on me by appointment June 28. He reported that he had received message from Mao Tse-tung and Chou En-lai assuring me that they would welcome me to Peiping if I wished to visit Yenching University. Background of this suggestion is as follows:

In early June Philip Fugh, in one of his conversations with Huang, asked casually, and not under instructions from me, if it would be possible for me to travel to Peiping to visit my old University as had been my habit in previous years on my birthday and Commencement. At that time Huang made no comment. However, 2 weeks later, June 18 to be precise, in discussing my return to Washington for consultation, Huang himself raised question with Fugh of whether time permitted my making trip to Peiping. Fugh made no commitment, commenting only that he himself had made this suggestion 2 weeks earlier. Neither Fugh nor I followed up this suggestion but apparently Huang did. Present message (almost an invitation) is reply.

Regardless whether initiation this suggestion is considered [by] Peiping to have come from me or from Communists, I can only regard Huang's message as veiled invitation from Mao and Chou to talk with them while ostensibly visiting Yenching. To accept would undoubtedly be gratifying to them, would give me chance to describe American policy; its anxieties regarding Communism and world revolution; its desires for China's future; and would enable me to carry to Washington most authoritative information regarding CCP intentions. Such trip would be step toward better mutual understanding and should strengthen more liberal anti-Soviet element in CCP. It would provide unique opportunity for American official to talk to top Chinese Communists in informal manner which may not again present itself. It would be imaginative, adventurous indication of US open-minded attitude towards changing political trends in China and would probably have beneficial effect on future Sino-American relations.

On negative side, trip to Peiping before my return to US on consultation would undoubtedly start rumors and speculations in China and might conceivably embarrass Department because of American criticism. It would probably be misunderstood by my colleagues in Diplomatic Corps who might feel that US representative was first to break united front policy which we have sponsored toward Communist regime and might prove beginning of trek of chiefs of mission to Peiping on one pretext or another. Trip to Peiping at this time invariably suggests idea of making similar one to Canton before my return to US.

While visiting both capitals might effectively dramatize American interest in Chinese people as a whole, it might also appear as peace-making gesture, unwarranted interference in China's internal affairs, and would probably be misunderstood by Chinese Communists, thus undoing any beneficial effects of visit north. Finally, trip of US Ambassador to Peiping at this time would enhance greatly prestige, national and international, of Chinese Communists and Mao himself and in a sense would be second step on our part (first having been my remaining Nanking) toward recognition Communist regime.

I received clear impression that Mao, Chou and Huang are very much hoping that I make this trip, whatever their motives. I, of course, gave Huang no answer to Mao's message, replying that, while I enjoyed going back to Yenching, this year had assumed it would be out of question, that I had already delayed longer than intended my departure for Washington; that travel on as yet incompletely restored railway line to Peiping might be taxing for "feeble old man," et cetera. Question of using my airplane was raised. Huang objected on ground danger from Communists' anti-aircraft batteries; that it would take couple days at least to give proper instructions and that there would always be some risk. He continued Peiping trip can now be made in less than 3 days by train, adding that all facilities of railway would be put at my disposal. I could, if thought desirable, make airplane travel condition to visit Peiping and it is not to be excluded that permission would be granted. There is consideration that prestige of travel Peiping my own plane would somewhat offset negative features outlined above.

I have made this rather full statement of case for Department's consideration and decision. I am, of course, ready to make journey by either means
should Department consider it desirable, and should be grateful for instructions earliest and nature of reply to Huang. . . .

Chou En-lai's (Zhou Enlai's) Demarche, 1949

Following message given Assistant Military Attaché [David D.] Barrett May
31 by reliable intermediary, origin being Chou En-lai. Chou desired message
be transmitted highest American authorities on top secret level without his
name being mentioned, said in fact that if it were attributed him he would
positively disavow it. Essential there be no leak his name to outside channels. Chou approved transmittal via Barrett who gave message me to transmit, but wanted name unmentioned even to Barrett. Chou desired what he
said be conveyed to British, expressed preference transmittal be through
Department.
 There were few disagreements in CCP Party [sic] during agrarian stage
revolution but with arrival at urban stage there have now developed disagreements of serious nature primarily re industrial-commercial policies and
questions international relations. There is still no actual split within party
but definite separation into liberal and radical wings, with Chou being of
liberal, and Liu Shao-chi of radical wing. Chou however said it would be
as big mistake to base any policy toward China on idea there would develop
major split in party as it was to attempt stop Communism in China by aiding
Kmt [Kuomintang or Nationalist Party] para-liberal group; feels that country
is in such bad shape that most pressing need is reconstruction without regard
political theories and that Mao Tse-tung concepts regarding private capital
should be effected. Group feels there should have been coalition with Kmt
because of party lack necessary knowledge regarding reconstruction, did not
favor coalition with elements Ho Ying-chin–Chen Li-fu type but felt that
without coalition reconstruction might be so delayed that party would lose
support people. Realistic coalition advocated by group failed after big dispute involving most of higher figures in party with exception Mao (Chou
was most careful in references to Mao). Coalition having failed, party must
make most of bad job and obtain aid from outside. USSR cannot give aid
which, therefore, must come from USA or possibly Britain. Chou favors
getting help from USA and does not accord Soviet attitude regarding USA.
Chou professedly sincere Communist but feels there has developed in USA
economy something which is outside Marxist theories and that present American economic situation is, therefore, not susceptible Marxian interpretation.
Therefore, Soviet attitude this respect wrong, feels American economy will
continue without internal collapse or revolution and that there is no real
bar to relations between USA and other governments, different political type.
Unequivocally opposed to American aid to Kmt but feels this was given
from mistaken motives altruism rather than American viciousness. Feels USA

has genuine interest in Chinese people which could become basis friendly relations between two countries.

Chou, speaking for liberal group, felt China should speedily establish *de facto* working relations with foreign governments.

This question will be prime issue in struggle between two wings. Radicals wish alliance with USSR, sort now existing between US and Britain, while liberals regard Soviet international policy as "crazy." Chou feels USSR is risking war which it is unable fight successfully and that good working relations between China and USA would have definite softening effect on party attitude toward Western countries. Chou desires these relations because he feels China desperately needs that outside aid which USSR unable give. Feels China on brink complete economic and physical collapse, by "physical" meaning breakdown physical well-being of people.

Chou feels USA should aid Chinese because: (1) China still not Communist and if Mao's policies are correctly implemented may not be so for long time; (2) democratic China would serve in international sphere as mediator between Western Powers and USSR; (3) China in chaos under any regime would be menace to peace Asia and world. Chou emphasized he spoke solely for certain people personally and not as member party, that he was not in position make formal or informal commitments or proposals. He hoped American authorities would recall wartime contacts with Communists and character and opinions of many whom they knew at that time. He hoped American authorities remembering this would believe there were genuine liberals in party who are concerned with everything connected with welfare Chinese people and "peace in our time" rather than doctrinaire theories. As spokesman for liberal wing he could say that when time came for Communist participation in international affairs his group would work within party for sensible solution impasse between USSR and west and would do its best make USSR discard policies leading to war. . . .

Chou emphasized that despite deficiencies, errors, disagreements, Communists had won military victory and in spite of same drawbacks would win future victory in reconstruction. Chou said Mao Tse-tung stands aside from party disputes using Chou, Liu Shao-chi and other liberals and radicals for specific purposes as he sees fit. Mao is genius in listening arguments various sides, then translating ideas into practical working policies.

Chou per source appeared very nervous and worried. . . .

The State Department's Response to the Demarche, 1949

US has traditionally maintained close and friendly relations with China and has thruout past 100 years Sino-US relations, particularly since end last century, taken lead in efforts obtain internatl respect for Chi territorial and administrative integrity to end that China might develop as stable, united and independent nation. Unique record US relations with China gives clear evidence US had no territorial designs on China and has sought no special privileges or rights which were not granted other fon nations; US has sought maintain relations on basis mutual benefit and respect. Basic US objectives and principles remain unchanged.

In present situation US hopes maintain friendly relations with China and continue social, economic and polit relations with that country insofar as these relations based upon principle mutual respect and understanding and principle equality and are to mutual benefit two nations. In absence these basic principles, it can hardly be expected that full benefit Sino–US relations can be attained.

In this connection, US Govt and people are naturally disturbed and seriously concerned over certain recent occurrences which represent significant departure from these principles and some of which, in fact, widely at variance with accepted internatl custom and practice: Repeated bitter propaganda misrepresenting US actions and motives in China and elsewhere in world; arbitrary restrictions on movement and denial communications ConGen Mukden and Commie failure reply to ConGen Peiping repeated representations this matter, including request withdraw ConGen and staff Mukden; and Commie failure take action release two US Marine flyers or reply ConGen Peiping representations this matter.

While we welcome expressions friendly sentiments, he must realize that they cannot be expected bear fruit until they have been translated into deeds capable of convincing American people that Sino–US relations can be placed upon solid basis mutual respect and understanding to benefit both nations. . . .

President Truman on the Demarche, 1949

I brought the President up to date with respect to the Chou En-lai *Démarche* and read to him the pertinent sections of our reply. He approved this course of action and directs us to be most careful not to indicate any softening toward the Communists but to insist on judging their intentions by their actions.

Dean Acheson in the "White Paper," 1949

When peace came the United States was confronted with three possible alternatives in China: (1) it could have pulled out lock, stock and barrel; (2) it could have intervened militarily on a major scale to assist the Nationalists to destroy the Communists; (3) it could, while assisting the Nationalists to assert their authority over as much of China as possible, endeavor to avoid a civil war by working for a compromise between the two sides.

The first alternative would, and I believe American public opinion at the time so felt, have represented an abandonment of our international responsibilities and of our traditional policy of friendship for China before we had made a determined effort to be of assistance. The second alternative policy, while it may look attractive theoretically and in retrospect, was wholly impracticable. The Nationalists had been unable to destroy the Communists during the 10 years before the war. Now after the war the Nationalists were, as indicated above, weakened, demoralized, and unpopular. They had quickly dissipated their popular support and prestige in the areas liberated from the Japanese by the conduct of their civil and military officials. The Communists on the other hand were much stronger than they had ever been and were in control of most of North China. Because of the ineffectiveness of the Nationalist forces which was later to be tragically demonstrated, the Communists probably could have been dislodged only by American arms. It is obvious that the American people would not have sanctioned such a colossal commitment of our armies in 1945 or later. We therefore came to the third alternative policy whereunder we faced the facts of the situation and attempted to assist in working out a *modus vivendi* which would avert civil war but nevertheless preserve and even increase the influence of the National Government. . . .

The reasons for the failures of the Chinese National Government appear in some detail in the attached record. They do not stem from any inadequacy of American aid. Our military observers on the spot have reported that the Nationalist armies did not lose a single battle during the crucial year of 1948 through lack of arms or ammunition. The fact was that the decay which our observers had detected in Chungking early in the war had fatally sapped the powers of resistance of the Kuomintang. Its leaders had proved incapable of meeting the crisis confronting them, its troops had lost the will to fight, and its Government had lost popular support. The Communists, on the other hand, through a ruthless discipline and fanatical zeal, attempted to sell themselves as guardians and liberators of the people. The Nationalist armies did not have to be defeated; they disintegrated. History has proved again and again that a regime without faith in itself and an army without morale cannot survive the test of battle. . . .

Fully recognizing that the heads of the Chinese Communist Party were ideologically affiliated with Moscow, our Government nevertheless took the view, in the light of the existing balance of forces in China, that peace could be established only if certain conditions were met. The Kuomintang would have to set its own house in order and both sides would have to make concessions so that the Government of China might become, in fact as well as in name, the Government of all China and so that all parties might function within the constitutional system of the Government. Both internal peace and constitutional development required that the progress should be rapid from one party government with a large opposition party in armed rebellion, to the participation of all parties, including the moderate non-communist elements, in a truly national system of government.

None of these conditions has been realized. The distrust of the leaders of both the Nationalist and Communist Parties for each other proved too deep-seated to permit final agreement, notwithstanding temporary truces and apparently promising negotiations. The Nationalists, furthermore, embarked in 1946 on an over-ambitious military campaign in the face of warnings by

General Marshall that it not only would fail but would plunge China into economic chaos and eventually destroy the National Government. General Marshall pointed out that though Nationalist armies could, for a period, capture Communist-held cities, they could not destroy the Communist armies. Thus every Nationalist advance would expose their communications to attack by Communist guerrillas and compel them to retreat or to surrender their armies together with the munitions which the United States has furnished them. No estimate of a military situation has ever been more completely confirmed by the resulting facts.

The historic policy of the United States of friendship and aid toward the people of China was, however, maintained in both peace and war. Since V–J Day, the United States Government has authorized aid to Nationalist China in the form of grants and credits totaling approximately 2 billion dollars, an amount equivalent in value to more than 50 percent of the monetary expenditures of the Chinese Government and of proportionately greater magnitude in relation to the budget of that Government than the United States has provided to any nation of Western Europe since the end of the war. In addition to these grants and credits, the United States Government has sold the Chinese Government large quantities of military and civilian war surplus property with a total procurement cost of over 1 billion dollars, for which the agreed realization to the United States was 232 million dollars. A large proportion of the military supplies furnished the Chinese armies by the United States since V–J Day has, however, fallen into the hands of the Chinese Communists through the military ineptitude of the Nationalist leaders, their defections and surrenders, and the absence among their forces of the will to fight.

It has been urged that relatively small amounts of additional aid—military and economic—to the National Government would have enabled it to destroy communism in China. The most trustworthy military, economic, and political information available to our Government does not bear out this view.

A realistic appraisal of conditions in China, past and present, leads to the conclusion that the only alternative open to the United States was full-scale intervention in behalf of a Government which had lost the confidence of its own troops and its own people. Such intervention would have required the expenditure of even greater sums than have been fruitlessly spent thus far, the command of Nationalist armies by American officers, and the probable participation of American armed forces—land, sea, and air—in the resulting war. Intervention of such a scope and magnitude would have been resented by the mass of the Chinese people, would have diametrically reversed our historic policy, and would have been condemned by the American people.

It must be admitted frankly that the American policy of assisting the Chinese people in resisting domination by any foreign power or powers is now confronted with the gravest difficulties. The heart of China is in Communist hands. The Communist leaders have foresworn their Chinese heritage and have publicly announced their subservience to a foreign power, Russia, which during the last 50 years, under czars and Communists alike, has been most assiduous in its efforts to extend its control in the Far East. In the recent past, attempts at foreign domination have appeared quite clearly to the Chinese people as external aggression and as such have been bitterly and in the long run successfully resisted. Our aid and encouragement have helped them to resist. In this case, however, the foreign domination has been masked behind the façade of a vast crusading movement which apparently has seemed to many Chinese to be wholly indigenous and national. Under these circumstances, our aid has been unavailing.

The unfortunate but inescapable fact is that the ominous result of the civil war in China was beyond the control of the government of the United States. Nothing that this country did or could have done within the reasonable limits of its capabilities could have changed that result; nothing that was left undone by this country has contributed to it. It was the product of internal Chinese forces, forces which this country tried to influence but could not. A decision was arrived at within China, if only a decision by default.

And now it is abundantly clear that we must face the situation as it exists in fact. We will not help the Chinese or ourselves by basing our policy on wishful thinking. We continue to believe that, however tragic may be the immediate future of China and however ruthlessly a major portion of this great people may be exploited by a party in the interest of a foreign imperialism, ultimately the profound civilization and the democratic individualism of China will reassert themselves and she will throw off the foreign yoke. I consider that we should encourage all developments in China which now and in the future work toward this end.

In the immediate future, however, the implementation of our historic policy of friendship for China must be profoundly affected by current developments. It will necessarily be influenced by the degree to which the Chinese people come to recognize that the Communist regime serves not their interests but those of Soviet Russia and the manner in which, having become aware of the facts, they react to this foreign domination. One point, however, is clear. Should the Communist regime lend itself to the aims of Soviet Russian imperialism and attempt to engage in aggression against China's neighbors, we and the other members of the United Nations would be confronted by a situation violative of the principles of the United Nations Charter and threatening international peace and security.

Meanwhile our policy will continue to be based upon our own respect for the Charter, our friendship for China, and our traditional support for the Open Door and for China's independence and administrative and territorial integrity.

Mao's Denunciation of American Imperialism, 1949

The war to turn China into a U.S. colony, a war in which the United States of America supplies the money and guns and Chiang Kai-shek the men to fight for the United States and slaughter the Chinese people, has been an important component of the U.S. imperialist policy of world-wide aggression since World War II. The U.S. policy of aggression has several targets. The three main targets are Europe, Asia and the Americas. China, the centre of gravity in Asia, is a large country with a population of 475 million; by seizing China, the United States would possess all of Asia. With its Asian front consolidated, U.S. imperialism could concentrate its forces on attacking Europe. U.S. imperialism considers its front in the Americas relatively secure. These are the smug over-all calculations of the U.S. aggressors.

But in the first place, the American people and the peoples of the world do not want war. Secondly, the attention of the United States has largely been absorbed by the awakening of the peoples of Europe, by the rise of the People's Democracies in Eastern Europe, and particularly by the towering presence of the Soviet Union, this unprecedentedly powerful bulwark of peace bestriding Europe and Asia, and by its strong resistance to the U.S. policy of aggression. Thirdly, and this is most important, the Chinese people have awakened, and the armed forces and the organized strength of the people under the leadership of the Communist Party of China have become more powerful than ever before. Consequently, the ruling clique of U.S. imperialism has been prevented from adopting a policy of direct, large-scale armed attacks on China and instead has adopted a policy of helping Chiang Kai-shek fight the civil war.

U.S. naval, ground and air forces did participate in the war in China. There were U.S. naval bases in Tsingtao, Shanghai and Taiwan. U.S. troops were stationed in Peiping, Tientsin, Tangshan, Chinwangtao, Tsingtao, Shanghai and Nanking. The U.S. air force controlled all of China's air space and took aerial photographs of all China's strategic areas for military maps. At the town of Anping near Peiping, at Chiutai near Changchun, at Tangshan and in the Eastern Shantung Peninsula, U.S. troops and other military personnel clashed with the People's Liberation Army and on several occasions were captured. Chennault's air fleet took an extensive part in the civil war. Besides transporting troops for Chiang Kai-shek, the U.S. air force bombed and sank the cruiser *Chungking,* which had mutinied against the Kuomintang. All these were acts of direct participation in the war, although they fell short of an open declaration of war and were not large in scale, and although the principal method of U.S. aggression was the large-scale supply of money, munitions and advisers to help Chiang Kai-shek fight the civil war.

The use of this method by the United States was determined by the objective situation in China and the rest of the world, and not by any lack of desire on the part of the Truman-Marshall group, the ruling clique of U.S. imperialism, to launch direct aggression against China. Moreover, at the outset of its help to Chiang Kai-shek in fighting the civil war, a crude farce was staged in which the United States appeared as mediator in the conflict between the Kuomintang and the Communist Party; this was an attempt to soften up the Communist Party of China, deceive the Chinese people and thus gain control of all China without fighting. The peace negotiations failed, the deception fell through and the curtain rose on the war.

Liberals or "democratic individualists" who cherish illusions about the United States and have short memories! Please look at Acheson's own words:

> When peace came the United States was confronted with three possible alternatives in China: (1) it could have pulled out lock, stock and barrel; (2) it could have intervened militarily on a major scale to assist the Nationalists to destroy the Communists; (3) it could, while assisting the Nationalists to assert their authority over as much of China as possible, endeavor to avoid a civil war by working for a compromise between the two sides.

Why didn't the United States adopt the first of these policies? Acheson says:

> The first alternative would, and I believe American public opinion at the time so felt, have represented an abandonment of our international responsibilities and of our traditional policy of friendship for China before we had made a determined effort to be of assistance.

So that's how things stand: the "international responsibilities" of the United States and its "traditional policy of friendship for China" are nothing but intervention against China. Intervention is called assuming international responsibilities and showing friendship for China; as to non-intervention, it simply won't do. Here Acheson defiles U.S. public opinion; his is the "public opinion" of Wall Street, not the public opinion of the American people.

Why didn't the United States adopt the second of these policies? Acheson says:

> The second alternative policy, while it may look attractive theoretically and in retrospect, was wholly impracticable. The Nationalists had been unable to destroy the Communists during the 10 years before the war. Now after the war the Nationalists were, as indicated above, weakened, demoralized, and unpopular. They had quickly dissipated their popular support and prestige in the areas liberated from the Japanese by the conduct of their civil and military officials. The Communists on the other hand were much stronger than they had ever been and were in control of most of North China. Because of the ineffectiveness of the Nationalist forces which was later to be tragically demonstrated, the Communists probably could have been dislodged only by American arms. It is obvious that the American people would not have sanctioned such a colossal commitment of our armies in 1945 or later. We therefore came to the third alternative policy. . . .

What a splendid idea! The United States supplies the money and guns and Chiang Kai-shek the men to fight for the United States and slaughter the Chinese people, to "destroy the Communists" and turn China into a U.S. colony, so that the United States may fulfill its "international responsibilities" and carry out its "traditional policy of friendship for China." . . .

What matter if we have to face some difficulties? Let them blockade us! Let them blockade us for eight or ten years! By that time all of China's problems will have been solved. Will the Chinese cower before difficulties when they are not afraid even of death? Lao Tzu said, "The people fear not death, why threaten them with it?" U.S. imperialism and its running dogs, the Chiang Kai-shek reactionaries, have not only "threatened" us with death but actually put many of us to death. Besides people like Wen Yi-to, they have killed millions of Chinese in the last three years with U.S. carbines, machine-guns, mortars, bazookas, howitzers, tanks and bombs dropped from aeroplanes. This situation is now coming to an end. They have been defeated. It is we who are going in to attack them, not they who are coming out to attack us. They will soon be finished. True, the few problems left to us, such as blockade, unemployment, famine, inflation and rising prices, are difficulties, but we have already begun to breathe more easily than in the past three years. We have come triumphantly through the ordeal of the last three years, why can't we overcome these few difficulties of today? Why can't we live without the United States?

When the People's Liberation Army crossed the Yangtse River, the U.S. colonial government at Nanking fled helter-skelter. Yet His Excellency Ambassador Stuart sat tight, watching wide-eyed, hoping to set up shop under a new signboard and to reap some profit. But what did he see? Apart from the People's Liberation Army marching past, column after column, and the workers, peasants and students rising in hosts, he saw something else—the Chinese liberals or democratic individualists turning out in force, shouting slogans and talking revolution together with the workers, peasants, soldiers and students. In short, he was left out in the cold, "standing all alone, body and shadow comforting each other." There was nothing more for him to do, and he had to take to the road, his briefcase under his arm.

There are still some intellectuals and other people in China who have muddled ideas and illusions about the United States. Therefore we should explain things to them, win them over, educate them and unite with them, so they will come over to the side of the people and not fall into the snares set by imperialism. But the prestige of U.S. imperialism among the Chinese people is completely bankrupt, and the White Paper is a record of its bankruptcy. Progressives should make good use of the White Paper to educate the Chinese people.

Leighton Stuart has departed and the White Paper has arrived. Very good. Very good. Both events are worth celebrating.

Senator William Knowland Argues Against Recognition, 1950

Mr. President and Members of the Senate, within the last 90 days two catastrophic events have taken place. These are the Soviet success in atomic development, as announced by the President of the United States on September 23, 1949, and the establishment of a Soviet-recognized Communist regime in China. Only in retrospect will we be able to finally determine which event will have the most far-reaching influence. Both have set off chain reactions that have not yet run their full course.

Fifty years of friendly interest on the part of our people and our Government in a free and independent China and the overwhelming contribution made by our Army, Navy, and Air Force in the Pacific during World War II gave us the power, the prestige, and the opportunity for constructive action no western nation had ever before possessed. We could have pioneered in exporting the ideals that inspired men who loved freedom everywhere following our own breakaway from colonial status.

All this opportunity has been frittered away by a small group of willful men in the Far Eastern Division of the State Department who had the backing of their superiors.

In Europe where the record of Soviet aims was clearly outlined in Poland, Czechoslovakia, Bulgaria, Hungary, Rumania, Latvia, Lithuania, and Estonia we finally stood up to communism in Greece, Turkey, Iran, Berlin, and western Germany.

Knowing that communism thrives on economic and political chaos we gave economic aid through the ECA and with the North Atlantic Pact and the arms-implementation legislation, we have given moral and material support for the protection of western Europe and the Middle East from overt aggression. In that area we have given hope and support to those advancing the cause of a free world of freemen.

Munich certainly should have taught us that appeasement of aggression, then as now, is but surrender on the installment plan. Mr. Chamberlain, Prime Minister of Great Britain 10 years ago, may have sincerely thought that he was gaining "peace in our time" by consenting to the destruction of a free and independent Czechoslovakia by Nazi Germany. We know now that paying such international blackmail only increased later demands that made World War II inevitable.

The men in the Kremlin are as power hungry as the Nazis, and their system is as destructive of human liberty as was Hitlerism with which they were bedfellows while Poland was being dismembered in 1939. They have, however, learned some new techniques.

Communism is destructive of human liberty everywhere in the world. It is no less destructive in China or Korea than it is in Poland, Czechoslovakia, Latvia, Estonia, Lithuania, Hungary, Rumania, or Bulgaria. The pattern may differ slightly. In Poland the opposition leader, Mikolajczyk, was forced to flee; in Bulgaria Petkov was hanged; in Rumania the King was given a 2-hour ultimatum to change the government regardless of the constitution; in Czechoslovakia Masaryk's life was forfeited when it became apparent that coalition with communism would not work.

A Chinese official put it clearly by saying to me recently that there can be no real coalition with a tiger unless you are inside the tiger.

The President's State of the Union message of January 4 was notable for its silence on the question of China. In what we hope will be a free world of freemen does the administration have less concern with human liberty in Asia than it does in Europe? On what basis does the administration write off freemen in China?

Let me reread the cold type of the President's message to the Congress:

> While great problems still confront us, the greatest danger has receded—the possibility which faced us 3 years ago that most of Europe and the Mediterranean area might collapse under totalitarian pressure. Today the free peoples of the world have new vigor and new hope for peace.

Why no concern regarding the 400,000,000 people of China who have been dragged behind the iron curtain? International communism has already gained more in manpower and resources in Asia than it has lost in Europe, and it is on the march to even greater victories.

At a press conference this morning, the President made it clear that he backs the Far Eastern Division and Acheson policy of stopping further military aid to the Republic of China.

In Europe we have had a foreign policy in which the Republicans and the Democrats have contributed to the initiation and formulation of doctrines that are understandable. In the Far East there has been no bipartisan foreign policy. The Republicans in Congress have not been consulted in the moves leading up to the bankrupt policy which now stands revealed in all its sorry detail. The administration, and it alone, has the full responsibility for the debacle which has taken place on the continent of Asia and which day by day and hour by hour is endangering the future peace of the world and the security of this country. . . .

Our long-standing far eastern policy was first compromised at Yalta. We gave to the Soviet Union vital rights in Manchuria which were not ours to give. It was done without the consent or approval of the American Congress or the American people. It was done in violation of the open-door policy of John Hay and of Woodrow Wilson's concept of "open covenants, openly arrived at." The Yalta agreement made Soviet domination of Manchuria and other border provinces inevitable. It made possible Chinese Communist domination of the balance of continental China and has opened the door to bringing the entire continent of Asia, with more than a billion people and vast resources, into the orbit of international communism. Sitting with our American delegation at Yalta was Alger Hiss.

Following VJ-day the representatives of our Department of State persistently tried to get the Government of the Republic of China to form a coalition with the Communists. When they refused we placed an embargo against the shipments of any arms or ammunition to the legal government of the country while during those same months the Soviet army of occupation in Manchuria, as the result of the Yalta agreement, was turning over to the Communist forces large amounts of captured Japanese war stocks.

Like a person with a bad conscience, the State Department on August 6 released the China white paper. All the blame was placed on the National Government, then with its back to the wall. It was apparently issued with the hope that our own sorry part and share of responsibility might be overlooked.

That the National Government of China made mistakes, has had more than their share of Benedict Arnolds, and men who betrayed their trust needed no underscoring from us in the way and at the time it was done. Our own history also has examples of men who have betrayed their trust from Cabinet members down to ward bosses. We have also been plagued with racketeers, highwaymen, and 5-percenters at various times.

The basic objective the United States should have kept constantly in mind was to preserve a free, independent, united non-Communist China. In the postwar illness of that nation we prescribed that the strychnine of communism be taken. The State Department having contributed greatly to the Chinese disaster, still proclaims that we must follow a hands off policy, or that we must wait for the dust to settle, or we must investigate some more. Are they preparing for a post mortem rather than a consultation? . . .

In a very well-written article in the January 7 issue of the Saturday Evening Post, Joseph Alsop has this to say about State Department excuses as contained in the China white paper:

> But there is also one carefully concealed defect in the State Department argument. If you have kicked a drowning friend briskly in the face as he sank for the second and third times, you cannot later explain that he was doomed anyway because he was such a bad swimmer. The question that must be answered is not whether the Chinese did their best to save themselves, which they most certainly did not. The question is whether we did our best to save China.
>
> The answer to this question is contained in the strange, still secret inner history of our China policy. And this true history for which the State Department could find no room in all the 1,054 pages of the white paper may be simply, if grimly, summarized:
>
> Throughout the fateful years in China, the American representatives there actively favored the Chinese Communists. They also contributed to the weakness, both political and military, of the National Government. And in the end they came close to offering China up to the Communists, like a trussed bird on a platter, over 4 years before the eventual Communist triumph. . . .

It is a sad commentary that Britain, which itself was in such a desperate plight after Dunkerque, which joined us in complaining of Mussolini's stab in the back when France was down but not quite out, should now be contemplating abandoning the Republic of China and giving recognition, aid, and comfort to the Communists who are so closely allied with the same international Communist conspiracy that threatens human freedom in Europe.

Like Mr. Chamberlain at Munich, there are some in this country and in Great Britain who believe that by appeasing the Communists they may change their way of life. This is naive, and such a viewpoint is dangerous to the peace of the world and the security of this country.

First, the Communists will not be satisfied with mere de facto recognition. That will merely be the opening wedge for full de jure approval. When that happens, China's seat in the United Nations and on the Security Council becomes a Communist one. Every Chinese embassy and consulate in this and other western nations will become centers of Communist espionage and fifth-column activity as in the case of similar Soviet establishments. At the peace conference with Japan, the Soviet bloc will have another voice and vote to help destroy the job Gen. Douglas MacArthur has so ably done in that country.

If or when the British or the United States give them full recognition, the Chinese Communists will then consider it unfriendly unless their economic rehabilitation is financed. Such action would, of course, also increase their war potential, for electric-power development, railroads, mines, ports, and factories are important in both peace and war. The United States is the only nation capable of such financing.

Are we to be called upon to pay out substantial sums to help stop communism in Europe while financing communism in Asia—and with serious budget problems of our own? Are we to give arms and guaranties to western Europe to save that area from going behind the iron curtain while we or they accelerate the spread of Communism in Asia?

It is my judgment that history will record the recognition of Communist China as being as great a betrayal of human freedom as was the pact of Munich. . . .

The question is asked "Can anything be done at this late date?" I believe that it can. While desperate, the situation is not more desperate than it was at the time of Dunkerque or Valley Forge.

First, of course, we need a foreign policy in the Far East. We have none there today. As a basis for such a foreign policy, I suggest the following:

First. That we make clear that we have no intention of recognizing the Communist regime in China at this time nor in the immediate future and that we make known to the powers associated with us that we do not look with favor upon such recognition by others.

It is of course not sufficient merely to delay our own recognition if, with a wink of the eye or tongue in cheek the State Department leaves doubt in the minds of others as to the course of action we may pursue.

Second. That we have a major shakeup in the Far Eastern Division of the State Department. We cannot expect to get inspired leadership for a new policy in the Far East from those who have been receivers of the bankrupt policy we have been following.

Third. Our policy itself, of course, will have to be set by our constitutional officers, the President, his advisers, and the Congress. Once we have a foreign policy there is great need for it to be coordinated in both its economic and defense phases. As coordinator, either Gen. Douglas MacArthur or some other comparable figure should be selected so that in that area of the world the right hand will know what the left is doing.

Fourth. We should give supervised aid to the legal Government of China in the same way we gave it to the legal Governments of Greece and Korea when they were threatened by communism. I have never favored giving unsupervised assistance. A mission headed by a man of the caliber of General Wedemeyer could supervise the requests for aid, be sure that the Chinese Government was properly training the troops in the use of equipment, and make certain from a logistical point of view that the supplies were received at the points where they were needed.

ESSAYS

Warren I. Cohen of Michigan State University argues in the first essay that
Dean Acheson hoped to drive a wedge between the Soviet Union and the People's
Republic of China, with recognition of the PRC as one means. But President
Truman, McCarthyism, and the outbreak of the Korean War wrecked his plans.
William W. Stueck, Jr., of the University of Georgia does not agree that Acheson
was willing to deal with the Chinese Communists. He notes the consequences of
the United States failure to talk and speculates about what might have come
from such discussions. The last essay, by Steven I. Levine of American University, doubts the chances for accommodation, given Chinese Communist hostility
toward the United States.

Acheson's Search for Accommodation

WARREN I. COHEN

Acheson was a commanding presence as secretary of state. Nothing seems
clearer than the fact that the opinion neither of his subordinates, of Congress,
nor of the public, could sway him once he had made up his mind. The
president, however, open to such influences, could and did on occasion reject,
modify, or otherwise impose his wishes on Acheson's recommendations.

Acheson had little interest in Chinese affairs. In 1946, however, he had
worked in support of Marshall's effort to avert the civil war and had shared
the frustration Marshall suffered in his dealings with Chiang. He had no
intention of enduring any such nonsense in 1949. He was aware that the
Communists were on the verge of victory, regretted the situation, but was
quite content to follow the course upon which Marshall had settled. As new
questions arose, he relied for information and analysis on [Walton] Butterworth, who became his assistant secretary for Far Eastern affairs; Dean
Rusk, his deputy undersecretary and later Butterworth's successor; and his
close friend and alter ego Philip C. Jessup, appointed ambassador-at-large.
Although he looked less to Policy Planning than had Marshall, Acheson often
received ideas from [George F.] Kennan and from John P. Davies, the PPS
specialist on China. In 1950 John Foster Dulles was brought into the department, at Rusk's suggestion, to attempt to salvage bipartisan support for
policy toward Asia. Despised by Acheson, Dulles nonetheless served him
loyally, working primarily with Rusk and, to a lesser extent, with Jessup.

Eager to contain Soviet influence everywhere, Acheson was, however, an

From "Acheson, His Advisors, and China, 1949–1950" in *Uncertain Years: Chinese-
American Relations, 1947–1950*, edited by Dorothy Borg and Waldo Heinrichs (New
York: Columbia University Press, 1980). Reprinted by permission of the publisher.

Atlanticist for whom Western Europe was the highest priority. His principal concerns in 1949 were European recovery and creation of the North Atlantic Treaty Organization. Stopping communism across the Pacific was also highly desirable, but a task of lesser importance. He had little interest in Asia beyond a determination to link Japan, like Germany, to the West. Jessup, Rusk, Kennan, and Davies were troubled by his neglect of East Asia, but they had little effect on his policy recommendations prior to the Korean War. He allowed them only symbolic acts, shows of concern—nothing that required a major commitment of American resources or power. . . .

Between the time Acheson took office and the onset of the Korean War, the department's concerns regarding China fell into three general areas. First, there was a need to determine policy toward the retreating Kuomintang and whatever factions emerged. Second, a decision had to be made about Formosa. Third, policy toward the emerging Communist regime had to be defined. In each area Acheson's intent was thwarted, in several instances by the perceived need for temporary delays in order to win a national consensus, and in every instance by the Korean War and the Sino-American conflict that developed from it.

Ten days before Acheson was sworn in, the National Security Council (NSC) agreed to continue efforts to prevent China from becoming "an adjunct of Soviet power." Council members also agreed that efforts toward China would be "of lower priority" than efforts where the benefits to American security were "more immediately commensurate" with the expenditure of resources.

By the end of January [1949] all of China north of the Yangtze was in Communist hands and Mao's legions were massing at the river. Chiang went home to Fenghua and left the government in the hands of Li Tsung-jen, who began peace overtures to the Communists. To Acheson and others in Washington it seemed clear that the time had come to stop aid. On February 3 the NSC recommended that the United States suspend shipments to China. Several days later, however, Congressional leaders urged the president not to take any formal action. That their concern was not for the fortunes of the Kuomintang but rather to soothe their colleagues and constituents was manifest in their willingness to have shipments delayed by informal action. Truman accepted the advice. Aid would not be suspended, but ways would be found to slow shipments. American political leaders feared that a public announcement of the cessation of aid would lead to the immediate collapse of the Kuomintang regime, and that they would be held responsible. Acheson had his orders.

By the end of February General Albert C. Wedemeyer, more sympathetic to Chiang than most American leaders, had concluded that it would be worse than useless to send aid to Chiang's forces: it would be seized almost immediately by the Communists. In mid-March Acheson wrote to Senator Tom Connally, chairman of the Senate Foreign Relations Committee, to oppose a bill calling for $1.5 billion in aid for China, insisting that even massive military assistance would not reverse the tide. But he agreed that it would be undesirable to cut off aid to Kuomintang-controlled areas "precipitously." Several days later, addressing the committee in executive session, Acheson was franker. He reported that he was persuaded by his advisers "that at the present time to continue aid to anybody in China is going to have the opposite result from what we want to achieve."

A few weeks later Acheson indicated confidence that he had won the support necessary to end aid to the Kuomintang and to seek an accommodation with the Chinese Communists. He told Ernest Bevin, the British foreign secretary, that Chiang's regime was "washed up," that the Communists now had a free hand in China. The Chinese people were tired and further aid to the Kuomintang would anger them. "We had," he explained to Bevin, "abandoned the idea of supporting the regime and were only extending to June 2 a further 58 million dollars under the China Aid Act." It was difficult to withdraw support publicly, but he thought "the extreme supporters of Chiang Kai-shek in Congress were gaining a better appreciation of realities." Most significantly, Acheson promised Bevin, "The U.S. henceforth will pursue a more realistic policy respecting China."

In mid-April Wellington Koo, near despair over his failure to win adequate American support for his government, met with Dulles. He reported finding Acheson preoccupied with Europe and blamed Marshall's influence for the State Department's indifference to China's plight. Dulles agreed and added that Senator Arthur H. Vandenberg, the key Republican foreign policy spokesman in the Senate, would no longer press for aid. The State Department had persuaded Vandenberg that the Kuomintang could not win, no matter how much aid the United States sent.

By the spring of 1949 Acheson was persuaded that the consensus necessary to withdraw support from the Kuomintang had been obtained. On June 2, when the China Aid Act expired, the United States would cease wasting its resources. Kuomintang China was dead. There remained only the need for last rites, to persuade the American people. Acheson turned to an earlier recommendation by Kennan that the public be informed of the reasons for American policy before it was misled by partisan criticism. Marshall had read the suggestion to the cabinet in November 1948, but Truman had rejected it. The people needed the facts, but to reveal Chiang's ineptness and the corruption of his regime would be tantamount to the United States' delivering the final blow. Nine months later, however, Truman agreed that the time had come. He supported Acheson over the objections of the secretary of defense and the Joint Chiefs, and "The China White Paper" was published. Awareness of the ties between Chiang's lobbyists and Republican critics may have facilitated the decision.

Acheson's determination to publish the White Paper, despite concern over Mao's "leaning to one side" speech, strong opposition from the Pentagon, reservations within the department and on Capitol Hill, and while the Kuomintang still held Canton, is explicable only as a decision to drive in the last nail. He was determined to end American involvement in the Chinese civil war, to quash in advance any new onslaught by Chiang's American friends, and to prepare for an accommodation with the Communist regime. Acheson failed, but not for want of trying. His *bête noire,* Chiang Kai-shek, escaped to Formosa and reopened the issue on a basis less susceptible to Acheson's arguments. . . .

The principal reason for Acheson's determination to cut off aid to Chiang and to acquiesce in the fall of Formosa was the desire to establish the best possible relationship with Mao's regime. The Communist victory posed dangers for the United States because of evident Soviet influence among Mao's colleagues. Acheson and his advisers were eager to lessen that influence and to develop among the Chinese Communist leaders a sense of a need for ties to the West.

The State Department considered trade, recognition, and Chinese representation on the UN Security Council as means of achieving tolerable relations with the Communists. Trade would be used as a weapon, to demonstrate the extent of Chinese dependence on the West. Eventual recognition was assumed, but it would not be automatic. Recognition, too, might be useful as a lever with which to gain advantage for the United States. Policy on the Security Council representation question would have to be more flexible. The People's Republic might well be seated without American approval. There would be no attempt to use the veto.

A variety of domestic restraints and Chinese Communist actions delayed recognition, but these were diminishing in importance. There were indications that the United States would grant recognition to the People's Republic after the elections of November 1950. "Formal, regularized relations . . . not intimate but proper" were anticipated. The department assumed that Peking's representatives would represent China in the UN as early as February or March 1950. But Acheson's preparations for overcoming public and Congressional opposition to an accommodation with the Communists were halted by the coming of war in Korea and abandoned after Chinese intervention in that war.

Kennan and his staff set the tone for dealing with the Chinese Communists in November 1948. The Kuomintang government would soon disappear, and the United States should determine its policy on recognition when that happened. Aid to Chiang was useless, but American ends in China might be achieved by using economic bargaining power to exact concessions, presumably from the successor Communist regime.

Butterworth reflected the same position in talks with British officials in January and February 1949. They agreed that trade and recognition provided opportunities for bargaining. Butterworth was also prepared to cut off all Economic Cooperation Administration (ECA) operations in Communist-controlled areas to make it "just as difficult for the Communists as possible, in order to force orientation to the West." On the other hand, he favored restoration of trade relations with Communist China as "the most feasible means of maintaining contact" and thought it desirable to allow the Communists to import petroleum products "in order that they might develop a sense of dependence on the West."

The department's premises were detailed in NSC 41, drafted by the State Department in late February 1949. The goal was to prevent "Soviet domination of China for strategic ends." The alternatives posed were political and economic warfare to isolate and intimidate the Chinese, or restoration of economic relations and efforts to divide the Chinese and Russian Communists. The department insisted that the first course would force Mao into complete subservience to the Soviet Union, was obviously undesirable, and should not be risked except in extremis. The second alternative might produce an independent regime and was the policy to be pursued.

Reports from the field, from Moscow as well as from offices in China, reinforced hope of an independent Communist regime. There was evidence of tension between Russian and Chinese leaders. There was suspicion that Russian-controlled Chinese Communists were worried by Mao's apparent interest in mutually beneficial relations with the United States. John M. Cabot, consul-general at Shanghai after a tour in Yugoslavia, sent a number of thoughtful letters and cables indicating his belief that a Sino-Soviet split was inevitable. The critical question of *when* might be affected by American policy. In March Acheson authorized Ambassador J. Leighton Stuart to approach Communist leaders. He was cautioned to avoid any ultimatums and any publicity. Acheson was eager to explore issues with Mao and Chou En-lai, but reports of talks were to be sent "eyes only for the secretary." The American public and the president were not quite ready to acknowledge the conquerors.

In April, as the People's Liberation Army poised to cross the Yangtze, Acheson advised diplomats in China not to demand recognition of their official consular status from the Communists. Such action would convey a sense of "de jure relations in which we [are] unable [to] reciprocate," presumably because the Kuomintang still controlled China south of the Yangtze. After the Yangtze defenses were breached, Acheson raised with Stuart the question of de facto recognition. He was concerned about Communist attitudes toward American officials and property. Was de facto recognition the best hope for protecting American interests, or would the Communists become more demanding? Would they immediately want de jure recognition "which the United States might be unprepared to grant in absence some sense of international responsibility?" Stuart conceded that de facto recognition would probably lead to a more correct attitude on the part of the Communists, but only if it were treated as tantamount to de jure recognition. Stuart clearly preferred sharper bargaining before dispensing what he saw as a reward for good behavior. Increasingly, discussions in the department on how to handle the Chinese Communists seemed liked a seminar on adolescent psychology.

On June 1, O. Edmund Clubb, the consul-general at Peking, reported an unusual initiative attributed to Chou En-lai. Chou indicated, as Mao had on previous occasions, that he was interested in American trade and investment on terms of mutual advantage. But he also noted that there were party leaders opposed to friendly relations with the United States. A more forthcoming attitude would be welcome, timely, and mutually advantageous.

Acheson was in Paris when the department received and formulated a response to Chou's message. Clubb and Stuart advised the acting secretary to be wary. Clubb suspected the Communists wanted the best of both worlds, to obtain American aid while supporting the Soviet Union. Stuart wanted the Chinese to demonstrate their desire for good relations by their actions. The president agreed emphatically: there was to be no indication of any softening toward the Communists. Nothing came of Chou's demarche.

In May and June Stuart met several times with Huang Hua, his former student who was serving as chief of the Communists' Office of Alien Affairs. These meetings culminated in an invitation for Stuart to visit Yenching University in Peking, where he could expect to be welcomed by Mao and Chou. Word of the invitation generated excitement within the Department of State, but Butterworth and Davies feared an adverse public reaction. Davies thought Stuart should accept the opportunity to berate Mao and Chou about proper behavior and believed the public would approve a trip for that purpose. Butterworth devised an elaborate scheme for disguising the trip as a mission to rescue the staff of the Mukden consulate-general. The president would have none of it; "under no circumstances" was Stuart to visit Peking. An extraordinary opportunity to explore terms of accommodation was brushed aside, apparently because the president did not wish to be held responsible for applying the *coup de grâce* to the Kuomintang. But this was only one of several times Truman resisted department recommendations designed to improve relations with the Communists. Indeed it was only with great difficulty that Acheson was able to dissuade Truman from ordering Stuart to visit Kuomintang headquarters at Canton instead of Peking.

In an unrelated action on the day Acheson informed Stuart of the president's decision, Mao contributed to the difficulty of reaching an accommodation. He denounced the United States and declared that China would lean to the side of the Soviet Union; it would not allow itself to become dependent on the West. Acheson expected such rhetoric and had tried to prepare Congress and the president for it. In mid-March he had predicted to the Senate Foreign Relations Committee that Chinese Communist leaders, as they gained control of China, would "go out of their way to show their sympathetic attitude of cooperation with the Russians. I think they are going to show a considerable amount of hostility to us and to the West." As Sino-Soviet tensions developed, he expected the Chinese to become even more insistent on their kinship with the Russians. He would be patient. But if Acheson was unperturbed by Mao's speech, it nevertheless increased his problems in persuading the president, Congress, and the public of the wisdom of his course.

The equanimity with which Acheson approached policy toward China was not shared by most of his advisers. Kennan, Davies, Rusk, and Jessup feared that the apparent inaction of the United States in East Asia was upsetting to Americans and Asians. In July Kennan called for a "change of climate" in policy toward East and South Asia. Rusk converted Kennan's idea into a forty-seven-point "action program" that included a "declaration of nonrecognition" of Communist China, continued support for Kuomintang China in the UN, and assistance to "non-Communist China." In August Kennan, Davies, and Jessup devised a twenty-one-point program containing a call for a policy of "frank hostility to the Chinese Communists." They wanted to demonstrate American willingness to use force, to react with strength, "with majesty and greatness." A week later Davies suggested bombing a few installations in Manchuria to demonstrate that the United States would not tolerate the Chinese behaving like "bandits and blackmailers."

Acheson refused to encourage Truman to play Teddy Roosevelt and continued preparing the country for the accommodation with the People's Republic that he assumed was inevitable. Nonetheless his aides persisted in efforts to manipulate trade and recognition policies in order to reform Chinese Communist behavior and appease public, Congressional, and presidential opinion. In September a high-level department meeting concluded that the British were eager to normalize relations with China. Rusk and Butterworth urged delay, and Acheson agreed to ask Bevin to exact satisfactory performance on China's international obligations. He indicated to Bevin that it was of great importance to the United States to let the dust settle, to let events rather than an act of the West proclaim a Communist victory. Clearly, Acheson was prepared to wait until after the annihilation of Chiang Kai-shek and his forces, another inevitability he did not wish to delay.

A number of remarks attributed to the president in the summer and fall of 1949 indicated his preference for more active opposition to the Chinese Communists than Acheson was advocating. At least once there was a suggestion in his remarks of doubt that the department was following his wishes. Several weeks after denying permission for Stuart to go to Peking, Truman began pressing for revision of NSC 41, which had precluded economic warfare against the new regime. On October 1 he "indicated strongly" his desire that the department do nothing to subvert the Kuomintang blockade of mainland ports. Acting Secretary James E. Webb reported that "the President stressed again the fact that his policy was to permit the blockade to work effectively, to which policy he expected strict adherence." Two days later he remarked that the United States should be in no hurry to recognize the People's Republic, noting that the country had waited many years to recognize the Russian regime. Not long afterward, when Consul-General Angus Ward was imprisoned in Manchuria, Truman contemplated using force to liberate the consular staff.

In these circumstances, Acheson's failure to respond to the Chinese interest in recognition was less remarkable than his success in restraining his colleagues and the president from more aggressive action. He delayed two months before responding to the president's call for revision of NSC 41, and then argued against a change of policy. No recommendation for a show of force against the People's Republic went forward from the department. Instead, Acheson had a study prepared on recognition policy, lectured congressmen on the meaning of recognition, and used Jessup as choreographer for a series of elaborate dances that consumed approximately six months, their only significant result. He was confident that time was on the side of sensible policy and that his opponents understood precisely what he was doing. Wellington Koo complained bitterly as Jessup and outside consultants studied policy and as Jessup embarked on a sea voyage to examine conditions in East Asia. Koo realized that the department was stalling until everyone agreed it was too late to help Kuomintang China.

Keeping the door open for recognition of the People's Republic was a more difficult, and ultimately impossible, task. Nonetheless, the record of Acheson's efforts is clear. Throughout 1949 and the first half of 1950 he persisted in his attempt to persuade Truman that efforts to detach the Peking regime from Moscow did not constitute appeasement, that harassment would be a mistake. No doubt reluctantly, apprehensively, Truman stayed with him. When confronted with outrageous Chinese behavior, Acheson argued that vital American interests had not been affected, that policies likely to drive Mao closer to Stalin were not warranted. In May 1949, before the Ward case came to a head, he argued that it be viewed as a special situation. In November, as Ward was brought to trial and public outrage verged toward explosion, Acheson stressed the fact that no Americans had been killed in Communist-controlled areas. He argued that, considering the circumstances of revolution and civil war and the refusal of the United States to recognize the regime, American consular posts had "on the whole not fared badly." The public explosion came, but the torrents of abuse did not move him and he held the president's support.

In January 1950 both the department and the Communist regime misplayed a minor problem in Peking to the benefit of opponents of Sino-American accommodation. Acheson thought he had given the Communists a clear signal of American intent to establish formal relations as soon as practicable. But the Chinese were impatient and pressed the United States and other regimes that still withheld recognition, threatening to requisition their property in Peking, including the consular premises of the governments involved. Acheson devised a compromise that seemed sensible. The Communists were informed that they could take a large part of the area, but not the building the United States planned to use for its chancellery. Such an arrangement might give the Communists face without creating an uproar in the United States. The Peking regime was warned, however, that seizure of the building in question would be unacceptable and result in the withdrawal of all American diplomatic personnel in China. The Chinese seized the building and American officials were ordered out of China. Each side apparently thought the other was bluffing. The results were unfortunate, but neither Edmund Clubb in Peking nor Acheson perceived the action as a final break. Indeed, withdrawal had long been advocated by Jessup and others in the department as a means of avoiding incidents that would inflame public opinion against the Chinese.

A few weeks after the incident Trygve Lie, secretary general of the UN, met with Acheson to express his fear about the consequences. Acheson's "let the dust settle" speech of January 12 had reassured him about American intentions, but he feared Peking's action might complicate and delay a settlement. He feared the United States might try to keep the People's Republic out of the UN, resulting in a permanent Russian withdrawal. Rusk, who was present, indicated his expectation that "in a matter of several weeks seven members of the Security Council will have recognized the communist regime and when that happens a communist representative will be seated on a procedural vote." Rusk left no doubt that the United States regarded the issue as procedural and that "we would neither ourselves exercise the veto nor acquiesce in a veto by anyone else."

Rather than being distraught about the prospects for normalization of relations with the People's Republic, Acheson was anticipating better opportunities when Mao returned from his protracted negotiations with Stalin. He planted rumors of Stalin's attempts at extortion with Cyrus Sulzberger, Paris-based correspondent for the *New York Times*. But the alliance Mao and Stalin signed in February was clearly a setback. In April Clubb's informants gave him little hope for an early open break between Peking and Moscow. There appeared to be but a slight chance for a more conciliatory attitude toward the United States for several years. Still Acheson was in no hurry. Kuomintang resistance on the mainland had been virtually eliminated. Chiang's flight to Formosa was another complication, but the CIA estimated that the problem would disappear before the end of the year. Perhaps the president would be ready to act after the November elections. In the interim, nonrecognition might please the French, who were worried about Chinese support for Ho Chi Minh in Indochina. So long as Chiang was destroyed, so long as there was no chance of further involving the United States in the Chinese civil war, Acheson could wait. There was no compelling reason for more immediate action.

The war in Korea brought an end to Acheson's complacency about East Asia. His position on Formosa was immediately undermined and his efforts to hold course on recognition, UN representation, and aid to the Kuomintang ended in failure after the Chinese intervened. . . .

Acheson's goal was to reach an accommodation with the People's Republic under the most advantageous terms for the United States. He hoped to encourage the Peking regime to distance itself from the Soviet Union and to recognize the importance of its historic ties to the West. The quest for advantage doubtless contributed to delay, and ultimately to failure. But Acheson saw no reason to be eager about the normalization of relations with the new regime. His determination to proceed deliberately was strengthened when Mao and Chou indicated a desire for American aid and voiced the doctrinaire assumption that American capitalism required trade with China to avoid depression. He assumed that the Russians could not provide the economic and technical assistance China needed and that it would be useful for the People's Republic to perceive that it needed the United States more than the United States needed it. Such as awareness might prompt good behavior.

He opposed overt involvement with Formosa because the aim of American policy was to separate the People's Republic from Moscow's control, in part by focusing on Soviet imperialism. It was essential not to provide the Communists with a concrete anti-American issue. His interest in even covert operations to save Formosa vanished when he realized that Chiang would soon be ensconced there, that the native independence movement lacked the power to throw out the Kuomintang.

Acheson's confidence in his passive policy toward Asia was founded on his indifference to the region. He was not persuaded that much of consequence to the United States could happen on the Asian mainland. He was much more interested in British and French opinion, in pacifying major allies, than in the fate of Chiang Kai-shek or Southeast Asia. When his advisers became frantic in their concern over his disinterest, he agreed to exercises in political theater—invitations to Asian leaders, statements of the importance of Asia, and Jessup's extended tour. When Jessup reported that no major expenditure of American power or resources was required, only a little aid and a little psychological warfare, he was telling the secretary precisely what he wanted to hear.

Acheson was also certain of his ability to cope with Congressional and public opinion. Indeed, public opinion polls showed a low regard for Chiang and little inclination to aid him—before the Korean War. The polls did indicate opposition to recognition of the Communist regime or a place for it in the UN, but it was reasonable to assume these reservations would disappear when Chiang did. Republican opposition to his policies and attacks by McCarthyites irritated Acheson, but he was not apprehensive. He had worked with Vandenberg and Dulles to surmount such problems in the past, and he assumed "the primitives" were still manageable.

The second important ingredient in American policy toward China appears to have been Truman's greater responsiveness to domestic pressures. Congressional leaders feared the disruptive influence of the China bloc, and Democrats concerned about reelection in 1950 were uneasy. Truman delayed the termination of aid to the Kuomintang and prevented steps that might have led to an early normalization of relations with the Communists. Acheson and Truman thought they had time, that foreign policy goals would not be jeopardized by obeisance to temporary domestic political needs.

In the spring of 1950 there seemed to be a race between Rusk's efforts to change policy and the tolling of the bells that would sound Chiang's doom. Delays caused by the inability to get the desired responses from Mao, by Truman, perhaps also by French apprehension about Peking's intentions in Southeast Asia allowed a third ingredient—war in Korea—to win a reprieve for Chiang. But even the coming of war in Asia did not preclude accommodation with the People's Republic. Acheson worked desperately to keep that option retrievable, and he might well have succeeded had it not been for the decision to send UN forces across the 38th parallel [in Korea]. Even then Acheson tried to stave off an association with Chiang that would prevent a settlement with the Chinese Communists.

Acheson's performance was not perfect, but it was perfectly creditable until the decision to cross the 38th parallel. Conceivably Rusk understated the danger of Chinese intervention. Perhaps Acheson deferred to a Pentagon led by Marshall and Deputy Defense Secretary Robert A. Lovett, two of the few men he respected. Or, most obviously, the temptation to disarm domestic critics by "liberating" Korea proved irresistible. But Acheson's response to Chinese intervention was senseless. He knew full well that the United States, thanks to MacArthur, was sending confusing signals to Peking. In the heat of battle and bearing a burden of guilt as Americans died at Chinese hands, he blamed the Chinese for their anger at the United States. He assumed it would take too long for the Sino-Soviet split to manifest itself. Mao might be independent, but he was intensely anti-American and his hostility had to be reciprocated, had to be the basis of policy. Nonetheless, Acheson refused alliance with Kuomintang China, leaving that mistake for the succeeding administration.

In 1951 Acheson and the Truman administration squared off against the plague of McCarthyism, a kind of public constraint he could never have imagined and could not ignore. By its disastrous decision to cross the 38th parallel the administration had rearmed the "primitives"—and it spent its last years staggering under McCarthy's attack.

The American Failure to Negotiate

WILLIAM W. STUECK, JR.

The issue of political relations with a Chinese Communist regime was closely tied to commercial matters. The Communists might survive a Western economic boycott, but State Department officials believed that the new masters of China would at least temporarily want trade with the capitalist powers. Yet, during late 1948 and early 1949, as the Communists moved into cities of Manchuria and North China in which American consular personnel resided, they refused to acknowledge the official standing of the representatives of foreign governments. Communist leaders also announced their intention to abrogate U.S. treaties with Nationalist China.

American officials deeply resented this attitude. Not only were representatives of the United States accustomed to favored treatment in China, they, as well as top policymakers in Washington, regarded the upholding of treaty obligations as "basic to relations among modern States." This view, together with the belief that, for commercial reasons, the Communists would soon adopt a less extreme course, produced a tough position regarding the formal recognition of Peking. As Ambassador Stuart put it, "the Communists, rather than nations with well-established tradition[s] and accepted international standards," should be placed "on trial." In early May 1949, Acheson decided that the United States should not initiate moves toward recognition, and he instructed American officials to impress upon Western European govern-

From The Road to Confrontation: American Policy Toward China and Korea, 1947–1950 by William W. Stueck, Jr. Copyright 1981 The University of North Carolina Press. By permission of the publisher.

ments the desirability of developing a "common front" on the issue. Weeks before the secretary, responding to political pressures at home, outlined publicly the criteria for establishing political relations, he privately had adopted the Jeffersonian model. A Communist regime would be judged in three areas: its capacity to control the territory it purported to govern, its "ability and willingness . . . to discharge its international obligations," and the "general acquiescence" of the people of the country under its rule.

This attitude led to rejection of an apparent opportunity for an American official to talk directly to Mao and other top men in Peking. Ironically, just after the United States moved to create a united front among the Western powers on the recognition question, Huang Hua, head of the Communist Alien Affairs Bureau in Nanking, approached Ambassador Stuart. On 13 May, the two men talked for nearly two hours. Raising the matter of recognition, Huang expressed much interest in Communist relations with the United States on a basis of "equality and mutual benefit." Stuart outlined the criteria recently established in Washington. The Chinese official then apologized for a recent incident in which Communist soldiers had trespassed on Stuart's living quarters.

Then, at the end of the month, Chou En-lai, a powerful figure in the Chinese Communist Party, made an indirect approach to the American consulate general at Peking through Michael Keon, an Australian journalist employed by the United Press. Chou talked of a division within the Communist camp between a liberal group, of which he was a leader, and a radical faction, headed by Liu Shao-chi. The liberals desired friendly relations with the Western democracies, especially the United States and Great Britain, as a means of obtaining the assistance necessary for economic reconstruction at home. The radicals demurred, desiring a close alliance with the Soviet Union. The State Department authorized O. Edmund Clubb, the consul general at Peking, to respond that Washington hoped for amicable relations with the new China on the basis of "mutual respect" and "equality," but was deeply disturbed by Communist treatment of American representatives in the country and propaganda attacks on the United States. President Truman approved this reply, though he emphasized that Clubb must avoid any indication of a "softening" American attitude toward the Communists. When Clubb sought to transmit the message directly to Chou or his secretary, however, the Communist leader abruptly broke off contact.

In the meantime, Stuart's talks with Huang in Nanking had continued. On 28 June, only days after Chou had squelched his own initiative in Peking, Huang told the ambassador that Mao would welcome him in the northern city if he wished to visit Yenching University. This proposal was a response to a query from Philip Fugh, Stuart's secretary and confidant, regarding the feasibility under present circumstances of the ambassador's annual July pilgrimage to his former school. Stuart immediately cabled Washington for instructions. In the State Department, both Butterworth and John Paton Davies considered the invitation to be significant, but they feared the domestic reaction if Stuart accepted. They proposed to skirt this problem. The ambassador could stop in Peking after traveling to Mukden to pick up Angus Ward, the American consul general there, who, along with his staff, was being held under house arrest; or Washington could announce that Stuart had gone to Peking to read Communist leaders "the riot act" regarding mistreatment of American diplomats.

On 1 July, however, Acheson wired Stuart and stated that a decision had been reached at the "highest level" against a journey to Peking. Communist attitudes toward American officials in China, of which the Ward case was only the most extreme expression, and toward treaties concluded by the National government, were foremost in reaching this verdict. On 16 June 1949, President Truman had instructed Webb to be "most careful not to indicate any softening toward the Communists but to insist on judging their intentions by their actions." A trip by Stuart to Peking also might have disrupted American efforts to unite Western governments on a cautious policy regarding recognition, and, to Acheson, a united front was a prerequisite to applying effective pressure on the Communists. Moreover, the Communists had not yet officially proclaimed themselves the government of China. The United States continued to recognize the National government. A trip to Peking by the American ambassador could not be kept secret, and Stuart was known to be inclined to deviate from instructions. His journey would detract from the already diminished prestige of the Nationalists and bolster the Communists at a time when their capacity to rule China remained uncertain. In a narrow legal sense, talks between the United States and a Chinese party, against the wishes of the recognized government, were inappropriate.

From the standpoint of politics in the United States, the trip would add fuel to the already intense attacks from Capitol Hill on Truman administration China policy. On 24 June, twenty-two Senators, including six Democrats, sent a letter to the president urging him to withhold recognition of the Communists. A week later, on the very day that the proposed Stuart trip to Peking was rejected, Acheson wrote to Senator Connally outlining the previously established criteria for recognition; the secretary assured him he would consult the Foreign Relations Committee before acting on the matter. The North Atlantic Treaty was then before the Senate, and the military assistance program, considered essential to give teeth to the pact, had not yet been sent to Congress. The specter, which had been so pervasive in late 1947 and early 1948, of a China bloc on Capitol Hill withholding support for critical enterprises in Europe, reappeared.

Yet domestic political concerns probably only reinforced Truman's and Acheson's inclination against the Huang overture. Had they believed that a major opportunity was at hand to advance American interests in China, they surely would have moved with less dispatch to stifle it. Certainly they would have explored the possibility of using Clubb at Peking to initiate talks with Communist leaders, a procedure that stood an excellent chance of remaining secret. If revealed to the public, it could be explained away, both to international lawyers and hostile politicians, far more easily than the Stuart trip. In all likelihood, Acheson advised Truman to reject the Huang initiative, and the president, already inclined in that direction, agreed. To them, a more positive response might encourage the Communists to persist in their aggressive behavior toward American officials in China, and undermine administration efforts to maintain a united Western front on recognition.

Both temperamentally and intellectually, Acheson was poorly suited to deal in an astute manner with the Communists. For one thing, he was preoccupied with the European theater. It was there, he felt, that the great issues of international politics would be played out. Furthermore, as Dean Rusk noted many years later, Acheson never had much respect for Asian peoples. He was a Europeanist not only in American foreign policy, but in culture as well. Finally, he had a passion for order. "In fact, I was always a conservative," he was to declare in 1969: "I sought to meet the Soviet menace and help create some order out of the world. I was seeking stability and never had much use for revolution. As a friend once said, we had plenty of chaos, but not enough to make a world." From this perspective, it was up to Communist China to demonstrate its worthiness to enter into the family of nations. Although the secretary of state was far from inflexible on China policy, neither was he anxious to explore every possible opportunity for constructive relations with the Communists. . . .

Few American decisions toward China in the postwar period were as unfortunate as the outright rejection of the Huang overture. To be sure, much of Communist behavior in preceding months evinced strong hostility toward the United States. Then, on 1 July—and probably unknown to Truman and Acheson at the time of their decision—Mao published an essay, "On People's Democratic Dictatorship," in which he asserted that the United States was the "one great imperialist power" remaining on earth. Because America sought "to enslave the world," he claimed, China must ally itself "with the Soviet Union, with every New Democratic country, and with the proletariat and broad masses in all other countries."

Such statements, however, do not eliminate the possibility that a careful probing of Peking's position in the summer of 1949 could have been useful to the United States. As John M. Cabot, the outspoken American consul general in Shanghai, observed, "Virulent anti-American propaganda is natural in view of our aid to the Nationalists." That aid was ineffectual in sustaining the Nationalists in China, but it added significantly to the anti-Communist resistance there. Even so, Communist leaders expressed interest in relations with the United States. On 15 June, Mao stated in a speech that his regime was

> willing to discuss with any foreign government the establishment of diplomatic relations on the basis of the principles of equality, mutual benefit and mutual respect for territorial integrity and sovereignty, provided it is willing to sever relations with the Chinese reactionaries, stops conspiring with them or helping them and adopts an attitude of genuine, and not hypocritical, friendship toward People's China.

Other evidence existed that the Communists were, as Stuart put it, "far from a Soviet Punch and Judy show." Clearly they were not anxious to eliminate the American presence in China. Throughout 1949, the Communist attitude toward American missionaries encouraged them to remain in China. Some American-owned businesses had similar experiences. Relations between the Peking regime and the Shanghai Power Company, for instance, remained smooth for months after the May 1949 Communist takeover of Shanghai.

Talks with Communist leaders could have served a variety of purposes. They could have been used to protest the treatment of American representatives in China. To avoid conveying a sense of American weakness or desperation, the United States could have held to a firm position on this issue. Top officials in Peking might well have demonstrated flexibility on the matter. It was by no means certain, after all, either then or later, that the harassment of American officials represented a centrally coordinated policy of the Communists or merely the independent acts of local forces.

Acheson could have minimized confusion and resentment among Western European nations by keeping their leaders informed of the proceedings. The mere fact of discussions in Peking need not have detracted from caution and unity on the recognition question. In fact, Peking talks might actually have strengthened Western harmony. If they went poorly, tendencies, already apparent in Great Britain and France, to open relations with the Communists once they formed a government, might have been weakened.

On the other hand, conversations in Peking might have been a basic step toward mutual toleration between Communist China and the West. Washington's failure to pursue discussions diminished such prospects. As Cabot noted, the out-and-out rejection of the Huang overture may "have placed those Communists favoring better relations with the West in an impossible situation." The American response was especially damaging because the ambassador's secretary had initiated the idea of a Stuart visit to Peking. The Communists probably viewed the suggestion as a concrete overture by the United States. When Washington squelched it, therefore, Peking was understandably embarrassed and displeased. Indeed, between July and September 1949 there emerged little new evidence that Communist leaders desired a "working relationship with the United States." Even Chou En-lai made strong anti-American speeches. And Communist officials in Mukden, who on 21 June had notified Ward that transportation facilities would be made available for him and his staff to leave the city, hardened their position toward the American diplomat. Although a variety of considerations may have dictated against Stuart traveling to Peking, Acheson should at least have communicated to the Communists that the United States desired talks but wanted, for the present, to pursue them through Clubb.

Direct contacts between the United States and the Communist Chinese were especially desirable in view of continued American aid to Chiang. In the absence of diplomatic exchanges between Peking and Washington, Communist leaders inevitably saw an American plot behind every Nationalist move. In late June, for example, in an effort to impede Communist efforts to rule China, the Nationalists blockaded Shanghai. The action consisted of both air and naval maneuvers to prevent foreign ships from unloading cargoes there. Although the United States did not approve the move, the Communists soon labeled it as American-inspired. This characterization may have been part of a Communist strategy of exploiting popular resentments against foreigners for the purpose of building unity at home. But past American support for the Nationalists—which continued, albeit at a low level—coupled with Washington's rejection of Peking's overtures, made it just as likely that the Communists truly believed that the United States was responsible for the blockade.

In addition to the possibility that talks would have increased Communist understanding of the American position, they also might have added to the Truman administration's grasp of events in China. Washington's perceptions of the Communists already had suffered from insufficient contact. Although the State Department had tentatively concluded—perhaps in part because of the recent example of Yugoslavia—that, in a positive sense, there was little the United States could or need do to influence Communist relations with the Soviet Union, more extensive knowledge might have led to a different judgment. As *New York Times* correspondent Seymour Topping has noted, even if the Truman administration could not have influenced Mao "to adopt a neutral position in the East-West struggle," conversations with the Communist leader might have "led at least to the establishment of a channel of communication between Peking and Washington." "If Americans had continued to talk to the Chinese Communists," Topping maintains, "many of the misunderstandings and much of the agony in Asia over the next two decades might have been averted." . . .

The administration's top priority was to maintain a united front against early recognition. The American effort faced serious difficulties, for the Labor government in Great Britain, in the face of pressures from commercial interests at home, leaned toward the establishment of relations with the Mao government. India's Prime Minister Jawaharlal Nehru also favored quick action. A succession of other Western European and Asian governments undoubtedly would follow the British and Indian lead. Rather than planning to move with the tide, Acheson summoned his persuasive powers in an attempt to reverse it. He failed in the endeavor; India recognized the People's Republic in December, and Great Britain took the same course a week later. By 18 January 1950, nine more non-Communist regimes had taken similar action.

Acheson's stand enjoyed widespread congressional and public support. Gallup polls of the summer and fall of 1949 indicated that Americans with opinions on the matter—only about 60 percent of those questioned—opposed recognition by more than a two to one margin. In late November, the Committee to Defend America by Aiding Anti-Communist China launched a "nationwide drive" against recognition with a rally at Carnegie Hall in New York. Several members of Congress attended the event. On 29 December, Senator Connally, following the overwhelming opinion expressed in letters to him from private citizens, announced his opposition to recognition.

James Reston, Washington correspondent for the *New York Times,* reported that State Department officials conceded in private that the domestic climate alone was delaying American recognition. As earlier, however, this consideration merely reinforced Acheson's inclinations, for Communist China's comportment in international matters genuinely disturbed him. On 24 October 1949, Angus Ward was jailed in Mukden for an alleged assault on a former Chinese servant at the American consulate. The State Department managed to obtain his release a month later, but Communist aggressiveness toward American officials and property in China did not end. On 14 January 1950, the Chinese government seized American consular compounds in Peking. In response to this action, and to the termination two months later of American radio communications with its representatives on the mainland, the United States withdrew completely from China. To the secretary of state, these were only the most overt manifestations of a generally intolerable state of mind that prevailed within the new government. Although he did not desire to slam the door permanently on American recognition, a halt to the "active abuse of us" in Peking was a prerequisite to a reevaluation of his position.

In early 1950, there was little movement on the question. Acheson toyed with the idea of using continued Nationalist air attacks on Shanghai—which often damaged American property—as a pretext for a total break with the Nationalist government, but such a break never occurred. In March, on the eve of Clubb's final departure from Peking, the secretary of state suggested that the consul general seek "an informal discussion with high Commie authorities of outstanding points of friction" between the United States and the new regime. Acheson emphasized, however, that Clubb must avoid "any inference [that] such [a] discussion constituted [a] move toward recognition or is a preliminary to such a move," or that the overture resulted from Communist "pressure" or American "weakness." Concern for American credibility abroad remained a barrier to flexible diplomacy.

In early April, Communist Chinese officials made it clear that termination of United States support for Chiang was a quid pro quo for talks on other issues. For all practical purposes, this exchange closed the matter. Clubb left China before the end of the month. Intent on avoiding any implication that Communist pressure could soften American policy, Acheson held firmly to the view that the Mao regime must submit to generally accepted standards of international conduct before the United States would talk about halting aid to the Nationalists and recognizing Peking. If the domestic political factor was critical, it was so only in an indirect sense: the American failure during 1949 to abandon the Nationalists completely—which was partially a result of pressures at home—influenced the Communist attitude toward the United States which, in turn, shaped the State Department position on relations with the Mao regime.

Another factor early in the fall of 1949 concerned pockets of armed resistance to the Communists in China. Although American officials recognized the probable futility of such activity, they did not want to openly discourage it. The desire remained strong to make the road to power of the Communists as rocky as possible. By mid-November, however, this consideration was no longer a significant impediment to recognition.

Concern for resistance to Communism on China's borders continued to influence Acheson's deliberations. On 16 December, he sent telegrams to his representatives in Southeast Asia requesting their views on the impact of American recognition. In the next two weeks, the secretary received replies from the consul general in Saigon, the chargé in Burma, and the ambassadors to Thailand and the Philippines. All of them emphasized the negative impact early recognition might have on efforts to bolster anti-Communist forces south and east of China's borders. This negative consideration took on decisive weight when combined with the prevailing State Department view that little could be done, in a positive vein, to alter the essentially hostile attitude of the Communists toward the United States.

From a domestic political standpoint, the Truman administration's best opportunity to talk to Peking was in the last months of 1949. The Communist government had been officially established, and the Atlantic pact and the Military Assistance Plan had passed Congress. Public and congressional opinion did not necessitate a negative policy on recognition. In October, for instance, the State Department's Office of Public Opinion Studies reported that "most observers" in the press, while seeing "little need for haste, . . . expected eventual *de facto* recognition as the most 'realistic' course." Even after the Ward case made headlines in late October, most commentators "did not discount the possibility or desirability of recognition at some time in the future." Most Asian experts in the academic community, most Protestant church organizations, and many businessmen with interests in China favored early recognition. Admittedly, Catholic organizations and much of organized labor disagreed, as did large pluralities of those Americans queried by pollsters. The firmness of much of this opposition, however, especially in the general citizenry, may be doubted. Recognizing Peking would not take money or jobs away from many Americans, nor would it lead directly to physical setbacks to the security of the United States. Surely a public-relations offensive by the administration in favor of recognition would have had some impact.

Furthermore, if the hostility of the Chinese Communists toward the United States was related to American hostility toward them, and if the antagonism of many Americans toward recognition derived in part from Peking's antagonism to the United States, then American overtures to Mao might have led ultimately to a decline of public opposition to relations with the new government. In the absence of American initiatives toward Peking, on the other hand, Communist hostility was virtually certain to continue, as was the tendency of the American public to oppose recognition. In fact, much can be said for the argument that the Truman administration's best chance of overcoming the charge that it had "lost" China rested in the cautious but active pursuit of rapprochement with the Communists.

What were the prospects for rapprochement? Although the hostile acts in

Mukden in late October 1949 and in Peking in the following January indicated to many the total hostility of the Communists, it remains uncertain that the incidents reflected decisions by a unified national leadership. One plausible explanation of the Ward affair is that Kao Kang, the pro-Russian head of the Northeastern People's Government, which was seated in Mukden—a government that had been established in late August and that temporarily maintained a degree of autonomy—took the action without prior approval from Peking. Clubb believed that the Soviet Union had instigated Ward's arrest in retaliation for the prosecution in the United States of Valentin Gubichev, a Russian citizen who the Kremlin asserted had diplomatic immunity. The State Department's Office of European Affairs suspected a direct connection between the Ward case and the October 1949 arrest in the United States of officials in the Soviet-owned Amtorg Trading Corporation for failing to register as foreign agents. Whatever the reasons for Ward's arrest, its occurrence so soon after Clubb had seen evidence that the Communists genuinely desired to establish relations with the United States suggests that powerful forces were pulling in opposite directions within China. Whether or not the United States could have influenced the situation remains a mystery. It is certain, however, that in October 1949 the State Department rejected an opportunity to explore the possibility.

Initially, Clubb, based on information from a "reliable source," interpreted events in Peking during January 1950 as representing a Communist effort to pressure the United States into recognizing the new regime. British consular property had not been confiscated, he observed, and this fact appeared to be related to London's recognition of the Communists. Years later, Clubb suggested that confiscation of American consular property was the brainstorm of a faction within the Chinese Communist party, rather than the act of a monolithic leadership. The move, after all, came while Mao was in Moscow attempting to negotiate a treaty of alliance with the Russians. The time it took to achieve this purpose—nearly two months—and the meager assistance received by China as a result of the Treaty of Friendship, Alliance, and Mutual Assistance that was signed on 14 February, indicates that all was not smooth in the Sino-Soviet relationship. Prior to the emergence of the pact, the State Department had reliable reports that Mao was seriously dissatisfied with the Soviet position on several points. During the previous fall, Clubb's contacts in Peking had indicated that the Chinese leader was a "moderate" on the question of relations with the United States. It is unlikely that such a man would choose the middle of tough discussions with the Kremlin to intentionally burn all bridges to Washington.

Sino-American talks in Peking in October 1949 would have run into difficulties in two areas: continued American assistance to the Nationalists and the status of treaties between the United States and the Chiang regime. Agreement could have come only through concessions on both sides. The United States undoubtedly would have been expected to end economic and military aid to Taiwan. Past Sino-American agreements would have needed to be renegotiated. Pressures from the pro-Soviet faction in China and the China bloc in the United States made flexibility difficult for either government.

Nevertheless, an exchange of views might have shown compromise to be possible. For instance, the United States might have offered to end all assistance to the Nationalists after 15 February 1950, the termination date for the commitment of funds through the China Aid Act. The United States might also have agreed to revise old pacts between the two countries, provided that changes were more of form than of substance. In a Sino-American agreement of 1943, the United States had renounced the most blatant privileges in the "unequal treaties" of the nineteenth and early twentieth centuries, but dissatisfaction remained among the Communists in certain areas, including the status of part of the United States consular compound in Peking, which had been seized in 1900 as a barracks for American troops in the foreign intervention against the Boxer Rebellion. A protocol of 1901 had given the United States title to this land, and the agreement of 1943, though calling for an end to all rights received in the earlier pact, provided for the continued American use of property allocated for its diplomatic quarters. It may be wondered here if relatively minor concessions by Washington would have satisfied Communist determination to remove all vestiges of "imperialist" domination. A demonstrated willingness on the part of the United States to discuss the matter might at least have prevented precipitous action such as occurred on 14 January 1950.

Perhaps the Communists, fearing the Kremlin's reaction, would have shied away from serious talks with the United States. The Soviets maintained a strong, possibly even dominant, presence in Manchuria, and—in the aftermath of Yugoslavia's revolt against Stalin's direction—were particularly sensitive to any Peking flirtations with the West. Walter McConaughy, who during the previous summer had replaced Cabot as consul general at Shanghai, had information that Mao's trip to Moscow was the result of a "strong and rather sudden . . . pressure" from the Kremlin in response to "moves" by Great Britain and other non-Communist nations toward recognition and an impending visit by Philip Jessup to the western Pacific. On the other hand, McConaughy also reported a "rapidly swelling tide [of] Chinese charges and bitterness re[garding] Soviet greed [and] encroachments" in Manchuria. Had Washington demonstrated greater flexibility toward the new regime, it might have evaluated its options somewhat differently.

But the cold war had so come to dominate Acheson's mentality that common bargaining was unthinkable with a Communist government that repudiated widely accepted standards of international conduct—standards, by the way, that China had had no role in constructing—and showed open allegiance to Moscow. To Acheson, there was little to discuss and nothing to concede. If "keeping a foot in the door" and avoiding the diversion of potential Chinese irredentist sentiments against Russia in the north were of sufficient worth to merit a degree of restraint on the part of the United States, they warranted little in the way of positive effort. And Acheson received little pressure within the administration, from either above or below, to loosen his stance.

No Lost Chance: Chinese Anti-Americanism

STEVEN M. GOLDSTEIN

The Communist armies that crossed the Yangtze in April 1949 were well disciplined, battle-hardened troops. They were euphoric as they finally entered China's great cities to garner the fruits of their victory. They were also highly politicized armies. For nearly three years the troops had been lectured on the indignities visited upon the Chinese nation by the imperialist United States. Awaiting them in the cities were workers who shared their intense anti-Americanism.

Anti-Americanism had been strong at the grass-roots level among the Chinese Communists ever since 1945–46. In August 1946, Chou En-lai candidly stated to Ambassador Stuart that resentment against the presence of American troops in China was "hotter among the lower classes than the higher classes of Communists." By the beginning of 1949 hostility to the United States was rampant among the masses, especially in the major Chinese cities that contained large foreign communities. Missionaries, according to their own accounts, had to bear the brunt of much popular ill will despite the restraining efforts of Communist leaders. In Nanking members of the United States Embassy were targets of anti-American outbursts from middle- and low-ranking Communist officials. In Shanghai the pent-up animosity of the workers toward the United States erupted in spontaneous demonstrations after the Communists took over the city. Leftist tendencies pervaded the workers' movement, anxious to settle scores with foreign and domestic entrepreneurs.

Prominent among the foreigners who had expected to stay in China after the Communists came to power were American businessmen in the main urban centers. Many were eager to do business with the new China. In their own eyes, they had been compassionate observers of the Chinese scene and were now prepared to make concessions to the Chinese Communists' sensitivities. Still, like most foreign residents in China they had, consciously or unconsciously, become accustomed to occupying a highly privileged position and were unprepared to cope with the broad-based antiforeign feeling that developed in 1949 and quickly led to the elimination of their special status. By the end of the year most of the American businessmen who originally intended to remain in China had returned to the United States.

Much of the anti-American and antiforeign outburst that occurred in 1949 was clearly contrary to the wishes of the CCP leadership. In the early months of 1949 the CCP had hoped to differentiate between the imperialist governments and their people. While warning the Communist troops before they entered the cities against hostile acts likely to be instigated by foreign governments they also instructed them "to protect the lives and property" of all

From "Chinese Communist Policy Toward the United States: Opportunities and Constraints, 1944–1950" in *Uncertain Years: Chinese-American Relations, 1947–1950,* edited by Dorothy Borg and Waldo Heinrichs (New York: Columbia University Press, 1980). Reprinted by permission of the publisher.

foreign nationals in China. In the spring of 1949 Mao himself wrote: "The Chinese people wish to have friendly cooperation with the people of all countries and to resume and expand international trade in order to promote economic prosperity."

The distinction between imperialist governments and their nationals proved, however, difficult to make in practice, especially in relation to the United States. Given the intensity of their feeling against the United States, the Chinese people were in no mood to draw fine lines between official and unofficial America. American nationals in China were beneficiaries of the unjust, imperialist system. If the CCP had been conciliatory toward individual American businessmen, many Chinese would have felt that the Party was violating one of its most vital tenets: the eradication of imperialism in China. To recognize or even merely to reform the old commercial system in China—a system which many Americans and other Westerners regarded as essential for the conduct of business—was patently a political impossibility. As a member of the Democratic League, one of the Chinese political parties then outlawed by the Kuomintang, reported to a U.S. official:

> General intransigence of labor whether under foreign or Chinese employment is exploiting opportunity to extent which Communists disapprove but cannot afford suppress, irrespective rights and wrongs, for fear seeming to champion capitalists, imperialists, and losing urgently needed mass support.

The Party leaders not only recognized the political dangers of modifying their anti-imperialist position but also realized the benefits that might be obtained from capitalizing on it. The civil war had entered a crucial phase. The Communists were now in the cities, the very places where they had the most to gain from demonstrating their loyalty to the anti-imperialist cause. Throughout the summer of 1949 the Chinese Communist press prominently published accounts of incidents in which Westerners, who had allegedly mistreated Chinese, were forced to pay compensation, indicating that the day of Western supremacy in China was over. Accounts of this nature merely intensified the public's hostility toward foreigners and thus committed the Party even more deeply to opposing the imperialists.

Domestic political considerations, therefore, left the CCP little room for making any adjustments in its relations with Americans. Moreover the actions of the United States Government, as interpreted by the CCP, most certainly did not justify any moderation of its anti-American policy. America's global policy continued to be bellicose, as evinced by the founding of NATO. Its China policy was seen as no different. As noted above, from the end of 1948 the Party leaders had predicted that the hostility of the United States government to the CCP would increase as the defeat of the Kuomintang drew nearer. By mid-summer of 1949 they felt their predictions had been substantiated to an alarming degree. The Truman administration was apparently acquiescing in the naval blockade imposed by the Kuomintang in June against the ports under Chinese Communist control and in August the State Department issued the famous White Paper.

From the Chinese Communists' point of view it would be difficult to imagine a more inflammatory document than the White Paper. The CCP immediately launched a massive "anti-White Paper" campaign. A large body of documentation was produced to substantiate the oft-made charge that the United States must bear a major share of the responsibility for the civil war in China. The campaign was above all an attack on the hope expressed in the White Paper that "democratic individualism" would emerge in China and that the Chinese Communists would follow the road of Titoism. This American approach intensified a long-held CCP concern, and the Chinese Communists asserted that in attempting to foster "democratic individualism" (which they translated as "democratic individualists") the United States was trying to construct a fifth column in China. They moreover took the occasion of a renewal of the anti-Tito campaign by the Soviet bloc to reemphasize their earlier position that to advocate Titoism was to be ensnared by an imperialist trick to win China over to the American side. In the international world, they were convinced, there was no middle ground between the reactionary and democratic camps. Any Chinese who favored neutrality was at best unpatriotic, at worse treasonous.

As 1949 developed there seemed to be little incentive for the CCP to change its anti-American posture. Domestic restraints existed and American actions—in China and the world—conformed to the adversary relationship the CCP anticipated would develop as their victory grew nearer. China would have to confront the forces of imperialism. . . .

The American side of the story is told elsewhere in this volume. As the civil war developed and the Communists gained the upper hand, the United States government was forced to keep its distance from the CCP. While public opinion was generally permissive, the pro-KMT lobby in Congress was strong—or at least appeared so to the policymakers in Washington. The president and the State Department were still reluctant to give a wartime ally the coup de grâce by dealing with its enemy. In addition the administration's options were limited by foreign policy commitments elsewhere. It was difficult to maintain simultaneously an anti-Communist posture in Europe and an accommodating position toward a major Communist movement in Asia. In short it was impossible, in 1949, for American policy makers to deal with the emerging Chinese regime as it was—a pro-Soviet, anti-imperialist movement, humiliating one of America's wartime allies and driving uncompromisingly against United States interests in China.

But what of the CCP? If Washington had not had these inhibitions, would the Chinese Communists have established friendly relations at this time? Could they have dealt with the United States as it was—a capitalist nation with significant economic and political stakes in China moving toward a global confrontation with the Soviet Union? I do not think so.

Unlike the pre-1947 period, in 1949 CCP statements about the United States were almost uniformly hostile. The animosity they reflected was strong and clear and any suggestions of possible ties with the United States were vague. There are, however, a few reports of Chinese Communists approaching American officials with a view to establishing friendly relations between the CCP and the Truman Administration. Of these, two have received considerable attention.

The first involves an alleged demarche by Chou En-lai through Michael Keon, an Australian journalist, in Peking in June 1949. Chou purportedly sent a "top secret" message through Keon to the American consul general in Peking for transmittal to the State Department. The message suggested inter alia that Chou was part of a "liberal" faction that was seeking ties with the United States and was eager to act as a mediating agency between America and the Soviet Union. In response the Acting Secretary of State, James E. Webb, drafted a statement of conditions for discussions with the CCP. Nothing materialized as Chou En-lai suddenly became elusive.

This story has evoked much skepticism. American specialists on China, who were in Peking at the time, strongly question its validity. A few months earlier Keon had been denounced by the Chinese Communists for reportorial distortions and would therefore seem an unlikely choice to serve as messenger on a mission of this nature. Moreover it is improbable that, in the period of Cominform opposition to Tito, Chou En-lai would have maintained that China's place was between the United States and the Soviet Union.

A second account of a demarche has somewhat more substance. On June 28, 1949, Huang Hua, then director of the Communist Alien Affairs Office in Nanking, suggested that Ambassador Stuart, who had been president of Yenching University for almost three decades, might consider returning to Peking for his annual birthday visit. Huang strongly implied that, while in Peking, Stuart could hold a meeting with Mao Tse-tung and Chou En-lai. Two days later, while Huang's suggestion was under consideration in Washington, Mao delivered his "lean to one side" speech. On July 1 the proposed trip was vetoed by the State Department, to all appearances under instructions from President Truman, bringing the episode to an end.

Some scholars have suggested that, if a meeting between Ambassador Stuart and the Chinese leaders had been held, it would have changed the course of history materially. There is little to substantiate such a thesis. Indeed if the constant exchanges in Nanking between American and Chinese officials in the period before late June 1949 are a guide, Ambassador Stuart, Mao Tse-tung, and Chou En-lai might well have found that neither side was willing to yield on matters perceived as essential. In the Nanking meetings the responses of the Chinese officials to American initiatives were tentative and evasive. Despite the greater stature of the leaders in Peking there is no ground for supposing their reaction would have been any different. The CCP simply did not believe existing domestic or international conditions permitted the establishment of positive relations with the United States.

The domestic conditions that in the CCP's judgment ruled out an understanding with the administration in Washington are apparent. As indicated earlier, when the Chinese Communists entered the cities and began to confront imperialism in its economic, social, and political reality, they were greatly impressed by the strength of the popular reaction to the anti-imperialist issue. In the summer of 1949 the Party leaders apparently feared that to relent on the strident anti-Americanism that had characterized the CCP's foreign policy for years would incur grave political costs in the urban areas. It might also create serious organizational problems, as there was considerable hostility to the United States throughout the Party and the army. Moreover the CCP leadership was deeply concerned with the effect that any lessening of tension between the Chinese Communists and the Truman Administration might have upon the Chinese intellectuals. Although the Chinese intellectuals were firmly opposed to American imperialism, they generally still admired the United States, especially in comparison with the Soviet Union. The CCP had long feared that, under certain circumstances, many Chinese intellectuals would consciously or unconsciously promote the interests of the American imperialists. A detente between the Chinese Communists and Washington could provide just such an opportunity.

While the domestic situation, in the CCP's view, therefore suggested that there was more to lose than to gain from reaching an understanding with the United States, the international situation in 1949 seemed to point to the same conclusion. The events after 1946 had only confirmed the Party's earlier judgment that revolutionary China's struggle with imperialism was inextricably bound to the global confrontation between the forces of reaction and of progress. As the Cold War quickened, the CCP became increasingly impressed with the benefits to be derived from a policy of leaning to the side of the Soviet Union.

Admittedly there had been developments following the war—especially Stalin's advice to the CCP to negotiate with the Nationalists and the Soviets' self-serving actions in Manchuria—that might have increased the CCP's misgivings regarding the Soviet Union. Yet it would be a serious mistake to conclude that Mao's relations with Stalin in 1949 contained more areas of discord than of agreement. The spirit of Communist interdependence remained strong. From 1947 to 1949, the CCP consistently supported the Soviets on matters of global policy. Such support was more than a mere gesture. The CCP adhered to its often unpopular alignment with Moscow at considerable domestic political cost. But it was obviously willing to pay the price. Whatever second thoughts the Party may have had concerning Soviet actions were more than offset by the increased American threat and the consequent importance of relying on the USSR.

It has often been stated that even if the Communists were committed to a lean-to-one-side policy they may still have been prepared to establish some limited economic or other ties with the United States. But there are a number of considerations that argue against such a thesis. In addition to the existing domestic situation and the CCP's assessment of the United States as a threat, the ideological trend within the international Communist movement in the late 1940s was against any association with the imperialist camp. The expulsion of Tito from the Cominform and the subsequent purges of other East European Communist leaders clearly conveyed the message that Stalin would not look with favor upon any dalliance with the bourgeois world. Under such circumstances the CCP was not likely to enter into any arrangements with the enemy which at best would achieve only marginal gains and might result in the alienation of the USSR, China's only real friend among the great powers. While the lean-to-one-side policy need not have precluded ties with the West, the CCP had long recognized that under certain circumstances it might do so. Such was the case in 1949–50.

It is common to view the crisis-ridden beginnings of Sino-American relations as the result of a "failure" of American diplomacy. While some impugn the motives of the Truman administration, more sympathetic proponents of this view depict the administration as severely constrained by political considerations of a domestic and international nature. Discussions of the Chinese side rarely mention comparable constraints. Mao and the CCP leadership often seem to be making policy in splendid isolation from such factors.

This paper asserts, to the contrary, that an appreciation of similar constraints on the CCP leaders is indispensable to an understanding of United States-China relations in the years from 1944 to 1950. Peking, too, was constrained in what it could do by the weight of past policies and perceptions and, more immediately, the pressures of domestic public opinion and international commitments. There was no "lost chance" for the simple reason that neither side was in a position to take a chance.

FURTHER READING

Robert M. Blum, *Drawing the Line* (1982)
Russell Buhite, *Patrick J. Hurley and American Foreign Policy* (1973)
——, *Soviet-American Relations in Asia, 1945–1954* (1982)
Warren I. Cohen, *America's Response to China* (1980)
John P. Davies, *Dragon by the Tail* (1972)
John K. Fairbank, *The United States and China* (1979)
Herbert Feis, *The China Tangle* (1953)
John Gittings, *The World and China, 1922–1972* (1974)
Akira Iriye, *The Cold War in Asia* (1974)
E. J. Kahn, Jr., *The China Hands* (1972)
Ross Koen, *The China Lobby in American Politics* (1974)
William Manchester, *American Caesar: Douglas MacArthur, 1880–1964* (1978)
Ernest R. May, ed., *The Truman Administration and China, 1945–1949* (1975)
Gary May, *China Scapegoat: The Diplomatic Ordeal of John Carter Vincent* (1979)
Thomas G. Paterson, "If Europe, Why Not China? The Containment Doctrine, 1947–49," *Prologue*, 13 (1981), 19–38
James Reardon-Anderson, *Yenan and the Great Powers* (1980)
Michael Schaller, *The U.S. Crusade in China, 1938–1945* (1978)
——, *The United States and China in the Twentieth Century* (1979)
Tang Tsou, *America's Failure in China, 1941–1950* (1963)

Barbara Tuchman, "If Mao Had Come to Washington," *Foreign Affairs,* 51 (1972), 44–64

——, *Stilwell and the American Experience in China, 1911–1945* (1971)

Nancy Tucker, *Patterns in the Dust: Chinese-American Relations and the Recognition Controversy, 1949–1950* (1983)

Paul Varg, *The Closing of the Door: Sino-American Relations, 1936–1947* (1973)

H. Bradford Westerfield, *Foreign Policy and Party Politics* (1955)

Donald Zagoria, "Choices in the Postwar World: Containment and China," in Charles Gati, ed., *Caging the Bear* (1974)

The Korean War

10

Before the outbreak of the Korean War in June 1950, the United States had launched a number of Cold War programs—the Truman Doctrine, the Marshall Plan, and NATO—and had weathered several crises: in Iran, Greece, and Berlin, for example. Yet in Asia, the American policy of containment faltered in China, where Mao Tse-tung's (Mao Zedong's) Communists unseated Chiang Kai-shek's (Jiang Jieshi's) Nationalists in late 1949 and created the People's Republic of China. Americans considered the new Chinese government a Soviet puppet.

Another shock wave hit the United States in August 1949, when the Soviet Union successfully exploded a nuclear device, thereby ending the American atomic monopoly. Many Americans jumped to the conclusion that the United States was losing the Cold War. The phenomenon of McCarthyism began in early 1950. Then the Korean War erupted. The Truman administration quickly decided to intervene—to draw the containment line.

Since then, questions have challenged contemporaries and scholars alike: Why did the Truman administration intervene? Should the United States have intervened? Was the Korean War an example of global Communist aggression? Or was it essentially a Korean civil war? Did Russia plan and order the North Korean invasion? Why did Truman decide to order American troops across the 38th parallel? What exactly was China's role, and why did it intervene? Why was General Douglas MacArthur fired? Should the Americans have conducted a "limited" war? The recent declassification of formerly closed documents permits historical scholarship on the Korean War to move increasingly from tentative answers to substantiated conclusions.

DOCUMENTS

On January 12, 1950, Secretary of State Dean Acheson delivered a speech, reprinted here, on United States policy toward Asia. In it he defined the American defense perimeter, which excluded Korea. Critics later charged that this omission gave the Soviet Union the incentive to use its North Korean allies to attack South Korea. The second document is the first North Korean statement on the outbreak of war in June 1950, blaming South Korea for provoking hostilities. During the opening days of the Korean crisis, President Harry S. Truman met with key advisers at Blair House, a building across the street from the White House. Reproduced as the third document is a record of the June 26, 1950, meeting, in which Acheson recommended several important policies, not only for Korea but also for the Philippines, Formosa, and Indochina.

At a meeting with Truman on Wake Island on October 15, 1950, General Douglas MacArthur assured the President that the Chinese would not enter the war even in the face of an American advance through North Korea toward the Chinese border. In a November 28, 1950, speech to the United Nations Security Council, Peoples Republic of China official Wu Hsiu-ch'üan explained why China felt compelled to join the Korean War. Truman summarized American policy in the enlarged war in a speech dated April 11, 1951, shortly after he relieved MacArthur of his command. The last document is MacArthur's rebuttal of April 19, delivered as a speech to Congress.

Dean Acheson on the Defense Perimeter in Asia, 1950

I hear almost every day someone say that the real interest of the United States is to stop the spread of communism. Nothing seems to me to put the cart before the horse more completely than that. Of course we are interested in stopping the spread of communism. But we are interested for a far deeper reason than any conflict between the Soviet Union and the United States. We are interested in stopping the spread of communism because communism is a doctrine that we don't happen to like. Communism is the most subtle instrument of Soviet foreign policy that has ever been devised, and it is really the spearhead of Russian imperialism which would, if it could, take from these people what they have won, what we want them to keep and develop, which is their own national independence, their own individual independence, their own development of their own resources for their own good and not as mere tributary states to this great Soviet Union.

Now, it is fortunate that this point that I made does not represent any real conflict. It is an important point because people will do more damage and create more misrepresentation in the Far East by saying our interest is merely to stop the spread of communism than any other way. Our real interest is in those people as people. It is because communism is hostile to that interest that we want to stop it. But it happens that the best way of doing both things is to do just exactly what the peoples of Asia want to do and what we want to help them to do, which is to develop a soundness of administration of these new governments and to develop their resources and their technical skills so that they are not subject to penetration either through ignorance, or because they believe these false promises, or because there is real distress in their areas. If we can help that development, if we can go forward with it, then we have brought about the best way that anyone knows of stopping this spread of communism.

It is important to take this attitude not as a mere negative reaction to communism but as the most positive affirmation of the most affirmative truth that we hold, which is in the dignity and right of every nation, of every people, and of every individual to develop in their own way, making their own mistakes, reaching their own triumphs but acting under their own responsibility. That is what we are pressing for in the Far East, and that is what we must affirm and not get mixed up with purely negative and inconsequential statements.

Now, let me come to another underlying and important factor which determines our relations and, in turn, our policy with the peoples of Asia. That is the attitude of the Soviet Union toward Asia, and particularly towards those parts of Asia which are contiguous to the Soviet Union, and with great particularity this afternoon, to north China.

The attitude and interest of the Russians in north China, and in these other areas as well, long antedates communism. This is not something that has come out of communism at all. It long antedates it. But the Communist regime has added new methods, new skills, and new concepts to the thrust of Russian imperialism. This Communistic concept and techniques have armed Russian imperialism with a new and most insidious weapon of penetration. Armed with these new powers, what is happening in China is that the Soviet Union is detaching the northern provinces [areas] of China from China and is attaching them to the Soviet Union. This process is complete in outer Mongolia. It is nearly complete in Manchuria, and I am sure that in inner Mongolia and in Sinkiang there are very happy reports coming from Soviet agents to Moscow. This is what is going on. It is the detachment of these whole areas, vast areas—populated by Chinese—the detachment of these areas from China and their attachment to the Soviet Union.

I wish to state this and perhaps sin against my doctrine of nondogmatism, but I should like to suggest at any rate that this fact that the Soviet Union is taking the four northern provinces of China is the single most significant, most important fact, in the relation of any foreign power with Asia.

What does that mean for us? It means something very, very significant. It means that nothing that we do and nothing that we say must be allowed to obscure the reality of this fact. All the efforts of propaganda will not be able to obscure it. The only thing that can obscure it is the folly of ill-conceived adventures on our part which easily could do so, and I urge all who are thinking about these foolish adventures to remember that we must not seize the unenviable position which the Russians have carved out for themselves. We must not undertake to deflect from the Russians to ourselves the righteous anger, and the wrath, and the hatred of the Chinese people which must develop. It would be folly to deflect it to ourselves. We must take the position we have always taken—that anyone who violates the integrity of China is the enemy of China and is acting contrary to our own interest. That, I suggest to you this afternoon, is the first and the greatest rule in regard to the formulation of American policy toward Asia.

I suggest that the second rule is very like the first. That is to keep our own purposes perfectly straight, perfectly pure, and perfectly aboveboard and do not get them mixed-up with legal quibbles or the attempt to do one thing and really achieve another.

The consequences of this Russian attitude and this Russian action in China are perfectly enormous. They are saddling all those in China who are proclaiming their loyalty to Moscow, and who are allowing themselves to be used as puppets of Moscow, with the most awful responsibility which they must pay for. Furthermore, these actions of the Russians are making plainer than any speech, or any utterance, or any legislation can make throughout all of Asia, what the true purposes of the Soviet Union are and what the true function of communism as an agent of Russian imperialism is. These I suggest to you are the fundamental factors, fundamental realities of attitude out of which our relations and policies must grow.

Now, let's in the light of that consider some of these policies. First of all, let's deal with the question of military security. I deal with it first because it is important and because, having stated our policy in that regard, we must clearly understand that the military menace is not the most immediate.

What is the situation in regard to the military security of the Pacific area, and what is our policy in regard to it?

In the first place, the defeat and the disarmament of Japan has placed upon the United States the necessity of assuming the military defense of Japan so long as that is required, both in the interest of our security and in the interests of the security of the entire Pacific area and, in all honor, in the interest of Japanese security. We have American—and there are Australian—troops in Japan. I am not in a position to speak for the Australians, but I can assure you that there is no intention of any sort of abandoning or weakening the defenses of Japan and that whatever arrangements are to be made either through permanent settlement or otherwise, that defense must and shall be maintained.

This defensive perimeter runs along the Aleutians to Japan and then goes to the Ryukyus. We hold important defense positions in the Ryukyu Islands, and those we will continue to hold. In the interest of the population of the Ryukyu Islands, we will at an appropriate time offer to hold these islands under trusteeship of the United Nations. But they are essential parts of the defensive perimeter of the Pacific, and they must and will be held.

The defensive perimeter runs from the Ryukyus to the Philippine Islands. Our relations, our defensive relations with the Philippines are contained in agreements between us. Those agreements are being loyally carried out and will be loyally carried out. Both peoples have learned by bitter experience the vital connections between our mutual defense requirements. We are in no doubt about that, and it is hardly necessary for me to say an attack on the Philippines could not and would not be tolerated by the United States. But I hasten to add that no one perceives the imminence of any such attack.

So far as the military security of other areas in the Pacific is concerned, it must be clear that no person can guarantee these areas against military attack. But it must also be clear that such a guarantee is hardly sensible or necessary within the realm of practical relationship.

Should such an attack occur—one hesitates to say where such an armed attack could come from—the initial reliance must be on the people attacked to resist it and then upon the commitments of the entire civilized world under the Charter of the United Nations which so far has not proved a weak reed to lean on by any people who are determined to protect their independence against outside aggression. But it is a mistake, I think, in considering Pacific and Far Eastern problems to become obsessed with military considerations. Important as they are, there are other problems that press, and these other problems are not capable of solution through military means. These other problems arise out of the susceptibility of many areas, and many countries in the Pacific area, to subversion and penetration. That cannot be stopped by military means. . . .

That leads me to the other thing that I wanted to point out, and that is the limitation of effective American assistance. American assistance can be effective when it is the missing component in a situation which might otherwise be solved. The United States cannot furnish all these components to solve the question. It can not furnish determination, it can not furnish will, and it can not furnish the loyalty of a people to its government. But if the will and if the determination exists and if the people are behind their government, then, and not always then, is there a very good chance. In that situation, American help can be effective and it can lead to an accomplishment which could not otherwise be achieved. . . .

Korea. In Korea, we have taken great steps which have ended our military occupation, and in cooperation with the United Nations, have established an independent and sovereign country recognized by nearly all the rest of the world. We have given that nation great help in getting itself established. We are asking the Congress to continue that help until it is firmly established, and that legislation is now pending before the Congress. The idea that we should scrap all of that, that we should stop half way through the achievement of the establishment of this country, seems to me to be the most utter defeatism and utter madness in our interests in Asia. . . .

So after this survey, what we conclude, I believe, is that there is a new day which has dawned in Asia. It is a day in which the Asian peoples are on their own, and know it, and intend to continue on their own. It is a day in which the old relationships between east and west are gone, relationships which at their worst were exploitation, and which at their best were paternalism. That relationship is over, and the relationship of east and west must now be in the Far East one of mutual respect and mutual helpfulness. We are their friends. Others are their friends. We and those others are willing to help, but we can help only where we are wanted and only where the conditions of help are really sensible and possible. So what we can see is that this new day in Asia, this new day which is dawning, may go on to a glorious noon or it may darken and it may drizzle out. But that decision lies within the countries of Asia and within the power of the Asian people. It is not a decision which a friend or even an enemy from the outside can decide for them.

North Korea Blames South Korea for Starting the War, 1950

Official announcement made by the Home Affairs Bureau of the Peoples Republic of Korea. The so-called "defense army" of the South Korea puppet regime started a surprise invasion of the north along the whole front of the 38th parallel line at dawn on the 25th. The enemy, who started the surprise operation, invaded the territory north of the 38th parallel line one to two kilometers at three points west of Haeju, Kumchon, and Chorwon. The Home Affairs Bureau of the Peoples Republic of Korea has issued an order to the security army of the Peoples Republic to repulse the enemy. At this moment, our security army is putting up stiff counter-operations against the enemy. The Peoples Republic army succeeded in repulsing the enemy force which penetrated into the north at Yangyang. In this connection, the Peoples Republic of Korea wishes to remind the South Korea puppet regime of the fact that, unless the puppets immediately suspend their adventurous military actions, the Peoples Republic will be obliged to resort to decisive counter-measures. At the same time the Peoples Republic entrusted the Home Affairs Bureau to call the attention of the South Korea puppet regime to the fact that the whole responsibility for the grave consequences arising from their reckless venture would squarely rest on the shoulders of the South Korea puppet regime.

"Blair House Meeting," June 26, 1950

GENERAL [HOYT S.] VANDENBERG reported that the First Yak plane had been shot down.

THE PRESIDENT remarked that he hoped that it was not the last.

GENERAL VANDENBERG read the text of the orders which had been issued to our Air Forces calling on them to take "aggressive action" against any planes interfering with their mission or operating in a manner unfriendly to the South Korean forces. He indicated, however, that they had been avoiding combat where the direct carrying-out of their mission was not involved.

MR. [DEAN] ACHESON suggested that an all-out order be issued to the Navy and Air Force to waive all restrictions on their operations in Korea and to offer the fullest possible support to the South Korean forces, attacking tanks, guns, columns, etc., of the North Korean forces in order to give a chance to the South Koreans to reform.

THE PRESIDENT said he approved this.

MR. [FRANK] PACE inquired whether this meant action only south of the 38th parallel.

MR. ACHESON said this was correct. He was making no suggestion for any action across the line.

GENERAL VANDENBERG asked whether this meant also that they should not fly over the line.

MR. ACHESON said they should not.

THE PRESIDENT said this was correct; that no action should be taken north of the 38th parallel. He added "not yet".

MR. PACE said that care should be used to avoid hitting friendly forces.

GENERAL [J. LAWTON] COLLINS agreed but suggested that the orders themselves should not put restrictions on the operation.

MR. ACHESON said that if it was considered useful the orders could add that the purpose which the orders would implement is to support South Korean forces in conformity with the resolution of the Security Council.

MR. ACHESON said that the second point he wished to bring up was that orders should be issued to the Seventh Fleet to prevent an attack on Formosa.

THE PRESIDENT said he agreed.

MR. ACHESON continued that at the same time the National Government of China should be told to desist from operations against the mainland and that the Seventh Fleet should be ordered to see that those operations would cease.

MR. ACHESON said his third point was an increase in the United States military forces in the Philippines and an acceleration of aid to the Philippines in order that we might have a firm base there.

THE PRESIDENT said he agreed.

MR. ACHESON said his fourth point was that aid to Indochina should be stepped up and that a strong military mission should be sent.

He suggested that on all these matters if orders were issued tonight it would be desirable for the President to make a statement tomorrow. He handed the President a rough draft of the type of statement which might be issued.

THE PRESIDENT said he would work on the statement tonight. The President continued that he wished consideration given to taking Formosa back as part of Japan and putting it under MacArthur's Command.

MR. ACHESON said that he had considered this move but had felt that it should be reserved for later and should not be announced at this time. It required further study.

THE PRESIDENT said that he had a letter from the Generalissimo about one month (?) ago to the effect that the Generalissimo might step out of the situation if that would help. He said this was a private letter and he had kept it secret. He said that we might want to proceed along those lines in order to get Chinese forces helping us. He thought that the Generalissimo might step out if MacArthur were put in.

MR. ACHESON said that the Generalissimo was unpredictable and that it was possible that he might resist and "throw the ball game". He said that it might be well to do this later.

THE PRESIDENT said that was alright. He himself thought that it was the next step.

MR. [LOUIS A.] JOHNSON said that the proposals made by the Secretary of State pleased him very much. He thought that if we hold the line as indicated that that was alright.

MR. ACHESON added in regard to the Formosan situation that he thought it undesirable that we should get mixed up in the question of the Chinese administration of the Island.

THE PRESIDENT said that we were not going to give the Chinese "a nickel" for any purpose whatever. He said that all the money we had given them is now invested in United States real estate.

MR. JOHNSON added or in banks in the Philippine Islands.

ADMIRAL [FORREST P.] SHERMAN said that the Command of the Seventh Fleet could be either under Admiral Radford at Pearl Harbor or under General MacArthur. He said that under the orders issued yesterday the Seventh Fleet had been ordered to proceed to Japan and placed under General MacArthur's Command. He said that the orders in regard to Formosa would be issued from the Joint Chiefs of Staff to General MacArthur so to employ the forces allocated by Admiral Radford to General MacArthur.

No objection was raised to this statement.

MR. ACHESON said that the Security Council would meet tomorrow afternoon and that the Department had prepared a further resolution for adoption. Our reports were that we would get full support. He noted that even the Swedes were now supporting us.

MR. [JOHN D.] HICKERSON read the draft of the Security Council resolution recommending that UN members render such assistance as was needed to Korea to repel the attack.

THE PRESIDENT said that was right. He said we wanted everyone in on this, including Hong Kong.

GENERAL [OMAR] BRADLEY reported that British Air Marshall Tedder had come to see him, was generally in accord with our taking the firm position, and gave General Bradley a full report of the forces which the British have in that area.

MR. [DEAN] RUSK pointed out that it was possible the Russians would come to the Security Council meeting and cast a veto. In that case we would still take the position that we could act in support of the Charter.

THE PRESIDENT said that was right. He rather wished they would veto. He said we needed to lay a base for our action in Formosa. He said that he would work on the draft of his statement tonight and would talk to the Defense and

State Departments in the morning regarding the final text.

MR. RUSK pointed out that it was Mr. Kennan's estimate that Formosa would be the next likely spot for a Communist move.

SECRETARY JOHNSON reported that SCAP's guess was that the next move would be on Iran. He thought there should be a check on this.

GENERAL COLLINS said that SCAP did not have as much global information as they have in Washington. He and Mr. Pace stated that they have asked for full reports all over the world in regard to any developments, particularly of Soviet preparations.

SECRETARY JOHNSON suggested to Mr. Acheson that it would be advisable to have some talks with the UK regarding possible action in Iran.

MR. ACHESON said he would talk with both the British and French.

MR. ACHESON asked Admiral Sherman whether he desired that any action should be taken regarding the utilization of the Sakishimas, south of Okinawa.

ADMIRAL SHERMAN said he would leave this to General MacArthur.

MR. ACHESON said it would be better to put any necessary supporting air forces on these Islands than to try to put them on Formosa itself.

MR. PACE inquired whether the State Department would inform Ambassador Muccio concerning the orders which were being given.

MR. ACHESON said from latest reports it would probably be impossible for us to contact Ambassador Muccio.

GENERAL COLLINS reported that they were in contact with Seoul through a ham radio operator there.

MR. PACE said that they could pass a message to Ambassador Muccio through General MacArthur.

MR. ACHESON suggested that the President might wish to get in Senator Connally and other members of the Senate and House and tell them what had been decided.

THE PRESIDENT said that he had a meeting scheduled for 10:00 tomorrow morning with the Big Four and that he would get in any others that the Secretary thought should be added. He suggested that Secretaries Acheson and Johnson should also be there.

MR. JOHNSON suggested that the majority and minority members of the two Armed Services Committees be included.

After the discussion it was agreed to set the meeting for 11:30.

THE PRESIDENT then read the following list of persons to be included in the meeting:

The Big Four (Lucas, Rayburn, McCormack—the Vice President will be out of town), Senators Connally, Wiley, George, Alexander Smith, Thomas of Utah, Tydings and Bridges; Congressmen Kee, Eaton, Vinson and Short.

MR. JOHNSON referred again to the draft statement for the President, said that it was very forthright, that he liked it very much and that the Joint Chiefs would consider it during the evening and make any suggestions in the morning.

GENERAL COLLINS stated that the military situation in Korea was bad. It was impossible to say how much our air can do. The Korean Chief of Staff has no fight left in him.

MR. ACHESON stated that it was important for us to do something even if the effort were not successful.

MR. JOHNSON said that even if we lose Korea this action would save the situation. He said this action "suits me". He then asked whether any of the military representatives had any objection to the course of action which had been outlined. There was no objection.

GENERAL VANDENBERG, in response to a question from Mr. Finletter, said that he bet a tank would be knocked out before dark.

THE PRESIDENT said he had done everything he could for five years to prevent this kind of situation. Now the situation is here and we must do what we can to meet it. He had been wondering about the mobilization of the National Guard and asked General Bradley if that was necessary now. If it was he must go to Congress and ask for funds. He was merely putting the subject on the table for discussion. He repeated we must do everything we can for the Korean situation—"for the United Nations".

GENERAL BRADLEY said that if we commit our ground forces in Korea we cannot at the same time carry out our other commitments without mobilization. He wondered if it was better to wait now on the question of mobilization of the National Guard. He thought it would be preferable to wait a few days.

THE PRESIDENT said he wished the Joint Chiefs to think about this and to let him know in a few days time. He said "I don't want to go to war".

GENERAL COLLINS stated that if we were going to commit ground forces in Korea we must mobilize.

MR. ACHESON suggested that we should hold mobilization in reserve.

MR. JOHNSON said he hoped these steps already authorized will settle the Korean question.

THE PRESIDENT said the next question would be the mobilization of the Fleet Reserve.

ADMIRAL SHERMAN said there must be a degree of balance.

THE PRESIDENT noted that there is some pretty good air in the National Guard. He had never been in favor of this and thought it should be like the Naval Reserve.

GENERAL VANDENBERG said he was very glad to hear the President say this.

ADMIRAL SHERMAN asked whether MacArthur could anchor the fleet in Formosan ports if necessary.

THE PRESIDENT asked Mr. Acheson what he thought about this.

MR. ACHESON said that they should go ahead and do it.

ADMIRAL SHERMAN said this would be the best procedure.

GENERAL COLLINS remarked that if we had had standing orders we could have stopped this. We must consider this problem for the future.

THE PRESIDENT said he agreed.

MR. JOHNSON said that if there was danger of a Russian veto in the Security Council the President's statement should be put out before the Security Council meets tomorrow.

MR. ACHESON agreed.

General MacArthur on the Chances for Chinese Intervention, 1950

THE PRESIDENT: What are the chances for Chinese or Soviet interference?

GENERAL MACARTHUR: Very little. Had they interfered in the first or second months it would have been decisive. We are no longer fearful of their intervention. We no longer stand hat in hand. The Chinese have 300,000 men in Manchuria. Of these probably not more than 100/125,000 are distributed along the Yalu River. Only 50/60,000 could be gotten across the Yalu River. They have no Air Force. Now that we have bases for our Air Force in Korea, if the Chinese tried to get down to Pyongyang there would be the greatest slaughter.

With the Russians it is a little different. They have an Air Force in Siberia and a fairly good one, with excellent pilots equipped with some jets and B–25 and B–29 planes. They can put 1,000 planes in the air with some 2/300 more from the Fifth and Seventh Soviet Fleets. They are probably no match for our Air Force. The Russians have no ground troops available for North Korea. They would have difficulty in putting troops into the field. It would take six weeks to get a division across and six weeks brings the winter. The only other combination would be Russian air support of Chinese ground troops. Russian air is deployed in a semicircle through Mukden and Harbin, but the coordination between the Russian air and the Chinese ground would be so flimsy that I believe Russian air would bomb the Chinese as often as they would bomb us. Ground support is a very difficult thing to do. Our Marines do it perfectly. They have been trained for it. Our own Air and Ground Forces are not as good as the Marines but they are effective. Between untrained Air and Ground Forces an air umbrella is impossible without a lot of joint training. I believe it just wouldn't work with Chinese Communist ground and Russian air. We are the best. . . .

The Chinese Case for Intervention, 1950

Under the pretext of the Korean civil war, which was of its own making, the United States Government launched armed aggression simultaneously against Korea and Taiwan. From the very outset the United States armed aggression against Korea gravely threatened China's security. Korea is about 5,000 miles away from the boundaries of the United States. To say that the civil war in Korea would affect the security of the United States is a flagrant, deceitful absurdity. But there is only a narrow river between Korea and China. The United States armed aggression in Korea inevitably threatens China's security. That the United States aggression forces in Korea have directly threatened China's security is fully borne out by the facts.

From 27 August to 10 November 1950, the military aircraft of the United States aggression forces in Korea have violated the territorial air of North-

East China ninety times; they have conducted reconnaissance activities, strafed and bombed Chinese cities, towns and villages, killed and wounded Chinese peaceful inhabitants and damaged Chinese properties. . . .

Now the United States forces of aggression in Korea are approaching our north-eastern frontiers. The flames of the war of aggression waged by the United States against Korea are swiftly sweeping towards China. Under such circumstances the United States armed aggression against Korea cannot be regarded as a matter which concerns the Korean people alone. No, decidedly not. The United States aggression against Korea gravely endangers the security of the People's Republic of China. The Korean People's Democratic Republic is a country bound by close ties of friendship to the People's Republic of China. Only a river separates the two countries geographically. The Chinese people cannot afford to stand idly by in the face of this serious situation brought about by the United States Government's aggression against Korea and the dangerous tendency towards the extension of the war. . . .

One of the master-planners of Japanese aggression, Tanaka, once said: to conquer the world, one must first conquer Asia; to conquer Asia, one must first conquer China; to conquer China, one must first conquer Manchuria and Mongolia; to conquer Manchuria and Mongolia, one must first conquer Korea and Taiwan.

Ever since 1895, the course of aggression taken by imperialist Japan has exactly corresponded to the Tanaka plan. In 1895, imperialist Japan invaded Korea and Taiwan. In 1931, imperialist Japan occupied the whole of North-East China. In 1937, imperialist Japan launched the war of aggression against the whole of China. In 1941, it started the war aimed at the conquest of the whole of Asia. Naturally, as everyone knows, before it had realized this design, Japanese imperialism collapsed. American imperialism, by its aggression against Taiwan and Korea, in practice plagiarizes Tanaka's memorandum and follows the beaten path of the Japanese imperialist aggressors. The Chinese people are maintaining a sharp vigilance over the progress of American imperialist aggression. They have already acquired the experience and learned the lesson from history as to how to defend themselves from aggression.

American imperialism has taken the place of Japanese imperialism. It is now following the old track of aggression against China and Asia on which Japanese imperialism set forth in 1894–95, only hoping to proceed with greater speed. But after all, 1950 is not 1895; the times have changed, and so have the circumstances. The Chinese people have arisen. The Chinese people who have victoriously overthrown the rule of Japanese imperialism and of American imperialism and its lackey, Chiang Kai-shek on China's mainland, will certainly succeed in driving out the United States aggressors and recover Taiwan and all other territories that belong to China. . . .

Truman Defends American Policy, 1951

I want to talk plainly to you tonight about what we are doing in Korea and about our policy in the Far East.

In the simplest terms, what we are doing in Korea is this: We are trying to prevent a third world war.

I think most people in this country recognized that fact last June. And they warmly supported the decision of the Government to help the Republic of Korea against the Communist aggressors. Now, many persons, even some who applauded our decision to defend Korea, have forgotten the basic reason for our action.

It is right for us to be in Korea. It was right last June. It is right today.

I want to remind you why this is true.

The Communists in the Kremlin are engaged in a monstrous conspiracy to stamp out freedom all over the world. If they were to succeed, the United States would be numbered among their principal victims. It must be clear to everyone that the United States cannot—and will not—sit idly by and await foreign conquest. The only question is: When is the best time to meet the threat and how?

The best time to meet the threat is in the beginning. It is easier to put out a fire in the beginning when it is small than after it has become a roaring blaze.

And the best way to meet the threat of aggression is for the peace-loving nations to act together. If they don't act together, they are likely to be picked off, one by one.

If they had followed the right policies in the 1930's—if the free countries had acted together, to crush the aggression of the dictators, and if they had acted in the beginning, when the aggression was small—there probably would have been no World War II.

If history has taught us anything, it is that aggression anywhere in the world is a threat to peace everywhere in the world. When that aggression is supported by the cruel and selfish rulers of a powerful nation who are bent on conquest, it becomes a clear and present danger to the security and independence of every free nation.

This is a lesson that most people in this country have learned thoroughly. This is the basic reason why we joined in creating the United Nations. And since the end of World War II we have been putting that lesson into practice— we have been working with other free nations to check the aggressive designs of the Soviet Union before they can result in a third world war.

That is what we did in Greece, when that nation was threatened by the aggression of international communism.

The attack against Greece could have led to general war. But this country came to the aid of Greece. The United Nations supported Greek resistance. With our help, the determination and efforts of the Greek people defeated the attack on the spot.

Another big Communist threat to peace was the Berlin blockade. That too could have led to war. But again it was settled because free men would not back down in an emergency.

The aggression against Korea is the boldest and most dangerous move the Communists have yet made.

The attack on Korea was part of a greater plan for conquering all of Asia. . . .

They want to control all Asia from the Kremlin.

This plan of conquest is in flat contradiction to what we believe. We believe that Korea belongs to the Koreans, that India belongs to the Indians—that all the nations of Asia should be free to work out their affairs in their own way. This is the basis of peace in the Far East and everywhere else.

The whole Communist imperialism is back of the attack on peace in the Far East. It was the Soviet Union that trained and equipped the North Koreans for aggression. The Chinese Communists massed 44 well-trained and well-equipped divisions on the Korean frontier. These were the troops they threw into battle when the North Korean Communists were beaten.

The question we have had to face is whether the Communist plan of conquest can be stopped without general war. Our Government and other countries associated with us in the United Nations believe that the best chance of stopping it without general war is to meet the attack in Korea and defeat it there.

That is what we have been doing. It is a difficult and bitter task.

But so far it has been successful.

So far, we have prevented World War III.

So far, by fighting a limited war in Korea, we have prevented aggression from succeeding and bringing on a general war. And the ability of the whole free world to resist Communist aggression has been greatly improved.

We have taught the enemy a lesson. He has found out that aggression is not cheap or easy. Moreover, men all over the world who want to remain free have been given new courage and new hope. They know now that the champions of freedom can stand up and fight and that they will stand up and fight.

Our resolute stand in Korea is helping the forces of freedom now fighting in Indochina and other countries in that part of the world. It has already slowed down the timetable of conquest.

In Korea itself, there are signs that the enemy is building up his ground forces for a new mass offensive. We also know that there have been large increases in the enemy's available air forces.

If a new attack comes, I feel confident it will be turned back. The United Nations fighting forces are tough and able and well equipped. They are fighting for a just cause. They are proving to all the world that the principle of collective security will work. We are proud of all these forces for the magnificent job they have done against heavy odds. We pray that their efforts may succeed, for upon their success may hinge the peace of the world.

The Communist side must now choose its course of action. The Communist rulers may press the attack against us. They may take further action which will spread the conflict. They have that choice, and with it the awful responsibility for what may follow. The Communists also have the choice of a peaceful settlement which could lead to a general relaxation of tensions in the Far East. The decision is theirs, because the forces of the United Nations will strive to limit the conflict if possible.

We do not want to see the conflict in Korea extended. We are trying to prevent a world war—not to start one. The best way to do that is to make it plain that we and the other free countries will continue to resist the attack.

But you may ask: Why can't we take other steps to punish the aggressor? Why don't we bomb Manchuria and China itself? Why don't we assist Chinese Nationalist troops to land on the mainland of China?

If we were to do these things we would be running a very grave risk of starting a general war. If that were to happen, we would have brought about the exact situation we are trying to prevent.

If we were to do these things, we would become entangled in a vast conflict on the continent of Asia and our task would become immeasurably more difficult all over the world.

What would suit the ambitions of the Kremlin better than for our military forces to be committed to a full-scale war with Red China?

It may well be that, in spite of our best efforts, the Communists may spread the war. But it would be wrong—tragically wrong—for us to take the initiative in extending the war.

The dangers are great. Make no mistake about it. Behind the North Koreans and Chinese Communists in the front lines stand additional millions of Chinese soldiers. And behind the Chinese stand the tanks, the planes, the submarines, the soldiers, and the scheming rulers of the Soviet Union.

Our aim is to avoid the spread of the conflict.

The course we have been following is the one best calculated to avoid an all-out war. It is the course consistent with our obligation to do all we can to maintain international peace and security. Our experience in Greece and Berlin shows that it is the most effective course of action we can follow.

First of all, it is clear that our efforts in Korea can blunt the will of the Chinese Communists to continue the struggle. The United Nations forces have put up a tremendous fight in Korea and have inflicted very heavy casualties on the enemy. Our forces are stronger now than they have been before. These are plain facts which may discourage the Chinese Communists from continuing their attack.

Second, the free world as a whole is growing in military strength every day. In the United States, in Western Europe, and throughout the world, free men are alert to the Soviet threat and are building their defenses. This may discourage the Communist rulers from continuing the war in Korea—and from undertaking new acts of aggression elsewhere.

If the Communist authorities realize that they cannot defeat us in Korea, if they realize it would be foolhardy to widen the hostilities beyond Korea, then they may recognize the folly of continuing their aggression. A peaceful settlement may then be possible. The door is always open.

Then we may achieve a settlement in Korea which will not compromise the principles and purposes of the United Nations.

I have thought long and hard about this question of extending the war in Asia. I have discussed it many times with the ablest military advisers in the country. I believe with all my heart that the course we are following is the best course.

I believe that we must try to limit the war to Korea for these vital reasons:

to make sure that the precious lives of our fighting men are not wasted; to see that the security of our country and the free world is not needlessly jeopardized; and to prevent a third world war.

A number of events have made it evident that General MacArthur did not agree with that policy. I have therefore considered it essential to relieve General MacArthur so that there would be no doubt or confusion as to the real purpose and aim of our policy.

It was with the deepest personal regret that I found myself compelled to take this action. General MacArthur is one of our greatest military commanders. But the cause of world peace is more important than any individual.

MacArthur's "No Substitute for Victory" Speech, 1951

I do not stand here as advocate for any partisan cause, for the issues are fundamental and reach quite beyond the realm of partisan consideration. They must be resolved on the highest plane of national interest if our course is to prove sound and our future protected. I trust, therefore, that you will do me the justice of receiving that which I have to say as solely expressing the considered viewpoint of a fellow American. I address you with neither rancor nor bitterness in the fading twilight of life with but one purpose in mind, to serve my country. . . .

While I was not consulted prior to the President's decision to intervene in the support of the Republic of Korea, that decision from a military standpoint proved a sound one. As I say, a brief and sound one as we hurled back the invaders and decimated his forces. Our victory was complete and our objectives within reach when Red China intervened with numerically superior ground forces. This created a new war and an entirely new situation, a situation not contemplated when our forces were committed against the North Korean invaders, a situation which called for new decisions in the diplomatic sphere to permit the realistic adjustment of military strategy. Such decisions have not been forthcoming.

While no man in his right mind would advocate sending our ground forces into continental China—and such was never given a thought—the new situation did urgently demand a drastic revision of strategic planning if our political aim was to defeat this new enemy as we had defeated the old.

Apart from the military need as I saw it to neutralize sanctuary, protection given to the enemy north of the Yalu, I felt that military necessity in the conduct of the war made necessary:

First, the intensification of our economic blockade against China.

Second, the imposition of a naval blockade against the China coast.

Third, removal of restrictions on air reconnaissance of China's coastal areas and of Manchuria.

Fourth, removal of restrictions on the forces of the Republic of China on Formosa with logistical support to contribute to their effective operation against the Chinese mainland.

For entertaining these views all professionally designed to support our forces committed to Korea and bring hostilities to an end with the least possible delay and at a saving of countless American and Allied lives, I have been severely criticized in lay circles, principally abroad, despite my understanding that from a military standpoint the above views have been fully shared in the past by practically every military leader concerned with the Korean campaign, including our own Joint Chiefs of Staff.

I called for reinforcements, but was informed that reinforcements were not available. I made clear that if not permitted to utilize the friendly Chinese force of some 600,000 men on Formosa; if not permitted to blockade the China coast to prevent the Chinese Reds from getting succor from without; and if there were to be no hope of major reinforcements, the position of the command from the military standpoint forbade victory. We could hold in Korea by constant maneuver and at an approximate area where our supply advantages were in balance with the supply line disadvantages of the enemy, but we could hope at best for only an indecisive campaign, with its terrible and constant attrition upon our forces if the enemy utilized his full military potential. I have constantly called for the new political decisions essential to a solution. Efforts have been made to distort my position. It has been said in effect that I was a warmonger. Nothing could be further from the truth. I know war as few other men now living know it, and nothing to me is more revolting. . . .

But once war is forced upon us, there is no other alternative than to apply every available means to bring it to a swift end. War's very object is victory—not prolonged indecision. In war, indeed, there can be no substitute for victory.

There are some who for varying reasons would appease Red China. They are blind to history's clear lesson. For history teaches with unmistakable emphasis that appeasement but begets new and bloodier war. It points to no single instance where the end has justified that means—where appeasement has led to more than a sham peace. Like blackmail, it lays the basis for new and successively greater demands, until, as in blackmail, violence becomes the only other alternative. Why, my soldiers asked of me, surrender military advantages to an enemy in the field? I could not answer. Some may say to avoid spread of the conflict into an all-out war with China; others, to avoid Soviet intervention. Neither explanation seems valid. For China is already engaging with the maximum power it can commit and the Soviet will not necessarily mesh its actions with our moves. Like a cobra, any new enemy will more likely strike whenever it feels that the relativity in military or other potential is in its favor on a world-wide basis.

The tragedy of Korea is further heightened by the fact that as military action is confined to its territorial limits, it condemns that nation, which it is our purpose to save, to suffer the devastating impact of full naval and air bombardment, while the enemy's sanctuaries are fully protected from such attack and devastation. Of the nations of the world, Korea alone, up to now, is the sole one which has risked its all against communism. The magnificence of the courage and fortitude of the Korean people defies description. They have chosen to risk death rather than slavery. Their last words to me were "Don't scuttle the Pacific."

I have just left your fighting sons in Korea. They have met all tests there and I can report to you without reservation they are splendid in every way. It was my constant effort to preserve them and end this savage conflict honorably and with the least loss of time and a minimum sacrifice of life. Its growing bloodshed has caused me the deepest anguish and anxiety. Those gallant men will remain often in my thoughts and in my prayers always.

I am closing my 52 years of military service. When I joined the Army even before the turn of the century, it was the fulfillment of all my boyish hopes and dreams. The world has turned over many times since I took the oath on the plain at West Point, and the hopes and dreams have long since vanished. But I since remember the refrain of one of the most popular barrack ballads of that day which proclaimed most proudly that—

"Old soldiers never die; they just fade away." And like the old soldier of that ballad, I now close my military career and just fade away—an old soldier who tried to do his duty as God gave him the light to see that duty.

Good-by.

ESSAYS

The first essay, by Barton J. Bernstein of Stanford University, poses a number of questions about the origins of the Korean War, which some scholars believe had the characteristics of a *civil* war among Koreans, North and South. He analyzes the American decision to intervene, the extent of Soviet involvement, and the momentous consequences of this conflict for American foreign policy. In his conclusion, he doubts the United States should have intervened. In the second essay, James T. Matray of New Mexico State University Press studies the American decision to unite the two Koreas by sending American troops across the 38th parallel. That decision and the military thrust into the North ultimately brought the Chinese into the war. Matray does not believe President Truman acted to improve his unsteady political standing at home. Nor does he think that the decision for the offensive sprang from the sense of optimism that Americans felt after the successful Inchon landing. Matray stresses instead Truman's commitment to the principle of self-determination and his hope that once military action ceased, the Koreans would be free to choose their own—preferably non-Communist—government.

American Military Intervention in the Korean Civil War

BARTON J. BERNSTEIN

At 4 a.m. on Sunday morning (Korean time), June 25, 1950, the Democratic People's Republic of Korea (DPRK) launched a bombardment against

"The Week We Went to War: American Intervention in the Korean Civil War," Parts I and II. Reprinted from the *Foreign Service Journal* (January and February 1977) by permission of Barton J. Bernstein.

the Republic of Korea (ROK), according to the ROK, and at about 6 a.m. crossed the 38th parallel to attack the South's armies. During the early hours, the reports from the battle area were piecemeal and often unsure, and did not conclusively indicate that it was a massive attack. At General Douglas MacArthur's headquarters in Tokyo, officers first judged the conflict another "incident"—one of the many ongoing border clashes between the forces of the North and South in the recently divided Korea. By late morning, however, Pyongyang charged that the ROK had initiated the attack and that the North Korean forces had responded strongly to the assault.

In Washington (14 hours behind Korean time), at 9:26 p.m. on Saturday, the State Department received from its Ambassador in Korea, John J. Muccio, its first official news of the attack: "According to [South] Korean Army reports which are partly confirmed by [US] Korean Military Advisory Group field advisor reports, North Korean forces invaded Republic of Korea territory at several points this morning at Ongjin, Kaesong, and Chunchon, and south of Kangnung. "It would appear from the nature of the attack and the manner in which it was launched," Muccio tentatively concluded, "that it constitutes an all-out offensive against the Republic of Korea."

Shortly before midnight, Secretary of State Dean Acheson telephoned President Harry S. Truman, then in Independence, Missouri. "I have very serious news," the Secretary reported. "The North Koreans have invaded South Korea." Acheson did not contend that it was a full-scale attack but he treated it as more than just another border clash. Upon the Secretary's advice, Truman decided not to rush back to Washington, because the information was still skimpy, but approved Acheson's strategy that the United States should bring the matter of the invasion before the United Nations Security Council on Sunday.

By early Sunday morning (Washington time), the situation in Korea was still confused, but not bleak. American officials could find evidence for their cherished notion that the South Korean forces could resist the invasion. Ambassador Muccio, who had warned in early June that the South's armies were weak, told Americans in Seoul that "Korean officials and Security Forces are handling the situation calmly and with ability. There is no reason for alarm. As yet, it cannot be determined whether the northern communists intend . . . all-out warfare." KMAG officers were widely quoted that the attack had been "virtually stopped." One South Korean official lamented, "Our only cause for dissatisfaction is that there has been no order to advance into the North. By tomorrow morning," he predicted, "we shall have defeated them completely."

During the next five days (June 26–30) these hopes slowly collapsed. In incremental steps, Truman committed American forces—first, the Air Force and Navy, then the Army—to the battle. By Friday, the 30th, America was substantially engaged in its first shooting war since 1945. It was an undeclared war ("a police action," said Truman) without formal congressional approval, but with widespread popular and informal Congressional support in the early months.

The war dramatically altered the course of American foreign policy, promptly spurring the Administration to redefine other commitments: to increase military aid to the French in Indo-China, to reverse its position (disengagement) on Formosa and to support Chiang Kai-shek, to expand its military aid to Europe and to push for substantial European rearmament, and to escalate its military budget—the enactment, in effect, of National Security Council (NSC) document 68. The Truman administration, following the counsel of Acheson, was girding for a long struggle with the Soviet Union and seeking to organize and strengthen the "free world." America would have to create an international environment in which the American system of democratic capitalism could flourish.

Even a quarter century after the outbreak of the war, many of the critical questions remain in dispute: Who started the war? If North Korea, as seems most likely, why? Did the Soviet Union know about the scheduled attack and even initiate the scheme? Why did American policy makers assume that the Soviets had conceived the scheme? Why did policy makers in June commit their nation to a large-scale armed intervention? After defining Korea as outside America's "defense perimeter" as late as January 1950, why did they reverse themselves in June? What was the role of NSC-68 in their thinking?

Did the North or South start the war? Some analysts suggest that the events in Korea on the 25th are too unclear to allow any conclusion. They point out that the accusations against the North depend basically on South Korean reports (not American or UN observers), and a few writers even contend that Syngman Rhee, president of the ROK, may have started the war to force the United States into buttressing his position both within the South and against the North.

These analysts are technically correct on some matters. There is no *impartial* direct evidence (reported observations) on who started the war. The reports by American and UN observers rely upon South Korea's claims for the critical period (4 a.m. to 6 a.m.) or describe events after the outbreak of the conflict. And it is true, the way matters turned out, that the embattled Rhee, whose party had just lost the election, gained greatly from American intervention.

Yet, the indirect evidence indicates that North Korea, not South, started the war on the 25th. A UN field report of the 24th (filed later) by two Australians who observed the South Korean army, concluded, it "is organized entirely for defense and is in no condition to carry out attack on large scale." The lack of air support, armor, and heavy artillery would make "any action with object of invasion . . . impossible." The report also noted that North Korea "had recently removed . . . civilians from areas adjoining the [38th] parallel [, that] there was increased [Northern] military activity . . . about four kilometers north parallel [, and that North Korea had taken possession of] salients on south side parallel, occupation in at least one case being of fairly recent date." This information, when viewed in retrospect, suggests DPRK preparation for an attack.

Even though Rhee had threatened repeatedly to unify the country by arms and had good reason to want to increase American support, it is unlikely that he initiated the war. Despite MacArthur's affection for him, and the friendly visit in June by John Foster Dulles, a special representative of the State Department, Rhee did not have ample evidence for believing that the United States would come to his aid with troops if the North attacked. In fact, there was substantial evidence to suggest that the United States would probably abandon him: the recent reluctance of Congress to provide military and economic aid; the Truman administration's suspicion of him and its pleas for less repression; the warning in May by Senator Tom Connally, chairman of the Senate Foreign Relations Committee, that the Communists would force the United States to quit South Korea; and Acheson's refusal the next day to "say whether the United States might have to abandon South Korea to Russia." In view of this evidence, Rhee had good reason to be cautious and fearful—unless he was suicidal, which he was not. His frantic pleas during the first week of war underline how unsure he was that Truman would commit troops to defend the South.

In the months before June, Rhee knew that his military forces would be at a decided disadvantage in any sustained battle with the North—a point that South Korean officials emphasized in the spring. In January 1950, according to official American sources, North Korea had begun rapidly expanding her formerly "defensive-type" army into an offensive force. The Russians supplied about 150 tanks, some heavy artillery, and a small tactical air force —equipment that made the North considerably stronger than the ROK, which lacked tanks and combat planes. Partly because the Truman administration feared that Rhee might attack the DPRK, he was left without adequate supplies for an invasion to unify the country.

Other evidence supports the conclusion that the North started the war and offers likely motives. Nikita Khrushchev's memoir reports that Kim Il Sung, premier of the DPRK, had informed Stalin in late 1949 that he wanted to act to unify Korea. "The North Koreans wanted to prod South Korea with the point of a bayonet. Kim Il Sung said that the first poke would touch off an internal explosion in South Korea and that the power of the people would prevail, that is, the power which ruled in North Korea."

Khrushchev's recollection, as well as some military evidence, indicates that the North Korean government expected that its strong attack, and its quick capture of Seoul, would unleash the anticipated revolution in the South. Probably for this reason, the North Korean government did not originally give its attacking divisions orders to go beyond Seoul, and the North did not await mobilization of its full army but used only seven of 13–15 divisions in the attack. Even Kim Il Sung's calls in earlier June for the overthrow of Rhee, unification, and elections can be interpreted within the framework of the anticipated revolution.

The South had long faced an internal revolutionary threat. An official American army history describes "an organized guerrilla movement" in the South, and notes by late 1949 that deserters from the ROK army, guerrillas from the South, and infiltrators from the North "were attacking villages and installations and becoming . . . a grave threat to the internal security of . . . [South] Korea." So great were the problems, according to a recently declassified KMAG report, that 30 per cent of the South's forces were engaged in trying to put down the rebellion in late 1949.

When Rhee's supporters suffered a massive defeat in the May elections, Kim Il Sung could find additional evidence that an upheaval in the South was likely: Rhee and his cohorts would be cast out of office, and the divided country would be reunited. "Kim had believed," according to Khrushchev, "that South Korea was blanketed with Party organizations and that the people would rise up in revolt when the Party gave the signal." According to a Japanese study, Communist agents from the South reported that the party was strong, that there were about 500,000 in the underground, and that "members were asking them to start a war and invade the ROK as soon as possible. This was a major reason why [Kim] decided to attack the ROK." Later, the leader of the Southern faction, Pak Honyong, was indicted by Kim for, among other charges, falsely reporting in 1950 that the South was ready to overthrow Rhee.

Undoubtedly North Korea did not expect a speedy—if any—armed American intervention in the civil war. If the expected revolution had developed in the South, such intervention would have lacked the patina of legitimacy and, more importantly, would have been logistically very difficult, if not impossible, because there would have been no safe landing area for American troops. Even aside from logistical difficulties, American intervention should have seemed unlikely to Kim Il Sung, as it did to Rhee. The American withdrawal of troops in mid-1949 implied that Korea was not an area of significant interest for the United States. The presence of a 500-member American military advisory group and the continuation of economic aid were inadequate, despite an Administration claim, "to deter overt moves on the part of neighboring powers." Statements by Acheson and MacArthur, among others, excluding Korea from the American defense perimeter seemed to confirm that Korea was of marginal concern to America. Who would have made much of Acheson's implication in his January 1950 speech that South Korea would have to rely for assistance "upon the commitments of the entire civilized world under . . . the United Nations," and that this action might mean American intervention? Moreover, with only four under-trained divisions in Japan, and a relatively small army already strained perilously thin by global obligations, the United States did not seem prepared for military intervention in Korea. In view of all this evidence, why then should not the North have sought to achieve what Rhee periodically threatened but could not accomplish—unification of the country? The civil war, abetted by the revolution in the South, promised speedy success.

Did the Soviets originate or accede to the North Korean attack? Khrushchev claims that Stalin "had his doubts about a North Korean attack but acceded to it . . . the war wasn't Stalin's idea but Kim Il Sung's." The prospects of uniting a divided country under communism, establishing a counterweight to Mao's China, emboldening Japan's communist party, assisting a liberation movement, and nibbling away at American power—all should have seemed attractive but not risky to the usually cautious Stalin. He thought, according to Khrushchev, that the United States would not intervene if the war was fought and won swiftly.

Did Stalin know when the North Koreans would attack? Or did Kim "jump the gun"? There are various reasons—indirect evidence—suggesting that Stalin was surprised by the early date of the attack. First, and most important, the Soviets did not even return to the United Nations and temporarily end their boycott (on the issue of seating Communist China) to block the American-sponsored resolutions on the 25th charging North Korea with a "breach of the peace" and on the 27th urging aid for the ROK. Had Stalin known the scheduled date for the attack, he would have probably prepared for the first meeting of the Security Council and most certainly for the second meeting. Given the Soviets' concern about legalism and their fear that the UN was an American-controlled instrument, Stalin had good reason to want to block these resolutions. It would not have been difficult. A simple strategy could have been devised. Since North Korea claimed that Rhee had started the war, the Soviets could easily have endorsed that charge, delayed a vote in the Security Council for a few days, and demanded that Kim's government, as well as Rhee's, be heard by the UN. Not only did the Soviets seem unprepared in the UN, but they seemed so surprised by the outbreak of the war that they even delayed a few days in commenting on its origins and, in line with Kim, charging Rhee with aggression. Had they known that the DPRK would attack on the 25th, they would not have floundered for a few days.

Why did American policy makers assume that the Soviets had planned the attack? Despite Acheson's earlier thoughts of ultimately prying China out of her alliance with the Soviet Union, American leaders assumed comfortably that the Soviet Union orchestrated nearly all major events in the Communist world—certainly matters of aggression. Since North Korea was a Soviet satellite, according to Washington, no one doubted that this analysis fit the events of late June.

NSC-68, of which Acheson was the spiritual father, confirmed and dramatized this mode of thinking. Put together primarily by Paul Nitze of the Policy Planning Staff in the winter and early spring of 1949–50, NSC-68 contended that "the Soviet Union, unlike previous aspirants to hegemony, is animated by a new fanatic faith . . . and seeks to impose its absolute authority over the rest of the world. . . . To that end Soviet efforts are now directed toward the domination of the Eurasian land mass." NSC-68 warned that "the Communist success in China, taken with the politico-economic situation in the rest of South and South-East Asia, provides a springboard for the further incursion in this troubled area." Indo-China and the Philippines, by implication, were in danger. With a minor revision, the general analysis, when stretched geographically, could easily include Korea as an endangered region.

The document foresaw the dangers of "piecemeal aggression," which the

United States lacked the conventional forces to resist. The Soviet Union— employing aggression by satellites or subversion—could nibble away at sections of the "free world." The United States, with her depleted conventional forces, would not be able to halt these encroachments. The choice for America would be painful—acquiescence or nuclear weapons.

For Acheson and Nitze, Stalin's goals were insatiable expansion, ultimate conquest of the rest of the world. He would probe and test, exploit areas of weakness, nibble at the West, and slowly spread the Communist menace. It was a doctrine in 1949–50 that sounded remarkably like the analysis of the famous "Mr. X" essay ("The Sources of Soviet Conduct"), published in 1947 by George Kennan. By 1949–50, however, Kennan and Charles Bohlen had modified—even repudiated—parts of the "Mr. X" analysis, and they objected to NSC-68 on various grounds. They viewed the Soviet Union, in Bohlen's words, as "largely motivated by its interests as a national state, and that the idea of spreading Communism was secondary to such considerations."

Despite these disagreements on the goals and nature of Soviet policy, none in the high ranks of government questioned the conclusion that Stalin had planned North Korea's attack; but some—notably Kennan and Bohlen— challenged Acheson's thesis that the war was part of some "grand design." They rejected that conception. "NSC-68's misconception of Soviet aims," wrote Bohlen, "misled . . . Dean Acheson and others in interpreting the Korean war." It was not, Bohlen and Kennan contended, the beginning of a new phase of Soviet policy: attacks by satellite armies elsewhere. "The Soviet action in Korea," in Bohlen's words, "was limited strictly to Korea."

Kennan argued that Stalin was responding primarily to the proposed American peace treaty with Japan, which excluded the Soviet Union and guaranteed a longterm, formidable American military presence in the Pacific. "For some reason this connection—the idea that in doing things disagreeable to our interests the Russians might be reacting to features of our own behavior —was one to which the mind of official Washington would always be strangely resistant," wrote Kennan. "Our adversaries had always to be demonic, monstrous," he complained. "It was unthinkable that we, by admitting that they sometimes reacted to what we did, should confess to a share in the responsibility for their behavior." At the time and later, Acheson deemed this analysis fanciful, bizarre, and wrong-headed, and in late June the Secretary also barred Kennan from the high-level meetings with Truman.

Even Kennan and Bohlen, who challenged some of the assumptions about the war, would not endorse what now seems a more reasonable interpretation of that conflict: it was a civil war, initiated by the North for its own purposes, and approved by Stalin, despite some doubts. It was not a Soviet-directed or initiated scheme. Much of the explanation of the war lies in an understanding of politics in Korea and especially in the DPRK. Unfortunately the Cold War thinking of 1949–50, with the assumptions that satellites in both the Soviet and American camps lacked the capacity to initiate bold ventures, made it impossible for most Americans—both policy makers and attentive citizens—to formulate an interpretation that rested upon an analysis of politics in Korea.

By Sunday, the 25th, in Washington, the evidence began to accumulate that the North Korean attack was not simply another border incident. MacArthur had already sent a firm report that suggested a crisis: "Enemy effort serious in strength and strategic intent and is undisguised act of war." When asked "for estimate of objective of current North Korean attack," Maj. Gen. Charles A. Willoughby, MacArthur's chief of intelligence, replied, "There is no evidence . . . that the North Koreans are engaged in a limited offensive or raid . . . the size of [their] forces, the depth of penetration, the intensity of the attack, and the landings made miles south of the parallel . . . indicate [they] are engaged in an all-out offensive to subjugate South Korea." This message dramatized the situation and probably sought to evoke the increased American commitment to Asia that MacArthur had long sought. The Korean war would initially give him the opportunities he wanted, and partly revise American policy in Asia to meet his hopes and sense of destiny.

On Sunday afternoon, when Acheson informed Truman that the military situation was worsening, the President decided to cut short his visit in Independence and to fly back to Washington. During the day, high-ranking officials from State and Defense planned courses of action. Even before the President's conference with his advisers that evening, the army informed MacArthur's headquarters of the likely results: "In event Security Council . . . calls on member nations to take direct action in Korea, to authorize and direct you to employ forces of your Command . . . to stabilize the battle situation including if feasible the restoration of original boundaries at 38 degrees parallel." The prediction, though hedged by the contingency of UN support, was clear: a commitment of ground, air, and naval forces to the war in Korea to roll back the North's troops. "Come over and join the fight," MacArthur's headquarters responded. "We are delighted with your lines of action. . . ."

At the Blair House meeting on Sunday evening, Truman conferred with Acheson, Under Secretary of State James Webb, the JCS, the four civilian secretaries of the military, and three other representatives from State. The President accepted five recommendations: that MacArthur should send military supplies to Korea beyond the foreign aid program (which he was already doing); that the Seventh Fleet should move to Japan; that the Air Force should provide air cover for the evacuation of American civilians from Korea; that the Air Force "should propose plans to wipe out all Soviet air bases in the Far East"; and that State and Defense should make a "careful calculation . . . [of where] Soviet action might take place" in other parts of the world. Truman's program represented an endorsement of most of Acheson's stated program, and the Secretary was the dominant adviser at the meeting.

The President did resist efforts on two important matters—interposing the Seventh Fleet between mainland China and Formosa, and increasing aid to Indo-China and the Philippines. So far, the President had avoided making commitments that would reverse American policy toward Formosa and involve the United States in the Chinese civil war, or expand American involvement in the anti-revolutionary struggles in Indo-China and the Philippines. The reasons for delaying decisions on these matters are unclear, but probably Truman did not want to move that evening on matters that could briefly wait. There was time. Neither set of issues required immediate action. In addition, in the case of Formosa, Acheson may still have had serious doubts about ending the policy of disengagement, and he and the President were probably both troubled by suddenly reversing this policy.

At the meeting, according to the recently declassified minutes, much of the discussion focused on likely Russian intentions and military capacity, and less frequently—often obliquely—on the wisdom of committing ground troops. Admiral Forrest Sherman, Chief of Naval Operations, "said that the Russians do not want war now but if they do they will have it. The present situation in Korea offers a valuable opportunity for us to act." General Hoyt Vandenberg, Air Force Chief of Staff, "agreed that we must stop the North Koreans but he would not base our action on the assumption that the Russians would not fight." When asked by Truman whether the United States could knock out Soviet air bases in the Far East, "Vandenberg replied that this might take some time . . . it could be done if we used A-bombs." General Omar Bradley, Chief of the JCS, agreed generally with Sherman, "that Russia is not yet ready for war. The Korean situation offered as good an occasion for action in drawing the line as anywhere else. . . ."

None who spoke at the meeting disagreed with Bradley's judgment that Korea was the place to draw "the line." What would that entail? Important questions were not systematically addressed: What would be the nature of the American commitment and on what conditions would they expand it? Should the United States go so far as to send ground troops? That night, only three participants spoke explicitly on committing ground troops, and they opposed such action. Bradley "questioned the advisability of putting in ground units [,] particularly if large numbers were involved." Supporting him, both Secretary of the Army Frank Pace and Secretary of Defense Louis Johnson, in the words of the minutes, "opposed . . . committing ground troops in Korea." The recently declassified record refutes Truman's 1955 claim that the group had agreed "that whatever had to be done to meet this aggression had to be done."

Earlier that day, Acheson had received a telegram from Dulles, an eminent Republican, and John Allison, director of the Office of North Asian Affairs, who were in Japan. American "forces should be used," they cabled, if South Korea cannot repel the attack. "To sit by while Korea is overrun by unprovoked armed attack would start a disastrous chain of events leading most probably to world war." This advice, echoing the perils of Munich, also conformed to Dulles's analysis in May, when he warned that "a series of disasters [in Asia] can be prevented if at some doubtful point we quickly take a dramatic and strong stand that shows our confidence and resolution," even if it is necessary to "risk war" with Russia.

Anxiety about Soviet intentions elsewhere in the world prompted State on Sunday evening to send a cable to American embassies throughout the world: "Possible that Korea is only the first of a series of coordinated actions on part of Soviet. Maintain utmost vigilance and report immediately any positive or negative information." Some predicted Formosa or Yugoslavia; MacArthur's headquarters said Iran, which was also Truman's guess. Others feared that Germany would be next.

Amid bleak reports from Korea, on Monday night the Blair House group again met. They agreed on escalation of American involvement—that the Navy and Air Force be directed "to offer the fullest possible support to the South Korean forces" by attacking the North's forces but not crossing the 38th parallel. "Not yet," said the President, who seemed to imply that he now foresaw in the next few days a wider and deeper American involvement.

On Acheson's advice, and without dissent from advisers, Truman made the decisions that he had deferred on Sunday—increase aid and military forces in the Philippines, increased aid and a military mission to Indo-China, and deployment of the Seventh Fleet to protect Formosa and to halt Chiang's attacks on the mainland. In the case of Indo-China, Truman's action was in line with the analyses, approved by the NSC in December 1949, that "Asia is an area of significant potential power—political, economic and military— [whose loss] would threaten the security of . . . the United States," for its conquest would strengthen Russia and destroy the "economic advantage . . . from our trade with non-Communist Asia," especially South and Southeast Asia.

By reversing American policy and intervening in the Chinese civil war, Truman was recognizing the domestic and international political costs if Formosa now fell. How could he defend Korea but let Chiang "go down the drain?" Johnson, MacArthur, and some military leaders would protest. Republican critics, often Chiang's strongest supporters, would not tolerate it. Americans would not understand. The blows to America's and the President's prestige would be too great in this time of crisis. Yet, as the official minutes indicate, Truman and Acheson remained hostile to Chiang. "We are not going to give the Chinese 'a nickel' for any purpose whatever," Truman stated, according to the summary. "He said that all the money we had given them is now invested in United States real estate." ("Mr. Johnson added or in the banks in the Philippines.")

The United States was moving into the war and an increased military commitment in the Far East, but the President and his advisers had not yet faced systematically what would prove to be the major decision: Should the United States commit ground troops? The official summary of their discussion discloses that they did not explore the objections raised on Sunday by Bradley, Johnson, and Pace, and that they maintained cohesion by avoiding the difficult question. Here is the relevant part of the recently declassified summary of Monday night's meeting:

> General [J. Lawton] Collins, [Army Chief of Staff,] stated that the military situation in Korea is bad . . . It was impossible to say how much our air [force] can do. . . .

Mr. Acheson stated that it was important for us to do something even if the effort were not successful.

Mr. Johnson said that even if we lose Korea this action would save the situation [and] "suits me." He then asked whether any of the military representatives had any objection to the course of action which had been outlined. There was no objection. . . .

The President said he had done everything he could for five years to prevent this kind of situation. Now the situation is here and we must do what we can to meet it. He had been wondering about mobilization of the National Guard . . . He repeated we must do everything we can for the Korean situation—"for the United Nations." . . . "I don't want to go to war."

They continued to hope, as Secretary Johnson phrased it, that "these steps already authorized will settle the Korean question." The bleak counsel of Collins was neglected, for it raised troubling questions—ones that the group wanted to avoid.

For Truman, there was a sense of desperation and exultation, of pride and fear, of the need to act (at least as far as he had) and of the danger of inaction. He was proud that the government had acted, relieved that the test was dramatic, yet still unsure of whether the next step—what would prove to be the critical step—would be necessary. He had indicated that he would take that next step and commit ground troops, even though others had raised doubts. The course of the Cold War, he believed, had long involved challenges to America and his leadership—especially Greece in 1947–48 and Berlin in 1948–1949. Each time, he had met the challenge.

Backing down now, if troops became necessary, would be too dangerous. "Korea is the Greece of the Far East," he told an adviser. "If we are tough enough now, if we stand up to them like [sic] we did in Greece three years ago, they won't take any steps. But if we just stand by, they'll move into Iran and they'll take over the whole Middle East. There's no telling what they'll do if we don't put up a fight now." For the President, Korea was the testing ground of American will, resolution, and credibility. The Soviets were probing, and the next place, if America failed in Korea, would probably be the Middle East. "We can lose half a world at this point if we lose heart," the New York Times warned, echoing many major newspapers early that week.

The chief significance of Korea, for Truman, was as a test case of America's ability to resist Soviet aggression by proxy (satellite). Korea also had a military-strategic value, though the JCS in earlier years had minimized this theme. Korea was, as Admiral Sherman had said, a dagger pointing at Japan, "a strategic threat to Japan." It was "an area of great importance to the security of American-occupied Japan," Acheson later emphasized. Japan, with the communist control of mainland China, had become the linchpin of American power in Asia, the bulwark of resisting Communism there. In Asia, as elsewhere, the policy of containment would be endangered if Korea fell. Valuable areas in Asia, essential to the American politico-economic system, would be swept out of the "free world," disrupting the international economy, encouraging communist forces, inspiring neutralism. Presumably, the revolutionary movements in Indo-China and the Philippines might be emboldened. Given this analysis Korea was the first of a series of dominoes.

When conferring with Congressional leaders on Tuesday, the 27th, Acheson and Truman relied upon the same general analysis. Acheson explained, according to the recently declassified summary, that the United States had taken a firm stand because "the governments of many Western European nations appeared to be in a state of near panic, as they watched to see whether the United States would act or not." America's resolution in Asia, he believed, was essential to maintaining the anti-communist alliance in Europe, to halting the forces of neutralism, disintegration, and anti-Americanism.

Truman relied upon the domino theory but, unlike the night before, sketched a slightly different pattern of spreading disaster—first most of Asia, then the Near East, then Europe. "If we let Korea down, the Soviet will keep right on going and swallow up one piece of Asia after another. We had to make a stand some time, or else let all Asia go by the board. If we were to let Asia go, the Near East would collapse and no telling what would happen in Europe. Therefore, the President concluded, he had ordered our forces to support Korea as long as we could—or as long as the Koreans put up a fight and gave us something we *could* support—and it was equally necessary for us to draw the line at Indo-China, the Philippines, and Formosa." The strategy of NSC-68 was triumphing.

In talking with the Congressional leaders, Truman had provided the rationale for American armed intervention but had still stopped short of committing ground troops to Korea. When Muccio reported that the situation in Korea "had deteriorated," at the NSC meeting on Wednesday the President resisted some efforts to escalate the war. Despite the pleas of General Vandenberg and Secretary of Air Thomas Finletter, Truman refused to let the Air Force operate above the 38th parallel. At the same time, the President admitted that he was worried that the present level of military assistance might not produce "quick results," and he said that he did not want to retreat from Korea unless military danger compelled him.

Slowly the American military commitment grew. On Thursday evening, at a two-hour meeting of the NSC, Truman authorized the use of naval and air forces "to support the ROK units and against targets in North Korea, the use of army service and communication units in Korea . . . , and combat units [in the Pusan area] to retain a port and an airfield [there.]" This decision, while cautious, meant that the service and communication units would be fired upon, and then the question would be whether they should be withdrawn or supported by more American soldiers. The commitment at Pusan, in the far south, where the DPRK forces had not yet reached, assured the United States that a major port and airfield for supplies, incoming troops, or evacuation would be kept open.

Even though the Administration had concluded that Russia was not likely to intervene militarily in the Korean conflict, the lurking fear of Russia lingered. The Administration recognized the need to keep MacArthur in tight reins "if Soviet forces intervened in Korea." His orders were blunt: "defend himself, take no action to aggravate the situation, and . . . report to Washington." MacArthur had already violated earlier orders and sent American planes against North Korea before the President had removed the ban on attacks above the 38th parallel.

MacArthur pressed Truman for a greater commitment. Early Friday morning (Washington time), the General telegraphed, on the basis of his own reconnaissance in Korea, that the South Korean army was incapable of organized action, that there was a great danger of another breakthrough. "If the enemy advance continues much further," MacArthur reported, "it will seriously threaten the fall of the Republic." To hold the present line and to keep open the possibility of regaining lost ground, the United States would have to commit ground troops into the battle area. "To continue to utilize the [air and naval forces] without an effective ground element cannot be decisive." MacArthur wanted immediately to move a regimental team to the battle area and to follow it with two (of his four) divisions from Japan. Muccio endorsed the plan in his message to State.

For Truman, the choices had been narrowed. None challenged MacArthur's assessment. Either Truman would have to accede to the request or risk abandoning Korea. So far as the recently declassified records disclose, there had never been a top-level discussion, involving Truman and Acheson, of what the commitment of ground forces might mean. MacArthur, in his characteristically cunning way, had implied that two divisions might be sufficient. But what did officials in Washington think? How many divisions ultimately—only two, or four, or ten. Maybe more? How long a war? At what cost in American lives—5,000 dead, 20,000, or more? The only tentative assurance was that the Soviets would not retaliate with troops.

At 4:57 a.m., on Friday, in response to a phone request from Secretary Pace, the President authorized the movement of one regimental team to the combat area. Later that morning, probably after conferring with advisers, he approved the sending of two divisions. MacArthur promptly ordered the 24th Division to Korea, where "it will at once . . . contact the enemy . . . and delay his advance."

The decision had been made, and it would be popular in the short run. Though no official publicly questioned the decision, John Foster Dulles, who had earlier argued for military intervention in the war, raised serious questions on July 1st. In a high-level conference that day with Acheson, Pace, and some others from State, Dulles warned that the North Korean army could be assisted by "the virtually unlimited resources controlled by the Soviet Union in East Asia, including Communist China. In that part of the world we could be an [air] and sea power but it was hazardous for us to challenge communist power on the mainland." He mentioned that General MacArthur "had remarked to me . . . , just before I left . . . Japan [on the 27th] that anyone who advocated that ought to have his head examined." Dulles wanted to know "whether the Defense Establishment estimated that [it] was possible to defeat the North Koreans on land [, or] if they thought it was impossible and would lead to a Dunkirk" or the dangerous depletion of American forces elsewhere. Perhaps partly for political reasons, Pace refused to give Dulles, a leading Republican advisor, "any reliable estimate of results." Dulles contended that it would be possible to limit the American commitment to "the use of sea and air power [in Korea.]" That was precisely the position that Truman, MacArthur, Acheson, and others had reluctantly abandoned. Apparently Dulles did not argue vigorously for his position, perhaps because he realized that troops were on the way and that Truman would have popular support for this new commitment.

It is unclear whether the President learned of Dulles's doubts. They would not have deeply troubled Truman, for he was convinced of the necessity and rectitude of his decision, and already dealing with other problems. He was very tempted by Chiang's offer to send about 30,000 Nationalist troops to the battle zone—a scheme opposed by Acheson, who both feared widening the war and judged that Chiang might need the troops on Taiwan. "We probably should use the Chinese ground troops," Truman told an associate. "What that will do to Mao Tse-Tung we do not know. We must be careful not to cause a general Asiatic war. Russia is figuring on an attack in the Black Sea and toward the Persian Gulf. Both are prizes Moscow has wanted since Ivan the Terrible . . . ." Ultimately, Acheson triumphed, and Truman decided not to accept Chiang's offer.

Matters with the Soviet Union were handled skillfully: to bar mediation but to appear conciliatory while winning propaganda victories for the United States. The American note, delivered on the 27th, called upon the Soviet Union to "disavow responsibility" for the attack and "to use its influence" with North Korean authorities to withdraw their invading forces. An earlier draft of the message (still classified) had implied or charged Soviet responsibility, and State had softened it when the American embassy in Moscow had protested the sharp wording. As the Department explained, according to a recently declassified telegram, the strategy of the note was to deter other aggression by satellites and to win a propaganda victory, not to end the war. If the Soviets could be identified with aggression by their satellites and have their prestige directly involved, State reasoned, they will be less likely to "utilize their satellites or stooges to take aggressive action." The American note would also help destroy the Soviet peace offensive, which "is assuming serious proportions and having a certain effect on public opinion in many critical areas." The peace offensive threatened to strengthen the forces of neutralism, to weaken resistance to communism, and possibly to raise doubts in America about the official analysis of the Cold War and the impossibility of meaningful negotiations.

To add legitimacy to American actions and to strengthen the American-dominated UN, Truman was eager to have MacArthur appear to be acting under UN, not American, orders. Though the President expected the General to follow American orders, Truman admitted to Congressmen in a private session, "I don't want it stated . . . that I am telling MacArthur what to do . . . It would spoil everything if we said he was just doing what we tell him to do." Congressmen, as well as the Administration, also wanted the appearance of widespread participation, from the nations of the "free world," in the war in support of the UN. That would contribute to the appearance of legitimacy and thereby also meet political needs at home.

Ironically, in unnecessary ways, the Administration undermined its own quest for legitimacy and long-run political support at home. Truman had not asked Congress for a declaration of war. Perhaps events had moved too fast in the early days, and possibly the Administration did fear that the issue of a declaration would inspire a time-consuming discussion in Congress and thereby delay what semed necessary action. As early as the 28th, the day after Truman first conferred with Congressional leaders, Senator Robert A. Taft and a few others had publicly questioned the constitutionality of the Administration's action (committing naval and air forces to combat) and wanted a declaration of war. It was quibbling, Acheson later sneered: it was a "typical Senatorial legalistic ground for differing with the President . . . ."

For reasons that remain unclear, Truman also chose to deceive Congressmen in his private meeting with them on Friday, the 30th. After he had sanctioned MacArthur's committing troops to combat to stop the North's onslaught, the President said, according to the official summary, "our plan [is] just to send base troops to Pusan to keep communications and supply lines open." "If there is any necessity for Congressional action," Truman told the select Congressmen at this meeting, "I will come to you. But I hope that we can get those bandits in Korea suppressed without that."

In June 1949, after building up South Korea's military forces, the United States withdrew its troops from the peninsula; despite Rhee's plea, the Administration would not commit itself to intervening with armed forces to protect the South in the event of an attack. Yet, in June 1950, within the course of a few days, the Administration reversed that policy. How does one explain that reversal?

In 1949, when the United States withdrew from the peninsula, American policy makers hoped, and therefore believed, that the South Korean forces might soon be strong enough to halt—and therefore to deter—a North Korean invasion. They had delayed withdrawal more than a year to build up the South's military. By late 1949, they seemed to be more worried about Rhee's launching an attack than about the North's doing so. Perhaps partly for this reason, they minimized the ample evidence of the South's military weakness and in 1950 usually stressed the capacity of the South to defend itself from the North.

Did policy makers think that America would fight to stop a North Korean invasion? While Bradley and the JCS discussed this issue in 1949 and decided against intervention under most conditions, Truman and Acheson did not address this question. They answered a different one: Should the United States firmly commit herself to defend the ROK "even to the extent of risking involvement in a major war in an area in which virtually all of the natural advantages would accrue to the USSR?" Their answer was to approve what the NSC termed "a middle course"—arms and money for the ROK to minimize the chances of her being brought under communist domination.

Usually, in 1949 and early 1950, when policy makers thought about war, they conceived of an all-out war, against the Soviet Union and involving nuclear weapons, so they did not dwell upon limited war and the unique problems it would create for the United States. And when Acheson did occasionally consider limited war, he worried about Europe and Southeast Asia, not Northern Asia. As a result, Acheson and Truman never explicitly confronted the question: Would they fight in a limited war against North Korea to defend the ROK?

In fact, events up to early 1950 had never forced Truman and Acheson to consider carefully whether they would commit American troops to a limited war. The three most notable cases of limited war had been, or were being, conducted without American forces. In Greece, the United States had supplied funds and military equipment, and some advisers, but not soldiers for war. In China, despite about 2,500 American marines, the United States had recognized that victory for Chiang was impossible—unless the administration committed millions of troops and billions of dollars. There had been no willingness to pay that price. In Indo-China, where the French were trying to defeat the revolution, the United States in early 1950 was edging toward military aid, not troops. The Administration's belief that the French could triumph prevented Truman, Acheson, and others from considering under what conditions the United States would intervene militarily in this limited war.

On June 25–30, 1950, the *apparent* facts (interpreted by ideology) thrust upon Truman and Acheson the question that they had not directly faced: whether to intervene with American forces in a limited Asian war to stop Soviet aggression by proxy? The main reason for the American commitment was that policy makers believed that they were being tested—that the Soviets would move elsewhere if the United States did not meet this challenge. Aggression, if halted in Korea, would not occur in Iran, or Europe, they concluded, in generalizing from Germany's and Japan's expansion in the '30s. Second, by 1950, Asia itself had become more important in American thinking, especially with the "loss" of China and the revolution in Indo-China. Mao's triumph, anticipated as early as 1947, had led to a shift in American policy, with Japan the new linchpin in the Pacific. Korea, deemed without significant strategic importance by the JCS, could have strategic importance if it fell into communist hands, for, as Admiral Sherman and Acheson acknowledged, it was a dagger pointing at Japan. For all these reasons, Korea —primarily as a symbol and secondarily for its substance—became for American leaders the place to draw the line, the place to make a stand.

Given this analysis, a tantalizing question remains: Would the United States have intervened in, say, July–August 1949, shortly after the withdrawal of her troops? Or had the situation for policy makers changed by mid-1950? It is impossible to answer definitively this "what might have been" question. Probably the United States would not have intervened in July– August, 1949. But, a year later, the context had changed. Events and analysis, in a subtle interplay, had transformed assumptions and strengthened resolve in ways that most men did not recognize until the "test" of Korea occurred. The Soviet development of the A-bomb in August 1949, coming a few years earlier than Americans then expected, and the work on NSC-68, prompted in part by the Soviet explosion, prepared policy makers by mid-1950 to do what they probably would not have done earlier. By the spring of 1950, they had started thinking about the threat of limited war, the need to resist Soviet "proxy" actions, and the weakness of the "free world" arsenal.

In this transformation of official thinking, in this preparation for further militarizing policy, Dean Acheson was a guiding spirit. It was not that he was consciously hankering for a crisis to justify his analysis and to mobilize America and the "free world," but his efforts to build a new policy prepared him to misinterpret the crisis and to seize upon it to justify that policy. Perhaps, also, the attacks by Republican critics, who blamed him unfairly for the "loss" of China, made him even more eager to prove his resolution: to have America forcefully and successfully resist communist expansion.

Acheson and Truman were the key figures in pushing the Administration to commit forces in Korea, and probably the President was acting upon the quiet education he had received from the Secretary in the preceding months. Throughout the week of crisis, it was also Acheson, of all the Presidential advisers, who most shaped the high-level dialogue and defined the agenda of basic issues. At least as early as Sunday afternoon, the 25th, according to his memoirs, Acheson states, "my mind was pretty clear on where the course we were about to recommend would lead and why it was necessary that we follow that course."

Truman's critical decision of June 26 to commit American air and naval troops was made primarily on the advice of Acheson. "The military neither recommended it nor opposed it," Secretary Johnson later emphasized. Military leaders had previously pointed out some "difficulties and limitations," according to Johnson, but on the 26th they went along with the President and Acheson. Whatever the continuing private doubts of military leaders (especially their doubts about ground troops), they had no desire to oppose Truman and Acheson, the Cabinet member whom the President most trusted and admired.

Speedily, within a few days, the Administration globalized containment, and prepared the way for the large military buildup that Acheson had wanted and that Johnson and Truman had earlier resisted. Analysts of this period often forget that the President, prior to the war, was devoted to a military budget of $13–14.5 billion per year, and that he and Johnson were actually cutting the budget, despite the pleas of the JCS. Without the Korean war, an essential part of NSC-68 (a military budget of $38–50 billion) would have failed. Korea, as Acheson later remarked, "came along and saved us . . . it is doubtful whether anything like what happened in the next few years could have been done had not the Russians been stupid enough to have instigated the attack against Korea. . . ."

The attack, as interpreted by Acheson, Truman, and others, seemed to confirm Acheson's analysis of the Soviet Union and made the President, who was fearful of large military budgets and of deficit spending, willing to endorse huge expenditures for the expanding military system that security seemed to require. Many others in America, including business leaders, accepted this analysis and were willing to endorse large military budgets. The result was a form of military Keynesianism that some feared would weaken the economy and others believed would promote necessary growth, but that most approved because they wanted the military system it could purchase. It would allow the Administration to build "positions of strength" —which, in Acheson's analysis, were essential to halting Soviet advances and to forcing a Soviet retreat. His aim was to save Europe and Asia for the American system, and to enable America to win the Cold War.

In retrospect, it seems appropriate to ask the troubling questions, critical of American policy, that some dissenting Americans raised in 1950. Should not the United States have stayed out of the Korean civil war? American policy makers were wrong to interpret it as a Soviet-devised or Soviet-instigated plot. In 1950, they should have followed their own earlier recommendations, outlined first in NSC-8 in 1948, and have allowed a communist triumph on the peninsula in the event of an attack. "The US should not become so irrevocably involved in the Korean situation," the Administration-approved NSC paper stated, "that any action taken by any faction in Korea could be considered a *casus belli* for the US." Even though the Administration concluded in 1948 that a communist triumph would "constitute a severe blow to the prestige and influence of the . . . US, . . . enhance the political and strategic position of the Soviet Union with respect to . . . Japan, and adversely affect the position of the US . . . throughout the Far East," the Administration did not intend to get sucked into a war to defend Rhee and the ROK. Acheson and others erred in 1950 when they reversed that analysis.

Had the United States stayed out of the war, America's prestige would have been briefly impaired in 1950. But there were ways of regaining prestige and of meeting the expectations of allied governments without going to war in 1950. In the longer run, the Administration would have strengthened its position in Europe and elsewhere by adhering to the policy of disengagement from Chiang and even moving toward recognition of Mao. Such policies would have met European needs and especially pleased Britain, whose economic interests seemed to require recognition of Mao.

"As a result of . . . erroneous judgment," Charles Bohlen later maintained, "the United States overinterpreted the Korean war and overextended our commitments." The results, he lamented, were a greatly expanded military budget, the squandering of resources, and the over-militarization of NATO. The United States pushed its European allies to build up their forces and to contribute to the Korean war, and thereby compelled them to shift their expenditures and to join in a war that soon became very unpopular. "It is no wonder," Bohlen wrote in 1969, "that we acquired a reputation as a militaristic state. . . ."

The Korean war also left another painful legacy: a large-scale sustained military intervention without a Congressional declaration of war. What Acheson derided as Senatorial quibbling, when in his judgment the President properly refused to seek Congressional authorization for involvement in the Korean war, a later generation—having experienced the Vietnam war and having developed an appreciation of Robert Taft's constitutional objections of 1950—would view as wise criticism of the "Imperial Presidency."

Ensuring Korea's Freedom: The Decision to Cross the 38th Parallel

JAMES I. MATRAY

Although historians have devoted considerable attention in recent years to Harry S. Truman's foreign policy, one incident has escaped significant controversy. Few writers challenge the conclusion that Truman's decision to cross the thirty-eighth parallel and seek forcible reunification of the Korean peninsula was ill-considered and disastrous. American military operations north of the parallel constituted a clear escalation of hostilities and prompted Chinese intervention in the Korean conflict. Subsequently, American involvement in the prolonged and costly military stalemate undermined Truman's leadership both at home and abroad.

Some scholars have argued that Truman's primary motive for ordering American combat forces across the thirty-eighth parallel was political gain. Popular happiness over Korean reunification would increase sharply the popularity of the Democratic party and lead to a sweep of the 1950 midterm congressional elections. Domestic politics may have been an important consideration, but Truman ultimately decided to cross the thirty-eighth parallel because he believed that the reunification of Korea would inflict a momentous defeat on the strategy of Soviet expansion. Once the United States destroyed the North Korean army, the administration was confident that a united Korea would reject the communist model for national development. In crossing the parallel, Truman sought to guarantee for all Koreans the right of national self-determination.

Truman's decision to cross the thirty-eighth parallel was in large part the outgrowth of past policy. Ever since the Cairo Conference in December 1943, Washington's objective in Korea had been the creation of an independent, united, western-oriented nation that would possess a progressive and democratic government. Following the death of Franklin D. Roosevelt, Truman devised a strategy that appeared to ensure the realization of this goal. If American forces liberated Korea unilaterally, Truman reasoned, then the United States could reconstruct this Asian nation without Soviet interference. Josef Stalin's decision to send the Red Army into Korea before the United

From James I. Matray, "Truman's Plan for Victory: National Self-Determination and the Thirty-Eighth Parallel Decision in Korea," *Journal of American History*, 66 (September 1979), 314–333. Reprinted by permission of the publisher.

States had an opportunity to land troops on the peninsula forced Truman to settle for a line dividing Korea at the thirty-eighth parallel into zones of occupation. The Soviet-American partition of Korea meant that only a diplomatic agreement among the great powers could produce peaceful reunification.

After World War II Truman sought to reunify Korea under a government that reflected the American rather than the Soviet model of political and economic development. At the Moscow Conference in December 1945, the United States and the Soviet Union appeared to agree on an international trusteeship as the best method for resolving the Korean problem. When Stalin refused to accept the American interpretation of the Moscow decision, Truman rejected further negotiations and ultimately turned to the policy of containment in an effort to break the deadlock. Truman's strategy for containing Soviet expansion in Korea, in contrast to western Europe, was limited and required only that the United States provide economic aid, technical advice, and small amounts of military assistance. If successful, containment in Korea would foster the emergence of a strong and stable government south of the thirty-eighth parallel closely allied with the United States and capable of self-defense.

American objectives in Korea were, however, far more grandiose, since Truman and his advisors believed that containment would act as a liberating force. Arthur C. Bunce, the American economic advisor in Korea, indicated the nature of Washington's expectations in a revealing letter that expressed his hope that the South Korean leaders "will institute a whole series of necessary reforms which will so appeal to the North Koreans that their army will revolt, kill all the nasty Communists, and create a lovely liberal democracy to the everlasting credit of the U.S.A.!" Once containment registered its first victory for national self-determination in Korea, many American leaders hoped that other Asian nations would reject communism as well and thereby frustrate Stalin's strategy for expansion.

Unfortunately, the administration submitted its aid bill for Korea to Congress at the height of the acrimonious debate over Truman's China policy. Republican critics of the administration voiced immediate opposition to the proposal, arguing that unless Truman increased the American commitment to prevent a communist victory in China, further assistance to South Korea would be pointless. Many of Truman's major advisors testified before the House Committee on Foreign Affairs in an effort to overcome Republican opposition, but by the end of 1949 Congress still had not approved the Korean aid bill. Secretary of State Dean G. Acheson's now famous National Press Club speech of January 12, 1950, was designed in part to convince Congress that passage of Truman's aid program was vital to South Korea's survival.

In analyzing the Press Club speech, scholars have pointed to Acheson's exclusion of Korea from America's "defensive perimeter" as evidence of the absence of an American commitment to defend South Korea. This argument has tended, however, to divert attention from Acheson's statement of the actual nature of Truman's Korea policy. Washington believed that it could achieve peace and stability, not only in Korea but elsewhere in Asia, without a positive guarantee of military protection. If Asian nations developed strong democratic institutions and stable economies, Acheson argued, they could withstand communist "subversion and penetration." The United States could best contribute to the growth of stability in Asia through providing economic aid, technical knowledge, and administrative advice. Such a strategy, Acheson stressed, would be particularly successful in Korea, because, in contrast to China, the Republic of Korea not only wanted American aid but would use it effectively. Acheson indicated the importance of Korea to America's strategy when he concluded that "we have a greater opportunity to be effective" in South Korea than anywhere else on the Asian mainland.

In May 1950 the administration decided to request approval from Congress for a substantial increase in military assistance to South Korea. The following month, Truman dispatched John Foster Dulles on a fact-finding mission to the Republic of Korea. In an address before the Korean legislature, Dulles proclaimed that South Korea was "in the front line of freedom." The Republic of Korea's "great strides" toward political liberty and economic prosperity proved that the task of opposing Soviet expansionism was not hopeless. Dulles then made specific reference to the power of containment as a liberating force, when he predicted that South Korea's "wholesome society of steadily expanding well-being . . . will set up a peaceful influence which will disintegrate the hold of Soviet communism on your fellows in the north and irresistibly draw them into unity with you." To American leaders containment represented a particularly attractive policy alternative, since it promised to achieve a great deal at a relatively limited cost in terms of men and material. While avoiding the necessity of resorting to military means, the United States could progressively reduce the Soviet sphere of influence and ultimately obtain victory in the Cold War. At least that was the hope.

Truman and his advisors were totally unprepared for the North Korean invasion of South Korea in June 1950. The logic of containment precluded the possibility that Moscow would revert to open military aggression to further its expansionist aims. During the senate hearings regarding the subsequent dismissal of General Douglas MacArthur, Acheson indicated the nature of the administration's assumptions: "The view was generally held that since the Communists had far from exhausted the potentialities for obtaining their objectives through guerilla and psychological warfare, political pressure and intimidation, such means would probably continue to be used rather than overt military aggression." Acheson explained that the administration recognized that the situation was serious, "but it was not believed that the attack would take place at that time." North Korea's decision to pursue forcible reunification had a decisive impact on Truman's strategy for ending the Korean partition. American economic assistance and military advice alone would not provide sufficient means for resolving the Korean problem on terms advantageous to the United States. Since the Soviet challenge was now essentially military and far more aggressive, Truman concluded that he had to alter his Korea policy accordingly.

American leaders relied heavily on a global interpretation of the Korean conflict in the formulation of subsequent policy alternatives. Dulles spoke for the administration when he exclaimed that "one thing is certain, they [the North Koreans] did not do this purely on their own but as part of the world strategy of international communism." He stressed that South Korea was making tremendous progress toward political freedom and economic stability just prior to the attack. For the Soviet Union, this "promising experiment in democracy" in Asia was a source of embarrassment. Stalin and his cohorts had "found that they could not destroy it by indirect aggression, because the political, economic, and social life of the Republic was so sound that subversive efforts, which had been tried, had failed." The Truman administration reasoned that the very success of containment in Korea forced Moscow to alter its tactics. Since Asians would reject communism if given a free choice, Stalin turned to open military conquest to expand the area of Soviet control.

Stalin's decision to use armed force for the destruction of "wholesome" nations appeared to justify, if not demand, an American willingness to employ its military power to counter the new Soviet strategy. As Dulles explained at the time, "The Korean affair shows that communism cannot be checked merely by building up sound domestic economies." Such an approach had only encouraged military aggression. Washington now feared that Moscow would initiate similar thrusts into such areas as Yugoslavia and Indochina. Perhaps more alarming, if Stalin had attacked South Korea because of its political and economic progress, there was a strong possibility of "Soviet application [of] similar reasoning to Western Europe. . . ." "Since international communism may not be deterred by moral principles backed by *potential* might," Dulles concluded, "we must back those principles with military strength-in-being, and do so quickly."

North Korea's invasion of South Korea also destroyed all basis for continued faith in the power of containment as a liberating force. Soon after the attack, the administration recognized that the United States could achieve reunification of Korea under a desirable government only if American forces crossed the thirty-eighth parallel and eliminated the communist regime by military means. Initially, however, American leaders stated that the objective in Korea was merely to restore the status quo ante bellum. During a meeting on June 27, 1950, George F. Kennan assured the North Atlantic Treaty Organization (NATO) ambassadors that the United States had no intention of pursuing forcible reunification. Two days later, Acheson declared publicly that American efforts in Korea were aimed only at upholding the rule of law in international affairs and preserving the credibility of the United Nations. He stated categorically that military action "is solely for the purpose of restoring the Republic of Korea to its status prior to the invasion from the north and of reestablishing the peace broken by that aggression."

Once the United States had intervened in the Korean conflict with combat troops, certain individuals in the administration began to press for an American commitment to cross the thirty-eighth parallel in pursuit of reunification. Perhaps the most vocal member of this group was John M. Allison, the director of the Office of Northeast Asian Affairs. In a statement dated July 1, 1950, he wrote:

> I understand that there has been some suggestion that in the speech which is being prepared for President Truman to make on the Korean situation there should be included a statement to the effect that United States forces and presumably South Korean forces will only attempt to drive the North Koreans back to the 38th parallel and will not go any farther. I most strongly urge that no such statement be included in the speech. In my opinion it would be fatal to what may be left of South Korean morale if such a statement were made. It would also appear to me to be most unrealistic in the present situation. I believe there is ample justification in the last part of the second Resolution of the Security Council for any action which may be deemed appropriate at the time which will contribute to the permanent restoration of peace and stability in that area. I am convinced that there will be no permanent peace and stability in Korea as long as the artificial division at the 38th parallel continues. I believe the time has come when we must be bold and willing to take even more risks than we have already and, while I certainly would not advocate saying in the speech that we would proceed beyond the 38th parallel, nevertheless we should not commit ourselves at this time not to do so.

Allison strongly recommended that the United States establish military control over the entire peninsula and then sponsor the free election of a government to rule a reunited Korea.

MacArthur clearly shared Allison's point of view with respect to the thirty-eighth parallel. During the first week of July, American forces were unable to halt the North Korean advance, yet MacArthur was already considering offensive action. On July 4, American military leaders in Tokyo began to discuss the feasibility of an amphibious landing behind enemy lines. MacArthur speculated that the operation could begin as early as July 22. Three days later, he informed Washington of his intention to halt the North Korean advance as soon as possible and then launch a counteroffensive in coordination with an amphibious landing behind enemy lines that would permit the United States to "compose and unite" Korea. . . .

Paul Nitze, head of the Policy Planning Staff, voiced strong opposition to forcible reunification and counseled against crossing the thirty-eighth parallel under any circumstances. The United Nations would never sanction the military conquest of North Korea, while the Soviet Union would perceive such an operation as a clear threat to its national security. Nitze's Policy Planning Staff favored instead an attempt to restrict the conflict to south of the parallel and thereby avoid the dangers involved in pursuing reunification by force: "The risks of bringing on a major conflict with the U.S.S.R. or Communist China, if U.N. military action north of the 38th parallel is employed in an effort to reach a 'final' settlement in Korea, appear to outweigh the political advantages that might be gained from such further military action." If Washington sought only to repel aggression and restore the status quo, the United States could gain a settlement more quickly and implement it with a smaller number of combat troops. The Policy Planning Staff recognized that a permanent peace would require positive guarantees for the security of South Korea. Such an approach would also entail certain political hazards, since "public and Congressional opinion in the United States might be dissatisfied with any conclusion falling short of what it would consider a 'final' settlement of the problem."

Allison found these recommendations unpalatable and registered his "emphatic dissent." If the United States fought only for the status quo ante bellum, the United Nations would be starting at the same point as in 1947. "The aggressor would be informed," Allison explained, "that all he had to fear from aggression was being compelled to start over again." Not only were the present actions of North Korea in clear violation of the will of the United Nations, but the very existence of the communist regime was a moral and factual illegality. Allison insisted that if "a correct solution of the immediate problem is not reached, a correct long term solution will be impossible." The United States possessed a moral obligation to destroy the North Korean army and implement the United Nations resolutions providing for Korea's reunification, even at the risk of global war. For Allison the issue was clear— the United States could either stand up to and defeat "raw aggression" or admit that the Soviet strategy for expansion had won.

Allison's objections forced the Policy Planning Staff to alter its position paper. The new draft stated plainly that the ultimate objective in Korea was reunification, but stressed that "we have no commitment to use armed force in the effort to bring about Korean independence and unity." Since no clear consensus existed on immediate war aims, the paper offered the following conclusions and recommendations:

> The Korean problem must be dealt with in the wider framework of the conflict between the communist and non-communist countries. The necessity to maintain a realistic balance between our military strength on the one hand and commitments and risks on the other hand, together with the need for additional information ..., make it impossible to make decisions now regarding our future course of action in Korea. It seems clear that our national security and interest will be best served at present by maintaining the greatest possible degree of flexibility and freedom of action.

Allison reluctantly approved the revised draft but continued to express dissatisfaction. Acheson, on the other hand, apparently supported the paper. At that point in the conflict, he would agree only that "no arbitrary prohibition against crossing the parallel should be imposed."

American military leaders initially voiced support for the Kennan-Nitze position. They were quite fearful of widening the war and opposed consideration of offensive action north of the thirty-eighth parallel. On July 21 the Joint Chiefs of Staff (JCS) submitted a policy paper that warned against any "excessive commitment of United States military forces and resources in those areas of operations which would not be decisive." Truman's military advisors were apprehensive that Moscow would exploit American involvement in Korea and stage new acts of aggression in areas of greater strategic importance to the United States. Even if the Soviet Union intervened militarily in support of North Korea, the JCS believed that "the U.S. should prepare to minimize its commitment in Korea and prepare to execute war plans." Events on the Korean battlefield appeared to warrant the adoption of a cautious approach. By July 18 the North Korean army had advanced one hundred miles south of Seoul and seemed to be on the verge of total victory.

Despite the desperate nature of the situation, MacArthur was urging the administration to grant early approval of his plan for an amphibious landing behind enemy lines at Inchon. On July 23 he supplied Washington with the details and expressed confidence that the operation would sever North Korea's "main line of communication and enable us to deliver a decisive and crushing blow." If the United States refused to implement such a plan, MacArthur warned, a costly and prolonged frontal assault would be the only other feasible alternative. It was obvious, however, that the JCS would not grant approval as long as the North Korean offensive continued. As a result, MacArthur traveled to Korea on July 26 and informed the Eighth Army commander Walton H. Walker that he would not tolerate further retreat. This "stand or die" order was evidently effective; battlelines stabilized during the first week of August. MacArthur's army rapidly consolidated its position and on August 7 launched its first counterattack. That same day, MacArthur wrote to former Secretary of War Robert P. Patterson that "in spite of great odds, I am sure that before too long a time has passed we will again be on the winning end."

MacArthur's successful halting of the North Korean military advance had a decisive impact on the administration's attitude toward crossing the thirty-eighth parallel. American leaders who had been reluctant to support forcible reunification now began to reconsider their position. Significantly, the JCS advised Truman on July 31 that the occupation of North Korea was desirable if the Soviet Union did not intervene and "the United States would mobilize sufficient resources to attain the objective and strengthen its military position in all other areas of strategic importance." Improved conditions on the Korean battlefield undoubtedly produced a new sense of optimism among Truman's civilian advisors as well. In all probability, Truman and his advisors decided during the second week of August to cross the thirty-eighth parallel in pursuit of a final settlement to the Korean problem. American actions at the United Nations provide strong support for such a conclusion.

On August 17 Ambassador Warren Austin delivered a pivotal speech to the General Assembly in response to an Indian request for an American statement of peace terms. At the outset Austin reminded his listeners that the United States supported Korea's freedom and independence and would not have intervened in the absence of North Korea's aggression. "The Security Council," he declared, "has set as its first objective the end of the breach of the peace. This objective must be pursued in such a manner that no opportunity is provided for another attempt at invasion." The United Nations had to establish complete individual and political freedom in Korea. The ambassador then proclaimed, "Shall only a part of the country be assured this freedom? I think not." The United Nations had a moral obligation to assist all Koreans in creating a reunited and democratic nation eligible for admission as a member of the international organization.

Having decided to pursue forcible reunification of the Korean peninsula, the Truman administration now turned its attention to formulating plans for the achievement of this objective. Despite its support for military ground operations north of the parallel, the JCS continued to emphasize the need for caution, particularly in regard to MacArthur's Inchon landing project. On August 19 [Army Chief of Staff J. Lawton] Collins and Navy Chief of Staff Forrest Sherman traveled to Tokyo and reminded MacArthur of the serious risks involved in his plan. All those present during the subsequent discussions agreed that Inchon would be an extremely dangerous operation, but MacArthur delivered an extemporaneous speech that by all accounts was a masterful job of persuasion. He convinced his audience that the element of surprise alone guaranteed success. "We shall land at Inchon," MacArthur perorated, "and I shall crush them."

Perhaps the most significant aspect of the conference, however, was that a consensus existed on the need to cross the thirty-eighth parallel. Collins, Sherman, and MacArthur agreed that the United States had to destroy the North Korean army completely or the threat of invasion would remain. Since the Soviet Union had not as yet intervened militarily in Korea, MacArthur expressed confidence that Moscow would not become involved in the future. MacArthur adopted the global perspective and focused attention on the wider importance of total victory in Korea when he argued: "The Oriental follows a winner. If we win, the Chinese will not follow the USSR." Upon their return to Washington, Collins and Sherman informed Truman of MacArthur's plans. The president now instructed his advisors to formulate a detailed course of action for the occupation of North Korea and the reunification of the peninsula.

On August 28 the JCS tentatively approved the Inchon landing project and set September 15 as the target date. The administration simultaneously completed work on its plans for an offensive across the thirty-eighth parallel. On September 1 the JCS submitted a memorandum predicting that the Soviet Union would probably attempt to retain possession of North Korea. Once the United Nations reached the thirty-eighth parallel, Moscow would either call for a ceasefire or intervene militarily "under the guise of . . . maintaining law and order." The JCS then outlined a course of action designed to forestall such an eventuality:

> Our objective of unifying Korea, however, can be accomplished if we forestall Soviet action by early entry of United Nations forces into North Korea. Such a maneuver would deny to the Soviets the initiative, deal them a major political rebuff, and, if properly timed, may not necessarily increase the risk of collision with Soviet troops.

For American military leaders, time was of the essence if the United States hoped to reunify Korea without at the same time starting a global war.

American leaders were also concerned that the Soviet Union would apply pressure on the United Nations to accept a compromise settlement in Korea. India had already demonstrated that it would ignore American opposition and respond favorably to such a Soviet proposal. To avoid a possible stalemate at the United Nations, the National Security Council (NSC) recommended that the State Department inaugurate immediate and "vigorous action on the psychological and diplomatic front." The United States had to prevail upon its allies to support postponement at the United Nations of consideration of a compromise settlement. Once MacArthur had launched a successful offensive for reunification, the entire issue would become academic.

American leaders summarized plans for Korean reunification in a NSC report. The document proceeded from the basic assumption that the United Nations, in three previous resolutions, had established as its "political objective" in Korea the achievement of a completely independent and united nation. "If the present United Nations action in Korea can accomplish this political objective without substantial risk of general war with the Soviet Union or Communist China," the paper continued, "it would be in our interest to advocate the pressing of the United Nations action to this conclusion." It would be ill-advised to pursue forcible reunification, however, if it led to global war or sacrificed American support at the United Nations. To reduce the possibility of either occurrence, the report recommended certain precautions. First, MacArthur would offer peace terms to the North Koreans prior to crossing the thirty-eighth parallel. Second, the JCS would instruct MacArthur to permit only Korean forces in the most northern provinces. Finally, the United States should obtain the explicit support of the United Nations for reunification.

The report emphasized that "a clear legal basis" existed for such American "military actions north of the thirty-eighth parallel as are necessary" to compel the North Korean army to withdraw from South Korea. The United Nations resolutions did not, however, authorize the pursuit of the political aim of establishing Rhee's control over the entire peninsula. To counter opposition in the United Nations to offensive action north of the parallel, the paper urged the administration to concentrate on the military disadvantages of merely restoring the status quo ante bellum. If the United Nations permitted North Korea to survive, it would also have to provide sufficient military power on the peninsula to enforce the ceasefire.

The report also advised the administration to expect the outbreak of global war and prepare for such an eventuality. Since American military capabilities remained relatively limited, the JCS should instruct MacArthur to cross the thirty-eighth parallel only if there were no apparent threat or indication of Soviet or Chinese intervention. If Moscow intervened, MacArthur should withdraw to the parallel and notify the United Nations. The international organization would then either increase its military commitment to achieve reunification or condemn the Soviet Union for aggression. If, however, the Chinese intervened, the JCS should instruct MacArthur to continue military operations "as long as action by UN military forces offers a reasonable chance of successful resistance."

Finally, the report discussed the reconstruction of a reunited Korea. It stressed that the American military force had to act as an army of "liberation" in order to maximize support for Rhee's government in North Korea. The United States had to withdraw its troops from the peninsula as soon as practicable after the conclusion of hostilities. The United Nations would supervise free elections throughout Korea and consult with the South Korean government regarding any problems hampering reunification. Washington would then press for the neutralization of Korea and the adoption of guarantees for the future sovereignty of the nation. The report also expressed hope that the United Nations would foster "the reorientation of the North Korean people toward the outlook of free peoples who accept the standards of international behavior set forth in the United Nations Charter." Korea would retain its independence and unity, the report concluded, only if the United Nations remained involved in the peninsula until its stability was secure.

On September 7, 1950, the JCS informed Truman of its strong support for the NSC recommendations. Thus American leaders abandoned their earlier opposition to crossing the thirty-eighth parallel and now advocated the pursuit of forcible reunification. Although Kennan and probably Nitze continued to warn against military action north of the parallel, Allison's views now appeared to represent the attitude of most of Truman's diplomatic advisors. During a radio interview on August 27, Ambassador-at-Large Philip C. Jessup emphasized that both the United States and the United Nations were committed to the creation of a free and united Korea. Although it was an entirely United Nations decision, Washington intended to impress upon the international organization that only strong action would deter further aggression and build confidence in the effectiveness of collective security.

Assistant Secretary of State Dean Rusk was perhaps the most influential advocate of crossing the thirty-eighth parallel. In a speech delivered on September 9, he pointed out that the United States was attempting to foster the triumph of national self-determination throughout Asia. Rusk then declared that American leaders "believe that the United Nations must have the opportunity to give effect to its long-standing policy in favor of a free and united Korea. . . . We have tried every other method to build peace—we must now make it clear to any aggressor that aggression carries with it their certain destruction." International security demanded that all nations rely upon peaceful and legal means to settle disputes. Rusk viewed it as imperative that the United Nations punish those governments refusing to follow established rules for proper conduct.

Truman approved the NSC report on September 11 after only minor alterations. MacArthur did not receive a complete copy of the paper until September 22, largely because Truman had just replaced Louis Johnson with George C. Marshall as secretary of defense. The United States was now committed to the pursuit of forcible reunification in Korea as long as military action north of the parallel did not ignite a major war. For Truman and his advisors, success in Korea was a matter of global importance. As State Department official H. Freeman Matthews revealed in a memorandum to the JCS, if the United States reunified Korea militarily, "the resultant defeat to

the Soviet Union and to the Communist world will be of momentous significance." It was Washington, then, and not MacArthur, that made the decision to seek the destruction of North Korea. When the general crossed the
thirty-eighth parallel, he "was not violating policy but putting it into effect."

Truman was careful not to admit publicly that he had instructed Mac-
Arthur to cross the thirty-eighth parallel. At a press conference on September
21, a newsman asked the president if he had reached a decision with respect
to military action in North Korea. Truman stated flatly: "No, I have not.
That is a matter for the United Nations to decide. That is a United Nations
force, and we are one of the many who are interested in that situation. It
will be worked out by the United Nations and I will abide by the decision
that the United Nations makes." Truman remained fearful that the Soviet
Union would be able to mobilize sufficient support at the United Nations for
a compromise settlement to block offensive action north of the parallel. It
was vital for the United States to avoid any appearance of unilateralism that
might undermine its position at the United Nations. Washington could forestall a prolonged debate at the General Assembly if crossing the thirty-eighth
parallel appeared to be a matter of military necessity.

American efforts to minimize the possibility of United Nations interference
in the military advance north of the thirty-eighth parallel are important in
understanding the administration's instructions to MacArthur during the final
week of September. Truman and his advisors demonstrated an acute sensitivity to any public reference to the parallel. In a cable to MacArthur on
September 29, for example, Secretary Marshall expressed alarm over rumors
that the Eighth Army commander had announced his intention to halt at the
parallel and await authorization from the United Nations to cross into
northern Korea. The secretary of defense then explained the reason for
Washington's displeasure: "We want you to feel unhampered tactically and
strategically to proceed north of 38th parallel. Announcement above referred
to may precipitate embarrassment in the UN where evident desire is not to be
confronted with necessity of a vote on passage, rather to find you have found
it militarily necessary to do so." In response, MacArthur assured Marshall that
the report was erroneous and the parallel was "not a factor in the mil[itary]
employment of our forces." "Unless and until the enemy capitulates," the general emphasized, "I regard all of Korea open for our mil[itary] operations."

MacArthur apparently failed to comprehend the basis for Washington's
concern. On October 1 he informed the JCS of his desire to issue a "dramatic"
statement announcing his intention to pursue and destroy North Korean forces
throughout the peninsula. The proclamation would warn the enemy that "the
field of our military operations is limited only by military exigencies and the
international boundaries of Korea." The JCS cabled MacArthur immediately
that Washington considered "it unwise to issue your statement. In accordance
with General Marshall's message . . . We desire that you proceed with your
operations without any further explanation or announcement and let action
determine the matter." The JCS continued: "Our Government desires to
avoid having to make an issue of the 38th parallel until we have accom-

plished our mission of defeating the North Korean forces." The Truman administration was probably following the advice of its allies in adopting such an approach. The strategy was successful; on October 7 the United Nations passed a resolution instructing MacArthur to "ensure conditions of stability throughout Korea."

Acheson later insisted that the administration never advocated as a war aim the achievement of an independent and united Korea. Washington's sole objective was to destroy the North Korean army and restore peaceful conditions in the area, which required the crossing of the thirty-eighth parallel. Only the Korean people themselves could realize the "political objective" of a united and democratic government through participation in free elections under the sponsorship of the United Nations. Critics subsequently maintained that Acheson was engaged in a feeble attempt to counter charges that Truman had abandoned reunification as a war aim after Chinese intervention. In reality, the secretary of state's explanation illustrates well the administration's perception of what would soon transpire.

Since 1945 Truman and his advisors had believed that the vast majority of the Korean populace favored reunification under a western-oriented, democratic government. The illegitimate North Korean regime had managed to deny its people freedom of choice until the application of containment in South Korea began to erode the foundations of communist control. North Korea's invasion of South Korea demonstrated that only the military destruction of the Soviet puppet would permit all Koreans to exercise the right of national self-determination. Most American leaders certainly recognized that elections, even in a united Korea, would not be truly free or democratic. Yet Truman was determined to impress upon the international community that, in crossing the thirty-eighth parallel, the United States sought not to compel, but to allow, the Korean people to choose the American model for political and economic development.

Truman's decision to pursue the complete destruction of North Korea was an extremely dangerous policy in both military and political terms. When the administration reverted to the restoration of the status quo ante bellum as its military objective early in 1951, the Republicans began to denounce Truman for engaging in appeasement. MacArthur also exploited popular dissatisfaction with Truman's apparent retreat. During the MacArthur hearings he stressed that his "mission was to clear out all North Korea, to unify it and to liberalize it." According to MacArthur, Truman placed unwarranted restrictions on his command and thereby prevented the fulfillment of his assignment. The administration found it difficult to counter these charges. General Omar N. Bradley insisted that Washington had never issued orders of a political nature and that MacArthur's sole mission was to destroy the North Korean army. Chinese intervention had forced the United States to abandon this "military objective," but the administration never wavered in its commitment to the creation of a united Korea through free elections. Bradley stressed that the United States had not altered its "political objective" in Korea.

Public criticism of the administration probably would have been even more severe had Truman refused to authorize military action across the parallel. Few Americans raised any words of opposition to MacArthur's offensive into North Korea. In fact, most commentators demanded a "final" settlement in Korea. In one senate speech the Democratic chairman of the Senate Foreign Relations Committee, Tom Connally, called upon the United Nations to reaffirm its commitment to the creation of a united Korea. Republicans were even more enthusiastic about the prospects for victory in Korea. Dulles explained in one private letter that "if we have the power to do otherwise, it would be folly to go back to the division of Korea at the 38th Parallel." Dulles conveyed his opinion to the administration in a memorandum to Nitze. "If we have the opportunity to obliterate the line as a political division," he reasoned, "certainly we should do so in the interest of 'peace and security in the area.' " Even liberals voiced support for crossing the thirty-eighth parallel and anticipated the establishment of a united, democratic, and reform-minded government in Korea.

In the final analysis, Truman's decision to order American forces across the thirty-eighth parallel was the culmination of America's persistent efforts to resolve the Korean predicament. MacArthur's offensive into North Korea sought to guarantee for all Koreans the right of national self-determination, which had been the primary aim of America's Korea policy since World War II. Truman's decision to cross the parallel was not the product of "military momentum" or "a surge of optimism" following the Inchon landing, since the president had adopted this course of action early in August. The Truman administration turned to military means as a last resort and only after concluding that force alone would ensure Korea's freedom to determine its own destiny.

If the United States had halted at the thirty-eighth parallel, it would have registered a significant victory. The successful defense of South Korea would have secured the interests of the United States by maintaining American international credibility and prestige. Unfortunately, the assumptions underlying American foreign policy prevented the administration from being satisfied with a mere restoration of the status quo. American leaders interpreted the Korean conflict in the larger context of the global Soviet-American competition and believed a decisive victory was within easy grasp.

Yet Truman and his advisors never perceived the American offensive north of the parallel as aggressive and struggled to avoid any indication that the United States intended to force its will on the Korean people. American leaders sought instead to portray the operation as essentially negative and designed only to create conditions in which all Koreans would enjoy, or at least appear to possess, freedom of choice. The election of a united Korean government, rather than the destruction of the North Korean army, would inflict a momentous defeat on the Soviet strategy of expansion. When a united Korea produced economic prosperity, social stability, and the appearance of democracy, Truman believed that the popularity of communism throughout the world would begin to wane. The international community would soon realize that only national self-determination could produce "final" settlements. Crossing the thirty-eighth parallel was then only the prelude to the fulfillment of Truman's plan for victory in Korea and around the globe.

FURTHER READING

Frank Baldwin, ed., *Without Parallel* (1975)

Ronald J. Caridi, *The Korean War and American Politics* (1969)

Bruce Cummings, ed., *Child of Conflict* (1983)

———, *The Origins of the Korean War* (1981)

Charles Dobbs, *The Unwanted Symbol* (1981)

Alexander L. George and Richard Smoke, *Deterrence in American Foreign Policy* (1974)

Joseph Goulden, *Korea* (1982)

Karunaker Gupta, "How Did the Korean War Begin?" *China Quarterly,* No. 52 (1972), 699–716. Critics' comments in No. 54 (1973), 354–368

Allen Guttmann, ed., *Korea: Cold War and Limited War* (1972)

Francis H. Heller, ed., *The Korean War* (1977)

Gabriel Kolko and Joyce Kolko, *The Limits of Power* (1972)

Donald Lach and Edmund S. Wehrle, *International Politics in East Asia Since World War II* (1975)

James I. Matray, "America's Reluctant Crusade: Truman's Commitment of Combat Troops in the Korean War," *The Historian,* 42 (1980), 437–455

Ernest R. May, *"Lessons" of the Past* (1973)

David McLellan, *Dean Acheson* (1976)

Yōnosuke Nagai and Akira Iriye, eds., *The Origins of the Cold War in Asia* (1977)

Glenn D. Paige, *The Korean Decision* (1968)

———, ed., *1950: Truman's Decision* (1970)

David Rees, *Korea: The Limited War* (1964)

Robert R. Simmons, *The Strained Alliance* (1975)

Gaddis Smith, *Dean Acheson* (1972)

John W. Spanier, *The Truman-MacArthur Controversy* (1959)

I. F. Stone, *The Hidden History of the Korean War* (1952)

William W. Stueck, Jr., *The Road to Confrontation* (1981)

John E. Wiltz, "Truman and MacArthur: The Wake Island Meeting," *Military Affairs,* 42 (1978), 169–176

Allen Whiting, *China Crosses the Yalu* (1960)

The Eisenhower-Dulles Foreign Policy

11

In 1953 the leadership of the two major antagonists of the Cold War changed hands. In Soviet Russia, Josef Stalin died and Nikita Khrushchev eventually took command. In the United States, Dwight D. Eisenhower won the 1952 election, entered the White House, and named John Foster Dulles his Secretary of State. The problems they faced were familiar: Korea, Indochina, Berlin, China, Eastern Europe, and the nuclear arms race. But new problems arose in the Third World, as emerging nations asserted their independence. The Middle East and Latin America became more unsettled and hence more dangerous to international stability.

The Eisenhower-Dulles team had to respond to both the old Cold War issues and the new realities. Their response has prompted questions about the foreign policy of the 1950s: Was there continuity or discontinuity between Truman diplomacy and Eisenhower-Dulles diplomacy? Who was most responsible for shaping foreign policy—Eisenhower or Dulles? What kind of President was Eisenhower? How realistic was their diplomacy? How moralistic? How ideological? Did the Eisenhower administration restrain or exacerbate the Cold War? How skillfully did American leaders handle the crises in the Third World, like that in Guatemala? Why were alternative policies rejected, such as the acceptance of neutralism?

DOCUMENTS

Before taking office, Secretary of State John Foster Dulles told the Senate Foreign Relations Committee that he favored the "liberation" of China and Eastern Europe from Communist domination. Neither his statement of January 15, 1953, nor others by him explained how he would accomplish this.

In 1954, when a leftist Guatemalan government under Jacobo Arbenz Guzmán expropriated lands owned by the mammoth United Fruit Company, President Eisenhower ordered the Central Intelligence Agency to topple Arbenz. One of the tactics was to use propaganda to depict him as a Communist. Guatemalan Guillermo Toriello Garido defended the integrity of his nation in a speech on March 5, 1954, reprinted here as the second document. On June 30 of the same year, after Arbenz had been forced from office by CIA-backed forces, Dulles cheered the change as a victory over "international communism."

The fourth document is a portion of Eisenhower's press conference of April 7, 1954, in which he spelled out what he meant by the "domino theory" and its relationship to Indochina. Walter Lippmann, noted journalist, commented on the Eisenhower administration's negative posture toward "neutralism" in a *Washington Post* column of July 17, 1956. The "Eisenhower Doctrine" was announced by the President in a speech on January 5, 1957; it sought to draw the containment line in the Middle East. The last document is Eisenhower's farewell address of January 17, 1961, which surprised many by including a warning against a "military-industrial complex."

John Foster Dulles on Liberation, 1953

THE CHAIRMAN: I am particularly interested in something I read recently, to the effect that you stated you were not in favor of the policy of containment. I think you advocated a more dynamic or positive policy.

Can you tell us more specifically what you have in mind? . . .

MR. DULLES: There are a number of policy matters which I would prefer to discuss with the committee in executive session, but I have no objection to saying in open session what I have said before: namely, that we shall never have a secure peace or a happy world so long as Soviet communism dominates one-third of all of the peoples that there are, and is in the process of trying at least to extend its rule to many others.

These people who are enslaved are people who deserve to be free, and who, from our own selfish standpoint, ought to be free because if they are the servile instruments of aggressive despotism, they will eventually be welded into a force which will be highly dangerous to ourselves and to all of the free world.

Therefore, we must always have in mind the liberation of these captive peoples. Now, liberation does not mean a war of liberation. Liberation can be accomplished by processes short of war. We have, as one example, not an ideal example, but it illustrates my point, the defection of Yugoslavia, under Tito from the domination of Soviet communism. Well, that rule of Tito is not one which we admire, and it has many aspects of despotism, itself; but at least it illustrates that it is possible to disintegrate this present monolithic structure which, as I say, represents approximately one-third of all the people that there are in the world.

The present tie between China and Moscow is an unholy arrangement which is contrary to the traditions, the hopes, the aspirations of the Chinese people. Certainly we cannot tolerate a continuance of that, or a welding of the 450 million people of China into the servile instruments of Soviet aggression.

Therefore, a policy which only aims at containing Russia where it now is, is, in itself, an unsound policy; but it is a policy which is bound to fail because a purely defensive policy never wins against an aggressive policy. If our only policy is to stay where we are, we will be driven back. It is only by keeping alive the hope of liberation, by taking advantage of that wherever opportunity arises, that we will end this terrible peril which dominates the world, which imposes upon us such terrible sacrifices and so great fears for the future. But all of this can be done and must be done in ways which will not provoke a general war, or in ways which will not provoke an insurrection which would be crushed with bloody violence, such as was the case, for example, when the Russians instigated the Polish revolt, under General Bor, and merely sat by and watched them when the Germans exterminated those who were revolting.

It must be and can be a peaceful process, but those who do not believe that results can be accomplished by moral pressures, by the weight of propaganda, just do not know what they are talking about.

I ask you to recall the fact that Soviet communism itself, has spread from controlling 200 million people some 7 years ago to controlling 800 million people today, and it has done that by methods of political warfare, psychological warfare and propaganda, and it has not actually used the Red Army as an open aggressive force in accomplishing that.

Surely what they can accomplish, we can accomplish. Surely if they can use moral and psychological force, we can use it; and, to take a negative defeatest attitude is not an approach which is conducive to our own welfare, or in conformity with our own historical ideas.

Guatemala Defends Its Reforms, 1954

The people of Guatemala are enormously disturbed to find that a respected people, freed of brutal tyrannies, eager to progress and to put in practice the most noble postulates of democracy; determined to put an end to the abuses of the past, trying to wipe out feudalism and colonial procedures and the iniquitous exploitation of its most humble citizens, finds itself faced with the dismaying reality that those who boast of encouraging other peoples to travel the road to economic and political liberty decide to bring them to a halt, only because the decisions and the efforts of these peoples injure unjust interests and because the highest interest of these peoples is incompatible with the maintenance of privileges granted by tyrants in evil times as a means of achieving impunity and a guarantee that they not be moved from the throne of their despotism. And these privileges are so important for the satisfaction of intemperate ambitions and the privileged ones are so powerful that, despite the noble postulates of Pan Americanism, they have unleashed against Guatemala the most iniquitous campaign, and have been unashamed to have recourse to the most cowardly weapons to defame, to deceive, to discredit one of the purest movements that this hemisphere has ever witnessed. . . .

What is the reason for this campaign of defamation? What is the real and effective reason for describing our Government as communist? From what source comes the accusation that we threaten continental solidarity and security? Why do they wish to intervene in Guatemala?

The answers are simple and evident. The plan of national liberation being carried out with firmness by my Government has necessarily affected the privileges of the foreign enterprises that are impeding the progress and the economic development of the country. The highway to the Atlantic, besides connecting the important productive zones it traverses, is destroying the monopoly of internal transportation to the ports now held by the Ferrocarriles Internacionales de Centro América (an enterprise controlled by the United Fruit Company), in order to increase foreign trade free of grievous and discriminatory charges. With construction of national ports and docks, we are putting an end to the monopoly of the United Fruit Company, and we will thus make it possible for the nation to increase and to diversify its foreign trade through the use of maritime transport other than the White Fleet, also belonging to the United Fruit Company, which now controls this essential instrument of our international commercial relations.

With the realization of the plan of national electrification, we shall put and [sic] end to foreign monopoly of electric power, indispensable to our industrial development, which has been delayed by the lack, the scarcity, or the distribution failures of that important means of production.

With our Agrarian Reform, we are abolishing the latifundia, including those of the United Fruit Company itself. Following a dignified policy, we have refused to broaden the concessions of that company. We have insisted that foreign investment be in accordance with our laws, and we have recovered and maintained absolute independence in our foreign policy. . . .

These bases and purposes of the Guatemalan revolution cannot be catalogued within a Communist ideology or policy: a political-economic platform like that put forward by the government of Guatemala, which is settling in rural areas thousands of individual landowners, individual farmers, can never be conceived of as a Communist plan. Far from that, we believe that raising the standard of living and the income of rural and urban workers alone stimulates the capitalistic economic development of the country and the sociological bases of a genuinely Guatemalan functional democracy. . . .

International reaction, at the same time it is pointing out Guatemala as a "threat to continental solidarity", is preparing vast interventionist plans, such as the one recently denounced by the Guatemalan government. The published documents—which the Department of State at Washington hastened to call Moscow propaganda—unquestionably show that the foreign conspirators and monopolistic interests that inspired and financed them sought to permit armed intervention against our country, as "a noble undertaking against communism." Let us emphasize before this Conference the gravity of these events. Non-intervention is one of the most priceless triumphs of Pan Americanism and the essential basis of inter-American unity, solidarity, and cooperation. It has been fully supported in various inter-American instruments, and specifically in Article 15 of the Charter of the Organization of American States. The Secretary General of the Organization, Dr. Alberto Lleras Camargo, in his report on the Ninth International Conference of American States, in commenting on this article, states categorically that with it "the doubt that seemed to arise recently, as to whether intervention carried out collectively would be so considered, has thus been dispelled".

Dulles on "International Communism" in Guatemala, 1954

For several years international communism has been probing here and there for nesting places in the Americas. It finally chose Guatemala as a spot which it could turn into an official base from which to breed subversion which would extend to other American Republics.

This intrusion of Soviet despotism was, of course, a direct challenge to our Monroe Doctrine, the first and most fundamental of our foreign policies. . . .

In Guatemala, international communism had an initial success. It began 10 years ago, when a revolution occurred in Guatemala. The revolution was not without justification. But the Communists seized on it, not as an opportunity for real reforms, but as a chance to gain political power.

Communist agitators devoted themselves to infiltrating the public and private organizations of Guatemala. They sent recruits to Russia and other Communist countries for revolutionary training and indoctrination in such institutions as the Lenin School at Moscow. Operating in the guise of "reformers" they organized the workers and peasants under Communist leadership. Having gained control of what they call "mass organizations," they moved on to take over the official press and radio of the Guatemalan Government. They dominated the social security organization and ran the agrarian reform program. Through the technique of the "popular front" they dictated to the Congress and the President.

The judiciary made one valiant attempt to protect its integrity and independence. But the Communists, using their control of the legislative body, caused the Supreme Court to be dissolved when it refused to give approval to a Communist-contrived law. Arbenz, who until this week was President of Guatemala, was openly manipulated by the leaders of communism.

Guatemala is a small country. But its power, standing alone, is not a measure of the threat. The master plan of international communism is to gain a solid political base in this hemisphere, a base that can be used to extend Communist penetration to the other peoples of the other American Governments. It was not the power of the Arbenz government that concerned us but the power behind it.

If world communism captures any American State, however small, a new and perilous front is established which will increase the danger to the entire free world and require even greater sacrifices from the American people.

This situation in Guatemala had become so dangerous that the American States could not ignore it. At Caracas last March the American States held their Tenth Inter-American Conference. They then adopted a momentous statement. They declared that "the domination or control of the political institutions of any American State by the international Communist movement . . . would constitute a threat to the sovereignty and political independence of the American States, endangering the peace of America."

There was only one American State that voted against this declaration. That State was Guatemala.

This Caracas declaration precipitated a dramatic chain of events. From their European base the Communist leaders moved rapidly to build up the military power of their agents in Guatemala. In May a large shipment of arms moved from behind the Iron Curtain into Guatemala. The shipment was sought to be secreted by false manifests and false clearances. Its ostensible destination was changed three times while en route.

At the same time, the agents of international communism in Guatemala intensified efforts to penetrate and subvert the neighboring Central American States. They attempted political assassinations and political strikes. They used consular agents for political warfare.

Many Guatemalan people protested against their being used by Communist dictatorship to serve the Communists' lust for power. The response was mass arrests, the suppression of constitutional guaranties, the killing of opposition leaders, and other brutal tactics normally employed by communism to secure the consolidation of its power.

In the face of these events and in accordance with the spirit of the Caracas declaration, the nations of this hemisphere laid further plans to grapple with the danger. The Arbenz government responded with an effort to disrupt the inter-American system. Because it enjoyed the full support of Soviet Russia, which is on the Security Council, it tried to bring the matter before the Security Council. It did so without first referring the matter to the American regional organization as is called for both by the United Nations Charter itself and by the treaty creating the American organization.

The Foreign Minister of Guatemala openly connived in this matter with the Foreign Minister of the Soviet Union. The two were in open correspondence and ill-concealed privity. The Security Council at first voted overwhelmingly to refer the Guatemala matter to the Organization of American States. The vote was 10 to 1. But that one negative vote was a Soviet veto. . . .

Throughout the period I have outlined, the Guatemalan Government and Communist agents throughout the world have persistently attempted to obscure the real issue—that of Communist imperialism—by claiming that the United States is only interested in protecting American business. We regret that there have been disputes between the Guatemalan Government and the United Fruit Company. We have urged repeatedly that these disputes be submitted for settlement to an international tribunal or to international arbitration. That is the way to dispose of problems of this sort. But this issue is relatively unimportant. All who know the temper of the U.S. people and Government must realize that our overriding concern is that which, with others, we recorded at Caracas, namely, the endangering by international communism of the peace and security of this hemisphere.

The people of Guatemala have now been heard from. Despite the armaments piled up by the Arbenz government, it was unable to enlist the spiritual cooperation of the people.

Led by Colonel Castillo Armas, patriots arose in Guatemala to challenge the Communist leadership—and to change it. Thus, the situation is being cured by the Guatemalans themselves.

Dwight D. Eisenhower Explains the "Domino Theory," 1954

QUESTION. Robert Richards, *Copley Press:* Mr. President, would you mind commenting on the strategic importance of Indochina to the free world? I think there has been, across the country, some lack of understanding on just what it means to us.

THE PRESIDENT: You have, of course, both the specific and the general when you talk about such things.

First of all, you have the specific value of a locality in its production of materials that the world needs.

Then you have the possibility that many human beings pass under a dictatorship that is inimical to the free world.

Finally, you have broader considerations that might follow what you would call the "falling domino" principle. You have a row of dominoes set up, you knock over the first one, and what will happen to the last one is the certainty that it will go over very quickly. So you could have a beginning of a disintegration that would have the most profound influences.

Now, with respect to the first one, two of the items from this particular area that the world uses are tin and tungsten. They are very important. There are others, of course, the rubber plantations and so on.

Then with respect to more people passing under this domination, Asia, after all, has already lost some 450 million of its peoples to the Communist dictatorship, and we simply can't afford greater losses.

But when we come to the possible sequence of events, the loss of Indochina, of Burma, of Thailand, of the Peninsula, and Indochina following, now you begin to talk about areas that not only multiply the disadvantages that you would suffer through loss of materials, sources of materials, but now you are talking really about millions and millions and millions of people.

Finally, the geographical position achieved thereby does many things. It turns the so-called island defensive chain of Japan, Formosa, of the Philippines and to the southward; it moves in to threaten Australia and New Zealand.

It takes away, in its economic aspects, that region that Japan must have as a trading area or Japan, in turn, will have only one place in the world to go—that is, toward the Communist areas in order to live.

So, the possible consequences of the loss are just incalculable to the free world.

Walter Lippmann on Neutralism, 1956

Mr. Dulles on neutralism has been behaving for all the world like the man who went into a dark room looking for a black cat that wasn't there. The black cat that Mr. Dulles has been looking for is a universal all-purpose definition of neutrality which will announce the exact temperature of our official moral disapproval. He seems to feel that it is somehow the business of the United States, and of himself as Secretary of State to pronounce a wholesale blanket verdict on all countries which do not belong to NATO, SEATO, or METO, on countries as diverse as India and Ireland, as Sweden and Egypt, as Switzerland and Yugoslavia. Because this cannot be done, he has within the past month or so found it necessary to contradict the President, to contradict the Vice President who had contradicted the President, and to contradict himself.

Such a thing ought not to happen in a well-conducted government. For it betrays a confusion of mind which is more damaging than the attack of our adversaries. On June 9, at Ames, Iowa, Mr. Dulles declared that, except under very exceptional circumstances, the principle of neutrality is obsolete, shortsighted, and immoral. This blanket verdict that they are all immoral irritated the nonjoiners who are a multitude in south Asia, the Middle East, and Europe. The trouble was compounded by Vice President Nixon's howler in attacking Indian policy when he was in Pakistan. So Mr. Dulles had to go back into the dark room looking for his black cat. Last Wednesday at his press conference he emerged with a new version of the Dulles doctrine. As of July 11 countries belonging to the UN (which includes all countries, excepting only Switzerland, that are able to get themselves admitted) are no longer immoral neutrals, and Switzerland is not an immoral neutral because it has been neutral for so long a time.

This reduces to absurdity the attempt to generalize about the morality of neutrals. For having started with a blanket disapproval, Mr. Dulles has ended with another generalization which leaves him with no neutrals to disapprove of. The official doctrine at the moment is that neutrality is immoral but that there are no neutrals who are immoral.

Now that we have arrived at this thundering anticlimax, the question is how did we become entangled in so stultifying and damaging an argument? This is the morning after, and we must try to remember what touched off last night's talking match.

Walter Lippmann, "The Black Cat," *Washington Post* and *Times Herald* (July 17, 1956). © I.H.T. Corporation. Reprinted by permission.

At the moment of it there is a truly perplexing and difficult situation. The basic assumption of the cold war, that the world is divided into two camps, has been overtaken by the course of events, and a great change has come upon the world situation. Among the developments which have caused this change the most influential have been the attainment of nuclear parity by the Soviet Union, the success of the forced industrialization of the Soviet Union followed by the reaction against Stalinism, the consolidation of the Red regime in China. These developments in their combined effect have worked for neutralism, have worked against the idea that nations which have no nuclear weapons can find security by joining one or the other of the two military coalitions.

In the face of this new situation there have arisen in Washington two schools of thought. The one, represented by Senator Knowland, would like to refuse American aid to any country which does not join one of our military alliances. The other, which has had encouragement from the President himself, would recognize that the weak and underdeveloped countries may have good reason for not joining military alliances, and would nevertheless give them economic aid.

Neither school of thought has as yet produced a policy which can be applied indiscriminately to all the neutrals. No one will ever produce such a policy. In the reality of things the question of how to treat Tito's Yugoslavia is distinct and specifically different from the question of how to treat Nasser's Egypt. In the Asian subcontinent we have a vital interest in being friends both in India and with Pakistan. But it is impossible to formulate a generalized policy which is equally good for both.

The root of the trouble about defining neutrals has been the practice, unfortunately rather common in our inexperienced diplomacy, of trying to deal with specific and diverse and hard problems by sweeping them under the rug of a moral generalization. This is a political vice which can be, and frequently has been, ruinous to an effective and realistic and genuinely moral policy. It is the business of the statesmen to work out an Egyptian policy, and a Yugoslav policy, and an Indian policy, and a Swedish policy, and an Irish policy, and to refrain from upsetting the applecart by pronouncing moral judgment on "neutrals" as such and in the abstract.

There are people who, when they hear an official use of the word "moral," feel that morality is being promoted and defended. It may not be so. Nobody thinks it to be moral and high-minded for a man to issue blanket moral judgment on his fellow man. He is likely to get himself thoroughly distrusted and disliked. For each of us expects to be treated as an individual person, not as part of a generalized lump.

So it is among nations. They are proud, as we are proud, and they resent, as we would resent, being put publicly on trial to be judged for their moral character. They resent it all the more when the judgment is generalized and when they are treated as faceless objects, having no distinct individuality of their own.

The Eisenhower Doctrine, 1957

The action which I propose would have the following features.

It would, first of all, authorize the United States to cooperate with and assist any nation or group of nations in the general area of the Middle East in the development of economic strength dedicated to the maintenance of national independence.

It would, in the second place, authorize the Executive to undertake in the same region programs of military assistance and cooperation with any nation or group of nations which desires such aid.

It would, in the third place, authorize such assistance and cooperation to include the employment of the armed forces of the United States to secure and protect the territorial integrity and political independence of such nations, requesting such aid, against overt armed aggression from any nation controlled by International Communism.

Eisenhower on the "Military-Industrial Complex," 1961

A vital element in keeping the peace is our military establishment. Our arms must be mighty, ready for instant action, so that no potential aggressor may be tempted to risk his own destruction.

Our military organization today bears little relation to that known by any of my predecessors in peacetime, or indeed by the fighting men of World War II or Korea.

Until the latest of our world conflicts, the United States had no armaments industry. American makers of plowshares could, with time and as required, make swords as well. But now we can no longer risk emergency improvisation of national defense; we have been compelled to create a permanent armaments industry of vast proportions. Added to this, three and a half million men and women are directly engaged in the defense establishment. We annually spend on military security more than the net income of all United States corporations.

This conjunction of an immense military establishment and a large arms industry is new in the American experience. The total influence—economic, political, even spiritual—is felt in every city, every State house, every office of the Federal government. We recognize the imperative need for this development. Yet we must not fail to comprehend its grave implications. Our toil, resources and livelihood are all involved; so is the very structure of our society.

In the councils of government, we must guard against the acquisition of unwarranted influence, whether sought or unsought, by the military-industrial complex. The potential for the disastrous rise of misplaced power exists and will persist.

We must never let the weight of this combination endanger our liberties or democratic processes. We should take nothing for granted. Only an alert and knowledgeable citizenry can compel the proper meshing of the huge industrial and military machinery of defense with our peaceful methods and goals, so that security and liberty may prosper together.

Akin to, and largely responsible for the sweeping changes in our industrial-military posture, has been the technological revolution during recent decades.

In this revolution, research has become central; it also becomes more formalized, complex, and costly. A steadily increasing share is conducted for, by, or at the direction of, the Federal government.

Today, the solitary inventor, tinkering in his shop, has been overshadowed by task forces of scientists in laboratories and testing fields. In the same fashion, the free university, historically the fountainhead of free ideas and scientific discovery, has experienced a revolution in the conduct of research. Partly because of the huge costs involved, a government contract becomes virtually a substitute for intellectual curiosity. For every old blackboard there are now hundreds of new electronic computers.

The prospect of domination of the nation's scholars by Federal employment, project allocations, and the power of money is ever present—and is gravely to be regarded.

Yet, in holding scientific research and discovery in respect, as we should, we must also be alert to the equal and opposite danger that public policy could itself become the captive of a scientific-technological elite.

It is the task of statesmanship to mold, to balance, and to integrate these and other forces, new and old, within the principles of our democratic system—ever aiming toward the supreme goals of our free society. . . .

Down the long lane of the history yet to be written America knows that this world of ours, ever growing smaller, must avoid becoming a community of dreadful fear and hate, and be, instead, a proud confederation of mutual trust and respect.

Such a confederation must be one of equals. The weakest must come to the conference table with the same confidence as do we, protected as we are by our moral, economic, and military strength. That table, though scarred by many past frustrations, cannot be abandoned for the certain agony of the battlefield.

Disarmament, with mutual honor and confidence, is a continuing imperative. Together we must learn how to compose differences, not with arms, but with intellect and decent purpose. Because this need is so sharp and apparent I confess that I lay down my official responsibilities in this field with a definite sense of disappointment. As one who has witnessed the horror and the lingering sadness of war—as one who knows that another war could utterly destroy this civilization which has been so slowly and painfully built over thousands of years—I wish I could say tonight that a lasting peace is in sight.

Happily, I can say that war has been avoided. Steady progress toward our ultimate goal has been made. But, so much remains to be done. As a private citizen, I shall never cease to do what little I can to help the world advance along that road.

ESSAYS

Townsend Hoopes, a Defense Department official in the 1960s and author of *The Devil and John Foster Dulles,* believes that Dulles was the chief architect of the foreign policy of the 1950s. Hoopes critically probes Dulles' thought, finds him excessively moralistic, faults him for ignoring opportunities for negotiations, and compares his diplomacy unfavorably to that of Dean Acheson and Harry S. Truman.

In a reassessment of the Eisenhower presidency, Fred I. Greenstein of Princeton University challenges the view that Dulles was the prime mover. Using recently declassified documents, Greenstein presents the picture of an energetic, skilled, and activist President in command of decision-making. Eisenhower's was a "hidden hand leadership."

The third essay, by Richard H. Immerman of the University of Hawaii, explores the Central Intelligence Agency's covert actions in Guatemala that led to the overthrow of the Arbenz government. Ordered by Eisenhower, this successful intervention provided lessons on coup-making that were later applied to Castro's Cuba.

A Critique of the Prime Mover, John Foster Dulles

TOWNSEND HOOPES

There were few people who held indifferent opinions of John Foster Dulles. President Eisenhower called him, in retrospect, "the greatest Secretary of State I have ever known," and added, "his calm approach, his comprehension of the important factors in every problem, his firm conclusions, and his moral courage were majestic." Winston Churchill called him "the only bull I know who carries his china closet with him"; and, noting the garrulous insistence on dominating the moving diplomatic dialogue, Churchill added: "Mr. Dulles makes a speech every day, holds a press conference every other day, and preaches on Sundays. All this tends to rob his utterances of any real significance." Alastair Buchan thought him "one of the most unattractive figures in modern history." Elliott Bell admitted that his friend Dulles was "not a man with a great deal of come-hither." Sir Oliver Franks, the British Ambassador to Washington in the early 1950's, said: "Three or four centuries ago, when Reformation and Counter-Reformation divided Europe into armed camps, in an age of wars of religion, it was not so rare to encounter men of the type of Dulles. Like them he came to unshakable convictions of a religious and theological order. Like them he saw the world as an arena in which forces of good and evil were continuously at

From Townsend Hoopes, "God and John Foster Dulles." Reprinted with permission from *Foreign Policy* 13 (Winter 1973–74). Copyright 1973 by the Carnegie Endowment for International Peace.

war." James Reston thought that, like many crusaders, Dulles possessed "a wide streak of hypocrisy," reflected in "the constant contradiction" between the "moralistic man" and the "shrewd political and diplomatic operator."

I might say a passing word on why I decided to spend two years thinking and writing about this man. In early 1968, when the Tet offensive and then Lyndon Johnson's withdrawal from further political combat tore away the final veil hiding the misperception and failure of America's freedom-defending and nation-building in South Vietnam, I faced, along with many others, the dawning realization that an era in American foreign policy had ended—an era of more than 20 years' duration in which the American people had found a large measure of their political *raison d'être,* as well as much moral comfort, in fusing their perception of the national interest with what seemed an unarguable ideological imperative: namely, the absolute need to confront and defeat (or at least oppose) every manifestation of Communism at every point on the globe. In 1970, amid the crumbled premises of that posture, it seemed necessary for one to ask how and why America had come to press its quite legitimate concern for freedom and world order to extremes that increasingly failed to meet the test of interest or reason, proportion or morality. The question led backward in time to a reexamination of the roots and tendrils and spreading branches of the cold war—hardly a new subject for reappraisal.

Yet, at least one element of truth seemed to have been overlooked or underappreciated in earlier appraisals. It was that, while the Truman Administration responded with boldness to the serious Russian threats to Western and Southern Europe, and to the attack on South Korea, in the main its efforts were guided by a conscious rhetorical restraint, by a determined effort to avoid setting in motion the runaway locomotive of a global ideological crusade. And that, conversely, it was in the ensuing period of the Eisenhower Presidency that the spirit, the policies, and the supporting deployments of the cold war spread pervasively in the United States. The Eisenhower years thus seemed the necessary place to look for answers to the basic question of why American foreign policy had lost its sense of proportion. An examination of the Eisenhower foreign policy led, of course, straight to an appraisal of John Foster Dulles. For while Eisenhower knew his own mind in foreign policy, and indeed demonstrated at critical junctures a humane and practical wisdom, and a firm restraint in the face of bellicose advice, Dulles was indisputably the conceptual fount and prime mover—the initiator, formulator, energizer, negotiator and operator—of American foreign policy during those years. Moreover, as he came not only to dominate but to personify this policy, it was in largest measure *his* legacy that was bequeathed to Presidents Kennedy and Johnson. To Americans under 30, Dulles is only a name in history. But his legacy cast a long shadow upon successive Presidents, foreign policy practitioners at every level, and the national psyche. And that legacy was formed in large part out of the character and personality of the man.

Born in 1888, John Foster Dulles grew up in the small northern village of Watertown, New York, near the St. Lawrence River, the oldest of five children. His father was a Presbyterian minister descended from a long line of vigorous churchmen and missionaries, one of whom had sailed 123 days in an open boat to carry God's word to the heathen in the Indian state of Madras and had stayed in South Asia long enough to be buried in Ceylon. His mother was the daughter of John W. Foster, a soldier, lawyer, and diplomat who served as Secretary of State during the last eight months of President Benjamin Harrison's Administration. Previously he had been Minister (which is to say, Ambassador) to Mexico, Spain, and Russia. He was a worldly and affluent man, and the fact that his daughter had grown up in the relative glitter of the international diplomatic swim was a strong source of her own ambition for her two sons, John Foster and Allen. Dulles was thus marked by both aspects of his dual heritage throughout the course of his life. On his father's side was the simple, devout, moderately intellectual, unmoneyed life of a small upstate parsonage. On his mother's side were relative affluence and sophistication—a fine house in Washington that saw the comings and goings of ambassadors, senators, congressmen, and other men of the world. There is no doubt that it was Grandfather Foster who proved the decisive influence on his life, both as an example and as a source of moral and financial support at each of several junctures. The twin aspects of his family heritage were not, however, easy to reconcile, and the inner conflict between them deeply affected Dulles' personality and manner.

He went to Princeton because all of his theological Dulles relations had gone there. (His uncle Joseph, who had baptized him, was librarian of the Princeton Theological Seminary when Dulles entered the university in 1904.) It was assumed, certainly by his father, probably by his mother, that his purpose at Princeton was to prepare for the ministry. He was only 16 years old when he arrived. At Princeton, at least until well into his senior year, Dulles was an obscure member of the undergraduate body—serious, shy, poor, and notably younger than those around him. And a number of colleagues and observers of his later life attribute the rigid, grave, and graceless manner with which he moved through most of his relationships to the strain of his circumstances at Princeton and later at law school. His tender years, they said, his puritanical background, his lack of spending money, had all made it very hard for him to make friends on an equal basis; and the pain and chagrin caused by these were deepened by a fierce awareness, indeed a subjective enlargement, of his heritage, which he considered not merely an upstate parsonage but the corridors of diplomatic power. Needing defenses to hide the gap between his sense of who he was and the apparent facts of the situation, he built up heavy layers of reserve. Arthur Krock, one of his Princeton classmates, remembered that Dulles "kept greatly to himself," gave intense concentration to his intellectual studies (which were mainly philosophical), and played chess. Such social and psychological pressures had the effect of forcing him to grow up unevenly and rather too fast, and made him a man of persisting social unease—devoid of a sound sense of situational nuance, and with a manner combining shyness and suspicion with arrogance. He could express warmth and a rather Victorian sentimentality with a few close and trusted friends. But he was notable for a flat hardness and striking insensitivity to other people.

Thrown in with older men during the years of his early manhood—not only in college and law school, but later in his law firm, and especially during his service at Versailles in 1919, where he served as legal counsel to Bernard Baruch, the United States representative on the Reparations Commission—Dulles further developed a manner of grave reserve and an operating style that managed to combine an attitude of moral superiority with the cold blankness of a professional poker player. Physically imposing, he conveyed in negotiations the impression of massive immovability, technical mastery, and (hovering just beneath the surface) an instinct for the jugular. He also developed, no doubt inadvertently, an extraordinary manner of speaking—slow, almost tortured, with long pauses in mid-sentence while he blinked his eyes and opened and closed his mouth, groping for the precise word or phrase. His friend Elliott Bell said that Dulles vividly conveyed the impression that cerebration is an intense physical act. Although the performance made his auditors uncomfortable, it appeared to give Dulles no embarrassment. Finally would come forth a well-formulated, carefully phrased comment that seemed to reflect the sense of the meeting, resolve the major issues, and lay out the logical next steps. Carefully dissected, these Dullesian formulations were found to be simple in conception, confined to basic issues, more tactical than fundamental in their approach to action, and cast in almost banal language. What gave them decisive weight with the men who heard them, however, was the sense of passionate conviction with which they were propounded, an impression reinforced by the evident physical labor that accompanied their gestation.

This gift for logical synthesis made him an effective advocate and arbiter, though hardly a dazzling public speaker. In small groups he was supreme; speaking at a rostrum before a large audience, he seemed merely wooden. The gift also led to a reputation for compulsive oversimplification. He was never guilty of complex legal formulations, and his law firm, Sullivan and Cromwell, possessed several better legal theoreticians. In a true sense, the law for Dulles was a vehicle for the growth and self-expression of a powerful mind and personality—powerful in logic, powerful in practicality, but quite narrow in range, and seeking always an immediate and a tangible result. Combined with an instinct to dominate, this cast of mind made him an advocate with an ever-present tendency to overstate his case, and it was a tendency he did not confine to the law, but extended readily to theology and foreign affairs. Reinhold Niebuhr was later to complain that "Mr. Dulles' moral universe makes everything quite clear, too clear. . . . self-righteousness is the inevitable fruit of simple moral judgments."

The ease of his accommodation to the values of Wall Street seemed another reflection of this simplicity, suggesting that the theological baggage Dulles brought with him from the Watertown parsonage was a good deal lighter than some had supposed. There was no reason to doubt the genuineness of his religious beliefs, but they boiled down to three rather thin elements: a generalized faith in a "universal moral law," which he failed anywhere to define, yet assumed every man could grasp and should obey; a conviction in the supreme worth of the individual; and a belief that religion has a role to play in the political process. The theologian John Coleman Bennett thought Dulles had evolved his own form of "secularized Calvinism." In his many speeches over the years on the subject of religion, and in the steady stream of his moralistic utterances as Secretary of State, Dulles rarely referred to the central theological problem of sin, made no admission that ethical decisions are fraught with moral ambiguity, and evidenced no understanding that the dimension of self-interest and self-preservation is implicit in every exercise of power. What he lacked in theology, however, he more than made up for in a self-certitude that seemed to grow steadily out of his mounting worldly success. As the years passed, and especially following his categorical commitment to anti-Communism, this quality seemed to fuse with his thin but firm religious tenets in an awesome self-righteousness, as though, someone said, he were acting as the agent of a Higher Power.

A case can be made for the view that a healthy percentage of Dulles' moral utterances were calculated and pragmatic appeals to the sanctified American myths of God and Motherhood, designed to secure public support for his policies. Yet if pressed too far, this theory founders on the truth—evidenced by the striking similarity of his public and private statements—that Dulles was not merely a pragmatist, but also a genuine religionist and ideologue. On the plane of goals and premises, he was a true moral believer; on the plane of action, he was a rather thoroughly amoral tactician.

A major point in understanding Dulles is to grasp the fact that he was an intellectual loner, a man who relied not merely in the last resort, but almost exclusively, in large matters and in small, on his own counsel. He appeared to develop his views through some elaborate, structured, yet wholly internalized process, whose result thus stood at the end of a long chain of logic. When finally arrived at, they were not easily reversed. Moreover, resistance to reversal was reinforced by Dulles' almost unlimited confidence in his own reasoning, his own judgment, and his own power of persuasion. . . .

As Secretary of State, Dulles performed like a one-man band, causing wide circulation of the cliché that he "carried the State Department in his hat." A loyal inner circle of subordinates fiercely disputed this, insisting that he conferred with all relevant sectors of the department. The truth is, he conferred very selectively and the consultations were of a rather special sort. His ideas being largely self-developed, he needed facts, and relished debate with those he considered informed and tough enough to defend their positions. But the purpose of the process was to produce, at most, minor refinements of his own handiwork. He was not much interested in ideas that failed to mesh with his own (Ambassador Bohlen once said, "You could almost hear the click as he turned off the mental hearing aid"), and he could be discourteous in dealings with very high people.

Many officers in the Department of State, finding him forbidding and unapproachable, could hardly avoid the contrast between the new Secretary and his immediate predecessor. Both Dulles and Dean Acheson were men of exceptional intellectual power and purpose, and tough inner fiber; there the similarity ended. Acheson projected the long lines and aristocratic bearing of a thoroughbred horse, a self-assured grace, an acerbic elegance of mind, and a charm whose chief attraction was perhaps its penetrating candor. Dulles projected the heavy opaqueness of a large bear—massive in physique, in energy, in capacity for work, in self-certitude. Where Acheson was swift-flowing and direct, Dulles was ponderous and Jesuitical; where Acheson was perceived as an eighteenth century rationalist ready to apply an irreverent wit to matters public and private, Dulles came across as an austere nineteenth century moralist, a one-dimensional man who could not relieve the self-conscious gravity of his every public utterance. . . .

In the period 1946–1950, Dulles became a fervent anti-Communist. For him, the world struggle had now moved from a sort of economic determinism to a sort of spiritual determinism; the principal source of war was now to be found in a confrontation of universalist faiths: Christianity vs. Communism. While millions of his angry and fearful countrymen shared this view, Dulles held a measurably more absolute, more vigorously logical, more uncompromising posture.

When Stalin died on March 4, 1953, opening up the prospect of a major shift toward what Malenkov, his immediate successor, called "peaceful coexistence and competition," the event found Dulles girded for uncompromising, permanent, global struggle. Indeed he seemed to require, temperamentally, a form of Communist opposition whose goal was not less than the total conquest of the world in the most literal and physical sense. The effort to formulate an American response revealed profound differences of instinct and feeling between Dulles and Eisenhower. The President stood instinctively on the side of hope, seeing in the new situation an opportunity for renewed appeal to common aspirations on both sides of the Iron Curtain. The Secretary of State stood sternly on the side of moral rectitude, seeing in the new situation an opportunity to pursue, indeed to reinforce, a policy of global pressure and liberation. Eisenhower saw hopeful signals in the Malenkov speeches; Dulles saw exploitable weakness and uncertainty in the Kremlin. When the President nevertheless decided to make a speech in April, taking note of Stalin's death as marking the end of an era, and appealing to the Russians for a mutual reduction of strategic nuclear arms, Dulles was opposed, feeling the United States would be taking the baited hook of a new Communist peace offensive. He feared and suspected any manifestation of American-Russian agreement, thinking it could only be a ruse that would cause the free world to "let down its guard," as well as a fatal discouragement to peoples in Eastern Europe.

The President's speech of April 16, before the American Society of Newspaper Editors and Publishers, was very favorably received. The *New York Times* called it "a magnificent and deeply moving initiative," and both *Pravda* and *Isvestia* reprinted it verbatim, which was both unusual and unusually favorable in the context of 1953. Dulles, whose relations with the President were not yet intimate, and who had accordingly muted his opposition to the speech during its formulation, now moved boldly to fit the President's speech within the frame of his own policy of pressure. Speaking to the same audience two days later, he said:

> When President Eisenhower first took office, a plea for peace such as he made this week might have been interpreted as a sign of weakness or a mere gesture of sentimentality . . . it was first necessary to demonstrate the will and capacity to develop foreign policies so firm, so fair, so just that Soviet leaders might find it expedient to live with these policies rather than to live against them.

This statement amounted to the unreal claim that the policies of the new Administration had transformed the international situation in the space of its first two months in office! Of graver import than the rather crass effort at credit-taking was the cynical distortion of Eisenhower's generous impulse. Believing Eisenhower naive, Dulles gave the clear signal that only a policy of pressure had made the President's speech possible, and that a policy of pressure would continue.

Bureaucratic resistance to change was formidable on both sides of the Iron Curtain, and Eisenhower's speech was thus a paper boat launched against the tide. But Charles Bohlen, who assumed his post as Ambassador in Moscow that same month, believed in retrospect that the spring of 1953 had presented a rare opportunity for Western diplomacy. There were serious rumors in Moscow that the Russians were considering "the possibility of giving up East Germany," and these tended to be confirmed by Khrushchev's later charge that both Malenkov and Beria had "plotted" such a policy. Bohlen thought that if the United States had accepted Churchill's plea for a quick and flexible Summit meeting in 1953, it could have led to "a very fruitful period" for Western diplomacy, and perhaps to "a radical solution in our favor on the German question." Dulles was absolutely opposed to such a Summit, and his stone-bottomed resistance prevailed.

Dulles' famous "massive retaliation" speech of January 12, 1954 was, on one level, the Administration's considered public announcement of the so-called "New Look" approach to defense. In essence, this emphasized the threat of nuclear punishment against centers of Communist power, and de-emphasized local efforts to block or contain Russian or Chinese Communist expansion at the peripheries. The primary consideration for the new approach was budgetary, President Eisenhower and his principal advisors being gravely concerned that a logical extension of American defense efforts on the scale of the Korean war would lead to American bankruptcy. On another level, however, the Dulles speech was a strikingly personal interpretation of the new policy, couching the threat of nuclear retaliation in far more vivid terms than it was formulated in the underlying policy document (NSC 162/2) and drawing almost verbatim from an article he had written nearly two years before.

It was necessary, Dulles said, "for the free world to develop the will and organize the means to retaliate instantly against open aggression by Red Armies . . . by means of our choosing." As nuclear retaliation was, however, already a vital component of the containment strategy (and the Strategic Air Command a force in being), Dulles was not really calling on the free world to "organize the means" for nuclear retaliation, but rather to "develop the will" to use it "instantly." Taken at face value, this was a proposal to transform the awesome nuclear hitting power from an instrument of last resort to one of first resort. Whether this was a sensible or credible proposition, four years after the Soviet Union had exploded its own nuclear weapons, was a question Dulles did not choose to explore. His argument was a lawyer's brief, more presentation than analysis, and avoided the logical weaknesses in his own case. It concentrated entirely on what the United States could do to an enemy, ignoring what an enemy could do in return to the United States, or indeed what a nuclear exchange would mean for peoples and nations who happened to be located near the presumed points of nuclear conflict. The public reaction was, not surprisingly, an uproar of confusion, consternation, and disbelief. Yet Dulles applied the new doctrine of nuclear retaliation to a variety of situations over the next five years.

The basic elements of what came to be the standard Dulles formula for brinkmanship were four: (1) an overstatement of the threat; (2) the development of an elaborate framework of authority (involving proxy commitments given in advance by Congress or allies) within which the President could take or avoid action at his absolute discretion; (3) ambiguous public warnings as to the likelihood of such action; and (4) extreme vagueness as to the military means that might be employed. The indispensable added ingredient came to be ambiguity, which permitted not only a possible carrying out of the dire threat, but also a practical withdrawal from an untenable situation.

During the Indochina crisis of March-April 1954, for example, Dulles sought to persuade Britain and France to sign on to an ambiguous formulation he called "united action." It was never clear whether this envisioned Americans fighting beside the French in an allied coalition, or a warning of American air attack against China if the Chinese directly entered the struggle, or merely an organizing point for a regional security alliance in Southeast Asia. Dulles vigorously avoided definition of the term, and its meaning thus ranged up and down the scale of potential action over the next three months, causing confusion and irritation almost everywhere. Ironically, he had started out in 1950 deploring the ambiguity of the Truman posture. It was not hard or clear enough, as he saw it, to avoid the serious risk that an enemy might miscalculate the American reaction to its intended depredation (e.g., the North Korean attack on South Korea). His overriding aim was thus to make United States intentions "crystal clear" so that a "potential aggressor" would not "miscalculate" the certainty and strength of the American response. Dulles probably drew a distinction between the certainty of an American response if a clear-cut warning were ignored, and the desirable ambiguity regarding the character of such a response. Yet when he came to his own formulations—"united action," the Formosa Resolution, the Eisenhower Doctrine—the distinction was lost and the result was a compounding of the uncertainties for friend and foe alike.

The underlying reasons were not hard to discover. Once the Russians had acquired a respectable nuclear striking power of their own, the certainty of any American response could not be assumed. Moreover, to make categorical threats against them was not credible, for the growing public awareness of the reality of nuclear stalemate generated heated political resistance to the use of such threats. In a sense, then, Dulles was forced (in the absence of an abandonment of a first resort nuclear retaliation policy) to manipulate not only the ambiguity of means but the ambiguity of whether American power would react at all in a particular crisis. Broadly speaking, Dulles and a majority of the Joint Chiefs of Staff (General Matthew Ridgway of the Army being a notable dissenter) were more ready to react than was President Eisenhower.

Twenty years after he entered office as Secretary of State and fourteen years after his death in 1959, what does John Foster Dulles look like? An impressive, headstrong man who was unquestionably the principal architect of foreign policy during the Eisenhower period, he nonetheless left behind no very distinguished or enduring monuments to his diplomatic handiwork, with the notable exception of the Japanese Peace Treaty (and that was fashioned while he was a consultant to the Truman Administration). In fairness, it must be said that the basic architecture of the postwar world—the containment strategy, the Truman Doctrine, the Marshall Plan, NATO, the philosophy of foreign economic and military aid—was already in place when the Eisenhower Administration came to office. And while there was no doubt room for new conceptions and new structures, the works of the Truman Administration proved to have been soundly built, leaving Dulles little choice but to accept and utilize major elements of the legacy. He tried hard to disguise this fact, employing a dramatic rhetoric and a hyperthyroid activism to convey an impression of his own bold innovation, but he succeeded chiefly in institutionalizing the attitudes and structures of the cold war in American life. Moved by his self-righteous and apocalyptic style, the country set out to ring the Soviet Union and China with a comprehensive set of multilateral and bilateral anti-Communist alliances, whose development led in turn to a proliferation of American military bases overseas and a dramatic rise in the flow of American military equipment for foreign armies. Bases must be manned and client armies trained and advised. In 1950, we had a few occupation troops in Germany, Austria, Japan, and Korea, and a few military base rights (with Iceland and Saudi Arabia). By 1959, more than a million American officials, military and otherwise, including their servitors and dependents, were stationed in some 42 countries. This vast formation represented unprecedented imperial power, yet that fact remained largely beyond the recognition of the American people, who were now thoroughly conditioned by the doctrinaire tendency of their leaders to elevate every issue of foreign policy to the level of deadly clash between opposed moral absolutes. Dulles had led in the building of a powerful posture of anti-Communist "deterrence." As he quit the scene, there was as yet only the first glimmering awareness that this posture also defined the limits of Dullesian diplomacy, that he possessed neither the perception of the opportunity, nor the will to move beyond it.

Today the essence of his legacy is more apparent. The slogans that have clung to his name—"agonizing reappraisal," "liberation," "massive retaliation," "brinkmanship"—all share the same sad connotation of emptiness, indeed of semifraud. The collective security alliances he planned or put together—SEATO and CENTO—were in the 1950's not very different from the makeshift arrangements they appear today; at no time did they significantly strengthen the Western posture or enhance the diplomatic landscape, and their continued survival today, in a moribund state, is attributable largely to the extraordinary strength of bureaucratic inertia. The Formosa Resolution and the Eisenhower Doctrine appear in retrospect as onetime devices formulated in haste to meet problems that were substantially misperceived (or misrepresented), and to generate congressional support for potential American actions that seemed unclear even in the minds of Dulles and the President. There is an *ad hoc* quality to the whole record.

Much of this may be explained by the fact that Dulles was far more a tactician than a systematic strategist and planner, but it is important to understand that he was a tactician who operated on fixed moral or religious premises. Moved by strong, but highly generalized, articles of faith, and lacking the managerial instinct to develop an orderly or systematic plan of operation, he showed a marked tendency to move directly from the faith to the tactic, from an abstract premise to its direct application in a very specific situation. As his premises appeared to him too basic to warrant reexamination, and as his preference was for action, he expended most of his intellectual and physical energy on the short-term tactical requirements of a problem. Lawyerlike, he applied formidable powers of concentration to a suddenly urgent or dangerous development, yet rarely aimed at more than temporary repair; and as he was insensitive to the interdependence of problems, he would frequently say or do things to help the immediate case, only dimly aware of the adverse effects he was producing on other, often more important, cases.

One key premise was that the Communist system was not only morally inferior to the West (which few doubted), but also inherently inferior in material terms (which a good many doubted). Impelled by faith in this premise, Dulles continued to pursue a policy of global pressure aimed at isolating, weakening, and eventually bringing down the major Communist adversaries in the world arena, trusting (as West German Ambassador Albrecht von Kessel said of him) "that Bolshevism was a product of the Devil and that God would wear out the Bolsheviks in the long run." He resisted any earnest search for accommodation, for his goal was not really coexistence based on calculated compromise and a balance of force; it was superiority and mastery based on a vague expectation that the West would maintain a permanent power preponderance. There may have been a real opportunity to negotiate a détente with the Soviet Union in the fluid period immediately following Stalin's death, and with the Chinese Communists in the long lull between mid-1955 and mid-1958. But Dulles was geared, ideologically and intellectually, for interminable struggle with the Devil, and he refused to reexamine his premise of inherent Western superiority long after the Soviet Union had developed military and industrial strength and exportable economic surplus of magnitudes that made his policy unrealistic and unproductive.

By 1957, for example, most of the major trading countries, including Japan, were moving toward normal economic relations with Communist China. This action by other countries reduced America's "total embargo" on China trade to a symbolic gesture, yet Dulles clung stubbornly to his shop-worn posture of total exclusion. "Whatever others may do," he said, the United States "ought not build up the military power of its potential enemy." Similarly, he refused to use the opportunity afforded by the long lull in the Formosa Strait (1955–1958) to clarify the U.S. commitment to the offshore islands, or to take any other measures that might prevent or mitigate a second, predictable explosion over those tiny bits of territory nearly touching the Chinese mainland. With regard to Peking, he remained totally inflexible, asserting (June 28, 1957) that "neither recognition, nor trade, nor cultural relations, nor all three would favorably influence the evolution of affairs in China." On the contrary, U.S. recognition of Peking would simply "enhance their ability to hurt us and our friends"; admission of Communist China to the United Nations would implant in that organization "the seeds of its own destruction." He deeply deplored the rising sentiment for change in U.S. China policy that emanated from the universities, the newspapers, and the moderate and liberal sectors of the Congress. In exasperation, he declared, "If Communism is stubborn for the wrong, let us be steadfast for the right." As a consequence of this mulish resistance to the fast-changing realities of the mid-1950's (which also included a rising determination of the Third World to achieve a position of genuine independence between the two major power blocs), the confident architect of pressure in the first Eisenhower term became the exhausted fire-fighter in the second, dashing distractedly from one blaze to another in a frenzied effort to stifle the flames of national rebellion and revolution in the Third World.

The tragedy of this situation is that there might well have been a different outcome. For the domestic political situation in the second Eisenhower term might well have sustained a different approach to the Third World, including China. Through a demonstration of trustworthiness and practical wisdom, and the exercise of ultimate control over several dangerous foreign policy crises, Eisenhower, by the end of 1956, had persuaded most of the congressional Republicans (who had oscillated between isolationism and imperialism) to support the foreign policies of an internationalist Republican President, and indeed to assume a measure of personal responsibility for them. Except for a few incorrigibles, the Republican party was being brought out of isolation to the threshold of responsible international behavior. The stage seemed set for constructive diplomacy. But the popular President suffered a diffusion of purpose and a waning of energy, while the unpopular Secretary of State continued to pursue his phantom goals.

The result was that Dulles imposed a tenacious continuity on U.S. policy at a time when conditions, at home and abroad, cried out for a searching reappraisal of basic premises, and when bold, clearheaded political leadership might have produced far-reaching change in American relations with the Soviet Union and China, at least as significant as that finally achieved by the Nixon-Kissinger initiatives of 1972. Philosophically, for example, Dulles was a strong anti-colonialist, but as Russian and Chinese offers of trade and aid gave

Third World countries a greater leverage vis-à-vis the West in their determined efforts to achieve unfettered independence, he continued in sterile opposition to neutralism and nonalignment. Neutralism, he reasoned, had adverse implications for regional alliance arrangements and American military base rights, and these were the main ingredients of his policy of pressure and encirclement. Also, because he failed to see the practical limits for Russian and Chinese imperialism in its encounters with the resistant strength of nationalism (including Communist manifestations of nationalism) in the newly independent countries, he continued to fear that *any* Communist presence among weak and backward peoples would lead to forms of subversion and takeover that could only enhance the power and influence of the Soviet Union or China at the expense of the United States.

There was, however, no doubting his dominant influence. Conviction, intellect, knowledge, and power of advocacy gave him a preeminent place with the President, the Cabinet, and in the wider public forums across the country and the world. His was the informing mind on American foreign policy; his speeches and policy statements—stamped with personal conviction, tight logic and moral fervor—provided a uniquely authoritative assessment of allies, adversaries, crises, and proposed courses of action. He was the undisputed spokesman on foreign policy, and because he spoke so often, because his words were frequently amplified by dramatic activity or dramatic inactivity, it is fair to say that what the average American citizen thought about the Communist system in the 1950's—the threats it posed, and how the United States should respond in a world of complexity and danger—was derived in no small part, directly or indirectly, from Dulles. For six years, his simple, fervent sermons and his bluntly righteous approach to defense in Western Europe, liberation in Eastern Europe, Russian influence in the Middle East, Peking's claim to Taiwan, and Communism's threat to Southeast Asia, strongly shaped American attitudes and cast a long shadow upon the decade of the 1960's. The attitudes and convictions he engendered, if not his diplomatic achievements, were enduring. To his credit (although greater credit was due to President Eisenhower's firm restraint), he avoided actual war, yet his strident approach to nearly every crisis divided the nation, weakened the trust and support of allies, and led at times to the almost total diplomatic isolation of the United States.

The rigidity of his moral stance and the power of his advocacy also defined the limits of his constructive statesmanship. And in the longer perspective, as history is ultimately measured, it is these qualities that seem likely to deny him a place among the greatest American or foreign statesmen. For his real gift lay in adversary proceedings, in tactics, in handling the urgent problem at hand, a problem not infrequently exacerbated by his own previous tactics. He lacked, in large measure, the statesman's vision, especially the statesman's dispassionate courage to peer across the angry divide to the bristling trenches of alien ideology, to identify there, and then to build upon, the hidden elements of possible reconciliation. On the whole, he was too much the believer, too much the advocate, too much the prudent political partisan to venture very far beyond the near-term interest of his client, or to perceive the wisdom of yielding minor outposts for the sake of reconciling an enemy or of building greater stability into the larger situation. Where he thought morality or ideology were engaged, he was a compulsive and righteous combatant (though not always in the end an unyielding one), and he had also concluded that in such a public stance lay his surest hope of retaining office. As one diplomat, who knew him well, put it, with more truth than tact or elegance, "Dulles was a curious cross between a 'Christer' and a shrewd and quite ruthless lawyer."

Eisenhower as Activist Leader

FRED I. GREENSTEIN

The administration of Dwight D. Eisenhower is commonly thought to be devoid of interest to those who seek insight into the range of feasible ways to conduct the presidency in the era since the responsibilities and demands of that office mushroomed under Franklin D. Roosevelt. Most of the scholarly and serious journalistic commentators on Eisenhower as president have characterized him as an aging hero who reigned more than he ruled and who lacked the energy, motivation, and political skill to have a significant impact on events. If Eisenhower was an exemplar, to their minds, it was in the negative sense of showing how one ought *not* to be president.

In recent years, however, there has been a slowly but steadily rising tide of Eisenhower revisionism. Some of the new interest in Eisenhower stems from nostalgia for the alleged placid, uncomplicated nature of the 1950s. Other interest derives from "postliberal" attraction to the kinds of policies he espoused—for example, curbs on defense spending, mildly incremental approaches to expanding welfare policies, and efforts to hold down inflation. A third category of revisionism, which might be called "instrumental revisionism," arises from reassessments of Eisenhower's performance as a political practitioner. In view of the debacles of his successors, the conduct in office of the only post-Twenty-second Amendment president to be elected to and complete two terms (and with continuingly high levels of public support at that) seems worthy of reconsideration on that ground alone.

Instrumental revisionist reexamination of Eisenhower's performance has to date been largely deductive. The two writers who have argued most forcefully that Eisenhower was not inept but instead a skilled politician who practiced the art of ruling in a deceptively veiled fashion are journalists who have relied heavily on close readings of the published record. Both have ingeniously reconstructed what seems to them the logic of Eisenhower's actions in various widely publicized events. They also have drawn on pas-

From "Eisenhower as an Activist President: A Look at New Evidence." Reprinted with permission from the *Political Science Quarterly,* 94 (Winter 1979–80), 575–583.

sages from writings of his contemporaries, such as the following by Richard Nixon in his 1962 memoir:

> [Eisenhower] was a far more complex and devious man than most people realized, and in the best sense of these words. Not shackled to a one-track mind, he always applied two, three or four lines of reasoning to a single problem and he usually preferred the indirect approach where it would serve him better than the direct attack on a problem.

The observations on Eisenhower's presidential style adduced in this article differ from those of previous instrumental revisionists in that they are inductive rather than deductive. They are based mainly on one of the many newly available primary sources on his presidency, namely the collection of several thousand documents in the Whitman File at the Eisenhower Library. This archival trove, which is named after Eisenhower's personal secretary, Ann Whitman, was opened for scholarly perusal in the mid-1970s. The Whitman File provides far more thorough documentation of Eisenhower's day-to-day activities than has been preserved for other presidencies, including: daily lists of the president's appointments; detailed minutes of formal meetings such as those of the cabinet, National Security Council (NSC), and legislative leaders; extensive notes and numerous transcripts of informal meetings between the president and other political figures; transcripts or summaries of his face-to-face and telephone conversations; texts of pre-press conference briefings; and many observations by Mrs. Whitman of comings and goings in the White House, of offhand remarks by the president, and even of fluctuations in his mood and temper.

The Whitman File also contains Eisenhower's copious comments on and interpolations in the numerous drafts of his speeches; his memoranda and notes to colleagues; an extraordinary number of "personal and confidential" letters he dictated to correspondents; and his private diary, which reaches back to Eisenhower's service in the 1930s as aide to General Douglas MacArthur in the Philippines and extends forward into his late retirement years. The Eisenhower presidency is further illuminated by the unpublished diaries and oral histories of his personal associates, many of whom are now more disposed to be interviewed than would have been the case shortly after the end of his administration.

The conclusions I draw from an extensive reading of the archival materials are more consistent with the inferences of the instrumental revisionists than with the traditional lore deprecating Eisenhower's leadership skills and efforts. Eisenhower was politically astute and informed, actively engaged in putting his personal stamp on public policy, and applied a carefully thought-out conception of leadership to the conduct of his presidency.

The term activism is commonly used to refer to three presidential attributes that in fact may vary independently of one another: sheer extent of activity; commitment to use the office so as to have an impact on public policy; and actual success in affecting policy. Despite the widespread belief that Eisenhower was not an activist president in any of these respects, he worked hard and both intended to and did have an impact on policy. Moreover, as will be illustrated throughout this essay, his activism has not been evident to many observers of his presidency due to the "low-profile" nature of his leadership style. I shall begin by considering the extent of activity of this president who often was portrayed as being more attentive to golf than to government.

The extent of Eisenhower's activity can be assessed by examining the lists of his appointments and meetings for each official day. The lists for some days can be supplemented by taking account of the prodigious amount of correspondence he dictated and other paper work he engaged in along with his numerous telephone conversations. Furthermore, oral histories and interviews with people who worked with him provide information on Eisenhower's activities during the time not covered by the appointment lists—between appointments and before and after his official day.

The appointment list for October 13, 1960, which falls at about the median in number of appointments, is quite instructive, because in addition to demonstrating the sheer extent of his activity, it suggests the distinctive nature and style of certain aspects of Eisenhower's activism. The conventional view of him as an inactive president is manifestly inaccurate. He arrived at his office at 8:12 A.M., but his work had begun much earlier. Before leaving the White House residential quarters, Eisenhower often held 7:30 meetings over breakfast. On many days, moreover, he chatted with his closest confidant, his brother Milton, who regularly spent three-day weekends living in Washington and using an office in the Executive Office Building. And by the time Milton Eisenhower, Press Secretary James Hagerty, and the staff members who each morning briefed President Eisenhower on intelligence matters saw him, he had closely read several newspapers—papers to which he paid particular attention were the *New York Times, New York Herald-Tribune,* and the *Christian Science Monitor*.

The October 13 log lists seventeen meetings during the morning and afternoon, ranging from brief exchanges with his appointments secretary to the weekly meeting of the National Security Council. The first part of the log continues from 8:12 A.M. to 5:13 P.M., with a forty-five minute preluncheon break for the rest and exercise prescribed by Eisenhower's doctors. Ordinarily, his work day would have continued for perhaps another hour, and there probably would have been a predinner hour session of informal business conducted over cocktails in the official residence. This last hour was when Eisenhower met with his major friendly adversaries, House Speaker Sam Rayburn and Senate Majority Leader Lyndon Johnson, and it often was an occasion for reflective discussion with John Foster Dulles or Milton Eisenhower.

But on this evening, Head of State ceremonies were scheduled. President and Mrs. Eisenhower attended a dinner given for them by King Frederick and Queen Ingrid of Denmark at the Danish embassy, along with a performance of the Danish Royal Ballet (with reception of guests during the intermission). The Eisenhowers dropped off the king and queen at Blair House at 11:32 P.M. and arrived at the Executive Mansion at 11:37 P.M.

If Eisenhower typically was as busy as the log of activities on October 13, 1960, suggests, how did the misimpression of his lassitude arise? For one thing, the administration did not release to the press full lists of Eisenhower's meetings. For another, it was not deemed appropriate that some of the meetings be announced—indeed this was the case with three of those held on the day under consideration, which were listed as officially "off-the-record." The nature of these meetings helps to alter the impression of Eisenhower as a passive, apolitical president who "delegated away" authority to make decisions on major issues. . . .

Whether Eisenhower "delegated away" powers he himself should have exercised is a question that meetings like the third off-the-record meeting of October 13, 1960, shed light on. This was a fifty-five-minute session with a variety of high national security and foreign-policy officials (for example, the secretaries of state and defense and the director of the Central Intelligence Agency) which immediately preceded the official meeting of the National Security Council. It falls into a class of decision-making conferences that have been described by Douglas Kinnard, who drew on the minutes of the regular pre-NSC meeting conference. The NSC meetings and administrative machinery were at that time being criticized by Washington insiders such as Senators Henry Jackson and John F. Kennedy for being an unimaginative bureaucratic setting in which routine presentation of turgid position papers occurred. [Professor Douglas] Kinnard has shown, however, that the preliminary sessions were occasions for genuine policy debate and policymaking. Indeed these sessions had a give-and-take quality quite like that recommended by scholars who call for the avoidance of "groupthink" in policy deliberations. (The official NSC meetings also were occasions for discussion, but their main function was that of "spreading the word," that is, promulgating administration policy to those who were to execute it.) Not only in pre-NSC conferences and cabinet meetings but also in general, Eisenhower favored discussions that were preceded by careful staff work, but in which contending advocates were brought together and asked to argue vigorously for their policy options. Eisenhower usually reserved comment until the other participants had spoken. Then he—not his subordinates—made the final choices, which were followed by systematic attention by staff aides to insure implementation.

Decision making by the president after vigorous debate among advisers was not a product of the so-called new Eisenhower of 1959–60; rather, this procedure was followed throughout his first six years in office as well. During those years, Eisenhower still had in his employ Sherman Adams and John Foster Dulles, to each of whom he is commonly believed to have abdicated fundamental policy-making powers. Eisenhower did strongly hold that the ability to delegate power and to utilize staff support was a necessary condition for effective leadership of large, complex organizations. As far back as 1942, immediately on assuming command of Allied forces in the European theater of World War II, he stressed in a briefing to his aides that they were "free to solve their own problems wherever possible and not to get in the habit of passing the buck up." But his delegation practices were informed by a well-developed sense of whom he could entrust with what amount of decision-making power and of the need to be vigilant about possible failures by line and staff officials to adhere to their chief's policies.

Eisenhower did entrust important responsibilities to Adams and Dulles. He prized the service of both men, but he was not awed by them. In his view, both were overly gruff and insensitive to their abrasive effect on others, but these shortcomings were more than compensated for by the high quality and prodigious quantity of their work. In numerous private diary entries Eisenhower made from time to time (much like the performance evaluations of military associates he made in World War II and immediately thereafter as chief of staff of the army), he registered judgments on their deficiencies as well as on their strengths. For example, in a note Eisenhower dictated to himself summing up accomplishments and disappointments in his first year as president, he said of Adams: "Honesty, directness, and efficiency have begun to win friends among people who initially were prone to curse him because he had no time for flattery or cajolery, or even pleasantries over the telephone." With respect to Dulles, Eisenhower wrote this assessment: "He is well informed and [on matters of foreign affairs] at least is deserving, I think, of his reputation as a 'wise' man. . . . But he is not particularly persuasive in presentation and, at times, seems to have a curious lack of understanding as to how his words and manner may affect another personality."

The evidence required for close, if not definitive, analysis of the Eisenhower-Dulles and Eisenhower-Adams relationships is now accessible. It includes not only the Eisenhower Library sources enumerated above, but also the several hundred oral histories in the Columbia University Eisenhower Administration collection, the papers and oral histories in the Princeton University John Foster Dulles collection, and Adams's papers in the library of Dartmouth College.

Richard Immerman has reported preliminary findings of a study of how Eisenhower and Dulles worked together. The evidence overwhelmingly indicates that their relationship was collaborative. The two men agreed in their basic policy goals as well as their assessments of the political realities of the time and the strategies appropriate to deal with them, although they differed from time to time on matters of tactics. Their common beliefs and perceptions were reinforced by daily contact—direct meetings when Dulles was in Washington, electronic communication when he was traveling. Eisenhower, it should be noted, conferred with and issued policy instructions to members of the foreign-policy community besides Dulles. He used Dulles partly as roving emissary, partly as official foreign-policy spokesman, and partly in his "wise man" capacity as a participant in a continuing dialogue on general and specific facets of foreign policy.

Eisenhower and Dulles practiced a division of labor resembling that of a client with his attorney—a client who has firm overall purposes and an attorney who is expected to help him devise ways to accomplish those purposes and to argue his case. The public impression that emanated from the quite different personal styles of these men—Dulles the austere cold warrior, Eisenhower the warm champion of peace—contributed to a further division of labor. Dulles was assigned the "get tough" side of foreign-policy enunciation, thus placating the fervently anti-Communist wing of the Republican party. Meanwhile, amiable Ike made gestures toward peace and international humanitarianism—for example, Atoms for Peace, Open Skies, and summitry at Geneva. . . .

In addition to the regular meetings with the cabinet and legislative leaders, the newspaper reading, conversations with his brother Milton, and intelligence briefings, Eisenhower had many other ways of seeking and receiving information. He read an extraordinary volume of official documents and maintained a voluminous "personal and confidential" correspondence with his extensive network of friends in the business and military communities and in other walks of life. His periodic stag dinners with carefully selected national figures were still another source of knowledge. Finally, it is instructive to note that although Adams had the impression that Eisenhower rarely used the telephone, the telephone logs for some days contain as many as a dozen calls in which Eisenhower sought information, gave instructions, rallied support, and made policy decisions.

Adams, in short, was an expediter of the president's policies and a like-minded agent, not a prime policy mover—this notwithstanding the not uncommon view that "O.K., S.A." was tantamount to adoption of a given course of action by "D.D.E." In this connection, the matter of "O.K., S.A." sheds light on a way that Adams's services had some of the same effect for Eisenhower as did Dulles's. The major policy papers and correspondence that went to the president did *not* bear this inscription. Rather, it was largely to be found on recommendations for minor patronage positions. Apart from being time consuming, such decisions are a notorious source of recrimination. It was much to Eisenhower's advantage that Adams take the blame for the bulk of them. (Eisenhower was able to benefit from those he informally arranged and then instructed Adams to implement.) More broadly, Adams's reputation as "abominable no man," like Dulles's as grim cold warrior, preserved Eisenhower's ability to appear as a benevolent national and international leader.

Stephen Hess has described Eisenhower's general approach to delegation of authority as one that "artfully constructed . . . an elaborate maze of buffer zones." Hess adds that "Eisenhower gave himself considerable freedom of action by giving his subordinates considerable latitude to act." It should be emphasized that Eisenhower's buffering practices did not consist exclusively of allowing subordinates to carry out the more controversial components of administration policy. But the division of labor in which the subordinate protected the president's ability to be perceived as being above the fray was in some instances a conscious strategy. For example, Press Secretary James

Hagerty (one of the staff members who had regular, direct access to the president) once reminisced:

> President Eisenhower would say, "Do it this way." I would say, "If I go to that press conference and say what you want me to say, I would get hell." With that, he would smile, get up and walk around the desk, pat me on the back and say, "My boy, better you than me."

The uses by Eisenhower and subordinates of this type of strategy are better described as acts of "pseudo-delegation" than of true delegation. In these cases the policy was Eisenhower's, but in its promulgation Eisenhower's hand was hidden. There is much further evidence of a variety of ways in which Eisenhower practiced what I shall designate as "hidden hand leadership."

Covert or hidden hand leadership is an alternative political tactic to seeking to enhance one's professional reputation. [Richard] Neustadt, it will be recalled, argues that the principal sources of presidential influence are the president's "professional reputation" among other politicians as a skilled leader, his prestige with the general public, and his use of formal powers. Eisenhower was prepared to sacrifice the first for the second. Further, he preferred informal to formal means of influence.

One type of hidden hand leadership Eisenhower practiced involved working through intermediaries. An example is provided by the following rough notes summarizing a telephone conversation in which Eisenhower charged Treasury Secretary Humphrey with the task of urging Eisenhower's friend, the Texas oil millionaire, Sid Richardson, to persuade Lyndon Johnson to be more cooperative.

> Called Secy. Humphrey—asking him to speak to Sid Richardson (who was really the angel for Johnson when he came in). Ask him what it is that Tex wants. We help out in drought, take tidelands matter on their side, & tax bill. But question is, how much influence has Sid got with Johnson? He tells Sid he's supporting us, then comes up here & disproves it (yesterday for instance). Perhaps Sid could get him into right channel, or threaten to get Shivers into primary & beat him for Senate. Humphrey says this is exactly the time to do it, too; & if he talks to Sid, it can't be said that DDE is taking advantage of long-time friendship. DDE admits Sid himself has helped us; but can't let Johnson do as he pleases. He nagged George on Bricker, now on this one. If Sid is friend of fine conservative govt., he'd better pull away from Johnson. Humphrey said Johnson's alibi to Sid this time was, "They wait until we are committed; then they come after us." But we just can't tell them things in advance—they always give it to the press. Sid understands rough language; Humphrey can use it, & will!

Another element of Eisenhower's deliberately unpublicized kind of activism consisted of exploitation of his putative lack of political skill. This is illustrated by an episode described in his private diary in which he took the blame for a diplomatic error on the part of Secretary of State Dulles. The diary entry was stimulated by a meeting with the retiring ambassador to the Court of St. James, "my good friend, Walter Gifford."

While Eisenhower was still at Supreme Headquarters Allied Powers Europe (SHAPE), he had learned of Gifford's plan to retire as soon as the next administration was in office. "With this knowledge, I of course was interested in the task of selecting a completely acceptable and useful successor. We started this job shortly after election in early November and it was not long before we determined that all things considered Winthrop Aldrich would be our best bet. This selection was made on the most confidential basis, but to our consternation it was soon public knowledge." Because Dulles felt the situation embarrassing and in need of public announcement, Eisenhower authorized this, but "put in my word of caution that Walter Gifford would have to be protected in every possible way."

In the haste to act quickly, Gifford's planned resignation and Aldrich's intended appointment were announced promptly, without clearing the matter with the British. Eisenhower continues:

> This upset the British government very badly—and I must say most under-standably. As Anthony Eden pointed out in his informal protest to Walter Gifford, this meant that Britain was being subjected to pretty rough treatment when there was no effort made to get the usual "agreement." He said that with this precedent, any small nation could pursue the same tactics and if Britain should protest, they could argue that since the United States had done this and Britain had accepted it, no real objection could be made. To guard against any such development as this, I am going to advise Anthony, when I see him next month, to lay the blame for this whole unfortunate occurrence squarely on me. He will have the logical explanation that my lack of formal experience in the political world was the reason for the blunder. Actually, I was the one who cautioned against anything like this happening, but mani-festly I can take the blame without hurting anything or anybody, whereas if the Secretary of State would have to shoulder it his position would be badly damaged.

Perhaps the most striking example of hidden hand leadership, at least in domestic politics, was Eisenhower's extensive behind-the-scenes participation in the sequence of events that culminated in the Senate's censure of Joseph McCarthy in December 1954. Working most closely with Press Secretary Hagerty, Eisenhower conducted a virtual day-to-day campaign via the media and congressional allies to end McCarthy's political effectiveness. The overall strategy was to avoid *direct mention* of McCarthy in the president's public statements, lest McCarthy win sympathy as a spunky David battling against the presidential Goliath. Instead Eisenhower systematically condemned the *types* of actions in which McCarthy engaged.

Hagerty arranged with sympathetic newspaper reporters, publishers, and broadcasters for coverage that underscored the president's implicit condemna-tion of McCarthy. In addition, an arrangement was made whereby an adminis-tration spokesman rather than McCarthy received network air-time on an occasion when Adlai Stevenson castigated the Republican party for McCarthyism. Finally, much attention was given to persuading congressional leaders to conduct the hearings evaluating McCarthy's conduct in a fashion that would vitiate McCarthy's usual means of defending himself against counterattack. Eisenhower's orchestration of the covert aspects of the events that led to McCarthy's censure even now have not been documented in the published literature on the period.

Eisenhower's published discourse was a principal source of the many deprecations of his fitness for presidential leadership. His unpublished discourse —both writings and transcripts of discussions—leads to an impression quite different from that conveyed by the published record. Eisenhower's critics derided his apparent inability to think and express himself clearly along with his seeming lack of knowledge. The evidence that gave rise to their view was the fuzzy and tangled prose in his answers at press conferences; his frequent professions of ignorance in response to reporters' questions about issues one would expect any self-respecting president to discuss knowledgeably; and the middle-brow, middle-America rhetoric of a large portion of his speeches.

Three kinds of evidence in the Whitman File make necessary a reevaluation of Eisenhower's level of knowledge and his rhetorical and cognitive styles: the transcripts of Eisenhower's conversations and conferences; his markups and insertions in the numerous drafts through which all of his major speeches went; and his personal correspondence. These sources reveal a skilled, sophisticated use of language on Eisenhower's part and extend my description of the nature and style of his activism.

A large number of the papers preserved in the Whitman File are transcripts or paraphrases of Eisenhower's conversations and conferences dealing with specifics of policy, in numerous instances matters that many people believed Eisenhower was neither interested in nor attentive to. An example is a transcribed paraphrase of a meeting with the chairman of the Council of Economic Advisers, in which the president requested a shift of emphasis in a passage of a draft of the 1959 Annual Economic Report. This document reveals the man who allegedly read only simplified one-page memos both reading and commenting upon a good many pages of complex subject matter.

> The President called Dr. Saulnier in and said that he had read the first two chapters of the proposed economic report. He liked them, but felt there was one very definite omission. He felt that in these two chapters there would be some account of the history of the weakness of the automobile market. He thinks it very important to say what caused this weakness—and he listed the causes as (1) lack of statesmanship in the search for market and (2) overextension in the use of credit terms. This latter had the effect of encouraging buying and unusual wage demands.

The transcripts of conversations and conferences also include minutes of pre-press conference briefings. Some of these explain one verbal regularity that led president-watchers to take it for granted that Eisenhower was poorly informed—his frequent statements in press conferences that he was unfamiliar with an issue. Eisenhower made such claims when he preferred not to discuss a matter. For example, in the July 31, 1957, briefing, Eisenhower was reminded that Egyptian President Nasser had made a series of speeches criticizing the United States and that the "Egyptians are trying to say [these speeches] have disturbed us." Eisenhower replied that if asked about Nasser's speeches he would state that he had not read them, whereas in fact hypothetical questions and answers on the topic were present in that session's briefing papers. It turned out, as was often the case with topics discussed in the preliminary conferences, that no journalist asked a question about Nasser's speeches.

Numerous similar assertions of Eisenhower's intention to deny knowledge of a sticky issue about which he was informed, or to say that he had not kept up with the technicalities of a matter, can be found in the pre-press conference transcripts. These assertions are borne out by abundant examples of followthrough. Virtually all of Eisenhower's press conferences include remarks such as "Well, this is the first I have heard about that," "You cannot expect me to know the legal complexities of that issue," and so on. No doubt all presidents have feigned ignorance or "stonewalled" occasionally, but out-and-out denials of knowledge are far more common in Eisenhower's press conferences than in those of the other modern presidents.

Insight into Eisenhower's confusing prose in press conferences is provided by the report, in his memoirs, of the following incident. In March 1955, two months after the passage of the Formosa Straits Resolution, reporters were still seeking unequivocal answers to such questions as whether, under what circumstances, and with what kinds of weapons the United States would defend the Nationalist Chinese-held islands of Quemoy and Matsu, if they were attacked from the mainland. In the March 16 conference, Eisenhower warned that in the event of a "general war" in Asia, the United States was prepared to use tactical nuclear weapons "on strictly military targets and for strictly military purposes." Just before the next week's conference, the State Department urgently requested, through Press Secretary James Hagerty, that the president refuse to discuss this delicate matter further.

> "Don't worry, Jim," I told him as we went out the door of my office, "if that question comes up, I'll just confuse them."
>
> One question on this subject came that morning from Joseph C. Harsch, of the *Christian Science Monitor:* "If we got into an issue with the Chinese, say, over Matsu and Quemoy, that we wanted to keep limited, do you conceive of using [atomic weapons] in that situation or not?"
>
> I said that I could not answer that question in advance. The only thing I knew about war was two things: the most unpredictable factor in war was human nature, but the only unchanging factor in war was human nature.
>
> "And the next thing," I said in answer to Mr. Harsch, "is that every war is going to astonish you in the way it occurred, and in the way it is carried out.
>
> "So that for a man to predict, particularly if he has the responsibility for making the decision, to predict what he is going to use, how he is going to do it, would I think exhibit his ignorance of war; that is what I believe.
>
> "So I think you just have to wait; and that this is the kind of prayerful decision that may some day face a President."

The July 17, 1957, pre-press conference briefing is illuminating on both the vagueness of his press conference statements and the nature of the Eisenhower-Dulles relationship. Eisenhower expressed to his staff annoyance that on the previous day the secretary of state, in his own press conference, had "wandered" into a discussion of a national security matter that Eisenhower felt should not have been commented upon at all, namely the disposition of American missiles in Europe. After checking by telephone with Dulles about precisely what had been said, Eisenhower informed his associates that if this matter were to arise in that day's press conference, "I will be evasive," as he in fact was.

Not only Eisenhower's claims of ignorance and ambiguous language, but also his fractured syntax led 1950s observers to deprecate his professional skills and, for that matter, his intelligence. Prudential calculation and personal style conspired to produce the garbled phrases quoted in so many writings drawing on Eisenhower's press conference utterances. The element of calculation is portrayed by Eisenhower in his memoirs, where he discusses the intra-administration objection to his decisions to release transcripts and later tapes on the ground that "an inadvertent misstatement in public would be a calamity." He explains that, "by consistently focusing on ideas rather than on phrasing, I was able to avoid causing the nation a serious setback through anything I said in many hours, over eight years, of intensive questioning."

The element of style involved a personal trait Eisenhower was well aware of, namely his tendency in spontaneous discourse to ramble and to stop and start. This trait derived from his tendency to have more ideas than he could readily convert into orderly sentences. Interestingly, in the absence of an audience waiting to seize upon controversial misstatements, he could dictate lengthy letters of noteworthy clarity. In press conferences, wary of misstatement and prone to a conversational mode of sputtering, he continually edited his discourse while talking. Overall, both the calculated and unintentional aspects of Eisenhower's press conference style had the same effect as his approach to delegation of authority: they damaged his reputation among the political cognoscenti, but protected his options as a decision maker and insulated him from blame by the wider public for controversial or potentially controversial utterances and actions.

Speech writing and editing were hardly novel experiences to Eisenhower when he entered partisan politics. For a number of the interwar years he had been speech writer for none other than Douglas MacArthur. His post-V-E Day Guild Hall speech in London had received wide acclaim for its eloquence. In view of this background, it should come as no surprise that as president, Eisenhower devoted great attention to his speeches. Mrs. Whitman estimates that twenty to thirty hours of the president's time, with much intervening response by speech writers, was spent on any speech of consequence.

The president's comments on the first draft of his 1954 State of the Union Message, of which thirty-eight were specific and four overarching, will serve to demonstrate his markups and insertions. The specific comments included two kinds of word changes and instructions to insert new paragraphs (which he dictated). The major purpose of one kind of Eisenhower's changes was to simplify language, striving to make the speeches more persuasive to the segment of the population to which he thought the Republican party ought to extend its appeal—members of normally Democratic population groups, such as white-collar workers and people who had completed high school but had not gone to college. To this end, Eisenhower eliminated phrases such as "substantial reductions in size and cost of Federal government" and "attacks on deficit financing," on the ground that the "man we are trying to reach" understands usages such as "purchasing power of the dollar" and stability "in the size of his market basket." Hence it was neither an accident nor an indicator of Eisenhower's own verbal limitations that when contrasted with the high-culture rhetoric of the principal Democratic spokesman of the time, Adlai Stevenson, Eisenhower's utterances seemed banal.

The second kind of change, editing with a view to perfecting diction and step-by-step progression of the exposition, probably was not necessary for rhetorical effectiveness with the general public. It was consistent with an enduring aspect of Eisenhower's cognitive style, namely intellectual precision. His demand for logical, carefully organized presentations is exemplified in the overarching recommendations concerning his 1954 message that he made to speech writer Bryce Harlow. They are the sort of recommendations one expects from experienced teachers of English composition: "Use blue pencil"; reexamine the structure of presentation by thinking through the sequence in which the paragraphs are put; "sections need to be more distinctly marked. Do not be afraid to say 'I come now to so-and-so'. . . . you cannot take the human mind from subject to subject . . . as quickly [as the present draft of this speech has attempted to do]." An illustration of the many suggestions for more precise diction is the instruction, accompanied by its rationale, to change a statement from "confidence has developed" to "constantly increasing confidence" in order to make clear that a "continuing action" is being described. (Eisenhower ranked tenth in his West Point class in English composition.)

Eisenhower's correspondence ranges from "personal and confidential" letters, many of which are quite long, to brief memoranda to aides and administration officials. In the long, confidential communications, the prose is crisp, the phrasing elaborate, and the reasoning logical and clear. It is remarkable that these highly focused letters were usually dictated in one draft that required little editing.

One such communication is a four-page, single-spaced, "eyes only" memorandum dated September 21, 1953, to Walter Bedell Smith (then undersecretary of state), concerning the defection of and subsequent award of bounty to a North Korean pilot who supplied the United Nations forces with a MIG aircraft. The gist of the episode is that defectors were no longer wanted, for as a result of recent defections of pilots in Europe there was nothing more to learn technically from a MIG plane. Eisenhower's concern was with the impact of the response by the United States on world propaganda. He had gone along with his advisers' proposal and the government had paid the bounty, kept the plane (in order to justify paying the bounty), and canceled the offer.

Eisenhower agreed that the bounty had to be paid and that the offer should be canceled. But he believed that the United States also should propose to return the plane, since a propaganda victory would attend that course of action—for the United States would be able "to stand before the world as a very honorable people, maintaining that while we had not been guilty of a real violation of the Armistice, we were anxious to avoid any implication of violating the spirit." The style and approach taken in the letter is more relevant in the present context than is the episode itself (a trivial way-station in the cold war).

In the memorandum, Eisenhower musters an orderly series of arguments that weigh the pros, cons, and probabilities of international propaganda gains against those of possible difficulties in justifying the action to the American people and of failing to take advantage of an opportunity to weaken the North Korean Air Force. In systematic progression, he considers fall-back positions the policymakers might take, depending upon anticipated responses to their initial actions. For example, if there is domestic criticism, he suggests that it be asserted that since the plane was inspected before it was returned, the United States was able to learn whether any recent changes in MIG design have been made. (Incidentally, several days after his memorandum was dispatched, the United States did offer to return the plane.)

Unlike the fairly long memoranda such as the one to Bedell Smith, much of Eisenhower's correspondence to aides and administration officials is quite brief, conveying suggestions or information rather than elaborate arguments. For instance, Eisenhower's comments on and proposed changes in drafts of his aides' letters and speeches were often phrased as polite suggestions or ideas he wanted his colleagues to consider, rather than as commands. Nonetheless, they appear to have been understood as directions, not suggestions. The passage that follows, an attempt to soften the dour tone of a Dulles speech draft, exemplifies the correspondence under consideration here.

> I have read the draft of your talk to the CIO and I must say that, in general, I enthusiastically approve. The suggestions that follow may have sufficient validity that you will want to consider them briefly:
>
> I. On page 6, at the point marked, I suggest that it might be well to expand your idea a little bit, somewhat as follows: "Based upon this clear understanding, the present Administration believes that the formulation and execution of a clear, positive, and effective American foreign policy are impossible except as it is presented against a background of American prosperity, well-being, and opportunity that extends from the most to the least fortunate among us. Specifically and concretely, this Administration is committed to the development of policies that will bring the greatest good to the greatest number. This means that appropriate governmental connection with our entire economy must be so adjusted as to develop and sustain a prosperous agriculture, manufacturing, and services, and above all such an equitable distribution of the resulting products that 60 million people will constitute always the finest advertisement for freedom." [Eisenhower makes four other suggestions and concludes], if any of the above suggestions prove helpful, I shall be pleased. If not, throw them away with a clear conscience.

Dulles revised the speech, incorporating Eisenhower's five proposed changes.

The CIA Intervention in Guatemala

RICHARD H. IMMERMAN

With the increasing accumulation of interpretive scholarship on international relations following World War II, most episodes in the cold war have been written and rewritten, evaluated and reevaluated. One striking exception, however, is the 1954 American intervention in Guatemala, which led to the overthrow of Jacobo Arbenz Guzman's constitutionally elected government. This article studies the antecedents, events, and consequences of that coup.

Analyses of hitherto unavailable archival data and of interviews with American participants in the coup who were privy to the covert aspects of the operation suggest that this event was a significant link in the unfolding chain of cold war history. Writings to date on the overthrow of Arbenz tend to be short on detailed documentation and analysis and to treat the coup illustratively. These accounts depict the United States intervention in Guatemala either as a background incident in the escalating cold war, as an example of the inordinate influence of economic interests (in this case the United Fruit Company [UFCO]) on American foreign policy, or as a way station in the evolution of the Central Intelligence Agency. These treatments fail to emphasize sufficiently that the coup typified the foundations of cold war diplomacy, providing a model to be emulated, and resisted, in subsequent years. . . .

Abiding by the constitutional limit of one six-year presidential term, Arevalo supported Arbenz, his minister of defense, in the 1950 national election. With the backing of all the parties in the governing coalition, Arbenz's election was all but assured. His chief opponent was Chief of the Armed Forces Francisco Javier Arana, the leading candidate of the conservatives, many of whom had sympathized with, and even encouraged, the more than twenty-five attempted coups which Arevalo had thwarted during his six-year administration. But Arana was assassinated in 1949, leaving only Miguel Ydigoras Fuentes to champion the opposition's cause. Long identified with some of the most repressive policies of Ubico's regime, Ydigoras Fuentes stood no chance, and Arbenz won an impressive victory. The possibility of his involvement in Arana's assassination, however, clouded his victory, muting the otherwise confident celebration over the peaceful and punctual transfer of executive power for the first time in the 130-year history of the Guatemalan Republic.

Arbenz was popular with the Guatemalan people. Tall and good looking, his fluent and vibrant voice made him the revolution's leading spokesman. Always Arevalo's foremost advocate, he campaigned [in 1950] on a platform of expanding the first administration's programs. Specifically, he spoke of the need to develop an autonomous economy that would no longer be subject to fluctuations in the international market. He explained that Guate-

From "Guatemala as Cold War History." Reprinted with permission from the *Political Science Quarterly*, 95 (Winter 1980–81), 629, 633–653.

mala had to exploit its own resources, increase the rate of employment of its population, and develop a diversified economy that was technologically innovative and fiscally sound. As Arbenz put it in his inaugural address, the fundamental objective of his administration would be "to convert Guatemala from a country bound by a predominantly feudal economy into a modern, capitalist one."

Having dedicated his government to this ambitious task of modernizing Guatemala, Arbenz put together an all-encompassing legislative program. It included the transformation of practically the country's entire economic infrastructure: the construction of factories, the improved exploitation and acquisition of mineral resources and other raw materials, the building of avenues of communication and transportation, and the further development of modern banking institutions and systems of credit. But comprehensive diversification required more basic changes. The latifundia-minifundia system that required so many agricultural laborers had to be eliminated in order to create an urban work force. More land had to be used to grow staple foods as opposed to export crops, since reliance on imports would continue to drive prices higher in the cities. And technology had to be applied to increase agricultural yields, thereby discouraging the traditional practice of leaving hundreds of acres fallow so that the soil could be replenished naturally.

To begin this process, in June 1952 Arbenz announced Decree 900, or the Agrarian Reform Bill. Certain of its components caused little difficulty— for example, the institution of new credit facilities, the careful monitoring of prices, the adjustment of tariff regulations, the provision of tax incentives, and the expansion of research programs. At the core of the program, however, was the expropriation and redistribution of land. The Ministry of Agriculture would expropriate and distribute the *idle* land of those latifundias with more than 223 acres. Almost immediately these guidelines were amended to permit those proprietors with holdings between 223 and 669 acres to keep one-third of their total fallow, and to exempt permanent pastures and woods that were being economically exploited and those fields with a slope in excess of 30 degrees. The controversy that ensued over this agrarian reform— especially as it applied to United Fruit—dramatically brought the Guatemalan Revolution to the attention of the American public. More importantly, it convinced any remaining skeptics in the Eisenhower administration that the programs of the Arbenz government were Communist inspired.

When Arevalo first became president [in 1945], few Americans feared his possible Communist affiliations. Edward Reed, charge d'affaires of the United States embassy in Guatemala, wrote the State Department that the new president "desired a moderately liberal and constitutionally stable form of government." Nevertheless, since Arevalo was relatively unknown in the United States, some extreme anti-Communists, such as former Assistant Secretary of State for Inter-American Affairs Spruille Braden, suspected that he had traveled among radical circles. As a precaution the State Department sought the opinion of the embassy in Argentina. Responding for this embassy John F. Griffiths wrote: "As far as are concerned the suspicions that might be had about Arevalo . . . it is my considered opinion that anyone even reasonably well informed about his teachings, writings and general activities would be inclined to pass over such suspicions as being so utterly without foundation as to call for no response."

But his vague doctrine of spiritual socialism, his enactment of sweeping reforms such as the 1947 Labor Code, and increased union agitation against major enterprises including United Fruit created a general uneasiness within the Truman administration. Under the direction of J. Edgar Hoover, the Federal Bureau of Investigation, charged at this time with foreign intelligence responsibilities for Latin America, investigated and compiled dossiers on Arevalo and many other prominent Guatemalans. The FBI agents focused their attention on labor leaders. Government experts reasoned that since unions in Guatemala were a post-Ubico phenomenon, any native organizer was unquestionably inexperienced and susceptible to the advice and manipulation of veteran Communists. These pundits particularly feared the influence of Vicente Lombardo Toledano of the Confederated Workers of Latin America (CTAL), which had many Communists within its ranks. Although based in Mexico, Lombardo Toledano made numerous trips to Guatemala to give aid and counsel to the nascent labor organizations.

Within a few years State Department officials extended their fear of Communist influence in Guatemalan unions to a more general concern for Communist influence in the Guatemalan government. They alleged Communists were active in all of the government propaganda outlets including the information offices, the official newspapers, and the government-owned radio stations. Even more worrisome was their contention that Arevalo positioned Communists high in his administration. Among those suspected was Augusto Charnaud MacDonald, Arevalo's minister of economy and labor, who charge d'affaires Milton K. Wells described as extremely hostile to foreign elements and the driving force behind the government's failure to defend aggressively United Fruit's interests. Wells and other observers considered the foreign ministry a particular locus of Communist sympathizers. For example, in evaluating Guatemala's ambassador to the United States, Jorge Garcia Granados, the FBI claimed that he had assumed a new name and, drawing on a traditional anti-Semitic aspersion, sought to impugn his political character by asserting that he was part Jewish and operated under the front of various Jewish organizations.

The notable aspect of this putative evidence of communism within the Guatemalan government is its dependence on McCarthy-like techniques to accuse supposed Communists. For example, the most widely cited indications of Communist penetration were the hardships encountered by the United Fruit Company. These difficulties first surfaced in the late 1940s, when the newly organized Guatemalan workers struck several UFCO operations. But the real challenge came after 1952, when Arbenz used the Agrarian Reform Bill to expropriate close to 400,000 acres of UFCO property. The law stipulated that compensation should be paid in twenty-five year guaranteed non-negotiable bonds and should be determined by the property's declared tax value—in this case close to $2 million. The expropriation and meager offer of compensation horrified UFCO and government officials. Like McCarthyite indictments of the State Department after the "fall" of China, experts believed that Communists had to be behind such an outrage.

Yet even President Eisenhower conceded that the expropriation was not conclusive proof. He wrote of Guatemala in his memoirs, "Expropriation in itself does not, of course prove Communism; expropriation of oil and agricultural properties years before in Mexico had not been fostered by Communists." For this reason Eisenhower buttressed his argument by adding more circumstantial evidence, in particular, Guatemala's reaction to the Korean War. He concluded that the Guatemalan government must have been in league with the Soviets and Chinese, for "it accepted the ridiculous Communist contention that the United States had conducted bacteriological warfare in Korea."

This coincidence between the Guatemalan allegations and similar ones by the Soviet Union was also a major determinant in John Moors Cabot's conviction that Guatemala had succumbed to the Communists and that some action was necessary. In a 1954 speech Eisenhower's assistant secretary of state for Latin American affairs condemned the Guatemalan government on the same charges the president would level nearly a decade later. His tenuous logic illustrates the nature of the reasoning used during this period: "We find it difficult, for example, to be patient, after all the blood and treasure we have poured out in Korea to safeguard the Free World, when the official Guatemalan newspaper follows the Communist line by accusing us in effect of bacteriological warfare just after our airmen have returned to tell us of the tortures to which they were subjected to extract fabricated confessions."

The prime illustration of this principle of guilt by association was the well-known "duck test." In 1950 Richard C. Patterson, Jr., then ambassador to Guatemala but already declared persona non grata by the Arevalo government and recalled to Washington, explained in a speech how to uncover Communists. His explanation is particularly instructive in that it makes explicit this "methodology" and how it could be applied to detect Communists and Communist influences.

> Many times it is impossible to prove legally that a certain individual is a communist; but for cases of this sort I recommend a practical method of detection—the "duck test." The duck test works this way: suppose you see a bird walking around in a farm yard. This bird wears no label that says "duck." But the bird certainly looks like a duck. Also, he goes to the pond and you notice he swims like a duck. Then he opens his beak and quacks like a duck. Well, by this time you have probably reached the conclusion that the bird is a duck, whether he's wearing a label or not.

When he testified to the House of Representatives in 1954, Patterson's successor John Peurifoy similarly relied on the duck test. Referring to Arbenz he stated, "I spent six hours with him one evening, and he talked like a Communist, and if he is not one, Mr. Chairman, he will do until one comes along. . . . He had all the earmarks."

The United Fruit Company effectively used this overarching fear of Communist subversion in order to evoke government and popular sympathy for its plight. Under the astute guidance of its prestigious public relations counsel, Edward Bernays, UFCO launched a massive publicity campaign. It sponsored junkets to Guatemala for leading newspaper and magazine reporters, and often also for their publishers. It enlisted prominent individuals such as former Assistant Secretary Braden, who had also been a long-time diplomat in Latin America, and ex-Roosevelt aide Thomas Corcoran to lobby among their influential friends in Washington. Understanding that the Communist threat overshadowed the expropriation controversy, these United Fruit agents emphasized the supposed international conspiracy, not particular economic grievances. They succeeded. In 1954 the *New York Times,* reflecting the dominant view within the White House, State Department, and Congress, wrote that the "constant harassment here [in Guatemala] to which the company [United Fruit] now is being subjected is largely a Communist tactic."

The approach taken by the United Fruit Company suggests that while policymakers were well aware of the difficulties faced by the UFCO, these difficulties in and of themselves were *not* sufficient reasons for the eventual decision to intervene. As Eisenhower noted in his memoirs, the Roosevelt administration protested Mexico's expropriations prior to World War II, but the appropriate policy was negotiation. But in Guatemala the expropriation of United Fruit's holdings became linked to the fear of a Communist outpost in the Western Hemisphere. This fear, more than the expropriation, led to the intervention.

This analysis of the Eisenhower administration's motives coincides with the president's personal views on relations with developing nations. He felt that policies that defended particular economic interests without considering the adverse effects such policies would have on nationalist movements were shortsighted and "victorian." Eisenhower argued that the Western powers should make gradual concessions to satisfy the spirit of nationalism in developing nations, thereby assuring their continued support. As he wrote in a letter to the *New York Herald Tribune*'s Executive Vice-President William Robinson a month after the Guatemalan coup, within these countries "there is a strong communist leaning among certain groups." If the United States constructed policies inimical to the economies of developing nations, he continued, "we will most certainly arouse more antagonism," and the possibility of these countries "turning communist would mount rapidly." But Eisenhower was a firm cold warrior, and once he determined a country *had* turned Communist, such as 1954 Guatemala, he sought to reverse the situation by any means feasible.

United Fruit's well-known connections within the White House, State Department, and Congress did help to create a sympathetic audience. Nevertheless, government officials brought with them an outlook on world politics that was fashioned by the cold war ethos. They assumed that communism threatened the fundamental American way of life, that foreign investment was essential for this way of life so any threat to this investment was concomitantly a threat to the national interest, and that any threat to the national interest was necessarily the result of Communist activity and a threat to national security.

By such logic, in spite of Eisenhower's distinction between nationalism and communism, Communists became scapegoats for virtually any program or policy that opposed United States interests. These interests incorporated strategic, political, and of course economic considerations. As Willard Barber, Truman's deputy assistant secretary of state for American republic affairs put it in 1949, combining ideological and material factors, Communist influences were those "alien to American ideals and which have affected Guatemala as a place for investment of capital." Even more specifically, less than two weeks before Castillo Armas's invasion of Guatemala, Secretary of State John Foster Dulles, in a televised press statement, explained to the American public the relationship between economic interests and national security. The expropriations were symptomatic of a greater danger. Dulles remarked: "If the United Fruit matter were settled, if they gave a gold piece for every banana, the problem would remain just as it is today as far as the presence of communist infiltration in Guatemala is concerned. That is the problem, not United Fruit."

It is difficult to pinpoint the exact date of the decision to intervene in Guatemala. Circumstances indicate that it came sometime in the middle of 1953, before the second expropriation of United Fruit property. At this time John Doherty replaced two former FBI operatives, Collins Almon and Birch O'Neill, as CIA station chief in Guatemala. Also during this period several envoys of Nicaragua's dictator Anastasio Somoza along with United Fruit's Corcoran contacted ex-CIA chief and current Undersecretary of State Walter Bedell Smith. They told Smith that the Communist danger in Guatemala had reached such proportions that certain neighboring nations, particularly Nicaragua and Honduras, were ready to act. These countries lacked sufficient resources by themselves and needed the help of the United States.

Another suggestion that this was the time of the decision is that in August 1953 Carlos Castillo Armas and Ydigoras Fuentes met in Tegucigalpa, Honduras, to sign a "gentleman's pact" promising to cooperate to overthrow Arbenz. Castillo Armas informed Ydigoras Fuentes that he had received assurances of American support, a claim supported by a letter he wrote to Somoza in September saying, "I have been informed by our friends here that the government of the North, recognizing the impossibility of finding another solution to the grave problem of my country, has taken the decision to permit us to develop our plans." Since Castillo Armas's plans required U.S. assistance, it is clear that the Eisenhower administration intended to do more than just look the other way.

A final indication as to the timing of the decision to intervene is that during the spring and summer of 1953 the Eisenhower administration began to look for a suitable ambassador to Guatemala who could coordinate State Department and CIA operations. Rudolph Schoenfeld, a career diplomat with some experience with Communist matters—he had been the American representative to Poland's government-in-exile during World War II and then became minister to Rumania—had succeeded Patterson, but the Guatemalan assignment required a less conventional individual. Eisenhower's close aide, C. D. Jackson, the head of the Psychological Strategy Board, met with CIA Deputy Director of Plans (DDP) Frank Wisner by himself and with Undersecretary Bedell Smith to discuss the candidacy of Whiting Willauer. Willauer had distinguished himself as an active opponent of communism while serving as General C. L. Chennault's right-hand man with the Flying Tigers in China. But Willauer was a Republican, and the administration wanted a Democrat who could take the blame should the project fail. Thus during Congress's August recess the White House decided on John E. Peurifoy, who while ambassador to Greece had earned the reputation of a plain-speaking, dynamic diplomat who could actively work to combat Communist influences. Peurifoy was also closely identified with the chief architect of Truman's foreign policy, Dean Acheson.

Whatever the precise date, the White House gave the CIA permission to develop a plan. It is impossible to determine how many officials knew of the decision, because the national security machinery was designed to assure security. The CIA's Richard Bissell asserted positively, however, that "there is no possible doubt that this operation was approved at the level of the secretary of state, the assistant secretary, and the president." This assertion supports Allen Dulles's response, in a 1965 television interview, to those who charged that the CIA acted independently: "At no time has the CIA engaged in any political activity or any intelligence that was not approved by the highest level." The telephone conversations between the two Dulles brothers before and during the coup testify to the CIA director's veracity.

Given the code name PBSUCCESS ("slug" in CIA jargon), the operation was begun. The CIA established a field headquarters at Opa Locka, Florida, near Miami. Estimates place the project's cost between $5 and $7 million, and it involved some 100 Americans as well as many mercenaries recruited from Guatemala and the surrounding Central American nations. For the first time a CIA organization was set up as an autonomous unit, distinct from one of the agency's regional divisions. The reasons are self-evident. The operation was of such magnitude that it would have been extremely confusing and inefficient to have the same desk officers handling other assignments simultaneously with those of Guatemala. PBSUCCESS received its own communications facilities, financial officers, support people, cover agents, and special powers to requisition confidential funds.

Virtually all of the CIA's chief officials played important roles. At the top was Allen Dulles. Bissell, Dulles's special assistant during the Guatemalan operation and deputy director of plans for the later attempt to oust Castro, states that Dulles "was closer to the Guatemala operation than he was to the Bay of Pigs." Wisner, the deputy director of plans in 1954, was directly in charge of preparations, and he received significant support from Tracy Barnes, another top assistant. In the field the major figures were Colonel J. C. King, who as head of the Western Hemisphere Division played only a paternal role; Al Haney, the "field commander"; and E. Howard Hunt, the chief of political action.

Under the instructions of Bedell Smith, a team of American diplomats aided the CIA. Peurifoy served as team leader, communicating constantly with the agency. Messages which originated in Washington were coordinated with the State Department and transmitted over the CIA channel to the agency's station in Guatemala. Once received, for security reasons, they were hand-carried or verbally conveyed by agents to the ambassador, who would subsequently contact the other members of the team: Willauer, who did become the ambassador to Honduras, Ambassador Robert Hill in Costa Rica, and Thomas Whelan, the American minister to Nicaragua.

Shortly before the operation took place Peurifoy returned to Washington to finalize the plans. He apparently learned that preparations were almost complete, for when asked about the prospects for Arbenz's regime he quipped, "We are making out our Fourth of July reception list, and we are not including any of the present administration." Two days after Arbenz's resignation Peurifoy flippantly lamented, "People are complaining that I was forty-five minutes off schedule."

Since the CIA guidelines ruled out a *direct* United States armed intervention, the initial assignment for the well-organized task force was to select a Guatemalan leader. Among the native conservative opposition, many regarded Ydigoras Fuentes as the rightful heir to the presidency. The ultimate selection, however, rested with the CIA, whose experts assessed Ydigoras Fuentes as too reactionary and likely to incur the hostility of both the international community and the majority of the Guatemalan people. They further considered his physical resemblance to a Spanish noble a distinct liability. E. Howard Hunt, who participated in the final decision, recalled: "These were the little things we had to take into consideration. You don't rally a country made up of mestizos with a Spanish don."

The first alternative was a civilian, Juan Cordova Cerna. Not only an implacable foe of Arbenz and a prominent coffee grower, Cordova Cerna had also been a legal adviser for the United Fruit Company. But he lacked the necessary military experience and, besides, at that time was undergoing treatment in New Orleans for throat cancer. The CIA thus decided upon the forty-year-old Castillo Armas.

A graduate of both the Escuela Politécnica, Guatemala's West Point, and the United States Army Staff School at Fort Leavenworth, Kansas, Castillo Armas was something of a folk hero. Wounded in a 1950 anti-Arevalo uprising, he was believed dead and taken off for burial. Only a fortuitous moan changed his destination to a hospital. Sentenced to prison after his recovery, he dramatically escaped on 11 June 1951 by tunneling to freedom. Subsequently, Castillo Armas traveled throughout Central America, contacting other conspirators, including Ydigoras Fuentes and Cordova Cerna. His military background, honest reputation, folk-hero image, and Mayan appearance made him a good choice to lead the invasion. By June 1954, he confidently asserted that he would "return very shortly" to his homeland.

The American government furnished Castillo Armas with all the requisites for the invasion. He received money and an "army," among whose ranks were many mercenaries recruited from the area. Edward Bernays notes in his memoirs that Evelyn Irons, an American reporter, hired a donkey and visited the training camp. She witnessed many soldiers "receiving wads of dollar bills passed out by men who were unmistakably American." Shipments of rifles and other small arms, machine guns, and ammunition found their way to rebel centers in Honduras and Nicaragua, one of which was located on a personal estate of Somoza. By June 1954, two months after the United States had concluded military agreements with both countries, the *New York Times,* although never explicitly implicating the American government in the plot, reported: "Militarily the United States is doing its utmost to draw a circle around this spot of Communist infection. . . . The charter aircraft business at Toncontin [Honduras] boomed so that it was virtually impossible to hire a private plane."

Several obsolete American bombers also landed at the airstrip. Once the invasion began, Castillo Armas lost two of these planes and asked the United States government for replacements. In his only acknowledgment of U.S. involvement, Eisenhower described in his memoirs a meeting in the Oval Office, attended by the Dulles brothers, Bedell Smith, and new Assistant Secretary for Inter-American Affairs Henry Holland. Holland opposed sending the additional planes but the others favored the request. The president asked Allen Dulles for his estimate of the situation. Dulles replied that Castillo Armas's chances were about 20 percent with the planes, and about zero without them. Eisenhower ordered that the planes be replaced. This is the only aspect of the operation to which Eisenhower admitted. It is also one of the few evidences of disagreement among the policymakers.

Ironically, in the context of the operation most of these military preparations amounted to little more than a show. The primary emphasis was not to be military but psychological. One essential project involved transmitting anti-Arbenz, pro-Castillo Armas broadcasts from the surrounding areas. On 1 May 1954 a team of Guatemalan exiles trained and financed by the CIA began broadcasting from the neighboring jungle across the Guatemalan borders. The choice of this international labor-day holiday assured as wide an audience as possible. Calling itself the "Voice of Liberation," the station adopted the slogan *"Trabajo Pan y Patria"*—work, bread and country. Adopted from the black propaganda techniques of World War II, it epitomized "The Big Lie." The broadcasters claimed they were operating from within Guatemala itself, even though they never set foot on its soil. Well camouflaged and free from observation, the exiles would simulate a raid by government troops, only to broadcast again the next day, allegedly from a new location. In this fashion they not only urged the population to support a rebel invasion, but also gave potential dissidents proof of Arbenz's ineptness. The "Voice of Liberation" sounded so authentic that many foreign correspondents, including those from the *New York Times* and *Life* magazine, believed it was located within Guatemala and accepted it as *the* source of information.

The CIA also arranged for propaganda leaflets to be dropped from aircraft throughout the countryside, criticizing the present government and preparing the rural populace for the forthcoming invasion. They persuaded Guatemalan Catholic leaders to hold clandestine meetings with members of their churches. These efforts resulted in a massive volume of anti-Arbenz pastoral messages delivered each Sunday, messages that received wide publicity in the local press. Military personnel required special attention. Henry Hecksher, a German exile who later became CIA station chief in Laos, disguised himself as a European businessman in order to gain better access to high officers in the armed forces. If Guatemalan military officers could not be convinced on principles to undermine their government, bribes were offered. Perhaps because of such efforts the *Hispanic American Report* wrote that prior to the invasion the CIA believed that "Arbenz would not be backed by his army in the event of an anti-communist revolution."

Concurrently, the State Department launched an extensive campaign to shape public opinion. It planted news stories throughout the hemisphere. In proposing an anti-Communist resolution at the Tenth Inter-American Conference held in Caracas, Venezuela, in March 1954, Secretary Dulles, after consulting with his brother on the wording, made headlines with his opening harangue on Communist aggression and its danger to the Americas. Only an hour after the resolution passed, the secretary of state, who was not an expert on Latin America, returned to Washington, soon to be on his way to Paris and Geneva in his continuing effort to keep the French fighting in Indochina.

Immediately following his opening statement Dulles introduced the United States draft proposal, "Declaration of Solidarity for the Preservation of the Political Integrity of the American States Against Communist Intervention," later termed the Declaration of Caracas. Denouncing communism as "alien intrigue and treachery," the resolution concluded by proposing that Communist domination or control of any country would justify "appropriate action in accordance with existing treaties." "Existing treaties" referred implicitly to the 1947 Rio Pact, which called for a Meeting of Consultation of the Foreign Ministers of the Organization of American States to determine acceptable measures for the common defense in the event of aggression. The State Department began to solicit support for such a meeting.

Several of the Latin American delegates expressed apprehension over the possibility of a nation construing such a declaration as legitimizing intervention in the internal affairs of another state. A number of amendments were proposed to allay these fears. During the ensuing discussion Dulles and Guatemalan Foreign Minister Guillermo Toriello engaged in a vitriolic debate. Toriello, like Dulles an accomplished speaker, drew loud applause when he condemned the resolution as "merely a pretext for the United States intervening in our internal affairs" and accused the Eisenhower administration of returning to "Big Stick" diplomacy, of projecting McCarthyism worldwide, and of seeking to use the Communist issue to suppress Latin American desires for economic independence.

In spite of the positive vocal reaction to Toriello's speech, the resolution passed by an overwhelming majority. Although this outcome satisfied the United States and certain Latin American dictatorships, it dismayed many of the other nations. Their representatives claimed that they withheld their opposition for fear that America would retaliate by cutting off economic or technological assistance. These "pangs of conscience" were so evident that *Time* and *Hispanic American Report,* two magazines that supported the U.S. position throughout the controversy, both quoted Uruguay's chief delegate as saying, "We voted for the resolution but without enthusiasm, without optimism, without joy, and without the feeling that we were contributing to the adoption of a constructive measure."

Concerned that the United States might use the declaration to justify an invasion and aware that preparations were already under way (in January 1954 Arbenz revealed his acquisition of the previously mentioned correspondence between Castillo Armas and Somoza), the Guatemalan government sought to prepare itself militarily. Traditionally the United States had supplied Guatemala with most of its armaments, but since the late 1940s it had instituted a boycott. After the State Department continued to reject his appeals to lift the arms embargo, Arbenz looked behind the Iron Curtain for help. Anticipating, at the very least, an opportunity to embarrass the United States, Soviet leaders eagerly complied. The Skoda factory in Czechoslovakia sent some 2000 tons of small arms and light artillery pieces to the East German Baltic port of Stettin. There they were loaded onto the Swedish freighter *Alfhem,* listed on the manifest as optical glass and laboratory supplies, and cleared for Dakar, Africa. The ship sailed directly for Puerto Barrios. That Arbenz risked infuriating the United States by purchasing military equipment from behind the Iron Curtain demonstrates his belief in the desperate predicament of his regime. Moreover, if he tried to use the arms to form a peasant militia, as some postulated he intended, he ran the additional risk of alienating his regular troops, whose support he required.

Before the *Alfhem* arrived in Puerto Barrios on 15 May, the CIA discovered its cargo. In Stettin an operative posing as a bird watcher spied what he thought were arms being loaded onto a ship. He wrote a seemingly innocuous letter to a French automobile parts concern in Paris, to which he substituted a microfilm dot for a period. The agent in Paris translated the microfilm message into code and transmitted it by shortwave to Washington. The key to the code was the twenty-second prayer of David in the Book of Psalms, which begins, "My God, my God, why has thou foresaken me." Decoded this meant that the shipment was enroute. Allen Dulles arranged for a surreptitious inspection as the *Alfhem* passed from the Baltic to the North Sea through the Kiel Canal, which confirmed the report, as did Henry Hecksher's conversations with senior officers on Arbenz's staff. The CIA intended to intercept the *Alfhem* on its way to Guatemala, but because agents had for a while mistakenly followed another vessel, the armament-laden ship managed to reach port. When it arrived at Puerto Barrios, American officials were waiting at the docks.

The *Alfhem*'s arrival determined the date for Castillo Armas's invasion.

Washington was in an uproar. Senate Foreign Relations Committee chairman Alexander Wiley called the shipment "part of the master plan of world Communism," and President Eisenhower claimed the quantity to exceed "any legitimate, normal requirements of the Guatemalan armed forces." Allen Dulles called an emergency session of the Intelligence Advisory Committee, which was composed of the heads of the army, navy, and air force intelligence networks; the intelligence officers of the Joint Chiefs of Staff, the Department of State, and the Atomic Energy Commission; and an FBI representative. The CIA director presented the CIA's assessment of the situation: since the shipment originated behind the Iron Curtain, the Soviet Union was blatantly disregarding the Monroe Doctrine and using Guatemala to establish itself firmly and actively in the Western Hemisphere. The following day Dulles reiterated his presentation to the National Security Council.

On 18 June 1954 Castillo Armas's forces crossed over the Honduran border to invade Guatemala. It would be inappropriate to claim that this force constituted an effective fighting unit capable of defeating Arbenz in combat. The so-called army entered Guatemala with only about 150 troops, most of whom had no prior military experience. The rebels settled down in the Church of the Black Christ, the country's major religious shrine, a mere six miles within the border. There they awaited the regime's collapse. The most serious military engagement leading up to the government's defeat resulted in the deaths of seventeen soldiers.

Arbenz lost, in the words of Bissell, "when his nerve cracked." He assumed that his previously expressed apprehensions had become a reality, that the small Army of Liberation—he never did know its actual size—was but a prelude to a much larger invasionary force. From the moment Castillo Armas set foot in Guatemala, the president believed that the months of preparation that had been going on across Guatemala's borders could only mean a large-scale effort. He never doubted the outcome. Arbenz reasoned that the United States's firmness at Caracas, its response to the arms shipment, and the documented help promised Castillo Armas by the "government of the North" indicated the Eisenhower administration's willingness to go to great lengths to assure the invasion's success, perhaps even to send American troops.

Arbenz miscalculated. There never was an American plan to escalate assistance. As Allen Dulles wrote Eisenhower in the midst of the invasion, "the entire effort is . . . dependent upon psychological impact rather than actual military strength." The CIA jammed Guatemalan radio communications so that the inhabitants of Guatemala City had little or no idea as to what was really happening at the "front." Wild rumors circulated, reporting major government defeats and the imminent arrival of well-equipped divisions of rebel troops. Arbenz aggravated the situation when, in an effort to silence the "Voice of Liberation," he ordered a total blackout of the capital and other large cities. The resultant silence increased the tension by making the threat seem more real. Nor was the blackout completely effective. Many of the poorer areas received their electricity from batteries or gasoline generators and continued to receive the antigovernment transmission. These primarily uneducated Guatemalans conveyed the news to the rest of the population. Incessant police sirens and curfew bells exacerbated the crisis atmosphere, as did the arrival of wounded soldiers and civilians, no matter how small the number. Hundreds fled the capital for the mountains, creating a scene of mass confusion. Anxiety prevailed everywhere, including within the National Palace.

Within this context Castillo Armas's air force became critical. But not for its military power. Except for a few small Cessnas it consisted totally of the antiquated planes received from the United States. This was sufficient, however, to frighten the people. Later commentators referred to the plans as *sulfatos,* the Guatemalan word for laxative, due to their psychological effect on the government and general population. The airplanes circled Guatemala City, dropping anything that caused a loud noise, such as blocks of dynamite attached to hand grenades. The citadel where the *Alfhem*'s munitions were stored was bombed, making an impressive explosion. In return, the only sounds coming from the government defenses were impotent machine gun bursts.

The additional use of the "Voice of Liberation" effectively negated Arbenz's air force, which was always very weak. The radio station broadcasted accounts of Soviet aviators who had defected to the West with their planes. When a Guatemalan pilot did the same, CIA agents implored him to appeal publicly to his countrymen to follow suit. At first he refused, but after being plied with alcohol, he agreed to make an imaginary appeal. This was secretly recorded, cut and spliced, and played over the CIA station. The results exceeded even the CIA's expectations. Former operative David Phillips remembers the situation: "From that moment the Guatemalan air force was grounded. Arbenz, fearing his pilots would defect with their planes, did not permit the flight of a single military aircraft during the duration of the conflict."

As the confusion and panic mounted, Arbenz finally considered arming the peasants and urban workers. By this time he felt he had no alternative. The prospect of this militia was the ultimate determinant in the army officers' decision to desert the revolutionary government. Not only were they, like everyone else, convinced of imminent defeat, but also they now perceived themselves and their traditionally privileged status as about to be seriously undercut, if not completely eliminated. They demanded Arbenz's resignation. Feeling extremely isolated and frightened, the president offered no resistance. On 27 June 1954, just ten years after the revolution began, Arbenz resigned and fled into exile.

The ease with which Arbenz conceded defeat, the ease with which the United States succeeded, contributed to the lack of any comprehensive analysis subsequent to the event. The rapidity of the government's capitulation presented little time, or reason, for investigation. Except for a few leftist journalists, the press treated the coup as a successful anti-Communist uprising. In the absence of investigative reporting, the American covert operation remained secret. Because the nature of the counterrevolution remained

unquestioned—Washington emphasized that it was a patriotic native insurrection—the premise that the Arbenz administration was unpopular and dominated by Communists was assumed correct. Few within the United States
doubted that Guatemala had become a center of Communist subversion and
a real threat to the entire hemisphere. Those Americans who followed the
coup believed that the Guatemalan people recognized the Communist infiltration and rooted it out. Within a few years the victory of Castillo Armas
became for the United States public a vague memory. Many even forgot the
Communist issue, remembering the coup only as another "banana revolt."

Within the intelligence and national security communities, however, policy-
makers developed a high confidence in the United States's capacity to engi-
neer coups. When an apparently similar situation arose in 1959 with the
Fidelistas' triumph in Cuba, the White House, State Department, and CIA
considered themselves well prepared. The Eisenhower administration first
conceived of the operation that eventually became the Bay of Pigs, and it
involved many of the individuals who participated in the Guatemalan venture.
Although these veterans understood the logistical differences between Guatemala and Cuba, they perceived marked similarities. They also perceived
similarities between Arbenz and Castro, both in terms of the possible dangers
they represented and the methods by which they could be eliminated. Since
American officials considered both leaders as puppetlike creatures of the
monolithic Communist conspiracy, they reasoned that the strategy that had
worked so perfectly in Guatemala could be to a large extent duplicated in
Cuba.

This reasoning led to the evolution of a plan for Cuba based essentially
on the Guatemalan strategy. The same people were used, the same operational mechanisms established, and the same blueprint mapped out. In the
words of Howard Hunt, "It [the Bay of Pigs operation] was done for the
same reason because we had a successful precedent. . . . We had no trouble
assuming our prior roles, knowing what it was all about, knowing what we
could do and how to do it." Different circumstances necessitated certain tactical modifications—for example, since Guatemala was surrounded by hostile
dictatorships friendly to the United States, there was no need for an amphibious landing—but the overall strategy was identical. Richard Bissell, who
was central to the plan, recalls that once the attacking exiles had secured a
beachhead, the CIA scenario projected "a possibly protracted period of
psychological and political warfare which would lead to the modification of
his [Castro's] regime." In other words, "The chance of true success—that is
the chance of toppling Castro—was predicated on the assumption that faced
with that kind of pressure, he would suffer the same loss of nerve [as Arbenz]."

Explanations for the failure of the Bay of Pigs project tend to concentrate
on the tactical weaknesses. They emphasize that since the strategy required
a successful beachhead, the operation should have been turned over to the
Pentagon, not left to the CIA. To be successful, tacticians theorize, the
invasion needed an armed expeditionary force with special weapons and
training, air support, and other military preparations.

The other major explanation for the Bay of Pigs fiasco emphasizes Kennedy's decision-making apparatus. According to this school, gross tactical miscalculations resulted from a failure of advisers to examine carefully options and contingencies. This failure stemmed from the administration's belief in U.S. superiority and the desire of key policymakers to avoid internal dissension. As a consequence, Kennedy's highest subordinates unquestionably accepted the CIA's simplistic assessment and proposal. Irving L. Janis, the leading exponent of this interpretation, states his findings most clearly:

> The failure of Kennedy's inner circle to detect any of the false assumptions behind the Bay of Pigs invasion can be at least partially accounted for by the group's tendency to seek concurrence at the expense of seeking information, critical appraisal, and debate. The concurrence-seeking tendency was manifested by shared illusions and other symptoms, which helped the members maintain a sense of group solidarity. Most crucial were the symptoms that contributed to complacent overconfidence in the face of vague uncertainties and explicit warnings.

Janis is correct in positing that a faulty decision-making process contributed to the failure to oust Castro. Likewise, tactical errors undoubtedly also contributed. But neither of these explanations accounts for Castro's ability to repel the invasion. The CIA's project to overthrow Arbenz called for less force than the Bay of Pigs operation. Yet it succeeded with hardly any resistance. There were no contingency plans in either case. Had Castro been as unprepared militarily, politically, and psychologically as Arbenz he might very well have suffered the same fate. But Castro was prepared. Due to an overconfidence stemming in a substantial part from the success in Guatemala, the CIA, State Department, and White House failed to consider adequately this distinction. The ease of Arbenz's overthrow "went to their heads." The tactical miscalculations resulted from misperceptions, not from gross negligence.

Whereas U.S. explanations for Castillo Armas's victory were superficial, Cuban revolutionaries analyzed the coup much more comprehensively. In 1960, Castro's chief lieutenant Ernesto "Che" Guevara addressed the Latin American Youth Congress in Havana. He paid tribute to Arbenz:

> We would like to extend a special greeting to Jacabo Arbenz, president of the first Latin American country which fearlessly raised its voice against colonialism; a country which gave expression to the hopes of the peasant masses. We would also like to *express our gratitude to him,* and to the democracy which gave way, for *the example they gave us* and for the *accurate estimate they enabled us to make of the weakness which that government was unable to overcome. This allows us to go to the root of the matter* and to behead those who hold power and their lackeys at a single stroke.

Guevara's speech explained to the Latin American youth, prior to the abortive Bay of Pigs invasion, that the Cubans understood the connection between Guatemala and Cuba, connections which Allen Dulles wrote of only in 1963. Guevara appropriately made the speech because he personified the connection. As a young, socially conscious medical student, he had come to

Guatemala in February 1954. Far from the dedicated revolutionary of his later years, his major involvement in the Guatemalan revolution derived from conversations with leaders such as former President Arevalo, and he scarcely played any role in the events themselves, remaining a concerned observer. Nevertheless, like so many others, Castillo Armas's victory forced him to seek asylum in the Argentine embassy in Guatemala City and then to flee to Mexico. There Guevara encountered a small community of Latin American radicals, many of whom had studied the coup with respect to their own native movements. Among those in Mexico was Raul Castro, who later introduced the young Guevara to his brother Fidel.

In this fashion the events in Guatemala directly influenced the emergence of Guevara's political personality, introducing him to radical theory and strategy. Before the government capitulated he told his friend Hilda Gadea that if Arbenz would repudiate his regular army and retreat to the mountains with a band of armed peasants, he could continue the fight indefinitely. Soon thereafter he wrote his first political article, "I saw the Fall of Jacabo Arbenz." Unfortunately the article has been lost, but according to Gadea, Guevara outlined his developing theories on guerilla warfare and revolutionary strategy. The article's final sentence read, "The struggle begins now."

Although the lessons Guevara drew from his personal experience in Guatemala did not guarantee that the Cubans could prevent the Bay of Pigs invasion from succeeding some seven years later, his speech reveals that unlike its counterpart in the United States, the Castro regime scrutinized the reasons for Arbenz's overthrow. It could thus make an "accurate estimate" of the "weakness which that government was unable to overcome." To Guevara and Castro, this weakness was the Arbenz administration's failure to transcend liberal reforms. The most extreme of the reforms, the agrarian legislation, called for the redistribution and private ownership of uncultivated land. There never was a program of nationalization or communization. In spite of Communist inroads, the traditional power structure remained intact. This was demonstrably evident within the army, which by failing to defend the government brought about Arbenz's resignation. Arbenz, himself a regular army officer of middle-class origin, refused, until it was too late, to arm the peasants and workers.

The Cuban administrators believed that by leaving the power structure essentially untouched, the Arbenz government failed "to go to the root of the matter." A strong case can therefore be made that Cuba's revolutionary leaders' perceptions of Arbenz's overthrow drove their policies farther to the left. This was the meaning of Guevara's 1960 speech. He, Castro, and the other Cuban radicals understood from the Guatemalan episode the paradox of reform in Latin America. Leaders in the United States such as President Eisenhower encouraged the development of Third World nations. This development necessarily entails agrarian reform. When this agrarian reform adversely affected American interests, as was the case with United Fruit in Guatemala, these same U.S. leaders interpreted the reforms as evidence of Communist ideology. They believed only Communists would oppose the notion that promoting U.S. enterprises and values benefited the entire world. Guevara and Castro realized that this logic could lead to U.S. intervention in Cuba, as it had in Guatemala.

This judgment of the Guatemalan coup influenced the Cuban leaders to go beyond Arbenz's programs. They believed that by enacting legislation that would alter the traditional power bases and eliminate those elements that might support a counterrevolutionary movement, they would make Cuba less vulnerable to the type of operation that had toppled the Guatemalan government. The agrarian reforms of 1959 and 1962 effectively destroyed the foreign and national entrepreneurs who controlled Cuba's agricultural economy. They did not merely redistribute the uncultivated land. Furthermore, unlike Arbenz, Castro rose to power relying on an irregular militia, and once he had succeeded he immediately dismantled the remaining army with its elite leadership and organized the peasantry for any future attacks. After the United States refused his request for aid, he readily accepted help from the Soviet Union. There were mass imprisonments, executions, expulsions, and public trials. The overthrow of the Arbenz government in Guatemala sharpened the antagonisms between Latin American nationalists and American cold warriors. Had U.S. strategists perceived this difference between Castro's and Arbenz's preparedness, and their ideological orientations, they certainly would not have miscalculated at the Bay of Pigs. Indeed, it is unlikely there would have been a Bay of Pigs.

The study of American involvement in Guatemala in 1954 is thus important not merely as a case study, but as an integral part of cold war history. It illustrates the manner in which the cold war ethos created within the Washington community an exaggerated perception of Communist subversion in Guatemala. The CIA project there had been a high-risk operation, and the ease with which it succeeded resulted largely from the nonmilitant nature of the 1944 revolution. American policymakers, rather than discerning these favorable circumstances, generalized from the particular. They concluded that a strategy based on a mixture of military threats, covert operations, and alliances with indigenous client groups could effectively thwart movements for political, economic, and social change. They underestimated the ability and motivation of these movements to resist, while increasing that ability and motivation. Misconstruing Arbenz's nationalism, liberalism, and eclectic idealism as militant communism, U.S. government leaders failed to recognize militancy where it existed. Castro, Guevara, and their allies understood that their success required this militancy. Their perception, tenaciousness, and ruthless dedication prevented a repeat of the Guatemalan coup.

FURTHER READING

Charles Alexander, *Holding the Line* (1975)
Stephen Ambrose, *Ike's Spies* (1981)
Blanche W. Cook, *The Declassified Eisenhower* (1981)
Robert A. Divine, *Eisenhower and the Cold War* (1981)
Alexander L. George and Richard Smoke, *Deterrence in American Foreign Policy* (1974)
Louis Gerson, *John Foster Dulles* (1968)
Richard Gould-Adams, *Time of Power* (1962)
Fred I. Greenstein, *The Hidden-Hand Presidency* (1982)
Michael Guhin, *John Foster Dulles* (1972)
Townsend Hoopes, *The Devil and John Foster Dulles* (1973)
Emmet J. Hughes, *The Ordeal of Power* (1963)
Richard H. Immerman, *The CIA in Guatemala* (1982)
———, "Eisenhower and Dulles: Who Made the Decisions?" *Political Psychology*, 1 (1979), 3–20
Burton I. Kaufman, *Trade and Aid: Eisenhower's Foreign Economic Policy, 1953–1961* (1982)
Douglas Kinnard, "President Eisenhower and the Defense Budget," *Journal of Politics*, 39 (1977), 596–623
Gabriel and Joyce Kolko, *The Limits of Power* (1972)
Walter LaFeber, *America, Russia, and the Cold War* (1980)
Peter Lyon, *Eisenhower* (1974)
Donald Neff, *Warriors at Suez* (1981)
Herbert S. Parmet, *Eisenhower and the Great Crusades* (1972)
Thomas G. Paterson, ed., *Containment and the Cold War* (1973)
Ronald W. Pruessen, *John Foster Dulles: The Road to Power* (1982)
George H. Quester, "Was Eisenhower a Genius?" *International Security*, 4 (1979), 159–179
Barry Rubin, "America and the Egyptian Revolution, 1950–1957," *Political Science Quarterly*, 97 (1982), 73–90
Bennett C. Rushkoff, "Eisenhower, Dulles and the Quemoy-Matsu Crisis, 1954–1955," *Political Science Quarterly*, 96 (1981), 465–480
Stephen Schlesinger and Stephen Kinzer, *Bitter Fruit: The Untold Story of the American Coup in Guatemala* (1982)
Thomas F. Soapes, "A Cold Warrior Seeks Peace: Eisenhower's Strategy for Nuclear Disarmament," *Diplomatic History*, 4 (1980), 55–71
I. F. Stone, *The Haunted Fifties* (1963)

Cuba and the Missile Crisis

12

*In October 1962, American U-2 reconnaissance planes photographed Soviet
missile sites in Cuba. For several days a chilling war scare gripped Washington
and the world. The Cuban Missile Crisis became one of the most dangerous
Cold War confrontations, bringing the world perilously close to nuclear
holocaust. After installation of an American naval blockade, a dramatic
television address by President John F. Kennedy, and an exchange of letters
between Kennedy and Soviet Premier Nikita Khrushchev, an agreement was
reached whereby Russia pledged to withdraw its missiles from Cuba and
the United States promised never again to invade Cuba (as it had done in
April 1961 at the Bay of Pigs).*

*Questions persist, and the answers will remain tentative until both Soviet
and American documentary archives are opened to scholars: Why did the
Soviets place missiles in Cuba? Why did the Cubans welcome the missiles?
Did American assassination plots against Fidel Castro, and other covert
operations, influence the Cuban and Soviet decisions? Did the missiles
affect seriously the strategic balance of power? Why did Kennedy shun
private negotiations? What alternatives existed, and why was the blockade
selected? Was the crisis necessary? What lessons were drawn from the
experience? What impact did the crisis have thereafter on international
relations?*

DOCUMENTS

The first document is part of a November 1975 report by the Senate Select
Committee to Study Governmental Operations with Respect to Intelligence

Activities. Some of the assassination plots against Fidel Castro are recounted here. In his memoirs published in 1970 Soviet Premier Nikita Khrushchev explained that the missiles were sent to Cuba to thwart American intervention. The third document is a speech by Cuban President Osvaldo Dorticós. Delivered to the United Nations on October 8, 1962, before the missile crisis, it defended a Cuban military build-up as necessary to counter United States "aggression."

The fourth document was written by White House assistant Theodore C. Sorensen for President John F. Kennedy on October 17, 1962, two days after the missiles were discovered in Cuba. The memorandum summarizes the questions and alternatives considered by the Executive Committee that Kennedy organized to advise him. The next document is Kennedy's October 22 television address to the nation, in which he announced an American naval "quarantine" of Cuba. In an October 27 letter, Khrushchev offered proposals to defuse the crisis. The President ignored this letter, which asked that American missiles be removed from Turkey, and answered an earlier, more moderate letter which had not mentioned such a swap.

The last document was written for *Time* magazine on the twentieth anniversary of the missile crisis by several men who had served with Kennedy in 1962: Dean Rusk, Robert McNamara, George W. Ball, Roswell L. Gilpatric, Theodore Sorensen, and McGeorge Bundy. They summarize the lessons they have drawn from the confrontation.

Assassination Plots Against Fidel Castro, 1960–1965

We have found concrete evidence of at least eight plots involving the CIA to assassinate Fidel Castro from 1960 to 1965. Although some of the assassination plots did not advance beyond the stage of planning and preparation, one plot, involving the use of underworld figures, reportedly twice progressed to the point of sending poison pills to Cuba and dispatching teams to commit the deed. Another plot involved furnishing weapons and other assassination devices to a Cuban dissident. The proposed assassination devices ran the gamut from high-powered rifles to poison pills, poison pens, deadly bacterial powders, and other devices which strain the imagination. . . .

Efforts against Castro did not begin with assassination attempts.

From March through August 1960, during the last year of the Eisenhower Administration, the CIA considered plans to undermine Castro's charismatic appeal by sabotaging his speeches. According to the 1967 Report of the CIA's Inspector General, an official in the Technical Services Division (TSD) recalled discussing a scheme to spray Castro's broadcasting studio with a chemical which produced effects similar to LSD, but the scheme was rejected because the chemical was unreliable. During this period, TSD impregnated a box of cigars with a chemical which produced temporary disorientation, hoping to induce Castro to smoke one of the cigars before delivering a speech. The Inspector General also reported a plan to destroy Castro's image as "The Beard" by dusting his shoes with thallium salts, a strong depilatory that would cause his beard to fall out. The depilatory was to be administered during a trip outside Cuba, when it was anticipated Castro would leave his shoes outside the door of his hotel room to be shined. TSD procured the chemical and tested it on animals, but apparently abandoned the scheme because Castro cancelled his trip. . . .

A notation in the records of the Operations Division, CIA's Office of Medical Services, indicates that on August 16, 1960, an official was given a box of Castro's favorite cigars with instructions to treat them with lethal poison. The cigars were contaminated with a botulinum toxin so potent that a person would die after putting one in his mouth. The official reported that the cigars were ready on October 7, 1960; TSD notes indicate that they were delivered to an unidentified person on February 13, 1961. The record does not disclose whether an attempt was made to pass the cigars to Castro.

In August 1960, the CIA took steps to enlist members of the criminal underworld with gambling syndicate contacts to aid in assassinating Castro. The origin of the plot is uncertain. According to the 1967 Inspector General's Report,

> Bissell recalls that the idea originated with J. C. King, then Chief of W. H. Division, although King now recalls having only had limited knowledge of such a plan and at a much later date—about mid-1962.

Bissell testified that:

> I remember a conversation which I would have put in early autumn or late summer between myself and Colonel Edwards [Director of the Office of Security], and I have some dim recollection of some earlier conversation I had had with Colonel J. C. King, Chief of the Western Hemisphere Division, and the subject matter of both of those conversations was a capability to eliminate Castro if such action should be decided upon.

The earliest concrete evidence of the operation is a conversation between DDP Bissell and Colonel Sheffield Edwards, Director of the Office of Security. Edwards recalled that Bissell asked him to locate someone who could assassinate Castro. Bissell confirmed that he requested Edwards to find someone to assassinate Castro and believed that Edwards raised the idea of contacting members of a gambling syndicate operating in Cuba.

Edwards assigned the mission to the Chief of the Operational Support Division of the Office of Security. The Support Chief recalled that Edwards had said that he and Bissell were looking for someone to "eliminate" or "assassinate" Castro.

Edwards and the Support Chief decided to rely on Robert A. Maheu to recruit someone "tough enough" to handle the job. Maheu was an ex-FBI agent who had entered into a career as a private investigator in 1954. A former FBI associate of Maheu's was employed in the CIA's Office of Security and had arranged for the CIA to use Maheu in several sensitive covert operations in which "he didn't want to have an Agency person or a government person get caught." Maheu was initially paid a monthly retainer by the CIA of $500, but it was terminated after his detective agency became more lucrative. The Operational Support Chief had served as Maheu's case officer since the Agency first began using Maheu's services, and by 1960 they had become close personal friends.

Sometime in late August or early September 1960, the Support Chief approached Maheu about the proposed operation. As Maheu recalls the conversation, the Support Chief asked him to contact John Rosselli, an underworld figure with possible gambling contacts in Las Vegas, to determine if he would participate in a plan to "dispose" of Castro. The Support Chief testified, on the other hand, that it was Maheu who raised the idea of using Rosselli.

Maheu had known Rosselli since the late 1950's. Although Maheu claims not to have been aware of the extent of Rosselli's underworld connections and activities, he recalled that "it was certainly evident to me that he was able to accomplish things in Las Vegas when nobody else seemed to get the same kind of attention."

The Support Chief had previously met Rosselli at Maheu's home. The Support Chief and Maheu each claimed that the other had raised the idea of using Rosselli, and Maheu said the Chief was aware that Rosselli had contacts with the gambling syndicate.

At first Maheu was reluctant to become involved in the operation because it might interfere with his relationship with his new client, Howard Hughes. He finally agreed to participate because he felt that he owed the Agency a commitment. The Inspector General's Report states that:

> Edwards and Maheu agreed that Maheu would approach Rosselli as the representative of businessmen with interests in Cuba who saw the elimination of Castro as the first essential step to the recovery of their investments.

The Support Chief also recalled that Maheu was to use this cover story when he presented the plan to Rosselli, but Rosselli said that the story was developed after he had been contacted, and was used as a mutual "cover" by him, the Chief, and Maheu in dealing with Cubans who were subsequently recruited for the project. The Support Chief testified that Maheu was told to offer money, probably $150,000, for Castro's assassination.

According to Rosselli, he and Maheu met at the Brown Derby Restaurant in Beverly Hills in early September 1960. Rosselli testified that Maheu told him that "high government officials" needed his cooperation in getting rid of Castro, and that he asked him to help recruit Cubans to do the job. Maheu's recollection of that meeting was that "I informed him that I had been asked by my Government to solicit his cooperation in this particular venture."

Maheu stated that Rosselli "was very hesitant about participating in the project, and he finally said that he felt that he had an obligation to his government, and he finally agreed to participate." Maheu and Rosselli both testified that Rosselli insisted on meeting with a representative of the Government.

A meeting was arranged for Maheu and Rosselli with the Support Chief at the Plaza Hotel in New York. The Inspector General's Report placed the meeting on September 14, 1960. Rosselli testified that he could not recall the precise date of the meeting, but that it had occurred during Castro's visit to the United Nations, which the New York Times Index places from September 18 through September 28, 1960.

The Support Chief testified that he was introduced to Rosselli as a business associate of Maheu. He said that Maheu told Rosselli that Maheu represented international business interests which were pooling money to pay for the assassination of Castro. Rosselli claimed that Maheu told him at that time that the Support Chief was with the CIA.

It was arranged that Rosselli would go to Florida and recruit Cubans for the operation. Edwards informed Bissell that contact had been made with the gambling syndicate.

During the week of September 24, 1960 the Support Chief, Maheu, and Rosselli met in Miami to work out the details of the operation. Rosselli used the cover name "John Rawlston" and represented himself to the Cuban contacts as an agent of ". . . some business interests of Wall Street that had . . . nickel interests and properties around in Cuba, and I was getting financial assistance from them."

Maheu handled the details of setting up the operation and keeping the Support Chief informed of developments. After Rosselli and Maheu had been in Miami for a short time, and certainly prior to October 18, Rosselli introduced Maheu to two individuals on whom Rosselli intended to rely: "Sam Gold," who would serve as a "back-up man," or "key" man and "Joe," whom "Gold" said would serve as a courier to Cuba and make arrangements there. The Support Chief, who was using the name "Jim Olds," said he had met "Sam" and "Joe" once, and then only briefly.

The Support Chief testified that he learned the true identities of his associates one morning when Maheu called and asked him to examine the "Parade" supplement to the *Miami Times*. An article on the Attorney General's ten-most-wanted criminals list revealed that "Sam Gold" was Momo Salvatore Giancana, a Chicago-based gangster, and "Joe" was Santos Trafficante, the Cosa Nostra chieftain in Cuba. The Support Chief reported his discovery to Edwards, but did not know whether Edwards reported this fact to his superiors. The Support Chief testified that this incident occurred after "we were up to our ears in it," a month or so after Giancana had been brought into the operation, but prior to giving the poison pills to Rosselli.

Maheu recalled that it was Giancana's job to locate someone in Castro's entourage who could accomplish the assassination, and that he met almost daily with Giancana over a substantial period of time. Although Maheu described Giancana as playing a "key role," Rosselli claimed that none of the Cubans eventually used in the operation were acquired through Giancana's contacts. . . .

The Inspector General's Report described conversations among Bissell, Edwards, and the Chief of the Technical Services Division (TSD), concerning the most effective method of poisoning Castro. There is some evidence that Giancana or Rosselli originated the idea of depositing a poison pill in Castro's drink to give the "asset" a chance to escape. The Support Chief recalled Rosselli's request for something "nice and clean, without getting into any kind of out and out ambushing," preferably a poison that would disappear without a trace. The Inspector General's Report cited the Support Chief as stating that the Agency had first considered a "gangland-style killing" in which Castro would be gunned down. Giancana reportedly opposed the idea because it would be difficult to recruit someone for such a dangerous operation, and suggested instead the use of poison.

Edwards rejected the first batch of pills prepared by TSD because they would not dissolve in water. A second batch, containing botulinum toxin, "did the job expected of them" when tested on monkeys. The Support Chief received the pills from TSD, probably in February 1961, with assurances that they were lethal, and then gave them to Rosselli.

The record clearly establishes that the pills were given to a Cuban for delivery to the island some time prior to the Bay of Pigs invasion in mid-April 1961. There are discrepancies in the record, however, concerning whether one or two attempts were made during that period, and the precise date on which the passage[s] occurred. The Inspector General's Report states that in late February or March 1961, Rosselli reported to the Support Chief that the pills had been delivered to an official close to Castro who may have received kickbacks from the gambling interests. The Report states that the official returned the pills after a few weeks, perhaps because he had lost his position in the Cuban Government, and thus access to Castro, before he received the pills. The Report concludes that yet another attempt was made in April 1961, with the aid of a leading figure in the Cuban exile movement.

Rosselli and the Support Chief testified that the Cuban official described by the Inspector General as having made the first attempt was indeed involved in the assassination plot, and they ascribed his failure to a case of "cold feet." Rosselli was certain, however, that only one attempt to assassinate Castro had been made prior to the Bay of Pigs, and the Support Chief and Maheu did not clarify the matter. It is possible then, that only one pre-Bay of Pigs attempt was made, and that the Cuban exile leader was the contact in the United States who arranged for the Cuban described in the Inspector General's Report to administer the poison.

In any event, Rosselli told the Support Chief that Trafficante believed a certain leading figure in the Cuban exile movement might be able to accomplish the assassination. The Inspector General's Report suggests that this Cuban may have been receiving funds from Trafficante and other racketeers interested in securing "gambling, prostitution, and dope monopolies" in Cuba after the overthrow of Castro. The Report speculated that the Cuban was interested in the assassination scheme as a means of financing the purchase of arms and communications equipment.

The Cuban claimed to have a contact inside a restaurant frequented by Castro. As a prerequisite to the deal, he demanded cash and $1,000 worth of communications equipment. The Support Chief recalled that Colonel J. C. King, head of the Western Hemisphere Division, gave him $50,000 in Bissell's office to pay the Cuban if he successfully assassinated Castro. The Support Chief stated that Bissell also authorized him to give the Cuban the requested electronics equipment. . . .

The attempt met with failure. According to the Inspector General's Report, Edwards believed the scheme failed because Castro stopped visiting the restaurant where the "asset" was employed. Maheu suggested an alternative reason. He recalled being informed that after the pills had been delivered to Cuba, "the go signal still had to be received before in fact they were administered." He testified that he was informed by the Support Chief sometime after the operation that the Cubans had an opportunity to administer the pills to Fidel Castro and either Che Guevarra or Raul Castro, but that the "go signal" never came. Maheu did not know who was responsible for giving the signal. The Cuban subsequently returned the cash and the pills.

The date of the Cuban operation is unclear. The Inspector General's Report places it in March-April 1961, prior to the Bay of Pigs. Shimon's testimony puts it around March 12, 1961. Bissell testified that the effort against Castro was called off after the Bay of Pigs, and Maheu testified that he had no involvement in the operation after the Bay of Pigs. The Support Chief however, was certain that it occurred during early 1962.

The Inspector General's Report divides the gambling syndicate operation into Phase I, terminating with the Bay of Pigs, and Phase II, continuing with the transfer of the operation to William Harvey in late 1961. The distinction between a clearly demarcated Phase I and Phase II may be an artificial one, as there is considerable evidence that the operation was continuous, perhaps lying dormant for the period immediately following the Bay of Pigs.

In early 1961, Harvey was assigned the responsibility for establishing a general capability within the CIA for disabling foreign leaders, including assassination as a "last resort." The capability was called Executive Action and was later included under the cryptonym ZR/RIFLE. . . .

In early April 1962, Harvey, who testified that he was acting on "explicit orders" from Helms, requested Edwards to put him in touch with Rosselli. The Support Chief first introduced Harvey to Rosselli in Miami, where Harvey told Rosselli to maintain his Cuban contacts, but not to deal with Maheu or Giancana, whom he had decided were "untrustworthy" and "surplus." The Support Chief recalled that initially Rosselli did not trust Harvey although they subsequently developed a close friendship.

Harvey, the Support Chief and Rosselli met for a second time in New York on April 8–9, 1962. A notation made during this time in the files of the Technical Services Division indicates that four poison pills were given to the Support Chief on April 18, 1962. The pills were passed to Harvey, who arrived in Miami on April 21, and found Rosselli already in touch with the same Cuban who had been involved in the pre-Bay of Pigs pill passage. He gave the pills to Rosselli, explaining that "these would work anywhere and at any time with anything." Rosselli testified that he told Harvey that the

Cubans intended to use the pills to assassinate Che Guevara as well as Fidel and Raul Castro. According to Rosselli's testimony, Harvey approved of the targets, stating "everything is all right, what they want to do."

The Cuban requested arms and equipment as a *quid pro quo* for carrying out the assassination operation. With the help of the CIA's Miami station which ran covert operations against Cuba (JM/WAVE), Harvey procured explosives, detonators, rifles, handguns, radios, and boat radar costing about $5,000. Harvey and the chief of the JM/WAVE station rented a U-Haul Truck under an assumed name and delivered the equipment to a parking lot. The keys were given to Rosselli, who watched the delivery with the Support Chief from across the street. The truckload of equipment was finally picked up by either the Cuban or Rosselli's agent. Harvey testified that the arms "could" have been for use in the assassination attempt, but that they were not given to the Cuban solely for that purpose.

Rosselli kept Harvey informed of the operation's progress. Sometime in May 1962, he reported that the pills and guns had arrived in Cuba. On June 21, he told Harvey that the Cuban had dispatched a three-man team to Cuba. The Inspector General's report described the team's mission as "vague" and conjectured that the team would kill Castro or recruit others to do the job, using the poison pills if the opportunity arose.

Harvey met Rosselli in Miami on September 7 and 11, 1962, The Cuban was reported to be preparing to send in another three-man team to penetrate Castro's bodyguard. Harvey was told that the pills, referred to as "the medicine," were still "safe" in Cuba.

Harvey testified that by this time he had grave doubts about whether the operation would ever take place, and told Rosselli that "there's not much likelihood that this is going anyplace, or that it should be continued." The second team never left for Cuba, claiming that "conditions" in Cuba were not right. During early January 1963, Harvey paid Rosselli $2,700 to defray the Cuban's expenses. Harvey terminated the operation in mid-February 1963. At a meeting with Rosselli in Los Angeles, it was agreed that Rosselli would taper off his communications with the Cubans. Rosselli testified that he simply broke off contact with the Cubans. However, he never informed them that the offer of $150,000 for Castro's assassination had been withdrawn.

The agency personnel who dealt with Rosselli attributed his motivation to patriotism and testified that he was not paid for his services. According to the Support Chief, Rosselli "paid his way, he paid his own hotel fees, he paid his own travel. . . . And he never took a nickel, he said, no, as long as it is for the Government of the United States, this is the least I can do, because I owe it a lot."

Edwards agreed that Rosselli was "never paid a cent," and Maheu testified that "Giancana was paid nothing at all, not even for expenses, and that Mr. Rosselli was given a pittance that did not even begin to cover his expenses." It is clear, however, that the CIA did pay Rosselli's hotel bill during his stay in Miami in October 1960. The CIA's involvement with Rosselli caused the Agency some difficulty during Rosselli's subsequent prosecutions for fraudulent gambling activities and living in the country under an assumed name.

As [for the question of authorization], both Helms and the high Kennedy Administration officials who testified agreed that no direct order was ever given for Castro's assassination and that no senior Administration officials, including McCone, were informed about the assassination activity. Helms testified, however, that he believed the assassination activity was permissible and that it was within the scope of authority given to the Agency. McCone and other Kennedy Administration officials disagreed, testifying that assassination was impermissible without a direct order and that Castro's assassination was not within the bounds of the MONGOOSE operation.

As DDP, Helms was in charge of covert operations when the poison pills were given to Rosselli in Miami in April 1962. Helms had succeeded to this post following Bissell's retirement in February 1962. He testified that after the Bay of Pigs:

> Those of us who were still [in the Agency] were enormously anxious to try and be successful at what we were being asked to do by what was then a relatively new Administration. We wanted to earn our spurs with the President and with other officers of the Kennedy Administration.

Khrushchev Recalls His Decision to
Deploy the Missiles (1962), 1970

Cuba's geographical position has always made it very vulnerable to its enemies. The Cuban coast is only a few miles from the American shore, and it is stretched out like a sausage, a shape that makes it easy for attackers and incredibly difficult for the island's defenders. There are infinite opportunities for invasion, especially if the invader has naval artillery and air support.

We were sure that the Americans would never reconcile themselves to the existence of Castro's Cuba. They feared, as much as we hoped, that a Socialist Cuba might become a magnet that would attract other Latin American countries to Socialism. Given the continual threat of American interference in the Caribbean, what should our own policy be? This question was constantly on my mind, and I frequently discussed it with the other members of the Presidium. Everyone agreed that America would not leave Cuba alone unless we did something. We had an obligation to do everything in our power to protect Cuba's existence as a Socialist country and as a working example to the other countries of Latin America. It was clear to me that we might very well lose Cuba if we didn't take some decisive steps in her defense.

The fate of Cuba and the maintenance of Soviet prestige in that part of

From *Khrushchev Remembers* by Nikita Khrushchev, with an Introduction, Commentary, and Notes by Edward Crankshaw, Translated and Edited by Strobe Talbott. Copyright © 1970 by Little, Brown and Company, Inc. By permission of Little, Brown and Company.

the world preoccupied me even when I was busy conducting the affairs of state in Moscow and traveling to the other fraternal countries. While I was on an official visit to Bulgaria, for instance, one thought kept hammering away at my brain: what will happen if we lose Cuba? I knew it would have been a terrible blow to Marxism-Leninism. It would gravely diminish our stature throughout the world, but especially in Latin America. If Cuba fell, other Latin American countries would reject us, claiming that for all our might the Soviet Union hadn't been able to do anything for Cuba except to make empty protests to the United Nations. We had to think up some way of confronting America with more than words. We had to establish a tangible and effective deterrent to American interference in the Caribbean. But what exactly? The logical answer was missiles. The United States had already surrounded the Soviet Union with its own bomber bases and missiles. We knew that American missiles were aimed against us in Turkey and Italy, to say nothing of West Germany. Our vital industrial centers were directly threatened by planes armed with atomic bombs and guided missiles tipped with nuclear warheads. As Chairman of the Council of Ministers, I found myself in the difficult position of having to decide on a course of action which would answer the American threat but which would also avoid war. Any fool can start a war, and once he's done so, even the wisest of men are helpless to stop it—especially if it's a nuclear war.

It was during my visit to Bulgaria that I had the idea of installing missiles with nuclear warheads in Cuba without letting the United States find out they were there until it was too late to do anything about them. I knew that first we'd have to talk to Castro and explain our strategy to him in order to get the agreement of the Cuban government. My thinking went like this: if we installed the missiles secretly and then if the United States discovered the missiles were there after they were already poised and ready to strike, the Americans would think twice before trying to liquidate our installations by military means. I knew that the United States could knock out some of our installations, but not all of them. If a quarter or even a tenth of our missiles survived—even if only one or two big ones were left—we could still hit New York, and there wouldn't be much of New York left. I don't mean to say that everyone in New York would be killed—not everyone, of course, but an awful lot of people would be wiped out. I don't know how many: that's a matter for our scientists and military personnel to work out. They specialize in nuclear warfare and know how to calculate the consequences of a missile strike against a city the size of New York. But that's all beside the point. The main thing was that the installation of our missiles in Cuba would, I thought, restrain the United States from precipitous military action against Castro's government. In addition to protecting Cuba, our missiles would have equalized what the West likes to call "the balance of power." The Americans had surrounded our country with military bases and threatened us with nuclear weapons, and now they would learn just what it feels like to have enemy missiles pointing at you; we'd be doing nothing more than giving them a little of their own medicine. And it was high time America learned what it feels like to have her own land and her own people threatened. . . .

All these thoughts kept churning in my head the whole time I was in Bulgaria. I paced back and forth, brooding over what to do. I didn't tell anyone what I was thinking. I kept my mental agony to myself. But all the while the idea of putting missiles in Cuba was ripening inside my mind. After I returned to Moscow from Bulgaria I continued to think about the possibility. Finally we convened a meeting and I said I had some thoughts to air on the subject of Cuba. I laid out all the considerations which I've just outlined. I presented my idea in the context of the counterrevolutionary invasion [Bay of Pigs] which Castro had just resisted. I said that it would be foolish to expect the inevitable second invasion to be as badly planned and as badly executed as the first. I warned that Fidel would be crushed if another invasion were launched against Cuba and said that we were the only ones who could prevent such a disaster from occurring.

In the course of discussions inside the Government, we decided to install intermediate-range missiles, launching equipment, and Il-28 bombers in Cuba. Even though these bombers were obsolete, they would be useful against an enemy landing force. The Il-28 was too slow to fly over enemy territory because it could easily be shot down, but was well suited for coastal defense. The Il-28 was our first jet bomber. In its time it had been god of the air, but by the time we gave military assistance to Cuba, the Il-28 had already been taken out of production. . . .

I want to make one thing absolutely clear: when we put our ballistic missiles in Cuba, we had no desire to start a war. On the contrary, our principal aim was only to deter America from starting a war. We were well aware that a war which started over Cuba would quickly expand into a world war. Any idiot could have started a war between America and Cuba. Cuba was eleven thousand kilometers away from us. Only a fool would think that we wanted to invade the American continent from Cuba. Our goal was precisely the opposite: we wanted to keep the Americans from invading Cuba, and, to that end, we wanted to make them think twice by confronting them with our missiles. This goal we achieved—but not without undergoing a period of perilous tension.

The Cuban Case, 1962

It was enough for us to promulgate laws which affected the United States monopolistic interests in our country, it was enough to promulgate the land reform act at a period when our revolutionary development was not yet shaped by socialist principles, for aggressive action against our homeland to be undertaken by the United States Government.

That was the start of the insolent diplomatic notes and piratical flights over our territory. Then the Cuban sugar quota was eliminated from the United States market, supplies of petroleum to our country were stopped, and diplomatic measures were taken aimed at isolating Cuba from the continent. Finally there was a whole series of eminently aggressive activities which generated this tension, long before—I repeat—long before we proclaimed that our revolution was a socialist one.

And what has happened since?

It would be unduly tedious, I think, to recapitulate all the acts of aggression committed by the United States against Cuba. Suffice it to mention all the efforts designed to subvert our country from within, the acts of sabotage, the attacks on persons and the espionage activities on our soil. In brief, suffice it to recall the armed invasion of our country by mercenary forces financed, trained in warfare, militarily protected and commanded by the Government of the United States: the invasion of Playa Girón [Bay of Pigs]. And what happened after Playa Girón, that ridiculous fiasco? Did they perchance learn a great lesson of history from it? Did they perchance have sufficient perception and knowledge to realize what immense forces can be marshalled by a nation firmly resolved to preserve its freedom and independence? That is not what happened. We immediately became the victims of further acts of aggression with the infiltration of agents landed on our coasts and trained by the Central Intelligence Agency, new attempts at sabotage, the military training of groups to carry out the hitherto unsuccessful internal subversion of our country and the increase of economic pressure on our homeland—tenaciously and doggedly applied in the hope that it would undermine our revolution and that, as a result, their sole objective would be attained: the downfall of the Revolutionary Government of Cuba. . . .

These aggressive acts continue, like the United States warships that lie near the coast off our harbours. Every day those of us who live in Havana must see with our own eyes these warships lurking around our island, making a show of war or of preparation for war.

This is the situation today but we can also say that it is qualitatively different from the situation which existed before the invasion of our country at Playa Girón, for the following reasons. Before Playa Girón, the Government of the United States had on more than one occasion stated that it had no aggressive intentions towards our country. It is obvious that after Playa Girón even the President of the United States publicly and officially acknowledged his responsibility and his sympathy and support for that invasion.

Today the situation is different, for while it is true that once again it is being asserted—as the Head of the United States delegation has stated here —that there are no aggressive designs on our country, on the other hand there are records, and there have been statements and official resolutions which authorize armed aggression against Cuba and seek to justify it in advance. The fact is that the object—as acknowledged recently in a statement by the State Department of the United States—of the foreign policy of the United States Government in regard to Cuba is clearly and obviously the overthrow of the revolutionary Government and the destruction of our glorious revolution. . . .

Cuba does not stand alone; it has friends, it can count on the solidarity of other nations and relies on friendly countries which must enable it to carry on its international trade.

But there is something more, something to which I emphatically wish to draw the attention of the Assembly. At the beginning of my address I said that the situation as regards Cuban-United States relations before the invasion at Playa Girón was qualitatively different from the present situation. And I said so because in the United States there have been statements and official resolutions designed to build up a case in advance for direct armed aggression against our country. By way of proof it is sufficient to take a brief look at the operative part of the joint resolution of the United States Congress.

"*Resolved by the Senate and House of Representatives of the United States of America in Congress assembled,*

"That the United States is determined

"(*a*) To prevent by whatever means may be necessary, including the use of arms"—I repeat, including the use of arms—"the Marxist-Leninist régime in Cuba from extending, by force or the threat of force, its aggressive or subversive activities to any part of this hemisphere." . . .

Of course we should have preferred to devote all those human and material resources, all the energies we have had to employ in strengthening our military defences, to the development of our economy and culture. We have armed ourselves against our wishes and contrary to our aspirations, because we were driven to strengthen our miiltary defences lest we should jeopardize the sovereignty of our nation and the independence of our homeland. We have armed ourselves because the people of Cuba have a legitimate right, sanctioned by history, to defend their sovereign decisions and to steer their country on the historic course which, in the exercise of their sovereignty, they have chosen.

I ask you, so that you may answer in all sincerity to your own consciences: what would have happened if we had not strengthened our military defences when a division armed and trained by the United States Government invaded our country at Playa Girón? Our revolution would not, of course have been defeated nor the tide of our history turned back; but no doubt the struggle would have been long and bloody, and many more lives and more wealth than our country actually lost would have been destroyed. We wiped out this invasion, this unjustified act of aggression and arrogance towards our country, in seventy-two hours, because we had exercised in time the right to strengthen our defensive military capability in order to safeguard our sovereignty, our independence and our revolution.

If the United States could give assurances, by word and by deed, that it would not commit acts of aggression against our country, we solemnly declare that there would be no need for our weapons and our armies, because we want peace and we want to carry on our work in peace. . . .

Cuba does not, as has been stated here, represent a problem between the East and the West. Cuba poses a problem of sovereignty and independence. The Cuban problem is a problem involving the sovereign decision of a people and the right of that people to self-determination. Cuba has not wanted to be drawn into the cold war. Cuba merely wants to pursue its economic and cultural development and to shape its own future in peace, and it is ready to demonstrate these intentions at any time. And if it is not true that there is an intention to attack our country—although we consider that such an intention certainly exists—we urge the head of the United States delegation specifically to guarantee before this Assembly that his Government does not intend to attack Cuba. We urge him, however, to back up these guarantees not merely by words, but more especially by deeds. Verbal guarantees were given before Playa Girón, and when the invasion took place, many Members of the Assembly heard the representative of the United States Government state that there was no such invasion and that his Government had not planned one; yet only a few days later, the President of the United States himself publicly and officially assumed the responsibility for that invasion.

Theodore C. Sorensen's Memorandum on Executive Committee Discussions, 1962

1. It is generally agreed that Soviet MRBM's—offensive weapons—are now in Cuba. While only one complex of three sites and no nuclear warheads have been spotted, it must be assumed that this is the beginning of a larger build-up.

2. It is generally agreed that these missiles, even when fully operational, do not significantly alter the balance of power—i.e., they do not significantly increase the potential megatonnage capable of being unleashed on American soil, even after a surprise American nuclear strike. The Soviet purpose in making this move is not understood—whether it is for purposes of diversion, harassment, provocation or bargaining.

3. Nevertheless it is generally agreed that the United States cannot tolerate the known presence of offensive nuclear weapons in a country 90 miles from our shore, if our courage and our commitments are ever to be believed by either allies or adversaries. Retorts from either our European allies or the Soviets that we can become as accustomed as they to accepting the nearby presence of MRBM's have some logic but little weight in this situation.

4. It is also agreed that certain of our NATO allies would be notified but not consulted immediately prior to any action by the United States; that certain Latin nations would at least be notified; and that, if there is to be military action, the President would hold announcing the existence of the missiles and the justification of our action until after that action had been completed.

5. The following possible tracks or courses of action have each been considered. Each has obvious diplomatic and military disadvantages, but none others as yet occur.

> Track A: Political action, pressure and warning, followed by a military strike if satisfaction is not received.
> Track B: A military strike without prior warning, pressure or action, accompanied by messages making clear the limited nature of this action.

Track C: Political action, pressure and warning, followed by a total naval blockade, under the authority of the Rio Pact and either a Congressional Declaration of War on Cuba or the Cuban Resolution of the 87th Congress.
Track D: Full-scale invasion, to "take Cuba away from Castro."

Obviously any one of these could lead to one of the others—but each represents a distinguishable approach to the problem.

6. Within Tracks A and C, the political actions, pressures and warnings could include one or more of the following:
    a. Letter to Khrushchev
        —Stating if ever offensive bases exist, they will be struck; or
        —Warning that we know they exist, and must be dismantled or they will be struck; or
        —Summoning him to a Summit, offering to withdraw our MRBM's from Turkey, etc.
    b. Letter to Castro
        —Warning him of action if bases not dismantled; and/or
        —Seeking to separate him from Soviets on grounds that they are willing to see him destroyed
    c. Take this threat to the peace before the UN, requesting inspection team, etc.
    d. Take this threat to the Hemisphere to the OAS and obtain authorization for action.

7. Within Tracks A and B, the most likely military alternatives aside from blockade and invasion include the following:
    a. A 50 sortie, 1 swoop air strike limited to the missile complex, followed by open surveillance and announcement that future missile sites would be similarly struck.
    b. Broadened air strikes to eliminate all Cuban air power or other retaliatory capacity, up to 200 sortie (one day's activities).
    c. Not yet considered: Commando raid, under air cover, by helicopter or otherwise, to take out missiles with bullets, destroy launches, and leave.
    d. Note: It is generally agreed that we must also be prepared to take further action to protect Guantanamo, from which dependents will have to be evacuated in advance.

8. Other questions or points of disagreement
    a. Whether Soviet reaction would be more intense to Tracks A, B, C or D
    b. Whether Moscow would be either able or willing to prevent Soviet missile commanders from firing on United States when attacked, or Castro and/or his Air Force or any part of it attacking U.S. mainland. This includes the further question of whether, if a military strike is to take place, it must take place before these missiles become operational in the next 2 weeks or so.
    c. Whether Soviets would make, or threaten in response to any note, an equivalent attack on U.S. missiles in Turkey or Italy—or attack

Berlin or somewhere else—or confine themselves to stirring up UN and world opinion.

d. What our response would be to such a Soviet attack—or a Soviet defiance of blockade—and what their response would be to our response

e. Whether Castro would risk total destruction by sending planes to U.S. mainland—or be able to control all his planes

f. Whether any Congressmen should be consulted, whether war need be declared, whether the President should cancel all remaining speeches

g. Whether NATO allies should be briefed at highest level by high-level spokesman

h. Fate of the 1100 prisoners under any alternative

i. Whether it would be helpful to obtain a public (UN) and private (Gromyko) denial

j. To what extent any advance notice—through political notes or pressure, etc.—makes more difficult the military's task, if in the meantime
   —the missiles are concealed; or
   —the missiles become operational

k. Whether, if missiles are taken out, the Soviets would bring in additional missiles—or, if aware of continued surveillance, would find "their bayonets had struck steel instead of mush" and therefore desist

l. Whether reservists call-up, National Emergency, or Declaration of War by a reconvened Congress are necessary

m. How successful we would be in justifying to world military action against Cuba

n. Whether the effect on our allies would be worse if we do strike or if we do not.

John F. Kennedy's Television Address, 1962

This Government, as promised, has maintained the closest surveillance of the Soviet military buildup on the island of Cuba. Within the past week unmistakable evidence has established the fact that a series of offensive missile sites is now in preparation on that imprisoned island. The purpose of these bases can be none other than to provide a nuclear strike capability against the Western Hemisphere.

Upon receiving the first preliminary hard information of this nature last Tuesday morning [October 16] at 9:00 A.M., I directed that our surveillance be stepped up. And having now confirmed and completed our evaluation of the evidence and our decision on a course of action, this Government feels obliged to report this new crisis to you in fullest detail.

The characteristics of these new missile sites indicate two distinct types of installations. Several of them include medium-range ballistic missiles capable of carrying a nuclear warhead for a distance of more than 1,000 nautical miles. Each of these missiles, in short, is capable of striking Washington, D.C., the Panama Canal, Cape Canaveral, Mexico City, or any other city in the southeastern part of the United States, in Central America, or in the Caribbean area.

Additional sites not yet completed appear to be designed for intermediate-range ballistic missiles capable of traveling more than twice as far—and thus capable of striking most of the major cities in the Western Hemisphere, ranging as far north as Hudson Bay, Canada, and as far south as Lima, Peru. In addition, jet bombers, capable of carrying nuclear weapons, are now being uncrated and assembled in Cuba, while the necessary air bases are being prepared.

This urgent transformation of Cuba into an important strategic base—by the presence of these large, long-range, and clearly offensive weapons of sudden mass destruction—constitutes an explicit threat to the peace and security of all the Americas, in flagrant and deliberate defiance of the Rio Pact of 1947, the traditions of this nation and hemisphere, the Joint Resolution of the 87th Congress, the Charter of the United Nations, and my own public warnings to the Soviets on September 4 and 13.

This action also contradicts the repeated assurances of Soviet spokesmen, both publicly and privately delivered, that the arms buildup in Cuba would retain its original defensive character and that the Soviet Union had no need or desire to station strategic missiles on the territory of any other nation.

The size of this undertaking makes clear that it has been planned for some months. Yet only last month, after I had made clear the distinction between any introduction of ground-to-ground missiles and the existence of defensive antiaircraft missiles, the Soviet Government publicly stated on September 11 that, and I quote, "The armaments and military equipment sent to Cuba are designed exclusively for defensive purposes," and, and I quote the Soviet Government, "There is no need for the Soviet Government to shift its weapons for a retaliatory blow to any other country, for instance Cuba," and that, and I quote the Government, "The Soviet Union has so powerful rockets to carry these nuclear warheads that there is no need to search for sites for them beyond the boundaries of the Soviet Union." That statement was false.

Only last Thursday, as evidence of this rapid offensive buildup was already in my hand, Soviet Foreign Minister Gromyko told me in my office that he was instructed to make it clear once again, as he said his Government had already done, that Soviet assistance to Cuba, and I quote, "pursued solely the purpose of contributing to the defense capabilities of Cuba," that, and I quote him, "training by Soviet specialists of Cuban nationals in handling defensive armaments was by no means offensive," and that "if it were otherwise," Mr. Gromyko went on, "the Soviet Government would never become involved in rendering such assistance." That statement also was false.

Neither the United States of America nor the world community of nations can tolerate deliberate deception and offensive threats on the part of any nation, large or small. We no longer live in a world where only the actual firing of weapons represents a sufficient challenge to a nation's security to constitute maximum peril. Nuclear weapons are so destructive and ballistic missiles are so swift that any substantially increased possibility of their use or any sudden change in their deployment may well be regarded as a definite threat to peace.

For many years both the Soviet Union and the United States, recognizing this fact, have deployed strategic nuclear weapons with great care, never upsetting the precarious *status quo* which insured that these weapons would not be used in the absence of some vital challenge. Our own strategic missiles have never been transferred to the territory of any other nation under a cloak of secrecy and deception; and our history, unlike that of the Soviets since the end of World War II, demonstrates that we have no desire to dominate or conquer any other nation or impose our system upon its people. Nevertheless, American citizens have become adjusted to living daily on the bull's eye of Soviet missiles located inside the U.S.S.R. or in submarines.

In that sense missiles in Cuba add to an already clear and present danger—although it should be noted the nations of Latin America have never previously been subjected to a potential nuclear threat.

But this secret, swift, and extraordinary buildup of Communist missiles—in an area well known to have a special and historical relationship to the United States and the nations of the Western Hemisphere, in violation of Soviet assurances, and in defiance of American and hemispheric policy—this sudden, clandestine decision to station strategic weapons for the first time outside of Soviet soil—is a deliberately provocative and unjustified change in the *status quo* which cannot be accepted by this country if our courage and our commitments are ever to be trusted again by either friend or foe.

The 1930's taught us a clear lesson: Aggressive conduct, if allowed to grow unchecked and unchallenged, ultimately leads to war. This nation is opposed to war. We are also true to our word. Our unswerving objective, therefore, must be to prevent the use of these missiles against this or any other country and to secure their withdrawal or elimination from the Western Hemisphere.

Our policy has been one of patience and restraint, as befits a peaceful and powerful nation, which leads a worldwide alliance. We have been determined not to be diverted from our central concerns by mere irritants and fanatics. But now further action is required—and it is underway; and these actions may only be the beginning. We will not prematurely or unnecessarily risk the costs of worldwide nuclear war in which even the fruits of victory would be ashes in our mouth—but neither will we shrink from that risk at any time it must be faced.

Acting, therefore, in the defense of our own security and of the entire Western Hemisphere, and under the authority entrusted to me by the Constitution as endorsed by the resolution of the Congress, I have directed that the following *initial* steps be taken immediately:

> *First:* To halt this offensive buildup, a strict quarantine on all offensive military equipment under shipment to Cuba is being initiated. All ships of any kind bound for Cuba from whatever nation or port will, if found to contain

cargoes of offensive weapons, be turned back. This quarantine will be extended, if needed, to other types of cargo and carriers. We are not at this time, however, denying the necessities of life as the Soviets attempted to do in their Berlin blockade of 1948.

Second: I have directed the continued and increased close surveillance of Cuba and its military buildup. The Foreign Ministers of the OAS in their communique of October 3 rejected secrecy on such matters in this hemisphere. Should these offensive military preparations continue, thus increasing the threat to the hemisphere, further action will be justified. I have directed the Armed Forces to prepare for any eventualities; and I trust that, in the interest of both the Cuban people and the Soviet technicians at the sites, the hazards to all concerned of continuing this threat will be recognized.

Third: It shall be the policy of this nation to regard any nuclear missile launched from Cuba against any nation in the Western Hemisphere as an attack by the Soviet Union on the United States, requiring a full retaliatory response upon the Soviet Union.

Fourth: As a necessary military precaution I have reinforced our base at Guantanamo, evacuated today the dependents of our personnel there, and ordered additional military units to be on a standby alert basis.

Fifth: We are calling tonight for an immediate meeting of the Organ of Consultation, under the Organization of American States, to consider this threat to hemispheric security and to invoke articles 6 and 8 of the Rio Treaty in support of all necessary action. The United Nations Charter allows for regional security arrangements—and the nations of this hemisphere decided long ago against the military presence of outside powers. Our other allies around the world have also been alerted.

Sixth: Under the Charter of the United Nations, we are asking tonight that an emergency meeting of the Security Council be convoked without delay to take action against this latest Soviet threat to world peace. Our resolution will call for the prompt dismantling and withdrawal of all offensive weapons in Cuba, under the supervision of U.N. observers, before the quarantine can be lifted.

Seventh and finally: I call upon Chairman Khrushchev to halt and eliminate this clandestine, reckless, and provocative threat to world peace and to stable relations between our two nations. I call upon him further to abandon this course of world domination and to join in an historic effort to end the perilous arms race and transform the history of man. He has an opportunity now to move the world back from the abyss of destruction—by returning to his Government's own words that it had no need to station missiles outside its own territory, and withdrawing these weapons from Cuba—by refraining from any action which will widen or deepen the present crisis—and then by participating in a search for peaceful and permanent solutions.

This nation is prepared to present its case against the Soviet threat to peace, and our own proposals for a peaceful world, at any time and in any forum— in the OAS, in the United Nations, or in any other meeting that could be useful —without limiting our freedom of action.

We have in the past made strenuous efforts to limit the spread of nuclear weapons. We have proposed the elimination of all arms and military bases in a fair and effective disarmament treaty. We are prepared to discuss new proposals for the removal of tensions on both sides—including the possibilities of a genuinely independent Cuba, free to determine its own destiny. We have no wish to war with the Soviet Union, for we are a peaceful people who desire to live in peace with all other peoples.

But it is difficult to settle or even discuss these problems in an atmosphere of intimidation. That is why this latest Soviet threat—or any other threat which is made either independently or in response to our actions this week—must and will be met with determination. Any hostile move anywhere in the world against the safety and freedom of peoples to whom we are committed—including in particular the brave people of West Berlin—will be met by whatever action is needed.

Finally, I want to say a few words to the captive people of Cuba, to whom this speech is being directly carried by special radio facilities. I speak to you as a friend, as one who knows of your deep attachment to your fatherland, as one who shares your aspirations for liberty and justice for all. And I have watched and the American people have watched with deep sorrow how your nationalist revolution was betrayed and how your fatherland fell under foreign domination. Now your leaders are no longer Cuban leaders inspired by Cuban ideals. They are puppets and agents of an international conspiracy which has turned Cuba against your friends and neighbors in the Americas—and turned it into the first Latin American country to become a target for nuclear war, the first Latin American country to have these weapons on its soil.

These new weapons are not in your interest. They contribute nothing to your peace and well-being. They can only undermine it. But this country has no wish to cause you to suffer or to impose any system upon you. We know that your lives and land are being used as pawns by those who deny you freedom.

Many times in the past the Cuban people have risen to throw out tyrants who destroyed their liberty. And I have no doubt that most Cubans today look forward to the time when they will be truly free—free from foreign domination, free to choose their own leaders, free to select their own system, free to own their own land, free to speak and write and worship without fear or degradation. And then shall Cuba be welcomed back to the society of free nations and to the associations of this hemisphere.

My fellow citizens, let no one doubt that this is a difficult and dangerous effort on which we have set out. No one can foresee precisely what course it will take or what costs or casualties will be incurred. Many months of sacrifice and self-discipline lie ahead—months in which both our patience and our will will be tested, months in which many threats and denunciations will keep us aware of our dangers. But the greatest danger of all would be to do nothing.

The path we have chosen for the present is full of hazards, as all paths are; but it is the one most consistent with our character and courage as a nation and our commitments around the world. The cost of freedom is always high—but Americans have always paid it. And one path we shall never choose, and that is the path of surrender or submission.

Our goal is not the victory of might but the vindication of right—not peace at the expense of freedom, but both peace *and* freedom, here in this hemisphere and, we hope, around the world. God willing, that goal will be achieved.

Khrushchev's Second Letter to the President, 1962

I understand your concern for the security of the United States, Mr. President, because this is the first duty of the president. However, these questions are also uppermost in our minds. The same duties rest with me as chairman of the USSR Council of Ministers. You have been worried over our assisting Cuba with arms designed to strengthen its defensive potential—precisely defensive potential—because Cuba, no matter what weapons it had, could not compare with you since these are different dimensions, the more so given up-to-date means of extermination.

Our purpose has been and is to help Cuba, and no one can challenge the humanity of our motives aimed at allowing Cuba to live peacefully and develop as its people desire. You want to relieve your country from danger and this is understandable. However, Cuba also wants this. All countries want to relieve themselves from danger. But how can we, the Soviet Union and our government, assess your actions which, in effect, mean that you have surrounded the Soviet Union with military bases, surrounded our allies with military bases, set up military bases literally around our country, and stationed your rocket weapons at them? This is no secret. High-placed American officials demonstratively declare this. Your rockets are stationed in Britain and in Italy and pointed at us. Your rockets are stationed in Turkey.

You are worried over Cuba. You say that it worries you because it lies at a distance of 90 miles across the sea from the shores of the United States. However, Turkey lies next to us. Our sentinels are pacing up and down and watching each other. Do you believe that you have the right to demand security for your country and the removal of such weapons that you qualify as offensive, while not recognizing this right for us?

You have stationed devastating rocket weapons, which you call offensive, in Turkey literally right next to us. How then does recognition of our equal military possibilities tally with such unequal relations between our great states? This does not tally at all.

It is good, Mr. President, that you agreed for our representatives to meet and begin talks, apparently with the participation of U.N. Acting Secretary General U Thant. Consequently, to some extent, he assumes the role of intermediary, and we believe that he can cope with the responsible mission if, of course, every side that is drawn into this conflict shows good will.

I think that one could rapidly eliminate the conflict and normalize the situation. Then people would heave a sigh of relief, considering that the statesmen who bear the responsibility have sober minds, an awareness of their responsibility, and an ability to solve complicated problems and not allow matters to slide to the disaster of war.

This is why I make this proposal: We agree to remove those weapons from Cuba which you regard as offensive weapons. We agree to do this and to state this commitment in the United Nations. Your representatives will make a statement to the effect that the United States, on its part, bearing in mind the anxiety and concern of the Soviet state, will evacuate its analogous weapons from

Turkey. Let us reach an understanding on what time you and we need to put this into effect.

After this, representatives of the U.N. Security Council could control on-the-spot the fulfillment of these commitments. Of course, it is necessary that the Governments of Cuba and Turkey would allow these representatives to come to their countries and check fulfillment of this commitment, which each side undertakes. Apparently, it would be better if these representatives enjoyed the trust of the Security Council and ours—the United States and the Soviet Union—as well as of Turkey and Cuba. I think that it will not be difficult to find such people who enjoy the trust and respect of all interested sides.

We, having assumed this commitment in order to give satisfaction and hope to the peoples of Cuba and Turkey and to increase their confidence in their security, will make a statement in the Security Council to the effect that the Soviet Government gives a solemn pledge to respect the integrity of the frontiers and the sovereignty of Turkey, not to intervene in its domestic affairs, not to invade Turkey, not to make available its territory as a place d'armes for such invasion, and also will restrain those who would think of launching an aggression against Turkey either from Soviet territory or from the territory of other states bordering on Turkey.

The U.S. Government will make the same statement in the Security Council with regard to Cuba. It will declare that the United States will respect the integrity of the frontiers of Cuba, its sovereignty, undertakes not to intervene in its domestic affairs, not to invade and not to make its territory available as place d'armes for the invasion of Cuba, and also will restrain those who would think of launching an aggression against Cuba either from U.S. territory or from the territory of other states bordering on Cuba.

Of course, for this we would have to reach agreement with you and to arrange for some deadline. Let us agree to give some time, but not to delay, two or three weeks, not more than a month.

The weapons on Cuba, that you have mentioned and which, as you say, alarm you, are in the hands of Soviet officers. Therefore any accidental use of them whatsoever to the detriment of the United States of America is excluded. These means are stationed in Cuba at the request of the Cuban Government and only in defensive aims. Therefore, if there is no invasion of Cuba, or an attack on the Soviet Union, or other of our allies then, of course, these means do not threaten anyone and will not threaten. For they do not pursue offensive aims.

If you accept my proposal, Mr. President, we would send our representatives to New York, to the United Nations, and would give them exhaustive instructions to order to come to terms sooner. If you would also appoint your men and give them appropriate instructions, this problem could be solved soon.

Why would I like to achieve this? Because the entire world is now agitated and expects reasonable actions from us. The greatest pleasure for all the peoples would be an announcement on our agreement, on nipping in the bud the conflict that has arisen. I attach a great importance to such understanding because it might be a good beginning and, specifically, facilitate a nuclear test ban agreement. The problem of tests could be solved simultaneously, not linking one with the other, because they are different problems. However, it is important to reach an understanding to both these problems in order to make a good gift to the people, to let them rejoice in the news that a nuclear test ban agreement has also been reached and thus there will be no further contamination of the atmosphere. Your and our positions on this issue are very close.

All this, possibly, would serve as a good impetus to searching for mutually acceptable agreements on other disputed issues, too, on which there is an exchange of opinion between us. These problems have not yet been solved but they wait for an urgent solution which would clear the international atmosphere. We are ready for this.

These are my proposals, Mr. President.

Dean Rusk and Other Leaders on the Lessons of the Missile Crisis, 1982

In the years since the Cuban missile crisis, many commentators have examined the affair and offered a wide variety of conclusions. It seems fitting now that some of us who worked particularly closely with President Kennedy during that crisis should offer a few comments, with the advantages both of participation and of hindsight.

First: The crisis could and should have been avoided. If we had done an earlier, stronger and clearer job of explaining our position on Soviet nuclear weapons in the Western Hemisphere, or if the Soviet government had more carefully assessed the evidence that did exist on this point, it is likely that the missiles would never have been sent to Cuba. *The importance of accurate mutual assessment of interests between the two superpowers is evident and continuous.*

Second: Reliable intelligence permitting an effective choice of response was obtained only just in time. It was primarily a mistake by policymakers, not by professionals, that made such intelligence unavailable sooner. But it was also a timely recognition of the need for thorough overflight, not without its hazards, that produced the decisive photographs. The usefulness and scope of inspection from above, also employed in monitoring the Soviet missile withdrawal, should never be underestimated. *When the importance of accurate information for a crucial policy decision is high enough, risks not otherwise acceptable in collecting intelligence can become profoundly prudent.*

Third: The President wisely took his time in choosing a course of action. A quick decision would certainly have been less carefully designed and could well have produced a much higher risk of catastrophe. The fact that the crisis did not become public in its first week obviously made it easier for

Dean Rusk et al., "The Lessons of the Cuban Missile Crisis," *Time Magazine*, 52 (September 27, 1982), 85–86. Reprinted by permission of Dean Rusk and McGeorge Bundy.

President Kennedy to consider his options with a maximum of care and a minimum of outside pressure. Not every future crisis will be so quiet in its first phase, but *Americans should always respect the need for a period of confidential and careful deliberation in dealing with a major international crisis.*

Fourth: The decisive military element in the resolution of the crisis was our clearly available and applicable superiority in conventional weapons within the area of the crisis. U.S. naval forces, quickly deployable for the blockade of offensive weapons that was sensibly termed a quarantine, and the availability of U.S. ground and air forces sufficient to execute an invasion if necessary, made the difference. American nuclear superiority was not in our view a critical factor, for the fundamental and controlling reason that nuclear war, already in 1962, would have been an unexampled catastrophe for both sides: the balance of terror so eloquently described by Winston Churchill seven years earlier was in full operation. No one of us ever reviewed the nuclear balance for comfort in those hard weeks. *The Cuban missile crisis illustrates not the significance but the insignificance of nuclear superiority in the face of survivable thermonuclear retaliatory forces. It also shows the crucial role of rapidly available conventional strength.*

Fifth: The political and military pressure created by the quarantine was matched by a diplomatic effort that ignored no relevant means of communication with both our friends and our adversary. Communication to and from our allies in Europe was intense, and their support sturdy. The Organization of American States gave the moral and legal authority of its regional backing to the quarantine, making it plain that Soviet nuclear weapons were profoundly unwelcome in the Americas. In the U.N., Ambassador Adlai Stevenson drove home with angry eloquence and unanswerable photographic evidence the facts of the Soviet deployment and deception.

Still more important, communication was established and maintained, once our basic course was set, with the government of the Soviet Union. If the crisis itself showed the cost of mutual incomprehension, its resolution showed the value of serious and sustained communication, and in particular of direct exchanges between the two heads of government.

When great states come anywhere near the brink in the nuclear age, there is no room for games of blindman's bluff. Nor can friends be led by silence. They must know what we are doing and why. *Effective communication is never more important than when there is a military confrontation.*

Sixth: This diplomatic effort and indeed our whole course of action were greatly reinforced by the fact that our position was squarely based on irrefutable evidence that the Soviet government was doing exactly what it had repeatedly denied that it would do. The support of our allies and the readiness of the Soviet government to draw back were heavily affected by the public demonstration of a Soviet course of conduct that simply could not be defended. In this demonstration no evidence less explicit and authoritative than that of photography would have been sufficient, and it was one of President Kennedy's best decisions that the ordinary requirements of secrecy in such matters should be brushed aside in the interest of persuasive exposition. *There are times when a display of hard evidence is more valuable than protection of intelligence techniques.*

Seventh: In the successful resolution of the crisis, restraint was as important as strength. In particular, we avoided any early initiation of battle by American forces, and indeed we took no action of any kind that would have forced an instant and possibly ill-considered response. Moreover, we limited our demands to the restoration of the *status quo ante,* that is, the removal of any Soviet nuclear capability from Cuba. There was no demand for "total victory" or "unconditional surrender." These choices gave the Soviet government both time and opportunity to respond with equal restraint. *It is wrong, in relations between the superpowers, for either side to leave the other with no way out but war or humiliation.*

Eighth: On two points of particular interest to the Soviet government, we made sure that it had the benefit of knowing the independently reached positions of President Kennedy. One assurance was public and the other private.

Publicly we made it clear that the U.S. would not invade Cuba if the Soviet missiles were withdrawn. The President never shared the view that the missile crisis should be "used" to pick a fight to the finish with Castro; he correctly insisted that the real issue in the crisis was with the Soviet government, and that the one vital bone of contention was the secret and deceit-covered movement of Soviet missiles into Cuba. He recognized that an invasion by U.S. forces would be bitter and bloody, and that it would leave festering wounds in the body politic of the Western Hemisphere. The no-invasion assurance was not a concession, but a statement of our own clear preference—once the missiles were withdrawn.

The second and private assurance—communicated on the President's instructions by Robert Kennedy to Soviet Ambassador Anatoli Dobrynin on the evening of Oct. 27—was that the President had determined that once the crisis was resolved, the American missiles then in Turkey would be removed. (The essence of this secret assurance was revealed by Robert Kennedy in his 1969 book *Thirteen Days,* and a more detailed account, drawn from many sources but not from discussion with any of us, was published by Arthur M. Schlesinger Jr. in *Robert Kennedy and His Times* in 1978. In these circumstances, we think it is now proper for those of us privy to that decision to discuss the matter.) This could not be a "deal"—our missiles in Turkey for theirs in Cuba—as the Soviet government had just proposed. The matter involved the concerns of our allies, and we could not put ourselves in the position of appearing to trade their protection for our own. But in fact President Kennedy had long since reached the conclusion that the outmoded and vulnerable missiles in Turkey should be withdrawn. In the spring of 1961 Secretary Rusk had begun the necessary discussions with high Turkish officials. These officials asked for delay, at least until Polaris submarines could be deployed in the Mediterranean. While the matter was not pressed to a conclusion in the following year and a half, the missile crisis itself reinforced the President's convictions. It was entirely right that the Soviet government should understand this reality.

This second assurance was kept secret because the few who knew about it at the time were in unanimous agreement that any other course would have had explosive and destructive effects on the security of the U.S. and its allies. If made public in the context of the Soviet proposal to make a "deal," the unilateral decision reached by the President would have been misread as an unwilling concession granted in fear at the expense of an ally. It seemed better to tell the Soviets the real position in private, and in a way that would prevent any such misunderstanding. Robert Kennedy made it plain to Ambassador Dobrynin that any attempt to treat the President's unilateral assurance as part of a deal would simply make that assurance inoperative.

Although for separate reasons neither the public nor the private assurance ever became a formal commitment of the U.S. Government, the validity of both was demonstrated by our later actions; there was no invasion of Cuba, and the vulnerable missiles in Turkey (and Italy) were withdrawn, with allied concurrence, to be replaced by invulnerable Polaris submarines. Both results were in our own clear interest, and both assurances were helpful in making it easier for the Soviet government to decide to withdraw its missiles.

In part this was secret diplomacy, including a secret assurance. Any failure to make good on that assurance would obviously have had damaging effects on Soviet-American relations. But it is of critical importance here that the President gave no assurance that went beyond his own presidential powers; in particular he made no commitment that required congressional approval or even support. The decision that the missiles in Turkey should be removed was one that the President had full and unquestioned authority to make and execute.

When it will help your own country for your adversary to know your settled intentions, you should find effective ways of making sure that he does, and a secret assurance is justified when a) you can keep your word, and b) no other course can avoid grave damage to your country's legitimate interests.

Ninth: The gravest risk in this crisis was not that either head of government desired to initiate a major escalation but that events would produce actions, reactions or miscalculations carrying the conflict beyond the control of one or the other or both. In retrospect we are inclined to think that both men would have taken every possible step to prevent such a result, but at the time no one near the top of either government could have that certainty about the other side. *In any crisis involving the superpowers, firm control by the heads of both governments is essential to the avoidance of an unpredictably escalating conflict.*

Tenth: The successful resolution of the Cuban missile crisis was fundamentally the achievement of two men, John F. Kennedy and Nikita S. Khrushchev. We know that in this anniversary year John Kennedy would wish us to emphasize the contribution of Khrushchev; the fact that an earlier and less prudent decision by the Soviet leader made the crisis inevitable does not detract from the statesmanship of his change of course. We may be forgiven, however, if we give the last and highest word of honor to our own President, whose cautious determination, steady composure, deep-seated compassion and, above all, continuously attentive control of our options and actions brilliantly served his country and all mankind.

ESSAYS

Arthur M. Schlesinger, Jr., is an historian who was a Kennedy aide. He has written two major chronicles of the 1960s, *A Thousand Days* (1965) and *Robert Kennedy and His Times* (1978). In the first essay, an excerpt from the latter book, he presents the Cuban-American story after the Bay of Pigs. In attempting to exonerate John and Robert Kennedy from wrongdoing toward Cuba before the missile crisis, Schlesinger studies Operation Mongoose and the assassination plots. For Schlesinger, the Central Intelligence Agency made mistakes, but he gives high marks to the Kennedys for their actions in the missile crisis.

One of the critics of the Kennedy administration's handling of the missile crisis whom Schlesinger attempts to refute is James A. Nathan of the University of Delaware. Nathan doubts that the crisis was managed well, suggests that domestic political considerations helped to determine the President's diplomacy, emphasizes the importance of "appearances," and concludes that American civilian leaders were so impressed with their performance that "toughness" thereafter became their watchword.

The Kennedys and Cuba

ARTHUR M. SCHLESINGER, JR.

"The Cuba matter is being allowed to slide," Robert Kennedy said on June 1 [1961]. "Mostly because nobody really has the answer to Castro. Not many are really prepared to send American troops in there at the present time but maybe that is the answer. Only time will tell." The Attorney General was unquestionably right on one point: nobody had the answer to Castro.

John Kennedy politely asked Richard Nixon, "What would you do now in Cuba?" "I would find a proper legal cover," Nixon replied (by his own account), "and I would go in." In mid-June the Cuba Study Group chimed in. "There can be no long-term living with Castro as a neighbor," Maxwell Taylor, Robert Kennedy and their associates solemnly concluded. The group saw two possible policies: either to hope that time and internal discontent would eventually end the threat, "or to take active measures to force its removal. . . . Neither alternative is attractive. . . . While inclining personally to a positive course of action against Castro without delay, we recognize the danger of dealing with the Cuban problem outside the context of the world Cold War situation."

Senator Mike Mansfield, who was regularly wiser on questions of foreign policy than most members of the National Security Council, offered the best answer. "If we yield to the temptation to give vent to our anger at our own failure," he wrote the President, "we will, ironically, strengthen Castro's position." Mansfield sensibly recommended "gradual disengagement of the U.S. government from anti-Castro revolutionary groups, . . . a taciturn resistance to the political blandishments or provocations from those at home who would urge that we act directly in Cuba, . . . a cessation of violent verbal attacks on Castro by officials of the government" and full steam ahead on the Alliance for Progress because without economic progress *"Castroism is likely to spread elsewhere in Latin America whether or not Castro remains in power in Cuba."* Robert Kennedy agreed over the long run. "If the Alliance for Progress goes into operation fully," he said in 1963, "if reforms, social, economic and political, are put into effect, then Communism and Castroism will collapse in Latin America." . . .

But neither the Alliance for Progress nor the diplomatic and economic isolation of Cuba promised immediate results. With his brother under Communist harassment in Berlin and Southeast Asia and under Republican harassment in the United States, with Castro's operatives plotting against democratic regimes in Latin America, Robert Kennedy was determined to find quicker ways of striking back. . . .

With sure bureaucratic instinct, the Agency [CIA] seized on the Cuban problem as the way of making its comeback from the Bay of Pigs. "We wanted to earn our spurs with the President," as Richard Helms said. But as usual it thought it alone knew how to do the job. The CIA wished to organize Castro's overthrow itself from *outside* Cuba, as against those in the White House, the Attorney General's office and State who wished to support an anti-Castro movement *inside* Cuba. The CIA's idea was to fight a war; the others hoped to promote a revolution. Any successful anti-Castro movement inside Cuba would have to draw on disenchanted Castroites and aim to rescue the revolution from the Communists. This approach, stigmatized as *Fidelismo sin Fidel,* was opposed by businessmen, both Cuban and American, who dreamed of the restoration of nationalized properties. But the CIA alternative was probably dictated less by business interests than by the Agency's preference for operations it could completely control—especially strong in this case because of the Cuban reputation for total inability to keep anything secret.

As I wrote in July 1961 to Richard Goodwin, the White House liaison for Cuba, the CIA's Cuban Covert Plan contemplated "a *CIA* underground formed on criteria of operational convenience rather than a *Cuban* underground formed on criteria of building political strength sufficient to overthrow Castro." The CIA specifications favored those Cubans "most willing to accept CIA identification and control" and discriminated against Cubans who insisted on running their own show. I had in mind the anti-Castro radical Manuel Ray, who was believed to have the most effective network on the island. "The practical effect," I concluded, "is to invest our resources in the people least capable of generating broad support within Cuba."

These disagreements were temporarily papered over at the end of August 1961 when the Cuba Task Force—which included George Ball and some Latin Americanists from State, Goodwin from the White House and a CIA delegation led by Richard Bissell—came up with a formula. They all agreed, as Goodwin reported to the President, on a campaign directed "toward the destruction of targets important to the economy, e.g., refineries, plants using U.S. equipment, etc." This was the CIA plank; but Goodwin also won nominal CIA acceptance of "the principle that para-military activities ought to be carried out through Cuban revolutionary groups which have a potential for establishing an effective political opposition to Castro within Cuba."

But the Goodwin plank was against the CIA's operational code. The Agency could not bring itself to trust those it could not control. In the early fall Bissell was told, perhaps in a meeting with the President and the Attorney General, to "get off your ass about Cuba." After a meeting with Bissell, Esterline and other Agency people on October 23, I noted: "At bottom, there is a conflict between operational interests and diplomatic interests. CIA wants to subordinate everything else to tidy and manageable operations; hence it prefers compliant people, like [Joaquin] Sanjenis [head of Operation 40, a right-wing clandestine group funded by the CIA] to proud and independent people, like Miro [Cardona, the head of the Cuban Revolutionary Council and Castro's first prime minister]." Hoping to bring the CIA into line, Goodwin proposed to the President in early November that Robert Kennedy "would be the most effective commander of the anti-Castro campaign." At just this point, the famed General Lansdale returned from a trip to Saigon. Robert Kennedy, remembering Lansdale's doctrine of pre-empting the revolution and aware that the Army did not want him in Vietnam, thought that the savior of Magsaysay might have the answer to Castro.

On November 4, 1961, Cuba was the subject of a White House meeting. Present, according to Robert Kennedy's handwritten notes, were

> McNamara, Dick Bissell, Alexis Johnson [the deputy under secretary of state for political affairs], Paul Nitze, Ed Lansdale (the Ugly American). McN said he would make latter available for me—I assigned him to make survey of situation in Cuba—the problems & our assets.
>
> My idea is to stir things up on island with espionage, sabotage, general disorder, run & operated by Cubans themselves with every group but Batistaites & Communists. Do not know if we will be successful in overthrowing Castro but we have nothing to lose in my estimate.

Lansdale made his survey. He recommended "a very different course" from the CIA "harassment" operations of the summer, conceived and led as they were by Americans. Instead, the United States, Lansdale argued, should seek out Cubans who had opposed Batista and then had become disillusioned with Castro. His theory was to work within Cuba, taking care not to "arouse premature actions, not to bring great reprisals on the people there." The objective was to depose Castro in the same way Castro had deposed Batista—to have "the people themselves overthrow the Castro regime rather than U.S. engineered efforts from outside Cuba."

The President decided in favor of the Goodwin-Lansdale thesis and against the CIA. At the end of November he put out a top secret instruction "to use our available assets . . . to help Cuba overthrow the Communist regime." Lansdale was appointed chief of operations, reporting to a new review committee known as the Special Group (Augmented). Operation Mongoose was born. . . .

Mongoose, like the baby in the old story, was attended at the cradle by good fairies with divergent wishes. The President's wish was that, as Taylor described it, "all actions should be kept in a low key." Since "anything big was going to be charged to the United States," Mongoose had to be kept small, functioning at what was known in intelligence circles as a low noise level. The American hand was to be concealed. Nor did the President wish undue activity to jeopardize the lives of the Bay of Pigs prisoners.

The Attorney General had a separate wish, as rendered in CIA notes of a meeting at Justice with Mongoose planners in January 1962: that "no time, money, effort—or manpower . . . be spared." Mongoose was "top priority." But he was never clear how the time, money, etc., were to be used.

Lansdale's wish was activity—a lot of it—leading to internal revolution. He had a multitude of ideas: nonlethal chemicals to incapacitate sugar workers; "gangster elements" to attack police officials; defections "from the top echelon of the Communist gang"; even (at least according to one witness before the Church committee; Lansdale later disclaimed the project) spreading word that Castro was anti-Christ and that the Second Coming was imminent—an event to be verified by star shells sent up from an American submarine off the Cuban coast ("elimination by illumination," a waspish critic called it). In February, Lansdale presented a six-phase plan designed to culminate the next October in an "open revolt and overthrow of the Communist regime." All this was a little rich for the Special Group (Augmented), which directed him instead to make the collection of intelligence the "immediate priority objective of U.S. efforts in the coming months." While the group was willing to condone a little concurrent sabotage, the acts "must be inconspicuous," it told Lansdale, and on a scale "short of those reasonably calculated to inspire a revolt." It further insisted that all "sensitive" operations, "sabotage, for example, will have to be presented in more detail on a case by case basis."

The Augmented Group could prescribe policy to Lansdale. It was harder for Lansdale to prescribe operations, which remained in the hands of CIA. Task Force W, the CIA unit for Mongoose, soon had four hundred American employees in Washington and Miami, over fifty proprietary fronts, its own navy of fast boats, a rudimentary air force and two thousand Cuban agents. The Miami headquarters became for a season the largest CIA station in the world. All this cost over $50 million a year. The CIA had its special wish for Mongoose too. Whereas the Special Group (Augmented) had accepted the presidential decision that "the one thing that was off limits was military invasion," the Agency persisted in seeing the objective as the creation of "internal dissension and resistance leading to eventual U.S. intervention"

(October 1962). The Agency, in short, was more bent than ever on fighting a war. It proved this by the men to whom it offered command of Task Force W.

Bissell's first choice, if Howard Hunt can be believed, was Hunt himself, an operative notorious in the Cuban community for his division of the exiles into (as one anti-Castro exile put it) the "good guys," who did his bidding, and the "bad guys," who "refused to be coerced into accepting his standard operating procedures." Hunt, however, declined the job on the ground that "it was obvious there was no serious interest in overthrowing Castro, and I was reluctant to conduct operations for their own sake, to give the appearance of activity."

The next CIA candidate was no more amenable to the Lansdale-Goodwin political strategy. William King Harvey had begun as an FBI counterespionage agent, renowned for having turned the Nazi spy William Sebold into a double agent during the Second World War. Fired by Hoover for drunkenness in 1947, he caught on with the CIA and became one of its celebrated operators. His great coup, the 'Berlin tunnel,' had enabled the CIA for many months in 1955–56 to intercept communications between East Berlin and Moscow. He was a histrionic fellow who always packed a gun, even in CIA headquarters in Langley. "If you ever know as many secrets as I do," he would say mysteriously, "then you'll know why I carry a gun." Far from wanting the independent Cuban movement envisaged by Lansdale, Harvey was determined to reduce his Cuban operatives to abject dependence. "Your CO [case officer] was like your priest," one of Harvey's Cubans said later. ". . . You learned to tell him everything, your complete life."

Lansdale found Harvey intensely secretive, almost paranoid. Lansdale finally said to him, "I'm not the enemy. You can talk to me." But the momentum of the overblown Miami establishment generated its own excesses. "Mostly the things we needed were not the things they wanted to do," Lansdale said later. "Still, if the equipment exists, the temptation to use it becomes irresistible." Lansdale would ask what they expected random hit-and-run raids to accomplish. They had no good answer. A bridge would be blown up. "Why did you do it?" Lansdale would say. "What communications were you trying to destroy?" Harvey would reply, "You never told us not to blow up the bridge." Lansdale made his directives increasingly precise in the hope of stopping aimless sabotage and saving courageous Cubans from pointless death.

Harvey protested to McCone about the "tight controls exercised by the Special Group" and the "excruciating detail" he was expected to provide. The controls must have had some effect. "They never let us fight as much as we wanted to," lamented Ramón Orozco, a Cuban commando, "and most of the operations were infiltrations and weapons drops." In October 1962 Robert Kennedy pointed out that, after almost a year of Mongoose, "there had been no acts of sabotage and that even the one which had been attempted [against the Matahambre copper mines] had failed twice." CIA itself complained that same month, "Policymakers not only shied away from the military intervention aspect but were generally apprehensive of sabotage proposals."

Still Harvey's Cubans evidently did more than Washington imagined. "The difficulties of control were so great," Taylor Branch and George Crile have written, "that the Agency [itself] often didn't know which missions were leaving in which directions." Harvey's people included soldiers of fortune like William (Rip) Robertson, a flamboyant figure who, in defiance of presidential orders, had landed on the beach at the Bay of Pigs. "When we didn't go [on missions]," said Orozco, "Rip would feel sick and get very mad." Once Robertson told Orozco "I'll give you $50 if you bring me back an ear." Orozco brought him two, and "he laughed and said, 'You're crazy,' but he paid me $100, and he took us to his house for a turkey dinner." They all sounded crazy. It was the 'dirty dozen' spirit, action for action's sake, without concern for the safety of the Cubans involved or for the reprisal effect or for political follow-up.

Lansdale, Robert Kennedy said in 1964, "came to cross purposes with CIA and they didn't like his interferences." "Revolutions have to be indigenous," Lansdale said in retrospect. ". . . We have a tendency as a people to want to see things done right—and, if they aren't, we step in and try to do them ourselves. That is fatal to a revolution." Harvey, however, had the decisive advantage of operational control. The political strategy fell by the wayside. As for Robert Kennedy, he found Harvey and his meaningless melodrama detestable. "Too much 'Gunsmoke stance' for the Attorney General," said Howard Hunt. "Why lose lives," Kennedy used to say to Taylor and to Lansdale, "if the return isn't clearly, clearly worth it?" As for Harvey, he "hated Bobby Kennedy's guts," said a CIA colleague, "with a purple passion."

The Attorney General was always dissatisfied with Mongoose. He wanted it to do more, the terrors of the earth, but what they were he knew not. He was wildly busy in 1962—a trip around the world in February, the steel fight in April, civil rights always, Ole Miss in September, organized crime, Hoffa, apportionment, fighting with Lyndon Johnson about minority employment, fighting with Edgar Hoover about everything. Castro was high on his list of emotions, much lower on his list of informed concerns. When he was able to come to meetings of Special Group (Augmented), as he did his best to do, he made up in pressure for what he lacked in knowledge. His style there, as everywhere, was to needle the bureaucracy. If there was a problem, there had to be a solution. He conveyed acute impatience and urgency. With the intelligence-collection phase ending in August 1962, the Mongoose group meditated a "stepped up Course B Plus" intended to inspire open revolt. Kennedy, who was away on the west coast, endorsed B Plus in a message to Taylor. "I do not feel," he said, "that we know yet what reaction would be created in Cuba for an intensified program. Therefore, I am in favor of pushing ahead rather than taking any step backward."

In October he urged the Augmented Group, in the name of the President, to give more priority to sabotage. The group responded by calling for "new and imaginative approaches with the possibility of getting rid of the Castro regime." The State Department recommended the use of Manuel Ray, the anti-Castro radical. "I do believe," Lansdale wrote Robert Kennedy on October 15, "we should make a real hard try at this—since helping Cubans to help themselves was the original concept of Mongoose and still has validity." But CIA had always rejected Ray as too independent. Lansdale added: "I believe you will have to hit CIA over the head personally. I can then follow through, to get the action desired." . . . On the same day, CIA experts were poring over photographs just taken by a U-2 plane over western Cuba. . . .

The CIA had yet another program against Castro, the one initiated in 1960 and dedicated to his death. The Agency had considered assassination within its purview since the early Eisenhower years when it gave a special unit responsibility for, among other things, kidnapping and murder. The Church committee found no evidence that this special unit tried to kill any foreign leaders. There are indications, however, that CIA operatives abroad tried, or at least wished, to kill Chou En-lai in 1955. But the fever seems not to have struck in full force until the last Eisenhower year. In August 1960 the CIA decided to kill Patrice Lumumba, the pro-Soviet Premier of the newly independent Congo, and delivered a bag of poison to Leopoldville for that purpose. (Lumumba's actual murder the following January was, however, the work of his fellow countrymen and not of the CIA.) In August also, the CIA set in motion the plot to kill Castro.

The early planning was evidently confided to a team of humorists. One idea was to dust Castro's shoes, if he chanced to leave them outside his hotel room, with thallium salts in the expectation that this would cause his beard to fall out and destroy his charisma. Another was to lace a box of cigars with a chemical that produced temporary disorientation and get Castro to smoke one before delivering a speech. Since Castro's speeches often gave an impression of disorientation anyway, it is not clear how much difference the toxic cigar would have made. By August 1960 the Agency had progressed to the project of impregnating cigars with botulinum, a poison so deadly that a man would die after putting one in his mouth. The cigars were ready in October and were delivered to an unidentified person the following February.

The Agency also may have recruited Marie Lorenz, a pretty German girl whom Castro had taken as a mistress in 1959 and later cast off. She fell in with Frank Fiorini, an adventurer who had fought beside Castro, but turned against him and went to work for CIA; under the name of Frank Sturgis, Fiorini figured in the Bay of Pigs and later in Watergate. The CIA, Lorenz claimed in 1976, appealed to her patriotism, promised her money for her old age and asked her to kill Castro. Sturgis gave her two poison capsules, which she secreted in a jar of cold cream. When she arrived in Havana, Castro greeted her warmly, took his phone off the hook, ordered food and coffee and then fell asleep on the bed with a cigar, evidently not a CIA model, in his mouth. Lorenz went to the bathroom and opened the cold cream. "I couldn't find the capsules," she said in 1976. "They had melted. It was like an omen. . . . I thought, 'To hell with it. Let history take its course.' "

The Agency decided to turn to experts. When Castro's revolution swept into Havana at the end of 1958, it swept out not only Batista but the dictator's partners in the North American mob. Batista and the criminal entrepreneur Meyer Lansky fled on the same day. The closing of the casinos, the bordellos and the drug traffic cost the mob perhaps $100 million a year. Back in God's country, Lansky was reputed to have persuaded his associates to join in a pledge of a million dollars for Castro's head. Frank Sturgis claimed in 1975 that the mob had offered him $100,000 in 1959 to kill Castro. The masterminds of CIA now decided the syndicate possessed uniquely both the motives and skills required to rid the world of the Cuban revolutionary. Since the mob had its own grudge against Castro, a gangland hit would be less likely to lead back to the American government.

The CIA commissioned Robert Maheu—a former FBI agent, later a private eye involved for a time with Hoffa's friend Eddie Cheyfitz and now working for Howard Hughes—to put out the contract. Maheu subsequently said that assassination was presented to him as "a necessary ingredient . . . of the overall invasion plan." Maheu brought in John Rosselli, a minor crook-about-town he had known in Las Vegas. Rosselli, who had no illusions about his middling rank in the underworld, brought in the Chicago big shot Sam Giancana, who was a don and could make the right connections. Giancana's vital connection for this purpose was Santos Trafficante, Jr., the boss of organized crime in Florida; not so long before, in Havana.

CIA case officers made their contact with the underworld notables before they informed their own chief, Allen Dulles. One would have supposed that an alliance between the CIA and the mob might have required prior approval at least by the CIA director, if not by the Special Group. That this was not the case suggests the liberties casually taken even by lesser CIA officials in the Agency's golden age.

In the fall of 1960, CIA installed Giancana and Rosselli in a Miami Beach hotel. The Agency stuck staunchly by Giancana even after J. Edgar Hoover sent Bissell in October a report that, "during recent conversations with several friends, Giancana stated that Fidel Castro was to be done away with shortly." For his part Giancana, plotting away in Miami and jealously apprehensive that his girl, the singer Phyllis McGuire, might have her own plots in Las Vegas, asked the CIA to arrange an illegal wiretap in the room of his putative rival, the comedian Dan Rowan. The Agency obliged: anything to keep Giancana happy. When the tap was discovered, the Agency did its best to stop prosecution.

As for Trafficante, he was a leader in his field. He had been a prime suspect in the barbershop murder of Albert Anastasia in 1957. Later that year he had been picked up at the Apalachian seminar. Havana was his base, and he was the only syndicate boss to stay on after the revolution. Castro imprisoned him in 1959. For an enemy of the people, Trafficante lived behind bars in surprising comfort. Chums from the mainland visited him, among them the Dallas hood Jack Ruby. On release in September 1959, Trafficante went to Tampa. With his Cuban business presumably destroyed, but with part of the gang still in Havana, Trafficante had both motives and men for the CIA job.

It may have been more complicated than that. Why, after all, had Castro let Trafficante go? A Federal Narcotics Bureau document in July 1961 reported rumors in the exile community that Castro had "kept Santo [sic] Trafficante, Jr., in jail to make it appear that he had a personal dislike for Trafficante, when in fact Trafficante is an agent of Castro. Trafficante is allegedly Castro's outlet for illegal contraband in the country. While banning drugs at home, Castro might have wished to earn foreign exchange by permitting them to flow through Cuba to the United States, as they had done so lucratively under Batista. He might also have hoped to promote drug addiction in the United States—even as Chou En-lai organized the export of Chinese opium in order to demoralize American troops in Vietnam. If Trafficante was indeed a double agent, one can see why Castro survived so comfortably the ministrations of the CIA. . . .

Their first idea was to slip some pills into Castro's drink shortly before the Bay of Pigs. After one batch of CIA pills failed to dissolve, a more soluble batch killed some innocent monkeys and was deemed suitable. The obliging Trafficante produced a Cuban who, he said, had access to one of Castro's favorite restaurants. Maheu gave the Cuban the pills and $10,000. Castro survived. A second attempt was made in April immediately before the Bay of Pigs. Castro survived.

After the Bay of Pigs, the Castro project was, in the CIA patois, "stood down"—i.e., suspended. In the meantime William K. Harvey had entered the picture. In January 1961, before Kennedy's inauguration, Bissell discussed with Harvey, and soon directed him to establish, an "executive action capability" for the disabling of foreign leaders, including assassination as a "last resort." No one has been able to discover that the executive-action crowd did much apart from Cuba. In April 1962, Richard Helms, who had now succeeded Bissell, ordered Harvey to reactivate the Castro project. Whatever else, Harvey was, he was a professional, and he found the six-link operation—CIA to Maheu to Rosselli to Giancana to a Cuban exile to a Cuban assassin—intolerably loose. He thereupon instructed Rosselli to cut out Maheu and Giancana. Now it all started again: poison pills in April 1962; a three-man assassination team in June; talk of a new team in September; Castro always in perfect health. Harvey began to doubt whether the operation was going anyplace. He finally terminated it in February 1963. The mob's conning of CIA came to an end.

CIA's stalking of Castro did not. Some genius proposed that James Donovan, during his negotiations for the Bay of Pigs prisoners, give Castro a scuba diving suit contaminated by a tubercle bacillus and dusted inside with a fungus designed to produce skin disease. Donovan, who knew nothing of this, innocently foiled the Agency by giving Castro a clean diving suit on his own. Then Desmond FitzGerald, who replaced Harvey as head of Task Force W in January 1963, suggested depositing a rare seashell, rigged to explode, in a place where Castro might skin-dive and pick it up. This inspiration proved beyond the Agency's technical capacity. . . .

Though the assassination plan was confided to Robert Maheu, though it became a staple of Sam Giancana's table talk and a joke among the mob, there is *no* evidence that any Agency official ever mentioned it to any President—Eisenhower in 1960, Kennedy after 1960, Johnson after 1963—except (in Johnson's case) for operations already terminated. The practice of "plausible denial" had, as Colonel William R. Corson, a veteran intelligence officer, put it, "degenerated to the point where the cover stories of presidential ignorance really are fact, not fiction."

Nor was the Castro murder plan submitted to the Special Group, the supposed control mechanism for covert action, either in 1960 or thereafter; nor to the Special Group (Augmented), sitting on top of Mongoose. Nor was it disclosed after the Bay of Pigs to Maxwell Taylor and his review board. Rusk, McNamara, Bundy, Taylor, Gilpatric, Goodwin, Rostow, all testified under oath that they had never heard of it (nor had Kenneth O'Donnell, nor, for that matter, had I). On every occasion in the Kennedy years when CIA officials might naturally have brought it up—Bissell's briefings of his old Yale friend Mac Bundy after the inauguration, the Bay of Pigs meeting, the Taylor board, the missile crisis—they studiously refrained from saying a word.

The argument that the Kennedys knew and approved of the assassination plan comes down, in the end, to the argument that they *must* have known—an argument that, of course, applies with equal force to Eisenhower and Johnson. The CIA, it is said, would never have undertaken so fearful a task without presidential authorization.

In John Kennedy's case, Bissell and Helms offered contradictory theories about the nature of that authorization. Bissell assumed the project had been cleared with Kennedy, as with Eisenhower, in ways that were tacit, "circumlocutious," camouflaged, leaving no record. Helms thought CIA's authority was derived, not from supposed "circumlocutious" talks, but from the "intense" pressure the Kennedys radiated against Castro. The CIA operators were undoubtedly misled by the urgency with which the Kennedys, especially Robert, pursued Mongoose. "We cannot overemphasize the extent," the CIA inspector general said in 1967, "to which responsible Agency officers felt themselves subject to the Kennedy Administration's severe pressure to do something about Castro and his regime." "It was the policy at the time to get rid of Castro," said Helms, "and if killing him was one of the things that was to be done in this connection, that was within what was expected." Having been asked "to get rid of Castro," Helms added, ". . . there were no limitations put on the means, and we felt we were acting well within the guidelines." No member of the administration told Helms to kill Castro, but no one had ever specifically ruled it out, so the Agency, he believed, could work for Castro's overthrow as it deemed best. Moreover, as Helms said, "Nobody wants to embarrass a President . . . by discussing the assassination of foreign leaders in his presence."

Still it seems singular that, even if the CIA people believed they had an original authorization of some yet undiscovered sort from Eisenhower, they never inquired of Kennedy whether he wished these risky and disagreeable adventures to continue. The project after all had begun as part of the Cuban invasion plan. In this context the murder of Castro had an arguably rational, if wholly repellent, function. After the Bay of Pigs and the abandonment of invasion fantasies, the radical change in context ought surely to have compelled reconsideration both of the project itself and of the alleged authorization. The Mongoose committee was demanding at this time that all "sensitive" operations be presented in "excruciating" detail, case by case. But the Agency, without consulting superior authority, resuscitated the assassination project on its own, the murder of Castro now becoming, without the invasion, an end in itself—a quite pointless end, too, in the unconsulted judgment of the CIA's Intelligence Branch. In October 1961 the Special Group asked for a contingency plan in the event Castro died from whatever cause. The CIA Board of Estimates responded that Castro's death "by assassination or by natural causes . . . would almost certainly not prove fatal to the regime." Its main effect would probably be to strengthen the Communist position in Cuba. Unfortunately the Intelligence Branch and the Clandestine Services were hardly on speaking terms.

It appears that the CIA regarded whatever authorization it thought it had acquired in 1960 as permanent, not requiring review and reconfirmation by new Presidents or, even more astonishingly, by new CIA directors. For neither Bissell nor Helms even told John McCone what his own Agency was up to. Harvey, after supplying Rosselli with a new batch of poison pills in 1962, briefed Helms and, according to the 1967 report by the CIA inspector general, "obtained Helms' approval not to brief the Director." "For a variety of reasons which were tossed back and forth," Harvey said later, "we agreed that it was not necessary or advisable to brief him."

The available evidence clearly leads to the conclusion that the Kennedys did not know about the Castro assassination plots before the Bay of Pigs or about the pursuit of those plots by the CIA after the Bay of Pigs. There is a final consideration. No one who knew John and Robert Kennedy well believed they would conceivably countenance a program of assassination. Like McCone, they were Catholics. Robert, at least, was quite as devout as McCone. Theodore Sorensen's statement about John Kennedy applied to them both: assassination "was totally foreign to his character and conscience, foreign to his fundamental reverence for human life and his respect for his adversaries, foreign to his insistence upon a moral dimension in U.S. foreign policy and his concern for this country's reputation abroad and foreign to his pragmatic recognition that so horrendous but inevitably counterproductive a precedent committed by a country whose own chief of state was inevitably vulnerable could only provoke reprisals." "I find," said McGeorge Bundy, "the notion that they separately, privately encouraged, ordered, or arranged efforts at assassination totally inconsistent with what I knew of both of them, . . . their character, their purposes, and their nature and the way they confronted international affairs." McNamara said it would have been "totally inconsistent with everything I knew about the two men." I too find the idea incredible that these two men, so filled with love of life and so conscious of the ironies of history, could thus deny all the values and purposes that animated their existence. . . .

But had the American secret war against Castro left the Russians no alternative but to send nuclear missiles secretly to Cuba? Certainly Castro had the best grounds for feeling under siege. Even if double agents had not told him the CIA was trying to kill him, the Mongoose campaign left little doubt that the American government was trying to overthrow him. It would hardly have been unreasonable for him to request Soviet protection. But did he request nuclear missiles?

The best evidence is that he did not. Castro's aim was to deter American aggression by convincing Washington that an attack on Cuba would be the same as an attack on the Soviet Union. This did not require nuclear missiles. "We thought," he told Jean Daniel of *L'Express* in November 1963, "of a proclamation, an alliance, conventional military aid." It was Khrushchev who thought of nuclear missiles. "The initial idea," Castro said, "originated with the Russians and with them alone." Khrushchev's proposal, Castro said to Daniel with emphasis, *"surprised us at first and gave us great pause."* No doubt he worried (rightly) that the Soviet missile bases in Cuba would be an intolerable provocation to Washington. So he resisted the missiles. "When Castro and I talked about the problem," Khrushchev recalled, "we argued and argued. Our argument was very heated. But, in the end, Fidel agreed with me." "We felt that we could not get out of it," Castro told Claude Julien of *Le Monde* the next March. "This is why we accepted them. It was not in order to ensure our own defense, but primarily to strengthen socialism on the international plane." "We finally went along," Castro told Daniel, "because on the one hand the Russians convinced us that the United States would not let itself be intimidated by conventional weapons and secondly because it was impossible for us not to share the risks which the Soviet Union was taking to save us. . . . It was, in the final analysis, a question of honor."

Why did Khrushchev wish to force nuclear weapons on Castro? In his memoirs he alleged the protection of Cuba as his primary motive. The thought, he wrote, was "hammering away at my brain; what will happen if we lose Cuba?"—much as in American brains the thought was starting to hammer away about the dire consequences if Washington 'lost' Vietnam. Losing Cuba, Khrushchev believed, would be a "terrible" blow, gravely diminishing Soviet influence throughout the Third World, especially in Latin America—the domino theory, I expect. It would also, though Khrushchev did not say this, expose the Soviet Union to devastating ideological attack by Peking.

Still, if the protection of Cuba had been the only point, this could have been done far more simply, as Castro had proposed, through a proclamation or an alliance or the stationing of Soviet troops on the island. If nuclear weapons were to be used, tactical weapons would have been easier to install, harder to detect and less likely to provoke. As Graham Allison later wrote in his careful study of the crisis: "It is difficult to conceive of a Soviet deployment of weapons less suited to the purpose of Cuban defense than the one the Soviets made." Long-range nuclear missiles, in short, served Russian, not Cuban, purposes. Khrushchev, as Castro told Herbert Matthews in 1967, "was acting solely in Russian interests and not in Cuban interests." The secret war against Castro was therefore *not* the cause of the Soviet attempt to make Cuba a nuclear missile base.

By 1962 Khrushchev was in a state of acute frustration—blocked in Berlin, at odds with Peking, stalled in the Third World, left badly behind by the inordinate American missile build-up. Inside the Soviet Union industrial growth was slowing down; agriculture was in its usual trouble; generals were demanding a larger share of limited resources for the military budget; old-line Stalinists were grumbling against internal liberalization. Khrushchev was desperate for a change of fortune.

The emplacement of nuclear missiles in Cuba would prove the Soviet ability to act with impunity in the very heart of the American zone of vital interest —a victory of high significance for the Kremlin, which saw the world in terms of spheres of influence and always inflexibly guarded its own. It would go far to close the Soviet Union's own missile gap, increasing by half again Soviet first-strike capacity against American targets. It would do so without the long wait and awful budgetary strain attendant on an intensified missile production program. Secrecy would conceal the missiles until they were deployed. Once they were operational, Kennedy, as a rational man, would not go to nuclear war in order to expel them. If they were discovered prematurely, the congressional elections, not to speak of Kennedy's past irresolution on Cuban matters, would delay the American response. With one roll of the nuclear dice, Khrushchev might redress the strategic imbalance, humiliate the Americans, rescue the Cubans, silence the Stalinists and the generals, confound the Chinese and acquire a potent bargaining counter when he chose to replay Berlin. The risks seemed medium; the rewards colossal.

A plunger, he plunged. He sent 42 medium-range (1100-mile) nuclear missiles, 24 intermediate-range (2200-mile) missiles (which never arrived), 42 IL-28 nuclear bombers, 24 antiaircraft missile sites (SAMs) and 22,000 Soviet troops and technicians. This was something, he bragged to Castro, Stalin would never have done. He explained his objective in his memoirs: "Our missiles would have equalized . . . 'the balance of power.' " As Mikoyan put it in a secret meeting with Communist diplomats in Washington on November 30, 1962, the purpose of the deployment was to achieve "a definite shift in the power relationship between the socialist and the capitalist worlds." . . .

Critics have called it a needless crisis. Kennedy's conduct, according to R. J. Walton, was "irresponsible and reckless to a supreme degree." Driven by "the *machismo* quality" in his character, by rage over deception, by egotistical concern over personal prestige, by fear of setbacks in the elections, by a spurious notion of international credibility, Kennedy exaggerated the danger, rejected a diplomatic resolution and instead insisted on a public showdown. His purpose was the conspicuous humiliation of Khrushchev—eyeball to eyeball. Pursuing so insensate a course, he risked the incineration of the world in order to satisfy his own psychic and political needs. . . .

R. J. Walton was an exception among the revisionists in conceding that, "given the political realities, Kennedy had to get the missiles removed." But he and others have asserted that, instead of negotiating them out, Kennedy manufactured a public crisis. Even if he had not sought a showdown in August, he definitely sought one in October: both for personal reasons—obsession with his image, Irish temper, machismo, etc.—and for political reasons—the November election. He should, say, have discussed the missiles when Andrei Gromyko, the Soviet foreign minister, called on him at the White House three days after their discovery. If the Executive Committee had not yet figured out what to do, why did he not call Gromyko back as soon as the decision was made and before instituting the quarantine? Why did he not yield to Khrushchev at once the things that would enable the Soviet leader to remove the missiles with dignity: a no-invasion guarantee for Cuba and the removal of American Jupiter missiles from Turkey?

Charles Bohlen, that brilliant aficionado of Soviet policy, attended the meetings on the first two days. Departing on the third day, to take up new duties as ambassador to France, he left Kennedy a valedictory memorandum. The missiles, Bohlen agreed, had to be eliminated; and "no one can guarantee that this can be achieved by diplomatic action—but it seems to me essential that this channel should be tested out before military action is employed." On the same day, Sorensen, summing up the discussion thus far, defined a choice between what he called "the Rusk or the Bohlen approaches." Rusk, he said, favored a limited strike without prior warning. Bohlen and "all blockade advocates" favored a "prompt letter to Khrushchev, deciding after the response whether we use air strike or blockade. . . . If you accept the Bohlen plan, we can then consider the nature of the letter to K[hrushchev]."

Critics claim that Kennedy rejected the "Bohlen plan." In fact Kennedy did his best to pursue the plan. For two days, at his direction, Sorensen and others worked on letters to the Kremlin. On October 20, Sorensen reported to the President: "No one has been able to devise a satisfactory message to Khrushchev to which his reply could not outmaneuver us"—by, for example, demanding submission of the dispute to the UN or to a summit meeting, thereby plunging the whole affair into a protracted diplomatic wrangle and making other forms of American reaction difficult while the missile bases were rushed to completion. The not unreasonable decision was therefore to announce the quarantine *before* beginning talks with the Russians. . . .

Why had Khrushchev given up? "This is a mystery," Castro said bitterly the next March. "Maybe historians will be able to clarify this twenty or thirty years hence. I don't know." The assurances about the Cuban guarantee [no future U.S. invasion] and the Turkish missiles [Robert Kennedy promised their withdrawal] undoubtedly helped sweeten his retreat. But the political concessions were face savers. The real reason Khrushchev pulled out was his hopeless military situation. In his explanation to the Supreme Soviet in December 1962, he emphasized that Cuba was to be attacked in two or three days. An American invasion of Cuba would have been a disaster for Khrushchev personally and for the Soviet claim to world revolutionary leadership—especially when Khrushchev's own recklessness had handed America the pretext. What Communist state would trust Soviet promises thereafter? And, if Kennedy were serious about invasion, Khrushchev could do nothing about it, short of nuclear war against a stronger nuclear power. He was not suicidal. "It would have been preposterous," Khrushchev said later, "for us to unleash a war against the United States from Cuba. Cuba was 11,000 kilometers from the Soviet Union. Our sea and air communications were so precarious that an attack against the U.S. was unthinkable." Lacking conventional superiority in the Caribbean, he could neither break the blockade nor protect Cuba against invasion. Lacking strategic superiority, Khrushchev could not safely retaliate elsewhere in the world. . . .

The record demands the revision of the conventional portraits of Kennedy during the crisis: both the popular view, at the time, of the unflinching leader fearlessly staring down the Russians until they blinked; and the later left-wing view of a man driven by psychic and political compulsions to demand unconditional surrender at whatever risk to mankind. Far from rejecting diplomacy in favor of confrontation, Kennedy in fact took the diplomatic path after arranging the military setting that would make diplomacy effective.

The hard-liners thought him fatally soft. Dean Acheson in another year: "So long as we had the thumbscrew on Khrushchev, we should have given it another turn every day. We were too eager to make an agreement with the Russians." Richard Nixon inevitably thought that Kennedy's doves had "enabled the United States to pull defeat out of the jaws of victory." Or Daniel Patrick Moynihan in 1977: "The Cuban Missile Crisis was actually a *defeat.* . . . When anybody puts missiles into a situation like that, he should expect to have a lot of trouble with the United States, and real trouble— and all that happened was the agreement: 'O.K., you can have your man down there permanently.' "

The revisionists, on the other hand, portrayed Kennedy as reckless and irresponsible. This was not the view of those in the best position to judge— neither of Khrushchev nor, in the end, of Castro himself. In a time of "serious confrontation," Khrushchev said, ". . . one must have an intelligent, sober-minded counterpart with whom to deal. . . . I believe [Kennedy] was a man who understood the situation correctly and who genuinely did not want war. . . . Kennedy was also someone we could trust. . . . He showed great flexibility and, together, we avoided disaster. . . . He didn't let himself become frightened, nor did he become reckless. . . . He showed real wisdom and statesmanship." In 1967 Castro told Herbert Matthews that he thought Kennedy had "acted as he did partly to save Khrushchev, out of fear that any successor would be tougher." And in 1975 Castro told George McGovern:

"I would have taken a harder line than Khrushchev. I was furious when he compromised. But Khrushchev was older and wiser. I realize in retrospect that he reached the proper settlement with Kennedy. If my position had prevailed, there might have been a terrible war. I was wrong."

In all this, Robert Kennedy was the indispensable partner. Without him, John Kennedy would have found it far more difficult to overcome the demand for military action. Even Senator Fulbright, in Kennedy's meeting with congressional leaders before his television speech, had advocated the invasion of Cuba as a "wiser course" than the quarantine. It was Robert Kennedy who oversaw the Executive Committee, stopped the air-strike madness in its tracks, wrote the reply to the Khrushchev letter, conducted the secret negotiations with Dobrynin. "Throughout the entire period of the crisis," McNamara said in 1968, "a period of the most intense strain I have ever operated under, he remained calm and cool, firm but restrained, never nettled and never rattled." "For this happy outcome to such long and agonizing negotiations," Adlai Stevenson wrote him, "I think you are entitled to our gratitude." Khrushchev, recalling the discussions during the crisis, said the Americans "had, on the whole, been open and candid with us, especially Robert Kennedy." "Looking back on it," said Harold Macmillan, "the way that Bobby and his brother played this hand was absolutely masterly.... What they did that week convinced me that they were both great men." ...

The Tragic Enshrinement of Toughness

JAMES A. NATHAN

Historians know there is a rhythm to their craft. Events are examined and orthodoxies are established. Then comes a chipping away of previously held convictions. New understandings emerge and stand, at least for a while; and then comes another tide of re-evaluation. The Kennedy Administration's shimmering hour—the Cuban missile crisis—has just begun to have its luster tarnished by critics. Yet few have subjected the event to a complex review of its meaning in terms of the assumptions, policy processes, and relationships of the cold war.

My contention is that the crisis became something of a misleading "model" of the foreign policy process. There are seven central tenets of this model, each of which was "confirmed" by the "lessons" of the Cuban crisis:

1. Crises are typical of international relations. The international environment is a constant collision of wills that is a surrogate of war and, at the same time, takes place at the doorstep of war. Crises are objective elements of the international system—but they also have a profoundly psychological element of "will" and "resolve."

James A. Nathan, "The Missile Crisis: His Finest Hour Now," *World Politics*, 27 (January 1975) 256–281. Copyright © 1975 by Princeton University Press. Reprinted by permission of Princeton University Press.

2. Crises are assumed to be manageable. The skills of personality, training, and organizational expertise that have been developed in the national security machinery during the past twenty-five years can be orchestrated by a vast bureaucracy in controlled and responsive movements.

3. Although crises are a characteristic of the international system, the domestic system is one of order and consensus, and is insulated from the necessities of international politics. Public opinion can be controlled to lend support for a particular foreign policy; but rarely do appurtenances of the domestic sector have their own imperatives.

4. Diplomacy is a mixture of the instrumentation of force and bargaining. An essential element of crisis management is the ability to reconcile the inherent forward dynamic of violence, threats of violence, and the instruments of violence with negotiation.

5. The United States can control the process of crisis negotiation to "win." "Winning" results in the conclusion of the events themselves. Political crises therefore terminate by definition, almost like medical crises.

6. The Soviets seldom negotiate serious matters except under extreme duress.

7. Military questions are too critical to be left in the hands of strictly military men and organizations that are not in step with the needs of crisis management. Crisis management can and must be a civilian enterprise.

After the Cuban missile crisis, there were the beginnings of détente with the Soviet Union. The test-ban treaty, the hot line, and a more civil exchange between the two powers are widely believed to stem from the favorable resolution of the missile crisis. Yet the model and the usual inherent assumptions on the meaning of Cuba can be challenged. Nevertheless, the Cuban missile crisis stands as a watershed of the cold war and in the history of the contemporary international system.

By far the most intense experience in East-West relations occurred in October 1962, when the Russians were discovered to have placed forty-two medium-range missiles in Cuba. In Khrushchev's apt description, it was a time when "a smell of burning hung heavy" in the air. Kennedy's apparently controlled and masterful way of forcing Khrushchev to withdraw the missiles in the thirteen-day crisis has become a paradigmatic example of the way force can be harnessed to a policy by an elaborate manipulation of threats and gambits, negotiation and intimidation. Academic and government analysts have viewed Kennedy's response as a highly calibrated dissection of alternatives instead of seeing his actions as largely an intuitive response to a threat to his administration's electoral future, pride, and strategic posture. As Hans J. Morgenthau, the eminent scholar and a critic of the Kennedy Administration, concluded: "The Cuban Crisis of 1962 . . . was the distillation of a collective intellectual effort of a high order, the like of which must be rare in history." Much of this analysis—so drenched in the cool light of hindsight—bears a suspicious resemblance to the logical and psychological fallacy of reasoning, *post hoc, ergo propter hoc*. Nevertheless, the dominant lesson Americans have drawn from the Cuban experience has been a joyous sense of the United States regaining mastery over history.

For many years Americans had felt threatened by the Soviet challenge to world order—especially since that challenge had been reinforced by growing Russian strategic capability. But after Cuba, the fears of precipitate expansion of a Soviet-American dispute into a final paroxysm of nuclear dust were dissipated. After Cuba, "escalation" became the *idée fixe* of academics and policy-makers —a vision of a ladder of force with rungs separated by equivalent spaces of destruction, each with its own "value," running out toward darkness. Escalation became the dominant metaphor of American officialdom. Each rung could be ascended or descended with the proper increment of will and control. Events and military machines could be mastered for diplomatic ends. As Robert McNamara exalted after the exciting and frightening Cuban climax: "There is no longer any such thing as strategy, only crisis management." Dennis Healy, the British Labor Party "shadow" Defense Minister called the Kennedy Administration's performance a "model in any textbook on diplomacy." Journalist Henry Pachter described Kennedy's execution of crisis management as "a feat whose technical elegance compelled the professionals' admiration." Similarly, the Wohlstetters made Cuba into a general historical principle about the use of force in times of great stress: "where the alternative is to be ruled by events with such enormous consequences, the head of a great state is likely to examine his acts of choice in crisis and during it to subdivide these possible acts in ways that make it feasible to continue exercising choice."

The decisions as to what steps should be taken to deal with the implantation of the missiles were hammered out in the ExCom meetings. Although court chroniclers of the Kennedy Administration have pored over each detail, the impression now is not one of all choices having been carefully weighed and considered. Rather, in retrospect, there appears to have been a gripping feeling of uncertainty and pressure. Robert Kennedy, for instance, at the height of the crisis, looked across at his brother and almost fainted at the horror of what they were contemplating: "Inexplicably, I thought of when he was ill and almost died; when he lost his child, when we learned that our oldest brother had been killed; of personal times of strain and hurt. The voices droned on, but I didn't seem to hear anything. . . ."

There were reports that one Assistant Secretary was so disconcerted and fatigued that he drove into a tree at 4 a.m. Robert Kennedy recalled, "The strain and the hours without sleep were beginning to take their toll. . . . That kind of pressure does strange things to a human being, even to brilliant, self-confident, mature, experienced men." And President Kennedy, although deliberately pacing himself, wondered if some of his principal advisors had not suffered mental collapse from the long hours and pressure. Tense, fearful, and exhausted men planned and held together the American policy response to the Russian missiles.

The consensus of most behavioral research is that men operating under such acute stress are scarcely capable of considered judgment. Strain and fatigue commonly produce actions which are "caricatures of day-to-day behavior." Although the stress of crisis decision-making concentrates and focuses the collective mind, it does not allow for the kind of elegant dissection of events that is now read into the Cuban affair. Events can take charge of decision-makers; on

October 25, 1962, Robert Kennedy reported that he felt, as Soviet ships drew near the edge of the American quarantine, that "[W]e were on the edge of a precipice with no way off. . . . President Kennedy had initiated the course of events, but he no longer had control over them." John F. Kennedy's calm public face, discipline, and cool control gave a sense of intellectual engagement in the crisis which yielded no hint of the mute wasteland he was contemplating. But his private anxiety is well recorded, and a case can be made that dispassionate analysis or problem-solving was all but precluded by the psychology of the situation.

It was very close. The military and the "hawks"—a term coined by journalistic descriptions of the ExCom deliberations—were pushing for actions ranging from a "surgical strike" to an all-out invasion of Cuba. Such options would have demanded the stark choice of an even greater Soviet humiliation or a Soviet response in kind. Ironically, a "surgical strike" was not really practical, for there was no guarantee that more than 90 percent of the missiles could be extirpated. Even after an American air attack, some of the missiles could have survived and been launched. And "surgical" always was a misnomer to describe an estimated 25,000 Cuban fatalities, not to speak of the 500 sorties which American planes would have had to run in order to "take out" the Soviet missiles and bombers. Nevertheless, if six out of fourteen members of the ExCom group had had their way, the blockade of Cuba would have been an attack, which Bobby Kennedy called a "Pearl Harbor in reverse." It is no wonder that President Kennedy estimated the world's chance of avoiding war at between one out of three and even.

The illusion of control derived from the crisis was perniciously misleading. Although many Americans shared the belief of historian Schlesinger that the Cuban crisis displayed to the "whole world . . . the ripening of an American leadership unsurpassed in the responsible management of power . . . [a] combination of toughness . . . nerve and wisdom, so brilliantly controlled, so matchlessly calibrated that [it] dazzled the world," President Kennedy's control was in fact far from complete. For example, the main instrument of pressure was the blockade run by the Navy. Following the suggestion of British Ambassador Ormsby-Gore, Kennedy decided to move the blockade closer to Cuba, from 800 miles to 500 miles, in order to give the Russian ships heading toward Cuba more time. The order was given but never carried out. The blockade remained at 800 miles.

McNamara had sensed the Navy's lack of responsiveness to civilian commands and had gone to the "Flag Plot," or Naval Operations Center, where he could talk to ship commanders directly by voice-scrambled radio. McNamara pointed to a map symbol indicating that a ship was in a spot where he had not wanted it. "What's that ship doing there?" he asked. Anderson confessed, "I don't know, but I have faith in my officers." McNamara's unease with the apparent lack of responsiveness of the Navy to civilian command prompted him to inquire what would happen if a Soviet captain refused to divulge his cargo to a boarding American officer. Chief of Naval Operations Anderson picked up a Manual of Naval Regulations and rose to defend the Navy against any implied slight about Navy procedure. "It's all in there," Anderson asserted. McNamara retorted, "I don't give a damn what John Paul Jones would have done. I want to know what you are going to do, now!" The last word—again, however—was the Navy's: Admiral Anderson patronizingly soothed the fuming Defense Secretary, "Now, Mr. Secretary, if you and your deputy will go to your offices, the Navy will run the blockade." As McNamara and his entourage turned to leave, Anderson called to him, "Don't worry, Mr. Secretary, we know what we are doing here."

Just when the first Soviet-American encounter at sea seemed imminent, William Knox, the president of Westinghouse International, who happened to be in Moscow, was surprised by an abrupt summons from Premier Khrushchev. The voluble Soviet leader, perhaps half-convinced that Wall Street really manipulated American policy, gave a frightening summary of the strategic situation in the Caribbean. He warned that if the U.S. Navy began stopping Soviet ships, the Soviet subs would start sinking American ships. That, Khrushchev explained, would lead to World War III.

Only a little later, the Navy began to force Soviet subs to the surface in order to defend its blockade—well before Kennedy had authorized contact with surface vessels. Kennedy was appalled when he learned that military imperatives are distinct from diplomatic necessities and can, all too often, conflict. When he found out that the Navy was intent on surfacing ships, he was horrified: "Isn't there some way we can avoid having our first exchange with a Russian submarine—almost anything but that?" McNamara replied, "No, there's too much danger to our ships. There is no alternative." The President's brother wrote that "all six Russian submarines then in the area or moving toward Cuba from the Atlantic were followed and harassed and, at one time or another, forced to surface in the presence of U.S. military ships." One can only wonder what would have happened if one of the Russian subs had refused to surface and had instead turned on its pursuers.

Events were only barely under control when at the height of the crisis, on October 26, an American U-2 plane fixed on the wrong star and headed back from the North Pole to Alaska via Siberia. To compound matters the Alaskan Air Command sent fighter-bombers to escort the plane home, and the U.S. fighters and the spy plane met over Soviet territory before proceeding back. To survive a Strangelove series of incidents like these, even given the assumptions of the day, can hardly be characterized as more than luck. It would not seem to be the mastery that Schlesinger and other court scribes delight in recalling and extolling.

Why was there a crisis in the first place? The answer is found, in part, in one of the unacknowledged necessities in the conduct of American international affairs—domestic political considerations. The Kennedy Administration's sense of its own precarious electoral position, the coming of the November mid-term elections, and the place Cuba had occupied in public debate, all augured for an immediate and forceful response, no matter what the strategic reality was of having Russian missiles near American borders. The imperatives of American domestic politics during an election year had been building for some time. On August 27, 1962, for example, Republican Senator Homer E. Capehart of Indiana declared, "It is high time that the American people demand that President Kennedy quit 'examining the situation' and start protecting the interests of the United States." Former Vice President Nixon, on the gubernatorial campaign stump in California, proposed that Cuban communism be "quarantined" by a naval blockade. Republicans in both Houses had warned the administration that Cuba would be "the dominant issue of the 1962 campaign." The chairman of the Republican National Committee jabbed at Kennedy's most sensitive spot—his concern for foreign policy "resolve": "If we are asked to state the issue in one word, that word would be Cuba—symbol of the tragic irresolution of the administration."

The pressure mounted. As the political campaign began, one observer spotted a sign at a Kennedy rally in Chicago which read, "Less Profile—More Courage." The widely respected and conservative London Economist reported that America had become "obsessed" by the "problem" of Cuba; and I. F. Stone despaired in his Weekly that Cuba was a bogey which shook Americans, in the autumn of 1962, even more than the thought of war. The domestic pressure on the American President was so intense that one member of Camelot, former Ambassador John Kenneth Galbraith, wrote: "once they [the missiles] were there, the political needs of the Kennedy administration urged it to take almost any risk to get them out." This skeptical view was shared by none other than former President Eisenhower, who suspected "that Kennedy might be playing politics with Cuba on the eve of Congressional elections."

Nor, as Ronald Steel pointed out, were the "principals"—the ExCom—insulated from domestic considerations in their deliberations. One Republican member of the crisis planners sent Theodore Sorensen—Kennedy's alter ego—a note that read: "Ted—have you considered the very real possibility that if we allow Cuba to complete installation and operational readiness of missile bases, the next House of Representatives is likely to have a Republican majority?" Similarly, McGeorge Bundy, chief advisor to two presidents, wondered, when the missiles were first reported, whether action could be deferred until after the election. If the missile installations were completed earlier, there would be, arguably, both a strategic and an electoral problem facing the administration.

What was the worrisome substance of change in the strategic balance represented by the placement of forty-two missiles? To Robert McNamara, the Secretary of Defense, it seemed that "A missile is a missile. It makes no great difference whether you are killed by a missile from the Soviet Union or from Cuba." About two weeks later, on television, Deputy Secretary of Defense Roswell Gilpatrick confirmed the debatable meaning of the missiles: "I don't believe that we were under any greater threat from the Soviet Union's power, taken in totality, after this than before." Indeed, Theodore Sorensen wrote in a memorandum to the President on October 17, 1962—five days before the blockade was ordered—that the presence of missiles in Cuba did not "significantly alter the balance of power." Sorensen explained, "They do not significantly increase the potential megatonnage capable of being unleashed on American soil, even after a surprise American nuclear strike." Sorensen confessed, in conclusion, that "Soviet motives were not understood."

To Khrushchev, the missiles offered the appearance of what former State Department analyst Roger Hilsman called a "quick fix" to the Soviet problem of strategic inferiority. Khrushchev was under enormous pressure from the Russian military who rejected his "goulash communism" and were pushing for a vast increase in the Soviet arms budget. The Cuban missile ploy was probably Khrushchev's response to the prospect of Russian strategic inferiority which was reported by the Kennedy Administration as it admitted that the Democratic preelection charge of a "missile gap" had not been based on fact. The American announcement that the "gap" had been closed was accompanied by a Defense Department plan, dated October 19, 1961, for production of over one thousand missiles by 1964.

One purpose of the Soviet moves in Cuba was, therefore, to gain the *appearance* of parity with the Americans. The employment of twenty-four MRBM's and eighteen IRBM's *seemed* to be a dramatic movement in that direction. But such an increase posed no real threat to American retaliatory strength, or to increasing American superiority. As Henry Kissinger noted at the time, "The bases were of only marginal use in a defensive war. In an offensive war their effectiveness was reduced by the enormous difficulty—if not impossibility —of coordinating a first strike from the Soviet Union and Cuba."

The U.S. Administration knew that the Soviets were not striving for more than an appearance of strategic equality. As Kennedy later reflected, they were not "intending to fire them, because if they were going to get into a nuclear struggle, they have their own missiles in the Soviet Union. But it would have politically changed the balance of power. It would have appeared to, and appearances contribute to reality." In the 1970's, by contrast, "appearances" were less important while the Americans were arranging a complex international order which verged on duopoly. Indeed, beginning in 1970, Soviet submarines and tenders began to visit Cuban ports. And by 1973, Soviet submarines with Polaris-type missiles were regularly stopping in Cuba. What protest there was by the Nixon Administration seemed so muted as to be almost inaudible.

Why was Kennedy so concerned about "appearances"? Perhaps he felt that the American people demanded an energetic response, given their purported frustration over Cuba. The administration's evaluation of the public mood supported the notion that firmness was a requisite of policy. Although repeated Gallup polls before the crisis showed 90 per cent of Americans opposing actual armed intervention in Cuba, Kennedy's own sense was, as his brother pointed out, that if he did not act, he would have been impeached.

Another explanation for Kennedy's concern that he would not "appear credible" to Khrushchev dates from the time, less than two years earlier, when he decided not to use air support for the Bay of Pigs invasion. According to James Reston's impression upon seeing Kennedy ten minutes after the two leaders had met in Vienna, "Khrushchev had studied the events of the Bay of Pigs; he would have understood if Kennedy had left Castro alone or destroyed him; but when Kennedy was rash enough to strike at Cuba but not bold enough to finish the job, Khrushchev decided he was dealing with an inexperienced young leader who could be intimidated and blackmailed." Similarly, George F. Kennan, then the United States Ambassador to Yugoslavia, met the President after the Vienna summit session and reported that he found Kennedy "strangely tongue-tied" during these talks. Later, he recalled for a Harvard oral history interviewer:

> I felt that he had not acquitted himself well on this occasion and that he had permitted Khrushchev to say many things which should have been challenged right there on the spot.
> I think this was definitely a mistake. I think it definitely misled Khrushchev; I think Khrushchev failed to realize on that occasion what a man he was up against and also that he'd gotten away with many of these talking points; that he had placed President Kennedy in a state of confusion where he had nothing to say in return.

Kennedy expressed concern to Reston and others that Khrushchev considered him but a callow, inexperienced youth and that he soon expected a "test." "It will be a cold winter," he was heard to mutter as he left the Vienna meeting. Khrushchev may indeed have been surprised at the forceful reaction of Kennedy, particularly after the young President had accepted the Berlin Wall in August 1961 with no military response and had temporized in Laos in 1961 and 1962.

Perhaps, as Hilsman has argued, the Soviets assumed that the fine American distinctions between "offensive and defensive" missiles were really a *de facto* acknowledgment of the Soviet effort in Cuba. One could conjecture that this was what led Khrushchev to promise, and to believe that Kennedy understood, that no initiatives would be taken before the elections. In any case, Kennedy's concern about his "appearance" and the national appearance of strength kept him from searching very far for Soviet motivation. His interpretation was that it was a personal injury to him and his credibility, as well as to American power. He explained this sentiment to *New York Post* reporter James Wechsler:

> What worried him was that Khrushchev might interpret his reluctance to wage nuclear war as a symptom of an American loss of nerve. Some day, he said, the time might come when he would have to run the supreme risk to convince Khrushchev that conciliation did not mean humiliation. "If Khrushchev wants to rub my nose in the dirt," he told Wechsler, "it's all over." But how to convince Khrushchev short of a showdown? "That son of a bitch won't pay any attention to words," the President said bitterly on another occasion. "He has to see you move."

The missile crisis illuminates a feature of the American character that came to be considered a requisite personality trait of the cold war: being "tough." Gritty American determination had become the respected and expected stance of American statesmen under stress in confrontations with the Soviets from the earliest days of the cold war. When Truman, for example, dispatched an aircraft carrier, four cruisers, a destroyer flotilla, and the battleship Missouri to counter Soviet pressure on the Turkish Straits, he told Acheson, "We might as well find out whether the Russians [are] bent on world conquest now as in five or ten years." Clark Clifford gave more formal expression to this sentiment when he advised Harry Truman, in a memo, in late 1946: "The language of military power is the only language which disciples of power politics understand. The United States must use that language in order that Soviet leaders will realize that our government is determined to uphold the interest of its citizens and the rights of small nations. Compromise and concessions are considered, by the Soviets, to be evidence of weakness and they are encouraged by our 'retreats' to make new and greater demands."

The American concern with its appearance of strength was a mark of the Kennedy Administration. One White House aide recalled that, especially after the failure of the Bay of Pigs, "Nobody in the White House wanted to be soft. ... Everybody wanted to show they were just as daring and bold as everybody else."

In the Cuban crisis, the cold-war ethic of being "tough" exacerbated the discrepancies between the necessities of force and the necessities of diplomacy and negotiation. As a result, diplomacy was almost entirely eclipsed. In fact, it was hardly tried. According to Adam Yarmolinsky, an inside observer of the Executive Committee of the National Security Council, "90 per cent of its time" was spent "studying alternative uses of troops, bombers and warships. Although the possibility of seeking withdrawal of the missiles by straightforward diplomatic negotiation received some attention within the State Department, it seems hardly to have been aired in the Ex-Com." Yarmolinsky confesses that it is curious that no negotiations were considered. Nor were economic pressures ever suggested by the foreign affairs bureaucracy. Only a series of military plans emerged, and they varied from a blockade to a preemptive strike.

Kennedy knew the Russians had deployed missiles on October 16. But, instead of facing Soviet Foreign Secretary Gromyko with the evidence while the Russian was giving the President false assurances that missiles were not being installed, the President blandly listened without comment. Whether or not the Russians believed that Kennedy must have known, the effect of the charade was an absence of serious negotiations. Instead of using private channels to warn the Russians that he knew and intended to act, Kennedy chose to give notice to the Russians in a nationwide TV address. After that, a Soviet withdrawal had to be in public and it almost had to be a humiliation. When the Soviets attempted nonetheless to bargain for a graceful retreat, their path was blocked. Kennedy refused Khrushchev's offer of a summit meeting "until Khrushchev first accepted, as a result *of our deeds* as well as our statements, the U.S. determination in the matter." A summit meeting, Kennedy concluded, had to be rejected; for he was intent on offering the Russians "nothing that would tie our hands." We would only negotiate with that which would "strengthen our stand." If there were to be any deals, Kennedy wanted them to seem a part of American munificence. He did not want a compromise to be tied to the central issue of what he conceived to be a test of American will and resolve. "[W]e must stand absolutely firm now. Concessions must come at the end of negotiation, not at the beginning," Robert Kennedy cautioned.

In other words, the Soviets had to submit to American strength before any real concessions could take place. When Khrushchev offered to exchange the Cuban missiles for the Jupiter missiles stationed in Turkey, Kennedy refused, even though he had ordered the missiles out months earlier; in fact, he had thought they were out when Khrushchev brought them to his attention. (The Jupiters were all but worthless. A marksman with a high-powered rifle could knock them out. They took a day to ready for firing and the Turks did not want them.) Kennedy, however, did not want to appear to yield to Soviet pressure even when he might give little and receive a great deal. An agreement would have confounded the issue of "will." As Kennedy's Boswell put it, the President wanted to "concentrate on a single issue—the enormity of the introduction of the missiles and the absolute necessity of their removal."

In the final act of the crisis, Kennedy accepted one of two letters sent almost simultaneously by Khrushchev. One contained the demand for removal of the Turkish missiles; the other did not. Kennedy accepted the latter. Khrushchev's second letter began with a long, heartfelt, personal communication and made no mention of a *quid pro quo*. Kennedy's response was a public letter to Khrushchev, temperate in tone, in which he accepted the more favorable terms he preferred and further detailed American conditions. It is said that Kennedy published his response "in the interests of both speed and psychology." But this procedure of publishing the private terms of an interchange with another head of state was a considerable departure from diplomacy. It was not negotiation; it was, in this context, a public demand. Public statements during a crisis lack flexibility. Compromise is almost foreclosed by such a device, because any bargaining after the terms have been stated seems to be a retreat which would diminish a statesman's reputation. Since reputation was the stake in Cuba as much as anything else, Kennedy's response was hardly more than a polite ultimatum. In private, Kennedy was even more forceful. Robert Kennedy told Soviet Ambassador Dobrynin, "We had to have a commitment by tomorrow that those bases would be removed. . . . If they did not remove those bases, we would remove them. . . . Time was running out. We had only a few more hours—we needed an answer immediately from the Soviet Union. . . . We must have it the next day."

As a result of the crisis, force and toughness became enshrined as instruments of policy. George Kennan observed, as he left forty years of diplomatic service: "There is no presumption more terrifying than that of those who would blow up the world on the basis of their personal judgment of a transient situation. I do not propose to let the future of mankind be settled, or ended, by a group of men operating on the basis of limited perspectives and short-run calculations."

In spite of occasional epistles from the older diplomatists, the new managers who proliferated after Cuba routed those who most favored negotiations. In an article in the *Saturday Evening Post,* one of the last "moderates" of the Kennedy Administration, Adlai Stevenson, was attacked for advocating "a Munich." The source of the story, it was widely rumored, was President Kennedy himself.

The policy of toughness became dogma to such an extent that nonmilitary solutions to political problems were excluded. A "moderate" in this circumstance was restricted to suggesting limited violence. Former Under Secretary of State Ball explained his "devil advocacy" in Vietnam, in which he suggested that there be a troop ceiling of 70,000 men and bombing be restricted to the South: "What I was proposing was something which I thought had a fair chance of being persuasive . . . if I had said let's pull out overnight or do something of this kind, I obviously wouldn't have been persuasive at all. They'd have said 'the man's mad.' "

This peculiar search for the middle ground of a policy defined in terms of force was abetted by the sudden sense on the part of Kennedy's national security managers that the military was filled with Dr. Strangeloves. There was some warrant for this fear. Time and time again, during the crisis, the military seemed obsessed by the opportunity to demonstrate its potential. When asked what the Soviet reaction would be to a surgical raid on their missiles and men, General Lemay snapped, "There will be no reaction." When the crisis ended on Sunday, October 25th, one of the Joint Chiefs suggested that they go ahead with a massive bombing the following Monday in any case. "[T]he military are mad," concluded President Kennedy. Robert Kennedy recalled acidly that "many times . . . I heard the military take positions which, if wrong, had the advantage that no one would be around at the end to know."

In part, it was as a result of the Cuban crisis that the civilians of the American defense and foreign policy bureaucracy grew to despise the military. Hilsman reports that later in the Kennedy Administration, an official prepared a mock account of a high-level meeting on Vietnam in which Averell Harriman "stated that he had disagreed for twenty years with General [Brute] Krulak [Commandant of the Marines] and disagreed today, reluctantly, more than ever; he was sorry to say that he felt General Krulak was a fool and had always thought so." It is reported that President Kennedy roared with laughter upon reading this fictitious account. Hilsman also delighted in telling a story about General Lemnitzer, Chairman of the Joint Chiefs of Staff, who once briefed President Kennedy on Vietnam: "This is the Mekong Valley. Pointer tip hit the map. Hilsman, watching, noticed something, the point tip was not on the Mekong Valley, it was on the Yangtze Valley." Hilsman's recollection of the general's error became a common office story.

Ironically, while the military was increasingly thought to be rather loutish and ill-prepared, civilians were starting to rely more and more on military instrumentalities in the application of which, with few exceptions, they were not trained, and whose command structure they despised as being second-rate at best. Civilian "crisis managers" felt, after Cuba, that they should have control and that the military could not be trusted and had to be made more responsive to the political and civilian considerations of policy. To many observers, as well as to these managers, the "failures" of the Cuban missile crisis were not failures of civilian judgment but of organizational responsiveness. The intelligence establishment, for instance, had not discovered the missiles until the last minute. McNamara never really secured control over the Navy. U-2 flights were sent near the Soviet Union to "excite" Soviet radar at the height of the crisis; until Kennedy ordered their dispersal, American fighters and bombers were wing to wing on the ground, almost inviting a preemptive Soviet blow. Moreover, American tactical nuclear weapons and nuclear-tipped IRBM's in Turkey and Italy were discovered to be unlocked and lightly guarded. All this led observers and policy-makers to believe that crisis management demanded the President's organizational dominance and control, because the military and intelligence organizations were inept and their judgment was not reliable or at times even sane.

After Cuba, confidence in the ability of U.S. armed superiority to command solutions to "crises" in a way that would favor American interests expanded in such a way that Americans again began to speak of the American century. For a period before the crisis there had been a national reexamination. There were fears of national decline in the face of startling Soviet economic growth. Advances in Russian rocketry had led Americans to believe that not only were they in a mortal competition with the Soviets, but that the outcome was uncertain. Now, however, most of these doubts seemed to have dissipated.

The Cuban missile crisis revived the sense of the American mission. Henry R. Luce once rhapsodized in a widely circulated *Life* editorial that Americans must "accept wholeheartedly our duty and opportunity as the most powerful and vital nation in the world and in consequence to exert upon the world the full impact of our influence for such purposes as we see fit, and by such means as we see fit." After the crisis, Arthur Schlesinger could lyrically resurrect this tradition: "But the ultimate impact of the missile crisis was wider than Cuba, wider than even the western hemisphere. . . . Before the missile crisis people might have feared that we would use our power extravagantly or not use it at all. But the thirteen days gave the world—even the Soviet Union—a sense of American determination and responsibility in the use of power which, if sustained, might indeed become a turning point in the history of the relations between east and west."

Similarly, Professor Zbigniew Brzezinski, then a member of the Planning Council of the Department of State, proclaimed that American paramountcy was the lesson of Cuba. Brzezinski explained, "The U.S. is today the only effective global military power in the world."

In contrast to the United States, Brzezinski declared, the Soviets were not a global power. Although Khrushchev may at one time have believed otherwise, the Cuban crisis demonstrated the limits of Soviet capabilities. "The Soviet leaders were forced, because of the energetic response by the United States, to the conclusion that their apocalyptic power [nuclear deterrent power] was insufficient to make the Soviet Union a global power. Faced with a showdown, the Soviet Union didn't dare to respond even in an area of its regional predominance—in Berlin. . . . It had no military capacity to fight in Cuba, or in Vietnam, or to protect its interests in the Congo." No doubt the historic American sense of divine purpose and the almost Jungian need to be the guarantor of global order received a strong fillip from the Cuban crisis. Brzezinski concluded: "What should be the role of the United States in this period? To use our power responsibly and constructively so that when the American paramountcy ends, the world will have been launched on a constructive pattern of development towards international stability. . . . The ultimate objective ought to be the shaping of a world of cooperative communities."

The overwhelming belief of policy-makers in American superiority seriously eroded deterrence. The Soviet Union reached the same conclusion as the United States—that a preponderance of military power, ranging across the spectrum of force from PT craft to advanced nuclear delivery systems, was the *sine qua non* of the successful exercise of political will. Before fall of 1962, Khrushchev's strategic policy, in the words of a Rand Kremlinologist, "amounted to settling for a second-best strategic posture." The missile crisis, however, manifestly demonstrated Soviet strategic weakness and exposed every Soviet debility that Khrushchev's verbal proclamation of superiority had previously covered.

After Cuba, the Soviet military, responding to the humiliating American stimulus, demanded a higher priority to strategic arms and a cutback on the agricultural and consumer sectors of the Soviet economy. Although Khrushchev and Kennedy were by then moving toward a détente—best symbolized by the signing of the test-ban accords of mid-1963—many in the Kremlin saw this as but a breathing spell in which the Chinese might be isolated and Soviet arms could catch up. Naval preparations, especially the building of Polaris-type submarines, were intensified. Soviet amphibian landing capability—something in which the Soviets had shown little interest before—was revitalized and expanded. As Wolfe noted, "From the time of the first test-launching . . . of 1957 to mid-1961 only a handful of ICBM's had been deployed. . . . After Cuba, the pace of deployment picked up, bringing the total number of operational ICBM launchers to around 200 by the time of Khrushchev's ouster." Although the West still outnumbered the Russians by four to one in numbers of launchers at the time, the Russians worked furiously, and by September 1968, they commanded a larger force than the United States. Worldwide "blue water" Soviet submarine patrols were initiated; and a decision was taken under Brezhnev and Kosygin to extend the Soviet navy to "remote areas of the world's oceans previously considered a zone of supremacy of the fleets of the imperialist powers."

After the missile crisis, the cold-war establishmentarian John McCloy, representing President Kennedy, was host to Soviet Deputy Foreign Minister V. V. Kuznetzov. McCloy secured an affirmation from Kuznetzov that the Soviets would indeed observe their part of the agreement to remove the missiles and bombers from Cuba. But the Soviet leader warned, "Never will we be caught like this again."

The Soviets were to yield again to U.S. strength in Vietnam and the Middle-East. But each time, the usable strategic leverage of the United States grew weaker. Thus, the structure of the international system and international stability was shaken in three ways.

First, the United States became confident that its power would prevail because global politics had become "unifocal." But American military primacy began to erode as soon as it was proclaimed, when the Soviets fought to gain at least a rough strategic parity.

Second, nations, once cowed, are likely to be less timid in the next confrontation. As Kennedy admitted some time later, referring to the Cuban missile crisis, "You can't have too many of those." Just as Kennedy feared he had appeared callow and faint-hearted in successive Berlin crises, and thus had to be tough over Cuba, the Soviets were likely to calculate that they must appear as the more rigid party in future confrontations or risk a reputation of "capitulationism." For weeks after the missile crisis, the Chinese broadcast their charges of Russian stupidity and weakness to the four corners of the globe. The Chinese labeled Khrushchev an "adventurist" as well as a "capitulationist," and therefore not fit for world Communist leadership. The Russian answer was to accuse the Chinese of being even "softer" than they for tolerating the Western enclaves of Macao and Hong Kong. The charge of who was the most capitulationist, the Chinese or the Russians, grew almost silly; but these puerile exchanges had their own dangers in terms of deterrence.

Third, once a threat is not carried out—even after an appearance of a willingness to carry it out has been demonstrated—the ante is upped just a bit more. Morgenthau described a two-step process in nuclear gamesmanship, "diminishing credibility of the threat and even bolder challenges to make good on it. . . . [T]he psychological capital of deterrence has been nearly expended and the policy of deterrence will be close to bankruptcy. When they reach that point, the nations concerned can choose one of three alternatives: resort to nuclear war, retreat, or resort to conventional war."

Morgenthau's observation captured the dilemma of American policy-makers after Cuba. The problem was that nuclear superiority had been useful, but each succeeding threat (since no nuclear threat has ever been carried out) would necessarily be weaker than the last. Yet, how could security managers translate military power into political objectives without such threats? Daniel Ellsberg recalled the quandary of U.S. security managers:

> McNamara's tireless and shrewd efforts in the early sixties, largely hidden from the public to this day, [were to] gradually control the forces within the military bureaucracy that pressed for the threat and use of nuclear weapons. [He had] a creditable motive for proposing alternatives to nuclear threats. . . . [I]n this hidden debate, there was strong incentive—indeed it seemed necessary—for the civilian leaders to demonstrate that success was possible in Indochina without the need either to compromise Cold War objectives or to threaten or use nuclear weapons.
>
> Such concerns remained semi-covert: (for it was seen as dangerous to lend substance to the active suspicions of military staffs and their Congressional allies that there were high Administration officials who didn't love the Bomb). . . .

But after the Cuban crisis, the option of "low-level violence" became more and more attractive. Conventional and limited deployments of force became increasingly necessary as conventional force was considered less forbidding than the nuclear abyss. After all, the symbolic or "psychological capital" of deterrence rested on the notion of resolve. And one way to demonstrate political will was through the resurrection of conventional force as an instrument of demonstrating "commitment"—a commitment whose alternative form was a threat of nuclear holocaust. The latter was bound to deteriorate with the advent of a viable Soviet retaliatory capability and the knowledge that the Soviets had collapsed once under a nuclear threat and might not be willing to be quite so passive again. Many national security managers found they could navigate between the Scylla of nuclear war and the Charybdis of surrender with the serendipitous discovery of the "lifeboat" of the 1960's—limited war. It would not prove to be a sturdy craft.

Of course, the assumptions of the planners of limited war—as they emerged victorious from the Cuban crisis—were as old as the cold war. They dated from the Truman Doctrine's Manichean presentation of a bipolar global confrontation where a gain to one party necessarily would be a loss to the other. A world order of diverse centers of power, with elements of superpower cooperation, where gains and losses would be less easily demonstrable, was not so demanding of military remedy. A multipolar world would be less congenial to the belief that the only options available to policy-makers were either military force or retreat. Maneuver and negotiation, in such a world, would again become part of diplomacy. But such a development was to come about only after the tragic failure of the military remedy had been demonstrated in Vietnam.

There were other effects related to the exuberant reaction to the Cuban crisis. As the United States began to feel that power and force were successful solvents to the more sticky problems of the cold war, the role of international law declined precipitously.

Moral pontifications appeared increasingly hypocritical after Cuba. But after all, hypocrisy, in the words of H. L. Mencken, "runs, like a hair in a hot dog, through the otherwise beautiful fabric of American life." The participants in the crisis knew the blockade was an act of war that had little basis in international law. After the crisis was over, even lawyers began to see law as but another instrumentality of American policy. The conclusion reached by American academics was that "International law is . . . a tool, not a guide to action. . . . It does not have a valid life of its own; it is a mere instrument, available to political leaders for their own ends, be they good or evil, peaceful or aggressive. . . . [The Cuban missile crisis] merely reconfirms the irrelevance of international law in major political disputes."

Dean Acheson summarized the code of the cold war as it was confirmed by the Cuban experience: "The power, prestige and position of the United States had been challenged. . . . Law simply does not deal with such questions of ultimate power. . . . The survival of states is not a matter of law."

George Ball, former Under Secretary of State, wrote: "No one can seriously contend that we now live under a universal system or, in any realistic sense, under the 'rule of law.' We maintain the peace by preserving a precarious balance of power between ourselves and the Soviet Union—a process we used to call 'containment' before the word went out of style. It is the preservation of that balance which, regardless of how we express it, is the central guiding principle of American foreign policy."

The UN was used in the Cuban Crisis, not as Kennedy had told the General Assembly the year before, as "the only true alternative to war," but as a platform where Adlai Stevenson, the eloquent American representative, could deal "a final blow to the Soviet case before world opinion."

Epitomized by Cuba, crisis after crisis pointed out the stark irony: Americans, who had so long stroked the talisman of international law, now seemed to do so only when their interests were not jeopardized. Otherwise, law became merely a rhetorical flourish of United States policy. International law was still a part of the admonition that "armed aggression" and "breaches of the peace" cease and desist. But, in back of these legalistic and moralistic injunctions, the armed cop became more and more apparent. As General de Gaulle had observed earlier, the conclusion that American idealism was but a reflection of the American will to power became almost inescapable after the Cuban crisis. Few obeisances about the need for law in international society disguised the sense that America had abandoned her ancient, liberal inheritance in the zesty pursuit of world order.

Another effect of the crisis was to differentiate the "great powers"—the United States and the Soviet Union—from other states which were literally frozen out of a major role in structuring global politics. After all, the major "chips" of big-power poker were simply not accessible to other governments—even those with modest and nominally independent nuclear forces. For no other nations had the capability of making even plausible calculations of either preemptive or second-strike blows against a great power, much less basing national strategies on such possibilities. As a result, Europeans were offered the appearance of some control in their nuclear lot with the ill-fated MLF. But the nuclear trigger was still in the hands of the United States, and so was the final squeeze. Not only were the weapons of great-power diplomacy increasingly inaccessible to other states, but the other tools of statecraft also receded from the grasp of those with modest resources. The spy, for instance, was largely replaced by satellite reconnaissance. Intellectual musings on great-power conflict became differentiated from other strategic thinking. Gradually, the Soviets and the Americans created a shared private idiom of force; and a curious dialogue began between the congressional budget messages of the Secretary of Defense and the periodic revisions of *Strategy* by Marshal Sokolovsky. Allies became mere appurtenances of power whose purpose, in the duopolistic structure of international society, was increasingly symbolic. Thus, for example, the OAS was asked to validate the U.S. blockade at the same time the American quarantine was announced.

Similarly, Dean Acheson flew to Paris and other European capitals to confer with American allies about the coming confrontation over Cuba.

"Your President does me great honor," de Gaulle said, "to send me so distinguished an emissary. I assume the occasion to be of appropriate importance." Acheson delivered President Kennedy's letter, with the text of the speech to be delivered at P-hour, 7 P.M. Washington time. He offered to summarize it. De Gaulle raised his hand in a delaying gesture that the long-departed Kings of France might have envied. "May we be clear before you start," he said. "Are you consulting or informing me?" Acheson confessed that he was there to inform, not to consult. "I am in favor of independent decisions," de Gaulle acknowledged.

For the Europeans, Gaullists and Leftists alike, it appeared that there was a high likelihood of nuclear annihilation without representation. In spite of European gestures of support, the alliance received a shock from which it did not recover. The British, in the midst of a vicious internal debate about whether or not to abandon nuclear weapons, decided they were necessary to buy even minimum consideration from their American allies. The French did not debate; they accelerated their nuclear programs while withdrawing from a military role in the alliance.

On the Soviet side, it was equally apparent that Russian interests would not be sacrificed to sister socialist states. Castro was plainly sold out. The weak promise tendered by the Kennedy Administration not to invade the island was probably cold comfort as Castro saw his military benefactors beat a hasty retreat from American power. Embarrassingly, Castro began to echo the "capitulationist" theme of Chinese broadcasts. Privately Castro said that if he could, he would have beaten Khrushchev to within an inch of his life for what he did. Soviet Foreign Minister Mikoyan was dispatched to Cuba and stayed there for weeks, not even returning to the bedside of his dying wife, but Castro's fury was unabated. Whatever the motive for Khrushchev's moves in Cuba, the Chinese were also enraged. Any attempts the Soviets had made prior to October 1962 to dissuade the Chinese from assuming a nuclear role lost their validity when it became obvious that the Russians would not risk their own destruction for an associate.

By 1963, a new era of East-West relations was unfolding. The United States still cultivated the asymmetrical assumptions of the cold war, but the Soviet Union was at least admitted as a junior partner in a duopolistic international system which began to be characterized as détente. The relaxation was favorable to Kennedy, who wanted to begin to deal with the Soviets without the ideological rancor that had poisoned previous relations, and who had a vision of Soviet "responsibility" which was to be enlarged upon by succeeding administrations. The Soviets, too, sought a détente. Given their acknowledged strategic inferiority, they could hardly expect to be successful in another series of confrontations. Moreover, the Chinese began to present formidable ideological and political difficulties for the Russians, whose new interest in improved relations with the United States caused intense fears in China of American-Soviet collusion. At the same time, the Soviets began to fear a Sino-American agreement that would be detrimental to their interests. As Michael Suslov, chief ideologue of the Soviet Union, explained in early 1964, "With a stubbornness worthy of a better cause the Chinese leaders attempt to prevent the improvement of Soviet-American relations, representing this as 'plotting with the imperialists.' At the same time the Chinese government makes feverish attempts to improve relations with Britain, France, Japan, West Germany, and Italy. It is quite clear that they would not refuse to improve relations with the United States but as yet do not see favorable circumstances for such an endeavor."

Thus, by 1964, the crisis had precipitated a change in the global structure of power. American paramountcy had been self-proclaimed; the seeds of détente had been sown by a shared vision of nuclear oblivion; and the ingredients for a great-power condominium were becoming clear. If it had not been for the war in Vietnam, the present framework of international affairs might have been with us ten years earlier. Tragically and ironically, the "lessons" of the Cuban missile crisis—that success in international crisis was largely a matter of national guts; that the opponent would yield to superior force; that presidential control of force can be "suitable," "selective," "swift," "effective," and "responsive" to civilian authority; and that crisis management and execution are too dangerous and events move too rapidly for anything but the tightest secrecy—all these inferences contributed to President Johnson's decision to use American air power against Hanoi in 1965. The Cuban crisis changed the international environment but riveted American expectations to the necessities of the diplomacy of violence. Even the language of the Gulf of Tonkin Resolution was almost identical to that which Kennedy's legal advisors had drawn up for the OAS in October of 1962. Although the Cuban crisis created substantial changes in distinguishing superpowers from other states, the realization of the equality of the superpowers and of the indications that they could join in a relationship which had some elements of condominium and some elements of the classic balance of power was suppressed until the American agony in Vietnam drew to a close.

FURTHER READING

Elie Abel, *The Missile Crisis* (1966)

Graham Allison, *Essence of Decision* (1971)

Barton J. Bernstein, "The Cuban Missile Crisis: Trading the Jupiters in Turkey?" *Political Science Quarterly,* 95 (1980), 97–125

———, "The Week We Almost Went to War," *Bulletin of the Atomic Scientists,* 30 (1976), 13–21

Cole Blasier, *The Hovering Giant* (1976)

Dan Caldwell, "A Research Note on the Quarantine of Cuba, October 1962," *International Studies Quarterly,* 22 (1978), 625–633

Fidel Castro, *Atlas Armas* (1963)

Abram Chayes, *The Cuban Missile Crisis: International Crisis and the Role of Law* (1974)

David Detzer, *The Brink* (1979)

Herbert Dinerstein, *The Making of a Missile Crisis: October 1962* (1976)

Robert A. Divine, ed., *The Cuban Missile Crisis* (1971)

Theodore Draper, *Castroism* (1965)

A. A. Gromyko, "The Caribbean Crisis," *Soviet Law and Government,* 11 (1972), 3–53

Donald L. Hafner, "Bureaucratic Politics and 'Those Frigging Missiles': JFK, Cuba, and U.S. Missiles in Turkey," *Orbis,* 21 (1977), 307–333

Maurice Halperin, *The Rise and Decline of Fidel Castro* (1972)

———, *The Taming of Fidel Castro* (1981)

Jim Heath, *Decade of Disillusionment* (1975)

Irving L. Janis, *Groupthink* (1982)

Haynes B. Johnson, et al., *The Bay of Pigs* (1964)

Robert F. Kennedy, *Thirteen Days* (1969)

David L. Larson, ed., *The Cuban Crisis of 1962* (1963)

Lee Lockwood, *Castro's Cuba, Cuba's Fidel* (1967)

Frank Mankiewicz and Kirby Jones, *With Fidel* (1975)

Lewis J. Paper, "The Moral Implications of the Cuban Missile Crisis," *American Scholar,* 41 (1972), 276–283

Henry M. Pachter, *Collision Course* (1963)

Herbert S. Parmet, *JFK* (1983)

Thomas G. Paterson, "Bearing the Burden: A Critical Look at JFK's Foreign Policy," *Virginia Quarterly Review,* 54 (1978), 193–212

Arthur M. Schlesinger, Jr., *A Thousand Days* (1965)

Ronald Steel, "Endgame," *New York Review of Books,* March 13, 1969, pp. 15–22

Tad Szulc and K.E. Meyer, *The Cuban Invasion* (1962)

Hugh Thomas, *Cuba* (1971)

Lucien S. Vandenbroucke, "Anatomy of a Failure: The Decision to Land at the Bay of Pigs," *Political Science Quarterly* (1983)

Richard Walton, *Cold War and Counterrevolution* (1972)

Peter Wyden, *Bay of Pigs* (1979)

The War in Vietnam

13

For thirty years after World War II, the United States was involved in the Indo-chinese country of Vietnam. In 1945 America tolerated the reimposition of French colonialism there; in 1950 the United States began giving massive aid to the French to quell the Vietnamese insurgency; from 1954 to 1961 America helped to organize and maintain a non-Communist regime in the South; in 1961 American military personnel began to fight in Vietnamese jungles; in 1964 American bombers began a tremendous campaign of raids against North Vietnam; in 1968 peace talks began; in 1973 a peace settlement was reached and the United States continued to support the South Vietnamese regime; and in 1975 the remaining Americans were driven pell-mell from Vietnam when the Viet Cong and North Vietnamese seized the southern capital of Saigon, re-naming it Ho Chi Minh City. Over 57,000 American servicemen died in Viet-nam, and the United States spent over $150 billion in Southeast Asia between 1950 and 1975.

In the 1960s, when the American military intervention escalated, peace dem-onstrations and debates swept the United States, putting pressure on politicians to reverse American policy and withdraw from the war. The question posed in the 1960s is the same as that asked by recent scholars: Why did the United States become so deeply involved in Vietnam for so long? The answers have varied greatly: security, containment of Communism, economic needs, lessons of the past, maintenance of international stature as the "number one" power, rampant globalism, imperialism, arrogance of power, immorality, inadvertence (the "quagmire" thesis), an imperial presidency, manipulation of public opin-ion, and bureaucratic imperatives.

It is not surprising that America's longest war in history should produce so many explanations, for the causes of the Vietnamese conflict were less clear-cut than those of previous wars in which the United States fought, and the tragedy and ultimate defeat were so wrenching.

DOCUMENTS

Resistance to foreigners is an enduring theme in Vietnamese history. During World War II, the Vietnamese battled the invading Japanese and looked toward independence. On September 2, 1945, Ho Chi Minh and other nationalists wrote a Declaration of Independence for the Democratic Republic of Vietnam. The document, reprinted below, resembled the 1776 American declaration. But independence was denied by the returning French, who reclaimed their colony. From 1945 to 1954 Vietnam was rocked by anti-colonial rebellion. The beleaguered French ultimately decided to withdraw, and at the Geneva Conference of May 8–July 21, 1954, the warring parties and their allies, including the United States, prepared peace terms and long-range plans for Indochina. The Geneva accords, which the United States refused to sign, were summarized in the Final Declaration. Thereafter, Ho's Communists governed "North Vietnam" and the United States backed a regime in the "South."

The Tonkin Gulf Resolution, which passed the Senate on August 10, 1964, with only two dissenting votes, authorized the President to use the force he deemed necessary in Vietnam. President Lyndon B. Johnson's vigorous speech at The John Hopkins University on April 7, 1965, explains the reasons why the United States was fighting in Vietnam. The next document was sent to the President by Undersecretary of State George Ball. Dated July 1, 1965, the then-secret document revealed Ball's pessimism toward American intervention and urged a compromise solution. Johnson rejected it. The next document is a portion of Chinese General Lin Piao's (Lin Biao's) 1965 statement that "people's war" would overcome American imperialism in the "testing ground" of Vietnam. Such views alarmed American leaders and led some to argue that the United States was drawing the line against "Red Chinese" aggression in Southeast Asia.

J. William Fulbright, chairman of the Senate Foreign Relations Committee, became a vocal critic of the Vietnam War. In a speech on May 5, 1966, he protested an American "arrogance of power." The next document is an excerpt from an article by Clark M. Clifford, Secretary of Defense, 1968–1969, recalling his disconcerting conferences with military leaders in the shattering aftermath of the early-1968 Tet Offensive. The last document is a transcript of a November 24, 1969, interview between Mike Wallace of the Columbia Broadcasting System and Vietnam veteran Private Paul Meadlo, who had participated in the 1968 massacre of Vietnamese civilians at My Lai.

The Vietnamese Declaration of Independence, 1945

All men are created equal. They are endowed by their Creator with certain inalienable rights, among these are Life, Liberty and the pursuit of Happiness.

This immortal statement was made in the Declaration of Independence of the United States of America in 1776. In a broader sense, this means: All the peoples on the earth are equal from birth, all the peoples have a right to live, to be happy and free.

The Declaration of the French Revolution made in 1791 on the Rights of Man and the Citizen also states: "All men are born free and with equal rights, and must always remain free and have equal rights."

Those are undeniable truths.

Nevertheless, for more than eighty years, the French imperialists, abusing the standard of Liberty, Equality and Fraternity, have violated our Fatherland and oppressed our fellow-citizens. They have acted contrary to the ideals of humanity and justice.

In the field of politics, they have deprived our people of every democratic liberty.

They have enforced inhuman laws; they have set up three distinct political regimes in the North, the Centre and the South of Viet Nam in order to wreck our national unity and prevent our people from being united.

They have built more prisons than schools. They have mercilessly slain our patriots; they have drowned our uprisings in rivers of blood.

They have fettered public opinion; they have practised obscurantism against our people.

To weaken our race they have forced us to use opium and alcohol.

In the field of economics, they have fleeced us to the backbone, impoverished our people and devastated our land.

They have robbed us of our ricefields, our mines, our forests and our raw materials. They have monopolized the issuing of banknotes and the export trade.

They have invented numerous unjustifiable taxes and reduced our people, especially our peasantry, to a state of extreme poverty.

They have hampered the prospering of our national bourgeoisie; they have mercilessly exploited our workers. . . .

For these reasons, we, members of the Provisional Government, representing the whole Vietnamese people, declare that from now on we break off all relations of a colonial character with France; we repeal all the international obligation[s] that France has so far subscribed to on behalf of Viet Nam and we abolish all the special rights the French have unlawfully acquired in our Fatherland.

The whole Vietnamese people, animated by a common purpose, are determined to fight to the bitter end against any attempt by the French colonialists to reconquer their country.

We are convinced that the Allied nations which at Teheran and San Francisco have acknowledged the principles of self-determination and equality of nations, will not refuse to acknowledge the independence of Viet Nam.

A people who have courageously opposed French domination for more than eighty years, a people who have fought side by side with the Allies against the fascists during these last years, such a people must be free and independent.

For these reasons, we, members of the Provisional Government of the Democratic Republic of Viet Nam, solemnly declare to the world that Viet Nam has the right to be a free and independent country—and in fact it is so already. The entire Vietnamese people are determined to mobilize all their physical and mental strength, to sacrifice their lives and property in order to safeguard their independence and liberty.

Final Declaration of the Geneva Conference on Indochina, 1954

1. The Conference takes note of the agreements ending hostilities in Cambodia, Laos and Viet Nam and organising international control and the supervision of the execution of the provisions of these agreements. . . .

4. The Conference takes note of the clauses in the agreement on the cessation of hostilities in Viet Nam prohibiting the introduction into Viet Nam of foreign troops and military personnel as well as of all kinds of arms and munitions. . . .

5. The Conference takes note of the clauses in the agreement on the cessation of hostilities in Viet Nam to the effect that no military base under the control of a foreign State may be established in the regrouping zones of the two parties [above and below the 17th parallel], the latter having the obligation to see that the zones allotted to them shall not constitute part of any military alliance and shall not be utilised for the resumption of hostilities or in the service of an aggressive policy. . . .

6. The Conference recognises that the essential purpose of the agreement relating to Viet Nam is to settle military questions with a view to ending hostilities and that the military demarcation line [at the 17th parallel] is provisional and should not in any way be interpreted as constituting a political or territorial boundary. The Conference expresses its conviction that the execution of the provisions set out in the present declaration and in the agreement on the cessation of hostilities creates the necessary basis for the achievement in the near future of a political settlement in Viet Nam.

7. The Conference declares that, so far as Viet Nam is concerned, the settlement of political problems, effected on the basis of respect for the principles of independence, unity and territorial integrity, shall permit the Vietnamese people to enjoy the fundamental freedoms, guaranteed by democratic institutions established as a result of free general elections by secret ballot. In order to ensure that sufficient progress in the restoration of peace has been made, and that all the necessary conditions obtain for free expression of the national will, general elections shall be held in July 1956, under the supervision of an international commission composed of representatives of the Member States of the International Supervisory Commission, referred to in the agreement on the cessation of hostilities. Consultations will be held on this subject between the competent representative authorities of the two zones from July 20, 1955, onwards. . . .

12. In their relations with Cambodia, Laos and Viet Nam, each member of the Geneva Conference undertakes to respect the sovereignty, the

independence, the unity and the territorial integrity of the above-mentioned States, and to refrain from any interference in their internal affairs. . . .

The Tonkin Gulf Resolution, 1964

To promote the maintenance of international peace and security in southeast Asia.

Whereas naval units of the Communist regime in Vietnam, in violation of the principles of the Charter of the United Nations and of international law, have deliberately and repeatedly attacked United States naval vessels lawfully present in international waters, and have thereby created a serious threat to international peace; and

Whereas these attacks are part of a deliberate and systematic campaign of aggression that the Communist regime in North Vietnam has been waging against its neighbors and the nations joined with them in the collective defense of their freedom; and

Whereas the United States is assisting the peoples of southeast Asia to protect their freedom and has no territorial, military or political ambitions in that area, but desires only that these peoples should be left in peace to work out their own destinies in their own way: Now, therefore, be it *Resolved by the Senate and House of Representatives of the United States of America in Congress assembled,* That the Congress approves and supports the determination of the President, as Commander in Chief, to take all necessary measures to repel any armed attack against the forces of the United States and to prevent further aggression.

SEC. 2. The United States regards as vital to its national interest and to world peace the maintenance of international peace and security in southeast Asia. Consonant with the Constitution of the United States and the Charter of the United Nations and in accordance with its obligations under the Southeast Asia Collective Defense Treaty, the United States is, therefore, prepared, as the President determines, to take all necessary steps, including the use of armed force, to assist any member or protocol state of the Southeast Asia Collective Defense Treaty requesting assistance in defense of its freedom.

SEC. 3. This resolution shall expire when the President shall determine that the peace and security of the area is reasonably assured by international conditions created by action of the United Nations or otherwise, except that it may be terminated earlier by concurrent resolution of the Congress.

Lyndon B. Johnson Explains
Why Americans Fight in Vietnam, 1965

Why must this nation hazard its ease, its interest, and its power for the sake of a people so far away?

We fight because we must fight if we are to live in a world where every country can shape its own destiny, and only in such a world will our own freedom be finally secure.

This kind of world will never be built by bombs or bullets. Yet the infirmities of man are such that force must often precede reason and the waste of war, the works of peace.

We wish that this were not so. But we must deal with the world as it is, if it is ever to be as we wish.

The world as it is in Asia is not a serene or peaceful place.

The first reality is that North Viet-Nam has attacked the independent nation of South Viet-Nam. Its object is total conquest.

Of course, some of the people of South Viet-Nam are participating in attack on their own government. But trained men and supplies, orders and arms, flow in a constant stream from North to South.

This support is the heartbeat of the war.

And it is a war of unparalleled brutality. Simple farmers are the targets of assassination and kidnaping. Women and children are strangled in the night because their men are loyal to their government. And helpless villages are ravaged by sneak attacks. Large-scale raids are conducted on towns, and terror strikes in the heart of cities.

The confused nature of this conflict cannot mask the fact that it is the new face of an old enemy.

Over this war—and all Asia—is another reality: the deepening shadow of Communist China. The rulers in Hanoi are urged on by Peking. This is a regime which has destroyed freedom in Tibet, which has attacked India and has been condemned by the United Nations for aggression in Korea. It is a nation which is helping the forces of violence in almost every continent. The contest in Viet-Nam is part of a wider pattern of aggressive purposes.

Why are these realities our concern? Why are we in South Viet-Nam?

We are there because we have a promise to keep. Since 1954 every American President has offered support to the people of South Viet-Nam. We have helped to build, and we have helped to defend. Thus, over many years, we have made a national pledge to help South Viet-Nam defend its independence.

And I intend to keep that promise.

To dishonor that pledge, to abandon this small and brave nation to its enemies, and to the terror that must follow, would be an unforgivable wrong.

We are also there to strengthen world order. Around the globe from Berlin to Thailand are people whose well being rests in part on the belief that they can count on us if they are attacked. To leave Viet-Nam to its fate would shake the confidence of all these people in the value of an American commitment and in the value of America's word. The result would be increased unrest and instability, and even wider war.

We are also there because there are great stakes in the balance. Let no one think for a moment that retreat from Viet-Nam would bring an end to conflict. The battle would be renewed in one country and then another. The central lesson of our time is that the appetite of aggression is never satisfied. To withdraw from one battlefield means only to prepare for the next. We must say in

Southeast Asia—as we did in Europe—in the words of the Bible: "Hitherto shalt thou come, but no further."

There are those who say that all our effort there will be futile—that China's power is such that it is bound to dominate all Southeast Asia. But there is no end to that argument until all of the nations of Asia are swallowed up.

There are those who wonder why we have a responsibility there. Well, we have it there for the same reason that we have a responsibility for the defense of Europe. World War II was fought in both Europe and Asia and when it ended we found ourselves with continued responsibility for the defense of freedom.

Our objective is the independence of South Viet-Nam and its freedom from attack. We want nothing for ourselves—only that the people of South Viet-Nam be allowed to guide their own country in their own way.

We will do everything necessary to reach that objective and we will do only what is absolutely necessary.

In recent months attacks on South Viet-Nam were stepped up. Thus, it became necessary for us to increase our response and to make attacks by air. This is not a change of purpose. It is a change in what we believe that purpose requires.

We do this in order to slow down aggression.

We do this to increase the confidence of the brave people of South Viet-Nam who have bravely borne this brutal battle for so many years with so many casualties.

And we do this to convince the leaders of North Viet-Nam—and all who seek to share their conquest—of a simple fact:

We will not be defeated.

We will not grow tired.

We will not withdraw, either openly or under the cloak of a meaningless agreement.

We know that air attacks alone will not accomplish all of these purposes. But it is our best and prayerful judgment that they are a necessary part of the surest road to peace.

We hope that peace will come swiftly. But that is in the hands of others besides ourselves. And we must be prepared for a long continued conflict. It will require patience as well as bravery—the will to endure as well as the will to resist.

I wish it were possible to convince others with words of what we now find it necessary to say with guns and planes: armed hostility is futile—our resources are equal to any challenge—because we fight for values and we fight for principle, rather than territory or colonies, our patience and our determination are unending.

Once this is clear, then it should also be clear that the only path for reasonable men is the path of peaceful settlement. . . .

These countries of Southeast Asia are homes for millions of impoverished people. Each day these people rise at dawn and struggle through until the night to wrestle existence from the soil. They are often wracked by diseases, plagued by hunger, and death comes at the early age of forty.

Stability and peace do not come easily in such a land. Neither independence nor human dignity will ever be won though by arms alone. It also requires the works of peace. The American people have helped generously in times past in these works, and now there must be a much more massive effort to improve the life of man in that conflict-torn corner of our world.

The first step is for the countries of Southeast Asia to associate themselves in a greatly expanded co-operative effort for development. We would hope that North Viet-Nam would take its place in the common effort just as soon as peaceful co-operation is possible.

The United Nations is already actively engaged in development in this area, and as far back as 1961 I conferred with our authorities in Viet-Nam in connection with their work there. And I would hope tonight that the Secretary General of the United Nations could use the prestige of his great office and his deep knowledge of Asia to initiate, as soon as possible, with the countries of that area, a plan for co-operation in increased development.

For our part I will ask the Congress to join in a billion dollar American investment in this effort as soon as it is underway.

And I would hope that all other industrialized countries, including the Soviet Union, will join in this effort to replace despair with hope and terror with progress.

The task is nothing less than to enrich the hopes and existence of more than a hundred million people. And there is much to be done.

The vast Mekong River can provide food and water and power on a scale to dwarf even our own T.V.A.

The wonders of modern medicine can be spread through villages where thousands die every year from lack of care.

Schools can be established to train people in the skills needed to manage the process of development.

And these objectives, and more, are within the reach of a cooperative and determined effort.

I also intend to expand and speed up a program to make available our farm surpluses to assist in feeding and clothing the needy in Asia. We should not allow people to go hungry and wear rags while our own warehouses overflow with an abundance of wheat and corn and rice and cotton.

So I will very shortly name a special team of outstanding, patriotic, and distinguished Americans to inaugurate our participation in these programs. This team will be headed by Mr. Eugene Black, the very able former president of the World Bank.

This will be a disorderly planet for a long time. In Asia, and elsewhere, the forces of the modern world are shaking old ways and uprooting ancient civilizations. There will be turbulence and struggle and even violence. Great social change—as we see in our own country—does not always come without conflict.

We must also expect that nations will on occasion be in dispute with us. It may be because we are rich, or powerful, or because we have made some mistakes, or because they honestly fear our intentions. However, no nation need ever fear that we desire their land, or to impose our will, or to dictate their institutions.

But we will always oppose the effort of one nation to conquer another nation.

We will do this because our own security is at stake.

But there is more to it than that. For our generation has a dream. It is a very old dream. But we have the power, and now we have the opportunity to make that dream come true.

For centuries nations have struggled among each other. But we dream of a world where disputes are settled by law and reason. And we will try to make it so.

For most of history men have hated and killed one another in battle. But we dream of an end to war. And we will try to make it so.

For all existence most men have lived in poverty, threatened by hunger. But we dream of a world where all are fed and charged with hope. And we will help to make it so.

George Ball Dissents, 1965

(1) *A Losing War:* The South Vietnamese are losing the war to the Viet Cong. No one can assure you that we can beat the Viet Cong or even force them to the conference table on our terms, no matter how many hundred thousand *white, foreign* (U.S.) troops we deploy.

No one has demonstrated that a white ground force of whatever size can win a guerrilla war—which is at the same time a civil war between Asians— in jungle terrain in the midst of a population that refuses cooperation to the white forces (and the South Vietnamese) and thus provides a great intelligence advantage to the other side. Three recent incidents vividly illustrate this point: (a) the sneak attack on the Da Nang Air Base which involved penetration of a defense perimeter guarded by 9,000 Marines. This raid was possible only because of the cooperation of the local inhabitants; (b) the B-52 raid that failed to hit the Viet Cong who had obviously been tipped off; (c) the search and destroy mission of the 173rd Air Borne Brigade which spent three days looking for the Viet Cong, suffered 23 casualties, and never made contact with the enemy who had obviously gotten advance word of their assignment.

(2) *The Question to Decide:* Should we limit our liabilities in South Vietnam and try to find a way out with minimal long-term costs?

The alternative—no matter what we may wish it to be—is almost certainly a protracted war involving an open-ended commitment of U.S. forces, mounting U.S. casualties, no assurance of a satisfactory solution, and a serious danger of escalation at the end of the road.

(3) *Need for a Decision Now:* So long as our forces are restricted to advising and assisting the South Vietnamese, the struggle will remain a civil war between Asian peoples. Once we deploy substantial numbers of troops in combat it will become a war between the U.S. and a large part of the

population of South Vietnam, organized and directed from North Vietnam and backed by the resources of both Moscow and Peiping.

The decision you face now, therefore, is crucial. Once large numbers of U.S. troops are committed to direct combat, they will begin to take heavy casualties in a war they are ill-equipped to fight in a non-cooperative if not downright hostile countryside.

Once we suffer large casualties, we will have started a well-nigh irreversible process. Our involvement will be so great that we cannot—without national humiliation—stop short of achieving our complete objectives. *Of the two possibilities I think humiliation would be more likely than the achievement of our objectives—even after we have paid terrible costs.*

(4) Compromise Solution: Should we commit U.S. manpower and prestige to a terrain so unfavorable as to give a very large advantage to the enemy— or should we seek a compromise settlement which achieves less than our stated objectives and thus cut our losses while we still have the freedom of maneuver to do so.

(5) Costs of a Compromise Solution: The answer involves a judgment as to the cost to the U.S. of such a compromise settlement in terms of our relations with the countries in the area of South Vietnam, the credibility of our commitments, and our prestige around the world. In my judgment, if we act before we commit substantial U.S. troops to combat in South Vietnam we can, by accepting some short-term costs, avoid what may well be a long-term catastrophe. I believe we tended grossly to exaggerate the costs involved in a compromise settlement. An appreciation of probable costs is contained in the attached memorandum.

(6) With these considerations in mind, I strongly urge the following program:

a. Military Program
   1. Complete all deployment already announced—15 battalions—but decide not to go beyond a total of 72,000 men represented by this figure.
   2. Restrict the combat role of the American forces to the June 19 announcement, making it clear to General Westmoreland that this announcement is to be strictly construed.
   3. Continue bombing in the North but avoid the Hanoi-Haiphong area and any targets nearer to the Chinese border than those already struck.

b. Political Program
   1. In any political approaches so far, we have been the prisoners of whatever South Vietnamese government that was momentarily in power. If we are ever to move toward a settlement, it will probably be because the South Vietnamese government pulls the rug out from under us and makes its own deal *or* because we go forward quietly without advance prearrangement with Saigon.
   2. So far we have not given the other side a reason to believe there is *any* flexibility in our negotiating approach. And the other side has been unwilling to accept what *in their terms* is complete capitulation.

3. Now is the time to start some serious diplomatic feelers looking towards a solution based on some application of a self-determination principle.
4. I would recommend approaching Hanoi rather than any of the other probable parties, the NLF, ——— or Peiping. Hanoi is the only one that has given any signs of interest in discussion. Peiping has been rigidly opposed. Moscow has recommended that we negotiate with Hanoi. The NLF has been silent.
5. There are several channels to the North Vietnamese, but I think the best one is through their representative in Paris, Mai van Bo. Initial feelers of Bo should be directed toward a discussion both of the four points we have put forward and the four points put forward by Hanoi as a basis for negotiation. We can accept all but one of Hanoi's four points, and hopefully we should be able to agree on some ground rules for serious negotiations—including no preconditions.
6. If the initial feelers lead to further secret, exploratory talks, we can inject the concept of self-determination that would permit the Viet Cong some hope of achieving some of their political objectives through local elections or some other device.
7. The contact on our side should be handled through a non-governmental cutout (possibly a reliable newspaper man who can be repudiated).
8. If progress can be made at this level a basis can be laid for a multinational conference. At some point, obviously, the government of South Vietnam will have to be brought on board, but I would postpone this step until after a substantial feeling out of Hanoi.

(7) Before moving to any formal conference we should be prepared to agree once the conference is started:

a. The U.S. will stand down its bombing of the North
b. The South Vietnamese will initiate no offensive operations in the South, and
c. The DRV will stop terrorism and other aggressive action against the South.

(8) The negotiations at the conference should aim at incorporating our understanding with Hanoi in the form of a multinational agreement guaranteed by the U.S., the Soviet Union and possibly other parties, and providing for an international mechanism to supervise its execution.

Lin Piao (Lin Biao) on People's War, 1965

Ours is the epoch in which world capitalism and imperialism are heading for their doom and socialism and communism are marching to victory. Comrade Mao Tse-tung's theory of people's war is not only a product of the Chinese revolution, but has also the characteristics of our epoch. The new experience gained in the people's revolutionary struggles in various countries since World

War II has provided continuous evidence that Mao Tse-tung's thought is a common asset of the revolutionary people of the whole world. This is the great international significance of the thought of Mao Tse-tung.

Since World War II, U.S. imperialism has stepped into the shoes of German, Japanese, and Italian fascism and has been trying to build a great American empire by dominating and enslaving the whole world. It is actively fostering Japanese and West German militarism as its chief accomplices in unleashing a world war. Like a vicious wolf, it is bullying and enslaving various peoples, plundering their wealth, encroaching upon their countries' sovereignty and interfering in their internal affairs. It is the most rabid aggressor in human history and the most ferocious common enemy of the people of the world. Every people or country in the world that wants revolution, independence and peace cannot but direct the spearhead of its struggle against U.S. imperialism.

Just as the Japanese imperialists' policy of subjugating China made it possible for the Chinese people to form the broadest possible united front against them, so the U.S. imperialists' policy of seeking world domination makes it possible for the people throughout the world to unite all the forces that can be united and form the broadest possible united front for a converging attack on U.S. imperialism.

At present, the main battlefield of the fierce struggle between the people of the world on the one side and U.S. imperialism and its lackeys on the other is the vast area of Asia, Africa, and Latin America. In the world as a whole, this is the area where the people suffer worst from imperialist oppression and where imperialist rule is most vulnerable. Since World War II, revolutionary storms have been rising in this area, and today they have become the most important force directly pounding U.S. imperialism. The contradiction between the revolutionary peoples of Asia, Africa, and Latin America and the imperialists headed by the United States is the principal contradiction in the contemporary world. The development of this contradiction is promoting the struggle of the people of the whole world against U.S. imperialism and its lackeys.

Since World War II, people's war has increasingly demonstrated its power in Asia, Africa, and Latin America. The peoples of China, Korea, Vietnam, Laos, Cuba, Indonesia, Algeria and other countries have waged people's wars against the imperialists and their lackeys and won great victories. The classes leading these people's wars may vary, and so may the breadth and depth of mass mobilization and the extent of victory, but the victories in these people's wars have very much weakened and pinned down the forces of imperialism, upset the U.S. imperialist plan to launch a world war, and become mighty factors defending world peace.

Today, the conditions are more favorable than ever before for the waging of people's wars by the revolutionary peoples of Asia, Africa, and Latin America against U.S. imperialism and its lackeys.

Since World War II and the succeeding years of revolutionary upsurge, there has been a great rise in the level of political consciousness and the degree of organization of the people in all countries, and the resources available to them for mutual support and aid have greatly increased. The whole capitalist-imperialist system has become drastically weaker and is in the process of increasing convulsion and disintegration. After World War I, the imperialists lacked the power to destroy the new-born socialist Soviet state, but they were still able to suppress the people's revolutionary movements in some countries in the parts of the world under their own rule and so maintain a short period of comparative stability. Since World War II, however, not only have they been unable to stop a number of countries from taking the socialist road, but they are no longer capable of holding back the surging tide of the people's revolutionary movements in the areas under their own rule.

U.S. imperialism is stronger, but also more vulnerable, than any imperialism of the past. It sets itself against the people of the whole world, including the people of the United States. Its human, military, material and financial resources are far from sufficient for the realization of its ambition of dominating the whole world. U.S. imperialism has further weakened itself by occupying so many places in the world, overreaching itself, stretching its fingers out wide and dispersing its strength, with its rear so far away and its supply lines so long. As Comrade Mao Tse-tung has said, "Wherever it commits aggression, it puts a new noose around its neck. It is besieged ring upon ring by the people of the whole world."

When committing aggression in a foreign country, U.S. imperialism can only employ part of its forces, which are sent to fight an unjust war far from their native land and therefore have a low morale, and so U.S. imperialism is beset with great difficulties. The people subjected to its aggression are having a trial of strength with U.S. imperialism neither in Washington nor New York, neither in Honolulu nor Florida, but are fighting for independence and freedom on their own soil. Once they are mobilized on a broad scale, they will have inexhaustible strength. Thus superiority will belong not to the United States but to the people subjected to its aggression. The latter, though apparently weak and small, are really more powerful than U.S. imperialism.

The struggles waged by the different peoples against U.S. imperialism reinforce each other and merge into a torrential world-wide tide of opposition to U.S. imperialism. The more successful the development of people's war in a given region, the larger the number of U.S. imperialist forces that can be pinned down and depleted there. When the U.S. aggressors are hard pressed in one place, they have no alternative but to loosen their grip on others. Therefore, the conditions become more favorable for the people elsewhere to wage struggles against U.S. imperialism and its lackeys.

Everything is divisible. And so is this colossus of U.S. imperialism. It can be split up and defeated. The peoples of Asia, Africa, Latin America and other regions can destroy it piece by piece, some striking at its head and others at its feet. That is why the greatest fear of U.S. imperialism is that people's wars will be launched in different parts of the world, and particularly in Asia, Africa and Latin America, and why it regards people's war as a mortal danger.

U.S. imperialism relies solely on its nuclear weapons to intimidate people. But these weapons cannot save U.S. imperialism from its doom. Nuclear weapons cannot be used lightly. U.S. imperialism has been condemned by the people of the whole world for its towering crime of dropping two atom bombs on Japan. If it uses nuclear weapons again, it will become isolated in the extreme. Moreover, the U.S. monopoly of nuclear weapons has long been broken; U.S. imperialism has these weapons, but others have them too. If it threatens other countries with nuclear weapons, U.S. imperialism will expose its own country to the same threat. For this reason, it will meet with strong opposition not only from the people elsewhere but also inevitably from the people in its own country. Even if U.S. imperialism brazenly uses nuclear weapons, it cannot conquer the people, who are indomitable.

However highly developed modern weapons and technical equipment may be and however complicated the methods of modern warfare, in the final analysis the outcome of a war will be decided by the sustained fighting of the ground forces, by the fighting at close quarters on battlefields, by the political consciousness of the men, by their courage and spirit of sacrifice. Here the weak points of U.S. imperialism will be completely laid bare, while the superiority of the revolutionary people will be brought into full play. The reactionary troops of U.S. imperialism cannot possibly be endowed with the courage and the spirit of sacrifice possessed by the revolutionary people. The spiritual atom bomb which the revolutionary people possess is a far more powerful and useful weapon than the physical atom bomb.

Vietnam is the most convincing current example of a victim of aggression defeating U.S. imperialism by a people's war. The United States has made South Vietnam a testing ground for the suppression of people's war. It has carried on this experiment for many years, and everybody can now see that the U.S. aggressors are unable to find a way of coping with people's war. On the other hand, the Vietnamese people have brought the power of people's war into full play in their struggle against the U.S. aggressors. The U.S. aggressors are in danger of being swamped in the people's war in Vietnam. They are deeply worried that their defeat in Vietnam will lead to a chain reaction. They are expanding the war in an attempt to save themselves from defeat. But the more they expand the war, the greater will be the chain reaction. The more they escalate the war, the heavier will be their fall and the more disastrous their defeat. The people in other parts of the world will see still more clearly that U.S. imperialism can be defeated, and that what the Vietnamese people can do, they can do too.

History has proved and will go on proving that people's war is the most effective weapon against U.S. imperialism and its lackeys. All revolutionary people will learn to wage people's war against U.S. imperialism and its lackeys. They will take up arms, learn to fight battles and become skilled in waging people's war, though they have not done so before. U.S. imperialism, like a mad bull dashing from place to place, will finally be burned to ashes in the blazing fires of the people's wars it has provoked by its own actions.

Senator J. William Fulbright on the
Arrogance of Power, 1966

The attitude above all others which I feel sure is no longer valid is the arrogance of power, the tendency of great nations to equate power with virtue and major responsibilities with a universal mission. The dilemmas involved are preeminently American dilemmas, not because America has weaknesses that others do not have but because America is powerful as no nation has ever been before and the discrepancy between its power and the power of others appears to be increasing. . . .

We are now engaged in a war to "defend freedom" in South Vietnam. Unlike the Republic of Korea, South Vietnam has an army which [is] without notable success and a weak, dictatorial government which does not command the loyalty of the South Vietnamese people. The official war aims of the United States Government, as I understand them, are to defeat what is regarded as North Vietnamese aggression, to demonstrate the futility of what the communists call "wars of national liberation," and to create conditions under which the South Vietnamese people will be able freely to determine their own future. I have not the slightest doubt of the sincerity of the President and the Vice President and the Secretaries of State and Defense in propounding these aims. What I do doubt—and doubt very much—is the ability of the United States to achieve these aims by the means being used. I do not question the power of our weapons and the efficiency of our logistics; I cannot say these things delight me as they seem to delight some of our officials, but they are certainly impressive. What I do question is the ability of the United States, or France or any other Western nation, to go into a small, alien, undeveloped Asian nation and create stability where there is chaos, the will to fight where there is defeatism, democracy where there is no tradition of it and honest government where corruption is almost a way of life. Our handicap is well expressed in the pungent Chinese proverb: "In shallow waters dragons become the sport of shrimps."

Early last month demonstrators in Saigon burned American jeeps, tried to assault American soldiers, and marched through the streets shouting "Down with the American imperialists," while one of the Buddhist leaders made a speech equating the United States with the communists as a threat to South Vietnamese independence. Most Americans are understandably shocked and angered to encounter such hostility from people who by now would be under the rule of the Viet Cong but for the sacrifice of American lives and money. Why, we may ask, are they so shockingly ungrateful? Surely they must know that their very right to parade and protest and demonstrate depends on the Americans who are defending them.

The answer, I think, is that "fatal impact" of the rich and strong on the poor and weak. Dependent on it though the Vietnamese are, our very strength is a reproach to their weakness, our wealth a mockery of their poverty, our success a reminder of their failures. What they resent is the disruptive effect of our strong culture upon their fragile one, an effect which we can no more avoid than a man can help being bigger than a child. What they fear, I think rightly, is that traditional Vietnamese society cannot survive the American economic and cultural impact. . . .

The cause of our difficulties in southeast Asia is not a deficiency of power but an excess of the wrong kind of power which results in a feeling of impotence when it fails to achieve its desired ends. We are still acting like boy scouts dragging reluctant old ladies across the streets they do not want to cross. We are trying to remake Vietnamese society, a task which certainly cannot be accomplished by force and which probably cannot be accomplished by any means available to outsiders. The objective may be desirable, but it is not feasible. . . .

If America has a service to perform in the world—and I believe it has—it is in large part the service of its own example. In our excessive involvement in the affairs of other countries, we are not only living off our assets and denying our own people the proper enjoyment of their resources; we are also denying the world the example of a free society enjoying its freedom to the fullest. This is regrettable indeed for a nation that aspires to teach democracy to other nations, because, as Burke said, "Example is the school of mankind, and they will learn at no other." . . .

There are many respects in which America, if it can bring itself to act with the magnanimity and the empathy appropriate to its size and power, can be an intelligent example to the world. We have the opportunity to set an example of generous understanding in our relations with China, of practical cooperation for peace in our relations with Russia, of reliable and respectful partnership in our relations with Western Europe, of material helpfulness without moral presumption in our relations with the developing nations, of abstention from the temptations of hegemony in our relations with Latin America, and of the all-around advantages of minding one's own business in our relations with everybody. Most of all, we have the opportunity to serve as an example of democracy to the world by the way in which we run our own society; America, in the words of John Quincy Adams, should be "the well-wisher to the freedom and independence of all" but "the champion and vindicator only of her own." . . .

If we can bring ourselves so to act, we will have overcome the dangers of the arrogance of power. It will involve, no doubt, the loss of certain glories, but that seems a price worth paying for the probable rewards, which are the happiness of America and the peace of the world.

Clark M. Clifford Remembers
His Post-Tet Questions (1968), 1969

I took office on March 1, 1968. The enemy's Tet offensive of late January and early February had been beaten back at great cost. The confidence of the American people had been badly shaken. The ability of the South Viet-

From "A Viet Nam Reappraisal: The Personal History of One Man's View and How It Evolved." Excerpted by permission of *Foreign Affairs*, July 1969. Copyright 1969 by the Council on Foreign Relations, Inc.

namese Government to restore order and morale in the populace, and discipline and esprit in the armed forces, was being questioned. At the President's direction, General Earle G. Wheeler, Chairman of the Joint Chiefs of Staff, had flown to Viet Nam in late February for an on-the-spot conference with General Westmoreland. He had just returned and presented the military's request that over 200,000 troops be prepared for deployment to Viet Nam. These troops would be in addition to the 525,000 previously authorized. I was directed, as my first assignment, to chair a task force named by the President to determine how this new requirement could be met. We were not instructed to assess the need for substantial increases in men and matériel; we were to devise the means by which they could be provided.

My work was cut out. The task force included Secretary Rusk, Secretary Henry Fowler, Under Secretary of State Nicholas Katzenbach, Deputy Secretary of Defense Paul Nitze, General Wheeler, CIA Director Richard Helms, the President's Special Assistant, Walt Rostow, General Maxwell Taylor and other skilled and highly capable officials. All of them had had long and direct experience with Vietnamese problems. I had not. I had attended various meetings in the past several years and I had been to Viet Nam three times, but it was quickly apparent to me how little one knows if he has been on the periphery of a problem and not truly in it. Until the day-long sessions of early March, I had never had the opportunity of intensive analysis and fact-finding. Now I was thrust into a vigorous, ruthlessly frank assessment of our situation by the men who knew the most about it. Try though we would to stay with the assignment of devising means to meet the military's requests, fundamental questions began to recur over and over.

It is, of course, not possible to recall all the questions that were asked nor all of the answers that were given. Had a transcript of our discussions been made—one was not—it would have run to hundreds of closely printed pages. The documents brought to the table by participants would have totalled, if collected in one place—which they were not—many hundreds more. All that is pertinent to this essay are the impressions I formed, and the conclusions I ultimately reached in those days of exhausting scrutiny. In the colloquial style of those meetings, here are some of the principal issues raised and some of the answers as I understood them:

"Will 200,000 more men do the job?" I found no assurance that they would.

"If not, how many more might be needed—and when?" There was no way of knowing.

"What would be involved in committing 200,000 more men to Viet Nam?" A reserve call-up of approximately 280,000, an increased draft call and an extension of tours of duty of most men then in service.

"Can the enemy respond with a build-up of his own?" He could and he probably would.

"What are the estimated costs of the latest requests?" First calculations were on the order of $2 billion for the remaining four months of that fiscal year, and an increase of $10 to $12 billion for the year beginning July 1, 1968.

"What will be the impact on the economy?" So great that we would face the possibility of credit restrictions, a tax increase and even wage and price controls. The balance of payments would be worsened by at least half a billion dollars a year.

"Can bombing stop the war?" Never by itself. It was inflicting heavy personnel and matériel losses, but bombing by itself would not stop the war.

"Will stepping up the bombing decrease American casualties?" Very little, if at all. Our casualties were due to the intensity of the ground fighting in the South. We had already dropped a heavier tonnage of bombs than in all the theaters of World War II. During 1967, an estimated 90,000 North Vietnamese had infiltrated into South Viet Nam. In the opening weeks of 1968, infiltrators were coming in at three to four times the rate of a year earlier, despite the ferocity and intensity of our campaign of aerial interdiction.

"How long must we keep on sending our men and carrying the main burden of combat?" The South Vietnamese were doing better, but they were not ready yet to replace our troops and we did not know when they would be.

When I asked for a presentation of the military plan for attaining victory in Viet Nam, I was told that there was no plan for victory in the historic American sense. Why not? Because our forces were operating under three major political restrictions: The President had forbidden the invasion of North Viet Nam because this could trigger the mutual assistance pact between North Viet Nam and China; the President had forbidden the mining of the harbor at Haiphong, the principal port through which the North received military supplies, because a Soviet vessel might be sunk; the President had forbidden our forces to pursue the enemy into Laos and Cambodia, for to do so would spread the war, politically and geographically, with no discernible advantage. These and other restrictions which precluded an all-out, no-holds-barred military effort were wisely designed to prevent our being drawn into a larger war. We had no inclination to recommend to the President their cancellation.

"Given these circumstances, how can we win?" We would, I was told, continue to evidence our superiority over the enemy; we would continue to attack in the belief that he would reach the stage where he would find it inadvisable to go on with the war. He could not afford the attrition we were inflicting on him. And we were improving our posture all the time.

I then asked, "What is the best estimate as to how long this course of action will take? Six months? One year? Two years?" There was no agreement on an answer. Not only was there no agreement, I could find no one willing to express any confidence in his guesses. Certainly, none of us was willing to assert that he could see "light at the end of the tunnel" or that American troops would be coming home by the end of the year.

After days of this type of analysis, my concern had greatly deepened. I could not find out when the war was going to end; I could not find out the manner in which it was going to end; I could not find out whether the new requests for men and equipment were going to be enough, or whether it would take more and, if more, when and how much; I could not find out how soon the South Vietnamese forces would be ready to take over. All I had was the statement, given with too little self-assurance to be comforting, that if we persisted for an indeterminate length of time, the enemy would choose not to go on.

And so I asked, "Does anyone see any diminution in the will of the enemy after four years of our having been there, after enormous casualties and after massive destruction from our bombing?"

The answer was that there appeared to be no diminution in the will of the enemy. . . .

And so, after these exhausting days, I was convinced that the military course we were pursuing was not only endless, but hopeless. A further substantial increase in American forces could only increase the devastation and the Americanization of the war, and thus leave us even further from our goal of a peace that would permit the people of South Viet Nam to fashion their own political and economic institutions. Henceforth, I was also convinced, our primary goal should be to level off our involvement, and to work toward gradual disengagement.

Private Paul Meadlo Explains
the My Lai Massacre, 1969

MEADLO: Captain Medina had us all in a group, and oh, he briefed us, and I can't remember all the briefing.

WALLACE: How many of them were you?   A. Well, with the mortar platoon, I'd say there'd be about 60–65 people, but the mortar platoon wasn't with us, and I'd say the mortar platoon had about 20–25—about 25 people in the mortar platoon. So we didn't have the whole company in the Pinkville [My Lai], no we didn't.

Q. There weren't about 40–45—   A. . . . right. . . .

Q. —that took part in all of this?   A. Right.

Q. Now you took off from your base camp.   A. . . . yes—Dolly.

Q. . . . Dolly. At what time?   A. I wouldn't know what time it was. . . .

Q. . . . in the early morning. . . .   A. . . . In the early morning. It was—it would have been a long time ago.

Q. And what had you been briefed to do when you got to Pinkville?

A. To search and to make sure that there weren't no N.V.A. in the village and expecting to fight—when we got there. . . .

Q. To expect to fight?   A. To expect to fight.

Q. Un-huh. So you took off and—in how many choppers?

A. Well, I'd say the first wave was about four of us—I mean four choppers, and. . . .

Q. How many men aboard each chopper?

A. Five of us. And we landed next to the village, and we all got in line and we started walking toward the village. And there was one man, one gook in the shelter, and he was all huddled up down in there, and the man called out and said there's a gook over here.

Q. How old a man was this? I mean was this a fighting man or an older man?

A. An older man. And the man hauled out and said that there's a gook over here, and then Sergeant Mitchell hollered back and said shoot him.

Q. Sergeant Mitchell was in charge of the 20 of you?   A. He was in charge of the whole squad. And so then the man shot him. So we moved on into the village, and we started searching up the village and gathering people and running through the center of the village.

Q. How many people did you round up?   A. Well, there was about 40–45 people that we gathered in the center of the village. And we placed them in there, and it was like a little island, right there in the center of the village, I'd say. And—

Q. What kind of people—men, women, children?

A. Men, women, children.

Q. Babies?

A. Babies. And we all huddled them up. We made them squat down, and Lieutenant Calley came over and said you know what to do with them, don't you? And I said yes so I took it for granted that he just wanted us to watch them. And he left, and came back about 10 to 15 minutes later, and said, how come you ain't killed them yet? And I told him that I didn't think you wanted us to kill them, that you just wanted us to guard them. He said, no, I want them dead. So—

Q. He told this to all of you, or to you particularly?

A. Well, I was facing him. So, but, the other three, four guys heard it and so he stepped back about 10, 15 feet, and he started shooting them. And he told me to start shooting. So I started shooting, I poured about four clips into the group.

Q. You fired four clips from your . . . .   A. M-16.

Q. And that's about—how many clips—I mean how many—

A. I carried seventeen rounds to each clip.

Q. So you fired something like 67 shots—   A. Right.

Q. And you killed how many? At that time?

A. Well, I fired them on automatic, so you can't—you just spray the area on them and so you can't know how many you killed 'cause they were going fast. So I might have killed ten or fifteen of them.

Q. Men, women and children?   A. Men, women and children.

Q. And babies?

A. And babies.

Q. Okay, then what?   A. So we started to gather them up, more people, and we had about seven or eight people, that we was gonna put into the hootch, and we dropped a hand grenade in there with them.

Q. Now you're rounding up more?

A. We're rounding up more, and we had about seven or eight people. And we was going to throw them in the hootch, and well, we put them in the hootch and then we dropped a hand grenade down there with them. And somebody holed up in the ravine, and told us to bring them over to the ravine, so we took them back out, and led them over to—and by that time, we already had them over there, and they had about 70–75 people all gathered up. So we threw ours in with them and Lieutenant Calley told me, he said, Meadlo, we got another job to do. And so he walked over to the people, and he started pushing them off and started shooting. . . .

Q. Started pushing them off into the ravine?

A. Off into the ravine. It was a ditch. And so we started pushing them off and we started shooting them, so altogether we just pushed them all off, and just started using automatics on them. And then—

Q. Again—men, women, children?   A. Men, women and children.

Q. And babies?

A. And babies. And so we started shooting them and somebody told us to switch off to single shot so that we could save ammo. So we switched off to single shot and shot a few more rounds. And after that, I just—we just—the company started gathering up again. We started moving out, and we had a few gooks that was in—as we started moving out, we had gooks in front of us that was taking point, you know.

Q. Uh-huh.   A. —and as we walked—

Q. Taking point. You mean out in front? To take any fire that might come.

A. Right. And so we started walking across that field. And so later on that day, they picked them up, and gooks we had, and I reckon they took them to Chu Lai or some camp that they was questioning them, so I don't know what they done with them. So we set up [indistinct] the rest of the night, and the next morning we started leaving, leaving the perimeter, and I stepped on a land mine next day, next morning.

Q. And you came back to the United States.   A. I came back to the United States, and lost a foot out of it.

Q. You feel—

A. I feel cheated because the V.A. cut my disability like they did, and they said that my stump is well healed, well padded, without tenderness. Well, it's well healed, but it's a long way from being well padded. And without tenderness? It hurts all the time. I got to work eight hours a day up on my foot, and at the end of the day I can't hardly stand it. But I gotta work because I gotta make a living. And the V.A. don't give me enough money to live on as it is.

Q. Veterans Administration.   A. Right. So—

Q. Did you feel any sense of retribution to yourself the day after?

A. Well, I felt that I was punished for what I'd done, the next morning. Later on in that day, I felt like I was being punished.

Q. Why did you do it?   A. Why did I do it? Because I felt like I was ordered to do it, and it seemed like that, at the time I felt like I was doing the right thing, because like I said I lost buddies. I lost a damn good buddy, Bobby Wilson, and it was on my conscience. So after I done it, I felt good, but later on that day, it was getting to me.

Q. You're married?   A. Right.

Q. Children?   A. Two.

Q. How old?   A. The boy is two and a half, and the little girl is a year and a half.

Q. Obviously, the question comes to my mind . . . the father of two little kids like that . . . how can he shoot babies?   A. I didn't have the little girl. I just had a little boy at the time.

Q. Uh-huh. How do you shoot babies?   A. I don't know. It's just one of them things.

Q. How many people would you imagine were killed that day?   A. I'd say about 370.

Q. How do you arrive at that figure?   A. Just looking.

Q. You say, you think, that many people, and you yourself were responsible for how many of them?   A. I couldn't say.

Q. Twenty-five? Fifty?   A. I couldn't say . . . just too many.

Q. And how many men did the actual shooting?   A. Well, I really couldn't say that, either. There was other . . . there was another platoon in there and . . . but I just couldn't say how many.

Q. But these civilians were lined up and shot? They weren't killed by cross-fire?

A. They weren't lined up . . . they [were] just pushed in a ravine or just sitting, squatting . . . and shot.

Q. What did these civilians—particularly the women and children, the old men —what did they do? What did they say to you?   A. They weren't much saying to them. They [were] just being pushed and they were doing what they was told to do.

Q. They weren't begging or saying, "No . . . no," or—   A. Right, they were begging and saying, "No, no." And the mothers was hugging their children and, but they kept right on firing. Well, we kept right on firing. They was waving their arms and begging. . . .

Q. Was that your most vivid memory of what you saw?   A. Right.

Q. And nothing went through your mind or heart?   A. Many a times . . . many a times. . . .

Q. While you were doing it?   A. Not while I was doing it. It just seemed like it was the natural thing to do at the time. I don't know . . . I was getting relieved from what I'd seen earlier over there.

Q. What do you mean?   A. Well, I was getting . . . like the . . . my buddies getting killed or wounded or—we weren't getting no satisfaction from it, so what it really was, it was just mostly revenge.

Q. You call the Vietnamese "gooks?"   A. Gooks.

Q. Are they people to you? Were they people to you?

A. Well, they were people. But it was just one of them words that we just picked up over there, you know. Just any word you pick up. That's what you call people, and that's what you been called.

Q. Obviously, the thought that goes through my mind—I spent some time over there, and I killed in the second war, and so forth. But the thought that goes through your mind is, we've raised such a dickens about what the Nazis did, or what the Japanese did, but particularly what the Nazis did in the second world war, the brutalization and so forth, you know. It's hard for a good many Americans to understand that young, capable, American boys could line up old men, women and children and babies and shoot them down in cold blood. How do you explain that?

A. I wouldn't know.

Q. Did you ever dream about all of this that went on in Pinkville?

A. Yes, I did . . . and I still dream about it.

Q. What kind of dreams?   A. About the women and children in my sleep. Some days . . . some nights, I can't even sleep. I just lay there thinking about it.

ESSAYS

James C. Thomson, Jr., now of Harvard University, was an Asian policymaker in the State Department and White House from 1961 to 1966. He became a dissenter from American policy. In his essay on why the United States committed itself to war in Vietnam, he stresses a number of factors, including the influence of lessons from the past, bureaucratic inertia, lack of expertise, and miscalculation.

Thomson's autopsy of the subject differs from the radical prespective of Gabriel Kolko of York University. Kolko does not believe that the war was an American mistake or that Washington was simply acting according to the containment doctrine—to check the advance of Communism. Rather, he argues that the United States deliberately intervened in Southeast Asia in order to maintain its economic hegemony in the Third World. Vietnam, Kolko concludes, became a symbolic test case of America's ability to continue its economic supremacy in the face of leftist opposition.

George C. Herring of the University of Kentucky, whose book *America's Longest War* (1979) is one of the best studies of American participation in the Vietnam War, asks why the United States failed to win. He questions those scholars, politicians, and publicists who came to argue that the United States could have won. He discusses the powerful current of Vietnamese nationalism, the deficiencies of American-backed governments, the destructive American conduct of the war, and the shortcomings of the containment doctrine. America, he suggests, was caught in a "no-win situation."

Historical Legacies and Bureaucratic Procedures

JAMES C. THOMSON, JR.

As a case study in the making of foreign policy, the Vietnam War will fascinate historians and social scientists for many decades to come. One question that will certainly be asked: How did men of superior ability, sound training, and

James C. Thomson, Jr., "How Could Vietnam Happen? An Autopsy," *Atlantic Monthly*, 221 (1968), 47–53.

high ideals—American policy-makers of the 1960s—create such costly and divisive policy?

As one who watched the decision-making process in Washington from 1961 to 1966 under Presidents Kennedy and Johnson, I can suggest a preliminary answer. I can do so by briefly listing some of the factors that seemed to me to shape our Vietnam policy during my years as an East Asia specialist at the State Department and the White House. I shall deal largely with Washington as I saw or sensed it, and not with Saigon, where I have spent but a scant three days, in the entourage of the Vice President, or with other decision centers, the capitals of interested parties. Nor will I deal with other important parts of the record: Vietnam's history prior to 1961, for instance, or the overall course of America's relations with Vietnam.

Yet a first and central ingredient in these years of Vietnam decisions does involve history. The ingredient was *the legacy of the 1950s*—by which I mean the so-called "loss of China," the Korean War, and the Far East policy of Secretary of State Dulles.

This legacy had an institutional by-product for the Kennedy Administration: in 1961 the U.S. government's East Asian establishment was undoubtedly the most rigid and doctrinaire of Washington's regional divisions in foreign affairs. This was especially true at the Department of State, where the incoming Administration found the Bureau of Far Eastern Affairs the hardest nut to crack. It was a bureau that had been purged of its best China expertise, and of far-sighted, dispassionate men, as a result of McCarthyism. Its members were generally committed to one policy line: the close containment and isolation of mainland China, the harassment of "neutralist" nations which sought to avoid alignment with either Washington or Peking, and the maintenance of a network of alliances with anti-Communist client states on China's periphery.

Another aspect of the legacy was the special vulnerability and sensitivity of the new Democratic Administration on Far East policy issues. The memory of the McCarthy era was still very sharp, and Kennedy's margin of victory was too thin. The 1960 Offshore Islands TV debate between Kennedy and Nixon had shown the President-elect the perils of "fresh thinking." The Administration was inherently leery of moving too fast on Asia. As a result, the Far East Bureau (now the Bureau of East Asian and Pacific Affairs) was the last one to be overhauled. Not until Averell Harriman was brought in as Assistant Secretary in December, 1961, were significant personnel changes attempted, and it took Harriman several months to make a deep imprint on the bureau because of his necessary preoccupation with the Laos settlement. Once he did so, there was virtually no effort to bring back the purged or exiled East Asia experts.

There were other important by-products of this "legacy of the fifties":

The new Administration inherited and somewhat shared *a general perception of China-on-the-march*—a sense of China's vastness, its numbers, its belligerence; a revived sense, perhaps, of the Golden Horde. This was a perception fed by Chinese intervention in the Korean War (an intervention actually based on appallingly bad communications and mutual miscalculation on the part of Washington and Peking; but the careful unraveling of that tragedy, which scholars have accomplished, had not yet become part of the conventional wisdom).

The new Administration inherited and briefly accepted *a monolithic conception of the Communist bloc*. Despite much earlier predictions and reports by outside analysts, policy-makers did not begin to accept the reality and possible finality of the Sino-Soviet split until the first weeks of 1962. The inevitably corrosive impact of competing nationalisms on Communism was largely ignored.

The new Administration inherited and to some extent shared *the "domino theory" about Asia*. This theory resulted from profound ignorance of Asian history and hence ignorance of the radical differences among Asian nations and societies. It resulted from a blindness to the power and resilience of Asian nationalisms. (It may also have resulted from a subconscious sense that, since "all Asians look alike," all Asian nations will act alike.) As a theory, the domino fallacy was not merely inaccurate but also insulting to Asian nations; yet it has continued to this day to beguile men who should know better.

Finally, the legacy of the fifties was apparently compounded by an uneasy sense of a worldwide Communist challenge to the new Administration after the Bay of Pigs fiasco. A first manifestation was the President's traumatic Vienna meeting with Khrushchev in June, 1961; then came the Berlin crisis of the summer. All this created an atmosphere in which President Kennedy undoubtedly felt under special pressure to show his nation's mettle in Vietnam —if the Vietnamese, unlike the people of Laos, were willing to fight.

In general, the legacy of the fifties shaped such early moves of the new Administration as the decisions to maintain a high-visibility SEATO (by sending the Secretary of State himself instead of some underling to its first meeting in 1961), to back away from diplomatic recognition of Mongolia in the summer of 1961, and most important, to expand U.S. military assistance to South Vietnam that winter on the basis of the much more tentative Eisenhower commitment. It should be added that the increased commitment to Vietnam was also fueled by a new breed of military strategists and academic social scientists (some of whom had entered the new Administration) who had developed theories of counterguerrilla warfare and were eager to see them put to the test. To some, "counter-insurgency" seemed a new panacea for coping with the world's instability.

So much for the legacy and the history. Any new Administration inherits both complicated problems and simplistic views of the world. But surely among the policy-makers of the Kennedy and Johnson Administrations there were men who would warn of the dangers of an open-ended commitment to the Vietnam quagmire?

This raises a central question, at the heart of the policy process: Where were the experts, the doubters, and the dissenters? Were they there at all, and if so, what happened to them?

The answer is complex but instructive.

In the first place, the American government was sorely *lacking in real Vietnam or Indochina expertise*. Originally treated as an adjunct of Embassy

Paris, our Saigon embassy and the Vietnam Desk at State were largely staffed from 1954 onward by French-speaking Foreign Service personnel of narrowly European experience. Such diplomats were even more closely restricted than the normal embassy officer—by cast of mind as well as language—to contacts with Vietnam's French-speaking urban elites. For instance, Foreign Service linguists in Portugal are able to speak with the peasantry if they get out of Lisbon and choose to do so; not so the French speakers of Embassy Saigon.

In addition, the *shadow of the "loss of China"* distorted Vietnam reporting. Career officers in the Department, and especially those in the field, had not forgotten the fate of their World War II colleagues who wrote in frankness from China and were later pilloried by Senate committees for critical comments on the Chinese Nationalists. Candid reporting on the strengths of the Viet Cong and the weaknesses of the Diem government was inhibited by the memory. It was also inhibited by some higher officials, notably Ambassador Nolting in Saigon, who refused to sign off on such cables.

In due course, to be sure, some Vietnam talent was discovered or developed. But a recurrent and increasingly important factor in the decision-making process was *the banishment of real expertise.* Here the underlying cause was the "closed politics" of policy-making as issues become hot: the more sensitive the issue, and the higher it rises in the bureaucracy, the more completely the experts are excluded while the harassed senior generalists take over (that is, the Secretaries, Undersecretaries, and Presidential Assistants). The frantic skimming of briefing papers in the back seats of limousines is no substitute for the presence of specialists; furthermore, in times of crisis such papers are deemed "too sensitive" even for review by the specialists. Another underlying cause of this banishment, as Vietnam became more critical, was the replacement of the experts, who were generally and increasingly pessimistic, by men described as "can-do guys," loyal and energetic fixers unsoured by expertise. In early 1965, when I confided my growing policy doubts to an older colleague on the NSC staff, he assured me that the smartest thing both of us could do was to "steer clear of the whole Vietnam mess"; the gentleman in question had the misfortune to be a "can-do guy," however, and is now highly placed in Vietnam, under orders to solve the mess.

Despite the banishment of the experts, internal doubters and dissenters did indeed appear and persist. Yet as I watched the process, such men were effectively neutralized by a subtle dynamic: *the domestication of dissenters.* Such "domestication" arose out of a twofold clubbish need: on the one hand, the dissenter's desire to stay aboard; and on the other hand, the nondissenter's conscience. Simply stated, dissent, when recognized, was made to feel at home. On the lowest possible scale of importance, I must confess my own considerable sense of dignity and acceptance (both vital) when my senior White House employer would refer to me as his "favorite dove." Far more significant was the case of the former Undersecretary of State, George Ball. Once Mr. Ball began to express doubts, he was warmly institutionalized: he was encouraged to become the inhouse devil's advocate on Vietnam. The upshot was inevitable: the process of escalation allowed for periodic requests to Mr. Ball to speak his piece; Ball felt good, I assume (he had fought for righteousness); the others felt good (they had given a full hearing to the dovish option); and there was minimal unpleasantness. The club remained intact; and it is of course possible that matters would have gotten worse faster if Mr. Ball had kept silent, or left before his final departure in the fall of 1966. There was also, of course, the case of the last institutionalized doubter, Bill Moyers. The President is said to have greeted his arrival at meetings with an affectionate, "Well, here comes Mr. Stop-the-Bombing . . ." Here again the dynamics of domesticated dissent sustained the relationship for a while.

A related point—and crucial, I suppose, to government at all times—was *the "effectiveness" trap,* the trap that keeps men from speaking out, as clearly or often as they might, within the government. And it is the trap that keeps men from resigning in protest and airing their dissent outside the government. The most important asset that a man brings to bureaucratic life is his "effectiveness," a mysterious combination of training, style, and connections. The most ominous complaint that can be whispered of a bureaucrat is: "I'm afraid Charlie's beginning to lose his effectiveness." To preserve your effectiveness, you must decide where and when to fight the mainstream of policy; the opportunities range from pillow talk with your wife, to private drinks with your friends, to meetings with the Secretary of State or the President. The inclination to remain silent or to acquiesce in the presence of the great men—to live to fight another day, to give on this issue so that you can be "effective" on later issues—is overwhelming. Nor is it the tendency of youth alone; some of our most senior officials, men of wealth and fame, whose place in history is secure, have remained silent lest their connection with power be terminated. As for the disinclination to resign in protest: while not necessarily a Washington or even American specialty, it seems more true of a government in which ministers have no parliamentary back-bench to which to retreat. In the absence of such a refuge, it is easy to rationalize the decision to stay aboard. By doing so, one may be able to prevent a few bad things from happening and perhaps even make a few good things happen. To exit is to lose even those marginal chances for "effectiveness."

Another factor must be noted: as the Vietnam controversy escalated at home, there developed *a preoccupation with Vietnam public relations as opposed to Vietnam policy-making.* And here, ironically, internal doubters and dissenters were heavily employed. For such men, by virtue of their own doubts, were often deemed best able to "massage" the doubting intelligentsia. My senior East Asia colleague at the White House, a brilliant and humane doubter who had dealt with Indochina since 1954, spent three quarters of his working days on Vietnam public relations: drafting presidential responses to letters from important critics, writing conciliatory language for presidential speeches, and meeting quite interminably with delegations of outraged Quakers, clergymen, academics, and housewives. His regular callers were the late A. J. Muste and Norman Thomas; mine were members of the Women's Strike for Peace. Our orders from above: keep them off the backs of busy policy-makers (who usually happened to be nondoubters). Incidentally, my most discouraging assignment in the realm of public relations was the preparation of a White House pamphlet entitled *Why Vietnam,* in September, 1965; in a gesture toward my conscience, I fought—and lost—a battle to have the title followed by a question mark.

Through a variety of procedures, both institutional and personal, doubt, dissent, and expertise were effectively neutralized in the making of policy. But what can be said of the men "in charge"? It is patently absurd to suggest that they produced such tragedy by intention and calculation. But it is neither absurd nor difficult to discern certain forces at work that caused decent and honorable men to do great harm.

Here I would stress the paramount role of *executive fatigue.* No factor seems to me more crucial and underrated in the making of foreign policy. The physical and emotional toll of executive responsibility in State, the Pentagon, the White House, and other executive agencies is enormous; that toll is of course compounded by extended service. Many of today's Vietnam policy-makers have been on the job for from four to seven years. Complaints may be few, and physical health may remain unimpaired, though emotional health is far harder to gauge. But what is most seriously eroded in the deadening process of fatigue is freshness of thought, imagination, a sense of possibility, a sense of priorities and perspective—those rare assets of a new Administration in its first year or two of office. The tired policy-maker becomes a prisoner of his own narrowed view of the world and his own clichéd rhetoric. He becomes irritable and defensive—short on sleep, short on family ties, short on patience. Such men make bad policy and then compound it. They have neither the time nor the temperament for new ideas or preventive diplomacy.

Below the level of the fatigued executives in the making of Vietnam policy was a widespread phenomenon: *the curator mentality* in the Department of State. By this I mean the collective inertia produced by the bureaucrat's view of his job. At State, the average "desk officer" inherits from his predecessor our policy toward Country X; he regards it as his function to keep that policy intact— under glass, untampered with, and dusted—so that he may pass it on in two to four years to his successor. And such curatorial service generally merits promotion within the system. (Maintain the status quo, and you will stay out of trouble.) In some circumstances, the inertia bred by such an outlook can act as a brake against rash innovation. But on many issues, this inertia sustains the momentum of bad policy and unwise commitments—momentum that might otherwise have been resisted within the ranks. Clearly, Vietnam is such an issue.

To fatigue and inertia must be added the factor of internal confusion. Even among the "architects" of our Vietnam commitment, there has been persistent *confusion as to what type of war we were fighting* and, as a direct consequence, *confusion as to how to end that war.* (The "credibility gap" is, in part, a reflection of such internal confusion.) Was it, for instance, a civil war, in which case counterinsurgency might suffice? Or was it a war of international aggression? (This might invoke SEATO or UN commitment.) Who was the aggressor —and the "real enemy"? The Viet Cong? Hanoi? Peking? Moscow? International Communism? Or maybe "Asian Communism"? Differing enemies dictated differing strategies and tactics. And confused throughout, in like fashion, was the question of American objectives; your objectives depended on whom you were fighting and why. I shall not forget my assignment from an Assistant Secretary of State in March, 1964: to draft a speech for Secretary McNamara which would, *inter alia,* once and for all dispose of the canard that the Vietnam conflict was a civil war. "But in some ways, of course," I mused, "it *is* a civil war." "Don't play word games with me!" snapped the Assistant Secretary.

Similar confusion beset the concept of "negotiations"—anathema to much of official Washington from 1961 to 1965. Not until April, 1965, did "unconditional discussions" become respectable, via a presidential speech; even then the Secretary of State stressed privately to newsmen that nothing had changed, since "discussions" were by no means the same as "negotiations." Months later that issue was resolved. But it took even longer to obtain a fragile internal agreement that negotiations might include the Viet Cong as something other than an appendage to Hanoi's delegation. Given such confusion as to the whos and whys of our Vietnam commitment, it is not surprising, as Theodore Draper has written, that policy-makers find it so difficult to agree on how to end the war.

Of course, one force—a constant in the vortex of commitment—was that of *wishful thinking.* I partook of it myself at many times. I did so especially during Washington's struggle with Diem in the autumn of 1963 when some of us at State believed that for once, in dealing with a difficult client state, the U.S. government could use the leverage of our economic and military assistance to make good things happen, instead of being led around by the nose by men like Chiang Kai-shek and Syngman Rhee (and, in that particular instance, by Diem). If we could prove that point, I thought, and move into a new day, with or without Diem, then Vietnam was well worth the effort. Later came the wishful thinking of the air-strike planners in the late autumn of 1964; there were those who actually thought that after six weeks of air strikes, the North Vietnamese would come crawling to us to ask for peace talks. And what, someone asked in one of the meetings of the time, if they don't? The answer was that we would bomb for another four weeks, and that would do the trick. And a few weeks later came one instance of wishful thinking that was symptomatic of good men misled: in January, 1965, I encountered one of the very highest figures in the Administration at a dinner, drew him aside, and told him of my worries about the air-strike option. He told me that I really shouldn't worry; it was his conviction that before any such plans could be put into effect, a neutralist government would come to power in Saigon that would politely invite us out. And finally, there was the recurrent wishful thinking that sustained many of us through the trying months of 1965–1966 after the air strikes had begun: that surely, somehow, one way or another, we would "be in a conference in six months," and the escalatory spiral would be suspended. The basis of our hope: "It simply can't go on."

As a further influence on policy-makers I would cite the factor of *bureaucratic detachment.* By this I mean what at best might be termed the professional callousness of the surgeon (and indeed, medical lingo—the "surgical strike" for instance—seemed to crop up in the euphemisms of the times). In Washington the semantics of the military muted the reality of war for the civilian policy-makers. In quiet, air-conditioned, thick-carpeted rooms, such terms as "systematic pressure," "armed reconnaissance," "targets of opportunity," and even "body count" seemed to breed a sort of games-theory detachment. Most memorable to me was a moment in the late 1964 target planning when the question under discussion was how heavy our bombing should be, and how extensive our strafing, at some midpoint in the projected pattern of systematic pressure. An Assistant Secretary of State resolved the point in the following words: "It seems to me that our orchestration should be mainly violins, but with periodic touches of brass." Perhaps the biggest shock of my return to Cambridge, Massachusetts, was the realization that the young men, the flesh and blood I taught and saw on these university streets, were potentially some of the numbers on the charts of those faraway planners. In a curious sense, Cambridge is closer to this war than Washington.

There is an unprovable factor that relates to bureaucratic detachment: the ingredient of *crypto-racism*. I do not mean to imply any conscious contempt for Asian loss of life on the part of Washington officials. But I do mean to imply that bureaucratic detachment may well be compounded by a traditional Western sense that there are so many Asians, after all; that Asians have a fatalism about life and a disregard for its loss; that they are cruel and barbaric to their own people; and that they are very different from us (and all look alike?). And I *do* mean to imply that the upshot of such subliminal views is a subliminal question whether Asians, and particularly Asian peasants, and most particularly Asian Communists, are really people—like you and me. To put the matter another way: would we have pursued quite such policies—and quite such military tactics—if the Vietnamese were white?

It is impossible to write of Vietnam decision-making without writing about language. Throughout the conflict, words have been of paramount importance. I refer here to the impact of *rhetorical escalation* and to the *problem of over-sell*. In an important sense, Vietnam has become of crucial significance to us *because we have said that it is of crucial significance*. (The issue obviously relates to the public relations preoccupation described earlier.)

The key here is domestic politics: the need to sell the American people, press, and Congress on support for an unpopular and costly war in which the objectives themselves have been in flux. To sell means to persuade, and to persuade means rhetoric. As the difficulties and costs have mounted, so has the definition of the stakes. This is not to say that rhetorical escalation is an orderly process; executive prose is the product of many writers, and some concepts—North Vietnamese infiltration, America's "national honor," Red China as the chief enemy—have entered the rhetoric only gradually and even sporadically. But there is an upward spiral nonetheless. And once you have *said* that the American Experiment itself stands or falls on the Vietnam outcome, you have thereby created a national stake far beyond any earlier stakes.

Crucial throughout the process of Vietnam decision-making was a conviction among many policy-makers: that Vietnam posed a *fundamental test of America's national will*. Time and again I was told by men reared in the tradition of Henry L. Stimson that all we needed was the will, and we would then prevail. Implicit in such a view, it seemed to me, was a curious assumption that Asians lacked will, or at least that in a contest between Asian and Anglo-Saxon wills, the non-Asians must prevail. A corollary to the persistent belief in will was a *fascination with power* and an awe in the face of the power America possessed as no nation or civilization ever before. Those who doubted our role in Vietnam were said to shrink from the burdens of power, the obligations of power, the uses of power, the responsibility of power. By implication, such men were soft-headed and effete.

Finally, no discussion of the factors and forces at work on Vietnam policy-makers can ignore the central fact of *human ego investment*. Men who have participated in a decision develop a stake in that decision. As they participate in further, related decisions, their stake increases. It might have been possible to dissuade a man of strong self-confidence at an early stage of the ladder of decision; but it is infinitely harder at later stages since a change of mind there usually involves implicit or explicit repudiation of a chain of previous decisions.

To put it bluntly: at the heart of the Vietnam calamity is a group of able, dedicated men who have been regularly and repeatedly wrong—and whose standing with their contemporaries, and more important, with history, depends, as they see it, on being proven right. These are not men who can be asked to extricate themselves from error.

The various ingredients I have cited in the making of Vietnam policy have created a variety of results, most of them fairly obvious. Here are some that seem to me most central:

Throughout the conflict, there has been *persistent and repeated miscalculation* by virtually all the actors, in high echelons and low, whether dove, hawk, or something else. To cite one simple example among many: in late 1964 and early 1965, some peace-seeking planners at State who strongly opposed the projected bombing of the North urged that, instead, American ground forces be sent to South Vietnam; this would, they said, increase our bargaining leverage against the North—our "chips"—and would give us something to negotiate about (the withdrawal of our forces) at an early peace conference. Simultaneously, the air-strike option was urged by many in the military who were dead set against American participation in "another land war in Asia"; they were joined by other civilian peace-seekers who wanted to bomb Hanoi into early negotiations. By late 1965, we had ended up with the worst of all worlds: ineffective and costly air strikes against the North, spiraling ground forces in the South, and no negotiations in sight.

Throughout the conflict as well, there has been *a steady give-in to pressures for a military solution* and only minimal and sporadic efforts at a diplomatic and political solution. In part this resulted from the confusion (earlier cited) among the civilians—confusion regarding objectives and strategy. And in part this resulted from the self-enlarging nature of military investment. Once air strikes and particularly ground forces were introduced, our investment itself had transformed the original stakes. More air power was needed to protect the ground forces; and then more ground forces to protect the ground forces. And needless to say, the military mind develops its own momentum in the absence of clear guidelines from the civilians. Once asked to save South Vietnam, rather than to "advise" it, the American military could not but press for escalation. In addition, sad to report, assorted military constituencies, once involved in Vietnam, have had a series of cases to prove: for instance, the utility not only of air power (the Air Force) but of supercarrier-based air power (the Navy). Also, Vietnam policy has suffered from one ironic byproduct of Secretary McNamara's establishment of civilian control at the Pentagon: in the face of such control, interservice rivalry has given way to a united front among the military—reflected in the new but recurrent phenomenon of JCS unanimity. In conjunction with traditional congressional allies (mostly Southern senators and representatives) such a united front would pose a formidable problem for any President.

Throughout the conflict, there have been *missed opportunities, large and small, to disengage ourselves from Vietnam on increasingly unpleasant but still acceptable terms.* Of the many moments from 1961 onward, I shall cite only one, the last and most important opportunity that was lost: in the summer of 1964 the President instructed his chief advisers to prepare for him as wide a range of Vietnam options as possible for postelection consideration and decision. He explicitly asked that all options be laid out. What happened next was, in effect, Lyndon Johnson's slow-motion Bay of Pigs. For the advisers so effectively converged on one single option—juxtaposed against two other, phony options (in effect, blowing up the world, or scuttle-and-run)—that the President was confronted with unanimity for bombing the North from all his trusted counselors. Had he been more confident in foreign affairs, had he been deeply informed on Vietnam and Southeast Asia, and had he raised some hard questions that unanimity had submerged, this President could have used the largest electoral mandate in history to de-escalate in Vietnam, in the clear expectation that at the worst a neutralist government would come to power in Saigon and politely invite us out. Today, many lives and dollars later, such an alternative has become an elusive and infinitely more expensive possibility.

In the course of these years, another result of Vietnam decision-making has been *the abuse and distortion of history.* Vietnamese, Southeast Asian, and Far Eastern history has been rewritten by our policy-makers, and their spokesmen, to conform with the alleged necessity of our presence in Vietnam. Highly dubious analogies from our experience elsewhere—the "Munich" sellout and "containment" from Europe, the Malayan insurgency and the Korean War from Asia—have been imported in order to justify our actions. And more recent events have been fitted to the Procrustean bed of Vietnam. Most notably, the change of power in Indonesia in 1965–1966 has been ascribed to our Vietnam presence; and virtually all progress in the Pacific region—the rise of regionalism, new forms of cooperation, and mounting growth rates—has been similarly explained. The Indonesian allegation is undoubtedly false (I tried to prove it, during six months of careful investigation at the White House, and had to confess failure); the regional allegation is patently unprovable in either direction (except, of course, for the clear fact that the economies of both Japan and Korea have profited enormously from our Vietnam-related procurement in these countries; but that is a costly and highly dubious form of foreign aid).

There is a final result of Vietnam policy I would cite that holds potential danger for the future of American foreign policy: *the rise of a new breed of American ideologues who see Vietnam as the ultimate test of their doctrine.* I have in mind those men in Washington who have given a new life to the missionary impulse in American foreign relations: who believe that this nation, in this era, has received a threefold endowment that can transform the world. As they see it, that endowment is composed of, first, our unsurpassed military might; second, our clear technological supremacy; and third, our allegedly invincible benevolence (our "altruism," our affluence, our lack of territorial aspirations). Together, it is argued, this threefold endowment provides us with the opportunity and the obligation to ease the nations of the earth toward modernization and stability: toward a full-fledged *Pax Americana Technocratica.* In reaching toward this goal, Vietnam is viewed as the last and crucial test. Once we have succeeded there, the road ahead is clear. In a sense, these men are our counterpart to the visionaries of Communism's radical left: they are technocracy's own Maoists. They do not govern Washington today. But their doctrine rides high.

Long before I went into government, I was told a story about Henry L. Stimson that seemed to me pertinent during the years that I watched the Vietnam tragedy unfold—and participated in that tragedy. It seems to me more pertinent than ever as we move toward the election of 1968.

In his waning years Stimson was asked by an anxious questioner, "Mr. Secretary, how on earth can we ever bring peace to the world?" Stimson is said to have answered: "You begin by bringing to Washington a small handful of able men who believe that the achievement of peace is possible.

"You work them to the bone until they no longer believe that it is possible.

"And then you throw them out—and bring in a new bunch who believe that it is possible."

To Master the Third World

GABRIEL KOLKO

There is no comprehensive theory of the contemporary world crisis. That both conventional academic or Left scholars have failed or been unable to assess the causes and meaning of the most significant events of our time in large part reflects their unwillingness to confront directly the nature of American interest and power. Theories of imperialism are now the dry-as-dust topics of academic tomes, and all too few have made a serious effort to scratch beneath the ideology of American expansion to define its larger needs, imperatives, and functions as a system.

Earlier studies of imperialism left no doubt as to what one had to examine in order to comprehend the role of a state in the world. Whether it was imperialist rivalries for economic and strategic power, the atavism of feudal ideologies, reaction and counterrevolution, or the desire to integrate and stabilize a world economy, the study of foreign policy was specific, real, and discounted the notion of error, myth, and exuberance as the sources of conduct as explanations sufficient only for national patriots. American scholars have not translated their ability to perceive correctly the roots of diplomacy in the past into a description of contemporary American policy, even though the same categories and analogies may be equally relevant today.

To understand the unique economic interests and aspirations of the United States in the world, and the degree to which it benefits or loses within the existing distribution and structure of power and the world economy, is to define a crucial basis for comprehending as well as predicting its role overseas. The nature of the international crisis, and the limited American responses to it, tell us why the United States is in Vietnam and why in fact American intervention inevitably colors the direction of the vast changes in the world political and social system which are the hallmarks of modern history. In brief, the manner in which the United States has expanded its problems and objectives overseas, transforming the American crisis into a global one, also explains its consistent interventionism.

It is critical, as part of a comprehensive theory of the world crisis, to study the control and organization of the international economy, who gains and who loses in it, and how we have arrived at the present impasse. We should neither dismiss nor make too much of the issue of ideology or the less systematic belief, as former Secretary of Defense James Forrestal once put it, that ". . . our security is not merely the capacity or ability to repel invasion, it is our ability to contribute to the reconstruction of the world. . . ." For American ideology is a vague synthesis that embodies, once its surface is scratched, economic and strategic objectives and priorities that a thin rhetoric rationalizes into doctrines more interesting for what they imply than for what they state. . . . I shall deal only with the structure and the material components of the world economy that set the context for the repeated local interventions and crises that are the major characteristics of the modern world scene.

The role of raw materials is qualitative rather than merely quantitative, and neither volume nor price can measure their ultimate significance and consequences. The economies and technologies of the advanced industrial nations, the United States in particular, are so intricate that the removal of even a small part, as in a watch, can stop the mechanism. The steel industry must add approximately thirteen pounds of manganese to each ton of steel, and though the weight and value of the increase is a tiny fraction of the total, a modern diversified steel industry *must* have manganese. The same analogy is true of the entire relationship between the industrial and so-called developing nations: The nations of the Third World may be poor, but in the last analysis the industrial world needs their resources more than these nations need the West, for poverty is nothing new to peasantry cut off from export sectors, and trading with industrial states has not ended their subsistence living standards. In case of a total rupture between the industrial and supplier nations, it is the population of the industrial world that proportionately will suffer the most.

Since the Second World War the leaders of the United States have been acutely aware of their vital reliance on raw materials, and the fact, to quote Paul G. Hoffman, former Marshall Plan administrator, that ". . . our own dynamic economy has made us dependent on the outside world for many critical raw materials." Successive Administrations have been incessantly concerned over the ability and necessity of the United States to develop these resources everywhere, given the paucity of local capital and technology, and their interest extends far beyond short-term profits of investment. In areas such as Africa this obsession has defined American policy on every major issue.

At the beginning of this century the United States was a net earner in the export of minerals and commodities, but by 1926–30 it had a vast annual deficit of crude materials, and in 1930 imported 5 percent of its iron ore, 64 percent of its bauxite (aluminum), 65 percent of its copper, 9 percent of its lead, and 4 percent of its zinc. Imports of these five critical metals by 1960 had increased to 32 percent for iron ore, 98 percent for bauxite, 35 percent for lead, and 60 percent for zinc, and only in the case of copper declined to 46 percent. As a percentage of the new supply, the United States in 1956 imported at least 80 percent of thirty-nine necessary commodities, 50 to 79 percent of fifteen commodities, 10 to 49 percent of twenty commodities, and less than 10 percent of another twenty-three—all with a total import value of $6.6 billion. There was no doubt, as one Senate report concluded in 1954, that Washington knew that should the mineral-rich nations cut off these sources, "To a very dangerous extent, the vital security of this Nation is in serious jeopardy."

By 1956–60 the United States was importing over half of all its required metals and almost 60 percent of its wool. It imported all tropical foodstuffs, such as cocoa, coffee, and bananas, as well as over half the sugar supply. When, in 1963, Resources for the Future completed its monumental survey of raw materials and projected American needs for the next forty years, it predicted a vast multiplication of American demands that made imperative, in its estimate, ". . . that in the future even larger amounts of certain items will have to be drawn from foreign sources if demand is to be satisfied without marked increases in cost." Its medium projections suggested immensely increased needs for nearly all metals, ranging as high as nine times for molybdenum to about two and one-half times for lead. Within three years, however, all of the critical output, consumption, and population assumptions upon which the Resources for the Future experts based their speculations proved to be far too conservative, the omnivorous demands of the economy were far greater than they had expected.

A critical shift in the location of the world's most vital mineral output and reserves has accompanied the imperative need for raw materials in the United States. In 1913 the developing nations accounted for 3 percent of the world's total iron ore output and 15 percent of its petroleum, as opposed to 37 percent and 65 percent, respectively, in 1965. Its share of bauxite output increased from 21 percent in 1928 to 69 percent in 1965. The United States share of world oil output fell from 61 percent in 1938 to 29 percent in 1964, as the known world reserves shifted toward the Middle East.

Despite the introduction of synthetics between 1938 and 1954, which reduced by about one-fifth the quantity of natural raw materials needed for the average constant quantity of goods produced in the industrial nations, the vast increase in world industrial output has more than compensated for the shift and greatly increased pressures on raw materials supplies from the industrial nations. In effect, the United States has become more dependent on imported raw materials as its share of the consumption of the world's total has declined sharply in the face of European and Japanese competition for supplies. The United States, which consumed slightly less than half of the world's total output of copper, lead, zinc, aluminum, and steel in 1948–50, consumed slightly over one-quarter in 1960, save for aluminum, where the percentage decline was still great. This essentially European demand, which has grown far more rapidly than in the United States, has challenged the American predominance in the world raw materials trade in a manner which makes the maintenance and expansion of existing sources in the ex-colonial regions doubly imperative to it.

American and European industry can find most of these future sources of supply, so vital to their economic growth, only in the continents in upheaval and revolution. Over half of United States iron ore imports in 1960 came from Venezuela and three equally precarious Latin American countries. Over half the known world reserves of manganese are in Russia and China, and most of the remainder is in Brazil, India, Gabon, and South Africa. South Africa and Rhodesia account for nearly all the world's chromium reserves, Cuba and New Caledonia for half the nickel, China for over two-thirds the tungsten, and Chile, Northern Rhodesia, Congo, and Peru for well over two-thirds of the foreign copper reserves. Guyana has about six times the American reserves of bauxite, and China has three times, while Malaya, Indonesia, and Thailand alone have two-thirds of the world tin reserves, with Bolivia and the Congo possessing most of the balance. Only zinc and lead, among the major metals, are in politically stable regions, from the American viewpoint.

It is extraordinarily difficult to estimate the potential role and value of these scarce minerals to the United States, but certain approximate definitions are quite sufficient to make the point that the future of American economic power is too deeply involved for this nation to permit the rest of the world to take its own political and revolutionary course in a manner that imperils the American freedom to use them. Suffice it to say, the ultimate significance of the importation of certain critical raw materials is not their cost to American business but rather the end value of the industries that *must* employ these materials, even in small quantities, or pass out of existence. And in the larger sense, confident access to raw materials is a necessary precondition for industrial expansion into new or existing fields of technology, without the fear of limiting shortages which the United States' sole reliance on its national resources would entail. Intangibly, it is really the political and psychological assurance of total freedom of development of national economic power that is vital to American economic growth. Beyond this, United States profits abroad are made on overseas investments in local export industries, giving the Americans the profits of the suppliers as well as the consumer. An isolated America would lose all this, and much more.

It is not enough, therefore, to state that nonfood raw materials imports doubled in value between 1953 and 1966, and that $16.6 billion in imports for the food and industrial users in 1966 was vitally necessary to American prosperity. More relevant is the fact that in 1963 the Census valued the iron and steel industry's shipments at $22.3 billion, the aluminum's at $3.9 billion, metal cans at $2.1 billion, copper at $3.1 billion, asbestos at a half billion, zinc at a half billion, coffee at $1.9 billion, sugar and chocolate at $1.7 billion—and that all of these industries and many others, to some critical extent, depended on their access to the world's supply of raw materials. Without the availability of such goods for decades, at prices favorable to the United States, the American economy would have been far different—and much poorer.

To suggest that the United States could solve its natural shortages by attempting to live within its raw materials limits would also require a drastic reduction in its exports of finished goods, and this the leaders of the American system would never voluntarily permit, for it would bring profound economic repercussions for a capitalist economy in the form of vast unemployment and lower profits. While only four or five percent of American steel mill products went to exports in 1955–60, this proportion reached nearly one-quarter in the aluminum and one-fifth in the copper industries. In this context the United States has become a processor of the world's raw materials in a number of fields not simply to satisfy domestic needs but also its global export trade and military ambitions. At home, a policy of self-sufficiency would, in the case of aluminum, seriously affect the building construction industry, consumer and producer durables, and transport industries. The same is true for copper, which is critical for producer durables, building construction, communications, and electric power. Minor metals, of which the United States is largely deficient, are essential to any technologically advanced nation, especially to the chemical, electrical, and electronics industries.

America's ability to procure at will such materials as it needs, and at a price it can afford, is one of the keystones of its economic power in this century. The stakes are vast, and its capacity to keep intact something like the existing integrated but unequal relations between the poor, weak nations and the United States is vital to the future of its mastery of the international economy.

The dominant interest of the United States is in world economic stability, and anything that undermines that condition presents a danger to its present hegemony. Countering, neutralizing and containing the disturbing political and social trends thus becomes the most imperative objective of its foreign policy. . . .

In their brilliant essay on the political economy of nineteenth century British imperialism, John Gallagher and Ronald Robinson have described a process that parallels the nature of United States expansion after 1945:

> Imperialism, perhaps, may be defined as a sufficient political function of this process of integrating new regions into the expanding economy; its character is largely decided by the various and changing relationships between the political and economic elements of expansion in any particular region and time. Two qualifications must be made. First, imperialism may be only indirectly connected with economic integration in that it sometimes extends beyond areas of economic development, but acts for their strategic protection. Secondly, although imperialism is a function of economic expansion, it is not a necessary function. Whether imperialist phenomena show themselves or not, is determined not only by the factors of economic expansion, but equally by the political and social organization of the regions brought into the orbit of the expansive society, and also by the world situation in general.
>
> It is only when the politics of these new regions fail to provide satisfactory conditions for commercial or strategic integration and when their relative weakness allows, that power is used imperialistically to adjust those conditions. Economic expansion, it is true, will tend to flow into the regions of maximum opportunity, but maximum opportunity depends as much upon political considerations of security as upon questions of profit. Consequently, in any particular region, if economic opportunity seems large but political security small, then full absorption into the extending economy tends to be frustrated until power is exerted upon the state in question. Conversely, in proportion as satisfactory political frameworks are brought into being in this way, the frequency of imperialist intervention lessens and imperialist control is correspondingly relaxed. It may be suggested that this willingness to limit the use of paramount power to establishing security for trade is the distinctive feature of the British imperialism of free trade in the nineteenth century, in contrast to the mercantilist use of power to obtain commercial supremacy and monopoly through political possession.

In today's context, we should regard United States political and strategic intervention as a rational overhead charge for its present and future freedom to act and expand. One must also point out that however high that cost may appear today, in the history of United States diplomacy specific American economic interests in a country or region have often defined the national interest on the assumption that the nation can identify its welfare with the profits of some of its citizens—whether in oil, cotton, or bananas. The costs to the state as a whole are less consequential than the desires and profits of specific class strata and their need to operate everywhere in a manner that, collectively, brings vast prosperity to the United States and its rulers.

Today it is a fact that capitalism in one country is a long-term physical and economic impossibility without a drastic shift in the distribution of the world's income. Isolated, the United States would face those domestic backlogged economic and social problems and weaknesses it has deferred confronting for over two decades, and its disappearing strength in a global context would soon open the door to the internal dynamics which might jeopardize the very existence of liberal corporate capitalism at home. It is logical to regard Vietnam, therefore, as the inevitable cost of maintaining United States imperial power, a step toward saving the future in something akin to its present form by revealing to others in the Third World what they too may encounter should they also seek to control their own development. That Vietnam itself has relatively little of value to the United States is all the more significant as an example of America's determination to hold the line as a matter of principle against revolutionary movements. What is at stake, according to the "domino" theory with which Washington accurately perceives the world, is the control of Vietnam's neighbors, Southeast Asia and, ultimately, Latin America.

The contemporary world crisis, in brief, is a by-product of United States response to Third World change and its own definitions of what it must do to preserve and expand its vital national interests. At the present moment, the larger relationships in the Third World economy benefit the United States, and it is this type of structure America is struggling to preserve. Moreover, the United States requires the option to expand to regions it has not yet penetrated, a fact which not only brings it into conflict with Third World revolutions but also with an increasingly powerful European capitalism. Where neo-colonial economic penetration via loans, aid, or attacks on balanced economic development or diversification in the Third World are not sufficient to maintain stability, direct interventions to save local *compradors* and oligarchies often follow. Frequently such encroachments succeed, as in Greece and the Dominican Republic, but at times, such as Vietnam, it is the very process of intervention itself that creates its own defeat by deranging an already moribund society, polarizing options, and compelling men to choose—and to resist. Even the returns to the United States on partial successes have warranted the entire undertaking in the form not just of high profit ratios and exports, but in the existence of a vast world economic sector which supplies the disproportionately important materials without which American prosperity within its present social framework would eventually dry up.

The existing global political and economic structure, with all its stagnation and misery, has not only brought the United States billions but has made possible, above all, a vast power that requires total world economic integration not on the basis of equality but of domination. And to preserve this form of world is vital to the men who run the American economy and politics at the highest levels. If some of them now reluctantly believe that Vietnam was not the place to make the final defense against tides of unpredictable revolutionary change, they all concede that they must do it somewhere, and the logic of their larger view makes their shift on Vietnam a matter of expediency or tactics rather than of principle. All the various American leaders believe in global stability which they are committed to defend against revolution that may threaten the existing distribution of economic power in the world. . . .

The intervention of the United States in Vietnam is the most important single embodiment of the power and purposes of American foreign policy since the

Second World War, and no other crisis reveals so much of the basic motivating forces and objectives—and weaknesses—of American global politics. A theory of the origins and meaning of the war also discloses the origins of an American malaise that is global in its reaches, impinging on this nation's conduct everywhere. To understand Vietnam is also to comprehend not just the present purposes of American action but also to anticipate its thrust and direction in the future.

Vietnam illustrates, as well, the nature of the American internal political process and decision-making structure when it exceeds the views of a major sector of the people, for no other event of our generation has turned such a large proportion of the nation against its government's policy or so profoundly alienated its youth. And at no time has the government conceded so little to democratic sentiment, pursuing as it has a policy of escalation that reveals that its policy is formulated not with an eye to democratic sanctions and compromises but rather the attainment of specific interests and goals scarcely shared by the vast majority of the nation.

The inability of the United States to apply its vast material and economic power to compensate for the ideological and human superiority of revolutionary and guerrilla movements throughout the world has been the core of its frustration in Vietnam. From a purely economic viewpoint, the United States cannot maintain its existing vital dominating relationship to much of the Third World unless it can keep the poor nations from moving too far toward the Left and the Cuban or Vietnamese path. A widespread leftward movement would critically affect its supply of raw materials and have profound long-term repercussions. It is the American view of the need for relative internal stability within the poorer nations that has resulted in a long list of United States interventions since 1946 into the affairs of numerous nations, from Greece to Guatemala, of which Vietnam is only the consummate example—but in principle no different than numerous others. The accuracy of the "domino" theory, with its projection of the eventual loss of whole regions to American direction and access, explains the direct continuity between the larger United States global strategy and Vietnam.

Yet, ironically, while the United States struggles in Vietnam and the Third World to retain its own mastery, or to continue that once held by the former colonial powers, it simultaneously weakens itself in its deepening economic conflict with Europe, revealing the limits of America's power to attain its ambition to define the preconditions and direction of global economic and political developments. Vietnam is essentially an American intervention against a nationalist, revolutionary agrarian movement which embodies social elements in incipient and similar forms of development in numerous other Third World nations. It is in no sense a civil war, with the United States supporting one local faction against another, but an effort to preserve a mode of traditional colonialism via a minute, historically opportunistic *comprador* class in Saigon. For the United States to fail in Vietnam would be to make the point that even the massive intervention of the most powerful nation in the history of the world was insufficient to stem profoundly popular social and national revolutions throughout the world. Such a revelation of American weaknesses would be tantamount to a demotion of the United States from its present role as the world's dominant superpower.

Why the United States Failed in Vietnam

GEORGE C. HERRING

During the past few months [of 1981], a new phrase has entered the American political vocabulary. It is called the "Vietnam syndrome." It was apparently coined by Richard Nixon. As employed by the Reagan administration, it presumably means that America's failure in Vietnam and the backlash from it have been primarily responsible for the malaise that has allegedly reduced the United States to a state of impotence in a menacing world. Doctor Reagan and his associates seem determined to cure the disease. Some of the administration's defenders have even justified intervention in El Salvador as essential to that end; and although the White House and State Department may not go that far, their public statements leave no doubt of their determination to exorcise the Vietnam syndrome.

The notion of a Vietnam syndrome presupposes a view of the war which, although rarely articulated in full, nevertheless clearly influences the administration's foreign policy. Reagan himself has stated—contrary to a long-prevailing view—that Vietnam was "in truth a noble war," an altruistic attempt on the part of the United States to help a "small country newly free from colonial rule" defend itself against a "totalitarian neighbor bent on conquest." He and Secretary of State Alexander M. Haig, Jr. have also insisted that it was a necessary war, necessary to check the expansionist designs of the Soviet Union and its client states and to uphold the global position of the United States. They have left no doubt that they regard it as a war that we should have won. America failed, Reagan recently stated, not because it was defeated but because the military was *"denied permission to win."* Haig has argued that the war could have been won at any of several junctures if American leaders had been willing to "apply the full range of American power to bring about a successful outcome." The defeat was thus self-inflicted, and the consequences have been enormous. "America is no longer the America it was," Haig has stated, and "that is largely attributable to the mistakes of Vietnam."

These views are not, of course, new, nor is it surprising that they have gained credence in recent years. The aggressiveness of the Soviets and the Hanoi regime have made it easier for us to justify our own actions morally and in terms of national security. An explanation of failure which places blame on ourselves rather than elsewhere is probably easier for us to live with. Scholars had begun to revise conventional dovish views of the war

From "The 'Vietnam Syndrome' and American Foreign Policy," © *Virginia Quarterly Review*, LVII (Fall, 1981). Reprinted by permission of the author and publisher.

well before Reagan took office, and films such as *The Deerhunter,* whatever their artistic merit, promoted a form of redemption. What *is* significant is that this now [1981] seems to be the official view and is also a partial basis for major policy decisions. Equally important, it is getting little challenge from Congress and the media, the centers of respectable dissent in the late 1960's and early 1970's. From all appearances, to apply an Oriental usage, 1981 is the year of the hawk.

It seems particularly urgent, therefore, that we examine this view critically in terms of the following very difficult questions: was Vietnam a just and necessary war as is now being proclaimed? Was it a winnable war, our failure primarily the result of our own mistakes? . . .

Let me begin with a caveat. The questions I have just raised cannot now be answered definitively. We are still very close to Vietnam, and it is difficult to appraise the war with the sort of detachment and perspective we would like. The evidence is far from complete. We have no more than roughly 15 percent of the documentation on the American side, and Hanoi has given no indication that it plans to initiate a freedom of information act. More important, some of the major questions concerning the war can never be answered with finality. We cannot know, for example, what would have happened if we had not intervened in Vietnam or if we had fought the war differently. We can do no more than speculate, an inexact science at best.

With these qualifications in mind, we can turn to the essential questions that have been raised about the war and its consequences. For many of those who experienced the Vietnam era, Reagan's "noble war" statement seemed so far off the wall that it could not be taken seriously. But it touched a responsive chord, and this is not surprising. The charges of American atrocities and war guilt that echoed across the land just a few years ago ran across the grain of our traditional sense of our own righteousness. Every war has its elements of nobility, moreover, and it is perhaps proper and even necessary for us to recognize the acts of heroism, sacrifice, and compassion that were as much a part of Vietnam as the atrocities. Certainly it was wrong for us to lay on the veterans the guilt which all of us share in one way or another, and Reagan's statement may have been addressing this point, at least obliquely.

His argument was based on the specific premise that we intervened in defense of a "free government" against "outside aggression," however, and this interpretation badly distorts the origins and nature of the war. In fact, we tried to contain an indigenous revolution that, although Communist led, expressed the deepest and most powerful currents of Vietnamese nationalism. The Vietnam conflict cannot be understood by looking at the situation in 1965, when the major U.S. commitments were made. It is necessary to go back to 1945 or even earlier. The revolution that erupted in Vietnam at the end of World War II sought to eliminate French colonialism and to unify a country that had been divided for several centuries. During the ensuing war against France, the revolution generated widespread popular support, and its leader, Ho Chi Minh, came to symbolize for many Vietnamese the spirit of national independence just as George Washington did for the revolutionary generation of Americans. Ho's Vietminh defeated the French in 1954, despite the massive aid given France by the United States. It would probably have unified Vietnam after 1954, had the United States not stepped in and helped to make permanent a division at the 17th parallel the Geneva Conference had intended to be temporary. The Vietcong revolution, which erupted spontaneously in the south in the late 1950's, and subsequent North Vietnamese support of it, were extensions of the revolution of 1945, a fact which explains their unusual staying power in the face of tremendous adversity. This is not to endow the revolution with a higher morality, as the rhetoric of the antiwar movement frequently did. Its leaders were ruthless in pursuit of their goals and were capable of great brutality toward their own people and others. The point rather is that throughout much of the 30-year war, Ho's revolution represented the most powerful political force in Vietnam, and we can talk of outside aggression only in the most narrow, ahistorical sense.

Moreover, the governments we supported—by and large our own creations—were free primarily in the sense that they were non-Communist. It should be recalled in this connection that our first crucial commitment in Vietnam came in 1950 in support of French colonialism. When the French departed after Geneva, we inherited what was left of the puppet government they had created in 1949. We grafted onto it the trappings of Western-style democracy and gave it a measure of international respectability. But in fact, the government of Ngo Dinh Diem and his successors were narrowly based oligarchies, held up mainly by American power, at times quite repressive, and generally unresponsive to the needs and concerns of the predominantly rural population of southern Vietnam. It can be argued, of course, that they were better than their counterpart in the north and provided an alternative to the many Vietnamese who did not want Communism. This may well be true, but it blurs the issue, and we should be wary in the aftermath of the war of endowing the governments we supported with qualities they did not have.

A third point that must be stressed is this: whatever our intent, the way we conducted the war had a devastating impact on the land and people we professed to be serving. In trying to ennoble our cause, we must not forget the consequences of our actions. We prolonged for as much as 20 years a war that might have ended much earlier, with losses of human lives that ran into the millions. The heavy bombing and artillery fire of the high-technology war we fought permanently scarred the landscape of southern Vietnam, obliterating an area roughly the size of Massachusetts and leaving an estimated 21 million craters. Along with Vietcong terrorism, our military operations made refugees of nearly one-third of the population of South Vietnam. We destroyed the economic and social fabric of the nation for which we had assumed responsibility. Despite the moral pretensions on both sides, it seems evident, as Henry Kissinger once observed, that in Vietnam, no one had a "monopoly of anguish and no one . . . had a monopoly of moral insight."

Finally, I would argue that the major American decisions in Vietnam were made primarily on the basis of self-interest, not altruism. This is a sticky wicket, to be sure. It is difficult to separate the two, and American policy makers certainly felt they were acting on the basis of principle as well as self-interest. To put it another way, however, had it been merely a matter of saving a free people from outside aggression, they would not have acted as they did. At every step along the way, they were convinced that the national interests of the United States required them to escalate the commitment.

What were these interests and why were they felt to be so compelling? From 1950 at least into the late 1960's, we viewed Vietnam primarily in terms of the Cold War and the doctrine of containment, the overarching principle of our Cold War foreign policies. The basic assumption of that policy was that we faced a monolithic, tightly unified world Communist movement, orchestrated by Moscow, and committed to world revolution. We viewed the world as split into two hostile blocs, irreconcilably divided by ideology and existing in a precarious equilibrium. Particularly after the fall of China to communism in 1949, we saw the Cold War as a zero sum game in which any gain for communism was automatically a loss for what we called the "free world." To contain the global Communist menace, we constructed a world-wide network of alliances, intervened freely in the affairs of other nations, and went to war in Korea.

From the beginning to near the end, we viewed the conflict in Vietnam primarily from this perspective. Because the revolution was led by Moscow-trained Communists, we assumed it was but an instrument of the Kremlin's drive for world domination. In the early stages, we felt it necessary to block Communist conquest of Vietnam lest it set off a domino effect which could cause the loss of all of Southeast Asia, with presumably incalculable strategic, political, and economic consequences for the United States. Later, we escalated the commitment because of a felt need to uphold our credibility. We had to prove that we would stand by our commitments to dissuade the Communists from further aggressions that could drastically undermine our global position or perhaps plunge us into a global war.

This leads directly to question number two: were these assumptions valid? Was the war necessary, as many now allege, to stop the advance of communism and uphold our world position? It is impossible to answer these questions with absolute certainty because we can never know precisely what would have happened if we had not intervened. It seems probable that there would have been war of some kind and that Vietnam would have been unified by force. What then? Would the dominoes have fallen in Southeast Asia? Would there have been a new wave of aggression elsewhere? Obviously, we can never know. I would argue, however, that we badly misperceived the nature of the struggle in Vietnam and that we may have exaggerated the possible consequences of a Communist victory.

The containment policy was misguided both generally and in its specific application to Vietnam. The simplistic, black and white assumptions from which it derived never bore much resemblance to reality. Soviet goals were (and remain) as much the product of traditional Russian nationalism as ideology, and they fell considerably short of world domination. The so-called Communist bloc was never a monolith—it was torn by divisions from the start, and the fragmentation has become more pronounced. In the Third World, nationalism and resistance to any form of outside influence have been the driving force. And there has never been a zero sum game. What appeared to be a major victory for the Soviet Union in China in 1949, for example, has turned out to be a catastrophic loss. In most parts of the world, neither the Soviet Union nor the United States has prevailed, and pluralism and fragmentation have been the norm.

In applying the containment policy to Vietnam, we drastically misjudged the internal dynamics of the conflict. We attributed the war to an expansionist communism bent on world domination. In fact, as I have suggested, it began as a revolution against French colonialism. Ho Chi Minh and his cohorts were Communists, to be sure, rigid and doctrinaire in their views and committed to structure their society along Marxist-Leninist lines. But they were never mere instruments of Moscow. The Soviet Union did not instigate the revolution and in fact exerted very little influence on it until after the United States initiated the bombing in 1965. The Chinese Communists exerted some influence in the early stages, but traditional Vietnamese suspicions of China, the product of a long history of Chinese imperialism, restricted the closeness of these ties. "I would rather sniff French dung for a few more years than eat Chinese for a lifetime," Ho Chi Minh once said, expressing Vietnam's deep-seated fear of its larger northern neighbor. Throughout the 30-year war, the Soviet Union and China supported Vietnam when it was expedient to do so, but they also abandoned it at several critical junctures. North Vietnam played the two off against each other for essentially Vietnamese ends—to rid the country of foreign influence and unify it under one government.

Our rigid application of the containment doctrine in Vietnam had fateful consequences. By placing ourselves against the strongest force in an otherwise politically fragmented country, first in the war against France, later on our own, we may have ensured our ultimate failure. By ascribing the war to international rather than local forces, we underestimated the enemy's commitment, a vital point to which I will return later. Our intervention probably gave the war an international significance it did not have at the outset. Indeed, we may have driven the Vietnamese closer into the arms of their Communist allies than they would have preferred to go.

I also believe that we exaggerated the possible consequences of nonintervention. We will never know whether the domino theory would have operated if Vietnam had fallen earlier, but there is reason to doubt that it would have. Nationalism has proven the most potent and enduring force in recent history, and the nations of Southeast Asia, with their long tradition of opposition to China and Vietnam, would have resisted mightily. By making the war a test case of our credibility, we may have made its consequences greater than they would otherwise have been. By rigidly adhering to a narrow, one-dimensional world view, without adequately taking into account the nature and importance of local forces, we may have placed ourselves in an untenable position.

Question number three: was Vietnam a winnable war, our failure there primarily the result of our mistakes, our lack of will, the disunity within our society? Because it has such profound implications for future policy decisions, this is the most important of our questions and deserves the most extended commentary. Those who argue that our defeat was self-inflicted focus on the misuse of our admittedly vast military power. Instead of using air power to strike a knockout blow against the enemy, they contend, Lyndon Johnson foolishly hedged it about with restrictions, applied it gradually, and held back from the sort of massive, decisive bombing attacks that could have assured victory. Similarly, they argue, had Johnson permitted U.S. ground forces to invade North Vietnamese sanctuaries in Laos, Cambodia, and across the 17th parallel, General Westmoreland's strategy of attrition could have worked and the war could have been won.

These criticisms are not without merit. Johnson's gradual expansion of the bombing did give North Vietnam time to disperse its resources and develop a highly effective air defense system, and the bombing may have encouraged the will to resist rather than crippled it as Johnson had intended. A strategy of attrition could not work as long as the enemy enjoyed sanctuary. If losses reached unacceptable proportions, the enemy could simply retreat to safety, regroup and renew the battle at times and places of his own choosing. He retained the strategic initiative.

To jump from here to the conclusion that the unrestricted use of American power could have produced victory at acceptable costs raises some troubling questions, however. Could an unrestricted bombing campaign have forced North Vietnam to accept a settlement on our terms? Obviously, there is no way we can ever know, but there is reason to doubt that it would have. The surveys conducted after World War II raised some serious doubts about the effect of bombing on the morale of the civilian population of Germany and Japan, and the capacity of air power to cripple a pre-industrial society such as North Vietnam may have been even more limited. There is evidence to suggest that the North Vietnamese were prepared to resist no matter what the level of the bombing, even if they had to go underground. The United States could probably have destroyed the cities and industries of North Vietnam, but what then? Invasion of the sanctuaries and ground operations in North Vietnam might have made the strategy of attrition more workable, but they would also have enlarged the war at a time when the United States was already stretched thin. Each of these approaches would have greatly increased the costs of the war without resolving the central problem—the political viability of South Vietnam.

We must also consider the reasons why Johnson refused to expand the war. He feared that if the United States pushed North Vietnam to the brink of defeat, the Soviet Union and/or China would intervene, broadening the war to dangerous proportions, perhaps to a nuclear confrontation. Johnson may, of course, have overestimated the risks of outside intervention, but the pressures would certainly have been large and he would have been irresponsible to ignore the dangers. And even if the United States had been able militarily to subdue North Vietnam without provoking outside intervention, it would still have faced the onerous, expensive, and dangerous prospect of occupying a hostile nation along China's southern border.

Those who argue that the war was winnable also emphasize the importance of American public opinion in sealing our defeat. They shift blame from those who waged the war to those who opposed it, contending that an irresponsible media and a treacherous antiwar movement turned the nation against the war, forcing Johnson and later Nixon to curtail U.S. involvement just when victory was in grasp. As much mythology has developed around this issue as any other raised by the war, and we probably know as little about it as any. Studies of public opinion do indicate that despite an increasingly skeptical media and noisy protest in the streets, the war enjoyed broad, if unenthusiastic support until that point early in 1968 when it became apparent that the costs might exceed any possible gains—and, even then, Nixon was able to prolong it for four more years. Until the early 1970's, moreover, the antiwar movement was probably counterproductive in terms of its own goals, the majority of Americans finding the protestors more obnoxious than the war. Indeed, it seems likely that the antiwar protest in a perverse way may have strengthened support for the government. After 1969, public opinion and Congress did impose some constraints on the government, and the media probably contributed to this. But to pin the defeat on the media or the antiwar movement strikes me as a gross oversimplification.

The problem with all these explanations is that they are too enthnocentric. They reflect the persistence of what a British scholar has called the illusion of American omnipotence, the traditional American belief that the difficult we do tomorrow, the impossible may take awhile. When failure occurs, it must be *our* fault, and we find scapegoats in our own midst: the poor judgment of our leaders, the media, or the antiwar movement. The flaw in this approach is that it ignores the other side of the equation, in this case, the Vietnamese dimension. I would contend that the sources of our frustration and ultimate failure rest primarily, although certainly not exclusively, in the local circumstances of the war: the nature of the conflict itself, the weakness of our ally, the relative strength of our adversary.

The Vietnam War posed extremely difficult challenges for Americans. It was fought in a climate and on a terrain that were singularly inhospitable. Thick jungles, foreboding swamps and paddies, rugged mountains. Heat that could "kill a man, bake his brains, or wring the sweat from him until he died of exhaustion," Philip Caputo tells us in [A] Rumor of War. "It was as if the sun and the land itself were in league with the Vietcong," Caputo adds, "wearing us down, driving us mad, killing us." Needless to say, those who had endured the land for centuries had a distinct advantage over outsiders, particularly when the latter came from a highly industrialized and urbanized environment.

It was a people's war, where the people rather than territory were the primary objective. But Americans as individuals and as a nation could never really bridge the vast cultural gap that separated them from all Vietnamese. Not knowing the language or the culture, they did not know what the people felt or even how to tell friend from foe. "Maybe the dinks got things mixed up," one of the novelist Tim O'Brien's bewildered G.I.s comments in *Going After Cacciato* after a seemingly friendly farmer bowed and smiled and pointed the Americans into a minefield. "Maybe the gooks cry when they're happy and smile when they're sad." Recalling the emotionless response of a group of peasants when their homes were destroyed by an American company, Caputo notes that they did nothing "and I hated them for it. Their apparent indifference made me feel indifferent." The cultural gap produced cynicism and even hatred toward the people Americans were trying to help. It led to questioning of our goals and produced a great deal of moral confusion among those fighting the war and those at home.

Most important, perhaps, was the formless, yet lethal, nature of guerrilla warfare in Vietnam. It was a war without distinct battlelines or fixed objectives, where traditional concepts of victory and defeat were blurred. It was, Caputo writes, "a formless war against a formless enemy who evaporated into the morning jungle mists only to materialize in some unexpected place." This type of war was particularly difficult for Americans schooled in the conventional warfare of World War II and Korea to fight. And there was always the gnawing question, first raised by John Kennedy himself— how can we tell if we're winning? The only answer that could be devised was the notorious body count, as grim and corrupting as it was unreliable as an index of success. In time, the strategy of attrition and the body count came to represent for sensitive G.I.s and for those at home killing for the sake of killing. And the light at the end of the tunnel never glimmered. "Aimless, that's what it is," one of O'Brien's G.I.s laments, "a bunch of kids trying to pin the tail on the Asian donkey. But no . . . tail. No . . . donkey."

Far more important in explaining our failure is the uneven balance of forces we aligned ourselves with in Vietnam. With the passage of time, it becomes more and more apparent that in South Vietnam we attempted a truly formidable undertaking on the basis of a very weak foundation. The "country" to which we committed ourselves in 1954 lacked most of the essential ingredients for nationhood. Had we looked all over the world, in fact, we could hardly have found a less promising place for an experiment in nation-building. Southern Vietnam lacked a viable economy. The French had destroyed the traditional political order, and their departure left a gaping vacuum, no firmly established political institutions, no native elite capable of exercising effective political leadership. Southern Vietnam was rent by a multitude of conflicting ethnic and religious forces. It was, in the words of one scholar, a "political jungle of war lords, bandits, partisan troops, and secret societies." When viewed from this perspective, there were probably built-in limits to what the United States or any outside nation could have accomplished there.

For nearly 20 years, we struggled to establish a viable nation in the face of internal insurgency and external invasion, but the rapid collapse of South Vietnam after our withdrawal in 1973 suggests how little was really accomplished. We could never find leaders capable of mobilizing the disparate population of southern Vietnam. We launched a vast array of ambitious and expensive programs to promote sound and effective government, win the support of the people, and wage war against the Vietcong. When our client state was on the verge of collapse in 1965, we filled the vacuum by putting in our own military forces. But the more we did, the more we induced a state of dependency among those we were trying to help. Tragically, right up to the fall of Saigon in 1975, the South Vietnamese elite expected us to return and save them from defeat. This is not to denigrate the leaders or people who sided with us or to make them scapegoats for our failure. The point rather is that given the history of southern Vietnam and the conditions that prevailed there in 1954, the creation of a viable nation by an outside power may have been an impossible task.

The second point central to understanding our failure is that we drastically underestimated the strength and determination of our adversary. I do not wish to imply here that the North Vietnamese and Vietcong were supermen. They made blunders. They paid an enormous price for their success. They have shown a far greater capacity for making war than for building a nation. In terms of the balance of forces in Vietnam, however, they had distinct advantages. They were tightly mobilized and regimented and fanatically committed to their goals. They were fighting on familiar soil, and they employed methods already perfected in the ten years' war against France. The Vietcong were close to the rural population of South Vietnam, adapted its ideology and tactics to traditional Vietnamese political culture, and used the American presence to exploit popular distrust of outsiders. North Vietnam skillfully employed the strategy of protracted war, perceiving that the Americans, like the French, could become impatient, and if they bled long enough they might tire of the war. "You will kill ten of our men, but we will kill one of yours," Ho once remarked, "and in the end it is you who will tire." The comment was made to a French general in 1946, but it could easily have been said of the Second Indochina War.

Our fatal error, therefore, was to underestimate our adversary. We rather casually assumed that the Vietnamese, rational beings like ourselves, would know better than to stand up against the most powerful nation in the world. It would be like a filibuster in Congress, Lyndon Johnson speculated, enormous resistance at first, then a steady whittling away, then Ho Chi Minh hurrying to get it over with. Years later, Henry Kissinger confessed great surprise with the discovery that his North Vietnamese counterparts were "fanatics." Since our own goals were limited and from our standpoint more than reasonable, we found it hard to understand the total, unyielding commitment of the enemy, his willingness to risk everything to achieve his objective.

The circumstances of the war in Vietnam thus posed a dilemma that we never resolved. To have achieved our goal of an independent non-Communist South Vietnam required means that were either morally repugnant to us, posed unacceptable risks, or were unlikely to work. Success would have required the physical annihilation of North Vietnam, but given our limited goals, this would have been distasteful and excessively costly, and it held out a serious threat of Soviet or Chinese intervention. The only other way was to establish a viable South Vietnam, but given the weak foundation we worked from and the cultural gap, not to mention the strength of the internal revolution, this was probably beyond our capability. To put it charitably, we may very well have placed ourselves in a classic, no-win situation.

FURTHER READING

Richard J. Barnet, *Intervention and Revolution* (1972)

Larry Berman, *Planning a Tragedy* (1982)

Peter Braestrup, *Big Story* (1977)

Bernard Brodie, *War and Politics* (1973)

Joseph Buttinger, *Vietnam: A Political History* (1970)

Michael Charlton and Anthony Moncrieff, eds., *Many Reasons Why* (1978)

Warren I. Cohen, *Dean Rusk* (1980)

Chester Cooper, *The Lost Crusade* (1970)

Bernard Fall, *The Two Vietnams* (1967)

———, *Vietnam Witness, 1953–1966* (1966)

Frances FitzGerald, *Fire in the Lake* (1972)

Robert L. Gallucci, *Neither Peace Nor Honor* (1975)

Stephen A. Garrett, *Ideals and Reality* (1978)

Leslie H. Gelb and Richard K. Betts, *The Irony of Vietnam* (1979)

Philip Geyelin, *Lyndon B. Johnson and the World* (1966)

Allen E. Goodman, *The Lost Peace* (1978)

David Halberstam, *The Best and the Brightest* (1972)

James P. Harrison, *The Endless War: Fifty Years of Struggle in Vietnam* (1982)

George C. Herring, *America's Longest War* (1979)

Stanley Hoffman, et al., "Vietnam Reappraised," *International Security,* 6 (1981), 3–26

Townsend Hoopes, *The Limits of Intervention* (1969)

George M. Kahin and J.W. Lewis, *The United States in Vietnam* (1969)

David E. Kaiser, "Vietnam: Was the System the Solution?" *International Security,* 4 (1980), 199–218

Paul M. Kattenburg, *The Vietnam Trauma in American Foreign Policy, 1945–1975* (1980)

Douglas Kinnard, *The War Managers* (1977)

Walter LaFeber, "The Last War, the Next War, and the New Revisionists," *Democracy,* 1 (1981), 93–103

Anthony Lake, ed., *The Vietnam Legacy* (1976)

Guenter Lewy, *America in Vietnam* (1978)

William L. Lunch and Peter W. Sperlich, "American Public Opinion and the War in Vietnam," *Western Political Quarterly,* 32 (1979), 21–44

Terry Nardin and Jerome Slater, "Vietnam Revised," *World Politics,* 33 (1981), 436–448

Robert E. Osgood, *Limited War Revisited* (1979)
Archimedes L.A. Patti, *Why Viet Nam?* (1980)
Norman Podhoretz, *Why We Were in Vietnam* (1982)
Peter Poole, *The United States and Indochina from FDR to Nixon* (1973)
Gareth Porter, *A Peace Denied* (1975)
Earl C. Ravenal, *Never Again* (1978)
Herbert Y. Schandler, *The Unmaking of a President: Lyndon Johnson and Vietnam* (1977)
Robert Shaplen, *A Turning Wheel* (1979)
———, *Time Out of Hand* (1970)
William Shawcross, *Sideshow: Kissinger, Nixon, and the Destruction of Cambodia* (1979)
James C. Thompson, *Rolling Thunder* (1980)
W. Scott Thompson and Donaldson D. Frizzill, eds., *The Lessons of Vietnam* (1977)
Marilyn B. Young, "Revisionists Revised: The Case of Vietnam," *The Society for Historians of American Foreign Relations Newsletter,* 10 (1979), 1–10

The Nixon-Kissinger Diplomacy

14

Most observers agree that Henry A. Kissinger was a central figure in the history of the 1970s. First as an influential adviser to President Richard M. Nixon on national security affairs (1969–1973) and then as a highly visible and active Secretary of State (1973–1977), Kissinger offered advice and made decisions that reverberated across the globe. In his quest for international stability based on big-power arrangements, Kissinger practiced a personalized diplomacy that made this witty, intelligent man the most travelled Secretary of State in American history. The Nixon-Kissinger policy of détente with both China and Russia suggested that the Cold War was being redefined. Kissinger's secret negotiations permitted American withdrawal from Vietnam. His "shuttle diplomacy" in the Middle East helped to cool Arab-Israeli hostility. His management of the Strategic Arms Limitation Talks led to major agreements.

But Kissinger's legacy was mixed, as the following selections indicate. Interventions and crises in Vietnam, Chile, Cyprus, Bangladesh, Angola, and elsewhere tarnished his record and raised questions about his sense of morality and judgment. His conduct of diplomacy in an administration noted for secrecy, the violation of constitutional rights, and political corruption has raised controversial questions about the Secretary of State's own participation in the "Watergate crisis."

DOCUMENTS

Richard M. Nixon, elected President in 1968, came to office with a reputation as a hard-line Cold Warrior. But the first document, from his memoirs, shows that he saw new opportunities through negotiations to contain the Soviet Union and

637

end the war in Vietnam. One method for doing so was the exploitation of the Sino-Soviet split, sometimes called the "China card." By ending the hostile isolation that had characterized Sino-American relations since 1949, he and Kissinger hoped to play the two Communist giants against one another and reduce their commitment to North Vietnam. The second document, from Kissinger's memoirs, recounts the American movement toward détente with the People's Republic of China. In 1972 the Soviet Union and the United States signed the Strategic Arms Limitation Talks agreements, or SALT-I. The third document is the United States Arms Control and Disarmament Agency's explanation of the two SALT pacts: the Anti-Ballistic Missile (ABM) Treaty and the Interim Agreement on offensive ballistic missile systems. In a September 19, 1974, appearance before the Senate Foreign Relations Committee, Kissinger defined détente and its accomplishments.

Chile became a trouble spot from the Nixon-Kissinger perspective in 1970 when a Marxist, Salvador Allende, was elected president of that South American nation. The United States had attempted to prevent his election. When those covert operations failed, the Nixon administration worked to destablilize his government. The fifth document is a 1975 report from the United States Senate Select Committee on Intelligence Activities—the "Church Committee"—on covert activities in Chile, 1963–1973. The last document is a January 13, 1977, editorial by Anthony Lewis of the *New York Times,* a writer who sharply indicted Kissinger's diplomatic record.

Richard Nixon Recalls His Initial Goals (1968), 1978

For twenty-five years, I had watched the changing face of communism. I had seen prewar communism, luring workers and intellectuals with its siren call of equality and justice, reveal itself as an aggressive imperialistic ideology during the postwar period of the Marshall Plan. Despite the most nobly ringing rhetoric, the pattern was tragically the same: as soon as the Communists came to power, they destroyed all opposition. I had watched the Soviets' phenomenal recovery from the devastation of war and their costly but successful struggle to achieve for communism the selling point of potential prosperity. At home I had seen the face of underground subversive communism when it surfaced in the Hiss case, reminding people not only that it existed, but that its purpose was deadly serious.

In the late 1940s and during the 1950s I had seen communism spread to China and other parts of Asia, and to Africa and South America, under the camouflage of parties of socialist revolution, or under the guise of wars of national liberation. And, finally, during the 1960s I had watched as Peking and Moscow became rivals for the role of leadership in the Communist world.

Excerpts from *RN: The Memoirs of Richard Nixon,* © 1978 by Richard Nixon. Reprinted by permission of Grosset & Dunlap, Inc.

Never once in my career have I doubted that the Communists mean it when they say that their goal is to bring the world under Communist control. Nor have I ever forgotten Whittaker Chambers's chilling comment that when he left communism, he had the feeling he was leaving the winning side. But unlike some anticommunists who think we should refuse to recognize or deal with the Communists lest in doing so we imply or extend an ideological respectability to their philosophy and their system, I have always believed that we can and must communicate and, when possible, negotiate with Communist nations. They are too powerful to ignore. We must always remember that they will never act out of altruism, but only out of self-interest. Once this is understood, it is more sensible—and also safer—to communicate with the Communists than it is to live in icy cold-war isolation or confrontation. In fact, in January 1969 I felt that the relationship between the United States and the Soviet Union would probably be the single most important factor in determining whether the world would live at peace during and after my administration.

I felt that we had allowed ourselves to get in a disadvantageous position vis-à-vis the Soviets. They had a major presence in the Arab states of the Middle East, while we had none; they had Castro in Cuba; since the mid-1960s they had supplanted the Chinese as the principal military suppliers of North Vietnam; and except for Tito's Yugoslavia they still totally controlled Eastern Europe and threatened the stability and security of Western Europe.

There were, however, a few things in our favor. The most important and interesting was the Soviet split with China. There was also some evidence of growing, albeit limited, independence in some of the satellite nations. There were indications that the Soviet leaders were becoming interested in reaching an agreement on strategic arms limitation. They also appeared to be ready to hold serious talks on the anomalous situation in Berlin, which, almost a quarter century after the war had ended, was still a divided city and a constant source of tension, not just between the Soviets and the United States, but also between the Soviets and Western Europe. We sensed that they were looking for a face-saving formula that would lessen the risk of confrontation in the Mideast. And we had some solid evidence that they were anxious for an expansion of trade.

It was often said that the key to a Vietnam settlement lay in Moscow and Peking rather than in Hanoi. Without continuous and massive aid from either or both of the Communist giants, the leaders of North Vietnam would not have been able to carry on the war for more than a few months. Thanks to the Sino-Soviet split, however, the North Vietnamese had been extremely successful in playing off the Soviets and the Chinese against each other by turning support for their war effort into a touchstone of Communist orthodoxy and a requisite for keeping North Vietnam from settling into the opposing camp in the struggle for domination within the Communist world. This situation became a strain, particularly for the Soviets. Aside from wanting to keep Hanoi from going over to Peking, Moscow had little stake in the outcome of the North Vietnamese cause, especially as it increasingly worked against Moscow's own major interests vis-à-vis the United States. While I understood that the Soviets were not entirely free agents where their support for North Vietnam was concerned, I nonetheless planned to bring maximum pressure to bear on them in this area. . . .

During the transition period Kissinger and I developed a new policy for dealing with the Soviets. Since U.S.–Soviet interests as the world's two competing nuclear superpowers were so widespread and overlapping, it was unrealistic to separate or compartmentalize areas of concern. Therefore we decided to link progress in such areas of Soviet concern as strategic arms limitation and increased trade with progress in areas that were important to us—Vietnam, the Mideast, and Berlin. This concept became known as linkage.

Lest there be any doubt of my seriousness in pursuing this policy, I purposely announced it at my first press conference when asked a question about starting SALT talks. I said, "What I want to do is to see to it that we have strategic arms talks in a way and at a time that will promote, if possible, progress on outstanding political problems at the same time—for example, on the problem of the Mideast and on other outstanding problems in which the United States and the Soviet Union acting together can serve the cause of peace."

Linkage was something uncomfortably new and different for the Soviets, and I was not surprised when they bridled at the restraints it imposed on our relationship. It would take almost two years of patient and hard-nosed determination on our part before they would accept that linkage with what we wanted from them was the price they would have to pay for getting any of the things they wanted from us. . . .

The most pressing foreign problem I would have to deal with as soon as I became President was the war in Vietnam. During the transition Kissinger began a review of all possible policies toward Vietnam, distilling them into specific options that ran the gamut from massive military escalation to immediate unilateral withdrawal. A strong case could be made for each option.

For example, it could be argued that military victory was still possible if I would remove the restrictions Johnson had placed on our commanders in the field and allow them to use our massive power to defeat the enemy. The most serious of these constraints was the bombing halt; because of it the Communists had been able to regroup their forces and amass supplies for a new offensive. Those who favored the escalation option argued that just the threat of an invasion of North Vietnam would tie down North Vietnamese troops along the DMZ; that mining Haiphong Harbor would cripple the enemy's supply lines; and that free pursuit of the Communist forces into Laos and Cambodia would blunt their ability to continue making hit-and-run attacks against our forces in South Vietnam. Renewed bombing would reinforce these other moves. That, in essence, was the escalation option. It was an option we ruled out very early.

The opinion polls showed a significant percentage of the public favored a military victory in Vietnam. But most people thought of a "military victory" in terms of gearing up to administer a knockout blow that would both end the war and win it. The problem was that there were only two such knockout blows available to me. One would have been to bomb the elaborate systems of irrigation dikes in North Vietnam. The resulting floods would have killed hundreds of thousands of civilians. The other possible knockout blow would have involved the use of tactical nuclear weapons. Short of one of these methods, escalation would probably have required up to six months of highly intensified fighting and significantly increased casualties before the Communists would finally be forced to give up and accept a peace settlement. The domestic and international uproar that would have accompanied the use of either of these knockout blows would have got my administration off to the worst possible start. And as far as escalating the conventional fighting was concerned, there was no way that I could hold the country together for that period of time in view of the numbers of casualties we would be sustaining. Resorting to the escalation option would also delay or even destroy any chance we might have to develop a new relationship with the Soviet Union and Communist China.

At the other end of the spectrum from escalation was the case for ending the war simply by announcing a quick and orderly withdrawal of all American forces. If that were done, the argument went, the Communists would probably respond by returning our POWs after the last American had departed. . . .

I began my presidency with three fundamental premises regarding Vietnam. First, I would have to prepare public opinion for the fact that total military victory was no longer possible. Second, I would have to act on what my conscience, my experience, and my analysis told me was true about the need to keep our commitment. To abandon South Vietnam to the Communists now would cost us inestimably in our search for a stable, structured, and lasting peace. Third, I would have to end the war as quickly as was honorably possible. . . .

The Vietnam war was complicated by factors that had never occurred before in America's conduct of a war. Many of the most prominent liberals of both parties in Congress, having supported our involvement in Vietnam under Kennedy and Johnson, were now trying to back off from their commitment. Senators and congressmen, Cabinet members and columnists who had formerly supported the war were now swelling the ranks of the antiwar forces. In 1969 I still had a congressional majority on war-related votes and questions, but it was a bare one at best, and I could not be sure how long it would hold. Another unusual aspect of this war was that the American news media had come to dominate domestic opinion about its purpose and conduct and also about the nature of the enemy. The North Vietnamese were a particularly ruthless and cruel enemy, but the American media concentrated primarily on the failings and frailties of the South Vietnamese or of our own forces. In each night's TV news and in each morning's paper the war was reported battle by battle, but little or no sense of the underlying purpose of the fighting was conveyed. Eventually this contributed to the impression that we were fighting in military and moral quicksand, rather than toward an important and worthwhile objective.

More than ever before, television showed the terrible human suffering and sacrifice of war. Whatever the intention behind such relentless and literal reporting of the war, the result was a serious demoralization of the home front, raising the question whether America would ever again be able to fight an enemy abroad with unity and strength of purpose at home. As *Newsweek* columnist Kenneth Crawford wrote, this was the first war in our history when the media was more friendly to our enemies than to our allies. I felt that by the time I had become President the way the Vietnam war had been conducted and reported had worn down America's spirit and sense of confidence.

As I prepared to enter the presidency, I regarded the antiwar protesters and demonstrators with alternating feelings of appreciation for their concerns, anger at their excesses, and, primarily, frustration at their apparent unwillingness to credit me even with a genuine desire for peace. But whatever my estimation of the demonstrators' motives—and whatever their estimate of mine—I considered that the practical effect of their activity was to give encouragement to the enemy and thus prolong the war. They wanted to end the war in Vietnam. So did I. But they wanted to end it immediately, and in order to do so they were prepared to abandon South Vietnam. That was something I would not permit.

Henry Kissinger on Rapprochement with China (1972), 1979

When we completed drafting the communiqué announcing my secret visit to China in July 1971, Chou En-lai remarked that the announcement would shake the world. He was right. Not only was it a sensation for the media; overnight it transformed the structure of international politics. After twenty bitter years of isolation an American emissary had stepped onto the mysterious soil of Peking; and his President would shortly follow. It was abrupt and astonishing, but behind the climax were thirty months of patient and deliberate preparation as each side felt its way, gingerly, always testing the ground so that a rebuff would not appear humiliating, graduating its steps so that exposure would not demoralize nervous allies or give a new strategic opportunity to those who did not wish them well.

We took even ourselves by surprise. Originally we had not thought reconciliation possible. We were convinced that the Chinese were fanatic and hostile. But even though we could not initially see a way to achieve it, both Nixon and I believed in the importance of an opening to the People's Republic of China.

Events came to our assistance, but I doubt whether the rapprochement could have occurred with the same decisiveness in any other Presidency. Nixon had an extraordinary instinct for the jugular. He was less interested in tactics or the meticulous accumulation of nuance; too much discussion of details of implementation, indeed, made him nervous. Once he had set a policy direction, he almost invariably left it to me to implement the strategy and manage the bureaucracy. But though I had independently come to the same judgment as Nixon, and though I designed many of the moves, I did not have the political strength or bureaucratic clout to pursue such a fundamental shift of policy on my own. Nixon viscerally understood the essence of the opportunity and pushed for it consistently. He had the political base on the right, which protected him from the charge of being "soft on Communism." And his administrative style lent itself to the secretive, solitary tactics the policy required. If the NSC system of elaborating options interested him for anything, it was for the intelligence it supplied him about the views of a bureaucracy he distrusted and for the opportunity it provided to camouflage his own aims.

There was a marginal difference in our perspectives. Nixon saw in the opening to China a somewhat greater opportunity than I to squeeze the Soviet Union into short-term help on Vietnam; I was more concerned with the policy's impact on the structure of international relations. Nixon tended to believe that ending the isolation of 800 million Chinese itself removed a great threat to peace. To me a China active in foreign policy would call for very skillful diplomacy to calibrate our policies in the more complicated context that would evolve and that would alter all international relationships. But these differences rested on the same fundamental judgment: that if relations could be developed with both the Soviet Union and China the triangular relationship would give us a great strategic opportunity for peace. . . .

Thus by the end of 1969, America's relationship with the Communist world was slowly becoming triangular. We did not consider our opening to China as inherently anti-Soviet. Our objective was to purge our foreign policy of all sentimentality. There was no reason for us to confine our contacts with major Communist countries to the Soviet Union. We moved toward China not to expiate liberal guilt over our China policy of the late 1940s but to shape a global equilibrium. It was not to collude against the Soviet Union but to give us a balancing position to use for constructive ends—to give each Communist power a stake in better relations with us. Such an equilibrium could assure stability among the major powers, and even eventual cooperation, in the Seventies and Eighties. . . .

. . . Nixon was exposed for the first time to the Chinese style of diplomacy. The Soviets tend to be blunt, the Chinese insinuating. The Soviets insist on their prerogatives as a great power. The Chinese establish a claim on the basis of universal principles and a demonstration of self-confidence that attempts to make the issue of power seem irrelevant. The Soviets offer their goodwill as a prize for success in negotiations. The Chinese use friendship as a halter in advance of negotiation; by admitting the interlocutor to at least the appearance of personal intimacy, a subtle restraint is placed on the claims he can put forward. The Soviets, inhabiting a country frequently invaded and more recently expanding its influence largely by force of arms, are too unsure of their moral claims to admit the possibility of error. They move from infallible dogma to unchangeable positions (however often they may modify them). The Chinese, having been culturally preeminent in their part of the world for millennia, can even use self-criticism as a tool. The visitor is asked for advice—a gesture of humility eliciting sympathy and support. This pattern also serves to bring out the visitor's values and aims; he is thereby committed, for the Chinese later can (and often do) refer to his own recommendations. The Soviets, with all their stormy and occasionally duplicitous behavior, leave an impression of extraordinary psychological insecurity. The Chinese stress, because they believe in it, the uniqueness of Chinese values. Hence they convey an aura of imperviousness to pressure; indeed, they preempt pressure by implying that issues of principle are beyond discussion.

In creating this relationship Chinese diplomats, at least in their encounters with us, proved meticulously reliable. They never stooped to petty maneuvers; they did not haggle; they reached their bottom line quickly, explained it reasonably, and defended it tenaciously. They stuck to the meaning as well as the spirit of their undertakings. As Chou was fond of saying: "*Our* word counts." . . .

The trip [by Richard Nixon to China, February 1972] was increasingly perceived as a great success. As the American public gained hope from the China visit, Vietnam became less an obsession and more a challenge to be mastered. The Administration that had revolutionized international relations could not so easily be accused of neglecting the deepest concern of the American people.

Once more, though, we encountered the curious phenomenon that success seemed to unsettle Nixon more than failure. He seemed obsessed by the fear that he was not receiving adequate credit. He constantly badgered his associates to press a public relations campaign that would call more attention to the China visit. He followed the press carefully, so that any criticism could be immediately countered. He read some commentator's criticism that the Chinese statements of their position in the Shanghai Communiqué were more aggressive than the statements of our position. On March 9, therefore, he sent me a memorandum asking me to make clear to the press the deep thought and analysis that lay behind this "decision" to state our position moderately. His preference for this approach dated back, he said, to a speech he gave in the Soviet Union in 1959, which he urged me to read in his book *Six Crises*. Though Chou En-lai had originally proposed the idea of separate and conflicting statements, though Chou and I had drafted almost all of that part of the text in October 1971 without reference to Washington, and though Nixon had learned of both the approach and the content only after I returned, he wanted me to explain to the press—and I believe had convinced himself—that he had conceived it:

You could begin by pointing out that I made the decision with regard to the tone of the statement of our position for two basic reasons. First, the more aggressive we stated our position the more aggressive the Chinese would have to be in stating their position. As a result of our presenting our position in a very firm, but non-belligerent manner, their position, while it was also uncompromising on principle, was not nearly as rough in its rhetoric as has been the case in previous statements they have issued over the years. . . .

I was determined that in this document, which would be the first time Chinese leaders, and cadres, and to a certain extent even Chinese masses, would ever hear the American position expressed, I had to make the strongest possible effort to set it in a tone which would not make it totally incredible when they heard it. It would not have been credible, of course, had we set forth our position in more aggressive terms because 22 years of propaganda at the other extreme would have made it impossible for the reader of the communiqué, or those who heard it read on radio, to believe it at all if the tone was too harsh.

Nixon, of course, deserves full credit for the Shanghai Communiqué. A President is always responsible for the policy, no matter who does the technical labors. A less courageous President could have pulled back from the separate statements, when I presented them to him upon my return in October, in favor of a more orthodox presentation. This trivial incident does not derogate from Nixon's boldness in his historic opening to China. What it illustrates, however, is the tendency for illusion to become reality, a brooding and involuted streak that, together with starker character traits, at first flawed, and later destroyed, a Presidency so rich in foreign policy achievements. . . .

The SALT-I Agreements, 1972

The ABM [Anti-Ballistic Missile] Treaty is a definitive long-term agreement which contributes in a fundamental way to our security. The possibility of nuclear war has been dramatically reduced by this Treaty. It sets forth at the outset the joint commitment not to build a nationwide ABM defense nor provide a base for such defense. In this undertaking both countries have, in effect, agreed not to challenge the credibility of each other's deterrent missile forces by deploying a widespread defense against them. This is the central consequence of this Treaty, and its importance to avoidance of nuclear war cannot be overestimated. Both major nuclear powers have agreed that they will not attempt to build a shield against penetration by the other's missile forces which serve to deter nuclear attack.

The ABM Treaty limits the United States and the Soviet Union to two ABM sites each—one for the protection of the national capital, and the other for the defense of an ICBM complex. At each site, there can be no more than 100 ABM launchers and 100 associated interceptor missiles. In addition to numerical limitations on ABM launchers and missiles at each complex, the areas permitted for ABM deployment are limited geographically and in size.

To assure that these two complexes do not form a basis for a nationwide ABM system, the two sides agreed that they must be separated by a distance of at least 1300 kilometers (800 miles). In addition, each ABM system deployment area is restricted to a radius of 150 kilometers (94 miles).

ABM radars are an essential element of an ABM system and are its long-lead-time component. Defining appropriate limits on ABM radars—a highly complex subject—occupied a great deal of time in the negotiations. In addition to the technical restrictions on ABM radars specified in the Treaty, there are limitations on the deployment of certain types of non-ABM radars in order to reduce the possibility of their use as elements of an ABM system.

In order to assure further that there would be adequate restraints on ABM capabilities, the Treaty provides for significant qualitative limitations on ABM systems. The two sides agreed not to develop, test, or deploy ABM launchers for launching more than one interceptor missile at a time, not to modify launchers to provide them with such a capability, nor to develop, test, or deploy automatic or semiautomatic or other similar systems for rapid reload of ABM launchers. It was also agreed that these prohibitions included a ban on more than one independently guided warhead for an ABM missile.

An additional important qualitative limitation is the prohibition on development and testing, as well as deployment, of sea, air, space-based and land-mobile ABM systems and components.

Another important element is the agreement that if future types of ABM systems or components based on physical principles different from present technology become feasible, specific limitations thereon will be a subject of discussion and agreement in accordance with treaty provisions regarding amendments. An example of such a future system would be one depending on the use of laser beams for destruction of missile reentry vehicles.

To avoid possible circumvention of the ban on a nationwide ABM defense through developments in non-ABM systems, e.g., antiaircraft surface-to-air missiles, the Parties agreed to prohibit conversion or testing of such other systems, or components thereof, to perform an ABM role. For much the same reasons, they also agreed to restrict certain categories of large phased-array radars. These provisions deal with what had come to be known in this country as the "SAM-upgrade problem" (upgrading surface-to-air defense missiles for an ABM role).

It has been the position of the United States that a limitation on ABMs alone would not make as great a contribution to stability and security as would limitations on both offensive and defensive strategic systems. However, problems over definition of strategic systems made clear that it would be extremely difficult to negotiate a single comprehensive agreement.

The Interim Agreement is essentially a holding action which freezes existing levels of land and sea-based offensive ballistic missile systems until a more complete agreement, taking into account the complex asymmetries and implications involved, can be reached. Both nations have expressed the belief that a permanent agreement limiting strategic offensive systems can be reached before the 5-year duration of the Interim Agreement has expired.

The May 20, 1971, understanding focused discussions of strategic offensive systems on ICBMs and SLBMs, setting aside consideration of bombers and forward based systems.

The inclusion of ICBMs was never at issue. However, SLBMs became the subject of intense discussions. The Soviet Union was engaged in a very rapid buildup of its nuclear-missile submarine fleet, deploying additional sea-based ballistic missiles at the rate of about 100 per year. In the U.S. view, it was inconsistent with the purpose of the interim offensive freeze to leave the Soviet buildup unconstrained. It was only in late April, 1972, however, that the Soviets agreed in principle to limit SLBMs in some way. The final details were worked out during the 4 weeks leading up to the Moscow Summit Meeting.

The Interim Agreement is limited in duration and scope. The first two Articles deal with ICBM launchers. The Parties commit themselves not to construct additional fixed land-based ICBM launchers or to relocate existing ICBM launchers. In addition, they commit themselves not to convert launchers for light or older ICBMs into launchers for modern heavy ICBMs. This constitutes an important qualitative constraint which prevents the Soviets from replacing older missiles with SS-9s, the largest and most powerful missile in the Soviet inventory. Unrestrained growth in the number of SS-9s has been a concern of U.S. strategic planners.

Under the terms of the agreement, both sides are allowed to continue to modernize their existing ICBM forces. However, an understanding was reached that the dimensions of land-based ICBM silos will not be significantly increased.

The negotiators were unable to reach full agreement on the definition of a "heavy" missile to supplement the prohibition on conversion of existing light missiles to heavy missiles. The United States therefore made a formal unilateral interpretation of this matter, stating that we "would consider any ICBM having a volume significantly greater than that of the largest light ICBM now operational on either side to be a heavy ICBM."

The agreement does not cover land-mobile ICBMs. The Soviet Union did not want them included in the temporary freeze, arguing that neither side presently had such a system. Although no agreement was reached on mobile systems, the United States served notice to the Soviets in a formal statement that deployment of operational land-mobile ICBMs during the interim period would be considered inconsistent with the objectives of the agreement.

SLBM launchers and modern ballistic submarines are dealt with in Article III of the Interim Agreement and in the Protocol which accompanies the Agreement.

Taking into account current levels of strategic submarine fleets on the two sides, together with other factors in the U.S.-Soviet strategic equation, SLBM limitations were arrived at as follows: For the U.S.S.R., a ceiling of

62 was set on the number of modern, nuclear-powered submarines, and a limit of 950 established for the total number of modern SLBM launchers on either nuclear or diesel-powered submarines. However, for every modern Soviet SLBM launcher over 740 and up to the agreed ceiling of 950, the Soviet Union must, under agreed procedures, retire older land-based launchers (SS-7s and SS-8s) or launchers on older nuclear submarines. In other words, the 741st SLBM launcher on a modern nuclear-powered submarine must be a replacement for a currently deployed launcher. The rapid buildup which, in recent times, had been taking place in the Soviet strategic submarine fleet was thus constrained.

The United States has, under these arrangements, the existing level of 656 SLBM launchers, and the right to have, through replacement of 54 Titan II ICBMs, up to 710 SLBM launchers on 44 modern submarines.

The conversion of U.S. ICBM launchers to handle Minuteman III missiles and the conversion of current Polaris submarines to handle Poseidon missiles are not affected by the freeze.

The undertakings in the ABM Treaty and in the Interim Agreement are to be verified by national technical means of verification. For the types of obligations contained in these agreements, national technical means of verification are practical and effective. Both Parties have made the commitment not to interfere with the national technical means of verification of the other. This would, for example, prohibit interference with a satellite in orbit used for verification purposes. In addition, the Parties have committed themselves not to use deliberate concealment measures to impede the effectiveness of national means of verification. These commitments are landmarks in the joint effort to bring the strategic confrontation under manageable control.

Related to the question of compliance is the provision for a Standing Consultative Commission. This Commission will meet on a regular basis to consider questions of compliance and other aspects of implementation of both the ABM Treaty and the Interim Agreement.

Kissinger on Détente, 1974

Since the dawn of the nuclear age the world's fears of holocaust and its hopes for peace have turned on the relationship between the United States and the Soviet Union.

Throughout history men have sought peace but suffered war; all too often deliberate decisions or miscalculations have brought violence and destruction to a world yearning for tranquility. Tragic as the consequences of violence may have been in the past, the issue of peace and war takes on unprecedented urgency when, for the first time in history, two nations have the capacity to destroy mankind.

The destructiveness of modern weapons defines the necessity of the task; deep differences in philosophy and interests between the United States and the Soviet Union point up its difficulty.

Paradox confuses our perception of the problem of peaceful coexistence: If peace is pursued to the exclusion of any other goal, other values will be compromised and perhaps lost; but if unconstrained rivalry leads to nuclear conflict, these values, along with everything else, will be destroyed in the resulting holocaust.

There can be no peaceful international order without a constructive relationship between the United States and the Soviet Union. There will be no international stability unless both the Soviet Union and the United States conduct themselves with restraint and unless they use their enormous power for the benefit of mankind.

Thus, we must be clear at the outset on what the term "détente" entails. It is the search for a more constructive relationship with the Soviet Union. It is a continuing process, not a final condition. And it has been pursued by successive American leaders though the means have varied as have world conditions.

Some fundamental principles guide this policy:

The United States does not base its policy solely on Moscow's good intentions. We seek, regardless of Soviet intentions, to serve peace through a systematic resistance to pressure and conciliatory responses to moderate behavior.

We must oppose aggressive actions, but we must not seek confrontations lightly.

We must maintain a strong national defense while recognizing that in the nuclear age the relationship between military strength and politically usable power is the most complex in all history.

Where the age-old antagonism between freedom and tyranny is concerned, we are not neutral. But other imperatives impose limits on our ability to produce internal changes in foreign countries. Consciousness of our limits is a recognition of the necessity of peace—not moral callousness. The preservation of human life and human society are moral values, too.

We must be mature enough to recognize that to be stable a relationship must provide advantages to both sides and that the most constructive international relationships are those in which both parties perceive an element of gain.

America's aspiration for the kind of political environment we now call détente is not new.

The effort to achieve a more constructive relationship with the Soviet Union is not made in the name of any one administration, or one party, or for any one period of time. It expresses the continuing desire of the vast majority of the American people for an easing of international tensions, and their expectation that any responsible government will strive for peace. No aspect of our policies, domestic or foreign, enjoys more consistent bipartisan support. No aspect is more in the interest of mankind.

In the postwar period repeated efforts were made to improve our relationship with Moscow. The spirits of Geneva, Camp David, and Glassboro were evanescent moments in a quarter century otherwise marked by tensions and by sporadic confrontation. What is new in the current period of relaxation of tensions is its duration, the scope of the relationship which has evolved and the continuity and intensity of contact and consultation which it has produced.

We sought to explore every avenue toward an honorable and just accommodation while remaining determined not to settle for mere atmospherics. We relied on a balance of mutual interests rather than Soviet intentions.

Our approach proceeds from the conviction that in moving forward across a wide spectrum of negotiations, progress in one area adds momentum to progress in other areas. We did not invent the interrelationship; it was a reality because of the range of problems and areas in which the interests of the United States and the Soviet Union impinge on each other. By acquiring a stake in this network of relationships with the West the Soviet Union may become more conscious of what it would lose by a return to confrontation. Indeed, it is our expectation that it will develop a self-interest in fostering the entire process of relaxation of tensions.

Cooperative relations, in our view, must be more than a series of isolated agreements. They must reflect an acceptance of mutual obligations and of the need for accommodation and restraints.

To set forth principles of behavior in formal documents is hardly to guarantee their observance. But they are reference points against which to judge actions and set goals.

The first of the series of documents is the Statement of Principles signed in Moscow in 1972. It affirms: (1) the necessity of avoiding confrontation; (2) the imperative of mutual restraint; (3) the rejection of attempts to exploit tensions to gain unilateral advantages; (4) the renunciation of claims of special influence in the world; and (5) the willingness, on this new basis, to coexist peacefully and build a firm long-term relationship.

An Agreement on the Prevention of Nuclear War based on these principles was signed in 1973. But it emphasizes that this objective presuppose the renunciation of any war or threat of war not only by the two nuclear superpowers against each other, but also against allies or third countries. In other words, the principle of restraint is not confined to relations between the United States and the U.S.S.R. It is explicitly extended to include all countries.

These statements of principles are not an American concession; indeed, we have been affirming them unilaterally for two decades. Nor are they a legal contract; rather, they are an aspiration and a yardstick by which we assess Soviet behavior. We have never intended to rely on Soviet compliance with every principle; we do seek to elaborate standards of conduct which the Soviet Union would violate only to its cost. And if over the long term the more durable relationship takes hold, the basic principles will give it definition, structure, and hope.

One of the features of the current phase of United States-Soviet relations is the unprecedented consultation between leaders either face to face or through diplomatic channels.

It was difficult in the past to speak of a United States-Soviet bilateral relationship in any normal sense of the phrase. Trade was negligible. Contacts between various institutions and between the peoples of the two countries were at best sporadic. Today, by joining our efforts even in such seemingly apolitical fields as medical research or environmental protection, we and the Soviets can benefit not only our two peoples, but all mankind.

Since 1972 we have concluded agreements on a common effort against cancer, on research to protect the environment, on studying the use of the ocean's resources, on the use of atomic energy for peaceful purposes, on studying methods for conserving energy, on examining construction techniques for regions subject to earthquakes, and on devising new transportation methods.

Each project must be judged by the concrete benefits it brings. But in their sum—in their exchange of information and people as well as in their establishment of joint mechanisms—they also constitute a commitment in both countries to work together across a broad spectrum.

During the period of the cold war economic contact between ourselves and the U.S.S.R. was virtually nonexistent.

The period of confrontation should have left little doubt, however, that economic boycott would not transform the Soviet system or impose upon it a conciliatory foreign policy. Throughout this period the U.S.S.R. was quite prepared to maintain heavy military outlays and to concentrate on capital growth by using the resources of the Communist world alone.

The question then became how trade and economic contact—in which the Soviet Union is obviously interested—could serve the purposes of peace.

We have approached the question of economic relations with deliberation and circumspection and as an act of policy not primarily of commercial opportunity. As political relations have improved on a broad basis, economic issues have been dealt with on a comparably broad front. A series of interlocking economic agreements with the U.S.S.R. has been negotiated, side by side with the political progress already noted. The 25-year-old lend-lease debt was settled; the reciprocal extension of the most-favored-nation treatment was negotiated, together with safeguards against the possible disruption of our markets and a series of practical arrangements to facilitate the conduct of business; our Government credit facilities were made available for trade with the U.S.S.R.; and a maritime agreement regulating the carriage of goods has been signed.

This approach commanded widespread domestic approval. It was considered a natural outgrowth of political progress. At no time were issues regarding Soviet domestic political practices raised. Indeed, not until after the 1972 agreements was the Soviet domestic order invoked as a reason for arresting or reversing the progress so painstakingly achieved.

This sudden, ex post facto form of linkage raises serious questions.

The significance of trade, originally envisaged as only one ingredient of a complex and evolving relationship, is inflated out of all proportion;

The hoped-for results of policy become transformed into preconditions for any policy at all.

We recognize the depth and validity of the moral concerns expressed by those who oppose—or put conditions on—expanded trade with the U.S.S.R. But a sense of proportion must be maintained about the leverage our economic relations give us.

Denial of economic relations cannot by itself achieve what it failed to do when it was part of a determined policy of political and military confrontation.

The economic bargaining ability of most-favored-nation status is marginal.

MFN grants no special privilege; it is a misnomer, since we have such agreements with over 100 countries. To continue to deny it is more a political than an economic act.

The actual and potential flow of credits from the United States represents a tiny fraction of the capital available to the U.S.S.R. domestically and elsewhere, including Western Europe and Japan.

Over time, trade, and investment may leaven the autarkic tendencies of the Soviet system, invite gradual association of the Soviet economy with the world economy, and foster a degree of interdependence that adds an element of stability to the political relationship.

We cannot expect to relax international tensions or achieve a more stable international system should the two strongest nuclear powers conduct an unrestrained strategic arms race. Thus, perhaps the single most important component of our policy toward the Soviet Union is the effort to limit strategic weapons competition.

The competition in which we now find ourselves is historically unique:

Each side has the capacity to destroy civilization as we know it.

Failure to maintain equivalence could jeopardize not only our freedom but our very survival.

The lead time for technological innovation is so long, yet the pace of change so relentless that the arms race and strategic policy itself are in danger of being driven by technological necessity.

When nuclear arsenals reach levels involving thousands of launchers and over 10,000 warheads, and when the characteristics of the weapons of the two sides are so incommensurable, it becomes difficult to determine what combination of numbers of strategic weapons and performance capabilities would give one side a military and political superiority. At a minimum clear changes in the strategic balance can be achieved only by efforts so enormous and by increments so large that the very attempt is highly destabilizing.

The prospect of a decisive military advantage, even if theoretically possible, is politically intolerable; neither side will passively permit a massive shift in the nuclear balance. Therefore, the probable outcome of each succeeding round of competition is the restoration of a strategic equilibrium, but at increasingly higher and more complex levels of forces.

The arms race is driven by political as well as military factors. While a decisive advantage is hard to calculate, the appearance of inferiority—whatever its actual significance—can have serious political consequences. Thus, each side has a high incentive to achieve not only the reality but the appearance of equality. In a very real sense each side shapes the military establishment of the other.

If we are driven to it, the United States will sustain an arms race. But the political or military benefit which would flow from such a situation would remain elusive. Indeed, after such an evolution it might well be that both sides would be worse off than before the race began.

The Soviet Union must realize that the overall relationship with the United States will be less stable if strategic balance is sought through unrestrained competitive programs. Sustaining the buildup requires exhortations by both sides that in time may prove incompatible with restrained international conduct. The very fact of a strategic arms race has a high potential for feeding attitudes of hostility and suspicion on both sides, transforming the fears of those who demand more weapons into self-fulfilling prophecies.

The American people can be asked to bear the cost and political instability of a race which is doomed to stalemate only if it is clear that every effort has been made to prevent it. That is why every President since Eisenhower has pursued negotiations for the limitation of strategic arms while maintaining the military programs essential to strategic balance.

SALT has become one means by which we and the Soviet Union could enhance stability by setting mutual constraints on our respective forces and by gradually reaching an understanding of the doctrinal considerations that underlie the deployment of nuclear weapons. SALT, in the American conception, is a means to achieve strategic stability by methods other than the arms race. . . .

To be sure, the process of détente raises serious issues for many people. We will be guided by these principles.

First, if détente is to endure, both sides must benefit.

Second, building a new relationship with the Soviet Union does not entail any devaluation of traditional alliance relations.

Third, the emergence of more normal relations with the Soviet Union must not undermine our resolve to maintain our national defense.

Fourth, we must know what can and cannot be achieved in changing human conditions in the East.

We shall insist on responsible international behavior by the Soviet Union. Beyond this, we will use our influence to the maximum to alleviate suffering and to respond to humane appeals. We know what we stand for, and we shall leave no doubt about it. . . .

United States Covert Action in Chile (1963–1973), 1975

The pattern of United States covert action in Chile is striking but not unique. It arose in the context not only of American foreign policy, but also of covert U.S. involvement in other countries within and outside Latin America. The scale of CIA involvement in Chile was unusual but by no means unprecedented. . . .

The most extensive covert action activity in Chile was propaganda. It was relatively cheap. In Chile, it continued at a low level during "normal" times, then was cranked up to meet particular threats or to counter particular dangers.

The most common form of a propaganda project is simply the development of "assets" in media organizations who can place articles or be asked to write them. The Agency provided to its field Stations several kinds of guidance about what sorts of propaganda were desired. For example, one CIA project in Chile supported from one to five media assets during the seven years it operated (1965–1971). Most of those assets worked for a major Santiago daily which was the key to CIA propaganda efforts. Those assets wrote articles or editorials favorable to U.S. interests in the world (for example, criticizing the Soviet Union in the wake of the Czechoslovakian invasion); suppressed news items harmful to the United States (for instance about Vietnam); and authored articles critical of Chilean leftists.

The covert propaganda efforts in Chile also included "black" propaganda —material falsely purporting to be the product of a particular individual or group. In the 1970 election, for instance, the CIA used "black" propaganda to sow discord between the Communists and the Socialists and between the national labor confederation and the Chilean Communist Party.

TABLE I   Techniques of Covert Action: Expenditures in Chile, 1963–73*

Techniques	Amount
Propaganda for elections and other support for political parties	$8,000,000
Producing and disseminating propaganda and supporting mass media	4,300,000
Influencing Chilean institutions (labor, students, peasants, women) and supporting private sector organizations	900,000
Promoting military coup d'etat	< 200,000

* Figures rounded to nearest $100,000.

In some cases, the form of propaganda was still more direct. The Station financed Chilean groups who erected wall posters, passed out political leaflets (at times prepared by the Station) and engaged in other street activities. Most often these activities formed part of larger projects intended to influence the outcomes of Chilean elections (see below), but in at least one instance the activities took place in the absence of an election campaign.

Of thirty-odd covert action projects undertaken [in] Chile by the CIA between 1961 and 1974, approximately a half dozen had propaganda as their principal activity. Propaganda was an important subsidiary element of many others, particularly election projects. (See Table I.) Press placements were attractive because each placement might produce a multiplier effect, being picked up and replayed by media outlets other than the one in which it originally came out.

In addition to buying propaganda piecemeal, the Station often purchased it wholesale by subsidizing Chilean media organizations friendly to the United States. Doing so was propaganda writ large. Instead of placing individual items, the CIA supported—or even founded—friendly media outlets which might not have existed in the absence of Agency support.

From 1953 through 1970 in Chile, the Station subsidized wire services, magazines written for intellectual circles, and a right-wing weekly newspaper. According to the testimony of former officials, support for the newspaper was terminated because it became so inflexibly rightist as to alienate responsible conservatives.

By far, the largest—and probably the most significant—instance of support for a media organization was the money provided to *El Mercurio,* the major Santiago daily, under pressure during the Allende regime. That support grew out of an existing propaganda project. In 1971 the Station judged that *El Mercurio,* the most important opposition publication, could not survive pressure from the Allende government, including intervention in the newsprint market and the withdrawal of government advertising. The 40 Committee [a Sub-Cabinet level body of the executive branch which reviewed covert plans] authorized $700,000 for *El Mercurio* on September 9, 1971, and added another $965,000 to that authorization on April 11, 1972. A CIA project renewal memorandum concluded that *El Mercurio* and other media outlets supported by the Agency had played an important role in setting the stage for the September 11, 1973, military coup which overthrew Allende.

Through its covert activities in Chile, the U.S. government sought to influence the actions of a wide variety of institutions and groups in Chilean society. The specific intent of those activities ran the gamut from attempting to influence directly the making of government policy to trying to counter communist or leftist influence among organized groups in the society. That most of these projects included a propaganda component is obvious.

From 1964 through 1968, the CIA developed contacts within the Chilean Socialist Party and at the Cabinet level of the Chilean government.

Projects aimed at organized groups in Chilean society had more diffuse purposes than efforts aimed at government institutions. But the aim was similar: influencing the direction of political events in Chile.

Projects were directed, for example, toward:

- Wresting control of Chilean university student organizations from the communists;
- Supporting a women's group active in Chilean political and intellectual life;
- Combating the communist-dominated *Central Unica de Trabajadores Chilenos* (CUTCh) and supporting democratic labor groups; and
- Exploiting a civic action front group to combat communist influence within cultural and intellectual circles.

Covert American activity was a factor in almost every major election in Chile in the decade between 1963 and 1973. In several instances the United States intervention was massive.

The 1964 presidential election was the most prominent example of a large-scale election project. The Central Intelligence Agency spent more than $2.6 million in support of the election of the Christian Democratic candidate, in part to prevent the accession to the presidency of Marxist Salvador Allende. More than half of the Christian Democratic candidate's campaign was financed by the United States, although he was not informed of this assistance. In addition, the Station furnished support to an array of pro-Christian Democratic student, women's, professional and peasant groups. Two other political parties were funded as well in an attempt to spread the vote.

In Washington, an inter-agency election committee was established, composed of State Department, White House and CIA officials. That committee was paralleled by a group in the embassy in Santiago. No special task force was established within the CIA, but the Station in Santiago was reinforced. The Station assisted the Christian Democrats in running an American-style campaign, which included polling, voter registration and get-out-the-vote drives, in addition to covert propaganda.

The United States was also involved in the 1970 presidential campaign. That effort, however, was smaller and did not include support for any specific candidate. It was directed more at preventing Allende's election than at insuring another candidate's victory. . . .

Most covert American support to Chilean political parties was furnished as part of specific efforts to influence election outcomes. However, in several instances the CIA provided subsidies to parties for more general purposes, when elections were not imminent. Most such support was furnished during the Allende years, 1970–1973, when the U.S. government judged that without its support parties of the center and right might not survive either as opposition elements or as contestants in elections several years away.

In a sequence of decisions in 1971 through 1973, the 40 Committee authorized nearly $4 million for opposition political parties in Chile. Most of this money went to the Christian Democratic Party (PDC), but a substantial portion was earmarked for the National Party (PN), a conservative grouping more stridently opposed to the Allende government than was the PDC. An effort was also made to split the ruling Popular Unity coalition by inducing elements to break away. . . .

As part of its program of support for opposition elements during the Allende government, the CIA provided money to several trade organizations of the Chilean private sector. In September 1972, for instance, the 40 Committee authorized $24,000 in emergency support for an anti-Allende businessmen's organization. At that time, supporting other private sector organizations was considered but rejected because of the fear that those organizations might be involved in anti-government strikes.

The 40 Committee authorized $100,000 for private sector organizations in October 1972, as part of the March 1973 election project. According to the CIA, that money was spent only on election activities, such as voter registration drives and get-out-the-vote drives. In August 1973, the Committee authorized support for private sector groups, but with disbursement contingent on the agreement of the Ambassador and State Department. That agreement was not forthcoming. . . .

United States covert efforts to affect the course of Chilean politics reached a peak in 1970: the CIA was directed to undertake an effort to promote a military coup in Chile to prevent the accession to power of Salvador Allende [a project known as "Track II"]. . . . A brief summary here will demonstrate the extreme in American covert intervention in Chilean politics.

On September 15, 1970—after Allende finished first in the election but before the Chilean Congress had chosen between him and the runner-up,

Alessandri,—President Nixon met with Richard Helms, the Director of Central Intelligence, Assistant to the President for National Security Affairs Henry Kissinger and Attorney General John Mitchell. Helms was directed to prevent Allende from taking power. This effort was to be conducted without the knowledge of the Department of State and Defense or the Ambassador. Track II was never discussed at a 40 Committee meeting.

It quickly became apparent to both White House and CIA officials that a military coup was the only way to prevent Allende's accession to power. To achieve that end, the CIA established contact with several groups of military plotters and eventually passed three weapons and tear gas to one group. The weapons were subsequently returned, apparently unused. The CIA knew that the plans of all groups of plotters began with the abduction of the constitutionalist Chief of Staff of the Chilean Army, General René Schneider. The Committee has received conflicting testimony about the extent of CIA/White House communication and of White House officials' awareness of specific coup plans, but there is no doubt that the U.S. government sought a military coup in Chile.

On October 22, one group of plotters attempted to kidnap Schneider. Schneider resisted, was shot, and subsequently died. The CIA had been in touch with that group of plotters but a week earlier had withdrawn its support for the group's specific plans.

The coup plotting collapsed and Allende was inaugurated President. After his election, the CIA and U.S. military attachés maintained contacts with the Chilean military for the purpose of collecting intelligence. Whether those contacts strayed into encouraging the Chilean military to move against Allende; or whether the Chilean military—having been goaded toward a coup during Track II—took encouragement to act against the President from those contacts even though U.S. officials did not intend to provide it: these are major questions which are inherent in U.S. covert activities in the period of the Allende government. . . .

In addition to providing information and cover to the CIA, multinational corporations also participated in covert attempts to influence Chilean politics. . . .

In 1970, the U.S. government and several multinational corporations were linked in opposition to the candidacy and later the presidency of Salvador Allende. This CIA-multinational corporation connection can be divided into two phases. Phase I comprised actions taken by either the CIA or U.S.-based multinational companies at a time when it was official U.S. policy not to support, even covertly, any candidate or party in Chile. During this phase the Agency was, however, authorized to engage in a covert "spoiling" operation designed to defeat Salvador Allende. Phase II encompassed the relationship between intelligence agencies and multinational corporations after the September 1970 general election. During Phase II, the U.S. government opposed Allende and supported opposition elements. The government sought the cooperation of multinational corporations in this effort.

A number of multinational corporations were apprehensive about the possibility that Allende would be elected President of Chile. Allende's public announcements indicated his intention, if elected, to nationalize basic industries and to bring under Chilean ownership service industries such as the national telephone company, which was at that time a subsidiary of ITT.

In 1964 Allende had been defeated, and it was widely known both in Chile and among American multinational corporations with significant interests in Chile that his opponents had been supported by the United States government. John McCone, a former CIA Director and a member of ITT's Board of Directors in 1970, knew of the significant American government involvement in 1964 and of the offer of assistance made at that time by American companies. Agency documents indicate that McCone informed Harold Geneen, ITT's Board Chairman, of these facts.

In 1970 leaders of American multinational corporations with substantial interests in Chile, together with other American citizens concerned about what might happen to Chile in the event of an Allende victory, contacted U.S. government officials in order to make their views known.

In July 1970, a CIA representative in Santiago met with representatives of ITT and, in a discussion of the upcoming election, indicated that Alessandri could use financial assistance. The Station suggested the name of an individual who could be used as a secure channel for getting these funds to the Alessandri campaign.

Shortly thereafter John McCone telephoned CIA Director Richard Helms. As a result of this call, a meeting was arranged between the Chairman of the Board of ITT and Chief of the Western Hemisphere Division of the CIA. Geneen offered to make available to the CIA a substantial amount of money to be used in support of the Alessandri campaign. In subsequent meetings ITT offered to make $1 million available to the CIA. The CIA rejected the offer. The memorandum indicated further that CIA's advice was sought with respect to an individual who might serve as a conduit of ITT funds to the Alessandri campaign.

The CIA confirmed that the individual in question was a reliable channel which could be used for getting funds to Alessandri. A second channel of funds from ITT to a political party opposing Allende, the National Party, was developed following CIA advice as to a secure funding mechanism utilizing two CIA assets in Chile. These assets were also receiving Agency funds in connection with the "spoiling" operation.

During the period prior to the September election, ITT representatives met frequently with CIA representatives both in Chile and in the United States and CIA advised ITT as to ways in which it might safely channel funds both to the Alessandri campaign and to the National Party. CIA was kept informed of the extent and the mechanism of the funding. Eventually at least $350,000 was passed by ITT to this campaign. A roughly equal amount was passed by other U.S. companies; the CIA learned of this funding but did not assist in it. . . .

The Journalist Anthony Lewis on Kissinger, 1977

Henry Kissinger is leaving office in a blaze of adulation. The National Press Club produces a belly dancer for him and gives standing applause to his views on world peace. The Harlem Globetrotters make him an honorary member. Senators pay tribute to his wisdom.

Historians of the next generation will find it all very puzzling. Because they will not have seen Mr. Kissinger perform, they will have to rely on the record. And the record of his eight years in Washington is likely to seem thin in diplomatic achievement and shameful in human terms.

The one outstanding accomplishment is Mr. Kissinger's Middle East diplomacy. He restored United States relations with the Arab world, and he set in motion the beginnings of an Arab-Israeli dialogue. Of course, the work is incomplete. But to start something after so many years of total failure was a great breakthrough and it was essentially the work of one man: Henry Kissinger.

The other undoubtedly positive entry on the record is the opening to China, but that was in good part Richard Nixon's doing. Also, the beginnings of a relationship with the People's Republic were not followed up as they might have been, and the failure may prove damaging.

With the Soviet Union, Mr. Kissinger took the familiar idea of easing tensions and glamorized it as détente. The glamor was dangerous. It fostered the illusion that détente could prevent conflict all over the world, and many Americans turned sour on the whole idea when it did not. At times Mr. Kissinger himself seemed to believe the illusion—and became apoplectic when it failed as in Angola. Détente's real achievements are scant; not much more than a halting step toward nuclear arms control.

Ignorance and ineptitude marked his policy in much of the rest of the world. In Cyprus, his blundering led to human tragedy and left America's reputation damaged in both Greece and Turkey. His insensitivity to Japanese feelings had traumatic effects on a most important ally.

In dealing with Portugal and its African territories Mr. Kissinger decided in succession that (1) the Portuguese were in Africa to stay, (2) the U.S. should help Portugal's dictatorship, (3) after the dictatorship's fall the Communists were bound to prevail in Portugal and (4) the U.S. could decide the outcome in Angola by covert aid. That parade of folly was matched in his African policy generally: years of malign neglect, then last-minute intervention for majority rule in Rhodesia.

He often talked about freedom, but his acts shows a pre-eminent interest in order. Millions lost their freedom during the Kissinger years, many to dictatorships that had crucial support from his policies, as in Chile and the Philippines. He expressed little open concern for the victims of Soviet tyranny, and he did little to enforce the human rights clauses of the Helsinki Agreement.

Anthony Lewis, "This Way to the Egress," *New York Times,* January 13, 1977, p. 37, © 1977 by The New York Times Company. Reprinted by permission.

The American constitutional system of checks and balances he treated as an irritating obstacle to power. In his valedictory to the Press Club his only reference to Watergate was an expression of regret at "the disintegration of Executive authority that resulted."

Secrecy and deceit were levers of his power; he had no patience for the democratic virtues of openness and consultation. By keeping all the facts to himself and a few intimates, he centralized control. He practiced deceit with a kind of gusto, from petty personal matters to "peace is at hand."

His conduct in the wiretapping of his own staff gave ugly insight into his character. He provided names for investigation—and then, when the story came out, wriggled and deceived in order to minimize his role. He never expressed regret, even to those who had been closest to him, for the fact that their family conversations had been overheard for months. But when someone ransacked his garbage, he said his wife had suffered "grave anguish."

History will remember him most of all for his policy in Indochina. In the teeth of evidence well known by 1969, this supposed realist pressed obsessively for indefinite maintenance of the status quo. To that end, in his time, 20,492 more Americans died in Vietnam and hundreds of thousands of Vietnamese. The war was expanded into Cambodia, destroying that peaceable land. And all for nothing.

With such a record, how is it that people vie to place laurels on the head of the departing Secretary of State? The answer became clear the other night during an extraordinarily thoughtful Public Broadcasting television program on Mr. Kissinger's career: He has discovered that in our age publicity is power, and he has played the press as Dr. Miracle played his violin. He is intelligent and hard-working and ruthless, but those qualities are common enough. His secret is showmanship.

Henry Kissinger is our P. T. Barnum—a Barnum who plays in a vastly larger tent and whose jokes have about them the air of the grave. That we honor a person who has done such things in our name is a comment on us.

ESSAYS

John G. Stoessinger, a political scientist and friend of Henry Kissinger, has written a sympathetic study of the Secretary of State, subtitled *The Anguish of Power.* He commends Kissinger's search for and partial success in achieving a stable world order. In the second essay, Stanley Hoffmann of Harvard University reviews the first volume of Kissinger's memoirs, delineating the diplomat's style, world view, and goals. Critical of Kissinger's anti-Soviet "grand design," Hoffmann also questions his behavior within the American political system. Finally, Hoffmann thinks Kissinger's global view of a Soviet threat obliged him to "universal intervention" and to a tragic misreading of the internal problems of other countries.

Kissinger and a Safer World

JOHN G. STOESSINGER

"I know I have a first-rate mind," Henry Kissinger once told me many years ago, "but that's no source of pride to me. Intelligent people are a dime a dozen. But I am proud of having character."

Henry Kissinger never had much patience with mediocrities or fools. But when, in the rolling cadences of his Bavarian accent, he would describe some luckless academic as a "characterless bastard," he meant to convey a bottomless contempt. Kissinger reserved this ultimate epithet for those unfortunates who did not have the courage to *act* on their convictions. A man who said one thing but did another was even more certain to incur his wrath than someone who had no convictions whatsoever. The move to Washington did little to change Kissinger's opinion. "The worst kinds of bastards in this town," he declared three years after he had come to power, "are those who hold high positions and then go out and say they really didn't believe in Administration policies. If anyone would ever say I didn't believe in what Nixon is doing, I would publicly dispute him. I like the President. I agree with him. We've gone through all this for three years, like two men in a foxhole. . . ."

"Character" to Kissinger, had little to do with intelligence. What he admired was a man's capacity to stand up for his convictions in the world of action, alone if necessary. When, in a rare unguarded moment, Kissinger had said, "I have always acted alone," he had revealed a deep emotional conviction. Even though his intellect reminded him that "a policy that was conceived in the mind of one, but resided in the hearts of none," was doomed to failure, this *emotional* preference for solitude remained. It is for this reason that Kissinger preferred Castlereagh to Metternich. Castlereagh had a grand design and, even though it had "outdistanced the experience of his people," he had found the moral courage to remain loyal to his vision. Metternich, on the other hand, despite his brilliance and his cunning, had never found the courage to "contemplate an abyss as a challenge to overcome or to perish in the process." Thus, he had ultimately doomed himself to sterility, and with him, Imperial Austria.

Among contemporary statesmen, Kissinger most admired those who had not only conceived a vision, but had found the courage to translate it into action, even in the face of anguish and adversity. The fact that most of the men who shared these qualities happened to be adversaries, did not deter him in the least. When as a scholar at Harvard, he was preoccupied with Europe, he had often expressed considerable admiration for the strength and steadfastness of Charles de Gaulle, the *bête noire* of the North Atlantic Treaty. After he had come to power, he spoke with genuine respect of Mao Tse-tung and Chou En-lai and of their courage in adversity. Among his fellow intellectuals, he was most drawn to Hans Morgenthau, even though the older scholar had often attacked his policies on Indochina and the Middle East. But he admired Morgenthau's vision in having been the first to oppose Indochina policy under Kennedy and Johnson and his courage in making that early opposition known despite official ridicule and even harassment.

In Kissinger's hierarchy of values, courage and decisiveness came first. Loyalty, too, was prized by him. Intelligence, even brilliance, he considered fairly commonplace. If they were coupled with indecisiveness and weakness in a man, that combination was sure to arouse Kissinger's contempt. Whether one chose to describe Kissinger's ideal in the romantic terms of Hegel's *Zeitgeist,* or in the more rustic image of an embattled cowboy in a Western town, its essence was the same: a man must know how to think and act *alone.*

A great deal has been written about Henry Kissinger's personal diplomacy. His insistence on conducting important negotiations personally and his habit of establishing close relationships with adversary leaders are well known characteristics of his statecraft. His low opinion of the bureaucracy has also been widely commented upon. This penchant for the solo performance has been variously attributed to Kissinger's "enormous ego," his "obsessive secrecy" or to his "elemental need for power and for glory."

I should like to submit another interpretation. I believe that, in order for Kissinger to succeed in his most historic diplomatic initiatives, he *had to* establish personal dominance over the bureaucracy. To establish such control moreover, he had to act decisively, often secretly, and, at times, alone.

Kissinger had never had much patience with bureaucracy. When a professor at Harvard, he had reserved his most acid comments for university administrators. His tolerance for bureaucracy in government was not much greater. After having studied the American "foreign policy-making apparatus" he had come to the conclusion that it was a kind of feudal network of competing agencies and interests, in which there was a "powerful tendency to think that a compromise among administrative proposals (was) the same thing as a policy." The bureaucratic model for making a decision, in Kissinger's opinion, was a policy proposal with three choices: the present policy bracketed by two absurd alternatives.

Kissinger had been a consultant to both the Kennedy and Johnson administrations. While he never said so publicly, he had been deeply disappointed. So much had been promised; so much less had been attempted and, in his judgment, so little had been done. He had had the opportunity to observe government decision-making from a fairly close perspective. What impressed him most was that the foreign policy bureaucracy had a way of smothering initiative by advocating a path of least resistance. The lawyers, businessmen, and former academics who ran the hierarchy generally seemed to place a premium on safety and acceptance rather than on creativity and vision. The result was that any innovative statesmanship tended to expire in the feudal fiefs of the bureaucracy or come to grief on the rocks of organizational inertia.

There was ample basis for Kissinger's impatience. SALT might have been initiated at the Glassboro summit in 1967, between Lyndon Johnson and the

Soviet leaders, but there had been no decisive leadership. Nor had there been a clear-cut stand on the possible limitation of strategic arms. Instead, there were endless arguments among the Joint Chiefs of Staff, the Pentagon, the State Department, and academic experts in the field of arms control. Similarly, the Arab-Israeli war of 1967 had presented opportunities for American diplomacy and mediation, but there had been no one with a plan, let alone the courage to place himself between competing claims. Instead, there emerged from the bowels of the bureaucracy countless position papers by learned academic experts. There was no agreement on an overall strategy for mediation in the Middle East, only an almost fatalistic sense of hopelessness and drift.

This was the reason why Kissinger decided, immediately after January 20, 1969, to establish personal control over the bureaucracy. Those whom he could not dominate, he would manipulate. And those whom he could not manipulate, he would try to bypass. He embarked on this course of action as a result of a rational decision. He simply feared that *unless* he dominated, bypassed, or manipulated, nothing would get done. He, too, would ultimately be submerged in a long twilight struggle of modern feudal baronies. This he was simply not prepared to accept.

In his position as Assistant for National Security Affairs, Kissinger came to dominate the bureaucracy as no other figure before him had done, and as no other is likely to do for a very long time to come. He promptly established his control through the establishment of a few small committees each of which he personally chaired. These were a number of interdepartmental groups: a Review Group, a Verification Panel for SALT, a Vietnam Special Studies Group, the Washington Special Actions Group for Crisis Control, and the Forty Committee which dealt with covert intelligence operations.

It was out of these committees that Kissinger forged the great initiatives that have assured his place in history: SALT I in 1969, the opening to China after his secret trip to Peking in 1971, and the diplomatic mediation in the Middle East after the October war in 1973. It is true, of course, that some of the more dubious decisions also had their genesis in this small elitist structure, particularly in the Forty Committee. The "destabilization" of the Allende government in Chile in 1971, alleged payments to Italian neo-fascists in 1972, and the denouement in Indochina are some of the more disturbing examples. Only history can provide the necessary distance for a balanced assessment of these various initiatives. But what can already be asserted with a fair amount of certainty is that Kissinger was right in his assumption that, in order to put into effect a coherent global policy, he would have to concentrate as much power in his hands as possible.

Kissinger's pursuit of power had a very clear-cut purpose. During two decades of reflection he had evolved a theory of global order which, in his judgment, would bring the world a few steps closer to stability and peace. Nothing was more important to him in 1969 than the chance to test that theory. He believed with the most absolute conviction that he was the one best qualified. On one occasion, in 1968, when Rockefeller's speech writers had made some changes in a Kissinger position paper, the author exclaimed furiously: "If

Rockefeller buys a Picasso, he doesn't hire four housepainters to improve on it." In Kissinger's own view, this was not an arrogant statement. It was merely the reflection of an enormous, though quite genuine, intellectual self-confidence. He believed, quite matter-of-factly, that he was the Picasso of modern American foreign policy.

Henry Kissinger believed that, in creating a design for world order, realism was more compassionate than romanticism. The great American moralists, in his judgment, had been failures. In the end, Woodrow Wilson had proved ineffectual and John Foster Dulles had turned foreign policy into a crusade that had led straight into the Indochina quagmire. Kissinger did not make peace or justice the objective of his policy nor was he particularly interested in "making the world safe for democracy." He merely wished to make the world safer and more stable. This was a lesser goal, one that offered no illusions, but also brought fewer disappointments. It was also not quite in the mainstream of American history. But then, Kissinger was a European in America, his thought rooted firmly in the European philosophical tradition.

There has been a great deal of confusion about Kissinger's intellectual debt to Metternich for his vision of stability. Kissinger himself has made it abundantly clear that he never looked to Metternich for guidance on *substantive problems* of statecraft: "Most people associate me with Metternich. And that is childish . . . there can be nothing in common between me and Metternich. He was chancellor and foreign minister at a time when it took three weeks to travel from Central Europe to the ends of the Continent, when wars were conducted by professional soldiers and diplomacy was in the hands of the aristocracy. . . ." What Kissinger admired in Metternich was the Austrian diplomat's *conceptual insight* in having recognized the revolutionary character of the Napoleonic challenge, the need to neutralize that challenge without humiliating retribution, and, having achieved that end, his commitment to stability and balance which ushered in a century without a global war.

If Castlereagh taught Kissinger that a statesman must create a vision and remain faithful to it even in adversity, Metternich taught him how to adjust that vision to reality. If Castlereagh taught him about courage and a grand design, Metternich taught him about cunning and manipulation. But when all was said and done, the lessons Kissinger could learn from these two nineteenth century aristocrats were limited. In the end, Kissinger, too, had to stand alone.

Henry Kissinger once told me that a statesman, to be successful, had to have some luck. He knew well that he was no exception to this rule. His appearance on the world stage coincided most fortuitously with a new nadir in the relations between China and the Soviet Union. By 1969, Mao Tse-tung and Brezhnev feared each other more than they feared America, and thus had become more concerned with moderating their relations with the United States than with the pursuit of revolutionary goals of conquest vis-à-vis the West. Thus, the timing of Kissinger's arrival as a world statesman could not have been more fortunate for the particular objective that he had in mind: a new stability in the relations among the world's three great powers.

The drawing up of any balance sheet on the centerpiece of Kissinger's foreign policy—détente with the Soviet Union—must remain a highly personal business on which thoughtful people may have widely differing opinions. Any such analysis must enter in the realm of competing values, since in creating that centerpiece, choices had to be made and a price had to be paid. Hence, it is only fair that, as we enter this discussion, I reveal the basis of my judgment and share my values and prejudices with the reader.

I believe that Henry Kissinger was right when he declared that the overriding reason for détente with Russia was the avoidance of a nuclear catastrophe. I believe that if such a world cataclysm has become less likely, this is in no small measure to be credited to Kissinger. I am fully aware that the American relationship with Russia leaves a great deal to be desired. But there is no question in my mind that the danger of nuclear war has substantially receded. It no longer intrudes into our daily lives the way it did when Kissinger and I were students. Mothers worried about radioactive waste and strontium-90 in their children's milk; and a decade later, John F. Kennedy almost went to nuclear war with Khrushchev over missiles in Cuba. Today, we argue with the Soviet Union about strategic arms control, trade, and human rights, but we no longer live in daily terror of a nuclear exchange. The fearful scenarios that were conjured up in Herman Kahn's *Thinking About the Unthinkable* today read almost like horrible anachronisms. In addition to the elements of luck and timing, it was also Kissinger's design and courage that made détente possible at all.

I know the price that Kissinger has paid on behalf of the United States has been enormous. But, to be fair, we must ask ourselves in each case whether the alternatives would have yielded better results. In strategic arms control, Kissinger's accusers have blamed him for his acceptance in SALT I of Soviet superiority in missile numbers. They have also been suspicious of his lack of interest in alleged evidence that the Soviet Union had violated the spirit and perhaps even the letter of SALT I. Critics have also taken umbrage at his reported willingness—during the SALT II negotiations—to exclude the Soviet Backfire bomber from an overall ceiling while including the American cruise missile.

But the critics, in my judgment, have never given a convincing answer to Kissinger's own question: "What in God's name," he asked in 1974, "is strategic superiority? What is the significance of it, politically, militarily, operationally, at these levels of numbers? What do you do with it?" Kissinger simply did not believe that a marginal "overkill" capacity on either side could be translated into a meaningful strategic or political advantage. To my mind, there is no conclusive evidence that such a translation can in fact be made.

The "great grain robbery" of 1972 was not one of Kissinger's proudest moments. The Russian harvest was so poor that the Soviet leadership probably would have paid a better price. As it turned out, however, the American taxpayer helped to underwrite the Soviet purchases and got in return only a few ephemeral benefits: a little Soviet help in Hanoi and Brezhnev's decision to meet with Nixon at the Moscow summit despite the President's decision to place mines in Haiphong harbor.

Kissinger was right, however, in my judgment, in his dispute with Senator

Henry Jackson over the linking of most-favored-nations status for the Soviet Union with emigration of Soviet Jews to Israel. It was unreasonable for Jackson to couple an international agreement with Russia to a demand for internal changes within the Soviet state. How would Jackson have responded if the Soviet leadership had linked the conclusion of SALT I to a demand for a lifting of all American immigration quotas? The point I am making is not that the demand was ethically unjustified, but that it was asymmetrical. A *quid pro quo* of Soviet cooperation in the Middle East would have been more sensible and would not have brought up the delicate issue of Soviet internal politics. To those who argued that he was insensitive to the human rights of Jews wishing to emigrate to Israel, Kissinger could point to his record with not inconsiderable pride. Before the Soviets cancelled the 1972 trade agreement in their anger over the Jackson amendment, the annual figure of Jewish emigrants from Russia reached 35,000. After Jackson made his public demands, this figure was cut by more than half. In this instance, without a doubt, private diplomacy tactfully conducted had yielded better results that open covenants stridently demanded.

The great paradox of Kissinger's conception of détente is in his relative tolerance vis-à-vis the Soviet Union, still the fountainhead of communism, and his combativeness toward local Communist movements in peripheral areas. How can Kissinger proclaim détente with the Soviet Union, the supporter of Communist causes everywhere, and yet fight communism to the death in Indochina, warn Western European heads of state against coalition governments with Communists, and demand action against the Communists in Angola?

The key to this riddle is to be found in Kissinger's primary commitment to stability. In the central relationship between the superpowers, there can be no decisive change in the power balance, short of nuclear war. The balance could be changed dramatically, however, if a minor nation shifted its allegiance from one side to the other and thus added appreciably to the strength of one of the two main contenders. The direct jockeying for mutual advantage between Russia and the United States was not likely to affect the global balance. But Communist advances elsewhere could, at least cumulatively, affect the balance of power in the world. Hence, Kissinger's concern with stemming Communist advances in peripheral areas.

This logic, however, runs into serious difficulties. It may stand up in an area such as Angola where thousands of Cuban troops were imported to do battle for the Communist cause. In such a case, there was at least good circumstantial evidence for direct Soviet-sponsored intervention. But there was little, if any evidence that the Soviet Union was very active in helping the Communists in Portugal, Italy, or France. The growth of the Italian Communist movement in Italy under Enrico Berlinguer might be attributable more to that Italian's "historic compromise" with democratic socialism than to subversion by the Soviet Union. Yet, Kissinger accused the Portuguese Foreign Minister of being a "Kerensky," quarantined Portugal from NATO, and had secret payments made to a neo-fascist Italian general. In such cases, a good argument can be made that, by his indiscriminate opposition to all local forms of communism,

Kissinger might force breakaway groups back into Moscow's arms and thus bring about the very developments he was so eager to prevent.

On a deeper level, Hans Morgenthau has made the most telling criticism:

> Since the causes and effects of instability persist, a policy committed to stability and identifying instability with communism is compelled by the logic of its interpretation of reality to suppress in the name of anticommunism all manifestations of popular discontent and stifle the aspirations for reform. Thus, in an essentially unstable world, tyranny becomes the last resort of a policy committed to stability as its ultimate standard.

This is how, in Morgenthau's opinion, Kissinger, despite his extraordinary brilliance, often failed. He tended to place his great gifts at the service of lost causes, and thus, in the name of preserving stability and order, aligned the United States on the wrong side of the great historic issues.

Morgenthau may be a little harsh in such a judgment. What if the Italian Communists renounced their "historic compromise", made common cause with Moscow, and other European countries followed suit? The result could well be a catastrophe for the United States. Morgenthau, as critic, does not have to make that awesome choice. But can a statesman dare to take such risks at a moment when he must base his decisions on conjecture rather than on facts? Here the scholar, in my judgment, owes the statesman a measure of empathy and tolerance.

In this entire realm of argument, Kissinger is most vulnerable, in my view, on his Indochina policy. No one, of course, can blame him for the escalation which he regarded as a national disaster. But I have always differed with his judgment that the presence of 500,000 Americans had settled the importance of Vietnam since credibility was now at stake. Rather, it was my impression that American credibility rose rather than fell when that suicidal commitment finally came to an end. I have also never understood Kissinger's answer to the argument that a negotiated settlement could have been attained in 1969 on terms at least as favorable as those that he finally negotiated in 1973. His explanation that, for three years the North Vietnamese had refused to accept his "double track" plan of separating military from political matters always struck me as rather unconvincing. Finally, the Cambodian invasion that dragged a neutral nation into a war that it might have been able to avoid, struck me as the greatest, and possibly most tragic, blunder. And, in the end, when Saigon fell in April 1975, Kissinger looked like all the other Americans who had come to Indochina to lose their reputation to Ho Chi Minh and the Vietcong.

There may be a psychological interpretation of Kissinger's paradoxical approach to Communism. It may be found in his profound suspicion of the revolutionary as the greatest threat to a stable world order. In theory, as Kissinger had made clear in an essay on Bismarck, it made little difference to him whether a revolutionary was "red" or "white". But in practice, he always feared the "red" revolutionary infinitely more. It is not that he approved of a Greek or Chilean junta, but he simply did not believe that it posed the kind of threat to international stability as that presented by a Cunhal, an Allende, a Castro, or a Ho Chi Minh. These were the types of leaders, rather than a Brezhnev or a Mao Tse-tung, who were most likely to upset the global balance. They still retained that messianic revolutionary quality that had a vast potential for dislocation and contagion. In relation to the Soviet Union and China, one could afford to take some chances without risk to equilibrium. But when it came to the smaller revolutionaries, Kissinger believed that the war-maker still made the most effective peacemaker.

The opening to China was probably Kissinger's most uncontaminated triumph in his tenure as a statesman. It was also his greatest diplomatic adventure. Once he perceived the depth of the rift between China and the Soviet Union, he became convinced that rapprochement with China might make the Soviet Union more receptive to a genuine détente. In short, China, in his view, had become the key to Russia. In addition to establishing this triangular linkage, Kissinger's secret trip to Peking in 1971, had made him the first messenger of reconciliation. Furthermore to discover that beyond the Himalayas, there were men who elicited his admiration and respect only added to his elation. One of the few times that I heard Kissinger happily admit that he had been wrong was an occasion when he discussed his change of heart about Mao Tse-tung and Chou En-lai. In 1966, during the "Cultural Revolution", he had perceived the Chinese leaders as the two most dangerous men on earth. Five years later, he had come to regard them as rational statesmen who pursued China's national interest in a manner not altogether inconsistent with the rules of international stability. But then it was Henry Kissinger who had once said about himself that while he had a first-rate mind, he had a third-rate intuition about people. In the case of China, fortunately, the reality turned out to be more pleasant than the fantasy.

As for the charge that Kissinger's relationships with adversaries were often better than his relationships with friends, I would hardly cloak this statement in a mantle of universal application. There is, however, ample evidence for it if one contemplates Kissinger's policies toward the continent where he was born. Europe brought out the darker side of his personal diplomacy and his reluctance to delegate responsibility. His declaration of a "Year of Europe" in 1973 had come almost as an afterthought in response to complaints by Western European statesmen that their capitals had become little more than refueling stops for Kissinger on his way to or back from Moscow. It reminded one European diplomat of an unfaithful husband's decision to declare a "year of the wife." Kissinger's outbursts of exasperation in moments of frustration did little to improve relations. When he exclaimed in a moment of anger that he "didn't care what happened to NATO," this momentary lapse was taken seriously by his NATO partners. And his lectures to the Portuguese aroused their anger and resentment. In many of these instances, Kissinger followed his own judgment and generally ignored the advice of experienced foreign service officers.

The case that combined all the weaknesses of personal diplomacy, of course, was Cyprus. Kissinger made policy decisions with regard to Cyprus almost absentmindedly. Distracted by the final act of Watergate, he paid only the most cursory attention to events on that tormented island. His dislike for Archbishop Makarios prompted him to lean toward the Greek extremist, Nikos Sampson, of whose reputation he knew little. When the Turks, predictably enough, responded by mounting an invasion, Kissinger did little to deter them even though a democratic government in the meantime had assumed control in Athens. Thus, Kissinger managed to alienate *both* Greece and Turkey in an amazingly short period of time. Perhaps even more serious, the failure of his Cyprus policy led directly to the first of many strictures to be imposed upon him by an increasingly suspicious and hostile Congress.

Since Kissinger's main objective has always been the pursuit of international stability, his attention had been focussed on the world's major power wielders. The pawns on the global chessboard seemed quite expendable to him, until quite suddenly and without warning, some of them decided to improve their lowly status. The Arab oil embargo and the demands for a "new international economic order" that swept through the Third World like a hurricane, convinced Kissinger that he finally would have to pay attention to the smaller nations of Africa, Latin America, and Asia. He quickly realized that his vision of stability would have to become bifocal. Unless he did so, his policies might prevent World War III, but they were certain to prepare the ground for World War IV.

When, in the spring of 1976, Kissinger declared his clear support for black majority rule in southern Africa, he reversed a long tradition of American equivocation. While this reversal was triggered primarily by the Soviet victory in Angola, it was also motivated by Kissinger's desire to build détente between the races and the rich and poor. And when he pledged a dedicated effort to "roll back the desert" in famine-stricken African lands, his promise had the ring of truth. This compassion for the world's dispossessed came late, but when it came, it was sincere.

For almost thirty years, the United Nations had existed in the suburbs of Henry Kissinger's consciousness. Its lack of authority and power had convinced him that he could ignore it with impunity. The increase of Third World bloc voting, however, and the rise of a "tyranny of the majority," made him pay attention. When this majority, having driven the United States into the role of opposition, finally passed an Orwellian resolution that equated Zionism with racism, Kissinger's antennae, always sensitive to power, registered an ominous alert.

Somber warnings that the United Nations might become an empty shell, coupled with Ambassador Moynihan's blunt rhetoric, placed the Third World nations on guard that they were not immune to Kissinger's favorite mixture of diplomacy and force. When Moynihan, however, engaged in so much bluntness that it began to resemble "overkill," Kissinger became alarmed. The differences between the two men finally led to the ambassador's resignation. Even a Kissinger weakened by mounting criticism and congressional opposition was still a formidable adversary.

We cannot say with certitude whether the critics of the step-by-step approach to peace in the Middle East were justified in their assertions that Kissinger avoided the heart of the conflict by refusing to address himself to the Palestinian problem. What the record does indicate, however, is that Kissinger has managed to narrow the differences between Israel and the Arabs more successfully than any other mediator in the long history of that tragic conflict.

The essence of Kissinger's Middle East diplomacy has been the avoidance of the appearance of victory. Convinced that only a stalemate could contain the seeds of peace, he steered the October war to an inconclusive end. In doing so, he resisted enormous pressure from each side hungering for military victory. It was in the aftermath of this military stalemate that he succeeded in negotiating the two disengagement accords, first between Israel and Egypt and then, between Israel and Syria. The two agreements were achieved in no small measure because of Kissinger's personal tenacity. The Sinai agreement which followed in September 1975, was the first accord reached by Israel and an Arab state that was not an armistice to end a war. It was a voluntary agreement reached in times of peace. Even when shortly afterward Syria temporarily linked its future to the PLO, Kissinger's approach of "peace by pieces" had already achieved remarkable results.

It is in the Middle East that Kissinger's intellectual courage had to undergo its acid test. It was not easy always to negotiate between a hammer and an anvil. His striving for balance and equilibrium was never popular with either side. As a Jew, he did not find it easy to deny victory to the state of Israel. Personally, he endured considerable suffering. Yet, he remained faithful to his intellectual conviction that a victor's peace would plant the seeds of yet another war. He might be mistaken in this belief though history provides considerable evidence to back him up. But while his judgment may be open to debate, his sincerity is not. Nowhere in his statesmanship has Henry Kissinger shown greater courage than in his quest for a Middle Eastern peace.

If there is any iron law of history, Kissinger once said, it is that no longing is ever completely fulfilled. His own pursuit of a stable world order is no exception to this general rule.

After Nixon's resignation Kissinger remained the only major figure in the government who had been closely associated with the former president. He now had to pay the price exacted by a resurgent Congress in the post-imperial presidency.

Kissinger's autocratic temperament, highly personal style, and persistent secrecy, now made him a natural target. What had been admired in him earlier now was questioned and condemned. Within one year, between 1974 and 1975, the Congress placed severe restrictions on his freedom to maneuver in virtually every single area of foreign policy, from Turkey to Angola. The man who could do nothing wrong now suddenly could do nothing right. As Kissinger himself observed, "I have been praised excessively, so now I am being blamed excessively." Seldom has a man been more exposed to the fickleness of popular acclaim.

While Kissinger was still widely perceived as an asset to the United States as a *nation* in its relationships abroad, many Americans, by 1976, were deeply ambivalent about his impact on America as a *people* at home. Kissinger himself has been consistent. He has never wavered in his striving for a stable world order. But he was fated to experience in practice what he had learned in theory a quarter of a century before: that a statesman who removes himself too much from the experience of his people may doom himself to disappointment and despair. In February 1976, he stated that America was more endangered by her "domestic divisions than by her overseas adversaries." "A great nation that does not shape history," he continued, "eventually becomes its victim." In his frustration with a Congress that had persistently disavowed his policies and had simply refused to heed his counsel on Angola, he sounded a bleak and somber warning:

> Unless the country ends its divisions, our only option is to retreat—to become an isolated fortress in a hostile and turbulent global sea, awaiting the ultimate confrontation with the only response we will not have denied ourselves— massive retaliation.

Once again, Kissinger walked as a loner, with the ghost of Oswald Spengler by his side. His career showed clearly that vision and courage may not be enough to ensure success. As he himself had written, popular support was essential as well. Luck and timing also played a crucial role. Thucydides had realized this long ago in ancient Athens when he had elevated fortune to the rank of goddess.

Perhaps the most haunting questions about Henry Kissinger's foreign policy are of a philosophical nature. What is the role of ethics in Kissinger's world of stability and power? What is the relationship between personal and political morality? What room does Kissinger's pursuit of a stable world order leave for justice? What should be our criterion for success—his intentions or the consequences of his actions? In short, what must concern us, in conclusion, is the problem of statesmanship and moral choice.

There is little doubt that Kissinger, when facing Goethe's dilemma—the choice "between justice and disorder, on the one hand, and injustice and order, on the other," has tended to prefer the latter. In Kantian terms Kissinger made the pursuit of a stable world order the categorical imperative of his foreign policy. If, in the process, the human element had to be sacrificed at times on the altar of stability or of a larger strategic vision, so be it, because without stability, peace could not be born at all and justice, too, would be extinguished. He felt that, in a tragic world, a statesman was not able to choose between good and evil, but only among different forms of evil. Indeed, whatever decision he would make, *some* evil consequences were bound to flow from it. All that a realistic statesman could do in such a world was to choose the lesser evil.

The competing claims of stability and justice permeate the world of Henry Kissinger. A few examples from the record will suffice to demonstrate the pervasiveness of this terrible dilemma.

In the Indochina war, the problem presented itself in its starkest form in the Nixon decision to mine the ports of North Vietnam and to order all-out bombing attacks on Hanoi and Haiphong in 1972. These actions, which were publicly supported by Kissinger, tested the determination of the Soviet Union and China to stand by their North Vietnamese ally. When no action was forthcoming either from Moscow or Peking, Nixon and Kissinger realized that they had managed to isolate North Vietnam. The war was therefore brought to an end for American combat soldiers, but at a price that aroused the moral indignation of many nations and that of many Americans as well. The question that remains is whether this brutal means was justified to attain the desired objective of a "peace with honor," a peace which, in the end, proved to be ephemeral. Could not another, less dreadful, way have been found?

In his relations with the Soviet Union, Kissinger has also been accused of indifference to the human element. As Richard Falk has observed in a thoughtful essay, "Kissinger's effectiveness in dealing with foreign governments arose from his capacity to avoid unpleasant criticisms about their domestic indecencies." Since most powerful states have skeletons hidden in their closets, most statesmen, Falk observed, "found Kissinger's Machiavellian posture a welcome relief." If, in short, a choice had to be made between détente and human rights within the borders of the Soviet Union, there was little doubt how Kissinger would choose.

When India went to war with Pakistan in 1971, Kissinger "tilted" toward Yahya Khan. Not only had the Pakistani president helped in the preparations for the secret trip to China, but an Indian alliance with the Soviet Union threatened to dismember a weakened Pakistan. When Yahya Khan turned on his Bengali fellow-Moslems in a ferocious civil war, and drove ten million of them into exile, Kissinger remained silent. The imperatives of the strategic balance, once again, had overshadowed the human tragedy.

Until the nations of the Third World gained a measure of power through the oil embargo and bloc alignments in the United Nations, Kissinger had little time for the problems of the small and poor. Until famines in the Third World reached catastrophic dimensions, they remained on the periphery of his political awareness. Falk observed of Kissinger's early attitude that "it was inconceivable that afflictions of this magnitude in the Northern Hemisphere would not have been perceived as a catastrophe of historic significance." "Kissinger's outlook," Falk continued, "presupposed that it (was) possible to manage international relations mainly by moderating conflictual relations among governments in the Northern Hemisphere." Once more, Kissinger stood accused of ignoring humanity in the name of order.

It would not be fair to Kissinger to let these judgments stand without giving him a hearing. On Indochina, the question he might ask is this: What is more merciful and more compassionate, an end with horror or a horror without end? On the problem of ignoring human rights in Russia, he might well respond by asking whether the avoidance of an atomic holocaust was not itself the highest moral imperative of our age. On India and Pakistan, he might query his accuser as to whether Soviet domination of the Indian sub-continent might not have been the greater evil. And on the matter of the world's poor and dispossessed, Kissinger could now respond that his numerous proposals to build bridges between the world's rich and poor more than compensated for his earlier indifference.

When Henry Kissinger entered Harvard as an undergraduate in 1946, another Jewish refugee, almost a generation older, had just published his first book in the United States. Hans Morgenthau's *Scientific Man versus Power Politics* contained a paragraph that foreshadowed Kissinger's dilemma in all its awesome starkness:

> We have no choice between power and the common good. To act successfully, that is, according to the rules of the political art, is political wisdom. To know with despair that the political act is inevitably evil, and to act nevertheless, is moral courage. To choose among several expedient actions the least evil one is moral judgment. In the combination of political wisdom, moral courage and moral judgment, man reconciles his political nature with his moral destiny. That this conciliation is nothing more than a *modus vivendi,* uneasy, precarious, and even paradoxical, can disappoint only those who prefer to gloss over and to distort the tragic contradictions of human existence with the soothing logic of a specious concord.

In such a world, is it not easier to abstain from any decision altogether? Kissinger has never thought so. He knew that abstention from evil did not affect the existence of evil in the world, but only destroyed the faculty of choice. As Albert Camus had said, not to choose, too, was a choice.

When history would make its judgment on the foreign policy of Henry Kissinger, the chronicle would not pay much attention to his personal anguish when forced to choose between competing claims. Its iron pen would merely register the objective consequences of his acts. Nor would history reveal its alternatives had he acted otherwise. He would never know where the road *not* taken might have led. The unending quest for meaningful choices in a tragic world in which the only certainty was risk simply was a statesman's lot. It was, therefore, in action in the present that courage and humanity were born.

When a quarter of a century ago, on that October day in 1950, I first met Henry Kissinger, I had a premonition that one day he might enter history. I think the world is a safer place today because of his courage and his vision. It might even be a little better. No mortal man could ask for more.

Kissinger's Flawed and Disastrous Design

STANLEY HOFFMANN

Some people owe their psychological or sociological insight exclusively to their resentments and their fears. This is not Kissinger's case. These may sharpen his wits, and dip his brush in acid. But he has three great gifts which serve him equally well in his writings and his statecraft.

One is an almost devilish psychological intuition, an instinct for grasping the hidden springs of character, of knowing what drives or what dooms another person. He was at his best as a face-to-face negotiator precisely because of this rare talent. Had he been less tempted by action and more capable of that "fantasy life" of "romantic imaginings" in which, he says, Nixon indulged, he might have been a good novelist. The gallery of portraits is the best part of the book. Each reader will have his own favorites (and all will notice that some statesmen with whom Kissinger had many dealings hardly appear, Willy Brandt being the most conspicuous). My favorites are the vivid portraits of Chou, Heath, Brezhnev, and Mao—who is described with a power and subtlety that seem worthy of him. As in his account of Nixon, for example, Kissinger backs up his incisive analysis of character with incisive anecdotes. We see Chou, late at night, taking Kissinger on a walk where they cross two bridges, without a word referring to a conversation months before when Kissinger had told Chou that he felt like a character in Kafka's *Castle*—the plumber who is summoned and denied entrance—because of the presence of soldiers guarding the bridges connecting the various guest cottages, and Brezhnev trying to make a toy cannon work during a conference and strutting "like a prizefighter who has knocked out his opponent" when the cannon finally went off.

All of the portraits convey the relation between a personality and the culture that has shaped it. And Kissinger's second gift is that of a man particularly attuned to the nuances of cultural difference (the word "nuance" is one of his favorites, along with "intangible," "comparison," "exalted," "insecure," "petty," and "unsentimental"). People who have been transplanted from one country into another, who have a certain distance both from the history and mores of the society from which they were uprooted and from the memories and rituals of their adopted country, often develop this sense. They lose it only if they are too eager to assimilate into the mainstream of their new culture—something that was never Kissinger's case.

Kissinger is very good at evoking atmospheres, and their relation to the business of power: Washington dinner parties and receptions, where "the relationships are created without which the machinery of government would soon stalemate itself," the president's lonely hideaway room, the villa filled with Fernand Léger paintings where Kissinger met the North Vietnamese, the peculiarities of protocol in each country he visited. One of the most fascinating sides of this book is the analysis of different political styles, molded by distinctive historical experiences and geographical imperatives. Kissinger thus compares brilliantly the Chinese and the Soviet styles of negotiation (not to mention cuisines). "The Soviets insist on their prerogatives as a great power. The Chinese establish a claim on the basis of universal principles and a demonstration of self-confidence that attempts to make the issue of power irrelevant." Mao and Chou represented a nation that "had absorbed conquerors and had proved its inward strength by imposing its social and intellectual style on them. Its leaders were aloof, self-assured, composed. Brezhnev represented a nation that had survived not by civilizing its conquerors but by outlasting them . . . he sought to obscure his lack of assurance by boisterousness."

The Vietnamese, he notes, have outlasted their conquerors by driving them insane. A Japanese leader "does not announce a decision, he evokes it." Japanese decision-making by consensus is endless, but execution is disciplined; in the US, it is the other way around. In the Middle East, "formal positions are like the shadows in Plato's cave—reflections of a transcendent reality almost impossible to encompass in the dry legalisms of a negotiating process."

Nobody has analyzed more pithily Western European ambivalence toward the US—the fear of American rigidity compounded by the fear either of American retreat or of superpower condominium. French foreign policy under the Fifth Republic was prickly but "serious and consistent," at times "steadier and more perceptive than our own," whereas British statesmen "were content to act as honored consultants to our deliberations." And "one sometimes could not avoid the impression that to discuss international affairs with [Italy's] foreign minister was to risk boring him." One could cull a bestiary of negotiating styles from this book.

One could also draw from it a vast monograph on the workings of American bureaucracy in foreign affairs, and a short Little Red (or rather White) Book, an appendix to *The Prince,* on the art of diplomatic bargaining. For Kissinger's third gift is one that puts into practice his insights into personalities and cultures: it is the gift for the manipulation of power—exploiting the weaknesses and strengths of character of his counterparts, either by neutralizing them (if they were adversaries) or turning them into allies or accomplices by addressing their needs and playing on their fears of other countries. This did not always work: his attempt at negotiating a textile agreement with the Japanese began as "an intricate Kabuki play" which "turned out to be more like a Kafka story."

Kissinger's prerequisite for the exercise of this gift, as he suggests throughout the book, is a firm control of the US bureaucracy—which is precisely what Nixon also wanted. The president "was determined to run foreign policy from the White House," and Kissinger devised the machinery that was supposed to make it possible. But it never worked well enough, and those who believe that confusion and cacophony began with the Carter administration are in for a surprise.

If there is one constant theme that runs through every chapter of this complex book, it is that of the battle for control between, on the one hand, Nixon and Kissinger and, on the other, the bureaucracy—the State Department, Defense, the CIA, the Treasury during Connally's "frontal assault on the White House staff system." It was a vicious circle: Nixon and Kissinger, exasperated by the bureaucrats' lack of imagination, frequent resistance, and propensity to leaks, reserved more and more control over the key issues to themselves, but this only compounded the problem, since the execution of policies had to be largely entrusted to departments that had not been consulted or even informed. More and more Kissinger carried on the real business of foreign policy through secretive "back channels"—with Dobrynin over SALT and all other Soviet-American relations, with Chou, with Ambassador Rabin and Golda Meir (at the expense of Foreign Minister Abba Eban), later with Sadat. But the same issues were being treated simultaneously by the State Department, or in the formal SALT negotiation at Helsinki.

This created frequent confusion when America's negotiators did not know the agreements in the making through the back channels; it also gave the Soviets opportunities to try to play one team against the other. It created deep resentments among American diplomats ignored or undercut by the White House. It even created suspicion in Moscow and Peking, for Soviet and Chinese diplomats wondered why the Americans wanted so much secrecy. It meant that vital decisions (for instance, those concerning Cambodia in April 1970) were taken behind the backs or against the opposition of Secretaries Rogers and Laird. It meant that at the summits in Peking and Moscow, set up without Roger's participation, Kissinger had to enlist the cooperation of Chou and of Gromyko in handling our own resentful State Department. (In China, this did not work: when the State Department, which had been kept in the dark, was informed of the text of what became the Shanghai communiqué, it demanded a host of changes—and obtained some, behaving exactly as Thieu was going to do, a few months later, when he was finally informed of the text of the peace agreement Kissinger had negotiated alone with Le Duc Tho.)

When Kissinger was charged with executing a policy, the sluggishness and opposition of the bureaucracy could complicate and delay, but no more. When responsibilities were shared, or supposedly belonged to the State Department but were subject to White House review, policy could become incoherent: for instance in the Middle East in 1969–1970, when Rogers launched peace plans which Nixon and Kissinger did not endorse, or during the Bangladesh crisis when Rogers opposed the "tilt" toward Pakistan. The bureaucracy, in what it deemed "its" domain, often failed to consult the White House! Nixon's startling announcement of August 15, 1971—the monetary and economic measures that provoked a crisis with Western Europe and Japan—was made without either Rogers or Kissinger being consulted.

> The Nixon method of government worked well when the military problem was relatively straightforward and could be carried out in one daring move. . . . It was effective also for purposeful solitary diplomacy conducted by a trusted associate working with a small staff. . . . Difficulties arose when a sustained military effort was needed . . . or when the diplomacy was too complex to be handled by the security adviser's office. . . . Then the absence of consensus or even understanding inhibited coherence and commitment.

Nixon's reluctance to impose his will perpetuated the lack of discipline, and drove him increasingly into secrecy and distrust. Thus his methods made possible some remarkable initiatives, but also led straight to the crisis which destroyed him in 1974, and weakened the presidency.

Kissinger was more than willing to overlook those risks, both when in office and in writing most of his memoir. For the brand of diplomacy he wanted to perform cannot tolerate pluralism in the various institutions concerned with foreign policy, or the long delays that building a consensus among them would entail. He concentrated on the games to be played with foreign interlocutors, not domestic bureaucrats. For him the job of the US bureaucracies was to give him the data for the decisions he and Nixon would make, and to carry out these decisions.

Bureaucratic maneuver annoys him. What fascinates him is diplomatic maneuver, as he makes clear in countless maxims and comments on the art of relating force to goals, on the advantages and perils of crises. These confer "an unusual capacity for creative action," but they must be "overpowered early." "One's actions must be sustained; they must appear relentless, inexorable." In the final phase one must resist "the natural temptation to relax and perhaps to ease the process by a gesture of goodwill. . . . The time for conciliation is after the crisis is surmounted."

He tells us the requirements of secret diplomacy, the way of linking issues in a bargain so as to extract advantages, and the way of delaying agreement on the issues which one's opponent is in a hurry to settle until he has given in on the others. One must never appear too eager, yet one should not (as the Soviets tend to do) compromise one's gains by being too greedy or by asking for something unattainable; one should not make any unilateral concessions, yet one ought to avoid excessive haggling.

Kissinger also instructs us on triangular diplomacy (which "must rely on the natural incentives and propensities of the players" and "avoid the impression that one is 'using' either of the contenders against the other"), on giving an opponent "a formal reassurance intended to unnerve as much as to calm; and which would defeat its purpose if it were actually believed," on the error of raising too soon an issue on which "readiness to compromise does not exist," on the occasional need to substitute boldness if one lacks power, on the uses of insolence, "the armor of the weak."

If there seems considerable self-satisfaction in such advice, it is true that during the period covered by this book he was rarely caught at his own game: pathetically, his only personal diplomatic defeat was inflicted by Thieu, in October 1972, when the South Vietnamese leader turned the deadline agreed upon by Kissinger and the North Vietnamese into a weapon against the whole agreement as brilliantly as Kissinger had used the deadline of the US election in order to extract a "cascade" of concessions from Hanoi. (Both Thieu and Le Duc Tho used insolence to "stonewall" when in positions of weakness. Kissinger in this book does the same in reply to criticism from the left and from liberals.) Like an athlete reminiscing about a game he won because he was in top form, Kissinger relives his tactical calculations and manipulations with relish, and thus reveals what sustains a master politician in the daily drudgery of dealing with "the contingent." But what was the design which all the ingenuity he so fondly recalls was supposed to serve? What strategy required these tactics?

Kissinger's tactical maxims leave no doubt: the professed disciple of Kant, he is a follower of Hobbes in his assessment of human nature and of the behavior of states in the international state of nature. (Twice he mentions, with some awe, that Pompidou, who helped him conduct his secret negotiations with the North Vietnamese, "never used these kindnesses to extract anything in return.") As he sees them, nations are driven by diffidence, greed, and glory; they are often propelled by the murderous certainties of ideology, compelled to use their power for their preservation or their expansion. What order can nations achieve in this "state or war" which Hobbes deemed bearable in his day, but which has become a threat to the common survival in the age (foreseen by Kant) when total destruction is possible and nations are so intimately interdependent?

Americans, Kissinger tells us, have had three traditions: "an idealistic tradition that sees foreign policy as a contest between evil and good," a pragmatic tradition of problem-solving, and a legalistic tradition. They had all failed. "Emotional slogans" had kept America oscillating from over-involvement to isolationism. The time had come when "moral exuberance" could no longer be condoned: "we were becoming like other nations in the need to recognize that our power, while vast, had limits." "It was my conviction that a concept of our fundamental national interests would provide a ballast of restraint and an assurance of continuity." What America needed, and Kissinger wanted to establish, was a geopolitical tradition. ("By 'geopolitical' I mean an approach that pays attention to the requirements of equilibrium.")

Kissinger the realist sounds here like Hans Morgenthau writing on the balance of power. But Morgthenthau has often been severely critical of Kissinger. The drama of this doctrine of realism is that, while it conceives of world order as the product of a careful balancing of power, as a set of restraints on excessive ambitions, and as a compromise between conflicting interests, it allows for many different versions of nirvana, and different evaluations of threats and opportunities. Containment too—as described by George Kennan, and as executed (not to Kennan's satisfaction) by Acheson and (not to Acheson's satisfaction) by Dulles—had been an attempt to teach realism to Americans. But Kissinger is critical of containment: it "treated power and diplomacy as distinct elements or phases of policy"; by concentrating on building "situations of strength" at a time when we were strong and the Soviets weak, we allowed them to catch up, and thus to be in a much more favorable position on the distant day of negotiation. "Treating force and diplomacy as discrete phenomena caused our power to lack purpose and our negotiations to lack force." We had to learn a better integration of power and policy in an age of nuclear weapons, competing ideologies, and diffusion of political power.

The question remains: for what purpose? What was the "geopolitical design"? It is here that surprises begin. In the first place, Kissinger's repeated assertions about the need for a policy purged of emotional excesses and reconciled "to imperfect choices, partial fulfillment, the unsatisfying tasks of balance and maneuver" are nowhere accompanied by a description of the kind of world Kissinger was trying to bring about. If there was a vision beyond the geopolitical game, if the complex manipulation of rewards and punishments needed to create equilibrium and to restrain the troublemakers was aimed at a certain ideal of world order, we are left free to guess what it might have been. Maybe it is Kissinger's horror of grand designs mass-produced by "the wayward representatives of American liberalism" which explains this reticence. At any rate, he is much more mysterious about his purposes than about his method, about his destination than about his approach.

Secondly, the approach itself reminds one that geopolitics was a German school of thought based on the notion of constant and inevitable struggle. And Kissinger now reminds one of Karl Schmitt's fundamental distinction—in which he saw the key to politics—between friends and foes. Kissinger recognizes that the nuclear stalemate between the superpowers results in a kind of fragmentation of world politics: there is both a global balance of nuclear power, and a series of regional balances (or imbalances). But at the heart of his conception there are two propositions.

The first is that the decisive and dominant issue is the conflict between the US and the Soviet Union. This extends to every part of the world and, given the nature of Soviet ideology, includes "the internal policies and social structures of countries" as well. Soviet policy, whatever its "ultimate aims" or the Soviet leaders' "real intentions" (wrong questions, says Kissinger), wants "to promote the attrition of adversaries by gradual increments." Soviet strategy is "one of ruthless opportunism." There is no "terminal point to international tension" that could be achieved by "sentimental conciliation" or "liturgical belligerence," for we are "dealing with a system too ideologically hostile for instant conciliation and militarily too powerful to destroy."

The second fundamental proposition is that "to foreclose Soviet opportunities is thus the essence of the West's responsibility." It is a permanent task, not (as containment was thought to be) "an exertion that has a foreseeable end." The nature of that task is the management of the balance of power, which requires "perseverance, subtlety, not a little courage, and above all understanding of its requirements."

What are these requirements? Above all, we must create in our adversary a perception of "an equality of power": if it is perceived, "it will not be tested." "Calculation must include potential as well as actual power, not only the possession of power but the will to bring it to bear." We must understand that our performance in any part of the world has an effect on this balance of real and perceived power; therefore, the way in which we respond to any local crisis ought to be related to, and determined by its relation to, the central contest.

Kissinger rigorously applied this maxim in cases such as Chile, where he saw in Allende's election "a challenge to our national interest" not only because of Allende's revolutionary and anti-American program but because it happened "against the backdrop of the Syrian invasion of Jordan" (Syria being a Soviet ally) "and our effort to force the Soviet Union to dismantle its installation for servicing nuclear submarines in the Caribbean." He acted in the same way in the Middle East, where in 1969 "delay was on the whole in our interest because it enabled us to demonstrate even to radical Arabs that we were indispensable to *any* progress and that it cannot be extorted from us by Soviet pressure." The division of the world into radicals and moderates is as important to Kissinger as the division between Moscow and Washington, Moscow being seen as the ally of the radicals, and Washington the protector of the moderates.

Vietnam was of course part of the same chain: he tells us many times that his "initiatives with Peking and Moscow would have been impossible had we simply collapsed in Vietnam." He supported Pakistan against India because Pakistan was our ally, and China's friend, whereas India had signed a treaty with Moscow, and India's war threatened "our geopolitical design." Our friends must be supported whatever they may do within their own countries: hence Kissinger's determination to stick by Yahya Khan, Thieu, Lon Nol, the Shah, etc. . . . Still, when their acts could adversely affect the central conflict, we must check their course: thus as Nixon "frostily" reminded Willy Brandt, we did not support his *Ostpolitik*, we merely "did not object"; but we gave "the inevitable a constructive direction" by linking it to America's own policy toward the Soviet Union, and thus we "became responsible for the ultimate success of Brandt's policy." Our enemies, defined as whoever aligns himself with the Soviets, must be resisted and frustrated; our friends must be guided.

Kissinger's notion of linkage applies not only to power relations among nations and entire regions but also to political issues arising with the Soviets. Not only are "the actions of a major power inevitably related," and not only do they have "consequences beyond the issue or region immediately concerned," but we must try to link "deliberately" separate objectives in a negotiation, "using one as a leverage on the other." Hence the efforts of the Nixon administration to make "progress in settling the Vietnam war something of a condition for advance in areas of interest to the Soviets, such as the Middle East, trade or arms limitation"; and we linked SALT to the Berlin negotiation, on whose success, in turn, the Soviet-West German treaty depended. "We saw linkage, in short, as synonymous with an overall strategic and geopolitical view. To ignore the interconnection of events was to undermine the coherence of all policy."

Linkage was part of the attempt to restrain the Soviets with a careful mixture of penalties and incentives. Trade, for instance, was treated as "a political instrument," to be favored "in measured doses" when the Soviets behaved cooperatively, and withheld otherwise. "Penalties for adventurism" include "military assistance to friends resisting Soviet or Cuban or radical pressures." They also include the use of force.

On this point, Kissinger is prolix: on the one hand, the "basic choice is to act or not to act": "there are no rewards for exhibiting one's doubts in vacillation: statesmen get no praise for failing with restraint. Once committed they must prevail." "Gradual escalation tempts the opponent to match every move"; a leader, once committed, has the "obligation to end the confrontation rapidly. For this he must convey implacability."

On the other hand, the purpose of force is to restore a balance of power, without which negotiations are bound to be counterproductive for one's own side. And it is best to resort to force quickly, when a major crisis can still be avoided and the adversary is not yet fully committed. The objective of this strategy is "an end of the constant Soviet pressure against the global balance of power," to which "in our minds efforts to reduce the danger of nuclear war by the control of arms had to be linked." Reacting strongly, violently if necessary, in the early stages of Soviet expansion would save us from having to choose between either "the collapse of the balance of power or a colossal confrontation."

It must be clear that Kissinger's geopolitical design is not at all adequately described by the word détente. It was a scheme for universal, permanent, and successful containment, marshaling all our instruments of power more effectively than before, and aiming at "an end to the constant probing for openings and the testing of every equilibrium." Kissinger, indeed, appears as the Compleat Cold Warrior. To be sure, he would allow for some cooperation with Moscow, but as a reward for good behavior, as an incentive to moderation, and because of the risks in the nuclear age.

Détente was a name for the forced Soviet acceptance of the status quo, obtained by "a firm application of psychological and physical restraints and determined resistance to challenge." It was also "a device to maximize Soviet dilemmas," a tactic aimed at demonstrating "to our public and to our allies that we were not the cause of conflict." "We could not permit the Soviets to monopolize the world's yearning for peace." SALT I made us give up one weapon—the ABM—Congress was going to destroy anyhow, but it froze the Soviet offensive build-up (a debatable point) while allowing us to to catch up. Triangular diplomacy has to serve the aim of containing the Soviets without provoking them into greater aggressiveness, and

> it was a three-dimensional game, but any simplification had the makings of catastrophe. If we appeared irresolute or leaning toward Moscow, Peking would be driven to accommodations with the Soviet Union. If we adopted the Chinese attitude, however, we might not even help Peking: we might, in fact, tempt a Soviet preemptive attack on China and thus be faced with decisions of enormous danger.

Kissinger asks whether the Soviet's shift to détente was a tactical maneuver —a question that could be put to him.

This was, as I have written elsewhere, a design of Bismarckian proportions. "Our relations to possible opponents should be such, I considered, that our options toward both of them were always greater than their options toward each other." The US was to be the supreme manipulator of the triangle, and of course the supreme beneficiary of détente: the Soviets would be contained all over the world, and rewarded with measured deliveries of grain. Their proxies would be either punished, or induced to turn to us, as in the Middle East, from where, Kissinger announced in 1969, we wanted to expel the Soviets. "Three years later," he now claims, "we made this prediction come true"—another debatable point. Balance of power and American hegemony become synonymous. Just as "it is up to *us* to define the limits of Soviet aims," it is up to us to teach everyone else the boundaries of the permissible, to trace the borders of their diplomatic and social experiments.

The problems with this ambitious strategy were legion, and Kissinger is singularly unwilling to confront them. In the first place, it assumed a far greater ability to force the Soviets to play "our" game than it was wise to expect. During the period in question Soviet military might and their capacity to project it grew, in no small part because the US was bogged down in Vietnam. Not only the weaknesses but the strengths of our own friends and allies created openings for Soviet influence—in the Middle East and in southern Africa, for example. Were we really in a position to deny them "all opportunities for expansion"? Since we wanted to keep them out of our *chasses gardées,* and since they wanted to preserve the autonomy of their political and economic system, how many chances "for genuine cooperation" could we dangle before their eyes so as to "inculcate habits of moderation and bring about a more constructive future?"

Kissinger had criticized the containment doctrine for its suggestion that creating situations of strength would ultimately lead to harmony. But his own strategy left room for only two options: a constant manning of barricades, permanent crisis management, an endless vista of confrontations and tests, or else Soviet acceptance of the inevitable US dominance. The latter was unlikely, for it presumed total success by the US, for which the conditions existed neither at home nor in the world. The former was bleak.

Let us assume that the design made sense. Was it compatible with the American system of government? First, it required an extraordinary capacity for acting swiftly and flexibly all over the globe. Centralization of command allows for speed and suppleness. But it also entails concentration on a few fronts: a small staff can't cope with everything. The beast in Kafka's fable can't run to all the corners of the burrow at once. Kissinger tells us that his plan for the Middle East, in 1969–1972, was, through intransigence—i.e., by our refusing to put pressure on Israel to make any accommodation whatever with Moscow and its allies—to get to the point where "some Arab state showed a willingness to separate from the Soviets, or the Soviets were prepared to dissociate from the maximum Arab program." By the early spring of 1972, *both* of these developments had occurred: the Soviets were hinting strongly at their desire to deviate from that program (although they could not initiate this deviation themselves). At the summit they agreed on a weak statement of principles (Kissinger says he "never understood" why they did so) which Sadat indeed interpreted as a Soviet breach of solidarity with the Arabs. And Sadat himself, disillusioned with the Soviets, had opened a secret channel to Kissinger and suggested an American initiative.

Even after Sadat's expulsion of the Soviets in July, 1972, however, the U.S. took no such initiative. Kissinger—in the only chapter that sounds faintly embarrassed—pleads unconvincingly that Soviet proposals were unacceptable because they assumed a permanent Soviet presence in the Middle East. And yet—knowing what was happening to their position in Egypt—the Russians had offered to withdraw in the event of a comprehensive settlement. As for Sadat, Kissinger recognizes that he thought for too long that Nasser's successor was still playing Nasser's game: "great men are so rare that they take some getting used to!" In other words, opportunities were missed (and the October war made more likely), partly by Kissinger's fixation on the Soviet angle of the Middle Eastern problem, partly by the simple fact that the summits and Vietnam left him little time, partly by the fact that 1972 was an election year: "I was too immersed in Vietnam and Nixon in the campaign to do any serious negotiating." This is far from the only case where Kissinger's conception and manipulation of grand strategy are shown as defective by his own evidence.

In the second place, Kissinger's strategy required that domestic politics allow American leaders to pursue their delicate game abroad without constraints or pressures. He denounces, from chapter to chapter, those who wanted to cut the military budget at a time when the Soviets were building large missiles, or who sympathized with India over Bangladesh, or who tried to limit the Executive's freedom of military action in Cambodia, Laos, and Vietnam. But there can be no guarantee that a policy whose success depends largely on secrecy and speed will be automatically supported by a public and a Congress that are simply told to wait for the results. Surely the secrecy of the 1969 bombing of the sanctuaries in Cambodia was due at least as much to the desire not to sharpen domestic opposition as to the desire to protect Sihanouk. The tools of Kissinger's strategy—linkage, the unrestrained use of force for specific objectives—could be effective only in the hands of one person. Yet their very nature tempted others, in Congress or in the public, to try to impose different ways (more crude or more moderate) of using them.

The style of Kissinger's strategy was itself an invitation to damaging leaks, which in turn would provoke more or less legal retaliation, such as the wiretaps or the onslaught on Daniel Ellsberg; and these measures in turn would make Congress and the public more restive. In this sense, Kissinger cannot escape all responsibility for Watergate, if we mean by Watergate a pattern of Executive abuses. Watergate became a personal tragedy for Kissinger not only because it was the price of having served Nixon but also because it symbolized the revolt of the very democracy on whose behalf the geopolitical battle was being waged.

We have assumed so far that the design at least made sense abroad. But this too is open to challenge. The problem is not *whether* Soviet designs ought to be thwarted; the debate is over *how* to do it, and about the conception of the world that underlies Kissinger's strategy. To Kissinger, the struggle between Moscow and Washington is not just global in scope, it absorbs, so to speak, every other conflict or issue. Peace, or containment, is therefore indivisible. Every crisis anywhere tests our ability to stand up to the Soviets. And the credibility of the US depends on our capacity to meet every test. Thus, in case after case, Kissinger's policy was to make the Soviets squarely responsible for what was happening, and to act in such a way that they would either put pressure on their clients to cease and desist, or dissociate themselves from their clients.

Is this the real world? Or does it not substitute for the real world an artificially simple and tidy one, in which friends and foes, radicals and moderates are neatly lined up, and in which nationalism—surely as important a force as communism—gets thoroughly discounted? If one sees the world as more complex and fluid than in Kissinger's scheme, if one realizes that most states are not simply the superpowers' proxies—India and Syria are described as waging "proxy wars" for the Soviets—but pursue their own interests, the notion of indivisible credibility and of a strategy geared exclusively to the Soviet Union becomes eminently questionable. A Soviet presence or privileged position is not necessarily permanent. We may have a good reason for being occasionally on the same side as the Soviets in order to prevent them from capturing a cause or movement. And we may have many incentives to deal with Soviet clients while they still are beholden to the Soviets, precisely because they may not want to mortgage their independence, or because their radicalism is rhetorical, or compatible with our concerns. Looking to Moscow for a key (as Kissinger did, in early 1969, when he wanted to send Cyrus Vance there with a peace plan for Vietnam) can be a mistake. On the other hand, as we discovered in Vietnam, some "proxies" are of such a hostile will of their own that neither Soviet pressure nor Soviet political disengagement helps us much.

Kissinger's conception can thus be criticized in the first place because—strange as it seems—it limits America's flexibility and may turn into a set of self-fulfilling prophecies. It obliges us to treat practically all unfavorable events as confrontations, and yet it may be very wise to avoid confrontations one can't win—and some situations (as in the Horn of Africa) offer little or no scope for American success. Kissinger wanted us to establish priorities. Yet in his design every incident must be treated seriously, since even if it has no great intrinsic significance, losing the test would encourage our adversary to test us again. But if the Soviets are indeed intent on seizing every good opportunity, why would they fail to exploit one just because we blocked them elsewhere earlier?

To treat countries allied to Moscow (for their own national reasons) merely as Soviet proxies risks tightening their bonds to Moscow (it was Chou En-lai who wisely advised Kissinger to end the Vietnam war rapidly so as to reduce Soviet influence in Indochina), or putting oneself on the losing side (as in the Bangladesh crisis), or missing opportunities (as with Sadat). Indeed, to treat one's own allies as proxies may bring rude awakenings: Thieu, in the last part of 1972, derailed our negotiations by asserting his own interests. And Kissinger has some trouble defending, in a footnote, our friend the Shah's decision to press for high oil prices through OPEC.

Kissinger's conception is one which, in its obsession with Moscow, discounts the internal problems of other countries, and dismisses local circumstances. This is a recipe for disaster. Thus he reduces the Chilean domestic situation of 1969 to a simple choice between revolutionary communism and democracy, either ignoring or misreading the complexities of the Allende coalition and the opposition to it. In 1972, Kissinger refused to support Brandt—who was having trouble getting his *Ostpolitik* treaties through the

Bundestag—because the Soviets weren't helpful in Vietnam: had Brandt lost, there would have been a major crisis in US-West German relations (Schmidt has been more generous in trying to help Carter with SALT II).

In the case of Bangladesh, Kissinger blames "the majority of informed opinion" for having "sought to judge the confrontation on the subcontinent on the merits of the issue that had produced the crisis." We had to stay associated with Pakistan because dissociation would have been tantamount "to the US-Soviet condominium so dreaded by Peking." There would therefore have been no Peking summit, and without it there could be no Moscow summit. But the one thing, it seems, we could not do was to ask Yahya Khan to release Mujib, without whom Kissinger's dream of a "peaceful" solution of the Bangladesh problem (after so much bloodshed) was bound to remain a mirage, at Indira Gandhi's mercy. "The merits of the issue" not only produce a crisis: they are also the key to a solution.

The signing by Sadat of a treaty with Moscow was wrongly seen by Kissinger as evidence of Soviet domination and confirmation of the conviction he expressed to Rabin (see the latter's *Memoirs,* p. 201) that no settlement could be concluded without a Soviet-American understanding—on our terms. The geopolitical vision Kissinger advocates looks above all at military balances. Yet in the Middle East, where the US provided huge military assistance to Israel, William Quandt rightly notes that "the military balance proved not to be the key to regional stability and the prevention of war."

Kissinger's conception can be criticized for another reason as well. Like Metternich, he is caught in a contradiction. He seeks an order of restraint, yet his global view obliges him to universal intervention. He wants the Soviets to separate their domestic ideology and practices from their external conduct, yet his very recognition of the fact that "a domestic upheaval in any country can cause a major shift in international alignments" leads him to justify as blatant an intervention in another nation's affairs as the attempt to prevent Allende from becoming president. Indeed, he regrets that the US did not use arms and economic assistance as political weapons earlier and better in Chile. Our failure to do so "transformed us by 1970 from the dominant element of 1964 into a sort of mother hen clucking nervous irrelevancies from the sidelines." Kissinger wants to "shape events in the light of our own purposes"—those events may be another nation's own political life. But of course, in Kissinger's view, nobody's affairs are exclusively his own.

The third criticism arises from the human cost of such a strategy—admittedly a "sentimental" concern. Kissinger's conception turns people into pawns, countries into tools. Kissinger and the CIA encouraged the Kurds to agitate in Iraq so as to divert Iraqi forces from the Arab-Israeli conflict. When, in 1975, the Shah decided to "settle the Kurdish problem with Iraq" (a nice unsentimental euphemism), we approved. Chile's General Schneider was killed as a result of a half-comic, half-serious confusion produced by the famous Forty Committee's orders (Frei, the former Chilean president, whom we had financed in the past, refused to play the part Kissinger had assigned to him). And the classic case of a people sacrificed is of course Cambodia.

Had we not intervened, Kissinger writes, "Vietnamization and American withdrawal would then come unstuck." "Cambodia was not a moral issue. . . . What we faced was essentially a tactical choice." "Strategically, Cambodia could not be considered a country separate from Vietnam."

This does not mean that Kissinger presents his strategy as amoral: morality is defined as the defense of our values and the resistance to totalitarianism. But this is an ethics of intentions, or purposes, which neglects consequences, and makes of "credibility," in effect, the highest value. Whether a nation ensures its credibility by fighting unwinnable wars, by intervening blatantly in the affairs of others, by turning secondary issues into tests of strength, and by sacrificing others to its design is, at least, an open question. De-Gaulle asked Kissinger in 1969 why the U.S. did not leave Vietnam; he answered that "a sudden withdrawal might give us a credibility problem." De Gaulle asked where; Kissinger mentioned the Middle East. "How very odd," de Gaulle replied. "It is precisely in the Middle East that I thought your enemies had the credibility problem."

Indivisible credibility is a recipe for political hubris, military overextension, and moral callousness. "Those without strong values cannot withstand the ambiguities, pressures, and anguish that are inseparable from great responsibility." But "strong values" can apparently carry you anywhere. In Kissinger's conception, the ends justify the means, and the end (in both meanings of the word)—the stable, balanced world where the radicals and the Soviets will have been tamed—is attractive enough to vindicate a great deal of misery on the way. Kissinger wanted to put an end to America's oscillations from one form of idealism—isolation—to another—crusades. But he fails to see both how his division of the world into friends and foes resembles the crusaders' itch to divide it into good and evil, and how the way in which he proposed "to teach our people to face their permanent responsibility" was bound to produce a new swing toward the sentimental liberalism he despises.

If Kissinger's book is, at times, oppressive, it is because the "historian's perspective" he says he brought with him to power is both so grim and so thin. This is a world in which power is all: equilibrium is not just the prerequisite to order, the precondition for justice, it *is* order, it amounts to justice. Inspiration is provided not by an ideal, not by the attractiveness of the outcome—unless one makes a fetish out of a condition (balance)—but by the magnitude of the stakes. Ultimately, it is not surprising if no substantial conception of world order emerges. Religions are poor at describing paradise: it is with this world that they deal. And geopolitics is Kissinger's religion—its god is the balance of power, its dogma is linkage, faith is credibility, the high priest is a United States acting on Henry Kissinger's maxims.

All the flaws in Kissinger's conception come together in his discussion of Vietnam and Cambodia. It fills one-third of the volume. Just as Kissinger's ultimate vision of world order is elusive, he does not begin by telling us what his and Nixon's policy in Vietnam was trying to achieve. He tells us what was to be avoided—we had "the duty" to prove that the North Vietnamese ambition of imposing communist rule (or a fake coalition government) in Saigon was wrong—and what was at stake: "the future of other people depended on their confidence in America." Thus we had to fight on "until Hanoi's perceptions of its possibilities changed." What did this mean?

There were never more than two possible outcomes when Kissinger was in office. One was a victory of Hanoi—either on the battlefield or at the conference table. The other was a defeat of Hanoi—the North Vietnamese accepting in effect the survival of the regime of Saigon, under American protection, just as South Korea has survived since 1953. The fundamental ambiguity in Kissinger's account is revealed when he talks of the agreement negotiated in 1972 as a compromise—which is why, he says, up to the "breakthrough" of October 1972, both sides had rejected his strategy: each one "still yearned for a decisive victory." But a compromise was ultimately impossible, because it was not acceptable in the long run to either side and it could be no more than a lull. Ultimately either Saigon or Hanoi had to be in control.

Consider what Kissinger calls a satisfactory compromise, one with which he was so happy in October 1972 that he pleaded with Nixon to let him sign it almost at once, and did not communicate the text to Thieu until the last moment in the belief that Thieu would be impressed by the magnitude of Hanoi's concessions. What he saw as a compromise provided Saigon not merely with a "decent interval" but with "a decent settlement: Saigon, "generously armed and supported by the United States," could cope with "moderate violations," the US "would stand by to enforce the agreement and punish major violations," Hanoi would be deterred by the prospect of such punishment and the incentives of economic aid. In other words, this was victory—not complete, since Hanoi did not have to withdraw its forces in the South, but it could not reinforce them and they occupied little ground.

The reason for Thieu's fury was not just that "the South Vietnamese, after eight years of American participation, simply did not feel ready to confront Hanoi without our direct involvement"—although the reluctance of much of the South Vietnamese population to fight on behalf of the ruling regime had long been a fundamental problem for the US. It is also that Thieu doubted that indirect American involvement would be forthcoming. Kissinger hoped that "joint exertions" between American and South Vietnamese would preserve the peace; he writes that "if doubts as to compliance were to be allowed to block a satisfactory agreement, then the war would never come to a negotiated end." But doubts were justified, both about compliance (by either Saigon or Hanoi), and about America's willingness permanently to act as policeman to exact compliance from Hanoi. Here again Watergate—and the decline in support for Nixon's Vietnam policy that accompanied it—serves Kissinger as a convenient excuse for failure.

But even without Watergate, there was no justification for believing that an agreement that "depended on the vigor with which it was enforced" could rely on the only effective deterrent: the certainty of US forces reintervening. Nixon promised this to Thieu, but it was not credible even before Watergate. For years Congress had been trying to accelerate America's withdrawal; the two escalations of 1972, which involved no ground forces, provoked storms at home; Vietnamization had been an attempt to meet such criticisms (in vain).

Kissinger condemns those domestic upheavals throughout his book. Either he knew that the internal balance of forces in US politics would not allow the US to restore the external one in South Vietnam if there were a violation by Hanoi, in which case Thieu's suspicions would be justified, and the agreement was no more than a time- and face-saving charade. Or else (and this is undoubtedly the case) he once again underestimated domestic battle fatigue, misjudged his ability to make Americans believe that their standing in the world depended on their persistence in a hopeless undertaking, and absurdly overestimated Nixon's capacity to repeat in the future the temporary rescue of Saigon in 1972.

When, after Thieu's request for sixty-three changes in the agreement, Hanoi in turn reopened many issues (with the rather obvious aim of forcing the US to return to the October text), Kissinger concluded that "they have not in any way abandoned their objectives or ambitions with respect to South Vietnam" (report to Nixon). How could he have believed they had, and if they hadn't, could he believe that "reestablishing a better balance of risks" (another euphemism for bombing) would be available forever? The Christmas bombing may not have been the horror some critics denounced at the time; nevertheless it killed at least hundreds of people simply because Thieu needed time and a psychological lift that would enable him to sign at last. Returning to the October text after Thieu had so violently rejected it would have been "tantamount to wrecking the South Vietnamese government." Kissinger writes that "though I considered the agreement a good one" in October, "intervening events would turn acceptance of it into a debacle." This was a bloody charade—we got Hanoi to accept trivial changes that made no difference at all in the end.

Is one more "credible" for recognizing the inevitable early, and cutting one's losses, or for pursuing a futile course, escalating not only the means but the stakes, and adding to the sufferings which the winner was going to impose at the end, those inflicted by the attempt to delay his inevitable victory? When Kissinger finally obtained the separation of Peking and Moscow from Hanoi, what the China initiative had started was completed: he had "reduced Indo-China to its proper scale—a small peninsula on a major continent." Yet even then he acted as if American credibility demanded the vindication of the policies we had pursued from Eisenhower to LBJ, just as his geopolitical design was meant to be an apotheosis of containment.

There are bad places for a fight. In Vietnam, we (and the hapless South Vietnamese) never had a good alternative. We could "bug out," either unilaterally or by negotiating a "coalition" formula to save some face. Or we could dig in and stick to our protégé in order to reassure our other allies— but our enemy would still be there, unless we destroyed him completely, something our values, as well as our calculation of risks, prevented us from doing. And in the meantime the futility of the effort would ensure that we'd look for a way out. At the end, the "honor" we had saved in 1973 was "lost" in 1975. Although Kissinger proclaims that "the security of free peoples everywhere would [have been] jeopardized by an essentially narcissistic act of abdication," our allies were less than delighted to see what we were doing for them. They doubted its worth, and they feared that our exertions in this dubious cause might drain us of energy for better ones. In Vietnam, geopolitics were against us, and neither linkage nor dissociation could help.

Having however declared our policy moral, and all alternatives immoral as well as geopolitically dangerous, Kissinger can indeed affirm that he had little choice when the Cambodian crisis of 1970 broke out. There is a mad logic at work here. The new Nixon-Kissinger strategy, aimed at the same old objective of saving Saigon, entailed a greater willingness to use force outside South Vietnam (remember Kissinger's strictures against gradualism). And it also entailed Vietnamization: the combination of American withdrawals and South Vietnamese build-up. Cambodia, whose neutrality had been dented by Hanoi (as had that of Laos)—no one denies it—was the natural victim of these changes. As early as January 8, Nixon ordered a report on "what, if anything, we are doing to destroy the buildup there": the secret bombing was at least as much caused by this desire to loosen old constraints as by the North Vietnamese offensive at the end of February 1969.

The bombing did, as William Shawcross has shown [in *Sideshow,* 1979], begin to undermine Sihanouk. Kissinger denies what General Abrams has acknowledged to a Senate Committee: the bombing and other operations started pushing the North Vietnamese deeper into Cambodia. When Lon Nol's coup occurred, the North Vietnamese, and Peking, tried to get an agreement from Lon Nol about the sanctuaries. Even though no direct aid was provided to him for several weeks, according to Kissinger, Lon Nol's ultimate intransigence must have had something to do with an expectation of American support.

On the other hand, Nixon authorized (contrary to Kissinger's wishes, he tells us) South Vietnamese attacks across the border; and several Khmer units trained in Vietnam were "launched on a grand scale into Cambodia." The North Vietnamese started moving westward. They must have known that the American command in Saigon was preparing an attack against one of the sanctuaries. Kissinger minimizes the importance of the South Vietnamese raids. When he says that "there had been no consideration of attacking the sanctuaries before April 21," he surely does not mean in Saigon, as is shown in the memo to Nixon which he quoted in an earlier version of his book and then removed. He claims that the North Vietnamese were threatening Phnom Penh, and that Sihanouk, by "effectively declaring war on the new government," had ceased to be a possible alternative: his "return would have meant not a restoration of neutrality but the victory of his new communist patrons, whom he had lost all capacity to control." But it was not to the North Vietnamese advantage to take charge of a vast and unfriendly country (in which Lon Nol was fostering massacres of Vietnamese); it was in their interest to have in power someone who would let them maintain their line of communication and their sanctuaries.

What made it impossible for us to deal with Sihanouk was neither Le Duc Tho's rhetoric (which supported Sihanouk) nor Sihanouk's alliance with his communist ex-foes but our "geopolitical" notion that whoever sides with the communists must be opposed, and above all the requirements of Vietnamization. The North Vietnamese in Cambodia were threatening a vital part of South Vietnam; we had to withdraw without endangering Saigon's survival; Nixon had expressed anger at the existence of the sanctuaries from the beginning. The fall of Sihanouk and the westward moves of the North Vietnamese provided the opportunity to embroil them in Cambodia—by our helping Lon Nol, as Nixon wanted to do almost at once—as well as the opportunity to hit them from South Vietnam.

For America's strategy, a restoration of Sihanouk under North Vietnamese "protection" would have been a major setback. But for the Cambodian people, it would have provided a far better alternative than the war that ravaged the country and allowed, at the end, the Khmer Rouge—not the North Vietnamese—to take over. In 1970, the Khmer Rouge were a handful, with no prospects of power. Kissinger several times attributes the devastation of Cambodia to the U.S. opponents of the war, who crippled the scope of US military assistance legally available for Lon Nol, and thus obliged the Cambodian forces "to rely on our planes as their only strategic reserve."

But he does not include in his account what Shawcross stressed: that it was Kissinger who chose the most ambitious strategic option for the war in Cambodia, and got it approved by the National Security Council in October 1970. This strategy, designed to help Vietnamization, became a liability, both because of Lon Nol's incompetence and because the South Vietnamese, to whom the departing Americans were entrusting ever bigger missions, had to overstretch their resources to keep the North Vietnamese from taking over Cambodia. Our way of helping "free Cambodia" by relentlessly destructive bombing for several years prolonged the agony and did much to prepare for Pol Pot's rule. Kissinger may be right in saying that the Nixon administration had inherited the war in Vietnam. But not only did it accept the legacy, it extended the war to Cambodia.

The same geopolitical needs, global and local, kept Kissinger from trying to deal with Sihanouk before the peace agreement in Vietnam (and, as Shawcross shows, not much more actively later): "negotiations with him could not succeed so long as he was titular head of the communist force, insisting on total victory." He "could not resume his pre-1970 balancing role unless there were two parties left to balance." But by 1973, Sihanouk could not have returned except as head of the anti-Lon Nol forces (which would have been far better for the Cambodians than Pol Pot). We remained inhibited both by the belief that the North Vietnamese could somehow "deliver" the Khmer Rouge—it took Kissinger a long time to recognize that their relation to Hanoi was rather like that of Hanoi to Peking—and by the fear that a negotiation with Sihanouk while the war in Cambodia persisted could undermine the shaky regime in Phnom Penh, and perhaps by the belief that a continuing war in Cambodia might provide relief for our ally in Saigon. Thus, as in Saigon, we stuck to our client, and encouraged him to persist; but in Cambodia we could not even obtain a cease-fire.

External triumphs destroyed by domestic tragedy: a president's weird character, an irresponsible Congress. This is one of the main themes of this volume, and it will undoubtedly be the thread of its successor. But the questions Kissinger's relentless and impressive work leaves in the reader's mind are quite different. To what extent were the successes proof of the validity of Kissinger's "geopolitical" design? Was the détente of 1972 a vindication of his approach, or a passing episode? Was it only an attempt by Brezhnev "to calm the threat from Russia's Western past so that he could deal with its Chinese future," rather than an assent to Kissinger's theory of linkages, networks, rewards, and penalties?

Was the China summit a triumph of triangular diplomacy, or a delicate marriage of convenience, in which one of the partners wants a far closer embrace than the other deems in his interest, although he may have to submit to it lest the more ardent partner should feel jilted and resume a flirtation with their mutual enemy? How wise was American policy in the Middle East and in Iran during those years? Was the colossal effort to find an "honorable" way out of Vietnam proportional to the results? Also, was the pursuit of so single-minded and intense a policy compatible with America's institutions, and if not, what were the alternatives open to us? Kissinger, immersed in tactics, recounting the bureaucratic battles, and imperturbable in his reading of history, does not raise these questions.

FURTHER READING

Robert J. Alexander, *The Tragedy of Chile* (1978)
Richard J. Barnet, *The Giants* (1977)
———, *The Lean Years* (1980)
Coral Bell, *The Diplomacy of Détente* (1977)
Henry Brandon, *The Retreat of American Power* (1973)
Seyom Brown, *The Crises of Power* (1979)
Thomas M. Franck and Edward Weisband, *Foreign Policy by Congress* (1979)
Edward Friedland et al., *The Great Détente Disaster* (1975)
Lloyd C. Gardner, ed., *The Great Nixon Turnaround* (1973)
Charles Gati and Toby Trister Gati, *The Debate over Détente* (1977)
Matti Golan, *The Secret Conversations of Henry Kissinger* (1976)
Stephen Graubard, *Kissinger: Portrait of a Mind* (1973)
Seymour M. Hersh, *The Price of Power: Kissinger in the White House* (1983)
Stanley Hoffmann, *Primacy or World Order* (1978)
———, "The Return of Henry Kissinger," *New York Review of Books,* 29 (April 29, 1982), pp. 14 ff

Gene T. Hsiao, ed., *Sino-American Détente and Its Policy Implications* (1974)
Alan M. Jones, Jr., *U.S. Foreign Policy in a Changing World* (1973)
Bernard Kalb and Marvin Kalb, *Kissinger* (1974)
Robert C. Johansen, *The National Interest and the Human Interest* (1980)
David Landau, *Kissinger: Uses of Power* (1972)
Thomas B. Larson, *Soviet-American Rivalry* (1978)
Michael Mandelbaum, *The Nuclear Question* (1979)
Roger Morris, *Uncertain Greatness: Henry Kissinger and American Foreign Policy* (1977)
Fred Warner Neal, ed., *Detente or Debacle* (1979)
John Newhouse, *Cold Dawn: The Story of SALT* (1973)
James Petras and Morris Morley, *The United States and Chile* (1975)
Richard Pipes, *U.S.–Soviet Relations in the Era of Détente* (1981)
Robert D. Schulzinger, "The Naive and Sentimental Diplomat: Henry Kissinger's Memoirs," *Diplomatic History,* 4 (1980), 303–315
Edward R.F. Sheehan, *The Arabs, Israelis, and Kissinger* (1976)
Paul E. Sigmund, *The Overthrow of Allende and the Politics of Chile, 1964–1976* (1977)
Lewis Sorley, *Arms Transfers Under Nixon* (1983)
Tad Szulc, "How Kissinger Did It: Behind the Vietnam Cease-Fire Agreement," *Foreign Policy,* No. 15 (1974), pp. 21–61
———, *The Illusion of Peace* (1978)
Adam B. Ulam, *Dangerous Relations: The Soviet Union in World Politics, 1970–1982* (1983)
Garry Wills, *Nixon Agonistes* (1970)